Critical Inquiries

Critical Inquiries

Readings on Culture and Community

JACQUELINE JONES ROYSTER
The Ohio State University

with

Rebecca G. Taylor
Gustavus Adolphus College
Associate Editor

and

Kalenda Eaton
Nels Highberg
Pamela Martin
Vic Mortimer
Jean C. Williams
Research Associates

New York Boston San Francisco
London Toronto Sydney Tokyo Singapore Madrid
Mexico City Munich Paris Cape Town Hong Kong Montreal

Senior Vice President and Publisher: Joseph Opiela
Acquisitions Editor: Lynn M. Huddon
Development Editor: Michael Greer
Marketing Manager: Ann Stypuloski
Supplements Editor: Donna Campion
Production Manager: Ellen MacElree
Project Coordination, Text Design, and Electronic Page Makeup: Electronic Publishing Services Inc., NYC
Cover Design Manager: John Callahan
Cover Designer: Kay Petronio
Cover Illustration: Joseph Barnell/SuperStock
Photo Researcher: Electronic Publishing Services Inc., NYC
Manufacturing Buyer: Al Dorsey
Printer and Binder: Maple-Vail Book Manufacturing Group
Cover Printer: Phoenix Color Corps.

For permission to use copyrighted material, grateful acknowledgment is made to the copyright holders on pages 603–606, which are hereby made part of this copyright page.

Library of Congress Cataloging-in-Publication Data
Royster, Jacqueline Jones.
Critical inquiries : readings in culture and community / Jacqueline Jones Royster ; with Rebecca G. Taylor, associate editor ; and Kalenda Eaton ... [et al.], research associates.
p. cm.
Includes bibliographical references and index.
ISBN 0-321-01586-X
1. College readers. 2. Readers—Culture. 3. Readers—Community life. 4. Community life—Problems, exercises, etc. 5. English language—Rhetoric—Problems, exercises, etc. 6. Report writing—Problems, exercises, etc. 7. Culture—Problems, exercises, etc. I. Taylor, Rebecca G. II. Title.
PE1127.S6 R69 2002
808'.0427—dc21

2002040650

Please visit our website at http://www.ablongman.com

ISBN 0-321-01586-X

1 2 3 4 5 6 7 8 9 10—MA—05 04 03 02

Detailed Contents

Preface for Instructors

This book is designed for college-level courses in composition that seek to offer students an intense writing, reading, and critical thinking experience. The aim of the collection is threefold in helping students to:

1. reflect on their lives and experiences;
2. expand their knowledge and understanding of various issues in light of the selections included in the text and the research that these selections inspire; and
3. experiment with various techniques and strategies as they think deliberately and directly about what it means for them to use language well in a complex world.

In the case of item 3, this book acknowledges that we face many challenges as individuals who must function harmoniously among others. In using readings about timeless topics—home, nation, (im)migration, education, health, and technology—the collection pays attention to the ways in which basic concerns of life and living often constitute occasions when values, beliefs, practices, and points of view have the potential to both connect and divide individuals. These occasions set in motion a need for mediation and personal decision making; in recent years, such moments have given rise frequently in composition courses to learning objectives focused on language use and issues of tolerance.

Further, because this book is a textbook about writing, it, of course, draws direct attention to the critical role language plays in reflecting on experience, in analyzing and articulating viewpoints, and in considering consequences of human actions and interactions. Language use is indeed the central concern of the book, and rhetorical principles, practices, and processes are the means of engagement consistently used throughout each chapter.

GENERAL ASSUMPTIONS ABOUT WRITING

Textbooks about writing can take different approaches to the teaching of writing. This book views writing as a process that has cognitive, social, and political dimensions. As a **cognitive** process, writing is about what students know already. By the time students get to college, they have had innumerable experiences that have formed what they know about language(s) and about how to use language knowledge (oral and textual) in different settings and situations for different purposes. While students are not always consciously aware of their own knowledge, they have it, nevertheless, and it is there and available to be used in writing classrooms as a base from which to learn more and to learn how to do more.

As a **social** process, writing, like all communicative and expressive forms, makes sense mainly in the presence of others. From this perspective, the purpose of writing is to speak expressively, informatively, even persuasively in text and to elicit desirable responses from others, a process by which students learn to sharpen abilities and enhance communicative success. Further, writing functions by conventions, by the ways that a particular group of people have agreed, in the interest of communicative exchange, to use it. Unlike speech, writing needs the flexibility of transcending both time and space—to convey thoughts, feelings, and ideas typically without the writer being physically present as readers read. Because of the potential of distance, writing involves the responsibility to be clear, precise, and accurate without the luxury of an immediate opportunity to explain or clarify.

In recognizing that the basic role of writing conventions is to enable effective expression, what seems worthy of emphasis is that the ability to be successful as a language user depends on an understanding of the habits and preferences of the particular communities in which we are engaging. In any community, seen as an arena for communication, there are typically conventions for everything from the way we choose and spell words, punctuate, and make sentences to the way we make decisions about what is appropriate to discuss, who our audiences are, how we establish credibility with those audiences, how we structure ideas, and how we use evidence for those ideas.

This is the point at which the **political** dimensions of writing come to the table. Again, values, habits, and preferences vary from community to community—and so do language practices, as such activities are defined amid the social and cultural fabric of any given community. The contentious point to recognize is that some communities have more political power and social prestige than others. In effect, in using the language practices of a community, we symbolically invoke that community with all of its social and political clout, or the lack thereof, and we convey images of ourselves (often stereotypical ones, both positive and negative) that are embedded within and shaped by social and political history. By such processes, language practices are categorized as prestigious or nonprestigious, respected or not respected, valued or not valued, and so forth, and so are the people who use the practices. Both are deemed effective or ineffective based on the ways in which a particular speaker or writer satisfies a sense of the norm—in following expectations and, sometimes, in creatively and innovatively subverting those expectations. In the world today, these habits of valuing within a community and across community boundaries create problems—that is, problems of equity and fairness in terms of access to possibility, social gains, and economic reward.

These three dimensions of writing (cognitive, social, political) make visible two concerns for the writing classroom and thereby for this book. One is a concern focused on helping students develop a framework for questioning cognitive, social, and political dimensions of writing. A second is a focus on helping students gain experience in using language for many purposes, in many forms, across many contexts, in acknowledgment of the interests and expectations of many audiences.

ACKNOWLEDGMENTS

In gathering these materials and in making decisions about supplementary resources and classroom activities, I have depended greatly on a special team of associates. First, Rebecca Greenberg Taylor, the associate editor, has been steadfast in filling multiple roles in the preparation of this book, from identifying reading selections to developing classroom strategies, testing materials with groups of students, and reviewing materials based on various sets of criteria.

Second, Kalenda Eaton, Nels Highberg, Pamela Martin, Vic Mortimer, and Jean Williams all served at different points during the process as research associates who shared not only their time and energy in collecting and selecting materials but also their insights as researchers and teachers in helping shape what the book became.

Third, Melinda Wright, the author of the instructor's guide, deserves special praise. It was affirming to have a colleague at my own institution to participate in this collaboration so enthusiastically, sharing her time, talents, and considerable experience in bringing an idea to good classroom use.

Also, I gratefully acknowledge Giles Patrick Royster, who served throughout the process as an emergency web surfer who could be counted on, especially when a computer keyboard is involved, to search for and find the troublesome little details that make the difference between a fully documented source and one that is not.

From the community of compositionists, I add to this list Chuck Schuster, whose initial advice helped me begin the project; Lisa Ede, whose affirmation of the approach was encouraging; and Julia K. Ferganchick-Neufang, who suggested articles that helped reshape the project. Thank you to the outside readers who reviewed the manuscript and offered advice that was critical to refocusing and refining the book: Rick Albright, Lehigh University; Kathryn N. Benzel, University of Nebraska—Kearney; Carol Bott, Miami University; Michael Bourne, University of Richmond; Stephen Byars, University of Southern California; Michael D. Donnelly, Temple University; Tim Engles, University of Georgia; Jane Holman,

Portland Community College; Kate Kessler, James Madison University; Janice Lauer, Purdue University; Daniel Lowe, Community College of Allegheny County; Susan McDermott, Hudson Valley Community College; JoAnna S. Mink, Minnesota State University; Catherine Rainwater, St. Edward's University; John Ruszkiewicz, University of Texas at Austin; Michelle Sidler, Pennsylvania State University—Berks; Scott Simkins, University of Southern Mississippi; Cynthia Stretch, Southern Connecticut State University; Vicki Stieha, Northern Kentucky University; John Trimbur, Worcester Polytechnic University; John Wegner, Angelo State University; and Lynn West, Spokane Community College.

In addition, my gratitude for the talented cohort of professionals at Longman runs deep. First among those I'd like to single out is Michael Greer, who during the final process of preparing the manuscript became my constant email companion as we worked together to revise and edit the text. There are others, however, including Anne Smith, Lynn Huddon, Ginny Blanford, Shannon Egan, and Ellen MacElree. My thanks to them all for their support.

—Jacqueline Jones Royster

INTRODUCTION

Frameworks for Rhetorical Decision Making

In contemporary society, it is not unusual to think of yourself as a member of several overlapping communities. At home, at school, at work, in social, professional, and community organizations, you are typically in the company of others whose relationships to you may vary. With some individuals, you may feel close and familiar; you may need to interact for various reasons with others with whom you do not feel close or familiar at all. Over a lifetime of social and professional encounters, it seems inevitable that you will need to use language flexibly to mediate the range of these relationships.

Learning to think and write amid such variability can be a complex undertaking. Writing classrooms, as sites designated to enhance students' language abilities, often function as venues for negotiation and experimentation. They become places where writers analyze, plan, and practice writing; reflect on their own writing performances, as well as the performances of others; and come to understand through well-focused experiments a range of ways that writing can be successful, effective, and sometimes even elegant.

Critical Inquiries is designed to support such activities by helping you to:

- **develop strategies for raising thought-provoking questions** about topics that have proven, over time, to have ongoing significance for life and living and to develop as well strategies for responding to these ongoing interests articulately, thoughtfully, and creatively;
- **use rhetorical principles** (e.g., an understanding of *context*, *audience*, and *purpose*) to analyze written texts and how they function in their areas of use;

- **examine your own points of view** on issues, to figure what your thoughts are, what has influenced your thinking, and what the implications of your habits and preferences might be with regard to specific issues, problems, and concerns;
- **use your rhetorical resources** (i.e., the knowledge and experiences that you have gained or are developing through language use) to express those points of view with a clearer understanding of how language works as a *cognitive, social,* and *political* process.

Critical Inquiries is based on the view that the effort to write well benefits from an understanding that language use has cognitive, social, and political dimensions. As a *cognitive process,* writing well is tied to individual language abilities—that is, to the talents and skills we have as individuals capable of using language. Effectiveness in writing, however, is also tied to language experience—that is, to the opportunities a person has had to write and to learn from the trials and errors of those writing experiences over time. Understanding the cognitive dimensions of writing means recognizing that by the time students get to college, they have had many, many experiences by which they have learned language(s) and learned to use language variously in speaking and writing in different settings and situations for different purposes. While students are not always consciously aware of their own knowledge, they have it, nevertheless, and it is there and available to be used in writing classrooms as the students continue to experiment, learn, and, indeed, to enhance their language abilities.

As a *social process,* writing, like other communicative and expressive forms, makes sense mainly in the presence of others. The purposes of writing are to use language expressively, informatively, even persuasively in text and to elicit response from others. Further, in fulfilling communal goals, writing functions by conventions, by the ways a particular group of people have agreed to use language to meet and mediate designated goals and purposes. An additional necessity for writing conventions, however, as compared with conventions for speaking, is to reach beyond the immediate interaction, in terms of both time and space, to communicate well despite the likelihood that the writer will not be physically present with readers to explain.

Generally, writing as a social process functions in the interest of forging connections between and among individuals who desire to interact. The habits and preferences (or conventions) that emerge via these social dimensions help reduce misunderstanding, enhance arbitration, and create sets of expectations not only for behavior but also for assigning meaning and value to behavior, a process that facilitates the development of relationships and the formation of communities. With writing, we have developed conventions for everything from the way we choose and spell words, punctuate, and make sentences to the way we make decisions about appropriate subject matter, who our audiences are, how we establish credibility with those audiences, and how we structure ideas and the evidence for them in informative or convincing ways. What seems worthy of emphasis here is not so much that we have the habit of prescribing writing behavior but that writing well, given our need for conventions, is greatly enhanced when we pay attention to the language conventions of the communities in which we seek to participate as writers.

At the point when social dimensions of writing come to the center of attention, so too do the *political dimensions.* First, understanding that writing is a process that is defined within a specific social context highlights the fact that such practices inevitably vary from community to community. Second, understanding that language is conventional and that conventional practices operate at all levels of language use, from placing commas to establishing credibility, help us see the ways conventions are actually mirrors for a given community in the way they encode and signal values, beliefs, and preferences. Language choices symbolically invoke the community out of which the language comes. What we have come to understand in recent years, then, is that language use has effects and consequences. Amid hierarchies of power, influence, and prestige, in keeping with the hierarchies that surround us in our daily relationships, we convey images of ourselves (often stereotypical ones, both positive and negative) that signal the social and political history of the community itself.

We have learned that language use operates as a mechanism for assigning value and credibility to both the language used and the people who use it. Both the practices and the people are deemed by conventional expectations effective or ineffective, prestigious or nonprestigious, respected or not respected, valued or not valued, and so forth, based on the ways in which the language practices satisfy (or not) a sense of the norm—in following expectations or sometimes in creatively and innovatively subverting those expectations. In a complex world filled with communities that vary in their language practices for all sorts of reasons, differences in value systems offer many challenges for the task of writing well, especially when the writer crosses community boundaries. If, therefore, you are to be successful as a writer who can expect to interact in many social and professional situations, you will need to be able to use well a broad range of strategies that can permit you to cross various boundaries (e.g., in terms of home culture, academic disciplines, or various institutional expectations) as you use language for many purposes, in many forms, across many contexts.

THE STRUCTURE OF THE BOOK

Critical Inquiries is organized thematically around seven topics: identity, home, nation, (im)migration, education, health, and technology. Each chapter begins with a reading or set of readings called "Framing the

Topic," intended to help you generate questions about the topic and engage critically with related issues. The central section of each chapter is called "Readings for Inquiry and Exploration." This section creates occasions for you to encounter and engage different views of the topic. These selections offer opportunities to think about different points of view, to discuss these ideas with your classmates, to consider carefully the decisions writers have made and can make in writing about these topics, and to clarify your own views.

In a manner intended to intensify this type of inquiry, the selections at the end of each chapter are labeled "Calls to Action and Response." These readings function as occasions from which various *calls to action* related to the topic might arise. Here, the focus is on *synthesis.* The readings were chosen to help you consider the implications of ideas, to raise questions that may not have been addressed by earlier readings or that call for further inquiry, and to think about the connections between language and action. The activities are designed to help you sort through the ideas presented in the chapter and craft writing capable of making an idea interesting, compelling, and even persuasive to others. They provide opportunities for you to focus more deliberately on composing your own ideas and operating as a writer (or sometimes, perhaps, as a writer/activist). For example, you might choose to speak out about something of direct or related interest to the topic, or you might choose to strike a more activist stance and set a goal to persuade or inspire a specific audience to action.

After each individual reading selection, are two sets of activities. One is called "Mapping the Text;" the other is "Writing to Inquire." Both are designed to accomplish the goals listed above, but as these goals relate more directly to the specific reading. The questions in "Mapping the Text" focus on the actual writing performance of a given selection by drawing attention to issues of language, form, and function as well as to issues related to a writer's *ethos, context, audience,* and *purpose.*

Ethos refers to the sense of self that a writer holds and also conveys to others through the choice of writing strategies. As a concept, ethos takes into account the writer's privilege of actually constructing a self-view in whatever way the writer deems it viable or meaningful to do so. It also considers external factors and conditions in the writer's environment that might influence that construction. In particular, it takes into account the decisions a writer makes and the strategies a writer uses in crafting a text to convey a particular view or image of self to various audiences.

Context refers to the circumstances, conditions, and features in the environment in which the writer is writing that affect or influence a writer's choices in creating a text. This concept takes into account social, political, economic, cultural, and other factors; the occasion for the writing, the event, or the circumstances that form the springboard or the reason for the writing; and issues of status, power, and privilege as a writer negotiates in the presence of others the challenges of crafting a piece of writing that works well.

Audience and *purpose* are terms that are generally more familiar. With these concepts in mind, a writer is immediately drawn to basic rhetorical questions: who says what to whom under what circumstances for what reasons and with what intent? What we have come to understand with contemporary research, however, is that none of these questions are as simple as they seem, and we are cautioned to be alert to the nuances that complicate choices and create greater challenge for writers. For example, from a simplistic point of view, the audience is the reader and the purpose is what the writer is trying to accomplish. However, even when a student is writing for a specific audience rather than a general audience, the characteristics, features, and contexts for this audience may not be neat and tidy. There may, indeed, be variations within the group that require the writer to balance competing interests rather than permit the assumption that there is agreement and consensus in the audience's beliefs and values. These terms and others you will see throughout the chapters are useful in building decision-making experience and learning to discriminate details, assess information, and make reasonable judgments about available options.

The structure for each chapter ("Framing the Topic," "Readings for Inquiry and Exploration," and "Calls to Action and Response") and the questions for each reading ("Mapping the Text" and "Writing to Inquire") are designed to help you develop strategies for asking thought-provoking questions of the readings, the ideas, yourself, and your classmates. A basic imperative is to help you read carefully in order to see what is there, not there, and might be there instead; to use specific terms and concepts in the consideration of viewpoints; to use reflection (i.e., learning to think back and to think again) productively in determining what you think and why. Most of all, the goal is to help you experiment with writing and to learn from those experiments. The basic idea is to help you see and understand some of the rhetorical decisions that writers make, to consider the impact of their choices, and to make decisions yourself based on your own thoughts and purposes.

SEEING AS A WRITER

A core value of this book is critical inquiry. The assumption is that in order to enhance your skills and abilities in using written language well, you need to understand what it means to see as a writer. This book suggests that seeing as a writer begins with a working vocabulary for discussing, analyzing, and writing about what you see. The imperative is to identify terms useful in analyzing the writing of others (ethos, context, audience, purpose; language, form, and function) so that these terms can be consistently applied in making writing decisions. In encouraging you to see as a writer, *Critical Inquiries* highlights the ways in which reading, critical thinking, writing, discussing writing, and writing about writing converge as writers concentrate on enhancing their abilities to use language well. This book emphasizes, therefore, the benefits of the writer's tools—a critical eye, an inquiring mind, a compassionate heart—as tools for deliberation and reflection. Writing well is a complex challenge, but we have excellent tools for managing the process and getting the job done well.

CHAPTER 1

Claiming Identity

One of the readings in this chapter begins, "I don't remember things." Rebecca Walker, like many of the writers gathered here, explores the complexity of the concept of identity, the difficulty of having or being a "self." She continues: "Without a memory that invests in information retention, without a memory that can remind me at all times of who I definitively am, I feel amorphous, missing the unbroken black outline around my body everyone else seems to have." While each writer in this chapter approaches the question of identity from a different angle, all seem to agree that identity is something that must be claimed and reclaimed, and that one of the ways we do this is through language, writing, and story. While others outside of us may appear to be drawn in neatly, with "the unbroken black line" of selfhood, our own identity turns out to be constantly changing and redefining itself in relation to family, history, culture, and place. Writing is one way of understanding this changing process. Walker's own work, for example, is subtitled "Autobiography of a Shifting Self."

The objective in Chapter 1 of focusing on identity is twofold. On one hand, our purpose is to show how identity matters in language use. This view suggests that a sense of self is complex rather than simple, that we benefit from thinking about the views of ourselves that we hold, and that we can bring such complications resourcefully to the task whenever we express ourselves, communicate with others, and use language to get various things done. A second imperative grows from the first. Centering on the idea of the self as a resourceful decision maker in language use, these readings become occasions to highlight some terms related to decision making that will be useful to you throughout this book in analyzing readings and in composing your own writing.

The chapter begins with an excerpt from Henry David Thoreau's *Walden*, a chapter entitled, "Where I Lived, and What I Lived For." Thoreau remains famous after more than 150 years for his decision to withdraw from modern social life and to take up a solitary residence at Walden Pond, an experience later chronicled in *Walden* (first published in 1854). "Our life," he wrote, "is frittered away by detail." Thoreau's legacy—"Simplicity, simplicity, simplicity!"—is still honored by many artists and environmentalists, among others. In the 1990s, for example, musician Don Henley organized a series of concerts to benefit efforts to preserve Walden Woods, just west of Boston, which at the time were threatened by the development of a new shopping center. "Civil Disobedience," one of Thoreau's best-known essays, continues to be invoked by activists and grassroots social movements of many kinds.

Thoreau discusses his choice to live at Walden Pond in Massachusetts and presents his beliefs and values in the context of this natural setting. He believes in the power of observation and poses the problem of the struggle for balance between nature and civilization. A primary concern for him is a search for balance, a balance between the science of observing and the insight and inspiration that a person can receive in the process. He helps us think not only about nature but also about personal values and identity and about ourselves as human beings in and part of a larger world.

In this way, Thoreau helps frame the topic of identity as a commitment to inquire systematically about "self" as we construct and reconstruct our selves in various circumstances for various expressive or communicative purposes. Each subsequent selection in the chapter raises additional questions and issues. They bring attention to how personal characteristics, culture, age, family history, and geographic place can enrich and complicate the ways that we view ourselves and how we relate to others. They help establish the concept of identity as a rich landscape of ideas to think and write about.

FRAMING THE TOPIC

Where I Lived, and What I Lived For (from *Walden*)

HENRY DAVID THOREAU

Henry David Thoreau (1817–1862) was an essayist who is best known for his collection *Walden, or Life in the Woods,* published in 1854. This collection, including the essay below, chronicles a two-year period when he lived in a cabin he built on Walden Pond near Concord, Massachusetts, and sought to fulfill his desire to live a simple life in a natural setting. His other writings include *A Week on the Concord and Merrimack Rivers* (1849) and several collections published posthumously with the assistance of his sister Sophia Thoreau: *Excursions* (1863), *The Maine Woods* (1864), *Cape Cod* (1865), *Letters to Various Persons* (1865, edited by his friend and mentor Ralph Waldo Emerson), and *A Yankee in Canada with Anti-Slavery and Reform Papers* (1866). During his lifetime, Thoreau was not recognized as a great writer, being much overshadowed by Emerson and other writers in the Transcendentalist group of which he was a part. However, in the twentieth century, with a rising interest in the care and maintenance of natural areas and in simplified lifestyles, his works have found and sustained a loyal readership.

At a certain season of our life we are accustomed to consider every spot as the possible site of a house. I have thus surveyed the country on every side within a dozen miles of where I live. In imagination I have bought all the farms in succession, for all were to be bought, and I knew their price. I walked over each farmer's premises, tasted his wild apples, discoursed on husbandry with him, took his farm at his price, at any price, mortgaging it to him in my mind; even put a higher price on it—took everything but a deed of it—took his word for his deed, for I dearly love to talk—cultivated it, and him too to some extent, I trust, and withdrew when I had enjoyed it long enough, leaving him to carry it on. This experience entitled me to be regarded as a sort of real-estate broker by my friends. Wherever I sat, there I might live, and the landscape radiated from me accordingly. What is a house but a *sedes,* a seat?—better if a country seat. I discovered many a site for a house not likely to be soon improved, which some might have thought too far from the village, but to my eyes the village was too far from it. Well, there I might live, I said; and there I did live, for an hour, a summer and a winter life; saw how I could let the years run off, buffet the winter through, and see the spring come in. The future inhabitants of this region, wherever they may place their houses, may be sure that they have been anticipated. An afternoon sufficed to lay out the land into orchard, wood-lot, and pasture, and to decide what fine oaks or pines should be left to stand before the door, and whence each blasted tree could be seen to the best advantage; and then I let it lie, fallow perchance, for a man is rich in proportion to the number of things which he can afford to let alone.

My imagination carried me so far that I even had the refusal of several farms—the refusal was all I wanted—but I never got my fingers burned by actual possession. The nearest that I came to actual possession was when I bought the Hollowell place, and had begun to sort my seeds, and collected materials with which to make a wheelbarrow to carry it on or off with; but before the owner gave me a deed of it, his wife—every man has such a wife—changed her mind and wished to keep it, and he offered me ten dollars to release him. Now, to speak the truth, I had but ten cents in the world, and it surpassed my arithmetic to tell, if I was that man who had ten cents, or who had a farm, or ten dollars, or all together. However, I let him keep the ten dollars and the farm too, for I had carried it far enough; or rather, to be generous, I sold him the farm for just what I gave for it, and, as he was not a rich man, made him a present of ten dollars, and still had my ten cents, and seeds, and materials for a wheelbarrow left. I found thus that I had been a rich man without any damage to my poverty. But I retained the landscape, and I have since annually carried off what it yielded without a wheelbarrow. With respect to landscapes,

> 'I am monarch of all I *survey*,
> My right there is none to dispute.'

I have frequently seen a poet withdraw, having enjoyed the most valuable part of a farm, while the crusty farmer supposed that he had got a few wild apples only. Why, the owner does not know it for many years when a poet has put his farm in rhyme, the most admirable kind of invisible fence, has fairly impounded it, milked it, skimmed it, and got all the cream, and left the farmer only the skimmed milk.

The real attractions of the Hollowell farm, to me, were: its complete retirement, being about two miles from the village, half a mile from the nearest neighbor, and separated from the highway by a broad field; its bounding on the river, which the owner said protected it by its fogs from frosts in the spring, though that was nothing to me; the gray color and ruinous state of the house and barn, and the dilapidated fences, which put such an interval between me and the last occupant; the hollow and lichen-covered apple trees, gnawed by rabbits, showing what kind of neighbors I should have; but above all, the recollection I had of it from my earliest voyages up the river, when the house was concealed behind a dense grove of red maples, through which I heard the house-dog bark. I was in haste to buy it, before the proprietor finished getting out some rocks, cutting down the hollow apple trees, and grubbing up some young birches which had sprung up in the pasture, or, in short, had made any more of his improvements. To enjoy these advantages I was ready to carry it on; like Atlas, to take the world on my shoulders—I never heard what compensation he received for that—and do all those things which had no other motive or excuse but that I might pay for it and be unmolested in my possession of it; for I knew all the while that it would yield the most abundant crop of the kind I wanted, if I could only afford to let it alone. But it turned out as I have said.

5 All that I could say, then, with respect to farming on a large scale—I have always cultivated a garden—was, that I had had my seeds ready. Many think that seeds improve with age. I have no doubt that time discriminates between the good and the bad; and when at last I shall plant, I shall be less likely to be disappointed. But I would say to my fellows, once for all, As long as possible live free and uncommitted. It makes but little difference whether you are committed to a farm or the county jail.

Old Cato, whose 'De Re Rusticâ' is my 'Cultivator,' says—and the only translation I have seen makes sheer nonsense of the passage—'When you think of getting a farm turn it thus in your mind, not to buy greedily; nor spare your pains to look at it, and do not think it enough to go round it once. The oftener you go there the more it will please you, if it is good.' I think I shall not buy greedily, but go round and round it as long as I live, and be buried in it first, that it may please me the more at last.

The present was my next experiment of this kind, which I purpose to describe more at length, for convenience putting the experience of two years into one. As I have said, I do not propose to write an ode to dejection, but to brag as lustily as chanticleer in the morning, standing on his roost, if only to wake my neighbors up.

When first I took up my abode in the woods, that is, began to spend my nights as well as days there, which, by accident, was on Independence Day, or the Fourth of July, 1845, my house was not finished for winter, but was merely a defence against the rain, without plastering or chimney, the walls being of rough, weather-stained boards, with wide chinks, which made it cool at night. The upright white hewn studs and freshly planed door and window casings gave it a clean and airy look, especially in the morning, when its timbers were saturated with dew, so that I fancied that by noon some sweet gum would exude from them. To my imagination it retained throughout the day more or less of this auroral character, reminding me of a certain house on a mountain which I had visited a year before. This was an airy and unplastered cabin, fit to entertain a travelling god, and where a goddess might trail her garments. The winds which passed over my dwelling were such as sweep over the ridges of mountains, bearing the broken strains, or celestial parts only, of terrestrial music. The morning wind forever blows, the poem of creation is uninterrupted; but few are the ears that hear it. Olympus is but the outside of the earth everywhere.

The only house I had been the owner of before, if I except a boat, was a tent, which I used occasionally when making excursions in the summer, and this is still rolled up in my garret; but the boat, after passing from hand to hand, has gone down the stream of time. With this more substantial shelter about me, I had made some progress toward settling in the world. This frame, so slightly clad, was a sort of crystallization around me, and reacted on the builder. It was suggestive somewhat as a picture in outlines. I did not need to go outdoors to take the air, for the atmosphere within had lost none of its freshness. It was not so much within-doors as behind a door where I sat, even in the rainiest weather. The Harivansa says, 'An abode without birds is like a meat without seasoning.' Such was not my abode, for I found myself suddenly neighbor to the birds; not by having imprisoned one, but having caged myself near them. I was not only nearer to some of those which commonly frequent the garden and the orchard, but to those wilder and more thrilling songsters of the forest which never, or rarely, serenade a villager—the wood thrush, the veery, the scarlet tanager, the field sparrow, the whip-poor-will, and many others.

I was seated by the shore of a small pond, about a mile and a half south of the village of Concord and somewhat higher than it, in the midst of an extensive wood between that town and Lincoln, and about two miles south of that our only field known to fame, Concord Battle Ground; but I was so low in the woods that the opposite shore, half a mile off, like the rest, covered with wood, was my most distant horizon. For the first week, whenever I looked out on the pond it impressed me like a tarn high up on the side of a mountain, its bottom far above the surface of other lakes, and, as the sun arose, I saw it throwing off its nightly clothing of mist, and here and there, by degrees, its soft ripples or its smooth reflecting surface was revealed, while the mists, like ghosts, were stealthily withdrawing in every direction into the woods, as at the breaking up of some nocturnal conventicle. The very dew seemed to hang upon the trees later into the day than usual, as on the sides of mountains.

This small lake was of most value as a neighbor in the intervals of a gentle rain-storm in August, when, both air and water being perfectly still, but the sky overcast, mid-afternoon had all the serenity of evening, and the wood thrush sang around, and was heard from shore to shore. A lake like this is never smoother than at such a time; and the clear portion of the air above it being shallow and darkened by clouds, the water, full of light and reflections, becomes a lower heaven itself so much the more important. From a hill-top near by, where the wood had been recently cut off, there was a pleasing vista southward across the pond, through a wide indentation in the hills which form the shore there, where their opposite sides sloping toward each other suggested a stream flowing out in that direction through a wooded valley, but stream there was none. That way I looked between and over the near green hills to some distant and higher ones in the horizon, tinged with blue. Indeed, by standing on tiptoe I could catch a glimpse of some of the peaks of the still bluer and more distant mountain ranges in the northwest, those true-blue coins from heaven's own mint, and also of some portion of the village. But in other directions, even from this point, I could not see over or beyond the woods which surrounded me. It is well to have some water in your neighborhood, to give buoyancy to and float the earth. One value even of the smallest well is, that when you look into it you see that earth is not continent but insular. This is as important as that it keeps butter cool. When I looked across the pond from this peak toward the Sudbury meadows, which in time of flood I distinguished elevated perhaps by a mirage in their seething valley, like a coin in a basin, all the earth beyond the pond appeared like a thin crust insulated and floated even by this small sheet of intervening water, and I was reminded that this on which I dwelt was but *dry land.*

Though the view from my door was still more contracted, I did not feel crowded or confined in the least. There was pasture enough for my imagination. The low shrub oak plateau to which the opposite shore arose stretched away toward the prairies of the West and the steppes of Tartary, affording ample room for all the roving families of men. 'There are none happy in the world but beings who enjoy freely a vast horizon'—said Damodara, when his herds required new and larger pastures.

Both place and time were changed, and I dwelt nearer to those parts of the universe and to those eras in history which had most attracted me. Where I lived was as far off as many a region viewed nightly by astronomers. We are wont to imagine rare and delectable places in some remote and more celestial corner of the system, behind the constellation of Cassiopeia's Chair, far from noise and disturbance. I discovered that my house actually had its site in such a withdrawn, but forever new and unprofaned, part of the universe. If it were worth the while to settle in those parts near to the Pleiades or the Hyades, to Aldebaran or Altair, then I was really there, or at an equal remoteness from the life which I had left behind, dwindled and twinkling with as fine a ray to my nearest neighbor, and to be seen only in moonless nights by him. Such was that part of creation where I had squatted;

> 'There was a shepherd that did live,
> And held his thoughts as high
> As were the mounts whereon his flocks
> Did hourly feed him by.'

What should we think of the shepherd's life if his flocks always wandered to higher pastures than his thoughts?

Every morning was a cheerful invitation to make my life of equal simplicity, and I may say innocence, with Nature herself. I have been as sincere a worshipper of Aurora as the Greeks. I got up early and bathed in the pond; that was a religious exercise, and one of the best things which I did.

They say that characters were engraven on the bathing tub of King Tching-thang to this effect: 'Renew thyself completely each day; do it again, and again, and forever again.' I can understand that. Morning brings back the heroic ages. I was as much affected by the faint hum of a mosquito making its invisible and unimaginable tour through my apartment at earliest dawn, when I was sitting with door and windows open, as I could be by any trumpet that ever sang of fame. It was Homer's requiem; itself an Iliad and Odyssey in the air, singing its own wrath and wanderings. There was something cosmical about it; a standing advertisement, till forbidden, of the ever-lasting vigor and fertility of the world. The morning, which is the most memorable season of the day, is the awakening hour. Then there is least somnolence in us; and for an hour, at least, some part of us awakes which slumbers all the rest of the day and night. Little is to be expected of that day, if it can be called a day, to which we are not awakened by our Genius, but by the mechanical nudgings of some servitor, are not awakened by our own newly acquired force and aspirations from within, accompanied by the undulations of celestial music, instead of factory bells, and a fragrance filling the air—to a higher life than we fell asleep from; and thus the darkness bear its fruit, and prove itself to be good, no less than the light. That man who does not believe that each day contains an earlier, more sacred, and auroral hour than he has yet profaned, has despaired of life, and is pursuing a descending and darkening way. After a partial cessation of his sensuous life, the soul of man, or its organs rather, are reinvigorated each day, and his Genius tries again what noble life it can make. All memorable events, I should say, transpire in morning time and in a morning atmosphere. The Vedas say, 'All intelligences awake with the morning.' Poetry and art, and the fairest and most memorable of the actions of men, date from such an hour. All poets and heroes, like Memnon, are the children of Aurora, and emit their music at sunrise. To him whose elastic and vigorous thought keeps pace with the sun, the day is a perpetual morning. It matters not what the clocks say or the attitudes and labors of men. Morning is when I am awake and there is a dawn in me. Moral reform is the effort to throw off sleep. Why is it that men give so poor an account of their day if they have not been slumbering? They are not such poor calculators. If they had not been overcome with drowsiness, they would have performed something. The millions are awake enough for physical labor; but only one in a million is awake enough for effective intellectual exertion, only one in a hundred millions to a poetic or divine life. To be awake is to be alive. I have never yet met a man who was quite awake. How could I have looked him in the face?

15 We must learn to reawaken and keep ourselves awake, not by mechanical aids, but by an infinite expectation of the dawn, which does not forsake us in our soundest sleep. I know of no more encouraging fact than the unquestionable ability of man to elevate his life by a conscious endeavor. It is something to be able to paint a particular picture, or to carve a statue,

and so to make a few objects beautiful; but it is far more glorious to carve and paint the very atmosphere and medium through which we look, which morally we can do. To affect the quality of the day, that is the highest of arts. Every man is tasked to make his life, even in its details, worthy of the contemplation of his most elevated and critical hour. If we refused, or rather used up, such paltry information as we get, the oracles would distinctly inform us how this might be done.

I went to the woods because I wished to live deliberately, to front only the essential facts of life, and see if I could not learn what it had to teach, and not, when I came to die, discover that I had not lived. I did not wish to live what was not life, living is so dear; nor did I wish to practise resignation, unless it was quite necessary. I wanted to live deep and suck out all the marrow of life, to live so sturdily and Spartan-like as to put to rout all that was not life, to cut a broad swath and shave close, to drive life into a corner, and reduce it to its lowest terms, and, if it proved to be mean, why then to get the whole and genuine meanness of it, and publish its meanness to the world; or if it were sublime, to know it by experience, and be able to give a true account of it in my next excursion. For most men, it appears to me, are in a strange uncertainty about it, whether it is of the devil or of God, and have *somewhat hastily* concluded that it is the chief end of man here to 'glorify God and enjoy him forever.'

Still we live meanly, like ants; though the fable tells us that we were long ago changed into men; like pygmies we fight with cranes; it is error upon error, and clout upon clout, and our best virtue has for its occasion a superfluous and evitable wretchedness. Our life is frittered away by detail. An honest man has hardly need to count more than his ten fingers, or in extreme cases he may add his ten toes, and lump the rest. Simplicity, simplicity, simplicity! I say, let your affairs be as two or three, and not a hundred or a thousand; instead of a million count half a dozen, and keep your accounts on your thumb-nail. In the midst of this chopping sea of civilized life, such are the clouds and storms and quicksands and thousand-and-one items to be allowed for, that a man has to live, if he would not founder and go to the bottom and not make his port at all, by dead reckoning, and he must be a great calculator indeed who succeeds. Simplify, simplify. Instead of three meals a day, if it be necessary eat but one; instead of a hundred dishes, five; and reduce other things in proportion. Our life is like a German Confederacy, made up of petty states, with its boundary forever fluctuating, so that even a German cannot tell you how it is bounded at any moment. The nation itself, with all its so-called internal improvements, which, by the way are all external and superficial, is just such an unwieldy and overgrown establishment, cluttered with furniture and tripped up by its own traps, ruined by luxury and heedless expense, by want of calculation and a worthy aim, as the million households in the land; and the only cure for it, as for them, is in a rigid economy, a stern and more than Spartan simplicity of life and elevation of purpose. It lives too fast. Men think that it is essential that the *Nation* have commerce, and export ice, and talk through a telegraph, and ride thirty miles an hour, without a doubt, whether *they* do or not; but whether we should live like baboons or like men, is a little uncertain. If we do not get out sleepers, and forge rails, and devote days and nights to the work, but go to tinkering upon our *lives* to improve *them,* who will build railroads? And if railroads are not built, how shall we get to heaven in season? But if we stay at home and mind our business, who will want railroads? We do not ride on the railroad; it rides upon us. Did you ever think what those sleepers are that underlie the railroad? Each one is a man, an Irishman, or a Yankee man. The rails are laid on them, and they are covered with sand, and the cars run smoothly over them. They are sound sleepers, I assure you. And every few years a new lot is laid down and run over; so that, if some have the pleasure of riding on a rail, others have the misfortune to be ridden upon. And when they run over a man that is walking in his sleep, a supernumerary sleeper in the wrong position, and wake him up, they suddenly stop the cars, and make a hue and cry about it, as if this were an exception. I am glad to know that it takes a gang of men for every five miles to keep the sleepers down and level in their beds as it is, for this is a sign that they may sometime get up again.

Why should we live with such hurry and waste of life? We are determined to be starved before we are hungry. Men say that a stitch in time saves nine, and so they take a thousand stitches today to save nine tomorrow. As for *work,* we haven's any of any consequence. We have the Saint Vitus' dance, and cannot possibly keep our heads still. If I should only give a few pulls at the parish bell-rope, as for a fire, that is, without setting the bell, there is hardly a man on his farm in the outskirts of Concord, notwithstanding that press of engagements which was his excuse so many times this morning, nor a boy, nor a woman, I might almost say, but would forsake all and follow that sound, not mainly to save property from the flames, but, if we will confess the truth, much more to see it burn, since burn it must, and we, be it known, did not set it on fire—or to see it put out, and have a hand in it, if that is done as handsomely; yes, even if it were the parish church itself. Hardly a man takes a half-hour's nap after dinner, but when he wakes he holds up his head and asks, 'What's the news?' as if the rest of mankind had stood his sentinels. Some give directions to be waked every half-hour, doubtless for no other purpose; and then, to pay for it, they tell what they have dreamed. After a night's sleep the news is as indispensable as the breakfast. 'Pray tell me anything new that has happened to a man anywhere on this globe'—and he reads it over his coffee and rolls, that a man has had his eyes gouged out this morning on the Wachito River; never dreaming the while that he lives in the dark unfathomed mammoth cave of this world, and has but the rudiment of an eye himself.

For my part, I could easily do without the post-office. I think that there are very few important communications made through it. To speak critically, I never received more than one or two letters in my life—I wrote this some years ago—that were worth the postage. The penny-post is, commonly, an institution through which you seriously offer a man that penny for his thoughts which is so often safely offered in jest. And I am sure that I never read any memorable news in a newspaper. If we read of one man robbed, or murdered, or killed by accident, or one house burned, or one vessel wrecked, or one steamboat blown up, or one cow run over on the Western Railroad, or one mad dog killed, or one lot of grasshoppers in the winter—we never need read of another. One is enough. If you are acquainted with the principle, what do you care for a myriad instances and applications? To a philosopher all *news,* as it is called, is gossip, and they who edit and read it are old women over their tea. Yet not a few are greedy after this gossip. There was such a rush, as I hear, the other day at one of the offices to learn the foreign news by the last arrival, that several large squares of plate glass belonging to the establishment were broken by the pressure—news which I seriously think a ready wit might write a twelvemonth, or twelve years, beforehand with sufficient accuracy. As for Spain, for instance, if you know how to throw in Don Carlos and the Infanta, and Don Pedro and Seville and Granada, from time to time in the right proportions—they may have changed the names a little since I saw the papers—and serve up a bull-fight when other entertainments fail, it will be true to the letter, and give us as good an idea of the exact state or ruin of things in Spain as the most succinct and lucid reports under this head in the newspapers; and as for England, almost the last significant scrap of news from that quarter was the revolution of 1649; and if you have learned the history of her crops for an average year, you never need attend to that thing again, unless your speculations are of a merely pecuniary character. If one may judge who rarely looks into the newspapers, nothing new does ever happen in foreign parts, a French revolution not excepted.

20 What news! how much more important to know what that is which was never old! 'Kieou-he-yu (great dignitary of the state of Wei) sent a man to Khoung-tseu to know his news, Khoung-tseu caused the messenger to be seated near him, and questioned him in these terms; What is your master doing? The messenger answered with respect: My master desires to diminish the number of his faults, but he cannot come to the end of them. The messenger being gone, the philosopher remarked: 'What a worthy messenger! What a worthy messenger?' The preacher, instead of vexing the ears of drowsy farmers on their day of rest at the end of the week—for Sunday is the fit conclusion of an ill-spent week, and not the fresh and brave beginning of a new one—with this one other draggle-tail of a sermon, should shout with thundering voice, 'Pause! Avast! Why so seeming fast, but deadly slow?'

Shams and delusions are esteemed for soundest truths, while reality is fabulous. If men would steadily observe realities only, and not allow themselves to be deluded, life, to compare it with such things as we know, would be like a fairy tale and the Arabian Nights' Entertainments. If we respected only what is inevitable and has a right to be, music and poetry would resound along the streets. When we are unhurried and wise, we perceive that only great and worthy things have any permanent and absolute existence, that petty fears and petty pleasures are but the shadow of the reality. This is always exhilarating and sublime. By closing the eyes and slumbering, and consenting to be deceived by shows, men establish and confirm their daily life of routine and habit everywhere, which still is built on purely illusory foundations. Children, who play life, discern its true law and relations more clearly than men, who fail to live it worthily, but who think that they are wiser by experience, that is, by failure. I have read in a Hindoo book, that 'there was a king's son, who, being expelled in infancy from his native city, was brought up by a forester, and, growing up to maturity in that state, imagined himself to belong to the barbarous race with which he lived. One of his father's ministers having discovered him, revealed to him what he was, and the misconception of his character was removed, and he knew himself to be a prince. So soul,' continues the Hindoo philosopher, 'from the circumstances in which it is placed, mistakes its own character, until the truth is revealed to it by some holy teacher, and then it knows itself to be *Brahme.*' I perceive that we inhabitants of New England live this mean life that we do' because our vision does not penetrate the surface of things. We think that that *is* which *appears* to be. If a man should walk through this town and see only the reality, where, think you, would the 'Mill-dam' go to? If he should give us an account of the realities he beheld there, we should not recognize the place in his description. Look at a meeting-house, or a court-house, or a jail, or a shop, or a dwelling-house, and say what that thing really is before a true gaze, and they would all go to pieces in your account of them. Men esteem truth remote, in the outskirts of the system, behind the farthest star, before Adam and after the last man. In eternity there is indeed something true and sublime. But all these times and places and occasions are now and here. God himself culminates in the present moment, and will never be more divine in the lapse of all the ages. And we are enabled to apprehend at all what is sublime and noble only by the perpetual instilling and drenching of the reality that surrounds us. The universe constantly and obediently answers to our conceptions; whether we travel fast or slow, the track is laid for us. Let us spend our lives in conceiving then. The poet or the artist never yet had so fair and noble a design but some of his posterity at least could accomplish it.

Let us spend one day as deliberately as Nature, and not be thrown off the track by every nutshell and mosquito's wing that falls on the rails. Let us rise early and fast, or break fast, gently and without perturbation; let company come and let company go, let the bells ring and the children cry—determined to make a day of it. Why should we knock under and go with the stream? Let us not be upset and overwhelmed in that terrible rapid and whirlpool called a dinner, situated in the meridian shallows. Weather this danger and you are safe, for the rest of the way is down hill. With unrelaxed nerves, with morning vigor, sail by it, looking another way, tied to the mast like Ulysses. If the engine whistles, let it whistle till it is hoarse for its pains. If the bell rings, why should we run? We will consider what kind of music they are like. Let us settle ourselves, and work and wedge our feet downward through the mud and slush of opinion, and prejudice, and tradition, and delusion, and appearance, that alluvion which covers the globe, through Paris and London, through New York and Boston and Concord, through Church and State, through poetry and philosophy and religion, till we come to a hard bottom and rocks in place, which we can call *reality*, and say, This is, and no mistake; and then begin, having a *point d'appui*, below freshet and frost and fire, a place where you might found a wall or a state, or set a lamp-post safely, or perhaps a gauge, not a Nilometer, but a Realometer, that future ages might know how deep a freshet of shams and appearances had gathered from time to time. If you stand right fronting and face to face to a fact, you will see the sun glimmer on both its surfaces, as if it were a cimeter, and feel its sweet edge dividing you through the heart and marrow, and so you will happily conclude your mortal career. Be it life or death, we crave only reality. If we are really dying, let us hear the rattle in our throats and feel cold in the extremities; if we are alive, let us go about our business.

Time is but the stream I go a-fishing in. I drink at it; but while I drink I see the sandy bottom and detect how shallow it is. Its thin current slides away, but eternity remains. I would drink deeper; fish in the sky, whose bottom is pebbly with stars. I cannot count one. I know not the first letter of the alphabet. I have always been regretting that I was not as wise as the day I was born. The intellect is a cleaver; it discerns and rifts its way into the secret of things. I do not wish to be any more busy with my hands than is necessary. My head is hands and feet. I feel all my best faculties concentrated in it. My instinct tells me that my head is an organ for burrowing, as some creatures use their snout and fore paws, and with it I would mine and burrow my way through these hills. I think that the richest vein is somewhere hereabouts; so by the divining-rod and thin rising vapors I judge; and here I will begin to mine.

Mapping the Text

1. The title of this essay is "Where I Lived, and What I Lived For." How, in your estimation, does Thoreau address these questions? Where does he consider himself having "lived"? What has he lived for? How does he explain his motives for withdrawing from the society of his times?
2. A writer has the option of choosing from among a variety of literary and nonliterary forms of expression or *genres*. Literary genres include fiction (novels, short stories), nonfiction (narratives, essays), poetry, and drama. In addition to literary forms, there are others that we typically do not

think of as literature; these include letters, journals, diaries, and reports. A particular choice depends on the writer's purpose, audience, context, and material conditions (such as access to technological resources). Thoreau chose the *essay.* Consider Thoreau's choice and answer the following questions:

a. Describe the *audience* to whom Thoreau seems to be speaking.
b. What does he seem to want to accomplish by writing this essay? What is his *purpose?*
c. How would you describe the *context* in which he was writing? What *conditions* permitted or constrained his ability to say what was on his mind?
d. What do you think that he was saying? What was his *message?*
e. By what means do you think Thoreau developed the comfort, confidence, or *authority* to write in public?
f. Having read this one essay, how would you describe Thoreau as a person? From what features of the essay itself do you receive this impression? In other words, what sort of *presence, sense of self,* or *ethos* does he convey to his readers? Given what he says and how he says it, what do we think of him? What does he seem to think of himself?

3. Look at the sentences below that are taken from Thoreau's essay. What do these sentences suggest about Thoreau's *attitude* toward the landscape?

> Wherever I sat, there I might live, and the landscape radiated from me accordingly. What is a house but a *sedes,* a seat?—better if a country seat.
>
> I retained the landscape, and I have since annually carried off what it yielded without a wheelbarrow.
>
> There was pasture enough for my imagination.
>
> I discovered that my house actually had its site in such a withdrawn, but forever new and unprofaned, part of the universe.

4. Apparently, Thoreau is complaining about something in this essay or speaking up about something that seems to be a concern for him. What is his complaint/concern? What sorts of *evidence* does he use to make you, the reader, see his point?

Writing to Inquire

1. Write a journal entry in which you describe "the spot," the ideal site where you would want to live. Explain what makes this site so appealing to you. Share your view of an ideal site with two classmates and discuss what your views have in common, and how they differ.

2. In building a cabin on the shore of a pond, Thoreau made an odd choice even for his own day. What made the choice odd? Would a person today be able to make the same choice? How would this person's actions be perceived by a contemporary community? Would issues of personal identity (race, class, gender, culture) matter in making such a choice today? Did Thoreau's race, class, gender, or culture make any difference in his ability to make his choice? For example, would he have been able to live and work as he did if he were female? working class? African-American or Native American?
3. Imagine yourself living in the era in which Thoreau was writing. How would someone with your personal history be living? What would the material conditions of his or her life be in terms of food, clothing, shelter; work and income level; possibilities for the future? What implications do you see of race and ethnicity, class, gender, cultural beliefs, sexual preferences, physical abilities, and so forth?
4. *Transcendentalism* was a popular movement during Thoreau's day. Do some research to explore the following questions: What was transcendentalism about? Who participated in this movement? What sorts of beliefs did its proponents hold? In what sorts of activities did they engage? Write a summary definition based on your research and share it with your classmates.
5. Transcendentalism was just one movement that was important during the nineteenth century. Others include *abolitionism, woman's suffrage,* the *clubwomen's movement,* the *labor movement,* and the *common school movement.* Choose one of these movements (or perhaps some other that you identify on your own) as a project for library research.
6. To what extent is the way we live today dictated by the social norms of the community? How free are we to live as we choose? What factors constrain our choices? How would Thoreau write about today's society?

READINGS FOR INQUIRY AND EXPLORATION

From *Life As We Know It*

MICHAEL BÈRUBÈ

Michael Bèrubè is a professor of English at Penn State. His published books include *The Employment of English: Theory, Jobs, and the Future of Literary Studies* (1998), *Higher Education Under Fire: Politics, Economics, and the Crisis of the Humanities* (1995), and *Public Access: Literary Theory and Cultural Politics* (1994). Bèrubè has been concerned throughout his work to account for the cultural value and importance of literary study, and at the same time to render literary studies accountable to broader public audiences and pressures. The excerpt below is the introduction to *Life As We Know It*, a book that chronicles Bèrubè's experiences as the parent of a young child with Down syndrome.

My little Jamie loves lists: foods, colors, animals, numbers, letters, states, classmates, parts of the body, days of the week, modes of transportation, characters who live on Sesame Street, and the names of the people who love him. Early last summer, I hoped his love of lists—and his ability to catalogue things *into* lists—would stand him in good stead during what would undoubtedly be a difficult "vacation" for anyone, let alone a three-year-old child with Down syndrome: a three-hour drive to Chicago, a rush-hour flight to LaGuardia, a cab to Grand Central, a train to Connecticut—and *then* smaller trips to New York, Boston, and Old Orchard Beach, Maine. Even accomplishing the first of these mission objectives—arriving safely at O'Hare—required a precision and teamwork I do not always associate with my family. I dropped off Janet and nine-year-old Nick at the terminal with the baggage, then took Jamie to long-term parking with me while they checked in, and then entertained Jamie all the way back to the terminal, via bus and shuttle train. We sang about the driver on the bus, and we counted all the escalator steps and train stops, and when we finally got to our plane, I told Jamie, *Look, there's Mommy and Nick at the gate! They're yelling that we're going to lose our seats! They want to know why it took us forty-five minutes to park the car!*

All went well from that point on, though, and in the end, I suppose you could say Jamie got as much out of his vacation as might any toddler being whisked up and down New England. He's a seasoned traveler, and he thrives on shorelines, family gatherings, and New Haven pizza. And he's good with faces and names.

Then again, as we learned toward the end of our brief stay in Maine, he doesn't care much for amusement parks. Not that Nick did either, at three. But apparently one of the attractions of Old Orchard Beach, for my wife and her siblings, was the small beachfront arcade and amusement park in town, which they associated with their own childhoods. It was an endearing strip, with a roller coaster just the right size for Nick—exciting, mildly scary, but with no loop-the-loops, rings of fire, or oppressive G forces. We strolled among bumper cars, cotton candy, games of chance and skill, and a striking number of French-Canadian tourists: perhaps the first time our two little boys had ever seen more than one Bérubé family in one place. James, however, wanted nothing to do with any of the rides, and though he loves to pretend-drive and has been on bumper cars before, he squalled so industriously before the ride began as to induce the bumper cars operator to let him out of the car and refund his two tickets.

Jamie finally settled in next to a train ride designed for children five and under or thereabouts, which, for two tickets, took its passengers around an oval layout and over a bridge four times. I found out quickly enough that Jamie didn't want to *ride* the ride; he merely wanted to stand at its perimeter, grasping the partition with both hands and counting the cars—one, two, three, four, five, six—as they went by. Sometimes, when the train traversed the bridge, James would punctuate it with tiny jumps, saying, "Up! up! up!" But for the most part, he was content to hang onto the metal bars of the partition, grinning and counting—and, when the train came to a stop, pulling my sleeve and saying, "More, again."

5 This went on for about half an hour, well past the point at which I could convincingly share Jamie's enthusiasm for tracking the train's progress. As it went on my spirits began to sink in a way I do not recall having felt before. Occasionally it will occur to Janet or to me that Jamie will always be "disabled," that his adult and adolescent years will undoubtedly be more difficult emotionally—for him and for us—than his early childhood, that we will never *not* worry about his future, his quality of life, whether we're doing enough for him. But usually these moments occur in the relative comfort of abstraction, when Janet and I are lying in bed at night and wondering what will become of us all. When I'm *with* Jamie, by contrast, I'm almost always fully occupied by taking care of his present needs rather than by worrying about his future. When he asks to hear the Beatles because he loves their cover of Little Richard's "Long Tall Sally," I just play the song, sing along, and watch him dance with delight; I do not concern myself with extraneous questions such as whether he'll ever distinguish early Beatles from late Beatles, Paul's songs from John's, originals from covers. These questions are now central to Nick's enjoyment of the Beatles, but that's Nick for you. Jamie is entirely sui generis, and as long as I'm with him I can't think of him as anything but Jamie.

I have tried. Almost as a form of emotional exercise, I have tried, on occasion, to step back and see him as others might see him, as an instance of a category, one item on the long list of human subgroups. *This is a child with Down syndrome,* I say to myself. *This is a child with a developmental disability.* It never works: Jamie remains Jamie to me. I have even tried to imagine him as he would have been seen in other eras, other places; *This is a retarded child.* And even: *This is a Mongoloid child.* This makes for unbearable cognitive dissonance. I can imagine that people might think such things, but I cannot imagine how they might think them in a way that prevents them from seeing Jamie *as* Jamie. I try to recall how I saw such children when I was a child, but here I guiltily draw a blank: I don't remember seeing them at all, which very likely means that I never quite saw them *as* children. Instead I remember a famous passage from Ludwig Wittgenstein's *Philosophical Investigations:* "'Seeing-as' is not part of perception. And for this reason it is *like* seeing, and then again *not* like." Reading Wittgenstein, I often think, is something like listening to a brilliant and cantankerous uncle with an annoying fondness for koans. But on this one, I know exactly what he means.

As Jamie counted the train cars and urged them up, up, up for maybe the sixteenth time, I actually began to see him differently—and then to catch myself doing it. Seeing, then seeing-as, then seeing. He was not like the other children his size, who were riding the train with the usual varieties of distress and delight, and he was *noticeably* different. I began to see other parents looking at him with solicitude, curiosity, pity . . . and I thought, well, it's better than fear or disgust, but I still don't like it. Once last year, on our way back from visiting a local apple orchard, Janet told me that she'd seen other parents looking at James with an expression she read as *So that's what they're like when they're little,* and she said she'd sent those parents telepathic messages saying, *Don't be looking at my child, who's perfectly well behaved; keep an eye on your own child, the one who's pushing everybody else out of the wagon.* But this was different. Here, at a ride for small children, Jamie seemed clearly . . . limited. Not just unwilling, but somehow *unable* to enjoy the ride as "normal" children were supposed to enjoy it.

Finally, one mother approached us and asked Jamie (I was glad she asked us by asking Jamie directly, instead of asking me) if he would like to ride the train with her daughter. "Would you like to go on the train with this little girl?" I said, hoisting him up. "Nooooooo," said James, arching his back and repelling as best he could. "Down, down," he added, pointing to the ground. "Thanks very much," I said to the girl's mother. "He just loves watching the train, but he really doesn't want to go on. It was very nice of you to ask." She stayed by us for the duration of her daughter's ride, during which I engaged Jamie in a discussion of whether his classmates might ride the train:

"Does Madison ride a train?"

10 Jamie nodded "hm" (a shorthand "yes" he learned from his mother), then cocked his head and went into his "list" mode: "How 'bout . . . um . . . Keegan." Sometimes when Jamie gets pensive and says, "How 'bout, um," he's really thinking hard; sometimes, I think, he's just going through a routine he's learned from watching what pensive people do.

"Oh yes, Keegan rides a train," I assured him.

"How 'bout . . . um . . . Thaniel."

"Yes, Nathaniel also rides a train." (Good *th,* I thought.)

"How 'bout . . . um . . . Timmy."

15 "Timmy can ride a train."

"Are those his friends?" the girl's mother asked me.

"Yeah," I replied. "I'm hoping he'll get the idea that he can go on the train, too. Failing that, I'll settle for reminding him that he goes back to day care next week." But by this time I couldn't care less whether he went on the damn train; I just wanted him to vary his routine, to stop clutching the bars and saying "up, up, up." Not only for his benefit, or for the benefit of anyone who might be looking at him, but for my benefit; I was getting thoroughly bored with Jamie's take on the amusement park.

Suddenly I realized why Jamie's demeanor had been bothering me, why he had begun to seem like a "limited" child, a mere member of a *genus;* He was reminding me of a passage in William Faulkner's *The Sound and the Fury,* an image of Benjy Compson clutching the front gate and watching the "normal" children fearfully pass him by:

> *Aint nothing going to quiet him, T.P. said. He think if he down to the gate, Miss Caddy come back.*
>
> *Nonsense, Mother said.*
>
> I could hear them talking. I went out the door and I couldn't hear them, and I went down to the gate, where the girls passed with their booksatchels. They looked at me, walking fast, with their heads turned. I tried to say, but they went on, and I went along the fence, trying to say, and they went faster. Then they were running and I came to the corner of the fence and I couldn't go any further, and I held to the fence, looking after them and trying to say.

And then I remembered the very young Benjy, held tenderly by his sister Caddy after their mother has called him a "poor baby";

> We stopped in the hall and Caddy knelt and put her arms around me and her cold bright face against mine. She smelled like trees.
>
> "You're not a poor baby. Are you. Are you. You've got your Caddy. Haven't you got your Caddy."

It's one of the novel's earliest portraits of Caddy Compson; unlike her obsessively self-dramatizing mother, she loves Benjy too much to allow herself the distance of pity. The scene could not be more important to the emotional drama of Faulkner's novel. Caddy is so compelling and sympathetic a character precisely because she alone, of all the Compsons, consistently treats Benjy with a tenderness and compassion that never descends to condescension. Benjy is in this sense the key to the novel's moral index; *Whatsoever you do to the least of my brothers* . . . and when Caddy is banished from the household Benjy loses the only blood relative who has empathy enough to understand his desires. Not for nothing are Caddy and Benjy among the most unforgettable characters in the literature of our century. For all its famous narrative pyrotechnics, *The Sound and the Fury* is at bottom a novel of characters; doomed Caddy, brooding Quentin, demonic Jason, stoic Dilsey, and retarded Benjy, whose primary senses and emotions are painfully acute but who has no sense of the passage of time, no sense of good or evil. Most of Faulkner's readers know that the title of the novel alludes to the final soliloquy of Shakespeare's *Macbeth;*

> *Life's but a walking shadow, a poor player*
> *That struts and frets his hour upon the stage,*
> *And then is heard no more. It is a tale*
> *Told by an idiot, full of sound and fury,*
> *Signifying nothing.*

And, I suppose plenty of people (though all too few of my students) know that Benjy is part of a noble lineage in Western Lit, from *King Lear* to Dostoyevsky to *Forrest Gump.* But not too many readers know that Faulkner based his portrait of Benjy Compson on a local Mississippi man with Down syndrome.

Later that night we went out for—what else?—seafood. Jamie loves fish, particularly salmon, and he is both entertained and perplexed by picture-book portraits of grizzly bears plucking and devouring live salmon from the river. "Are you like a hungry bear?" I ask James. "Do you gobble the salmon all up?" "Hm," Jamie nods, and he's not kidding: we've seen him pack away half a pound of salmon at a sitting, all the while putting one index finger to pursed lips and saying, "More."

20 So James had a great time at dinner, as we expected. Then, after dinner, he felt like tooling around the restaurant a little. It was a large place and touted itself as a "family" restaurant, which meant it allowed for a lot of high chairs, booster seats, small portions, spills, dropped utensils, and noise. I figured a wandering toddler, supervised by Dad, wouldn't constitute a breach of decorum. Luckily, a whole section of the restaurant lay empty—about ten tables against the wall, on a platform raised two steps above the rest of the floor, punctuated by a bar and a TV. For now, the area was serving as a station for waitresses on break and hockey fans watching game four of the Stanley Cup finals between Detroit and New Jersey. "Well, I know you want to see the game," Janet said to me. "Why don't you just shepherd him over there?"

So I kept one eye on the Stanley Cup finals and one eye on Jamie, as he methodically walked to each table, babbled spiritedly to himself, and shuttled back and forth to a small slate fireplace—dormant, of course, in late June. But it wasn't until he got to a table near me that I overheard some of his babbling: "Taco," he was saying. "Hm. Chicken. Okay." He nodded, and then off he went to the fireplace.

I frowned. *No, it can't be.* But then, he *is* awfully mimetic, isn't he? Doesn't he pretend to make coffee in the morning? Doesn't he try to toss the salad, set the table, and sweep up all the debris under his chair after dinner? *But he wouldn't come up with something so elaborate. Not at three years of age.* Well, wait. Here he comes. He stops at one table, then proceeds to another where he seems, by his account, to be depositing pizza and burgers. I know the menu; all of these are items from his list of favorite foods. I abandon the hockey game, take a seat at a nearby table, and call him over. "Jamie?" He walks over. "Are you the waiter?"

"Hm," he hms brightly, eyes wide, clearly delighted that I've picked up on this.

"Can you get me . . . let's see . . . a tuna sandwich?"

"Tuna!" he half-shouts in a hoarse little voice, and heads back to the fireplace. Did I imagine him pretending to write that down? I must have imagined it. He's extraordinarily mimetic, all right, as so many children are, but he doesn't usually get the tiny details; he's more comfortable with the general idea. I mean, he moves the dustbuster around, but he doesn't get *all* the rice, not by a long shot. He knows the route Janet traverses to make coffee, but he doesn't understand that the water has to go *into* the coffee pot. He's three years old, and like the Cat in the Hat, he makes a mess. But I know I *wanted* to think he wrote down my order.

He eventually got back to my table, but I don't remember whether he remembered that I'd asked for a tuna sandwich. By this point I was lost in the same kind of reverie that had possessed me at the amusement park, only this time I knew Jamie had no literary antecedents. He had decided that this wing of the restaurant was his, that these tables were peopled by customers wanting tacos, chicken, pizza, burgers, fries, and tuna (no green beans, no peach melba, no broccoli, no strawberries), that the fireplace was the kitchen, and that he was the waiter. This was the child who'd seemed so "limited" at the amusement park? The adults who'd seen him that afternoon may have seen him as a retarded child, as a disabled child, as a child to be pitied; and the children, if they were children like the child I was, may not have "seen" him at all. They certainly wouldn't have seen the distinct little person with whom I went to the restaurant that evening—a three year old whose ability to imitate is intimately tied to his remarkable ability to imagine, and whose ability to imagine, in turn, rests almost entirely on his capacity to imagine *other people.* Sure, his imagination has its limits; they're evident in the menu. He imagines people who order *his* list of foods, and yes, that list is (by any nutritionist's standards) limited. But the ability to imagine what other people might like, what other people might need—that seems to me a more crucial, more *essential* ability for human beings to cultivate than the ability to ride trains round and round. After we got back to our motel, after New Jersey had won the Cup, after the kids were finally asleep, I looked out over the beach and wondered whether Janet and I would always be able to understand what Jamie wants and needs, and whether our ability to imagine his desires will be commensurate with his ability to imagine ours.

Meanwhile, as Jamie was fussing about bumper cars, serving entrees to imaginary diners, and splashing in the waves, the 104th U.S. Congress was debating how to balance the federal budget by slashing programs for the disabled and the mentally handicapped; electricians and construction workers in New Haven were putting the final touches on preparations for the 1995 Special Olympics World Games; researchers with the Human Genome Project were trying to locate the biochemical basis for all our variances; and millions of ordinary human beings, all of them women, were undergoing prenatal testing for "severe" genetic defects like Down syndrome.

Jamie has no idea what a busy intersection he's landed in; statutes, allocations, genetics, reproduction, representation—all meeting at the crossroads of individual idiosyncrasy and sociopolitical construction. "Value" may be something that can only be determined socially, by collective and chaotic human deliberation; but individual humans like James are compelling us daily to determine what *kind* of "individuality" we will value, on what terms, and why. Perhaps those of us who can understand this intersection have an obligation to "represent" the children who can't; perhaps we have an obligation to inform our children about the traffic, and to inform the traffic about our children. As those children grow, perhaps we need to foster their abilities to represent themselves—and to listen to them as they do. I strongly suspect that we do have those obligations. I am not entirely sure what they might entail. But it is part of my purpose, in writing this book, to represent Jamie as best I can—just as it is part of my purpose, in representing Jamie, to ask about our obligations to each other, individually and socially, and about our capacity to imagine other people. I cannot say why it is that we possess the capacity to imagine others, let alone the capacity to imagine that we might have *obligations* to others; nor do I know why, if we possess such things, we so habitually act as if we do not. But I do know that Jamie has compelled me to ask these questions anew, just as I know how crucial it is that we collectively cultivate our capacities to imagine our obligations to each other.

Mapping the Text

1. Bèrubè describes some different ways of looking at his young son Jamie. What are some of the different perspectives he might take? What role

does language play in these differences? What difference does it make to call Jamie "retarded"? "Mongoloid"?

2. How does Bèrubè create a persona for himself in this selection? How does it matter to you as a reader that he is writing from his own experience as a father? How would this essay have been different if he were writing about someone else's child? About disabled children in general?

5. What are the obligations to others that we might have, according to Bèrubè? How does this essay define and explore those obligations? What cultural and social obligations do we have to children like Jamie?

Writing to Inquire

1. Research the history of medical and social attitudes toward people with Down syndrome. How has our view of these people changed? What still needs to change?

2. Explore the language used historically to describe mental disabilities. How has language change been related to broader changes in social attitudes and public policy? Does language make a difference in the identities and lives of children like Jamie? How? Why?

The God of Small Feasts

Shoba Narayan

Shoba Narayan (1968–) is a freelance journalist who covers finance, technology, food, and culture. She has published articles in several newspapers and magazines, including the *Wall Street Journal,* the *New York Times,* the *Boston Globe, Newsweek, House Beautiful,* and several others. The essay below appeared in *Gourmet* and won the James Beard Foundation's M.F.K. Fisher Distinguished Writing Award in 2001, the most prestigious food writing award in the United States.

"Here," said my mother, pressing a dark-brown slab of one of her mysterious cooking ingredients into my hands. "Smell this."

I was nine. I obeyed.

"It smells stinky," I said, wrinkling my nose as I turned over the hard, pock marked resin in my palm. "Like a ...," I giggled, unable to say the rude word.

My mother smiled, as if I had understood some fundamental cooking concept. "It's asafetida," she said. "You sprinkle it on foods like beans and lentils so they won't give you gas."

5 We were standing in our cavernous kitchen, the mosaic-tiled floor cool against my bare feet, my mother in her starched cotton sari and me in my

pigtails and skirt, ready to flee. On the raw cement walls, smoke from the wood-burning stove left stains in Rorschach-like blotches. My mother was making yet another attempt to reveal to me the mysteries of South Indian cooking. I was more interested in fighting with the boys over cricket balls.

Cooking—and eating—in India is a communal activity governed by a complex system of rules, rituals, and beliefs. My mother recited examples to me whenever she got the chance. Cumin and cardamom arouse, so eat them only after you get married, she instructed. Fenugreek tea makes your hair lustrous and increases breast milk, so drink copious amounts when you have babies. Coriander seeds cool the body during summer; mustard and sesame seeds lend heat during winter. Cardamom aids digestion, cinnamon soothes, and lentils build muscles. Every feast should have the three P's; *pappadams, pachadi,* and *payasam* (lentil wafers, yogurt salad, and sweet pudding). Any new bride should be able to make a decent *rasam* (*dal*-and-tomato soup). If you cannot make *rasam,* do not call yourself the lady of the house. And so it went.

At nine, I had little interest in such matters. The kitchen was merely a place I might dart into between aiming catapults at sleepy chameleons and playing under the banyan tree in our overgrown garden. And, in a household headed by my grandmother and teeming with 14 cousins, four pairs of aunts and uncles, numerous servants, and any number of visiting relatives, there were always plenty of others to do the cooking.

The only time we youngsters were conscripted into helping out in the kitchen was during the annual *shraadam,* a daylong ceremony, celebrated on the anniversary of my grandfather's death, when the entire clan gathered to pay obeisance to our ancestors. The servants were given the day off, and the women cooked an elaborate 24-course feast—enough food to feed not just the family but 12 Brahman priests, our two cows, and all the crows in the neighborhood. The women would lay down banana leaves in the grass, arranging food as carefully for the birds as they did for the guests indoors. Crows are believed to carry the souls of forebears. The more crows we fed, the better it would be for our lineage.

On *shraadam* day, the whole household awoke before dawn. My grandmother stood in the middle of the kitchen, bellowing orders like an army general. There were strict rules. Everything had to be fresh and prepared according to a menu that had been decided on generations ago. Dairy and grains couldn't mix and were placed at opposite ends of the kitchen. Later, hands had to be washed after touching leftovers.

10 Blurred figures rushed about within the smoky mists, boiling water, stirring the *ghee,* grinding coconut, roasting spices. Coal embers glowed like beacons under heavy bronze cauldrons filled with rice. My cousins and I scampered between pantry and kitchen, ferrying ingredients back and forth. My mother and aunts chopped vegetables at a furious pace as my grandmother presided over the stove.

There were many such feasts in our household. After a meal's end, the curtains were drawn in the living room. As the ceiling fan swirled lazily overhead, the women sat cross-legged on bamboo mats, a brass betel tray in the center. In it were stacks of betel leaves, chewed as digestives, surrounded by crushed betel nuts, tobacco paste, and an assortment of fragrant spices—sugar-coated fennel, nutmeg, and cardamom wrapped in pieces of silver foil.

The women brushed the tender betel leaves with tobacco paste, filled them with the nuts and spices, then folded the leaves into triangles called *paan*. They popped these into their mouths, chewing gently until their tongues and teeth were stained red from the opiate combination.

With each *paan* they chewed, their jokes grew more risqué, their gossip more personal, and their bodies more horizontal. Soon, the room would be full of red-toothed, shrieking, laughing, swaying women that I hardly recognized as the same harassed housewives who were constantly shooing us children out of the way.

I would rest my head on my grandmother's squishy abdomen and feel her soft flesh rumble as she belly-laughed her way to tears. Although I didn't realize it at the time, this would be the closest I'd ever come to feeling totally at peace.

15 Inevitably, however, the conversation would turn toward errant offspring and how young girls ought to learn cooking as preparation for later life. I would sneak a betel leaf and scurry away. I had no intention of being court-martialed by a bevy of relatives trying to entice, entreat, or threaten me into the kitchen.

I continued to spurn cooking into my adolescence. When I reached 14, by some mysterious alchemy—was it genes? destiny?—a passion for the sensuality of food slowly, slowly began to take root. Ever the rebel, I kept it a secret.

Madras, India, 1986. At 18, I have just been accepted into Mount Holyoke College, in South Hadley, Massachusetts, but the consensus in my family is that I shouldn't go. America is full of muggers and all kinds of criminals, my teenage pest of a brother proclaims. No unmarried girl should venture into such a promiscuous society, my septuagenarian grandmother adds. Why go abroad to study when there are world-class Indian institutions to choose from here? an uncle asks. Get married first, my mother says with finality—then go to Timbuktu if you want.

After days of pleading, the elders relent a bit. I am to cook them a vegetarian feast with the perfect balance of spices and flavors. It is a test, one they are sure I will fail. And in it lies my destiny. If my meal is a success, I can go to the United States.

The elders pick a Friday, considered an auspicious day by many Hindus, for my debut as a cook. Though they've given me this advantage, they try to hide their smirks as they inform me that I need not stretch myself. They are not looking for complex *masalas* or complicated curries, merely good food.

20 I begin with tender green beans, forgiving and flexible, which I cut into small pieces and sauté in oil with mustard seeds and *urad dal*. I sprinkle the

beans with desiccated coconut, watching as the thin strips flutter downward: falling tea leaves foretelling my future.

I chop cucumbers, tomatoes, and red onions for the *pachadi* and douse them in thick yogurt, over which I arrange fresh green cilantro in concentric swirls. Under the yogurt-white landscape the red onions appear like bluish veins. Red tomatoes, white yogurt, and blue onions. Red, white, and blue. Is it an omen, or just my imagination?

I tease some spinach over a low flame until it blossoms into a green as deep and bright as the eye of the ocean—and smile with secret satisfaction. The spinach is for *palak paneer,* the one dish in my menu that is not from South India and that will stand out as a misfit. Renegade food made by a rebel; the thought pleases me. I purée the spinach and stir in asafetida, tomatoes, pearl onions, and cubes of creamy fried *paneer*—fresh cheese with the texture of warm tofu—suppressing a bubble of laughter.

Tomatoes brew in tamarind water with turmeric and salt as I cook red lentils. I blend them in, garnishing the *rasam* with cilantro, mustard seeds, and roasted cumin. The scent of cilantro perfumes the air and soothes my soul.

Tomato *rasam* is the vegetarian's equivalent of chicken soup. It's the only comfort food I know. When the monsoons ravaged the red earth of my homeland, my grandmother would purée the *rasam* with sticky rice and add a spoonful of warm *ghee.* We would watch the swaying trees arch under the sheets of rain, contentedly spooning the *rasam*-rice mixture from silver bowls.

25 I hover over virgin rice, cooking it until each grain is softened but doesn't stick. I stir in turmeric soaked in lemon juice, then ginger, peanuts, and curry leaves I've fried in oil. The rice looks like a painter's palette. Cadmium yellow speckled with burnt sienna.

As sweet butter turns into golden *ghee,* the food of gods, the litany I learned at my mother's knee echoes in my head; *Ghee* promotes growth, ginger soothes, garlic rejuvenates. My grandfather eluded the cholesterol police by drinking a tumblerful daily and living till 104.

Dessert is a simple *payasam,* rice pudding, with roasted pistachios, plump raisins, and strands of saffron strewn on top. The feast ends with aromatic South Indian coffee, a mixture of ground plantation and peaberry beans with a dash of chicory. I filter the coffee powder through a muslin cloth, then mix it with boiling cow's milk that froths on top and, following my mother's prescription, just enough sugar to take out the bitterness but add nothing to the taste.

The elders arrive, resplendent as peacocks in their silk saris and gleaming white dhotis made from spun Madras cotton. Even my teenage cousins are dressed to kill. They survey the ancient rosewood table that totters under the weight of the stainless-steel containers I have filled. I arrange banana leaves on the floor and invite everyone to sit down on the bamboo mats.

My guests pick and sample, judiciously at first. They don't want to eat, but they can't stop themselves. They fight over the last piece of *paneer,* taste overtaking caution. Grandma leans back and belches unapologetically.

30 I can go to America.

Mapping the Text

1. When we pay attention to the cultural practices of a group of people, we can begin to see how its members create a meaningful *context* for the things that they do. Make a list of things that you learn about the family in this narrative from the rules, rituals, and beliefs that the author shares.
2. Narayan writes her narrative for readers of an American magazine. What elements—words, phrases, sentences, images, metaphors—in the narrative show evidence that she is writing for an *audience* who did not grow up the way that she did?
3. What is the *effect* of Narayan's choice to talk about herself and her family through an explanation of some of their cooking and eating rituals? How is the reader affected?
4. What *message*(s) do you take from this narrative? What more do you wonder about?
5. Having read this narrative, how would you describe the author? From what features of the narrative do you receive this impression? What *sense of self* or *ethos* does she convey to her readers?

Writing to Inquire

1. What views of women do you get from this narrative—the author herself, her mother, her grandmother, others? How are these views of women like or different from your own?
2. Many people have family stories or stories about friendships that relate to eating or cooking rituals. Write a narrative about a food ritual and explain how the memory or experience is meaningful to you. Does this ritual suggest anything about your own sense of identity?

Phenomenal Woman

MAYA ANGELOU

Maya Angelou (1928–), Reynolds Professor of American Studies at Wake Forest University in Winston-Salem, North Carolina, is the author of many best-selling books. She began her career in the arts as a dancer but over the course of her life has been a singer, actress, composer, choreographer, script writer, journalist, and a multigenre creative writer. Her publications include *I Know Why the Caged Bird Sings* (1970), *Just Give Me a Drink of Water 'Fore I Die* (1971), *Gather Together in My Name* (1974), *Singin' and Swingin' and Gettin' Merry Like Christmas* (1976), *And Still I Rise* (1978), *The Heart of a Woman,* (1981), *All God's Children Need Traveling Shoes* (1986), *A Song Flung Up to Heaven* (2002). She has been recognized for many of her talents, being nominated for a National Book Award, a Pulitzer Prize for Poetry, a Tony award, and an Emmy. Her highest honor, however, was bestowed by the forty-second president of the United States, William J. Clinton, who named her Inaugural Poet at his inaugural ceremony in 1992.

Pretty women wonder where my secret lies.
I'm not cute or built to suit a fashion model's size
But when I start to tell them,
They think I'm telling lies.
I say,
It's in the reach of my arms,
The span of my hips,
The stride of my step,
The curl of my lips.
I'm a woman
Phenomenally.
Phenomenal woman,
That's me.

I walk into a room
Just as cool as you please,
And to a man,
The fellows stand or
Fall down on their knees.
Then they swarm around me,
A hive of honey bees.
I say,
It's the fire in my eyes,
And the flash of my teeth,
The swing in my waist,
And the joy in my feet,
I'm a woman
Phenomenally.
Phenomenal woman,
That's me.

Men themselves have wondered
What they see in me.
They try so much

But they can't touch
My inner mystery.
When I try to show them
They say they still can't see.
I say,
It's in the arch of my back,
The sun of my smile,
The ride of my breasts,
The grace of my style.
I'm a woman
Phenomenally.
Phenomenal woman,
That's me.

Now you understand
Just why my head's not bowed.
I don't shout or jump about
Or have to talk real loud.
When you see me passing
It ought to make you proud.
I say,
It's in the click of my heels,
The bend of my hair,
the palm of my hand,
The need for my care.
'Cause I'm a woman
Phenomenally.
Phenomenal woman,
That's me.

Mapping the Text

1. Maya Angelou titles this poem "Phenomenal Woman." Which *words* and *images* in the poem help define what she means by "phenomenal"?
2. Consider your own knowledge about the experiences of African-Americans, African-American women, and women generally. What circumstances and conditions do you think Angelou might have been reacting to in the social or political environment when she wrote this poem? What do you think Angelou's *purpose* or *intention* might have been in wanting to write the poem? What do you think she wanted to accomplish as a poet? as a representative or spokeswoman for a broader social group? Describe your own reaction to the poem. In reading the poem, what did you think? How did you feel?

Writing to Inquire

1. On one hand, you might consider this poem a celebration of African-American womanhood. On another, you might consider it a statement of resistance and activism. Write an essay in which you agree or disagree with one of these *points of view.* You may offer as evidence of the rationality of your choice: what Angelou actually says in the poem, your own experiences as they are similar to or different from hers and, if you choose, related data that you collect from sources that you establish as valid and credible.

Eleven

SANDRA CISNEROS

Sandra Cisneros (1954–), a writer of novels, short stories, and essays, was among the first Hispanic writers to achieve commercial success. Her first book, *The House on Mango Street* (1983), for which she received the American Book Award from the Before Columbus Foundation, remains her most critically acclaimed work. Her other publications include *Bad Boys* (1980), *My Wicked Wicked Ways* (1987), *Woman Hollering Creek and Other Stories,* which won the PEN Center West Award for Best Fiction of 1991, and *Loose Woman* (1994). In 1995, Cisneros won a prestigious MacArthur Foundation fellowship. "Eleven," from *Woman Hollering Creek,* is told in the childish narrative voice that Cisneros employs in several of her stories.

What they don't understand about birthdays and what they never tell you is that when you're eleven, you're also ten, and nine, and eight, and seven, and six, and five, and four, and three, and two, and one. And when you wake up on your eleventh birthday you expect to feel eleven, but you don't. You open your eyes and everything's just like yesterday, only it's today. And you don't feel eleven at all. You feel like you're still ten. And you are—underneath the year that makes you eleven.

Like some days you might say something stupid, and that's the part of you that's still ten. Or maybe some days you might need to sit on your mama's lap because you're scared, and that's the part of you that's five. And maybe one day when you're all grown up maybe you will need to cry like if you're three, and that's okay. That's what I tell Mama when she's sad and needs to cry. Maybe she's feeling three.

Because the way you grow old is kind of like an onion or like the rings inside a tree trunk or like my little wooden dolls that fit one inside the other, each year inside the next one. That's how being eleven years old is.

You don't feel eleven. Not right away. It takes a few days, weeks even, sometimes even months before you say Eleven when they ask you. And you don't feel smart eleven, not until you're almost twelve. That's the way it is.

5 Only today I wish I didn't have only eleven years rattling inside me like pennies in a tin Band-Aid box. Today I wish I was one hundred and two instead of eleven because if I was one hundred and two I'd have known what to say when Mrs. Price put the red sweater on my desk. I would've known how to tell her it wasn't mine instead of just sitting there with that look on my face and nothing coming out of my mouth.

"Whose is this?" Mrs. Price says, and she holds the red sweater up in the air for all the class to see. "Whose? It's been sitting in the coatroom for a month."

"Not mine," says everybody. "Not me."

"It has to belong to somebody," Mrs. Price keeps saying, but nobody can remember. It's an ugly sweater with red plastic buttons and a collar and sleeves all stretched out like you could use it for a jump rope. It's maybe a thousand years old and even if it belonged to me I wouldn't say so.

Maybe because I'm skinny, maybe because she doesn't like me, that stupid Sylvia Saldívar says, "I think it belongs to Rachel." An ugly sweater like that, all raggedy and old, but Mrs. Price believes her. Mrs. Price takes the sweater and puts it right on my desk, but when I open my mouth nothing comes out.

10 "That's not, I don't, you're not . . . Not mine," I finally say in a little voice that was maybe me when I was four.

"Of course it's yours," Mrs. Price says. "I remember you wearing it once." Because she's older and the teacher, she's right and I'm not.

Not mine, not mine, not mine, but Mrs. Price is already turning to page thirty-two, and math problem number four. I don't know why but all of a sudden I'm feeling sick inside, like the part of me that's three wants to come out of my eyes, only I squeeze them shut tight and bite down on my teeth real hard and try to remember today I am eleven, eleven. Mama is making a cake for me for tonight, and when Papa comes home everybody will sing Happy birthday, happy birthday to you.

But when the sick feeling goes away and I open my eyes, the red sweater's still sitting there like a big red mountain. I move the red sweater to the corner of my desk with my ruler. I move my pencil and books and eraser as far from it as possible. I even move my chair a little to the right. Not mine, not mine, not mine.

In my head I'm thinking how long till lunchtime, how long till I can take the red sweater and throw it over the schoolyard fence, or leave it hanging on a parking meter, or bunch it up into a little ball and toss it in the alley. Except when math period ends Mrs. Price says loud and in front of everybody, "Now, Rachel, that's enough," because she sees I've shoved the red sweater to the tippy-tip corner of my desk and it's hanging all over the edge like a waterfall, but I don't care.

15 "Rachel," Mrs. Price says. She says it like she's getting mad. "You put that sweater on right now and no more nonsense."

"But it's not—"

"Now!" Mrs. Price says.

This is when I wish I wasn't eleven, because all the years inside of me—ten, nine, eight, seven, six, five, four, three, two, and one—are pushing at the back of my eyes when I put one arm through one sleeve of the sweater that smells like cottage cheese, and then the other arm through the other and stand there with my arms apart like if the sweater hurts me and it does, all itchy and full of germs that aren't even mine.

That's when everything I've been holding in since this morning, since when Mrs. Price put the sweater on my desk, finally lets go, and all of a sudden I'm crying in front of everybody. I wish I was invisible but I'm not. I'm eleven and it's my birthday today and I'm crying like I'm three in front of everybody. I put my head down on the desk and bury my face in my stupid clown-sweater arms. My face all hot and spit coming out of my mouth because I can't stop the little animal noises from coming out of me, until there aren't any more tears left in my eyes, and it's just my body shaking like when you have the hiccups, and my whole head hurts like when you drink milk too fast.

20 But the worst part is right before the bell rings for lunch. That stupid Phyllis Lopez, who is even dumber than Sylvia Saldivar, says she remembers the red sweater is hers! I take it off right away and give it to her, only Mrs. Price pretends like everything's okay.

Today I'm eleven. There's a cake Mama's making for tonight, and when Papa comes home from work we'll eat it. There'll be candles and presents and everybody will sing Happy birthday, happy birthday to you, Rachel, only it's too late.

I'm eleven today. I'm eleven, ten, nine, eight, seven, six, five, four, three, two, and one, but I wish I was one hundred and two. I wish I was anything but eleven, because I want today to be far away already, far away like a runaway balloon, like a tiny *o* in the sky, so tiny-tiny you have to close your eyes to see it.

Mapping the Text

1. Restate in your own words the *theme* of this story.
2. Cite some examples of the *language*—vocabulary, phrasing, structure, or other elements of language—that Cisneros uses to create a character who "sounds" eleven years old.
3. Choose at least one passage that you think illustrates problems and challenges related to the specific *identity* of the *narrator.* How do her age, social class, and family history frame her sense of self?
4. In the final passage, Cisneros writes:

> I'm eleven today. I'm eleven, ten, nine, eight, seven, six, five, four, three, two, and one, but I wish I was one hundred and two. I wish I was anything but eleven, because I want today to be far away already, far away

> like a runaway balloon, like a tiny *o* in the sky, so tiny-tiny you have to close your eyes to see it.

How does Cisneros help her reader to see and understand the *experience* that she is narrating in this story? Describe the *viewpoint* that she, apparently, wants readers to notice. What problems, issues, and concerns become visible from this view?

Writing to Inquire

1. What *response* does Cisneros seem interested in generating in her *audience?* What was your own response? What did you think, feel, believe, want to do or say? To whom? Why?
2. Consider youth or age as an identity, as a vital part of who and how you are. What age would you choose as the ideal age? How would you describe the sense of self that comes with this stage of life? What does being this age enable or prevent in terms of personal, social, or public action?

Genealogy: Quacks, Cures, and Ancestors

MYRA VANDERPOOL GORMLEY

Myra Vanderpool Gormley is a certified genealogist who has done extensive historical work on her own family and who writes about the process of conducting family research using various resources. Gormley and Julie Case are coeditors of *Missing Links Newsletter,* a weekly genealogy e-zine at [RootsWeb.com]. In this essay, Gormley discusses contextual history that can emerge and be useful in genealogical work.

Health and medical records can be a valuable source of information for those researching family histories. Whether you are compiling a family tree to aid future generations, or trying to discover how or why an ancestor died, studying these records yields a great deal of information about our forebears and how they lived.

Facing diseases, injuries, and the well-meaning, but not always enlightened, efforts of physicians and lay healers, our ancestors were lucky to survive to adulthood. The estimated life expectancy for Americans in the late 18th century was only about 35 years. One in three babies died before its sixth birthday, and fewer than half reached the age of 16. Medical care was primitive by today's standards, and most physicians had little or no formal education in the field.

The first American medical school, the Medical Department of the College of Philadelphia (now the University of Pennsylvania School of

Medicine), was established in 1765. At that time there were no meaningful licensing requirements for physicians in the 13 original colonies and no way to know if a doctor was competent. The first major advances in modern medicine did not occur until about the turn of the 19th century; a rudimentary understanding of germs and their effects on the body did not come until the end of the 19th century.

By about 1850, the American medical profession was composed of three groups; those who had studied at the medical schools located in Philadelphia, New York, Boston, Baltimore, and Lexington, Kentucky; those who were products of the preceptor system (young men who apprenticed with an established physician, usually for three years); and those who simply took the title of doctor without any special training.

5 In 1847, when medical schools still varied widely in quality and instruction standards, the newly formed American Medical Association established a committee to study medical training and, with this step, medical education improved significantly. In 1869, Harvard extended the school year of the medical college to nine months, required written and oral examinations, and established a three-year curriculum. However, not until Johns Hopkins University opened in 1876 was clinical work required as an integral part of medical training.

Meanwhile, on the frontiers of America, professional medical help was sometimes miles away, if it was available at all. Childbirth (often assisted by midwives) and childbed fever claimed many lives. Today, midwife licenses and records that can be found in county auditor offices, state archives, and historical societies are used by researchers to place a person in a time or location—especially women, who often are lost in history due to name changes when they married.

Guided by books like *Gunn's Domestic Medicine* (1837) or family recipes, our ancestors often tried to cure themselves with home remedies. Recipes can be found in old diaries, ledgers, and plantation books, many of which are in archives and historical society collections. Doctors also had their own cures and their account records and daybooks have preserved their diagnoses, treatments, and fees. In 1671, Zerolabel Endicott, who dabbled in medicine like his father, John Endicott (governor of Massachusetts, intermittently, from 1644 to 1664), revealed the ingredients for his cures for deafness: "the juice of radishes, the fat of a mole, an eel, and the juice of onion, all soaked in wine and roasted." However, it is unclear whether this mixture was swallowed or dropped into the ear.

From Colonial days through the middle of the 20th century, most of the so-called medicines or cures contained generous amounts of alcohol. One famous cure was Lydia Pinkham's Vegetable Tonic, which contained about 20 percent alcohol. In addition, remedies were sometimes laced with cocaine, caffeine, opium, or morphine.

Mortality and census schedules, death certificates, and obituaries can assist genealogists in learning about the diseases and disorders that afflicted and killed their ancestors and also aid in compiling family health trees. However, while studying these records along with old letters, diaries, doctor account- and day-books, military pension applications, and death records, researchers encounter some medical terms that are not common today. Examples include:

AGUE—usually malaria, but also applied to any fever with chills.

CHOREA (St. Vitus' Dance)—used to identify any nervous disorder.

CONSUMPTION—(phthisis pulmonalia)—a term for tuberculosis in the days when there was no effective treatment for it; characterized by a gradual wasting away of the body.

DROPSY—denoted any type of swelling.

INANITION—most commonly signified the death of infants and the elderly from the inability to assimilate food.

LA GRIPPE—known today as the flu.

MILKSICK—not a disease, but a form of poisoning. Cows that ate the leaves of the white snakeroot plant passed along its toxin in their milk.

POTTS DISEASE—the degeneration of the vertebrae, often resulting in curvature of the spine.

QUINSY—an attack of tonsillitis resulting in abscessing near the tonsils.

SEPTICEMIA—blood poisoning.

SUMMER COMPLAINT—highly infectious and a euphemism for dysentery. It earned its name from its frequent occurrence in summer.

TYPHOID FEVER—caused by unsanitary water and contaminated food or milk and carried by flies.

10 More definitions of medical terms encountered in historical references can be found in genealogical dictionaries such as *The New A to Zax* by Barbara Jean Evans and *What Did They Mean By That?* by Paul Drake. Additionally, an article in *National Genealegical Society Quarterly* (volume 76, number 4, December 1988) entitled "Disease and Death in the Nineteenth Century; Genealogical Perspective," by James Byars Carter, M.D., explains many old medical terms and provides information on their importance to genealogists.

Mapping the Text

1. The *essay* is a nonfiction *genre* that is used often *to inform* readers about something. Answer the following questions:
   a. In this essay, Gormley actually names *one audience*. Who does she name?
   b. How does she *structure* this essay to be especially informative for this group?

c. A historical *point of view* is important in this essay. How does Gormley make historical knowledge meaningful and useful in this essay?

2. The choice of words in a piece of writing helps create the *tone* and *style* of the piece. Describe the tone of the Gormley essay. When you read the essay, what kind of voice do you "hear"? For example, does it sound formal or informal; angry, serious, or humorous; professional or nonprofessional? How does the tone help you envision the person speaking? describe the person that you imagine? Based on the tone, what impression do you have of the writer? What *adjectives* would you choose to describe the *style* of the essay? What words, phrases, types of sentences help generate these impressions?

Writing to Inquire

1. Based on Gormley's essay, make a list of questions that you would ask about the history of, attitudes toward, and the names of diseases in your own family or community.
2. Think about your own efforts to maintain a healthy self. What principles for health do you or should you pay attention to? In light of such principles, what, if any, challenges do you face in upholding them? To what extent do you think health and wellness should matter to individuals? to a society? Do such *values* affect a person's sense of self or identity?

From *Black, White, and Jewish; Autobiography of a Shifting Self*

REBECCA WALKER

Rebecca Walker (1969–) is a businesswoman, activist, and writer. She founded the Third Wave Foundation, a philanthropic organization for the benefit of young women between the ages of 15 and 30. Her writing has appeared in numerous anthologies and magazines, including the *New York Times Magazine, Harper's, Elle, Ms., Utne Reader, Vibe,* and *Spin.* In *Black, White, and Jewish: Autobiography of a Shifting Self* (2001), Walker writes about growing up as the daughter of internationally renowned author Alice Walker and Mel Leventhal. The selection below is excerpted from that autobiography.

I don't remember things. Like the names of streets and avenues I have driven down a hundred times, like the stories behind Jewish holidays I have celebrated since I was eleven, like the date of my father's birthday. At a funeral for a favorite uncle, I do not remember the names of cousins I played with as a child. For a few minutes, I do not remember the name of my dead uncle's wife. On her porch I stand blankly between her outstretched arms, my head spinning, suddenly unsure even of the ground upon which I stand. Who am I and why am I here? I cannot remember how we all are related.

There are thousands of large and small omissions, bits of information I swear normal people have built into their DNA; the speed of light, so-and-so's running mate twelve years ago, the capital of Wyoming, the way Treasury bills work. Mostly, I'm not bothered by my mind's resistance to what it considers meaningless, but sometimes I feel oddly off balance, like the whole world has figured out how to cope, how to master life on the grid, but me. Without a memory that invests in information retention, without a memory that can remind me at all times of who I definitively am, I feel amorphous, missing the unbroken black outline around my body that everyone else seems to have.

A good friend has decided that Soul is Mind, that Mind describes and encompasses the larger idea of Spirit. "You cannot Be without Mind," she says, referring to something which includes, but is much larger than, her brain. Knowing well the limitations of my own mind, I am skeptical, disapproving. "It's the heart," I say, laying my flat palm over my beating organ, feeling the heat grow between skin and skin, through the cotton of my tee shirt. "You cannot have Soul without heart." I, too, am referring to something ineffable, something much larger than the muscle in my chest.

We are talking about God, I think, and memory.

5 She shakes her head no as I look at her, wanting to remember how she looks to me on this Sunday afternoon in my living room with the sun streaming through the big old windows. My mind ticks away, registering her waffled army-green tee shirt, thick silver hoops, and brown, almond-shaped eyes. I sum her up, compare her today with her another day, piece her psyche together from all the strands of her childhood that I know. My eyes do all they can and then, as if considering a collage by Bearden or a painting by van Gogh, push the task gratefully onto my dumb, mute heart.

Because when it comes time to remember this woman it will not be all perfectly articulated platitudes or carefully constructed diagnoses. When it is time to remember her after she leaves it will be my heart—lazy, slow, decidedly not smart—that will pull and yearn and twist around like a dog in dirt. It will be my heart that will force my mind to remember her face, the way she felt lying next to me in the dark, the way she looked sitting on the sofa, telling me that Mind, to her, is everything. My heart will have registered the deeper meaning snaking and elusive beneath her disparate pieces; my heart alone will allow me to remember her whole.

I remember airports. The new one with the stained-glass-windowed, art-deco waiting room in Rochester, the one with tinted light blue glass and a super-efficient McDonald's in Manchester, Pittsburgh's airport-cum-shopping center; the Sky Mall. I remember Chicago's hyper-industrial steel-and-glass-corridored O'Hare, the pink and yellow neo-Aztec pyramid in

Puerto Vallarta, the hazy, dirty carpeted halls and frenzied, wind-whipped baggage claim at LAX. I remember the SkyTel Pager booth at Atlanta International, the women in black sitting on the periphery of the giant flattened rectangle of Cairo's concrete Bedouin tent. I remember the bougainvillea bushes spilling out from clay pots at Nairobi, the Italian Modern with portholes in Milan, and the hushed, airy cathedral of blond wood and brushed aluminum in Hamburg.

I am more comfortable in airports than I am in either of the houses I call, with undeserved nostalgia, Home. I am more comfortable in airports than I was in any of the eight different schools where I learned all of the things I now cannot remember. Airports are limbo spaces—blank, undemanding, neutral. Expectations are clear. I am the passenger. I am coming or going. I am late, on time, or early. I must have a ticket. I must have identification. I must not carry a weapon. Beyond these qualifications, I do not have to define this body. I do not have to belong to one camp, school, or race, one fixed set of qualifiers, adjectives based on someone else's experience. I do not have to remember who I, or anyone else, thinks I am. I am transitional space, form-shifting space, place of a thousand hellos and a million goodbyes.

Another friend tells me hyperbolically that she enjoyed a six-month stay in jail, and that on some days she comes dizzyingly close to checking herself into the asylum. "I need to be confined," she says, and I know what she means. There is safety in four walls, in rituals boiled down into rules. Freedom can feel overwhelming. I would not trade it, but sometimes I want to be told what to do. I want to know constraints, boundaries. I want to know the limits of who I am. Tell me what I cannot do. Let me master myself within articulated limitations. Without these, I feel vast, out of control. Like I can too easily slip outside of my own life and into someone else's. Like if I am not careful, I could, as my friend who liked jail wishes to do often, close my eyes and disappear.

10 Growing up I did not, ever, feel contained. I never felt the four walls of my room or my apartment or my house or my town or my culture close around me; I never knew the feeling of the extended womb. My parents did not hold me tight, but encouraged me to go. They did not buffer, protect, watch out for, or look after me. I was watered, fed, admired, stroked, and expected to grow. I was mostly left alone to discover the world and my place in it. From the houses and apartments in which I lived, I remember most of all the doors and how they opened for me. I remember the windows and how I never looked out of them longingly, for outside was never kept from me. I remember coming and going, going and coming. That, for me, was home.

...

When they meet in 1965 in Jackson, Mississippi, my parents are idealists, they are social activists, they are "movement folk." They believe in ideas, leaders, and the power of organized people working for change. They believe in justice and equality and freedom. My father is a liberal Jew who believes these abstractions can be realized through the swift, clean application of the Law. My mother believes they can be cultivated through the telling of stories, through the magic ability of words to redefine and create subjectivity. She herself is newly "Black." She and my father comprise an "interracial couple."

By the time they fall in love, my parents do not believe in the über-sanctity of family. They do not believe that blood must necessarily be thicker than water, because water is what they are to each other, and they will be together despite the objection of blood. In 1967, when my parents break all the rules and marry against laws that say they can't, they say that an individual should not be bound to the wishes of their family, race, state, or country. They say that love is the tie that binds, and not blood. In a photograph from their wedding day, they stand, brown and pale pink, inseparable, my mother's tiny five-foot-one-inch frame nestled birdlike within my father's protective embrace. Fearless, naive, breathtaking, they profess their shiny, outlaw love for all the world to see.

I am not a bastard, the product of a rape, the child of some white devil. I am a Movement Child. My parents tell me I can do anything I put my mind to, that I can be anything I want. They buy me Erector sets and building blocks, Tinkertoys and books, more and more books. Berenstain Bears, Dr. Seuss, Hans Christian Andersen. We are middle class. My mother puts a colorful patterned scarf on her head and throws parties for me in our backyard, under the carport, and beside the creek. She invites all of my friends over and watches over us as we roast hot dogs. She makes Kool-Aid and laughs when one of us kids does something cute or funny.

I am not tragic.

15 Late one night during my first year at Yale, a WASP-looking Jewish student strolls into my room through the fire-exit door. He is drunk, and twirling a Swiss Army knife between his nimble, tennis-champion fingers. "Are you really black and Jewish?" he asks, slurring his words, pitching forward in an old raggedy armchair my roommate has covered with an equally raggedy white sheet. "How can that be possible?"

Maybe it is his drunkenness, or perhaps he is actually trying to see me, but this boy squints at me then, peering at my nose, my eyes, my hair. I stare back at him for a few moments, eyes flashing with rage, and then take the red knife from his tanned and tapered fingers. As he clutches at the air above him, I hold it back and tell him in a voice I want him to be sure is black that I think he'd better go.

But after he leaves through the (still) unlocked exit door, I sit for quite a while in the dark.

Am I possible?

Mapping the Text

1. From reading these selections from Walker's autobiography, what evidence do you find of *rhetorical decisions* she has made? For example, how would you describe Walker's *structure* and *style?*
2. In the opening of this selection, Walker talks about not being able to remember things. What sorts of things does she fail to remember? What does she indicate are the consequences of her forgetting? What is lost or gained?
3. The title of Walker's book, *Black, White, and Jewish: Autobiography of a Shifting Self,* clearly asserts that *identity* is something that for her is unstable, or perhaps more fluid than static. What does she suggest shifts as she moves from "Black" to "White" to "Jewish"? What conclusion does she draw, given this excerpt, about this state of being? What is your reaction to this view of identity? Do you agree, disagree, have a different perspective altogether?
4. Autobiography as a genre suggests in very direct ways that there is a *speaking self.* What is your impression of the self that comes through in this selection? Describe this person. What *words* and *images* work to create this impression?

Writing to Inquire

1. This selection is taken from Rebecca Walker's *autobiography.* Autobiography is a *nonfiction genre* in which *interpretation* is important. As a genre, autobiography emerges from reflection, from looking back over one's life in order to make sense of it and to narrate it with some sort of *expressive intention.* Think about your own life. Choose one moment that you would be able to share with others, and answer the following questions;

   a. What about the moment that you have chosen seems to make it have potential as a good one to think again about and share with someone?
   b. With whom does it make sense to share it? Who is the best *audience* for it?
   c. What *tone of voice* would you choose? Should you be serious, humorous, lighthearted but not comedic, mysterious?
   d. Is there a particular *message* that you would want to make clear?
   e. Would you narrate the story yourself, or would you choose a *narrator* different from yourself? In other words, would you invent a *speaking self,* as the autobiographical narrator, or would you choose a different *genre*—a poem, a personal essay (rather than a narrative), a letter, a journal entry? Would you prefer to *fictionalize* the story?

   Choose a generic form (essay, story, or poem) and share your autobiographical moment. Write your piece. Prepare a short statement to accompany the piece in which you explain your rhetorical choices.

CALLS TO ACTION AND RESPONSE

C.P. Ellis

STUDS TERKEL

Studs Terkel (1912–) has spent most of his life as an outspoken advocate of ordinary people. He was trained as a lawyer but built his career in broadcast journalism. He is perhaps best known for a series of books in which he collected and edited interviews of everyday people about their lives, work, hopes, and dreams. His narratives capture in a compelling way the "American experience," an accomplishment that has been recognized by two of the nation's most prestigious awards. His book *Working: People Talk About What They Do All Day and How They Feel About What They Do* (1974) was nominated for the National Book Award, and *The Good War: An Oral History of World War II* (1986), the fifth in his series of oral histories, won the Pulitzer Prize. His most recent book, *My American Century* (1997), demonstrates his continuing, in the eighth decade of his life, to share insights about people and conditions. The profile below is one of Terkel's edited interviews; it first appeared in *American Dreams, Lost and Found* (1980).

We're in his office in Durham, North Carolina. He is the business manager of the International Union of Operating Engineers. On the wall is a plaque: "Certificate of Service, in recognition to C. P. Ellis, for your faithful service to the city in having served as a member of the Durham Human Relations Council. February 1977."

At one time, he had been president (exalted cyclops) of the Durham chapter of the Ku Klux Klan.

He is fifty-three years old.

My father worked in a textile mill in Durham. He died at forty-eight years old. It was probably from cotton dust. Back then, we never heard of brown lung. I was about seventeen years old and had a mother and sister depending on somebody to make a livin'. It was just barely enough insurance to cover his burial. I had to quit school and go to work. I was about eighth grade when I quit.

My father worked hard but never had enough money to buy decent clothes. When I went to school, I never seemed to have adequate clothes to wear. I always left school late afternoon with a sense of inferiority. The other kids had nice clothes, and I just had what Daddy could buy. I still got some of those inferiority feelin's now that I have to overcome once in a while.

I loved my father. He would go with me to ball games. We'd go fishin' together. I was really ashamed of the way he'd dress. He would take this money and give it to me instead of putting it on himself. I always had the feeling about somebody looking at him and makin' fun of him and makin' fun of me. I think it had to do somethin' with my life.

My father and I were very close, but we didn't talk about too many intimate things. He did have a drinking problem. During the week, he would work every day, but weekend he was ready to get plastered. I can understand when a guy looks at his paycheck and looks at his bills, and he's worked hard all the week, and his bills are larger than his paycheck. He'd done the best he could the entire week, and there seemed to be no hope. It's an illness thing. Finally you just say: "The heck with it. I'll just get drunk and forget it."

5 My father was out of work during the depression, and I remember going with him to the finance company uptown, and he was turned down. That's something that's always stuck.

My father never seemed to be happy. It was a constant struggle with him just like it was for me. It's very seldom I'd see him laugh. He was just tryin' to figure out what he could do from one day to the next.

After several years pumping gas at a service station, I got married. We had to have children. Four. One child was born blind and retarded, which was a real additional expense to us. He's never spoken a word. He doesn't know me when I go to see him. But I see him, I hug his neck. I talk to him, tell him I love him. I don't know whether he knows me or not, but I know he's well taken care of. All my life, I had work, never a day without work, worked all the overtime I could get and still could not survive financially. I began to say there's somethin' wrong with this country. I worked my butt off and just never seemed to break even.

I had some real great ideas about this great nation. (Laughs.) They say to abide by the law, go to church, do right and live for the Lord, and everything'll work out. But it didn't work out. It just kept gettin' worse and worse.

I was workin' a bread route. The highest I made one week was seventy-five dollars. The rent on our house was about twelve dollars a week. I will never forget: outside of this house was a 265-gallon oil drum, and I never did get enough money to fill up that oil drum. What I would do every night, I would run up to the store and buy five gallons of oil and climb up the ladder and pour it in that 265-gallon drum. I could hear that five gallons when it hits the bottom of that oil drum, splatters, and it sounds like it's nothin' in there. But it would keep the house warm for the night. Next day you'd have to do the same thing.

10 I left the bread route with fifty dollars in my pocket. I went to the bank and I borrowed four thousand dollars to buy the service station. I worked seven day a week, open and closed, and finally had a heart attack. Just

about two months before the last payments of that loan. My wife had done the best she could to keep it runnin'. Tryin' to come out of that hole, I just couldn't do it.

I really began to get bitter. I didn't know who to blame. I tried to find somebody. I began to blame it on black people. I had to hate somebody. Hatin' America is hard to do because you can't see it to hate it. You gotta have somethin' to look at to hate. (Laughs.) The natural person for me to hate would be black people, because my father before me was a member of the Klan. As far as he was concerned, it was the savior of the white people. It was the only organization in the world that would take care of the white people. So I began to admire the Klan.

I got active in the Klan while I was at the service station. Every Monday night, a group of men would come by and buy a Coca-Cola, go back to the car, take a few drinks, and come back and stand around talkin'. I couldn't help but wonder: Why are these dudes comin' out every Monday? They said they were with the Klan and have meetings close-by. Would I be interested? Boy, that was an opportunity I really looked forward to! To be part of somethin'. I joined the Klan, went from member to chaplain, from chaplain to vice-president, from vice-president to president. The title is exalted cyclops.

The first night I went with the fellas, they knocked on the door and gave the signal. They sent some robed Klansmen to talk to me and give me some instructions. I was led into a large meeting room, and this was the time of my life! It was thrilling. Here's a guy who's worked all his life and struggled all his life to be something, and here's the moment to be something. I will never forget it. Four robed Klansmen led me into the hall. The lights were dim, and the only thing you could see was an illuminated cross. I knelt before the cross. I had to make certain vows and promises. We promised to uphold the purity of the white race, fight communism, and protect white womanhood.

After I had taken my oath, there was loud applause goin' throughout the buildin', musta been at least four hundred people. For this one little ol' person. It was a thrilling moment for C. P. Ellis.

15 It disturbs me when people who do not really know what it's all about are so very critical of individual Klansmen. The majority of 'em are low-income whites, people who really don't have a part in something. They have been shut out as well as the blacks. Some are not very well educated either. Just like myself. We had a lot of support from doctors and lawyers and police officers.

Maybe they've had bitter experiences in this life and they had to hate somebody. So the natural person to hate would be the black person. He's beginnin' to come up, he's beginnin' to learn to read and start votin' and run for political office. Here are white people who are supposed to be superior to them, and we're shut out.

I can understand why people join extreme right-wing or left-wing groups. They're in the same boat I was. Shut out. Deep down inside, we want to be part of this great society. Nobody listens, so we join these groups.

At one time, I was state organizer of the National Rights party. I organized a youth group for the Klan. I felt we were getting old and our generation's gonna die. So I contacted certain kids in schools. They were havin' racial problems. On the first night, we had a hundred high school students. When they came in the door, we had "Dixie" playin'. These kids were just thrilled to death. I begin to hold weekly meetin's with 'em, teachin' the principles of the Klan. At that time, I believed Martin Luther King had Communist connections. I began to teach that Andy Young was affiliated with the Communist party.

I had a call one night from one of our kids. He was about twelve. He said; "I just been robbed downtown by two niggers." I'd had a couple of drinks and that really teed me off. I go downtown and couldn't find the kid. I got worried. I saw two young black people. I had the .32 revolver with me. I said; "Nigger, you seen a little young white boy up here? I just got a call from him and was told that some niggers robbed him of fifteen cents." I pulled my pistol out and put it right at his head. I said: "I've always wanted to kill a nigger and I think I'll make you the first one." I nearly scared the kid to death, and he struck off.

20 This was the time when the civil rights movement was really beginnin' to peak. The blacks were beginnin' to demonstrate and picket downtown stores. I never will forget some black lady I hated with a purple passion. Ann Atwater. Every time I'd go downtown, she'd be leadin' a boycott. How I hated—pardon the expression, I don't use it much now—how I just hated that black nigger. (Laughs.) Big, fat, heavy woman. She'd pull about eight demonstrations, and first thing you know they had two, three blacks at the checkout counter. Her and I have had some pretty close confrontations.

I felt very big, yeah. (Laughs.) We're more or less a secret organization. We didn't want anybody to know who we were, and I began to do some thinkin'. What am I hidin' for? I've never been convicted of anything in my life. I don't have any court record. What am I, C. P. Ellis, as a citizen and a member of the United Klansmen of America? Why can't I go to the city council meeting and say: "This is the way we feel about the matter? We don't want you to purchase mobile units to set in our schoolyards. We don't want niggers in our schools."

We began to come out in the open. We would go to the meetings, and the blacks would be there and we'd be there. It was a confrontation every time. I didn't hold back anything. We began to make some inroads with the city councilmen and county commissioners. They began to call us friend. Call us at night on the telephone; "C. P., glad you came to that meeting last night." They didn't want integration either, but they did it secretively, in order to get elected. They couldn't stand up openly and say it, but they were glad somebody was sayin' it. We visited some of the city leaders in their home and talked to 'em privately. It wasn't long before councilmen would call me up; "The blacks are comin' up tonight and makin' outrageous demands. How about some of you people showin' up and have a little balance?" I'd get on the telephone: "The niggers is comin' to the council meeting tonight. Persons in the city's called me and asked us to be there."

We'd load up our cars and we'd fill up half the council chambers, and the blacks the other half. During these times, I carried weapons to the meetings, outside my belt. We'd go there armed. We would wind up just hollerin' and fussin' at each other. What happened? As a result of our fightin' one another, the city council still had their way. They didn't want to give up control to the blacks nor the Klan. They were usin' us.

I began to realize this later down the road. One day I was walkin' downtown and a certain city council member saw me comin'. I expected him to shake my hand because he was talkin' to me at night on the telephone. I had been in his home and visited with him. He crossed the street. Oh shit, I began to think, somethin's wrong here. Most of 'em are merchants or maybe an attorney, an insurance agent, people like that. As long as they kept low-income whites and low-income blacks fightin', they're gonna maintain control.

I began to get that feeling after I was ignored in public. I thought: Bullshit, you're not gonna use me any more. That's when I began to do some real serious thinkin'.

The same thing is happening in this country today. People are being used by those in control, those who have all the wealth. I'm not espousing communism. We got the greatest system of government in the world. But those who have it simply don't want those who don't have it to have any part of it. Black and white. When it comes to money, the green, the other colors make no difference. (Laughs.)

I spent a lot of sleepless nights. I still didn't like blacks, I didn't want to associate with 'em. Blacks, Jews, or Catholics. My father said: "Don't have anything to do with 'em." I didn't until I met a black person and talked with him, eyeball to eyeball, and met a Jewish person and talked to him, eyeball to eyeball. I found out they're people just like me. They cried, they cussed, they prayed, they had desires. Just like myself. Thank God, I got to the point where I can look past labels. But at that time, my mind was closed.

I remember one Monday night Klan meeting. I said something was wrong. Our city fathers were using us. And I didn't like to be used. The reactions of the others was not too pleasant: "Let's just keep fightin' them niggers."

I'd go home at night and I'd have to wrestle with myself. I'd look at a black person walkin' down the street, and the guy'd have ragged shoes or his clothes would be worn. That began to do somethin' to me inside. I went through this for about six months. I felt I just had to get out of the Klan. But I wouldn't get out.

Then something happened. The state AFL-CIO received a grant from the Department of HEW, a $78,000 grant: how to solve racial problems in the school system. I got a telephone call from the president of the state AFL-CIO. "We'd like to get some people together from all walks of life." I said; "All walks of life? Who you talkin' about?" He said: "Blacks, whites, liberals, conservatives, Klansmen, NAACP people."

I said: "No way am I comin' with all those niggers. I'm not gonna be associated with those type of people." A White Citizens Council guy said: "Let's go up there and see what's goin' on. It's tax money bein' spent." I walk in the door, and there was a large number of blacks and white liberals. I knew most of 'em by face 'cause I seen 'em demonstratin' around town. Ann Atwater was there. (Laughs.) I just forced myself to go in and sit down.

The meeting was moderated by a great big black guy who was bushy-headed. (Laughs.) That turned me off. He acted very nice. He said: "I want you all to feel free to say anything you want to say." Some of the blacks stand up and say it's white racism. I took all I could take. I asked for the floor and I cut loose. I said: "No, sir, it's black racism. If we didn't have niggers in the schools, we wouldn't have the problems we got today."

I will never forget. Howard Clements, a black guy, stood up. He said: "I'm certainly glad C. P. Ellis come because he's the most honest man here tonight." I said: "What's that nigger tryin' to do?" (Laughs.) At the end of that meeting, some blacks tried to come up shake my hand, but I wouldn't do it. I walked off.

Second night, same group was there. I felt a little more easy because I got some things off my chest. The third night, after they elected all the committees, they want to elect a chairman. Howard Clements stood up and said: "I suggest we elect two co-chairpersons." Joe Beckton, executive director of the Human Relations Commission, just as black as he can be, he nominated me. There was a reaction from some blacks. Nooo. And, of all things, they nominated Ann Atwater, that big old fat black gal that I had just hated with a purple passion, as co-chairman. I thought to myself: Hey, ain't no way I can work with that gal. Finally, I agreed to accept it, 'cause at this point, I was tired of fightin', either for survival or against black people or against Jews or against Catholics.

35 A Klansman and a militant black woman, co-chairmen of the school committee. It was impossible. How could I work with her? But after about two or three days, it was in our hands. We had to make it a success. This give me another sense of belongin', a sense of pride. This helped this inferiority feelin' I had. A man who has stood up publicly and said he despised black people, all of a sudden he was willin' to work with 'em. Here's a chance for a low-income white man to be somethin'. In spite of all my hatred for blacks and Jews and liberals, I accepted the job. Her and I began to reluctantly work together. (Laughs.) She had as many problems workin' with me as I had workin' with her.

One night, I called her: "Ann, you and I should have a lot of differences and we got 'em now. But there's somethin' laid out here before us, and if it's gonna be a success, you and I are gonna have to make it one. Can we lay aside some of these feelin's?" She said: "I'm willing if you are." I said: "Let's do it."

My old friends would call me at night: "C. P., what the hell is wrong with you? You're sellin' out the white race." This begin to make me have guilt feelin's. Am I doin' right? Am I doin' wrong? Here I am all of a sudden makin' an about-face and tryin' to deal with my feelin's, my heart. My mind was beginnin' to open up. I was beginnin' to see what was right and what was wrong. I don't want the kids to fight forever.

We were gonna go ten nights. By this time, I had went to work at Duke University, in maintenance. Makin' very little money. Terry Sanford give me this ten days off with pay. He was president of Duke at the time. He knew I was a Klansman and realized the importance of blacks and whites getting along.

I said: "If we're gonna make this thing a success, I've got to get to my kind of people." The low-income whites. We walked the streets of Durham, and we knocked on doors and invited people. Ann was goin' into the black community. They just wasn't respondin' to us when we made these house calls. Some of 'em were cussin' us out. "You're sellin' us out, Ellis, get out of my door. I don't want to talk to you." Ann was gettin' the same response from blacks: "What are you doin' messin' with that Klansman?"

One day, Ann and I went back to the school and we sat down. We began to talk and just reflect. Ann said: "My daughter came home cryin' every day. She said her teacher was makin' fun of me in front of the other kids." I said: "Boy, the same thing happened to my kid. White liberal teacher was makin' fun of Tim Ellis's father, the Klansman. In front of other peoples. He came home cryin'." At this point—(he pauses, swallows hard, stifles a sob)—I begin to see, here we are, two people from the far ends of the fence, havin' identical problems, except hers bein' black and me bein' white. From that moment on, I tell ya, that gal and I worked together good. I begin to love the girl, really. (He weeps.)

The amazing thing about it, her and I, up to that point, had cussed each other, bawled each other, we hated each other. Up to that point, we didn't know each other. We didn't know we had things in common.

We worked at it, with the people who came to these meetings. They talked about racism, sex education, about teachers not bein' qualified. After seven, eight nights of real intense discussion, these people, who'd never talked to each other before, all of a sudden came up with resolutions. It was really somethin', you had to be there to get the tone and feelin' of it.

At that point, I didn't like integration, but the law says you do this and I've got to do what the law says, okay? We said: "Let's take these resolutions to the school board." The most disheartening thing I've ever faced was the school system refused to implement any one of these resolutions. These were recommendations from the people who pay taxes and pay their salaries. (Laughs.)

I thought they were good answers. Some of 'em I didn't agree with, but I been in this thing from the beginning, and whatever comes of it, I'm gonna support it. Okay, since the school board refused, I decided I'd just run for the school board.

45 I spent eighty-five dollars on the campaign. The guy runnin' against me spent several thousand. I really had nobody on my side. The Klan turned against me. The low-income whites turned against me. The liberals didn't particularly like me. The blacks were suspicious of me. The blacks wanted to support me, but they couldn't muster up enough to support a Klansman on the school board. (Laughs.) But I made up my mind that what I was doin' was right, and I was gonna do it regardless what anybody said.

It bothered me when people would call and worry my wife. She's always supported me in anything I wanted to do. She was changing, and my boys were too. I got some of my youth corps kids involved. They still followed me.

I was invited to the Democratic women's social hour as a candidate. Didn't have but one suit to my name. Had it six, seven, eight years. I had it cleaned, put on the best shirt I had and a tie. Here were all this high-class wealthy candidates shakin' hands. I walked up to the mayor and stuck out my hand. He give me that handshake with that rag type of hand. He said "C. P., I'm glad to see you." But I could tell by his handshake he was lyin' to me. This was botherin' me. I know I'm a low-income person. I know I'm not wealthy. I know they were sayin' "What's this little ol' dude runnin' for school board?" Yet they had to smile and make like they're glad to see me. I begin to spot some black people in that room. I automatically went to 'em and that was a firm handshake. They said: "I'm glad to see you, C. P." I knew they meant it—you can tell about a handshake.

Every place I appeared, I said I will listen to the voice of the people. I will not make a major decision until I first contacted all the organizations in the city. I got 4,640 votes. The guy beat me by two thousand. Not bad for eighty-five bucks and no constituency.

The whole world was openin' up, and I was learnin' new truths that I had never learned before. I was beginning' to look at a black person, shake hands with him, and see him as a human bein'. I hadn't got rid of all this stuff. I've still got a little bit of it. But somethin' was happenin' to me.

50 It was almost like bein' born again. It was a new life. I didn't have these sleepless nights I used to have when I was active in the Klan and slippin' around at night. I could sleep at night and feel good about it. I'd rather live now than at any other time in history. It's a challenge.

Back at Duke, doin' maintenance, I'd pick up my tools, fix the commode, unstop the drains. But this got in my blood. Things weren't right in this country, and what we done in Durham needs to be told. I was so miserable at Duke, I could hardly stand it. I'd go to work every morning just hatin' to go.

My whole life had changed, I got an eighth-grade education, and I wanted to complete high school. Went to high school in the afternoons on a program called PEP—Past Employment Progress. I was about the only white in class, and the oldest. I begin to read about biology. I'd take my books home at night, 'cause I was determined to get through. Sure enough, I graduated. I got the diploma at home.

I come to work one mornin' and some guy says: "We need a union." At this time I wasn't pro-union. My daddy was anti-labor too. We're not gettin' paid much, we're havin' to work seven days in a row. We're all starvin' to death. The next day, I meet the international representative of the Operating Engineers. He give me authorization cards. "Get these cards out and we'll have an election." There was eighty-eight for the union and seventeen no's. I was elected chief steward for the union.

Shortly after, a union man come down from Charlotte and says we need a full-time rep. We've got only two hundred people at the two plants here. It's just barely enough money comin' in to pay your salary. You'll have to get out and organize more people. I didn't know nothin' about organizin' unions, but I knew how to organize people, stir people up. (Laughs.) That's how I got to be business agent for the union.

55 When I began to organize, I began to see far deeper. I began to see people again bein' used. Blacks against whites. I say this without any hesitancy: management is vicious. There's two things they want to keep: all the money and all the say-so. They don't want these poor workin' folks to have none of that. I begin to see management fightin' me with everything they had. Hire antiunion law firms, badmouth unions. The people were makin' a dollar ninety-five an hour, barely able to get through weekends. I worked as a business rep for five years and was seein' all this.

Last year, I ran for business manager of the union. He's elected by the workers. The guy that ran against me was black, and our membership is seventy-five percent black. I thought: Claiborne, there's no way you can beat that black guy. People know your background. Even though you've made tremendous strides, those black people are not gonna vote for you. You know how much I beat him? Four to one. (Laughs.)

The company used my past against me. They put out letters with a picture of a robe and a cap: Would you vote for a Klansman? They wouldn't deal with the issues. I immediately called for a mass meeting. I met with the ladies at an electric component plant. I said: "Okay, this is Claiborne Ellis. This is where I come from. I want you to know right now, you black ladies here, I was at one time a member of the Klan. I want you to know, because they'll tell you about it."

I invited some of my old black friends. I said: "Brother Joe, Brother Howard, be honest now and tell these people how you feel about me." They done it. (Laughs.) Howard Clements kidded me a little bit. He said: "I don't know what I'm doin' here, supportin' an ex-Klansman." (Laughs.)

He said: "I know what C. P. Ellis come from. I knew him when he was. I knew him as he grew, and growed with him. I'm tellin' you now: follow, follow this Klansman." (He pauses, swallows hard.) "Any questions?" "No," the black ladies said. "Let's get on with the meeting, we need Ellis." (He laughs and weeps.) Boy, black people sayin' that about me. I won one thirty-four to forty-one. Four to one.

It makes you feel good to go into a plant and butt heads with professional union busters. You see black people and white people join hands to defeat the racist issues they use against people. They're tryin' the same things with the Klan. It's still happenin' today. Can you imagine a guy who's got an adult high school diploma runnin' into professional college graduates who are union busters? I gotta compete with 'em. I work seven days a week, nights and on Saturday and Sunday. The salary's not that great, and if I didn't care, I'd quit. But I care and I can't quit. I got a taste of it. (Laughs.)

I tell people there's a tremendous possibility in this country to stop wars, the battles, the struggles, the fights between people. People say: "That's an impossible dream. You sound like Martin Luther King." An ex-Klansman who sounds like Martin Luther King. (Laughs.) I don't think it's an impossible dream. It's happened in my life. It's happened in other people's lives in America.

I don't know what's ahead of me. I have no desire to be a big union official. I want to be right out here in the field with the workers. I want to walk through their factory and shake hands with that man whose hands are dirty. I'm gonna do all that one little ol' man can do. I'm fifty-two years old, and I ain't got many years left, but I want to make the best of 'em.

When the news came over the radio that Martin Luther King was assassinated, I got on the telephone and begin to call other Klansmen. We just had a real party at the service station. Really rejoicin' 'cause that son of a bitch was dead. Our troubles are over with. They say the older you get, the harder it is for you to change. That's not necessarily true. Since I changed, I've set down and listened to tapes of Martin Luther King. I listen to it and tears come to my eyes 'cause I know what he's sayin' now. I know what's happenin'.

POSTSCRIPT: *The phone rings. A conversation.*

"This was a black guy who's director of Operation Breakthrough in Durham. I had called his office. I'm interested in employin' some young black person who's interested in learnin' the labor movement. I want somebody who's never had an opportunity, just like myself. Just so he can read and write, that's all."

Mapping the Text

1. *Who* is C.P. Ellis? Given the details that Terkel presents:
   a. Describe the impression that you receive of Ellis as a person, a worker, a member of his community, a citizen.

b. How does he conform or not conform to the *norms,* the conventions of behavior, beliefs, and values in his community?

c. Go through the *narrative* and circle the personal pronouns (I, you, our, we, them, their). Describe Ellis's personal, social, and public *boundaries* as suggested by these pronouns (I/we, you/they).

2. What changes for Ellis over the course of his story? How and why do his behavior, attitudes, expectations, and relationships change?
3. Think about Terkel's crafting of this narrative. What does he do to create impressions, to reveal character, to convey a particular *message?* Does Terkel have a message in this narrative? What does his *purpose* seem to be? What does he seem to be trying to do as a writer? Does he fulfill this purpose?

Writing to Inquire

1. C.P. Ellis found ways to struggle through his problems. What were his solutions? In what ways do you feel his actions were effective or ineffective? If you faced a similar situation—one in which you needed to forge an alliance with a former enemy, for example, in order to succeed—what do you think that you would you do, and how do you think you might do it? Would you take advice from Ellis's narrative? If so, what advice would you take? If you wouldn't take his advice, why wouldn't you? What would you do instead?
2. Choose a character in the narrative other than Ellis. Write your own narrative of this situation from that person's point of view. After you have finished your narrative, consider the shift that you have made from Terkel's *profile* to your own fictionalized account. Write a memo about your piece to explain the shift that you make (the *rhetorical decisions* that you made in order to create your narrative). Point out in your explanatory memo any difference that you see in what your readers might understand about this situation based on the point of view that you present instead of Terkel's view by itself.

INQUIRY: WHO AM I?

1. Think about yourself as a person who has used language and related skills in a variety of ways all of your life, every day. In fact, you have a long history as a language user. We all do. Think about this history and consider at the same time what you believe it really means to use language thoughtfully and well both orally and in writing. Take the short inventory below of your skills and abilities.
   a. What strengths do you have in the areas below? Describe what you believe you do reasonably well.
      —writing
      —speaking
      —reading critically
      —thinking analytically
      —listening
      —interacting with others
      —posing, finding, and solving various types of questions
   b. Is there any skill or ability on the above list on which you think that you need to improve? Describe what you believe any weakness(es) to be.

To what extent do you see yourself in this image? What markers of identity are visible in this photograph? What identities are silent or invisible here?

c. If you could set one goal for yourself in terms of writing and related skills, what would it be?

2. Think about yourself and about others around you as people with beliefs, habits, and preferences. Think about how such factors contribute to the various views that you hold of yourself; who you are, what sorts of character and behavior traits you exhibit, what your personal, social, and public identities are. Think about how among all of these factors there are some dimensions of yourself that you think about as markers of a status or value and other dimensions of yourself that you rarely even notice except under special or unusual circumstances.

   a. In a discussion with two or three classmates, generate a list of your personal, social, and public identities that might offer, deny, or measure status in our society. Think about organzations you participate in, your relationship to family, social, and church groups, sports, or other group activities. You might consider other identities also, such as physical stature, athletic or other performance ability, being honest or friendly, being a wife or husband, and so forth.

   b. Examine each item on your group's list to determine whether it seems to be a marker of identity that is inherited (ethnic origins, physical stature), assigned (identities by which we label an individual based on social or political habits, racial identity, and social class), or apprenticed (deliberately chosen and learned by the individual, such as being a dancer, musician, or athlete).

3. Listed below are two types of relationships. Think about your own identities in these terms. Generate a list of your own relationships that seem to fit into each category.

   a. *in-group relationships* that signal groups to which you seem to *belong* and that feel rather natural or that feel close and most familiar (family, friends, teams, colleagues, organizations). In other words, these groups are ones to which you feel some degree of loyalty and that you are pretty conficent are loyal to you.

   b. *reference groups,* groups where you *value* membership in the group whether your membership in them is inherited, assigned, or apprenticed (See activity 2, above). Choose one of your reference groups and think about the *norms* of the group, its expectations for how its members behave, the language they use, or the beliefs that they hold.

4. Consider the ways in which pronouns (I, we, you, they) signal *boundaries* in your relationships with others. How would you describe your own personal, social, and public boundaries? What, in general terms, constitutes your clearest sense, if you have such a sense, of "I/you" and "we/they"? What implications do you draw based on your answers to these questions with regard to concepts such as *respect, appreciation, tolerance, intolerance,* or *bigotry?*

5. In the United States, the terms *race, gender, class,* and *culture* are frequently used in social or public arenas to explain who we are and to offer some view of the sense of self that we hold. Describe yourself using whatever vocabulary seems meaningful to you. Can this vocabulary be categorized by the terms race, gender, class, and culture? Discuss whether you consider these categories (race, gender, class, culture) adequate to describe and explain yourself. If your view is that such categories are inadequate, add a section in which you remedy the inadequacy by offering more information or different information in terms that seem to you more appropriate.
6. Consider each of the readings in this chapter (Thoreau, Bérubé, Narayan, Angelou, Cisneros, Gormley, Walker, and Terkel). Choose one reading to explore in detail in a written response. You may choose a writer whose view is close to your own, or you may want to write about a reading with which you strongly disagree or differ. How would you characterize the similarities and differences between your own perspectives and experiences and those of the writer? What is similar in your thinking? What is different? What is left unsaid that seems to or should matter?

CHAPTER 2

A Place Called "Home"

Who are you? Where do you come from? Questions like these often help start a conversation or make a human connection. They can initiate the process of meeting and interacting with others. They help you locate yourself, not only in a world of experiences but also in a world of thoughts and ideas. You place yourself in time and space, a process that permits, if not demands, that you account for yourself in some way as a person who exists among others and as someone who has inevitably participated in various groups or social settings—personal, social, and public or institutional.

Asking yourself these kinds of questions can help you prepare to express yourself in writing. In reflecting on who you are, where you came from, what you care about, and how you came to be the way you are, you increase your capacity as a writer to craft a meaningful place to stand (a point of view). You also build the power and authority to speak. A fundamental benefit is that you have a way to anchor yourself as you make decisions about your writing task and raise a voice, in speaking or writing, that is clear, articulate, and confident. You recognize more clearly the experiences and abilities that you can communicate to your readers and the world. You can consider your strengths in a more concrete way and develop a vocabulary for thinking about your reflections. As you build a language for talking about writing, you discover a new set of tools and techniques to enhance your strengths as a writer and to reduce whatever weaknesses you may identify. By starting with a clearer sense of place, where you are located physically, experientially, and ideologically (in the broad sense of your core values and beliefs), you get your moorings as a writer and gain the authority to speak.

In focusing on the topic of *place,* Chapter 2 is designed to help you think about your relationships to the world around you and to other human beings. The assumption here is that where you are in geographical space matters. We all have places that have witnessed our development as human beings and that often serve as touchstones of various sorts: where we think best, where we feel most comfortable or loved, where we find peace or beauty, where we find our clearest sense of self and meaning.

The two writers included in the first section, "Framing the Topic," open up different ways of looking at the connections between home and place, story and community, history and self. In "Homeplace (a site of resistance)," bell hooks describes the journey she made as a young girl traveling across town to her grandmother's house. Reflecting on that personal journey becomes, for hooks, an occasion to speak for a "political commitment to homeplace" and on behalf of "young women who are struggling for self-definition." Barry Lopez, in "Landscape and Narrative," explores in a different way the relationship between stories and places. Describing the "inexplicable renewal of enthusiasm" that comes from storytelling, Lopez links two landscapes: the external landscape outside the self, and the interior landscape, "a kind of projection within a person of a part of the exterior landscape." Both hooks and Lopez compel readers to revisit home and place in their own experiences, in a context made larger by the deep connections to history and the environment.

The seven selections in "Readings for Inquiry and Exploration" present such linkages from other points of view, with some of the writers raising complementary issues, such as what it means to take care of the places that we love and on which we depend. Two contrasting readings are included in the final section, "Calls to Action and Response." Each addresses issues concerning humans' role in changing the ecological landscape. A selection from Rachel Carson's influential 1962 book, *Silent Spring,* often credited with initiating a new environmentalism, is counterbalanced by a chapter from Dave Foreman's controversial *Confessions of an Eco-Warrior.*

All of the writers can help you see yourself in place and ask more boldly: Where is "home"? How does this place help shape who I am? What do I take away from it? What do I leave behind? What and how have I learned in this context? Who has been a part of this scene? To whom or what in this place am I grateful? What sense can I make from being in this place, of it, or from it? What obligations do I have to the places that surround me? How am I responsible for the earth?

FRAMING THE TOPIC

Homeplace

BELL HOOKS

bell hooks (1952–), Distinguished Professor of English at City College in New York, has written several books, including *Ain't I a Woman: Black Women and Feminism* (1981); *Feminist Theory: From Margin to Center* (1984); *Talking Back: Thinking Feminist, Thinking Black* (1989); *Yearning: Race, Class, and Cultural Politics* (1990); *Art on My Mind: Visual Politics* (1995); and *Remembered Rapture: The Writer at Work* (1999). Born in Hopkinsville, Kentucky, as Gloria Watkins, hooks uses her great-grandmother's name as a pseudonym and chooses, therefore, not to capitalize it as her own proper name. As bell hooks, she writes often about the need for critical consciousness in a racist, sexist, and classist society. In "Homeplace," hooks explores the notion of home as both domestic and political space.

When I was a young girl the journey across town to my grandmother's house was one of the most intriguing experiences. Mama did not like to stay there long. She did not care for all that loud talk, the talk that was usually about the old days, the way life happened then—who married whom, how and when somebody died, but also how we lived and survived as black people, how the white folks treated us. I remember this journey not just because of the stories I would hear. It was a movement away from the segregated blackness of our community into a poor white neighborhood. I remember the fear, being scared to walk to Baba's (our grandmother's house) because we would have to pass that terrifying whiteness—those white faces on the porches staring us down with hate. Even when empty or vacant, those porches seemed to say "danger," "you do not belong here," "you are not safe."

Oh! that feeling of safety, of arrival, of homecoming when we finally reached the edges of her yard, when we could see the soot black face of our grandfather, Daddy Gus, sitting in his chair on the porch, smell his cigar, and rest on his lap. Such a contrast, that feeling of arrival, of homecoming, this sweetness and the bitterness of that journey, that constant reminder of white power and control.

I speak of this journey as leading to my grandmother's house, even though our grandfather lived there too. In our young minds houses belonged to women, were their special domain, not as property, but as places where all that truly mattered in life took place—the warmth and comfort of shelter, the feeding of our bodies, the nurturing of our souls. There we learned dignity, integrity of being; there we learned to have faith. The folks who made this life possible, who were our primary guides and teachers, were black women.

Their lives were not easy. Their lives were hard. They were black women who for the most part worked outside the home serving white folks, cleaning their houses, washing their clothes, tending their children—black women who worked in the fields or in the streets, whatever they could do to make ends meet, whatever was necessary. Then they returned to their homes to make life happen there. This tension between service outside one's home, family, and kin network, service provided to white folks which took time and energy, and the effort of black women to conserve enough of themselves to provide service (care and nurturance) within their own families and communities is one of the many factors that has historically distinguished the lot of black women in patriarchal white supremacist society from that of black men. Contemporary black struggle must honor this history of service just as it must critique the sexist definition of service as women's "natural" role.

5 Since sexism delegates to females the task of creating and sustaining a home environment, it has been primarily the responsibility of black women to construct domestic households as spaces of care and nurturance in the face of the brutal harsh reality of racist oppression, of sexist domination. Historically, African-American people believed that the construction of a homeplace, however fragile and tenuous (the slave hut, the wooden shack), had a radical political dimension. Despite the brutal reality of racial apartheid, of domination, one's homeplace was the one site where one could freely confront the issue of humanization, where one could resist. Black women resisted by making homes where all black people could strive to be subjects, not objects, where we could be affirmed in our minds and hearts despite poverty, hardship, and deprivation, where we could restore to ourselves the dignity denied us on the outside in the public world.

This task of making homeplace was not simply a matter of black women providing service; it was about the construction of a safe place where black people could affirm one another and by so doing heal many of the wounds inflicted by racist domination. We could not learn to love or respect ourselves in the culture of white supremacy, on the outside; it was there on the inside, in that "homeplace," most often created and kept by black women, that we had the opportunity to grow and develop, to nurture our spirits. This task of making a homeplace, of making home a community of resistance, has been shared by black women globally, especially black women in white supremacist societies.

I shall never forget the sense of shared history, of common anguish. I felt when first reading about the plight of black women domestic servants in South Africa, black women laboring in white homes. Their stories evoked vivid memories of our African-American past. I remember that one of the black women giving testimony complained that after traveling in the wee hours of the morning to the white folks' house, after working there all day, giving her time and energy, she had "none left for her own." I knew this story. I had read it in the slave narratives of African-American women who, like Sojourner Truth, could say, "When I cried out with a mother's grief none but Jesus heard." I knew this story. I had grown to womanhood hearing about black women who nurtured and cared for white families when they longed to have time and energy to give to their own.

I want to remember these black women today. The act of remembrance is a conscious gesture honoring their struggle, their effort to keep something for their own. I want us to respect and understand that this effort has been and continues to be a radically subversive political gesture. For those who dominate and oppress us benefit most when we have nothing to give our own, when they have so taken from us our dignity, our humanness that we have nothing left, no "homeplace" where we can recover ourselves. I want us to remember these black women today, both past and present. Even as I speak there are black women in the midst of racial apartheid in South Africa, struggling to provide something for their own. "We . . . know how our sisters suffer" (Quoted in the petition for the repeal of the pass laws, August 9, 1956). I want us to honor them, not because they suffer but because they continue to struggle in the midst of suffering, because they continue to resist. I want to speak about the importance of homeplace in the midst of oppression and domination, of homeplace as a site of resistance and liberation struggle. Writing about "resistance," particularly resistance to the Vietnam war, Vietnamese Buddhist monk Thich Nhat Hahn says:

> . . . resistance, at root, must mean more than resistance against war. It is a resistance against all kinds of things that are like war. . . . So perhaps, resistance means opposition to being invaded, occupied, assaulted and destroyed by the system. The purpose of resistance, here, is to seek the healing of yourself in order to be able to see clearly. . . I think that communities of resistance should be places where people can return to themselves more easily, where the conditions are such that they can heal themselves and recover their wholeness.

Historically, black women have resisted white supremacist domination by working to establish homeplace. It does not matter that sexism assigned them this role. It is more important that they took this conventional role and expanded it to include caring for one another, for children, for black men, in ways that elevated our spirits, that kept us from despair, that taught some of us to be revolutionaries able to struggle for freedom. In his famous 1845 slave narrative, Frederick Douglass tells the story of his birth, of his enslaved black mother who was hired out a considerable distance from his place of residence. Describing their relationship, he writes:

> I never saw my mother, to know her as such more than four or five times in my life; and each of these times was very short in duration, and at night. She was hired by Mr. Stewart, who lived about twelve miles from my house. She made her journeys to see me in the night, traveling the whole distance on foot, after the performance of her day's work. She was a field hand, and a whipping is the penalty of not being in the field at sunrise . . . I do not recollect of ever seeing my mother by the light of day. She was with me in the night. She would lie down with me and get me to sleep, but long before I waked she was gone.

10 After sharing this information, Douglass later says that he never enjoyed a mother's "soothing presence, her tender and watchful care" so that he received the "tidings of her death with much the same emotions I should have probably felt at the death of a stranger." Douglass surely intended to impress upon the consciousness of white readers the cruelty of that system of racial domination which separated black families, black mothers from their children. Yet he does so by devaluing black womanhood, by not even registering the quality of care that made his black mother travel those twelve miles to hold him in her arms. In the midst of a brutal racist system, which did not value black life, she valued the life of her child enough to resist that system, to come to him in the night, just to hold him.

Now I cannot agree with Douglass that he never knew a mother's care. I want to suggest that his mother, who dared to hold him in the night, gave him at birth a sense of value that provided a groundwork, however fragile, for the person he later became. If anyone doubts the power and significance of this maternal gesture, they would do well to read psychoanalyst Alice Miller's book, *The Untouched Key: Tracing Childhood Trauma in Creativity and Destructiveness.* Holding him in her arms, Douglass's mother provided, if only for a short time, a space where this black child was not the subject of dehumanizing scorn and devaluation but was the recipient of a quality of care that should have enabled the adult Douglass to look back and reflect on the political choices of this black mother who resisted slave codes, risking her life, to care for her son. I want to suggest that devaluation of the role his mother played in his life is a dangerous oversight. Though Douglass is only one example, we are currently in danger of forgetting the powerful role black women have played in constructing for us homeplaces that are the site for resistance. This forgetfulness undermines our solidarity and the future of black liberation struggle.

Douglass's work is important, for he is historically identified as sympathetic to the struggle for women's rights. All too often his critique of male domination, such as it was, did not include recognition of the particular circumstances of black women in relation to black men and families. To me one of the most important chapters in my first book, *Ain't I a Woman;*

Black Women and Feminism, is one that calls attention to "Continued Devaluation of Black Womanhood." Overall devaluation of the role black women have played in constructing for us homeplaces that are the site for resistance undermines our efforts to resist racism and the colonizing mentality which promotes internalized self-hatred. Sexist thinking about the nature of domesticity has determined the way black women's experience in the home is perceived. In African-American culture, there is a long tradition of "mother worship." Black autobiographies, fiction, and poetry praise the virtues of the self-sacrificing black mother. Unfortunately, though positively motivated, black mother worship extols the virtues of self-sacrifice while simultaneously implying that such a gesture is not reflective of choice and will, rather the perfect embodiment of a woman's "natural" role. The assumption then is that the black woman who works hard to be a responsible caretaker is only doing what she should be doing. Failure to recognize the realm of choice, and the remarkable re-visioning of both woman's role and the idea of "home" that black women consciously exercised in practice, obscures the political commitment to racial uplift, to eradicating racism, which was the philosophical core of dedication to community and home.

Though black women did not self-consciously articulate in written discourse the theoretical principles of decolonization, this does not detract from the importance of their actions. They understood intellectually and intuitively the meaning of homeplace in the midst of an oppressive and dominating social reality, of homeplace as site of resistance and liberation struggle. I know of what I speak. I would not be writing this essay if my mother, Rosa Bell, daughter to Sarah Oldham, granddaughter to Bell Hooks, had not created homeplace in just this liberatory way, despite the contradictions of poverty and sexism.

In our family, I remember the immense anxiety we felt as children when mama would leave our house, our segregated community, to work as a maid in the homes of white folks. I believe that she sensed our fear, our concern that she might not return to us safe, that we could not find her (even though she always left phone numbers, they did not ease our worry). When she returned home after working long hours, she did not complain. She made an effort to rejoice with us that her work was done, that she was home, making it seem as though there was nothing about the experience of working as a maid in a white household, in that space of Otherness, which stripped her of dignity and personal power.

15 Looking back as an adult woman, I think of the effort it must have taken for her to transcend her own tiredness (and who knows what assaults or wounds to her spirit had to be put aside so that she could give something to her own). Given the contemporary notions of "good parenting" this may seem like a small gesture, yet in many post-slavery black families, it was a gesture parents were often too weary, too beaten down to make. Those of us who were fortunate enough to receive such care understood its value.

Politically, our young mother, Rosa Bell, did not allow the white supremacist culture of domination to completely shape and control her psyche and her familial relationships. Working to create a homeplace that affirmed our beings, our blackness, our love for one another was necessary resistance. We learned degrees of critical consciousness from her. Our lives were not without contradictions, so it is not my intent to create a romanticized portrait. Yet any attempts to critically assess the role of black women in liberation struggle must examine the way political concern about the impact of racism shaped black women's thinking, their sense of home, and their modes of parenting.

An effective means of white subjugation of black people globally has been the perpetual construction of economic and social structures that deprive many folks of the means to make homeplace. Remembering this should enable us to understand the political value of black women's resistance in the home. It should provide a framework where we can discuss the development of black female political consciousness, acknowledging the political importance of resistance effort that took place in homes. It is no accident that the South African apartheid regime systematically attacks and destroys black efforts to construct homeplace, however tenuous, that small private reality where black women and men can renew their spirits and recover themselves. It is no accident that this homeplace, as fragile and as transitional as it may be, a makeshift shed, a small bit of earth where one rests, is always subject to violation and destruction. For when a people no longer have the space to construct homeplace, we cannot build a meaningful community of resistance.

Throughout our history, African-Americans have recognized the subversive value of homeplace, of having access to private space where we do not directly encounter white racist aggression. Whatever the shape and direction of black liberation struggle (civil rights reform or black power movement), domestic space has been a crucial site for organizing, for forming political solidarity. Homeplace has been a site of resistance. Its structure was defined less by whether or not black women and men were conforming to sexist behavior norms and more by our struggle to uplift ourselves as a people, our struggle to resist racist domination and oppression.

That liberatory struggle has been seriously undermined by contemporary efforts to change that subversive homeplace into a site of patriarchal domination of black women by black men, where we abuse one another for not conforming to sexist norms. This shift in perspective, where homeplace is not viewed as a political site, has had negative impact on the construction of black female identity and political consciousness. Masses of black women, many of whom were not formally educated, had in the past been able to play a vital role in black liberation struggle. In the contemporary situation, as the paradigms for domesticity in black life mirrored white bourgeois norms (where home is conceptualized as politically neutral space), black people began to overlook and devalue the importance of black female labor in teaching critical consciousness in domestic space. Many black women, irrespective of class status, have responded to this crisis of meaning by imitating leisure-class sexist notions of women's role, focusing their lives on meaningless compulsive consumerism.

Identifying this syndrome as "the crisis of black womanhood" in her essay. "Considering Feminism as a Model for Social Change," Sheila Radford-Hill points to the mid-sixties as that historical moment when the primacy of black woman's role in liberation struggle began to be questioned as a threat to black manhood and was deemed unimportant. Radford-Hill asserts:

> Without the power to influence the purpose and the direction of our collective experience, without the power to influence our culture from within, we are increasingly immobilized, unable to integrate self and role identities, unable to resist the cultural imperialism of the dominant culture which assures our continued oppression by destroying us from within. Thus, the crisis manifests itself as social dysfunction in the black community—as genocide, fratricide, homicide, and suicide. It is also manifested by the abdication of personal responsibility by black women for themselves and for each other . . .The crisis of black woman hood is a form of cultural aggression: a form of exploitation so vicious, so insidious that it is currently destroying an entire generation of black women and then families.

20 This contemporary crisis of black womanhood might have been avoided had black women collectively sustained attempts to develop the latent feminism expressed by their willingness to work equally alongside black men in black liberation struggle. Contemporary equation of black liberation struggle with the subordination of black women has damaged collective black solidarity. It has served the interests of white supremacy to promote the assumption that the wounds of racist domination would be less severe were black women conforming to sexist role patterns.

We are daily witnessing the disintegration of African-American family life that is grounded in a recognition of the political value of constructing homeplace as a site of resistance; black people daily perpetuate sexist norms that threaten our survival as a people. We can no longer act as though sexism in black communities does not threaten our solidarity; any force which estranges and alienates us from one another serves the interests of racist domination.

Black women and men must create a revolutionary vision of black liberation that has a feminist dimension, one which is formed in consideration of our specific needs and concerns. Drawing on past legacies, contemporary black women can begin to reconceptualize ideas of homeplace, once again considering the primacy of domesticity as a site for subversion and resistance. When we renew our concern with homeplace, we can address political issues that most affect our daily lives. Calling attention to the skills and resources of black women who may have begun to feel that they have no meaningful contribution to make, women who may or may not be formally educated but who have essential wisdom to share, who have practical experience that is the breeding ground for all useful theory, we may begin to bond with one another in ways that renew our solidarity.

When black women renew our political commitment to homeplace, we can address the needs and concerns of young black women who are groping for structures of meaning that will further their growth, young women who are struggling for self-definition. Together, black women can renew our commitment to black liberation struggle, sharing insights and awareness, sharing feminist thinking and feminist vision, building solidarity.

With this foundation, we can regain lost perspective, give life new meaning. We can make homeplace that space where we return for renewal and self-recovery, where we can heal our wounds and become whole.

Mapping the Text

1. Find sentences in the hooks essay that indicate how she is defining *homeplace*. Using the ideas represented in these statements, draft your own definition and share it with two or three members of the class as they share their definitions with you. Consider the similarities and differences in the definitions. Is hooks's view of homeplace adequate? Would you change anything or add anything?
2. As a writer of essays, hooks is often categorized as a critical theorist. She uses this genre as an analytical instrument to interrogate problems and concerns and pose solutions. What are the problems that she interrogates in "Homeplace"? What solutions does she pose? In your own assessment of the problems or concerns that she raises, what is the extent to which you agree or disagree with hooks's view?
3. Consider hooks's basic rhetorical decisions. *Who* is she presenting herself as in the essay? What impressions of her as the writer of the essay do you receive from what she says? What *message(s)* come through as you read this text? What *purpose* do you think hooks is fulfilling in writing such an essay? To *whom* does she seem to be speaking directly, or maybe indirectly? How would you describe the *context* in which hooks is writing? In other words, what are the conditions and circumstances that seem to be the springboard that offers the inspiration for her wanting or needing to write?

Writing to Inquire

1. hooks identifies women's rights and feminist struggle as an issue of concern. Conduct a library search to gather several definitions of feminism. Document your sources. Write an essay in which you explain hooks's view of either women's rights or feminist struggle in light of one of more of your definitions. Consider, for example, how she enacts the definition, or ignores it, or extends it, or perhaps subverts it.

Landscape and Narrative

BARRY LOPEZ

Barry Lopez (1945–) writes both fiction and nonfiction; he is perhaps best known for his work as an essayist. His earliest book, *Desert Notes: Reflections in the Eye of a Raven* (1976), was the first of a trilogy that includes *River Notes: The Dance of Herons* (1979) and *Field Notes: The Grace Note of the Canyon Wren* (1994). Other works include *Crossing Open Ground* (1978); *Of Wolves and Men* (1978); and *Arctic Dreams* (1986). In "Landscape and Narrative," Lopez writes about the relationship between human culture and nature.

One summer evening in a remote village in the Brooks Range of Alaska, I sat among a group of men listening to hunting stories about the trapping and pursuit of animals. I was particularly interested in several incidents involving wolverine, in part because a friend of mine was studying wolverine in Canada, among the Cree, but, too, because I find this animal such an intense creature. To hear about its life is to learn more about fierceness.

Wolverines are not intentionally secretive, hiding their lives from view, but they are seldom observed. The range of their known behavior is less than that of, say, bears or wolves. Still, that evening no gratuitous details were set out. This was somewhat odd, for wolverine easily excite the imagination; they can loom suddenly in the landscape with authority, with an aura larger than their compact physical dimensions, drawing one's immediate and complete attention. Wolverine also have a deserved reputation for resoluteness in the worst winters, for ferocious strength. But neither did these attributes induce the men to embellish.

I listened carefully to these stories, taking pleasure in the sharply observed detail surrounding the dramatic thread of events. The story I remember most vividly was about a man hunting a wolverine from a snow machine in the spring. He followed the animal's tracks for several miles over rolling tundra in a certain valley. Soon he caught sight ahead of a dark spot on the crest of a hill—the wolverine pausing to look back. The hunter was catching up, but each time he came over a rise the wolverine was looking back from the next rise, just out of range. The hunter topped one more rise and met the wolverine bounding toward him. Before he could pull his rifle from its scabbard the wolverine flew across the engine cowl and the windshield, hitting him square in the chest. The hunter scrambled his arms wildly, trying to get the wolverine out of his lap, and fell over as he did so. The wolverine jumped clear as the snow machine rolled over, and fixed the man with a stare. He had not bitten, not even scratched the man. Then the wolverine walked away. The man thought of reaching for the gun, but no, he did not.

The other stories were like this, not so much making a point as evoking something about contact with wild animals that would never be completely understood.

When the stories were over, four or five of us walked out of the home of our host. The surrounding land, in the persistent light of a far northern summer, was still visible for miles—the striated, pitched massifs of the Brooks Range; the shy, willow-lined banks of the John River flowing south from Anaktuvuk Pass; and the flat tundra plain, opening with great affirmation to the north. The landscape seemed alive because of the stories. It was precisely these ocherous tones, this kind of willow, exactly this austerity that had informed the wolverine narratives. I felt exhilaration, and a deeper confirmation of the stories. The mundane tasks which awaited me I anticipated now with pleasure. The stories had renewed in me a sense of the purpose of my life.

This feeling, an inexplicable renewal of enthusiasm after storytelling, is familiar to many people. It does not seem to matter greatly what the subject is, as long as the context is intimate and the story is told for its own sake, not forced to serve merely as the vehicle for an idea. The tone of the story need not be solemn. The darker aspects of life need not be ignored. But I think intimacy is indispensable—a feeling that derives from the listener's trust and a storyteller's certain knowledge of his subject and regard for his audience. This intimacy deepens if the storyteller tempers his authority with humility, or when terms of idiomatic expression, or at least the physical setting for the story, are shared.

I think of two landscapes—one outside the self, the other within. The external landscape is the one we see—not only the line and color of the land and its shading at different times of the day, but also its plants and animals in season, its weather, its geology, the record of its climate and evolution. If you walk up, say, a dry arroyo in the Sonoran Desert you will feel a mounding and rolling of sand and silt beneath your foot that is distinctive. You will anticipate the crumbling of the sedimentary earth in the arroyo bank as your hand reaches out, and in that tangible evidence you will sense a history of water in the region. Perhaps a black-throated sparrow lands in a paloverde bush—the resiliency of the twig under the bird, that precise shade of yellowish-green against the milk-blue sky, the fluttering whir of the arriving sparrow, are what I mean by "the landscape." Draw on the smell of creosote bush, or clack stones together in the dry air. Feel how light is the desiccated dropping of the kangaroo rat. Study an animal track obscured by the wind. These are all elements of the land, and what makes the landscape comprehensible are the relationships between them. One learns a landscape finally not by knowing the name or identity of everything in it, but by perceiving the relationships in it—like that between the sparrow and the twig. The difference between the relationships and the elements is the same as that between written history and a catalog of events.

The second landscape I think of is an interior one, a kind of projection within a person of a part of the exterior landscape. Relationships in the exterior landscape include those that are named and discernible, such as the nitrogen cycle, or a vertical sequence of Ordovician limestone, and others that are uncodified or ineffable, such as winter light falling on a particular kind of granite, or the effect of humidity on the frequency of a blackpoll warbler's burst of song. That these relationships have purpose and order, however inscrutable they may seem to us, is a tenet of evolution. Similarly, the speculations, intuitions, and formal ideas we refer to as "mind" are a set of relationships in the interior landscape with purpose and order; some of these are obvious, many impenetrably subtle. The shape and character of these relationships in a person's thinking, I believe, are deeply influenced by where on this earth one goes, what one touches, the patterns one observes in nature—the intricate history of one's life in the land, even a life in the city, where wind, the chirp of birds, the line of a falling leaf, are known. These thoughts are arranged, further, according to the thread of one's moral, intellectual, and spiritual development. The interior landscape responds to the character and subtlety of an exterior landscape; the shape of the individual mind is affected by land as it is by genes.

In stories like those I heard at Anaktuvuk Pass about wolverine, the relationship between separate elements in the land is set forth clearly. It is put in a simple framework of sequential incidents and apposite detail. If the exterior landscape is limned well, the listener often feels that he has heard something pleasing and authentic—trustworthy. We derive this sense of confidence I think not so much from verifiable truth as from an understanding that lying has played no role in the narrative. The storyteller is obligated to engage the reader with a precise vocabulary, to set forth a coherent and dramatic rendering of incidents—and to be ingenuous.

10 When one hears a story one takes pleasure in it for different reasons—for the euphony of its phrases, an aspect of the plot, or because one identifies with one of the characters. With certain stories certain individuals may experience a deeper, more profound sense of well-being. This latter phenomenon, in my understanding, rests at the heart of storytelling as an elevated experience among aboriginal peoples. It results from bringing two landscapes together. The exterior landscape is organized according to principles or laws or tendencies beyond human control. It is understood to contain an integrity that is beyond human analysis and unimpeachable. Insofar as the storyteller depicts various subtle and obvious relationships in the exterior landscape accurately in his story, and insofar as he orders them along traditional lines of meaning to create the narrative, the narrative will "ring true." The listener who "takes the story to heart" will feel a pervasive sense of congruence within himself and also with the world.

Among the Navajo and, as far as I know, many other native peoples, the land is thought to exhibit a sacred order. That order is the basis of ritual. The rituals themselves reveal the power in that order. Art, architecture, vocabulary, and costume, as well as ritual, are derived from the perceived natural order of the universe—from observations and meditations on the exterior landscape. An indigenous philosophy—metaphysics, ethics, epistemology, aesthetics, and logic—may also be derived from a people's continuous attentiveness to both the obvious (scientific) and ineffable (artistic) orders of the local landscape. Each individual, further, undertakes to order his interior landscape according to the exterior landscape. To succeed in this means to achieve a balanced state of mental health.

I think of the Navajo for a specific reason. Among the various sung ceremonies of this people—Enemyway, Coyoteway, Red Antway, Uglyway—is one called Beautyway. In the Navajo view, the elements of one's interior life—one's psychological makeup and moral bearing—are subject to a persistent principle of disarray. Beautyway is, in part, a spiritual invocation of the order of the exterior universe, that irreducible, holy complexity that manifests itself as all things changing through time (a Navajo definition of beauty, hózhǫ́ǫ́). The purpose of this invocation is to recreate in the individual who is the subject of the Beautyway ceremony that same order, to make the individual again a reflection of the myriad enduring relationships of the landscape.

I believe story functions in a similar way. A story draws on relationships in the exterior landscape and projects them onto the interior landscape. The purpose of storytelling is to achieve harmony between the two landscapes, to use all the elements of story—syntax, mood, figures of speech—in a harmonious way to reproduce the harmony of the land in the individual's interior. Inherent in story is the power to reorder a state of psychological confusion through contact with the pervasive truth of those relationships we call "the land."

These thoughts, of course, are susceptible to interpretation. I am convinced, however, that these observations can be applied to the kind of prose we call nonfiction as well as to traditional narrative forms such as the novel and the short story, and to some poems. Distinctions between fiction and nonfiction are sometimes obscured by arguments over what constitutes "the truth." In the aboriginal literature I am familiar with, the first distinction made among narratives is to separate the authentic from the inauthentic. Myth, which we tend to regard as fictitious or "merely metaphorical," is as authentic, as real, as the story of a wolverine in a man's lap. (A distinction is made, of course, about the elevated nature of myth—and frequently the circumstances of myth-telling are more rigorously prescribed than those for the telling of legends or vernacular stories—but all of these narratives are rooted in the local landscape. To violate *that* connection is to call the narrative itself into question.)

15 The power of narrative to nurture and heal, to repair a spirit in disarray, rests on two things: the skillful invocation of unimpeachable sources and

a listener's knowledge that no hypocrisy or subterfuge is involved. This last simple fact is to me one of the most imposing aspects of the Holocene history of man.

We are more accustomed now to thinking of "the truth" as something that can be explicitly stated, rather than as something that can be evoked in a metaphorical way outside science and Occidental culture. Neither can truth be reduced to aphorism or formulas. It is something alive and unpronounceable. Story creates an atmosphere in which it becomes discernible as a pattern. For a storyteller to insist on relationships that do not exist is to lie. Lying is the opposite of story. (I do not mean to confuse ignorance with deception, or to imply that a storyteller can perceive all that is inherent in the land. Every storyteller falls short of a perfect limning of the landscape—perception and language both fail. But to make up something that is not there, something which can never be corroborated in the land, to knowingly set forth a false relationship, is to be lying, no longer telling a story.)

Because of the intricate, complex nature of the land, it is not always possible for a storyteller to grasp what is contained in a story. The intent of the storyteller, then, must be to evoke, honestly, some single aspect of all that the land contains. The storyteller knows that because different individuals grasp the story at different levels, the focus of his regard for truth must be at the primary one—with who was there, what happened, when, where, and why things occurred. The story will then possess similar truth at other levels—the integrity inherent at the primary level of meaning will be conveyed everywhere else. As long as the storyteller carefully describes the order before him, and uses his storytelling skill to heighten and emphasize certain relationships, it is even possible for the story to be more successful than the storyteller himself is able to imagine.

I would like to make a final point about the wolverine stories I heard at Anaktuvuk Pass. I wrote down the details afterward, concentrating especially on aspects of the biology and ecology of the animals. I sent the information on to my friend living with the Cree. When, many months later, I saw him, I asked whether the Cree had enjoyed these insights of the Nunamiut into the nature of the wolverine. What had they said?

"You know," he told me, "how they are. They said, 'That could happen.'"

20 In these uncomplicated words the Cree declared their own knowledge of the wolverine. They acknowledged that although they themselves had never seen the things the Nunamiut spoke of, they accepted them as accurate observations, because they did not consider story a context for misrepresentation. They also preserved their own dignity by not overstating their confidence in the Nunamiut, a distant and unknown people.

Whenever I think of this courtesy on the part of the Cree I think of the dignity that is ours when we cease to demand the truth and realize that the best we can have of those substantial truths that guide our lives is metaphorical—a story. And the most of it we are likely to discern comes only when we accord one another the respect the Cree showed the Nunamiut. Beyond this—that the interior landscape is a metaphorical representation of the exterior landscape, that the truth reveals itself most fully not in dogma but in the paradox, irony, and contradictions that distinguish compelling narratives—beyond this there are only failures of imagination: reductionism in science; fundamentalism in religion; fascism in politics.

Our national literatures should be important to us insofar as they sustain us with illumination and heal us. They can always do that so long as they are written with respect for both the source and the reader, and with an understanding of why the human heart and the land have been brought together so regularly in human history.

Mapping the Text

1. In "Landscape and Narrative," Barry Lopez makes a connection between the landscape and storytelling by identifying two landscapes, one outside of the self and another inside the self. Read through his essay to find sentences where he explains the difference between these external and internal views. How does he talk about the external landscape? How does he talk about the internal landscape? Then look for other binary relationships in the essay (e.g., fiction and nonfiction). See if you can determine a pattern for how he places these ideas side by side. When your analysis is complete, think about what, given the title of his essay, seems to be Lopez's most important connection and discuss with two or three members of your class how your group thinks he establishes relationships between the landscape and storytelling, and why.

Writing to Inquire

1. Consider your own landscapes, the physical world that surrounds you. Describe this landscape. Do these landscapes seem to inspire or suggest stories or memories, or to shape in any way the views of yourself that you hold?
2. Taking to heart the connections that Lopez makes between the physical land and our mental scapes, what do you think that the people of the twenty-second century might be like given the places that we are likely to leave behind to surround them?

READINGS FOR INQUIRY AND EXPLORATION

Taking a Visitor to See the Ruins

PAULA GUNN ALLEN

Paula Gunn Allen (1939–) is a Native American novelist, poet, and literary critic. Her first book, *Blind Lion Poems,* was published in 1974. Her critical work includes the edited collection *Studies of American Indian Literature: Critical Essays and Course Designs* (1983). Other publications include *Skin and Bones: Poems, 1979–1987* (1988); *The Woman Who Owned the Shadows* (1992); *The Sacred Hoop: Recovering the Feminine in American Indian Traditions* (1992); *Life Is a Fatal Disease: Collected Poems, 1962–1995* (1996); *Off the Reservation: Reflections on Boundary-Busting, Border-Crossing Loose Cannons* (1998); and *As Long As the Rivers Flow: The Stories of Nine Native Americans* (with Patricia Clark Smith, 2001), as well as numerous articles about Native American literature. Allen's poem "Taking a Visitor to See the Ruins" explores a provocative view of cultural expectations.

for Joe Bruchac

He's still telling about the time he came west
and was visiting me. I knew he
wanted to see some of the things

everybody sees when they're in the wilds of New Mexico.
So when we'd had our morning coffee
after he'd arrived, I said,

Would you like to go see some old Indian ruins?
His eyes brightened with excitement,
he was thinking, no doubt,

of places like the ones he'd known where he came from,
sacred caves filled with falseface masks,
ruins long abandoned, built secure

into the sacred lands; or of pueblos
once home to vanished people but peopled still
by their ghosts, connected still with the bone-old land.

Sure, he said. I'd like that a lot.
Come on, I said, and we got in my car,

drove a few blocks east, toward the towering peaks

of the Sandias. We stopped at a tall
high-security apartment building made of stone,
went up a walk past the pond and pressed the buzzer.

They answered and we went in,
past the empty pool room, past the empty party room,
up five flights in the elevator, down the abandoned hall.

Joe, I said when we'd gotten inside the chic apartment,
I'd like you to meet the old Indian ruins
I promised.

My mother, Mrs. Francis, and my grandmother, Mrs. Gottlieb.
His eyes grew large, and then he laughed
looking shocked at the two

women he'd just met. Silent for a second, they laughed too.
And he's still telling the tale of the old
Indian ruins he visited in New Mexico,

the two who still live pueblo style in high-security dwellings
way up there where the enemy can't reach them
just like in the olden times.

Mapping the Text

1. Consider the word *ruin* in Paula Gunn Allen's poem. What meanings of this word does Allen take advantage of in this poem? What meanings does she pit her view against? What meanings does she push her view toward? What effect does she create in her use of this type of language play?
2. Allen's poem is subtly filled with cultural information about the people represented in the poem. She dedicates the poem to Joe Bruchac (another writer who writes about his Native American heritage). Assume that he is the "he" in the poem. What information does Allen give about *who* he is? What information does she suggest about New Mexico? What information does she suggest about the narrator in the poem?

Writing to Inquire

1. Allen paints a provocative image of relationships, values, and expectation in her poem. She also alludes to provocative issues. Join two or three other students to look closely and critically at the poem. What issues do you detect embedded in the poem? Use the poem as a springboard for a further consideration of one of the issues. What genre seems

appropriate for the expression of this next consideration? Would you write another poem? a narrative? an essay? a research paper? What choice would you make?

2. The writers in this chapter each convey some dimension of a self in geographical and often ideological space. What is your view of the self that Paula Gunn Allen conveys and the space in which she defines this self?

The Memory Place

BARBARA KINGSOLVER

Barbara Kingsolver (1995–), a native of Kentucky who now lives in Arizona, writes fiction and essays. Among her many publications are *Animal Dreams* (1991); *The Bean Trees: A Novel* (1998); *The Poisonwood Bible* (1998); *Pigs in Heaven* (1999); and *Prodigal Summer* (2000). Her articles have appeared in a variety of publications, including the *Nation,* the *New York Times,* and *Smithsonian,* and many of them are included in the collection *High Tide in Tucson: Essays from Now or Never* (1996). "The Memory Place," included in *High Tide,* makes important connections between our most private places for personal reflection and public issues involving the environment.

This is the kind of April morning no other month can touch: a world tinted in watercolor pastels of redbud, dogtooth violet, and gentle rain. The trees are beginning to shrug off winter; the dark, leggy maple woods are shot through with gleaming constellations of white dogwood blossoms. The road winds through deep forest near Cumberland Falls, Kentucky, carrying us across the Cumberland Plateau toward Horse Lick Creek. Camille is quiet beside me in the front seat, until at last she sighs and says, with a child's poetic logic, "This reminds me of the place I always like to think about."

Me too, I tell her. It's the exact truth. I grew up roaming wooded hollows like these, though they were more hemmed-in, keeping their secrets between the wide-open cattle pastures and tobacco fields of Nicholas County, Kentucky. My brother and sister and I would hoist cane fishing poles over our shoulders, as if we intended to make ourselves useful, and head out to spend a Saturday doing nothing of the kind. We haunted places we called the Crawdad Creek, the Downy Woods (for downy woodpeckers and also for milkweed fluff), and—thrillingly, because we'd once found big bones there—Dead Horse Draw. We caught crawfish with nothing but patience and our hands, boiled them with wild onions over a campfire, and ate them and declared them the best food on earth. We collected banana-scented paw-paw fruits, and were tempted by fleshy, fawn-colored mushrooms but left those alone. We watched birds whose names we didn't know build nests in trees whose names we generally did. We witnessed the unfurling of hickory and oak and maple leaves in the springtime, so tender as to appear nearly edible; we collected them and pressed them with a hot iron under waxed paper when they blushed and dropped in the fall. Then we waited again for spring, even more impatiently than we waited for Christmas, because its gifts were more abundant, needed no batteries, and somehow seemed more exclusively *ours.* I can't imagine that any discovery I ever make, in the rest of my life, will give me the same electric thrill I felt when I first found little righteous Jack in his crimson-curtained pulpit poking up from the base of a rotted log.

These were the adventures of my childhood: tame, I guess, by the standards established by Mowgli the Jungle Boy or even Laura Ingalls Wilder. Nevertheless, it was the experience of nature, with its powerful lessons in static change and predictable surprise. Much of what I know about life, and almost everything I believe about the way I want to live, was formed in those woods. In times of acute worry or insomnia or physical pain, when I close my eyes and bring to mind the place I always like to think about, it looks like the woods in Kentucky.

Horse Lick Creek is a tributary to the Rockcastle River, which drains most of eastern Kentucky and has won enough points for beauty and biological diversity to be named a "wild river." The Nature Conservancy has chosen Horse Lick as a place to cherish particularly, and protect. The creek itself is 16 miles long, with a watershed of 40,000 acres; of this valley, 8,000 acres belong to the Forest Service, about 1,500 to the Nature Conservancy, and the remainder to small farms, whose rich bottoms are given over to tobacco and hay and corn, and whose many steep, untillable slopes are given to forest. The people who reside here have few choices about how they will earn a living. If they are landless, they can work for the school system or county government, they can commute to a distant city, or they can apply for food stamps. If they do have land, they are cursed and blessed with farming. It's rough country. The most lucrative crop that will grow around here is marijuana, and while few would say they approve, everybody knows it's the truth.

5 Sand Gap, the town at the upper end of the valley, is the straggling remains of an old mining camp. Gapites, as the people of Sand Gap call themselves, take note of us as we pass through. We've met up now with Jim Hays, the Nature Conservancy employee who oversees this holding and develops prospects for purchasing other land to improve the integrity of the preserve. I phoned him in advance and he has been kind enough, on a rainy morning, to show us the way into the preserve. Camille and I jostle in the cab of his pickup like pickled eggs in a jar as we take in the territory, bouncing around blind curves and potholes big enough to swallow at least a good laying hen. We pass a grocery store with a front porch, and

the Pony Lot Holiness Church. Jesus loves you, Bond welcomes you, declares a sign in another small settlement.

Jim grew up here, and speaks with the same hill cadences and turns of phrase that shaped my own speech in childhood. Holding tight to the wheel, he declares, "This is the hatefulest road in about three states. Everybody that lives on it wrecks." By way of evidence we pass a rusted car, well off the road and headed down-hollow; its crumpled nose still rests against the tree that ended its life, though it's hard to picture how it got there exactly. Between patches of woods there are pastures, tobacco fields, and houses with mowed yards and flower gardens and folkloric lawn art. Many a home has a "pouting house" out back, a tarpaper shack where a person can occasionally seek refuge from the rest of the family.

Turner's General Merchandise is the local landmark, meeting place, and commercial hub. It's an honest-to-goodness general store, with a plank floor and a pot-bellied stove, where you can browse the offerings of canned goods, brooms, onion sets, and more specialized items like overalls and cemetery wreaths. A pair of hunters come in to register and tag the wild turkey they've killed—the fourth one brought in today. It's opening day of turkey season, which will last two and a half weeks or until the allotted number of carcasses trail in, whichever comes first. If the season was not strictly controlled, the local turkey population would likely be extinct before first snowfall.

Nobody, and everybody, around here would say that Horse Lick Creek is special. It's a great place to go shoot, drive off-road vehicles, and camp out. In addition to the wild turkeys, the valley holds less conspicuous riches: limestone cliffs and caves that shelter insectivorous bats, including the endangered Indiana bat; shoals in the clear, fast water where many species of rare mussels hold on for their lives. All of this habitat is threatened by abandoned strip mines, herbicide and pesticide use, and literally anything that muddies the water. So earthy and simple a thing as *mud* might not seem hazardous, but in fact it is; fine silt clogs the gills of filter-feeding mussels, asphyxiates them, and this in turn starves out the organisms that depend on the filter feeders. Habitat destruction can be more subtle than a clear-cut or a forest fire; sometimes it's nearly invisible. Nor is it necessarily ugly. Many would argue that the monoculture of an Iowa cornfield is more beautiful than the long-grass prairie that made way for it. But when human encroachment alters the quality of a place that has supported life in its particular way for millions of years, the result is death, sure and multifarious. The mussels of Horse Lick evolved in clear streams, not muddy ones, and so some of the worst offenders here are not giant mining conglomerates but cattle or local travelers who stir up daily mudstorms in hundreds of spots where the road crosses the creek. Saving this little slice of life on earth—like most—will take not just legislation, but change at the level of the pickup truck.

Poverty rarely brings out the most generous human impulses, especially when it comes to environmental matters. Ask a hungry West African about the evils of deforestation, or an unemployed Oregon logger about the endangered spotted owl, and you'll get just about the same answer: I can't afford to think about that right now. Environmentalists must make a case, again and again, for the possibility that we can't afford *not* to think about it. We point to our wildest lands—the Amazon rain forests, the Arctic tundra—to inspire humans with the mighty grace of what we haven't yet wrecked. Those places have a power that speaks for itself, that seems to throw its own grandeur as a curse on the defiler. Fell the giant trees, flood the majestic canyons, and you will have hell and posterity to pay.

10 But Jackson County, Kentucky, is nobody's idea of wilderness. I wonder, as we bounce along: Who will complain, besides the mute mussels and secretive bats, if we muddy Horse Lick Creek?

Polly and Tom Milt Lakes settled here a hundred years ago, in a deep hollow above the creek. Polly was the county's schoolteacher. Tom Milt liked her looks, so he saved up to buy a geography book, then went to school and asked her to marry him. Both were in their late teens. They raised nine children on the banks of Horse Lick. We pass by their homestead, where feral jonquils mark the ghost-boundaries of a front porch long gone.

Their main visible legacy is the Lakes family cemetery, hidden in a little glade. Camille and I wander quietly, touching headstones where seventy or more seasons of rain have eroded the intentions of permanent remembrance. A lot of babies lie here; Gladys, Colon, and Ollie May Lakes all died the same day they were born. A pair of twins, Tomie and Tiny, lived one and two days, respectively. Life has changed almost unimaginably since the mothers of these children grieved and labored here.

But the place itself seems relatively unaltered—at least at first glance. It wasn't a true wilderness even then, but a landscape possessed by hunters and farmers. Only the contents of the wildcat dumps have changed: the one I stopped earlier to inventory contained a hot-water heater, the headboard of a wooden bed, an avocado-green toilet, a playpen, and a coffee maker.

We make our way on down the valley. The hillside drops steeply away from the road, so that we're looking up at stately maple trunks on the left, and down into their upper branches on the right. The forest is unearthly: filtered light through maple leaves gives a green glow to the creek below us. Mayapples grow in bright assemblies like crowds of rain-slick umbrellas; red trilliums and wild ginger nod from the moss-carpeted banks. Ginseng grows here too—according to Jim, many a young man makes his truck insurance payments by digging "sang."

15 Deep in the woods at the bottom of a hollow we find Cool Springs, a spot where the rocky ground yawns open to reveal a rushing underground stream. The freshet merely surfaces and then runs away again, noisily, under a deeply undercut limestone cliff. I walk back into the cave as far as

I can, to where the water roars down and away, steep and fast. I can feel the cold slabs of stone through the soles of my shoes. Turning back to the light, I see sunlit spray in a bright, wide arc, and the cave's mouth framed by a fringe of backlit maidenhair ferns.

Farther down the road we find the "swirl hole"—a hidden place in a rhododendron slick where the underground stream bubbles up again from the deep. The water is nearly icy and incredibly blue as it gushes up from the bedrock. We sit and watch, surrounded by dark rhododendrons and hemlocks, mesmerized by the repetitious swirling of the water. Camille tosses in tiny hemlock cones; they follow one another in single file along a spiral path, around and around the swirl hole and finally away, downstream, to where this clear water joins the opaque stream of Horse Lick Creek itself.

The pollution here is noticeable. Upstream we passed wildcat strip mines, bulldozed flats, and many fords where the road passes through the creek. The traffic we've seen on this road is recreational vehicles. At one point we encountered two stranded young men whose Ford pickup was sunk up to its doors in what they called a "soup hole," an enormous pothole full of water that looked like more fun than it turned out to be. We helped pull them out, but their engine only choked and coughed muddy water out the tailpipe—not a good sign. When we left them, they were headed back to town on foot.

When Tom Milt and Polly Lakes farmed and hunted this land, their lives were ruled by an economy that included powerful obligations to the future. If the land eroded badly, or the turkeys were all killed in one season, they and their children would not survive. Rarely does any creature have the luxury of fouling its own nest beyond redemption.

But now this territory is nobody's nest, exactly. It's more of a playground. The farmers have mostly gone to the cities for work, and with their hard-earned wages and leisure time they return with off-road vehicles. Careless recreation, and a failure of love for the land, are extracting their pound of flesh from Horse Lick Creek.

20 A map of this watershed is a jigsaw puzzle of public and private property. The Conservancy's largest holding lies at the lower end of the valley. We pass through Forest Service land to get to it, and park just short of a creek crossing where several tiny tributaries come together. Some of the streams are stained with iron ore, a deep, clear orange. I lean against the truck eating my sandwich while Camille stalks the butterflies that tremble in congregations around the mud puddles—tiger swallowtails. She tries to catch them with her hands, raising a languid cloud of yellow and black. They settle, only mildly perturbed, behind us, as we turn toward the creek.

We make our way across a fallow pasture to the tree-lined bank. The water here is invisibly clear in the shallows, an inviting blue green in the deeper, stiller places. We are half a mile down-stream from one of the largest mussel shoals. Camille, a seasoned beachcomber, stalks the shoreline with the delicate thoroughness of a sandpiper, collecting piles of shells. I'm less thrilled than she by her findings, because I know they're the remains of a rare and dying species. The Cumberland Plateau is one of the world's richest sites of mussel evolution, but mussels are the most threatened group in North America. Siltation is killing them here, rendering up a daily body count. Unless the Conservancy acquires some of the key lands where there is heavy creek crossing, these species will soon graduate from "endangered" to "extinct."

Along the creekbanks we spot crayfish holes and hear the deep, throaty clicking of frogs. The high bank across from us is a steep mud cliff carved with round holes and elongated hollows; it looks like a miniature version of the windswept sandstone canyons I've come to know in the West. But everything here is scaled down, small and humane, sized for child adventures like those I pursued with tireless enthusiasm three decades ago. The hay fields beyond these woods, the hawk circling against a mackerel sky, the voices of frogs, the smells of mud and leaf mold, these things place me square in the middle of all my childhood memories.

I recognize, exactly, Camille's wide-eyed thrill when we discover a trail of deer tracks in the soft mud among bird-foot violets. She kneels to examine a cluster of fern fiddleheads the size of her own fist, and is startled by a mourning cloak butterfly (which, until I learned to read field guides, I understood as "morning cloak"). Someone in my childhood gave me the impression that fiddleheads and mourning cloaks were rare and precious. Now I realize they are fairly ordinary members of eastern woodland fauna and flora, but I still feel lucky and even virtuous—a gifted observer—when I see them.

For that matter, they probably *are* rare, in the scope of human experience. A great many people will live out their days without ever seeing such sights, or if they do, never *gasping.* My parents taught me this—to gasp, and feel lucky. They gave me the gift of making mountains out of nature's exquisite molehills. The day I captured and brought home a giant, luminescent green luna moth, they carried on as if it were the Hope diamond I'd discovered hanging on a shred of hickory bark. I owned the moth as my captive for a night, and set it free the next, after receiving an amazing present: strands of tiny green pearls—luna moth eggs—laid in fastidious rows on a hickory leaf. In the heat of my bedroom they hatched almost immediately, and I proudly took my legion of tiny caterpillars to school. I was disappointed when my schoolmates didn't jump for joy.

25 I suppose no one ever taught them how to strike it rich in the forest. But I know. My heart stops for a second, even now, here, on Horse Lick Creek, as Camille and I wait for the butterfly to light and fold its purple, gold-bordered wings. "That's a morning cloak," I tell her. "It's *very rare.*"

In her lifetime it may well be true; she won't see a lot of these butterflies, or fern fiddleheads, or banks of trillium. She's growing up in another place, the upper Sonoran desert. It has its own treasures, and I inflate their importance as my parents once did for me. She signals to me at the breakfast table and we both hold perfectly still, watching the roadrunner outside our window as he raises his cockade of feathers in concentration while stalking a lizard. We gasp over the young, golden coyotes who come down to our pond for a drink. The fragile desert becomes more precious to me as it becomes a family treasure, the place she will always like to think about, after she's grown into adult worries and the need for imaginary refuge.

A new question in the environmentalist's canon, it seems to me, is this one: who will love the *imperfect* lands, the fragments of backyard desert paradise, the creek that runs between farms? In our passion to protect the last remnants of virgin wilderness, shall we surrender everything else in exchange? One might argue that it's a waste of finite resources to preserve and try to repair a place as tame as Horse Lick Creek. I wouldn't. I would say that our love for our natural home has to go beyond finite, into the boundless—like the love of a mother for her children, whose devotion extends to both the gifted and the scarred among her brood.

Domesticated though they are, I want the desert boundary lands of southern Arizona to remain intact. I believe in their remnant wildness. I am holding constant vigil over my daughter's memory place, the land of impossible childhood discovery, in hopes that it may remain a place of real refuge. I hope in thirty years she may come back from wherever she has gone to find the roadrunner thickets living on quietly, exactly as she remembered them. And someone, I hope, will be keeping downy woods and crawdad creeks safe for me.

Mapping the Text

1. Barbara Kingsolver says:

> Much of what I know about life, and almost everything I believe about the way I want to live, was formed in those woods. In times of acute worry or insomnia or physical pain, when I close my eyes and bring to mind the place I always like to think about, it looks like Kentucky.

   Think of a place that you like to think about. Describe this place and explain how it connects in some way to what you know about life or something that you believe about the way that you want to live. How is your place similar to or different from Kingsolver's place?

2. Of the rhetorical decisions that Kingsolver makes in this essay with respect to *context, purpose, audience,* and *genre,* which decisions do you find most interesting?

Writing to Inquire

1. In this essay, Kingsolver reminisces about returning with her daughter, Camille, to the place where she grew up. Camille is enjoying and

appreciating this place for the first time. Imagine that Camille is not with Kingsolver. Given what you perceive about the way Kingsolver is thinking in the essay, write a letter, mother to daughter, that Kingsolver might write. What are the points that you think Kingsolver would want to make to Camille? What would be her message? What view and voice do you think she would use?

2. At the end of the essay, Kingsolver asks, "Who will love our imperfect lands?" How does the notion of "imperfection" rather than "perfection" make a difference in how we conceive of environmental protection?

Just Past Shiprock

LUCI TAPAHANSO

Luci Tapahanso (1953–) writes stories and poems that blend Navajo cultural values and forms with the English language. Her works include *One More Shiprock Night: Poems* and *Seasonal Woman* (both published in 1981); *A Breeze Swept Through* (1987); *Saanii Dahataal: The Women Are Singing* (1993); *Blue Horses Rush In* (1997); and *Songs of Shiprock Fair* and *Navajo ABC: A Dine Alphabet Book* (both published in 1999). Raised on the largest Navajo reservation in the United States, Tapahonso examines what it means to be a Navajo in the twentieth and twenty-first centuries. In "Just Past Shiprock," she draws from a storytelling tradition to bring a place and a culture to life.

When I was a child, our family traveled often to Oak Springs, Arizona. Oak Springs is on the eastern slope of the Carriso Mountains, about fifty miles west of Shiprock. My father grew up there, and we have many relatives in the area. Our family has a plot of land with a hogan and storage cellar there.

On one occasion, we were going to Oak Springs, and there were perhaps six or seven children in the back of the pickup and Mary, an older cousin. Mary's father and my mother are siblings, so she is considered our sister. She is considerably older than we are and did not take part in the noisy playing we were involved in. Since she was the oldest one in the back of the pickup, she was responsible for our behavior or misbehavior.

As we went past Shiprock, there were flat mesas, gentle sandhills, and a few houses scattered at distances. Mary pointed to a mesa as we rounded a curve and asked. "See those rocks at the bottom?" We stopped playing and moved around her to listen. The question was the opening for a story. The rocks she pointed at were midway between the ground and the top of the rock pile. The mesa loomed behind, smooth and deep ochre. The rocks were on the shaded side of the mesa. Then Mary told this story:

They said a long time ago, something happened where those rocks are. When I was little, they told me that one time before there were cars or even roads around here, there was a family traveling through here on horseback. They had a little baby girl who was sick. As they came near here, the baby became sicker, and she kept getting worse. They finally stopped. They knew it was no use going on. They just stopped and held the baby. By then, she was hardly breathing, and then finally she just stopped breathing. They just cried and walked around with her.

5 In those days, people were buried differently. The mother and father wrapped her in a pelt of sheepskin and looked for a place to bury her. They prayed, sang a song, then put the baby inside. They stacked rocks over this place so that the animals wouldn't bother her. Of course, they were crying as they rode home.

Later on, whenever they passed by those rocks, they would say, "Our baby daughter is right there," or "She would have been an older sister now." They wiped their tears, remembering her. A lot of people knew that the baby was buried there—that she was their baby and that they still missed her. They knew that and thought of the baby as they passed through here.

So that's why when we come through here, remember those rocks and the baby who was buried there. She was just a newborn. Think about her and be quiet. Those rocks might look like any others, but they're special.

We listened to the story, and since that time we have told the story many times ourselves. Decades later, those particular rocks hold the haunting and lasting memory of a little baby girl. This land that may seem arid and forlorn to the newcomer is full of stories which hold the spirits of the people, those who live here today and those who lived centuries and other worlds ago. The nondescript rocks are not that at all, but rather a lasting and loving tribute to the death of a baby and the continuing memory of her family.

Mapping the Text

1. Luci Tapahonso makes the following statement in "Just Past Shiprock":

> This land that may seem arid and forlorn to the newcomer is full of stories which hold the spirits of the people, those who live here today and those who lived centuries and other worlds ago.

Consider this quotation and answer the questions below:

a. Do the landscapes that you know seem to hold the spirits of the people who live there in a fashion similar to that indicated by Tapahonso in her story?

b. Do these places inspire or suggest stories, or memories, or a sense of self, or ways of knowing the self?

2. Outline the structure of Tapahonso's story. Think about the brevity of the story. What kinds of details does Tapahonso use to convey meaning? What meaning(s) does she convey? How do you assess the quality of this story as a story? On what basis do you make this judgment? Consider the extent to which your assessment might be related to the ways that stories are told and function in your own community. Is this story similar or different, or a little of both?

Writing to Inquire

1. Think of the physical spaces that you currently occupy and the experiences you have in these spaces. Imagine yourself 10 or 20 years from now returning to one of them and reflecting on your life. What did you leave behind? What in the space will function as the trigger for your memories? Are memories like ghosts?

Chicago

CARL SANDBURG

Carl Sandburg (1878–1967) was a poet, folklorist, novelist, and historian. He began his career as a writer when he moved to Chicago in 1913, and he may be best known for his 1916 collection, *Chicago Poems*. Sandburg's works include two biographies of Abraham Lincoln, one of which won the Pulitzer Prize; *Cornhuskers* (1918); *Smoke and Steel* (1920); *Pigeons* (1923); *Country* (1929); *The People, Yes* (1936); *Complete Poems* (1950); and *Honey and Salt* (1963). His poem "Chicago" uses metaphor to invoke the spirit of the city in which he spent much of his life.

Hog Butcher for the World,
Tool Maker, Stacker of Wheat,
Player with Railroads and the Nation's Freight
    Handler;
Stormy, husky, brawling,
City of the Big Shoulders:
They tell me you are wicked and I believe them, for I
    have seen your painted women under the gas lamps
    luring the farm boys.
And they tell me you are crooked and I answer: Yes, it
    is true I have seen the gunman kill and go free to
    kill again.
And they tell me you are brutal and my reply is: On the
    faces of women and children I have seen the marks

of wanton hunger.
And having answered so I turn once more to those who
sneer at this my city, and I give them back the sneer
and say to them:
Come and show me another city with lifted head singing
so proud to be alive and coarse and strong and cun-
ning.
Flinging magnetic curses amid the toil of piling job on
job, here is a tall bold slugger set vivid against the
little soft cities:
Fierce as a dog with tongue lapping for action, cunning
as a savage pitted against the wilderness,
Bareheaded,
Shoveling,
Wrecking,
Planning,
Building, breaking, rebuilding,
Under the smoke, dust all over his mouth, laughing with
white teeth,
Under the terrible burden of destiny laughing as a young
man laughs,
Laughing even as an ignorant fighter laughs who has
never lost a battle,
Bragging and laughing that under his wrist is the pulse,
and under his ribs the heart of the people,
Laughing!
Laughing the stormy, husky, brawling laughter of
Youth, half-naked, sweating, proud to be Hog
Butcher, Tool Maker, Stacker of Wheat, Player with
Railroads and Freight Handler to the Nation.

Mapping the Text

1. Create two lists of images. In one list, jot down the images of Chicago that you identify in Carl Sandburg's poem. In the second list, jot down any images that you may have of Chicago from other sources or that you would have of any twenty-first-century city. You may notice when you compare the lists that Chicago has changed since the days when Sandburg was writing. What has changed about Chicago? about cities? about ways of life in the United States in general?
2. Choose one image from Sandburg's poem to explore. What is the image? How does it seem to work in the poem? What context does Sandburg seem to invoke with the image? What does the image indicate about Sandburg's Chicago?

3. Read Sandburg's poem closely and carefully. What evidence do you see in the poem about Sandburg's feelings toward Chicago? Does he like or not like this city?

Writing to Inquire

1. What is your favorite city, town, or village? Create snapshots through words and images of your view of this place so that the words make a sort of mental collage of it, or create a visual collage through photographs or drawings or a collection of relevant symbols, etc. Then write an essay in which you use the collage as a springboard from which to convey to an audience that you specify a particular idea about this place that you wish to share.

A Small Place

JAMAICA KINCAID

Jamaica Kincaid (1949–) is a native of the island of Antigua, where she was born Elaine Potter Richardson. Kincaid's works include *Annie John (1986), The Autobiography of My Mother (1996),* and *At the Bottom of the River (1992),* all of which examine the relationships between mothers and daughters. Kincaid writes often about issues of identity and power, such as colonialism and feminism. In "A Small Place," (1998) Kincaid pushes readers to examine their own colonizing impulses by exploring the behaviors and attitudes of tourists in a colonized land.

If you go to Antigua as a tourist, this is what you will see. If you come by aeroplane, you will land at the V. C. Bird International Airport. Vere Cornwall (V. C.) Bird is the Prime Minister of Antigua. You may be the sort of tourist who would wonder why a Prime Minister would want an airport named after him—why not a school, why not a hospital, why not some great public monument? You are a tourist and you have not yet seen a school in Antigua, you have not yet seen the hospital in Antigua, you have not yet seen a public monument in Antigua. As your plane descends to land, you might say, What a beautiful island Antigua is—more beautiful than any of the other islands you have seen, and they were very beautiful, in their way, but they were much too green, much too lush with vegetation, which indicated to you, the tourist, that they got quite a bit of rainfall, and rain is the very thing that you, just now, do not want, for you are thinking of the hard and cold and dark and long days you spent working in North America (or, worse, Europe), earning some money so that you could stay in this place (Antigua) where the sun always shines and where the climate is deliciously hot and dry for the four to ten days you are going to be staying there; and since you are on your holiday, since you are a tourist, the thought of what it might be like for someone who had to live day in, day out in a place that suffers constantly from drought, and so has to watch carefully every drop of fresh water used (while at the same time surrounded by a sea and an ocean—the Caribbean Sea on one side, the Atlantic Ocean on the other), must never cross your mind.

You disembark from your plane. You go through customs. Since you are a tourist, a North American or European—to be frank, white—and not an Antiguan black returning to Antigua from Europe or North America with cardboard boxes of much needed cheap clothes and food for relatives, you move through customs swiftly, you move through customs with ease. Your bags are not searched. You emerge from customs into the hot, clean air: immediately you feel cleansed, immediately you feel blessed (which is to say special); you feel free. You see a man, a taxi driver; you ask him to take you to your destination; he quotes you a price. You immediately think that the price is in the local currency, for you are a tourist and you are familiar with these things (rates of exchange) and you feel even more free, for things seem so cheap, but then your driver ends by saying, "In U.S. currency." You may say, "Hmmmm, do you have a formal sheet that lists official prices and destinations?" Your driver obeys the law and shows you the sheet, and he apologises for the incredible mistake he has made in quoting you a price off the top of his head which is so vastly different (favouring him) from the one listed. You are driven to your hotel by this taxi driver in his taxi, a brand-new Japanese-made vehicle. The road on which you are travelling is a very bad road, very much in need of repair. You are feeling wonderful, so you say, "Oh, what a marvellous change these bad roads are from the splendid highways I am used to in North America." (Or, worse, Europe.) Your driver is reckless; he is a dangerous man who drives in the middle of the road when he thinks no other cars are coming in the opposite direction, passes other cars on blind curves that run uphill, drives at sixty miles an hour on narrow, curving roads when the road sign, a rusting, beat-up thing left over from colonial days, says 40 MPH. This might frighten you (you are on your holiday; you are a tourist); this might excite you (you are on your holiday; you are a tourist), though if you are from New York and take taxis you are used to this style of driving: most of the taxi drivers in New York are from places in the world like this. You are looking out the window (because you want to get your money's worth); you notice that all the cars you see are brand-new, or almost brand-new, and that they are all Japanese-made. There are no American cars in Antigua—no new ones, at any rate; none that were manufactured in the last ten years. You continue to look at the cars and you say to yourself, Why, they look brand-new, but they have an awful sound, like an old car—a very old, dilapidated car. How to account for that? Well, possibly it's because they use leaded gasoline in these brand-new cars whose engines were built to use non-leaded gasoline, but you musn't ask the person driving the car if this is so, because he or she has never heard of unleaded gasoline. You look closely at the car; you see that it's a model of a Japanese car that you might hesitate to buy; it's a model that's very expensive; it's a model that's quite impractical for a person who has to work as hard as you do and who watches every penny you earn so that you can afford this holiday you are on. How do they afford such a car? And do they live in a luxurious house to match such a car? Well, no. You will be surprised, then, to see that most likely the person driving this brand-new car filled with the wrong gas lives in a house that, in comparison, is far beneath the status of the car; and if you were to ask why you would be told that the banks are encouraged by the government to make loans available for cars, but loans for houses not so easily available; and if you ask again why, you will be told that the two main car dealerships in Antigua are owned in part or outright by ministers in government. Oh, but you are on holiday and the sight of these brand-new cars driven by people who may or may not have really passed their driving test (there was once a scandal about driving licences for sale) would not really stir up these thoughts in you. You pass a building sitting in a sea of dust and you think, It's some latrines for people just passing by, but when you look again you see the building has written on it PIGOTT'S SCHOOL. You pass the hospital, the Holberton Hospital, and how wrong you are not to think about this, for though you are a tourist on your holiday, what if your heart should miss a few beats? What if a blood vessel in your neck should break? What if one of those people driving those brand-new cars filled with the wrong gas fails to pass safely while going uphill on a curve and you are in the car going in the opposite direction? Will you be comforted to know that the hospital is staffed with doctors that no actual Antiguan trusts; that Antiguans always say about the doctors, "I don't want them near me"; that Antiguans refer to them not as doctors but as "the three men" (there are three of them); that when the Minister of Health himself doesn't feel well he takes the first plane to New York to see a real doctor; that if any one of the ministers in government needs medical care he flies to New York to get it?

It's a good thing that you brought your own books with you, for you couldn't just go to the library and borrow some. Antigua used to have a splendid library, but in The Earthquake (everyone talks about it that way—The Earthquake; we Antiguans, for I am one, have a great sense of things, and the more meaningful the thing, the more meaningless we make it) the library building was damaged. This was in 1974, and soon after that a sign was placed on the front of the building saying, THIS BUILDING WAS DAMAGED IN THE EARTHQUAKE OF 1974. REPAIRS ARE PENDING. The sign hangs there, and hangs there more than a decade later, with its unfulfilled promise of repair, and you might see this as a sort of quaintness on the part of these islanders, these people descended from slaves—what a strange, unusual perception of time they have. REPAIRS ARE PENDING, and here it is many years later, but perhaps in a world that is twelve miles long and nine miles wide (the size of Antigua) twelve years and twelve minutes and twelve days are all the same. The library is one of those splendid old buildings from colonial times, and the sign telling of the repairs is a splendid old sign from colonial times. Not very long after The Earthquake Antigua got its independence from Britain, making Antigua a state in its own right, and Antiguans are so proud of this that each year to mark the day, they go to church and thank God, a British God, for this. But you should not think of the confusion that must lie in all that and you must not think of the damaged library. You have brought your own books with you, and among them is one of those new books about economic history, one of those books explaining how the West (meaning Europe and North America after its conquest and settlement by Europeans) got rich: the West got rich not from the free (free—in this case meaning got-for-nothing) and then undervalued labour, for generations, of the people like me you see walking around you in Antigua but from the ingenuity of small shopkeepers in Sheffield and Yorkshire and Lancashire, or wherever; and what a great part the invention of the wristwatch played in it, for there was nothing noble-minded men could not do when they discovered they could slap time on their wrists just like that (isn't that the last straw; for not only did we have to suffer the unspeakableness of slavery, but the satisfaction to be had from "We made you bastards rich" is taken away, too), and so you needn't let that slightly funny feeling you have from time to time about exploitation, oppression, domination develop into full-fledged unease, discomfort; you could ruin your holiday. They are not responsible for what you have; you owe them nothing; in fact, you did them a big favour, and you can provide one hundred examples. For here you are now, passing by Government House. And here you are now, passing by the Prime Minister's Office and the Parliament Building, and overlooking these, with a splendid view of St. John's Harbour, the American Embassy. If it were not for you, they would not have Government House, and Prime Minister's Office, and Parliament Building and embassy of powerful country. Now you are passing a mansion, an extraordinary house painted the colour of old cow dung, with more aerials and antennas attached to it than you will see even at the American Embassy. The people who live in this house are a merchant family who came to Antigua from the Middle East less than twenty years ago. When this family first came to Antigua, they sold dry goods door to door from suitcases they carried on their backs. Now they own a lot of Antigua; they regularly lend money to the government, they build enormous (for Antigua), ugly (for Antigua), concrete buildings in Antigua's capital, St. John's, which the government then rents for huge sums of money; a member of their family is the Antiguan Ambassador to Syria; Antiguans hate them. Not far from this mansion is another mansion, the home of a drug smuggler. Everybody knows he's a drug smuggler, and if just as you were driving by he stepped out of his door your driver might point him out to you as the notorious person that he is, for this drug smuggler is so rich people say he buys cars in tens—ten of this one, ten of that one—and that he bought a house (another mansion) near Five Islands, contents included, with cash he carried in a suitcase: three hundred and fifty thousand American dollars, and, to the surprise of the seller of the house, lots of American dollars were left over. Overlooking the drug smuggler's mansion is yet another mansion, and leading up to it is the best paved road in all of Antigua—even better than the road that was paved for the Queen's visit in 1985 (when the Queen came, all the roads that she would travel on were paved anew, so that the Queen might have been left with the impression that riding in a car in Antigua was a pleasant experience). In this mansion lives a woman sophisticated people in Antigua call Evita. She is a notorious woman. She's young and beautiful and the girlfriend of somebody very high up in the government. Evita is notorious because her relationship with this high government official has made her the owner of boutiques and property and given her a say in cabinet meetings, and all sorts of other privileges such a relationship would bring a beautiful young woman.

Oh, but by now you are tired of all this looking, and you want to reach your destination—your hotel, your room. You long to refresh yourself; you long to eat some nice lobster, some nice local food. You take a bath, you brush your teeth. You get dressed again; as you get dressed, you look out the window. That water—have you ever seen anything like it? Far out, to the horizon, the colour of the water is navy-blue; nearer, the water is the colour of the North American sky. From there to the shore, the water is pale, silvery, clear, so clear that you can see its pinkish-white sand bottom. Oh, what beauty! Oh, what beauty! You have never seen anything like this. You are so excited. You breathe shallow. You breathe deep. You see a beautiful boy skimming the water, godlike, on a Windsurfer. You see an incredibly unattractive, fat, pastrylike-fleshed woman enjoying a walk on the beautiful sand, with a man, an incredibly unattractive, fat, pastrylike-fleshed man; you see the pleasure they're taking in their surroundings. Still standing, looking out the window, you see yourself lying on the beach, enjoying the amazing sun (a sun so powerful and yet so beautiful, the way it is always overhead as if on permanent guard, ready to stamp out any cloud that dares to darken and so empty rain on you and ruin your holiday; a sun that is your personal friend). You see yourself taking a walk on that beach, you see yourself meeting new people (only they are new in a very limited way, for they are people just like you). You see yourself eating some delicious, locally grown food. You see yourself, you see yourself . . . You must not wonder what exactly happened to the contents of your lavatory when you flushed it. You must not wonder where your bathwater went when you pulled out the stopper. You must not wonder what happened when you brushed your teeth. Oh, it might all end up in the water you are thinking of taking a swim in; the contents of your lavatory might, just might, graze gently against your ankle as you wade carefree in the water, for you see, in Antigua, there is no proper sewage-disposal system. But the Caribbean Sea is very big and the Atlantic Ocean is even bigger; it would amaze even you to know the number of black slaves this ocean has swallowed up. When you sit down to eat your delicious meal, it's better that you don't know that most of what you are eating came off a plane from Miami. And before it got on a plane in Miami, who knows where it came from? A good guess is that it came from a place like Antigua first, where it was grown dirt-cheap, went to Miami, and came back. There is a world of something in this, but I can't go into it right now.

Mapping the Text

1. Review Jamaica Kincaid's narrative and answer the following questions:
   - Who does Kincaid present as the narrator of the story?
   - Why does Kincaid seem to be writing this narrative? What do you think she wants to accomplish by writing this piece?
   - Who do you think she is writing to and for?
   - What message(s) do you think she wants her readers to take away?
   - If you were going to place Kincaid's view in the context of a larger issue, what would the issue be?
2. Jamaica Kincaid is a writer from Antigua who lives in the United States. She writes about "home" away from home. How do you think that this distance might affect what she sees and says?
3. Read through Kincaid's narrative to find images or descriptions of her "small place" that you consider powerful or interesting or provocative in some way. Recount one of your choices and explain the way you see the passage and what your response to it is.

Writing to Inquire

1. Define the word *tourist.* Create a list of both positive and negative stereotypes of tourists and positive and negative roles for tourism in an area. Identify a tourist area and gather data on the impact of tourists and tourism on this area. Write a paper in which you use these data to justify and explain your decision either to be a tourist in the area or not.

The Quare Gene

TONY EARLEY

Tony Earley (1961–) is an assistant professor at Vanderbilt University. Both his first novel, *Jim the Boy,* (2000) and his first collection of essays, *Somehow Form a Family,* (2001) earned critical acclaim. His short stories have been anthologized in the *Best American Short Stories* series, and he is author of a collection of stories titled *Here We Are in Paradise* (1994). In "The Quare Gene," Earley considers the complex relationship between language practices and geographical and cultural communities.

I do not like, I have never liked, nor do I expect to like watermelon. For the record, I consider this a private, dietary preference, not a political choice, neither a sign of railing character nor a renunciation of Southern citizenship. I simply do not like watermelon. Nor, for that matter, do I like grits, blackberries, cantaloupe, buttermilk, okra, baked sweet potatoes, rhubarb, or collard greens. Particularly collard greens. I don't even like to look at collard greens. But, because I am a Southerner—a North Carolinian, of Appalachian, Scots-Irish descent, the offspring of farming families on both sides—my family finds my refusal to like the foods they like some how distressing. When I eat at my grandmother's redroofed, high-ceilinged Victorian barn of a house, in Polk County, North Carolina, my relatives earnestly strive to persuade me that I am making a big mistake by not sampling this or that, that I should just *try* the greens, have just a little *slice* of watermelon, a small *bite* of cantaloupe. They tell me that I will get used to the seeds in blackberries, the mealiness of grits, the swampy odor of greens boiled too long in a big pot. And when I passionately and steadfastly refuse, as I have done for the last thirty-seven years, they stare at me for a few seconds as if they didn't know me, their mouths set sadly, before looking down at their plates as if preparing to offer up a second grace. Then my grandmother pronounces. "Tony Earley, you're just quare."

According to my edition of the Shorter Oxford English Dictionary, "quare" is an Anglo-Irish adjective from the early nineteenth century meaning "queer, strange, eccentric." Most other dictionaries, if they list the word at all, will tell you that it is dialectical, archaic, or obsolete, an anachronism, a muted, aging participant in the clamoring riot of the English language. But when spoken around my grandmother's table, by my parents and aunts and uncles and cousins, "quare" is as current as the breath that produces it, as pointed as a sharpened stick. In my family's lexicon, "quare" packs a specificity of meaning which "queer," "strange," "eccentric," "odd," "unusual," "unconventional," and "suspicious" do not. The only adjective of synonymous texture would be "squirrelly," but we are a close bunch and would find the act of calling one another squirrelly impolite. So, in my grandmother's dining room when "quare" is the word we need "quare" is the word we use.

Nor is "quare" the only word still hiding out in my grandmother's house which dictionaries assure us lost currency years ago. If I brought a quare person to Sunday dinner at Granny's and he ate something that disagreed with him, we might say that he looked a little peaked. Of course, we might decide that he was peaked not because he had eaten something that disagreed with him but because he had eaten a bait of something he liked. We would say, Why, he was just too trifling to leave the table. He ate almost the whole mess by himself. And now we have this quare, peaked, trifling person on our hands. How do we get him to leave? Do we job him in the stomach? Do we hit him with a stob? No, we are kinder than that.

We tell him, "Brother, you liked to have stayed too long." We put his dessert in a poke and send him on his way.

When I was a child, I took these words for granted. They were part of the language 1 heard around me, and I breathed them in like air. Only when I began to venture, away from the universe that revolved around my grandmother's table did I come to realize that the language of my family was not the language of the greater world. I was embarrassed and ashamed when my town-bred classmates at Rutherfordton Elementary School corrected my speech, but by the time I entered college and signed up for an Appalachian-studies class I wasn't surprised to learn that my family spoke a dialect. I had begun to suspect as much, and was, by that time, bilingual. I spoke in the Appalachian vernacular when I was with my family and spoke standard English when I wasn't. This tailoring of speech to audience, which still feels a shade ignoble to me, is not uncommon among young people from my part of the world. In less generous regions of the greater American culture, the sound of Appalachian dialect has come to signify ignorance, backwardness, intransigence, and, in the most extreme examples, toothlessness, rank stupidity, and an alarming propensity for planting flowers in painted tractor tires.

5 This is not some sort of misguided, Caucasian appeal for ethnicity, nor is it a battle cry from the radical left against the patriarchal oppression of grammar, but the fact is that for me standard English has always been something of a second language. I have intuitively written it correctly from the time I started school, but speaking it still feels slightly unnatural, demands just enough conscious thought on my part to make me question my fluency. When I am introduced to a stranger, when I meet a more showily educated colleague in the English department at Vanderbilt, when I go to parties at which I feel unsure of my place in the evening's social pecking order, I catch myself proofreading sentences before I speak them—adding "g"s to the ends of participles, scanning clauses to make sure they ain't got no double negatives, clipping long vowels to affectless, Midwestern dimensions, and making sure I use "lay" and "lie" in a manner that would not embarrass my father-in-law, who is a schoolteacher from California. Occasionally, even my wife, whose Southern accent is significantly more patrician than my own, will smile and ask, "What did you just say?" And I'll realize that I have unwittingly slipped into the language of my people, that I have inadvertently become "colorful." I'll rewind my sentence in my head so that I can save it as an example of how not to speak to strangers. Only in the sanctity of Granny's house can I speak my mother tongue with anything resembling peace of mind.

In 1904, a librarian and writer named Horace Kephart, having recently left his wife and children and suffered a nervous breakdown, moved to the mountains around Bryson City, North Carolina. Although he travelled there initially to distance himself from human contact, he soon recovered enough to take an active interest in the world in which he found himself. An avid gatherer of information and a compulsive list-maker, Kephart spent the rest of his life compiling exhaustive journals and records detailing the geography, history, culture, and language of the southern Appalachians—a pursuit that resulted in countless magazine articles, a celebrated handbook, "Camping and Woodcraft," and two editions of a book entitled "Our Southern Highlanders."

Although Kephart had chosen the Appalachians over the deserts of the Southwest somewhat randomly, he arrived in western North Carolina at a particularly fortuitous time for a man of his particular talents. In the roadless hollows of the Blue Ridge and the Smokies, Kephart found a people isolated by their hostile, vertical geography and living largely as their ancestors had, in the later half of the eighteenth century, when the great Scots-Irish migration out of Pennsylvania first filled the region with people of European descent.

"No one can understand the attitude of our highlanders toward the rest of the earth," Kephart wrote,

> until he realizes their amazing isolation from all that lies beyond the blue, hazy skyline of their mountains. Conceive a shipload of emigrants cast away on some unknown island, far from the regular track of vessels, and left there for five or six generations, unaided and untroubled by the growth of civilization. Among the descendants of such a company we would expect to find customs and ideas unaltered from the time of their forefathers. . . . The mountain folk still live in the eighteenth century. The progress of mankind from that age to this is no heritage of theirs.

Because the Scots-Irish settlers had spoken to and been influenced by so few outsiders, the language they brought with them from Scotland and Ireland, by way of Pennsylvania, had been preserved remarkably intact. And the English dialect that Kephart encountered in North Carolina was in many ways closer to the Elizabethan English of Shakespeare or the Middle English of Chaucer than to anything that had been spoken in England for centuries. Coincidentally, had Kephart come to these mountains a generation later, his research would have been less definitive. Within a few years after his death, in 1931, road-building initiatives, radio, and the Sears, Roebuck catalogue had begun to open even the darkest hollows of the Appalachians to twentieth-century America. In a very short time, the resulting cultural homogenization had turned the southern highlands into a vastly different world from the one that Kephart had originally discovered.

10 When I first read "Our Southern Highlanders," late last year, it held for me the power of revelation. It told me who I was—or at least where I came from—in a way that I had never fully understood before. All the words I had thought specific to my family had entries in a dictionary compiled from Kephart's research. And all of them—with the exception of "quare," which is a mere two hundred years old—were words of Middle English origin, which is to say anywhere from five hundred to eight hundred years

old. Although most of the people I meet today wouldn't have any idea what it's like to eat a bait, Chaucer would have.

Of course, words of Middle English origin are mere babes compared with the words of Latin, Greek, and Hebrew etymology that constitute much of our language. The Latin and Greek roots of the words "agriculture" and "barbarian" were old long before the primitive tribes of the British Isles painted their faces blue and grunted in a dialect resembling English. So I am less taken by the age of the words of the Appalachian vernacular which found their way into my grandmother's house than I am by the specific history they hold.

The word "quare," for me, contains sea voyages and migrations. It speaks of families stopping after long journeys and saying, for any one of a thousand reasons, "This is far enough." It speaks to me of generations of farmers watching red dirt turn below plow blades, of young men stepping into furrows when old men step out. It speaks to me of girls fresh from their mothers' houses crawling into marriage beds and becoming mothers themselves. It bears witness to the line of history, most of it now unmappable, that led to my human waking beneath these particular mountains. If language is the mechanism through which we inherit history and culture, then each individual word functions as a type of gene, bearing with it a small piece of the specific information that makes us who we are, and tells us where we have been. My first cousin Greg and I came down with the same obscure bone disease in the same knee at the same age. For us, the word "quare" is no less a genetic signifier of the past than the odd, bone-eating chromosome carried down through history by one wonders how many limping Scots-Irish.

The last time I remember talking to my great-grandfather Womack, he was well into his nineties, and our whole family had gathered on the porch of the house he built as a young man, along Walnut Creek, in the Sunny View community of Polk County. When I tell this story, I choose to remember it as a spring day—although it may not have been—simply because I like to think that the daffodils in his yard were blooming. (My grandmother, who is eighty-three now, helped him plant them when she was a little girl.) At some point, everyone else got up and went inside, leaving Paw Womack and me alone on the porch. I was in high school, a freshman or sophomore, and was made self-conscious by his legendary age. He had been born in another century. His father had been wounded at Gettysburg. A preacher's son, he had never uttered a swear word or tasted alcohol. He had farmed with a mule until he was well into his eighties, and he had never got another car after one that he bought in 1926 wore out. He voted for Woodrow Wilson. He was *historical.* I felt that the family had somehow chosen me to sit with him; I felt that I needed to say something. I got out of my chair and approached him as one would a sacred relic. I sat down on the porch rail facing him. I remember his immense, knotted farmer's hands spread out on the arms of his rocker. We stared at each other for what seemed like a long time. Eventually, I blushed. I smiled at him and nodded. He smiled back and said, "Who *are* you?"

I said, "I'm Reba's boy. Clara Mae's grandson."

15 "Oh," he said. "Reba's boy."

If we ever spoke again, I don't remember it.

It seems significant to me now that when I told Paw Womack who I was I didn't give him my name. My position as an individual was secondary to my place in the lineage that had led to my sitting on his porch. I identified myself as a small part of a greater whole. *Who are you?* I'm Reba's boy, Clara Mae's grandson, Tom Womack's great-grandson. *Where are you from?* Over yonder. *Why don't you like watermelon?* I don't know. I guess I'm just quare.

Ironically, just as I have learned to appreciate the history contained in the word "quare," I have also had to accept the fact that it is passing out of my family with my generation. Neither I nor my cousins use it outside Granny's house unless we temper it first with irony—a sure sign of a word's practical death within a changing language. Of course, no language is a static property: the life cycles of words mirror the life cycles of the individuals who speak them. Every language, given enough time, will replace each of its words, just as the human body replaces each of its cells every seven years. The self-appointed guardians of English who protest that the word "celibate" means "unmarried," and not "abstaining from sexual intercourse," are wasting their time. "Sounds are too volatile and subtle for legal restraints," Samuel Johnson wrote in the 1755 Preface to his "Dictionary of the English Language"; "to enchain syllables, and to lash the wind, are equally the undertakings of pride."

I tell myself that the passing of Appalachian vernacular from my family's vocabulary is not a tragedy, or a sign of our being assimilated into a dominant culture, but simply the arrival of an inevitable end. "Tongues, like governments," Dr. Johnson wrote, "have a natural tendency to degeneration." I tell myself that it is a natural progression for my children to speak a language significantly different from that of my ancestors, but the fact that it has happened so suddenly, within the span of a single generation—my generation—makes me wonder if I have done something wrong, if I have failed the people who passed those words down. Sometimes the truest answer to the question "Who are you?" is "I don't know."

20 Words and blood are the double helix that connect us to our past. As a member of a transitional generation, I am losing those words and the connection they make. I am losing the small comfort of shared history. I compensate, in the stories I write, by sending people up mountains to look, as Horace Kephart did, for the answers to their questions, to look down from a high place and see what they can see. My characters, at least, can still say the words that bind them to the past without sounding queer, strange, eccentric, odd, unusual, unconventional, or suspicious. "Stories," says the writer Tim O'Brien, "can save us." I have put my faith in the idea that

words, even new ones, possess that kind of redemptive power. Writers write about a place not because they belong there, but because they want to belong. It's a quare feeling.

Mapping the Text

1. In "The Quare Gene," Tony Earley presents several words that he posits are distinctive within the community in which he grew up and that are generally not shared outside. Make a list of these words and identify any one with which you are familiar. In your estimation, what is the significance of having words such as these that exist within a community but are not part of the general knowledge and use of others? Is it important or not? How so? To what extent does it matter or not?
2. Earley suggests there are connections between language, heritage, and place. What connections do you see him making in his account of his own history?

Writing to Inquire

1. What does *vernacular* mean? Can *slang* be categorized as a vernacular? How many other words can you find that we use to describe language use, whether formal (e.g., the language with which Earley says he writes) or informal (e.g., the language that Earley grew up using and still hears among his family)? What do such words suggest about our attitudes toward various uses of language? How do you think we form such attitudes? What causes us to hold our values and assumptions about various vernaculars?

from *Jazz*

TONI MORRISON

Toni Morrison (1931–) is the Robert F. Goheen Professor, Council of the Humanities, at Princeton University, and a highly respected novelist and literary theorist. The excerpts here are from her novel *Jazz* (1992); she also wrote six other novels: *The Bluest Eye* (1970); *Sula* (1973); *Song of Solomon* (1977); *Tar Baby* (1981); *Beloved* (1987); and *Paradise* (1998). She is the author of a collection of critical essays, *Playing in the Dark: Whiteness and the Literary Imagination* (1992), and the editor of another such collection, *Race-ing Justice, En-gendering Power: Essays on Anita Hill, Clarence Thomas, and the Construction of Social Reality* (1992). Among her numerous honors and awards, Morrison has received the 1978 National Book Critics Circle Award for fiction, the 1988 Pulitzer Prize for fiction, and the 1993 Nobel Prize for Literature. The excerpts below illustrate Morrison's appreciation for detail and texture as she sets her narrative in place. In *Jazz,* the place is Harlem, New York City, in the critical era between the world wars and before the invention of jazz as a revolutionary musical form.

I'm crazy about this City.

Daylight slants like a razor cutting the buildings in half. In the top half I see looking faces and it's not easy to tell which are people, which the work of stonemasons. Below is shadow where any blasé thing takes place: clarinets and lovemaking, fists and the voices of sorrowful women. A city like this one makes me dream tall and feel in on things. Hep. It's the bright steel rocking above the shade below that does it. When I look over strips of green grass lining the river, at church steeples and into the cream-and-copper halls of apartment buildings, I'm strong. Alone, yes, but top-notch and indestructible—like the City in 1926 when all the wars are over and there will never be another one. The people down there in the shadow are happy about that. At last, at last, everything's ahead. The smart ones say so and people listening to them and reading what they write down agree: Here comes the new. Look out. There goes the sad stuff. The bad stuff. The things-nobody-could-help stuff. The way everybody was then and there. Forget that. History is over, you all, and everything's ahead at last. In halls and offices people are sitting around thinking future thoughts about projects and bridges and fast-clicking trains underneath. The A&P hires a colored clerk. Big-legged women with pink kitty tongues roll money into green tubes for later on, then they laugh and put their arms around each other. Regular people corner thieves in alleys for quick retribution and, if he is stupid and has robbed wrong, thieves corner him too. Hoodlums hand out goodies, do their best to stay interesting, and since they are being watched for excitement, they pay attention to their clothes and the carving out of insults. Nobody wants to be an emergency at Harlem Hospital but if the Negro surgeon is visiting, pride cuts down the pain. And although the hair of the first class of colored nurses was declared unseemly for the official Bellevue nurse's cap, there are thirty-five of them now—all dedicated and superb in their profession.

Nobody says it's pretty here; nobody says it's easy either. What it is is decisive, and if you pay attention to the street plans, all laid out, the City can't hurt you.

I haven't got any muscles, so I can't really be expected to defend myself. But I do know how to take precaution. Mostly it's making sure no one knows all there is to know about me. Second, I watch everything and everyone and try to figure out their plans, their reasonings, long before they do. You have to understand what it's like, taking on a big city: I'm exposed to all sorts of ignorance and criminality. Still, this is the only life for me. I like the way the City makes people think they can do what they want and get away with it. I see them all over the place: wealthy whites, and plain ones too, pile into mansions decorated and redecorated by black women richer than they are, and both are pleased with the spectacle of the other. I've seen the eyes of black Jews, brimful of pity for everyone not themselves, graze the food stalls and the ankles of loose women, while a breeze stirs the white plumes on the helmets of the UNIA men. A colored man floats down out of the sky blowing a saxophone, and below him, in the space between two buildings, a girl talks earnestly to a man in a straw hat. He touches her lip to remove a bit of something there. Suddenly she is quiet. He tilts her chin up. They stand there. Her grip on her purse slackens and her neck makes a nice curve. The man puts his hand on the stone wall above her head. By the way his jaw moves and the turn of his head I know he has a golden tongue. The sun sneaks into the alley behind them. It makes a pretty picture on its way down.

5 Do what you please in the City, it is there to back and frame you no matter what you do. And what goes on on its blocks and lots and side streets is anything the strong can think of and the weak will admire. All you have to do is heed the design—the way it's laid out for you, considerate, mindful of where you want to go and what you might need tomorrow.

I lived a long time, maybe too much, in my own mind. People say I should come out more. Mix. I agree that I close off in places, but if you have been left standing, as I have, while your partner overstays at another appointment, or promises to give you exclusive attention after supper, but is falling asleep just as you have begun to speak—well, it can make you inhospitable if you aren't careful, the last thing I want to be.

Hospitality is gold in this City; you have to be clever to figure out how to be welcoming and defensive at the same time. When to love something and when to quit. If you don't know how, you can end up out of control or controlled by some outside thing like that hard case last winter. Word was that underneath the good times and the easy money something evil ran the streets and nothing was safe—not even the dead.

. . .

The wave of black people running from want and violence crested in the 1870s; the '80s; the '90s but was a steady stream in 1906 when Joe and Violet joined it. Like the others, they were country people, but how soon country people forget. When they fall in love with a city, it is for forever, and it is like forever. As though there never was a time when they didn't love it. The minute they arrive at the train station or get off the ferry and glimpse the wide streets and the wasteful lamps lighting them, they know they are born for it. There, in a city, they are not so much new as themselves: their stronger, riskier selves. And in the beginning when they first arrive, and twenty years later when they and the City have grown up, they love that part of themselves so much they forget what loving other people was like—if they ever knew, that is. I don't mean they hate them, no, just that what they start to love is the way a person is in the City, the way a schoolgirl never pauses at a stoplight but looks up and down the street before stepping off the curb; how men accommodate themselves to tall buildings and wee porches, what a woman looks like moving in a crowd, or how shocking her profile is against the backdrop of the East River. The restfulness in kitchen chores when she knows the lamp oil or the staple is just around the corner and not seven miles away; the amazement of throwing open the window and being hypnotized for hours by people on the street below.

Little of that makes for love, but it does pump desire. The woman who churned a man's blood as she leaned all alone on a fence by a country road might not expect even to catch his eye in the City. But if she is clipping quickly down the big-city street in heels, swinging her purse, or sitting on a stoop with a cool beer in her hand, dangling her shoe from the toes of her foot, the man, reacting to her posture, to soft skin on stone, the weight of the building stressing the delicate, dangling shoe, is captured. And he'd think it was the woman he wanted, and not some combination of curved stone, and a swinging, high-heeled shoe moving in and out of sunlight. He would know right away the deception, the trick of shapes and light and movement, but it wouldn't matter at all because the deception was part of it too. Anyway, he could feel his lungs going in and out. There is no air in the City but there is breath, and every morning it races through him like laughing gas brightening his eyes, his talk, and his expectations. In no time at all he forgets little pebbly creeks and apple trees so old they lay their branches along the ground and you have to reach down or stoop to pick the fruit. He forgets a sun that used to slide up like the yolk of a good country egg, thick and red-orange at the bottom of the sky, and he doesn't miss it, doesn't look up to see what happened to it or to stars made irrelevant by the light of thrilling, wasteful street lamps.

10 That kind of fascination, permanent and out of control, seizes children, young girls, men of every description, mothers, brides, and barfly women, and if they have their way and get to the City, they feel more like themselves, more like the people they always believed they were. Nothing can pry them away from that; the City is what they want it to be: thriftless, warm, scary and full of amiable strangers. No wonder they forget pebbly creeks and when they do not forget the sky completely think of it as a tiny piece of information about the time of day or night.

But I have seen the City do an unbelievable sky. Redcaps and dining-car attendants who wouldn't think of moving out of the City sometimes go on at great length about country skies they have seen from the windows of trains. But there is nothing to beat what the City can make of a nightsky. It can empty itself of surface, and more like the ocean than the ocean itself, go deep, starless. Close up on the tops of buildings, near, nearer than the cap you are wearing, such a citysky presses and retreats, presses and retreats, making me think of the free but illegal love of sweethearts before they are discovered. Looking at it, this nightsky booming over a glittering city, it's possible for me to avoid dreaming of what I know is in the ocean, and the bays and tributaries it feeds: the two-seat aeroplanes, nose down in the muck, pilot and passenger staring at schools of passing bluefish;

money, soaked and salty in canvas bags, or waving their edges gently from metal bands made to hold them forever. They are down there, along with yellow flowers that eat water beetles and eggs floating away from thrashing fins; along with the children who made a mistake in the parents they chose; along with slabs of Carrara pried from unfashionable buildings. There are bottles too, made of glass beautiful enough to rival stars I cannot see above me because the citysky has hidden them. Otherwise, if it wanted to, it could show me stars cut from the lamé gowns of chorus girls, or mirrored in the eyes of sweethearts furtive and happy under the pressure of a deep, touchable sky.

But that's not all a citysky can do. It can go purple and keep an orange heart so the clothes of the people on the streets glow like dance-hall costumes. I have seen women stir shirts into boiled starch or put the tiniest stitches into their hose while a girl straightens the hair of her sister at the stove, and all the while heaven, unnoticed and as beautiful as an Iroquois, drifts past their windows. As well as the windows where sweethearts, free and illegal, tell each other things.

. . .

And when spring comes to the City people notice one another in the road; notice the strangers with whom they share aisles and tables and the space where intimate garments are laundered. Going in and out, in and out the same door, they handle the handle; on trolleys and park benches they settle thighs on a seat in which hundreds have done it too. Copper coins dropped in the palm have been swallowed by children and tested by gypsies, but it's still money and people smile at that. It's the time of year when the City urges contradiction most, encouraging you to buy street food when you have no appetite at all; giving you a taste for a single room occupied by you alone as well as a craving to share it with someone you passed in the street. Really there is no contradiction—rather it's a condition: the range of what an artful City can do. What can beat bricks warming up to the sun? The return of awnings. The removal of blankets from horses' backs. Tar softens under the heel and the darkness under bridges changes from gloom to cooling shade. After a light rain, when the leaves have come, tree limbs are like wet fingers playing in woolly green hair. Motor cars become black jet boxes gliding behind hoodlights weakened by mist. On sidewalks turned to satin figures move shoulder first, the crowns of their heads angled shields against the light buckshot that the raindrops are. The faces of children glimpsed at windows appear to be crying, but it is the glass pane dripping that makes it seem so.

. . .

Blues man. Black and bluesman. Blacktherefore blue man.
Everybody knows your name.
Where-did-she-go-and-why man. So-lonesome-I-could-die man.
Everybody knows your name.

Mapping the Text

1. Consider Toni Morrison's description of Harlem. How would you describe her appreciation of this city? What spirit of the place and people does she convey? What words and phrases help to convey this feeling?
2. Identify two or three images of the city that Morrison presents in these excerpts. Consider the ideas and experiences she invokes with these images. Assume that not everyone shares her view. Choose one of the images and write a view of the city that contrasts with Morrison's.

Writing to Inquire

1. Morrison writes about a particular time in Harlem's history. Do a library search and find other accounts of Harlem or New York more generally during this era, often referred to as the *Harlem Renaissance*. For example, search for information about immigrant communities, or employment opportunities across various social classes, or the nature of schooling, or the world of art, literature, and music, or the history of Wall Street as a center of finance, banking, and investments. What was this world?
2. The excerpts here constitute just a small segment of Morrison's larger novel about relationships within the context of this city. Read the full novel. Discuss how Morrison uses the setting to help create the story she wants to tell. How vital is the setting to the story?

CALLS TO ACTION AND RESPONSE

The Obligation to Endure

RACHEL CARSON

Rachel Carson (1907–1964) was one of the most important ecocritics of our time. A prolific writer, Carson published her first story, "A Battle in the Clouds," as a fourth grader in *St. Nicholas* magazine. Her works include *Under the Sea Wind* (1941) and *The Sea Around Us* (1951), which established her as a scientist and a writer. She is perhaps best known for her 1962 book *Silent Spring*. This book greatly influenced the contemporary environmental movement.

The history of life on earth has been a history of interaction between living things and their surroundings. To a large extent, the physical form and the habits of the earth's vegetation and its animal life have been molded by the environment. Considering the whole span of earthly time, the opposite effect, in which life actually modifies its surroundings, has been relatively slight. Only within the moment of time represented by the present century has one species—man—acquired significant power to alter the nature of his world.

During the past quarter century this power has not only increased to one of disturbing magnitude but it has changed in character. The most alarming of all man's assaults upon the environment is the contamination of air, earth, rivers, and sea with dangerous and even lethal materials. This pollution is for the most part irrecoverable; the chain of evil it initiates not only in the world that must support life but in living tissues is for the most part irreversible. In this now universal contamination of the environment, chemicals are the sinister and little-recognized partners of radiation in changing the very nature of the world—the very nature of its life. Strontium 90, released through nuclear explosions into the air, comes to earth in rain or drifts down as fallout, lodges in soil, enters into the grass or corn or wheat grown there, and in time takes up its abode in the bones of a human being, there to remain until his death. Similarly, chemicals sprayed on croplands or forests or gardens lie long in soil, entering into living organisms, passing from one to another in a chain of poisoning and death. Or they pass mysteriously by underground streams until they emerge and, through the alchemy of air and sunlight, combine into new forms that kill vegetation, sicken cattle, and work unknown harm on those who drink from once pure wells. As Albert Schweitzer has said, "Man can hardly even recognize the devils of his own creation."

It took hundreds of millions of years to produce the life that now inhabits the earth—eons of time in which that developing and evolving and diversifying life reached a state of adjustment and balance with its surroundings. The environment, rigorously shaping and directing the life it supported, contained elements that were hostile as well as supporting. Certain rocks gave out dangerous radiation; even within the light of the sun, from which all life draws its energy, there were short-wave radiations with power to injure. Given time—time not in years but in millennia—life adjusts, and a balance has been reached. For time is the essential ingredient; but in the modern world there is no time.

The rapidity of change and the speed with which new situations are created follow the impetuous and heedless pace of man rather than the deliberate pace of nature. Radiation is no longer merely the background radiation of rocks, the bombardment of cosmic rays, the ultraviolet of the sun that have existed before there was any life on earth; radiation is now the unnatural creation of man's tampering with the atom. The chemicals to which life is asked to make its adjustment are no longer merely the calcium and silica and copper and all the rest of the minerals washed out of the rocks and carried in rivers to the sea; they are the synthetic creations of man's inventive mind, brewed in his laboratories, and having no counterparts in nature.

5 To adjust to these chemicals would require time on the scale that is nature's; it would require not merely the years of a man's life but the life of generations. And even this, were it by some miracle possible, would be futile, for the new chemicals come from our laboratories in an endless stream; almost 500 annually find their way into actual use in the United States alone. The figure is staggering and its implications are not easily grasped—500 new chemicals to which the bodies of men and animals are required somehow to adapt each year, chemicals totally outside the limits of biologic experience.

Among them are many that are used in man's war against nature. Since the mid-1940's over 200 basic chemicals have been created for use in killing insects, weeds, rodents, and other organisms described in the modern vernacular as "pests"; and they are sold under several thousand different brand names.

These sprays, dusts, and aerosols are now applied almost universally to farms, gardens, forests, and homes—nonselective chemicals that have the power to kill every insect, the "good" and the "bad," to still the song of birds and the leaping of fish in the streams, to coat the leaves with a deadly film, and to linger on in soil—all this though the intended target may be only a few weeds or insects. Can anyone believe it is possible to lay down such a barrage of poisons on the surface of the earth without making it unfit for all life? They should not be called "insecticides," but "biocides."

The whole process of spraying seems caught up in an endless spiral. Since DDT was released for civilian use, a process of escalation has been going on in which ever more toxic materials must be found. This has happened because insects, in a triumphant vindication of Darwin's principle of the survival of the fittest, have evolved super races immune to the particular insecticide used, hence a deadlier one has always to be developed—and then a deadlier one than that. It has happened also because, for reasons to be described later, destructive insects often undergo a "flareback," or resurgence, after spraying, in numbers greater than before. Thus the chemical war is never won, and all life is caught in its violent crossfire.

Along with the possibility of the extinction of mankind by nuclear war, the central problem of our age has therefore become the contamination of man's total environment with such substances of incredible potential for harm—substances that accumulate in the tissues of plants and animals and even penetrate the germ cells to shatter or alter the very material of heredity upon which the shape of the future depends.

10 Some would-be architects of our future look toward a time when it will be possible to alter the human germ plasm by design. But we may easily be doing so now by inadvertence, for many chemicals, like radiation, bring about gene mutations. It is ironic to think that man might determine his own future by something so seemingly trivial as the choice of an insect spray.

All this has been risked—for what? Future historians may well be amazed by our distorted sense of proportion. How could intelligent beings seek to control a few unwanted species by a method that contaminated the entire environment and brought the threat of disease and death even to their own kind? Yet this is precisely what we have done. We have done it, moreover, for reasons that collapse the moment we examine them. We are told that the enormous and expanding use of pesticides is necessary to maintain farm production. Yet is our real problem not one of *overproduction?* Our farms, despite measures to remove acreages from production and to pay farmers *not* to produce, have yielded such a staggering excess of crops that the American taxpayer in 1962 is paying out more than one billion dollars a year as the total carrying cost of the surplus-food storage program. And is the situation helped when one branch of the Agriculture Department tries to reduce production while another states, as it did in 1958, "It is believed generally that reduction of crop acreages under provisions of the Soil Bank will stimulate interest in use of chemicals to obtain maximum production on the land retained in crops."

All this is not to say there is no insect problem and no need of control. I am saying, rather, that control must be geared to realities, not to mythical situations, and that the methods employed must be such that they do not destroy us along with the insects.

The problem whose attempted solution has brought such a train of disaster in its wake is an accompaniment of our modern way of life. Long before the age of man, insects inhabited the earth—a group of extraordinarily varied and adaptable beings. Over the course of time since man's advent, a small percentage of the more than half a million species of insects have come into conflict with human welfare in two principal ways: as competitors for the food supply and as carriers of human disease.

Disease-carrying insects become important where human beings are crowded together, especially under conditions where sanitation is poor, as in time of natural disaster or war or in situations of extreme poverty and deprivation. Then control of some sort becomes necessary. It is a sobering fact, however, as we shall presently see, that the method of massive chemical control has had only limited success, and also threatens to worsen the very conditions it is intended to curb.

Under primitive agricultural conditions the farmer had few insect problems. These arose with the intensification of agriculture—the devotion of immense acreages to a single crop. Such a system set the stage for explosive increases in specific insect populations. Single-crop farming does not take advantage of the principles by which nature works; it is agriculture as an engineer might conceive it to be. Nature has introduced great variety into the landscape, but man has displayed a passion for simplifying it. Thus he undoes the built-in checks and balances by which nature holds the species within bounds. One important natural check is a limit on the amount of suitable habitat for each species. Obviously then, an insect that lives on wheat can build up its population to much higher levels on a farm devoted to wheat than on one in which wheat is intermingled with other crops to which the insect is not adapted.

The same thing happens in other situations. A generation or more ago, the towns of large areas of the United States lined their streets with the noble elm tree. Now the beauty they hopefully created is threatened with complete destruction as disease sweeps through the elms, carried by a beetle that would have only limited chance to build up large populations and to spread from tree to tree if the elms were only occasional trees in a richly diversified planting.

Another factor in the modern insect problem is one that must be viewed against a background of geologic and human history the spreading of thousands of different kinds of organisms from their native homes to invade new territories. This worldwide migration has been studied and graphically described by the British ecologist Charles Elton in his recent book *The Ecology of Invasions.* During the Cretaceous Period, some hundred million years ago, flooding seas cut many land bridges between continents and living things found themselves confined in what Elton calls "colossal separate nature reserves." There, isolated from others of their kind, they developed many new species. When some of the land masses were joined again, about 15 million years ago, these species began to move out into new territories—a movement that is not only still in progress but is now receiving considerable assistance from man.

The importation of plants is the primary agent in the modern spread of species, for animals have almost invariably gone along with the plants, quarantine being a comparatively recent and not completely effective innovation. The United States Office of Plant Introduction alone has introduced almost 200,000 species and varieties of plants from all over the world. Nearly half of the 180 or so major insect enemies of plants in the United States are accidental imports from abroad, and most of them have come as hitchhikers on plants.

In new territory, out of reach of the restraining hand of the natural enemies that kept down its numbers in its native land, an invading plant or animal is able to become enormously abundant. Thus it is no accident that our most troublesome insects are introduced species.

These invasions, both the naturally occurring and those dependent on human assistance, are likely to continue indefinitely. Quarantine and massive chemical campaigns are only extremely expensive ways of buying time. We are faced, according to Dr. Elton, "with a life-and-death need not just to find new technological means of suppressing this plant or that animal"; instead we need the basic knowledge of animal populations and their relations to their surroundings that will "promote an even balance and damp down the explosive power of outbreaks and new invasions."

Much of the necessary knowledge is now available but we do not use it. We train ecologists in our universities and even employ them in our governmental agencies but we seldom take their advice. We allow the chemical death rain to fall as though there were no alternative, whereas in fact there are many, and our ingenuity could soon discover many more if given opportunity.

Have we fallen into a mesmerized state that makes us accept as inevitable that which is inferior or detrimental, as though having lost the will or the vision to demand that which is good? Such thinking, in the words of the ecologist Paul Shepard, "idealizes life with only its head out of water, inches above the limits of toleration of the corruption of its own environment . . . Why should we tolerate a diet of weak poisons, a home in insipid surroundings, a circle of acquaintances who are not quite our enemies, the noise of motors with just enough relief to prevent insanity? Who would want to live in a world which is just not quite fatal?"

Yet such a world is pressed upon us. The crusade to create a chemically sterile, insect-free world seems to have engendered a fanatic zeal on the part of many specialists and most of the so-called control agencies. On every hand there is evidence that those engaged in spraying operations exercise a ruthless power. "The regulatory entomologists . . . function as prosecutor, judge and jury, tax assessor and collector and sheriff to enforce their own orders," said Connecticut entomologist Neely Turner. The most flagrant abuses go unchecked in both state and federal agencies.

It is not my contention that chemical insecticides must never be used. I do contend that we have put poisonous and biologically potent chemicals indiscriminately into the hands of persons largely or wholly ignorant of their potentials for harm. We have subjected enormous numbers of people to contact with these poisons, without their consent and often without their knowledge. If the Bill of Rights contains no guarantee that a citizen shall be secure against lethal poisons distributed either by private individuals or by public officials, it is surely only because our forefathers, despite their considerable wisdom and foresight, could conceive of no such problem.

25 I contend, furthermore, that we have allowed these chemicals to be used with little or no advance investigation of their effect on soil, water, wildlife, and man himself. Future generations are unlikely to condone our lack of prudent concern for the integrity of the natural world that supports all life.

There is still very limited awareness of the nature of the threat. This is an era of specialists, each of whom sees his own problem and is unaware of or intolerant of the larger frame into which it fits. It is also an era dominated by industry, in which the right to make a dollar at whatever cost is seldom challenged. When the public protests, confronted with some obvious evidence of damaging results of pesticide applications, it is fed little tranquilizing pills of half truth. We urgently need an end to these false assurances, to the sugar coating of unpalatable facts. It is the public that is being asked to assume the risks that the insect controllers calculate. The public must decide whether it wishes to continue on the present road, and it can do so only when in full possession of the facts. In the words of Jean Rostand, "The obligation to endure gives us the right to know."

Mapping the Text

1. Go through Rachel Carson's essay and highlight the descriptive words and phrases she uses to present her point of view. Look at your list and consider the impression they make on you as the reader. What are the types of experiences from which these words draw? What images do they create in your mind? What impressions are they designed to convey?
2. From the traditions of classical rhetoric, we have learned that compositions appeal to various sensibilities in readers. These rhetoricians labeled their *appeals* as *logical* arguments, designed to appeal to a reader's ability to reason; *ethical,* designed to appeal to a reader's sense of honor, justice, and good character; and *pathetic,* designed to appeal to a reader's emotions. During the days of ancient Greece and Rome, audiences assigned top priority to logical appeals, but they recognized that the other appeals were also important in making a *persuasive* case that might actually change a reader's point of view or course of action. Rhetoricians today still value this knowledge about speaking and writing. However, we have begun thinking less abstractly about these categories and more concretely in terms of which body parts a writer seeks to involve in responding to the text. In terms of logical appeals, think about whether Carson is talking to your *head,* your mind. In terms of ethics, is she talking to your *backbone* or your *hands?* In terms of emotional appeals, is she talking to your *heart* or perhaps your *stomach?* Does she want you to think or act or feel? Where are her desires for the reader signaled most clearly or subtly? Create a chart of the types of appeals she seems to use. Can you

identify a pattern in these types of arguments? Which of these arguments seem most convincing to you? How successful do you think Carson is in presenting her case?

3. How do you think Carson intends for readers to respond to this text? What type of *impact* does she seek to make on the reader? For example, what does she want readers to think about, to change in their thinking or behavior, or to feel or do?

Writing to Inquire

1. In 1962, a time when environmentalism was not a common interest, Carson raised provocative challenges to chemical companies and the United States government. What government agency regulates the use of pesticides? Whom and what do they protect? What sorts of general policies and regulations does this agency have in place? What is the process for monitoring compliance with the policies?
2. The DDT case was prominent three decades ago. What has happened with DDT since then? Are there still pesticides that pose environmental problems and are (or perhaps should be) contested by concerned citizens?
3. Is this society dealing with environmental issues adequately? Who are the leaders and participants in these public causes? What examples do you see of good actions or actions that are not so good and that should be lobbied against? Is too much attention paid to the environment at the cost of other competing interests, such as jobs or food production?

Putting the Earth First

DAVE FOREMAN

Dave Foreman (1946–) is a founding member of several ecocritical movements, including the Wildlands Project and Earth First! He is the author of *Ecodefense; A Field Guide to Monkeywrenching* (1993), a hands-on how-to manual for (occasionally illegal) environmentalist actions; and *Confessions of an Eco-Warrior* (1991), an autobiography, from which this excerpt is taken.

These are the times that try men's souls; the summer soldier and the sunshine patriot will, in this crisis, shrink from the service of his country, but he that stands it now, deserves the love and thanks of man and woman.

—THOMAS PAINE

In July 1987, seven years after the campfire gathering that spawned Earth First!, I rose among the Ponderosa Pines and scattered shafts of sunlight on the North Rim of the Grand Canyon and mounted a stage festooned with Earth First! banners and American flags. Before me sat several hundred people: hippies in tie-dyed shirts and Birkenstocks, rednecks for wilderness in cowboy boots and hats, middle-class hikers in waffle stompers, graybeards and children. The diversity was impressive. The energy was overpowering. Never in my wildest dreams had I imagined the Earth First! movement would attract so many. Never had I hoped that we would have begun to pack such a punch. We were attracting national attention; we were changing the parameters of the debate about ecological issues; we had become a legend in conservation lore.

Yet, after seven years, I was concerned we were losing some of our clarity of purpose, and blurring our focus. In launching Earth First!, I had said, "Let our actions set the finer points of our philosophy." But now I was concerned that the *what* of our actions might be overwhelming the *why.* For some of those newly attracted to Earth First!, action seemed to be its own justification. I felt a need to return to wilderness fundamentalism, to articulate what I thought were the principles that defined the Earth First! movement, that gave it a specific identity. The response to the principles I offered that day was so overwhelmingly positive that I elaborated on them in the *Earth First! Journal* later that fall. Here they are.

A placing of Earth first in all decisions, even ahead of human welfare if necessary. Our movement is called "Earth First!" not "People First!" Sometimes what appears to be in the short-term interest of human beings as a whole, a select group of human beings, or individual human beings is detrimental to the short-term or long-term health of the biosphere (and to the actual long-term welfare of human beings). Earth First! does not argue that native diversity should be preserved if it can be done without negatively impacting the material "standard of living" of a group of human beings. We simply state that native diversity should be preserved, that natural diversity a-building for three and a half billion years should be left unfettered. Human beings must adjust to the planet; it is supreme arrogance to expect the planet and all it contains to adjust to the demands of humans. In everything human society does, the primary consideration should be for the long-term health and biological diversity of Earth. After that, we can consider the welfare of humans. We should be kind, compassionate, and caring with other people, but Earth comes first.

A refusal to use human beings as the measure by which to value others. An individual human life has no more intrinsic value than does an individual (Grizzly Bear life. Human suffering resulting from drought and famine in Ethiopia is tragic, yes, but the destruction there of other creatures and habitat is even more tragic. This leads quickly into the next point:

An enthusiastic embracing of the philosophy of Deep Ecology or biocentrism. This philosophy states simply and essentially that all living creatures and communities possess intrinsic value, inherent worth. Natural things live for their own sake, which is another way of saying they have value. Other beings (both animal and plant) and even so-called "inanimate" objects such as rivers and mountains are not placed here for the convenience of human beings. Our biocentric worldview denies the modern concept of "resources." The dominant philosophy of our time (which contains Judeo-Christianity, Islam, capitalism, Marxism, scientism, and secular humanism) is anthropocentrism. It places human beings at the center of the universe separates them from nature and endows them with unique value. EF!ers are in direct opposition to that philosophy. Ours is an ecological perspective that views Earth as a community and recognizes such apparent enemies as "disease" (e.g., malaria) and "pests" (e.g., mosquitoes) not as manifestations of evil to be overcome but rather as vital and necessary components of a complex and vibrant biosphere.

A realization that wilderness is the real world. The preservation of wilderness is the fundamental issue. Wilderness does not merely mean backpacking parks or scenery. It is the natural world, the arena for evolution, the caldron from which humans emerged, the home of the others with whom we share this planet. Wilderness is the real world; our citics, our computers, our airplanes, our global business civilization all are but artificial and transient phenomena. It is important to remember that only a tiny portion of the history of the human species has occurred outside of wilderness. The preservation of wildness and native diversity is *the* most important issue. Issues directly affecting only humans pale in comparison. Of course, ecology teaches us that all things are connected, and in this regard all other matters become subsets of wilderness preservation—the prevention of nuclear war, for example—but the most important campaigns being waged today are those directly on behalf of wilderness.

A recognition that there are far too many human beings on Earth. There are too many of us everywhere—in the United States, in Nigeria; in cities, in rural areas; with digging hoes, with tractors. Although there is obviously an unconscionable maldistribution of wealth and the basic necessities of life among humans, this fact should not be used—as some leftists are wont to do—to argue that overpopulation is not the problem. It *is* a large part of the problem; there are far too many of us *already*—and our numbers continue to grow astronomically. Even if inequitable distribution could be solved, six billion human beings converting the natural world to material goods and human food would devastate natural diversity.

This basic recognition of the overpopulation problem does not mean that we should ignore the economic and social causes of overpopulation, and shouldn't criticize the accumulation of wealth in fewer and fewer hands, the maldistribution of "resources," and the venality of multinational corporations and Third World juntas alike, but simply that we must understand that Great Blue Whales, Jaguars, Black Rhinoceroses, and rain forests are not compatible with an exploding human population.[1]

A deep questioning of, and even an antipathy to, "progress" and "technology." In looking at human history, we can see that we have lost more in our "rise" to civilization than we have gained. We can see that life in a hunter-gatherer society was on the whole healthier, happier, and more secure than our lives today as peasants, industrial workers, or business executives. For every material "achievement" of progress, there are a dozen losses of things of profound and ineffable value. We can accept the pejoratives of "Luddite" and "Neanderthal" with pride. (This does not mean that we must immediately eschew all the facets of technological civilization. We are *of* it, and use it; this does not mean that we can't critique it.)

A refusal to accept rationality as the only way of thinking. There is room for great diversity within Earth First! on matters spiritual, and nowhere is tolerance for diversity more necessary. But we can all recognize that linear, rational, logical left brain thinking represents only part of our brain and consciousness. Rationality is a fine and useful tool, but it is just that—a tool, one way of analyzing matters. Equally valid, perhaps more so, is intuitive, instinctive awareness. We can become more cognizant of ultimate truths by sitting quietly in the wild than by studying in a library. Reading books, engaging in logical discourse, and compiling facts and figures are necessary in the modern context, but they are not the only ways to comprehend the world and our lives. Often our gut instincts enable us to act more effectively in a crisis than does careful rational analysis. An example would be a patient bleeding to death in a hospital emergency room—you can't wait for all the tests to be completed. Your gut says, "Act!" So it is with Earth First!'s actions in Earth's current emergency.

A lack of desire to gain credibility or "legitimacy" with the gang of thugs running human civilization. It is basic human nature to want to be accepted by the social milieu in which you find yourself. It hurts to be dismissed by the arbiters of opinion as "nuts," "terrorists," "wackos," or "extremists." But we are not crazy; we happen to be sane humans in an insane human society in a sane natural world. We do not have "credibility" with Senator Mark Hatfield or with Maxxam

[1]Two excellent books on the population issue that are also sensitive to social and economic issues are William R. Catton, Jr.'s *Overshoot: The Ecological Basis of Revalutionary Change* (Urbana, Ill., and Chicago; University of Illinois Press, 1982), and *The Population Explosion*, by Paul and Anne Ehrlich (New York; Simon and Schuster, 1990). No one concerned with the preservation of biological diversity should be without these.

chairman Charles Hurwitz—but they do not have credibility with us! (We do have their attention, however.) They are madmen destroying the pure and beautiful. Why should we "reason" with them? We do not share the same worldview or values. There is, however, a dangerous pitfall here that some alternative groups fall into. That is that we gain little by being consciously offensive, by trying to alienate others. We can be strong and unyielding without being obnoxious.

The American system is very effective at co-opting and moderating dissidents by giving them attention and then encouraging them to be "reasonable" so their ideas will be taken seriously. Putting a critic on the evening news, on the front page of the newspaper, in a national magazine—all of these are methods the establishment uses to entice one to share their worldview and to enter the negotiating room to compromise. The actions of Earth First!—both the bold and the comic—have gained attention. If they are to have results, we must resist the siren's offer of credibility, legitimacy, and a share in the decision-making. We are thwarting the system, not reforming it. While we are therefore not concerned with political credibility, it most be remembered that the arguments and actions of Earth First! are based on the understandings of ecology. It is vitally important that we have biological credibility.

An effort to go beyond the tired, worn-out dogmas of left, right, and middle-of-the-road. These doctrines, whether blaming capitalism, communism, or the devil for all the problems in the world, merely represent internecine squabbles between different factions of humanism. Yes, multinational corporations commit great evil (the Soviet Union is essentially a state-run multinational corporation); there is a great injustice in the world; the rich are getting richer and the poor poorer—but all problems cannot be simplistically laid at the feet of evil capitalists in the United States, Europe, and Japan. Earth First! is not left or right; we are not even in front. Earth First! should not be in the political struggle between humanist sects at all. We're in a wholly different game.

An unwillingness to set any ethnic, class, or political group of humans on a pedestal and make them immune from questioning. It's easy, of course, to recognize that white males from North America and Europe (as well as Japanese males) hold a disproportionate share of responsibility for the mess we're in: that upper and middle-class consumers from the First World take an excessive portion of the world's "resources" and therefore cause greater per capita destruction than do other peoples. But it does not follow that everyone else is blameless.

The Earth First! movement has great affinity with aboriginal groups throughout the world. They are clearly in the most direct and respectful relationship with the natural world. Earth First! should back such tribes in the common struggle whenever possible without compromising our ideals. For example, we are supportive of the Dine (Navajo) of Big Mountain against relocation, but this does not mean we overlook the severe overgrazing by domestic sheep on the Navajo Reservation. We may be supportive of subsistence life-styles by natives in Alaska, but we should not be silent about clearcutting old-growth forest in southeast Alaska by native corporations, or about the Eskimo Doyon Corporation's push for oil exploration and development in the Arctic National Wildlife Refuge. It is racist either to condemn or to pardon someone based on their ethnic background.

Similarly, we are inconsistent when we castigate Charles Hurwitz for destroying the last wilderness redwood forest, yet feel sympathy for the loggers working for him. Industrial workers, by and large, share the blame for the destruction of the natural world. They may be yoked by the big-money boys, but they are generally willing servants who share the worldview of their bosses that Earth is a smorgasbord of resources for the taking. Sometimes, in fact, it is the sturdy yeoman from the bumpkin proletariat who holds the most violent and destructive attitudes toward the natural world (and toward those who would defend it).[2] Workers are victims of an unjust economic system, but that does not absolve them of what they do. This is not to deny that some woods workers oppose the destruction of ancient forests, that some may even be Earth First!ers, but merely that it is inappropriate to overlook abuse of the natural world simply because of the rung the perpetrators occupy on the economic ladder.

Some argue that workers are merely struggling to feed their families and are not delighting in destroying the natural world. They say that unless you deal with the needs of loggers to make a living, you can't save the forest. They also claim that loggers are manipulated by their bosses to express anti-wilderness viewpoints. I find this argument to be patronizing to loggers and other workers. When I read comments from timber fellers expressing hatred toward pristine forests and toward conservationists, it is obvious that they willingly buy into the worldview of the lumber barons. San Francisco's *Image Magazine* reports on a letter to the editor written by one logger: "Working people trying to feed their families have little time to be out in the woods acting like children and making things hard for other working people. . . . Anyone out there have a recipe for spotted owl?

[2]A case in point involves the Spotted Owl, a Threatened species dependent on ancient forests. These little owls are easily attracted by playing tapes of their call. Loggers in the Northwest are going into old-growth forests with tape recorders and shotguns to exterminate Spotted Owls. They feel that if they do so, they will eliminate a major reason to stop the logging of these pristine forests.

Food stamps won't go far, I'm afraid. And since they're always being shoved down my throat, I thought I'd like mine fried."[3] Bumper stickers proclaiming "Kill an owl. Save a logger." are rife in the Northwest. I at least respect the logger who glories in felling a giant tree and who hunts Spotted Owls enough to grant him the mental ability to have his own opinions instead of pretending he is a stupid oaf, manipulated by his bosses and unable to think for himself.

Of course the big timber companies do manipulate their workers with scare tactics about mill closings and wilderness lockups, but many loggers (or cat-skinners, oilfield workers, miners, and the like) simply bate the wild and delight in "civilizing" it. Even educating workers about ecological principles will not necessarily change the attitudes of many; there are basic differences of opinion and values. Conservationists should try to find common ground with loggers and other workers whenever possible, but the sooner we get rid of Marxist views about the noble proletariat, the better.

A willingness to let our actions set the finer points of our philosophy and a recognition that we must act. It is possible to debate endlessly the finer points of dogma, to feel that every nuance of something must be explored before one can act. Too often, political movements become mere debating societies where the participants engage in philosophical masturbation and never get down to the vital business at hand. Others argue that you have no right to argue for environmental preservation until you are living a pure, non-impacting life-style. We will never figure it all out, we will never be able to plan any campaign in complete detail, none of us will ever entirely transcend a polluting life-style—but we can act. We can act with courage, with determination, with love for things wild and free. We can't be perfect, but we can *act*. We are warriors. Earth First! is a warrior society. We have a job to do.

An acknowledgment that we must change our personal life-styles to make them more harmonious with natural diversity. We must eschew surplusage. Although to varying degrees we are all captives of our economic system and cannot break entirely free, we must practice what we preach to the best of our ability. Arne Naess, the Norwegian philosopher and originator of the term "Deep Ecology," points out that we are not able to achieve a true "Deep Ecology" life-style, but it is the responsibility of each of us to move in that direction. Most of us still need to make a living that involves some level of participation in "the system." Even for activists, there are trade-offs—flying in a jetliner to help hang a banner on the World Bank in Washington,

[3]Jane Kay. "Tree Wars," *San Francisco Examiner Image Magazine* (December 17, 1989).

D.C., in order to bring international attention to the plight of tropical rain forests: using a computer to write a book printed on tree pulp that will catalyze people to take action; driving a pickup truck down a forest road to gain access to a proposed timber sale for preventive maintenance. We need to be aware of these trade-offs, and to do our utmost to limit our impact.

A commitment to maintaining a sense of humor, and a joy in living. Most radicals are a dour, holier-than-thou, humorless lot. Earth First!ers strive to be different. We aren't rebelling against the system because we're losing in it. We're fighting for beauty, for life, for joy. We kick up our heels in delight in the wilderness, we smile at a flower and a hummingbird. We laugh. We laugh at our opponents—and, more important, we laugh at ourselves.

An awareness that we are animals. Human beings are primates, mammals, vertebrates. EF!ers recognize their animalness; we reject the New Age eco-la-la that says we must transcend our base animal nature and take charge of our evolution in order to become higher, moral beings. We believe we must return to being animal, to glorying in our sweat, hormones, tears, and blood. We struggle against the modern compulsion to become dull, passionless androids. We do not live sanitary, logical lives; we smell, taste, see, hear, and feel Earth; we live with gusto. We *are* Animal.

An acceptance of monkeywrenching as a legitimate tool for the preservation of natural diversity. Not all Earth First!ers monkeywrench, perhaps not even the majority, but we generally accept the idea and practice of monkeywrenching. Look at an EF! T-shirt. The monkeywrench on it is a symbol of resistance, an heir of the *sabot*—the wooden shoe dropped in the gears to stop the machine, from whence comes the word *sabotage.* The mystique and lore of "night work" pervades our tribe, and with it a general acceptance that strategic monkeywrenching is a legitimate tool for defense of the wild.

And finally: Earth First! is a warrior society. In addition to our absolute commitment to and love for this living planet, we are characterized by our willingness to defend Earth's abundance and diversity of life, even if that defense requires sacrifices of comfort, freedom, safety, or, ultimately, our lives. A warrior recognizes that her life is not the most important thing in her life. A warrior recognizes that there is a greater reality outside her life that must be defended. For us in Earth First!, that reality is Earth, the evolutionary process, the millions of other species with which we share this bright sphere in the void of space.

Not everyone can afford to make the commitment of being a warrior. There are many other roles that can—and must—be played in defense of Earth. One may not constantly be able to carry the burden

> of being a warrior; it may be only a brief period in one's life. There are risks and pitfalls in being a warrior. There may not be applause, there may not be honors and awards from human society. But there is no finer applause for the warrior of the Earth than the call of the loon at dusk or the sigh of wind in the pines.

Later that evening as I looked out over the darkening Grand Canyon, I knew that whatever hardships the future might bring, there was nothing better and more important for me to do than to take an intransigent stand in defense of life, to not compromise, to continue to be a warrior for the Earth. To be a warrior for the Earth regardless of the consequences.

Mapping the Text

1. What does David Foreman mean by the advice that we should "put the earth first"? How does he suggest we do that? Given your experiences, do you consider his suggestions reasonable?
2. Compare Foreman's view of home and the obligations to care for home. How is he similar to or different from the other writers in this chapter?
3. In this excerpt, Foreman considers the impact of people on the environment. Does he consider the impact of the environment on people?
4. Foreman places the earth at the center of his thinking and uses this view as the lens through which he makes his arguments. What effect does this shift in viewpoint create? What does it make visible? What does it cast in shadow?

Writing to Inquire

1. Foreman considers himself an "eco-warrior." What is his "war"? What behavior marks him as a warrior? What will let him know the war is over? What do you think the world might look like if Foreman's view of environmental success prevails?

INQUIRY: WHAT IS HOME?

1. Choose one writer from this chapter whose sentiments you share or with whom you disagree. How does this person's view of home resonate with your own or push you to think more or differently?
2. In recent years, increased attention has been paid to the environment. Participation in public dialog has come in many forms, counting everything from Saturday morning cartoons to restrictions on garbage pickup to the information on various products that tells us about the percentage of recycled materials used to books, articles, and public protests. In fact, we might comfortably say that most of us have experienced at least a general awakening to the existence of these issues and some are quite passionately committed to solving environmental problems. On a continuum of aware but not active to well informed and dedicated to specific issues, where do you place yourself and why?
3. Consider your own community. Generate a list of local environmental concerns. Rank-order these concerns based on your own interests. Compare your list with those of your classmates or friends and/or family. Choose one topic to research and develop a paper that documents your view of the problem and the solutions you think are appropriate.

Where is your home located, in geographical terms? How is home also a matter of linguistic address—how you are spoken to, and by whom? From what standpoint do you look out on the world? the environment?

4. Think about the environment in as broad and as concrete terms as you can. Consider, for example, air quality, land use, garbage disposal, water quality, materials for everyday use (such as paper or other wood products, gas, oil, etc.), air traffic noise, or noise made by other machines. Write about one way in which you are personally affected by an environmental issue.
5. What do future generations have to look forward to in terms of the quality of the environment? Is today's society operating now with an eye and a conscience that look toward this future? Who should take responsibility for this future? What can individuals, or groups, or society as a whole do to be appropriately responsive to our common needs?
6. What environmental issues, beyond preserving the rain forests in Brazil and reducing smokestack pollution from industries in the United States, are identified as global concerns? How are nations cooperating to address the global consequences of environmental issues?
7. Identify one endangered species and describe the circumstances of its endangerment. Where was the natural habitat for this species? Where will/can the habitat be for its future existence? How many of these animals remain? What strategies for preservation are currently underway?
8. What sorts of day-to-day habits can ordinary citizens develop to help sustain the quality of our environment? What sorts of public issues should we be vigilant about in support of the common interests of the society?
9. Review all of the writers in this chapter to generate a master list of the issues that concern them. How are their attitudes and beliefs similar? How are they different? With what view of "home" do you most agree or disagree? Why?

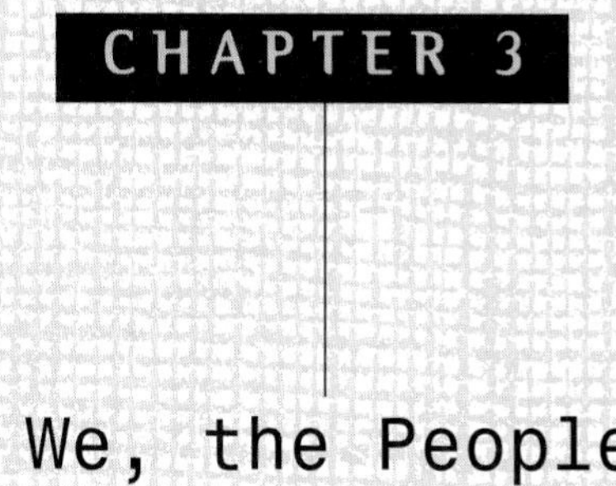

CHAPTER 3

We, the People

One of the most intriguing questions that we can ask about the concept of the United States as a *nation* is: Who counts as *the people?* Who actually do we and should we have in mind when we think of something as basic as *we, the people?* Like all nations, whether we talk about it or not, the United States operates with a sense of collective reality; we view ourselves as a group *together* in geographical space, not necessarily of *one* mind or body, but together, nonetheless, under *one flag*. We are *a nation*. We have views, various though they may be, of what the nation is and how it should function. Beyond a sense of local community, we have symbols of nationhood (such as the flag and the Constitution), and we have vested interests in *national* values, policies, and practices that exist in the name of *the people*—in *our* name. These are shared values that we often articulate with words like *freedom, justice, equality,* and *democracy.* In some fundamental ways we consistently establish the claim, in language and in action, that we *belong* to the nation and that the nation *belongs* to us.

Since September 11, 2001, these questions have taken on a renewed sense of urgency. New proposals to limit immigration, to develop a national identification system, or to limit the freedoms of noncitizens living and working within U.S. borders have been debated. At times, national security and individual rights and liberties have been cast as mutually incompatible. The nation's relationships with other countries have been tested and redefined, and our status on the global stage continues to be reshaped in a new and complex world. Much in the way that the 1941 bombing of Pearl Harbor propelled the United States into worldwide conflict and a new role as "global superpower," so too have the echoes of 11 September changed our perspectives on who we are and where we are situated on the international scene.

So we turn again to a fundamental question: Who are *we, the people?* As the readings in this chapter demonstrate, this question has a long history. It can be addressed in many ways. We have a habit of starting with the diverse places from which we "originally" came and the multiple pathways by which we made North America our land and the United States our nation. These places of origin and pathways to nationhood signal the histories, experiences, ways of being, and ways of doing that we all bring with us to the *American pot,* whether we consider that pot a melting pot, a stewpot, a container for salad, or something else. The miracle, perhaps, is that in the midst of variety and difference, we have actually forged a *union* and, likewise, over the years amid variety we have also formed a multivariant sense of *national identity.*

We manifest our various views of national identity, as demonstrated by the selections in this chapter, individually, through the stories we tell of struggle, adventure, and achievements, and collectively, through the documents we create. By such means, we make opportunities for people not previously connected with us to become aware of our presence, to learn about us, and to negotiate how we and they will exist together in time and space. These written expressions of self and society show us the many ways we have experienced being *American,* past, present, future. They constitute a fabric of *American-ness* and demonstrate that through language we have perhaps our best chance to discover and acknowledge *who* we are, negotiate our similarities and differences, find common ground, identify common concerns, and learn to act respectfully in the presence of others.

The selections in this chapter are about definitions. From Thomas Jefferson to Mary Crow Dog, they showcase beliefs, values, and goals that individuals and groups embrace in the name of nation, freedom, justice, equity, and equality. They speak to the issues that divide us and the circumstances that complicate our lives. They raise for questioning the ways and means by which we create national common ground, often as the writers define themselves in contrast to such notions, on the margins of these views rather than at the center. They demonstrate how language functions dramatically in articulating a sense of nation and also how simultaneously language itself can be a problematic symbol. Together, these writers offer opportunities for you to think about what you mean when you invoke the word *American* and how, indeed, you mean it.

FRAMING THE TOPIC

What Is an American?

J. HECTOR ST. JEAN DE CREVECOEUR

J. Hector St. Jean de Crevecoeur (1735–1813) is best known as the author of *Letters from an American Farmer: Describing Certain Provincial Situations, Manners, and Customs, Not Generally Known; and Conveying Some Idea of the Late and Present Interior Circumstances of the British Colonies of North America* (1782). This text helped the British reading public understand the nature of the experiences of the colonists in North America. "What Is an American?" is included among the sketches. In the excerpt from it below, de Crevecoeur considers the ways that life in the rural colonies affects the identities of the European immigrants who inhabit the colonies.

I wish I could be acquainted with the feelings and thoughts which must agitate the heart and present themselves to the mind of an enlightened Englishman when he first lands on this continent. He must greatly rejoice that he lived at a time to see this fair country discovered and settled; he must necessarily feel a share of national pride when he views the chain of settlements which embellish these extended shores. When he says to himself, "This is the work of my countrymen, who, when convulsed by factions, afflicted by a variety of miseries and wants, restless and impatient, took refuge here. They brought along with them their national genius, to which they principally owe what liberty they enjoy and what substance they possess." Here he sees the industry of his native country displayed in a new manner and traces in their works the embryos of all the arts, sciences, and ingenuity which flourish in Europe. Here he beholds fair cities, substantial villages, extensive fields, an immense country filled with decent houses, good roads, orchards, meadows, and bridges where an hundred years ago all was wild, woody, and uncultivated! What a train of pleasing ideas this fair spectacle must suggest; it is a prospect which must inspire a good citizen with the most heart-felt pleasure. The difficulty consists in the manner of viewing so extensive a scene. He is arrived on a new continent; a modern society offers itself to his contemplation, different from what he had hitherto seen. It is not composed, as in Europe, of great lords who possess everything and of a herd of people who have nothing. Here are no aristocratical families, no courts, no kings, no bishops, no ecclesiastical dominion, no invisible power giving to a few a very visible one, no great manufactures employing thousands, no great refinements of luxury. The rich and the poor are not so far removed from each other as they are in Europe. Some few towns excepted, we are all tillers of the earth, from Nova

Scotia to West Florida. We are a people of cultivators scattered over an immense territory, communicating with each other by means of good roads and navigable rivers, united by the silken bands of mild government, all respecting the laws without dreading their power, because they are equitable. We are all animated with the spirit of an industry which is unfettered and unrestrained, because each person works for himself. If he travels through our rural districts, he views not the hostile castle and the haughty mansion, contrasted with the clay-built hut and miserable cabin, where cattle and men help to keep each other warm and dwell in meanness, smoke, and indigence. A pleasing uniformity of decent competence appears throughout our habitations. The meanest of our log-houses is a dry and comfortable habitation. Lawyer or merchant are the fairest titles our towns afford; that of a farmer is the only appellation of the rural inhabitants of our country. It must take some time ere he can reconcile himself to our dictionary, which is but short in words of dignity and names of honour. There, on a Sunday, he sees a congregation of respectable farmers and their wives, all clad in neat homespun, well mounted, or riding in their own humble waggons. There is not among them an esquire, saving the unlettered magistrate. There he sees a parson as simple as his flock, a farmer who does not riot on the labour of others. We have no princes for whom we toil, starve, and bleed; we are the most perfect society now existing in the world. Here man is free as he ought to be, nor is this pleasing equality so transitory as many others are. Many ages will not see the shores of our great lakes replenished with inland nations, nor the unknown bounds of North America entirely peopled. Who can tell how far it extends? Who can tell the millions of men whom it will feed and contain? For no European foot has as yet travelled half the extent of this mighty continent!

The next wish of this traveller will be to know whence came all these people. They are a mixture of English, Scotch, Irish, French, Dutch, Germans, and Swedes. From this promiscuous breed, that race now called Americans have arisen. The eastern provinces must indeed be excepted as being the unmixed descendants of Englishmen. I have heard many wish that they had been more intermixed also; for my part, I am no wisher and think it much better as it has happened. They exhibit a most conspicuous figure in this great and variegated picture; they too enter for a great share in the pleasing perspective displayed in these thirteen provinces. I know it is fashionable to reflect on them, but I respect them for what they have done; for the accuracy and wisdom with which they have settled their territory; for the decency of their manners; for their early love of letters; their ancient college, the first in this hemisphere; for their industry, which to me who am but a farmer is the criterion of everything. There never was a people, situated as they are, who with so ungrateful a soil have done more in so short a time. Do you think that the monarchical ingredients which are more prevalent in other governments have purged them from all foul stains? Their histories assert the contrary.

In this great American asylum, the poor of Europe have by some means met together, and in consequence of various causes; to what purpose should they ask one another what countrymen they are? Alas, two thirds of them had no country. Can a wretch who wanders about, who works and starves, whose life is a continual scene of sore affliction or pinching penury—can that man call England or any other kingdom his country? A country that had no bread for him, whose fields procured him no harvest, who met with nothing but the frowns of the rich, the severity of the laws, with jails and punishments, who owned not a single foot of the extensive surface of this planet? No! Urged by a variety of motives, here they came. Everything has tended to regenerate them: new laws, a new mode of living, a new social system; here they are become men: in Europe they were as so many useless plants, wanting vegetative mould and refreshing showers; they withered, and were mowed down by want, hunger, and war; but now, by the power of transplantation, like all other plants they have taken root and flourished! Formerly they were not numbered in any civil lists of their country, except in those of the poor; here they rank as citizens. By what invisible power hath this surprising metamorphosis been performed? By that of the laws and that of their industry. The laws, the indulgent laws, protect them as they arrive, stamping on them the symbol of adoption; they receive ample rewards for their labours; these accumulated rewards procure them lands; those lands confer on them the title of freemen, and to that title every benefit is affixed which men can possibly require. This is the great operation daily performed by our laws. Whence proceed these laws? From our government. Whence that government? It is derived from the original genius and strong desire of the people ratified and confirmed by the crown. This is the great chain which links us all, this is the picture which every province exhibits, Nova Scotia excepted. There the crown has done all; either there were no people who had genius or it was not much attended to; the consequence is that the province is very thinly inhabited indeed; the power of the crown in conjunction with the musketos has prevented men from settling there. Yet some parts of it flourished once, and it contained a mild, harmless set of people. But for the fault of a few leaders, the whole was banished. The greatest political error the crown ever committed in America was to cut off men from a country which wanted nothing but men!

What attachment can a poor European emigrant have for a country where he had nothing? The knowledge of the language, the love of a few kindred as poor as himself, were the only cords that tied him; his country is now that which gives him his land, bread, protection, and consequence; *Ubi panis ibi patria* is the motto of all emigrants. What, then, is the American, this new man? He is either an European or the descendant of an European; hence that strange mixture of blood; which you will find in no other country. I could point out to you a family whose grandfather was an Englishman, whose wife was Dutch, whose son married a French woman, and whose present four sons have now four wives of different nations. *He* is an American, who, leaving behind him all his ancient prejudices and manners, receives new ones from the new mode of life he has embraced, the new government he obeys, and the new rank he holds. He becomes an American by being received in the broad lap of our great Alma Mater. Here individuals of all nations are melted into a new race of men, whose labours and posterity will one day cause great changes in the world. Americans are the western pilgrims who are carrying along with them that great mass of arts, sciences, vigour, and industry which began long since in the East; they will finish the great circle. The Americans were once scattered all over Europe; here they are incorporated into one of the finest systems of population which has ever appeared, and which will hereafter become distinct by the power of the different climates they inhabit. The American ought therefore to love this country much better than that wherein either he or his forefathers were born. Here the rewards of his industry follow with equal steps the progress of his labour; his labour is founded on the basis of nature, self-interest; can it want a stronger allurement? Wives and children, who before in vain demanded of him a morsel of bread, now, fat and frolicsome, gladly help their father to clear those fields whence exuberant crops are to arise to feed and to clothe them all, without any part being claimed, either by a despotic prince, a rich abbot, or a mighty lord. Here religion demands but little of him: a small voluntary salary to the minister and gratitude to God; can he refuse these? The American is a new man, who acts upon new principles; he must therefore entertain new ideas and form new opinions. From involuntary idleness, servile dependence, penury, and useless labour, he has passed to toils of a very different nature, rewarded by ample subsistence. This is an American.

Mapping the Text

1. Go through the text and pull out all the adjectives that de Crevecoeur uses to describe Americans. How would you categorize these words? What about the nature and character of the people with whom he is interacting is de Crevecoeur noticing? What do they suggest is the opposite "Old World" view?
2. Review the details of de Crevecoeur's sketch. What evidence is there that de Crevecoeur either likes or dislikes Americans, or is intrigued or impatient with them?

Writing to Inquire

1. Do a library search of eighteenth-century England to use art, literature, music, and history to gain a sense of what de Crevecoeur's British reading public was like. What about the scene in Great Britain or about the relationship between Great Britain and the United States might have been de Crevecoeur's incentive(s) for writing this sketch?
2. Over two centuries have passed since de Crevecoeur wrote his sketch. In your view, what is the same about Americans? What is different?

What to the Slave Is the Fourth of July?

FREDERICK DOUGLASS

Frederick Douglass (1817–1895), a leader of the Abolitionist movement, was born into slavery in Maryland. He escaped and went on to achieve great acclaim as a public speaker, first at the invitation of the American Anti-Slavery Society. His first autobiography, *Narrative of the Life of Frederick Douglass: An American Slave Written by Himself* (1845), earned him worldwide fame. He was also publisher of an antislavery paper, the *North Star,* and he served as adviser to President Lincoln during the Civil War. "What to the Slave Is the Fourth of July?" is a speech Douglass delivered in Corinthian Hall, Rochester, New York, July 5, 1852. It was reprinted in his 1855 autobiography, *My Bondage and My Freedom.* In the excerpted version below, Douglass invites readers to ponder the relationship of the United States to those who live here—free and enslaved.

Fellow-Citizens—pardon me, and allow me to ask, why am I called upon to speak here to-day? What have I, or those I represent, to do with your national independence? Are the great principles of political freedom and of natural justice, embodied in that Declaration of Independence, extended to us? and am I, therefore, called upon to bring our humble offering to the national altar, and to confess the benefits, and express devout gratitude for the blessings, resulting from your independence to us?

Would to God, both for your sakes and ours, that an affirmative answer could be truthfully returned to these questions! Then would my task be light, and my burden easy and delightful. For who is there so cold that a nation's sympathy could not warm him? Who so obdurate and dead to the claims of gratitude, that would not thankfully acknowledge such priceless benefits? Who so stolid and selfish, that would not give his voice to swell the hallelujah of a nation's jubilee, when the chains of servitude had been torn from his limbs? I am not that man. In a case like that, the dumb might eloquently speak, and the "lame man leap as an hart."[1]

But, such is not the state of the case. I say it with a sad sense of the disparity between us. I am not included within the pale of this glorious anniversary! Your high independence only reveals the immeasurable distance between us. The blessings in which you this day rejoice, are not enjoyed in common. The rich inheritance of justice, liberty, prosperity, and independence, bequeathed by your fathers, is shared by you, not by me. The sunlight that brought life and healing to you, has brought stripes and death to me. This Fourth of July is *yours,* not *mine. You* may rejoice, *I* must mourn. To drag a man in fetters into the grand illuminated temple of liberty, and call upon him to join you in joyous anthems, were inhuman mockery and sacrilegious irony. Do you mean, citizens, to mock me, by asking me to speak to-day? If so, there is a parallel to your conduct. And let me warn you that it is dangerous to copy the example of a nation whose crimes, towering up to heaven, were thrown down by the breath of the Almighty, burying that nation in irrecoverable ruin! I can to-day take up the plaintive lament of a peeled and woe-smitten people.

"By the rivers of Babylon, there we sat down. Yea! we wept when we remembered Zion. We hanged our harps upon the willows in the midst thereof. For there, they that carried us away captive, required of us a song; and they who wasted us required of us mirth, saying, Sing us one of the songs of Zion. How can we sing the Lord's song in a strange land? If I forget thee, O Jerusalem, let my right hand forget her cunning. If I do not remember thee, let my tongue cleave to the roof of my mouth."[2]

5 Fellow-citizens, above your national, tumultuous joy, I hear the mournful wail of millions, whose chains, heavy and grievous yesterday, are today rendered more intolerable by the jubilant shouts that reach them. If I do forget, if I do not faithfully remember those bleeding children of sorrow this day, "may my right hand forget her cunning, and may my tongue cleave to the roof of my mouth!" To forget them, to pass lightly over their wrongs, and to chime in with the popular theme, would be treason most scandalous and shocking, and would make me a reproach before God and the world. My subject then, fellow-citizens, is AMERICAN SLAVERY. I shall see this day and its popular characteristics from the slave's point of view. Standing there, identified with the American bondman, making his wrongs mine, I do not hesitate to declare, with all my soul, that the character and conduct of this nation never looked blacker to me than on this Fourth of July. Whether we turn to the declarations of the past, or to the professions of the present, the conduct of the nation seems equally hideous and revolting. America is false to the past, false to the present, and solemnly binds herself to be false to the future. Standing with God and the crushed and bleeding slave on this occasion, I will, in the name of humanity which is outraged, in the name of liberty which is fettered, in the name of the constitution and the bible, which are disregarded and trampled upon, dare to call in question and to denounce, with all the emphasis I can command, everything that serves to perpetuate slavery—the great sin and shame of America! "I will not equivocate; I will not excuse;"[3] I will use the severest language I can command; and yet not one word shall escape me that any man, whose judgment is not blinded by prejudice, or who is not at heart a slaveholder, shall not confess to be right and just.

But I fancy I hear some one of my audience say, it is just in this circumstance that you and your brother abolitionists fail to make a favorable impression on the public mind. Would you argue more, and denounce less, would you persuade more and rebuke less, your cause would be much more likely to succeed. But, I submit, where all is plain there is nothing to be argued. What point in the anti-slavery creed would you have me argue? On what branch of the subject do the people of this country need light? Must I undertake to prove that the slave is a man? That point is conceded already. Nobody doubts it. The slaveholders themselves acknowledge it in the enactment of laws for their government. They acknowledge it when they punish disobedience on the part of the slave. There are seventy-two crimes in the state of Virginia, which, if committed by a black man, (no matter how ignorant he be,) subject him to the punishment of death; while only two of these same crimes will subject a white man to the like punishment. What is this but the acknowledgment that the slave is a moral, intellectual, and responsible being. The manhood of the slave is conceded. It is admitted in the fact that southern statute books are covered with enactments forbidding, under severe fines and penalties, the teaching of the slave to read or write. When you can point to any such laws, in reference to the beasts of the field, then I may consent to argue the manhood of the slave. When the dogs in your streets, when the fowls of the air, when the cattle on your hills, when the fish of the sea, and the reptiles that crawl, shall be unable to distinguish the slave from a brute, then will I argue with you that the slave is a man!

For the present, it is enough to affirm the equal manhood of the negro race. Is it not astonishing that, while we are plowing, planting, and reaping, using all kinds of mechanical tools, erecting houses, constructing bridges, building ships, working in metals of brass, iron, copper, silver, and gold; that, while we are reading, writing, and cyphering, acting as clerks, merchants, and secretaries, having among us lawyers, doctors, ministers, poets, authors, editors, orators, and teachers; that, while we are engaged in all manner of enterprises common to other men—digging gold in California, capturing the whale in the Pacific, feeding sheep and cattle on the hillside, living, moving, acting, thinking, planning, living in families as husbands, wives, and children, and, above all, confessing and worshiping the christian's God, and looking hopefully for life and immortality beyond the grave,—we are called upon to prove that we are men!

Would you have me argue that man is entitled to liberty? that he is the rightful owner of his own body? You have already declared it. Must I argue the wrongfulness of slavery? Is that a question for republicans? Is it to be settled by the rules of logic and argumentation, as a matter beset with great difficulty, involving a doubtful application of the principle of justice, hard to be understood? How should I look to-day in the presence of Americans, dividing and subdividing a discourse, to show that men have a natural right to freedom, speaking of it relatively and positively, negatively and affirmatively? To do so, would be to make myself ridiculous, and to offer an insult to your understanding. There is not a man beneath the canopy of heaven that does not know that slavery is wrong *for him.*

What! am I to argue that it is wrong to make men brutes, to rob them of their liberty, to work them without wages, to keep them ignorant of their relations to their fellow men, to beat them with sticks, to flay their flesh with the lash, to load their limbs with irons, to hunt them with dogs, to sell them at auction, to sunder their families, to knock out their teeth, to burn their flesh, to starve them into obedience and submission to their masters? Must I argue that a system, thus marked with blood and stained with pollution, is wrong? No; I will not. I have better employment for my time and strength than such arguments would imply.

What, then, remains to be argued? Is it that slavery is not divine; that God did not establish it; that our doctors of divinity are mistaken? There is blasphemy in the thought. That which is inhuman cannot be divine. Who can reason on such a proposition! They that can, may; I cannot. The time for such argument is past.

At a time like this, scorching irony, not convincing argument, is needed. Oh! had I the ability, and could I reach the nation's ear, I would to-day pour out a fiery stream of biting ridicule, blasting reproach, withering sarcasm, and stern rebuke. For it is not light that is needed, but fire; it is not the gentle shower, but thunder. We need the storm, the whirlwind and the earthquake. The feeling of the nation must be quickened; the conscience of the nation must be roused; the propriety of the nation must be startled; the hypocrisy of the nation must be exposed; and its crimes against God and man must be proclaimed and denounced.

What to the American slave is your Fourth of July? I answer, a day that reveals to him, more than all other days in the year, the gross injustice and cruelty to which he is the constant victim. To him, your celebration is a sham; your boasted liberty, an unholy license; your national greatness, swelling vanity; your sounds of rejoicing are empty and heartless; your denunciations of tyrants, brass-fronted impudence; your shouts of liberty and equality, hollow mockery; your prayers and hymns, your sermons and thanksgivings, with all your religious parade and solemnity, are to him mere bombast, fraud, deception, impiety, and hypocrisy—a thin veil to cover up crimes which would disgrace a nation of savages. There is not a nation on the earth guilty of practices more shocking and bloody, than are the people of these United States, at this very hour.

Go where you may, search where you will, roam through all the monarchies and despotisms of the old world, travel through South America, search out every abuse, and when you have found the last, lay your facts by the side of the every-day practices of this nation, and you will say with me, that, for revolting barbarity and shameless hypocrisy, America reigns without a rival.

Notes

[1] The biblical reference is Isaiah 35:6.

[2] Douglass draws directly from Psalms 137:1–6.

[3] Douglass quotes from William Lloyd Garrison's opening editorial in the first issue of The Liberator, 1 Jan. 1831: "I am in earnest—I will not equivocate—I will not excuse—I will not retreat a single inch—and I will be heard."

Mapping the Text

1. In this speech, Douglass names his audience "Fellow-Citizens." On what basis does Douglass claim this authority? By using this label, what specifically do you think that he is claiming? Given what Douglass says next, how does this label set up the issue he identifies? What is the issue?
2. This speech is frequently anthologized in textbooks, which would suggest that it is perceived to have enduring value. Do you agree or disagree that it has enduring value for students? On what basis do you make your assertion?
3. What do you think Douglass's purpose was in making this speech? What do you think he wanted to accomplish?

Writing to Inquire

1. Consider the context and time in which Douglass was speaking in 1852. From one point of view, you could argue that he spoke provocatively on behalf of African-Americans, free and enslaved. Think about the lives of others during this era. Can you identify any other group whose experiences and point of view might have been similar? How so?

READINGS FOR INQUIRY AND EXPLORATION

The Declaration of Independence

THOMAS JEFFERSON

Thomas Jefferson (1743–1826) was the third president of the United States. He was a statesman, a writer, an architect, and an owner and father of slaves. Among his many accomplishments, Jefferson is credited with two actions in particular that were significant to the development of the nation. One was drafting the Declaration of Independence. Another was effecting the Louisiana Purchase, which added a considerable amount of territory to the United States by purchase from France rather than by war.

When, in the course of human events, it becomes necessary for one people to dissolve the political bonds which have connected them with another, and to assume among the powers of the earth, the separate and equal station to which the laws of nature and of nature's God entitle them, a decent respect to the opinions of mankind requires that they should declare the causes which impel them to the separation.

We hold these truths to be self-evident, that all men are created equal, that they are endowed by their Creator with certain unalienable rights, that among these are life, liberty and the pursuit of happiness. That to secure these rights, governments are instituted among men, deriving their just powers from the consent of the governed. That whenever any form of government becomes destructive to these ends, it is the right of the people to alter or to abolish it, and to institute new government, laying its foundation on such principles and organizing its powers in such form, as to them shall seem most likely to effect their safety and happiness. Prudence, indeed, will dictate that governments long established should not be changed for light and transient causes; and accordingly all experience hath shown that mankind are more disposed to suffer, while evils are sufferable, than to right themselves by abolishing the forms to which they are accustomed. But when a long train of abuses and usurpations, pursuing invariably the same object evinces a design to reduce them under absolute despotism, it is their right, it is their duty, to throw off such government, and to provide new guards for their future security.

Such has been the patient sufferance of these colonies; and such is now the necessity which constrains them to alter their former systems of government. The history of the present King of Great Britain is a history of repeated injuries and usurpations, all having in direct object the establishment of an absolute tyranny over these states. To prove this, let facts be submitted to a candid world.

He has refused his assent to laws, the most wholesome and necessary for the public good.

He has forbidden his governors to pass laws of immediate and pressing importance, unless suspended in their operation till his assent should be obtained; and when so suspended, he has utterly neglected to attend to them.

He has refused to pass other laws for the accommodation of large districts of people, unless those people would relinquish the right of representation in the legislature, a right inestimable to them and formidable to tyrants only.

He has called together legislative bodies at places unusual, uncomfortable, and distant from the depository of their public records, for the sole purpose of fatiguing them into compliance with his measures.

He has dissolved representative houses repeatedly, for opposing with manly firmness his invasions on the rights of the people.

He has refused for a long time, after such dissolutions, to cause others to be elected; whereby the legislative powers, incapable of annihilation, have returned to the people at large for their exercise; the state remaining in the meantime exposed to all the dangers of invasion from without, and convulsions within.

He has endeavored to prevent the population of these states; for that purpose obstructing the laws for naturalization of foreigners; refusing to pass others to encourage their migration hither, and raising the conditions of new appropriations of lands.

He has obstructed the administration of justice, by refusing his assent to laws for establishing judiciary powers.

He has made judges dependent on his will alone, for the tenure of their offices, and the amount and payment of their salaries.

He has erected a multitude of new offices, and sent hither swarms of officers to harass our people, and eat out their substance.

He has kept among us, in times of peace, standing armies without the consent of our legislature.

He has affected to render the military independent of and superior to civil power.

He has combined with others to subject us to a jurisdiction foreign to our constitution, and unacknowledged by our laws; giving his assent to their acts of pretended legislation:

- For quartering large bodies of armed troops among us.
- For protecting them, by mock trial, from punishment for any murders which they should commit on the inhabitants of these states.
- For cutting off our trade with all parts of the world.
- For imposing taxes on us without our consent.
- For depriving us in many cases, of the benefits of trial by jury.

- For transporting us beyond seas to be tried for pretended offenses.
- For abolishing the free system of English laws in a neighboring province, establishing therein an arbitrary government, and enlarging its boundaries so as to render it at once an example and fit instrument for introducing the same absolute rule in these colonies.
- *For taking away our charters, abolishing our most valuable laws, and altering fundamentally the forms of our governments.*
- *For suspending our own legislatures, and declaring themselves invested with power to legislate for us in all cases whatsoever.*

He has abdicated government here, by declaring us out of his protection and waging war against us.

He has plundered our seas, ravaged our coasts, burned our towns, and destroyed the lives of our people.

He is at this time transporting large armies of foreign mercenaries to complete the works of death, desolation and tyranny, already begun with circumstances of cruelty and perfidy scarcely paralleled in the most barbarous ages, and totally unworthy the head of a civilized nation.

He has constrained our fellow citizens taken captive on the high seas to bear arms against their country, to become the executioners of their friends and brethren, or to fall themselves by their hands.

He has excited domestic insurrections amongst us, and has endeavored to bring on the inhabitants of our frontiers, the merciless Indian savages, whose known rule of warfare, is undistinguished destruction of all ages, sexes and conditions.

In every stage of these oppressions we have petitioned for redress in the most humble terms: our repeated petitions have been answered only by repeated injury. A prince, whose character is thus marked by every act which may define a tyrant, is unfit to be the ruler of a free people.

Nor have we been wanting in attention to our British brethren. We have warned them from time to time of attempts by their legislature to extend an unwarrantable jurisdiction over us. We have reminded them of the circumstances of our emigration and settlement here. We have appealed to their native justice and magnanimity, and we have conjured them by the ties of our common kindred to disavow these usurpations, which, would inevitably interrupt our connections and correspondence. We must, therefore, acquiesce in the necessity, which denounces our separation, and hold them, as we hold the rest of mankind, enemies in war, in peace friends.

We, therefore, the representatives of the United States of America, in General Congress, assembled, appealing to the Supreme Judge of the world for the rectitude of our intentions, do, in the name, and by the authority of the good people of these colonies, solemnly publish and declare, that these united colonies are, and of right ought to be free and independent states; that they are absolved from all allegiance to the British Crown, and that all political connection between them and the state of Great Britain, is and ought to be totally dissolved; and that as free and independent states, they have full power to levy war, conclude peace, contract alliances, establish commerce, and to do all other acts and things which independent states may of right do. And for the support of this declaration, with a firm reliance on the protection of Divine Providence, we mutually pledge to each other our lives, our fortunes and our sacred honor.

John Hancock, President
Attested, Charles Thomson, Secretary

NEW HAMPSHIRE
Josiah Bartlett
William Whipple
Matthew Thornton

MASSACHUSETTS BAY
Samuel Adams
John Adams
Robert Treat Paine
Elbridge Gerry

RHODE ISLAND
Stephen Hopkins
William Ellery

CONNECTICUT
Roger Sherman
Samuel Huntington
William Williams
Oliver Wolcott

GEORGIA
Button Gwinnett
Lyman Hall
Geo. Walton

MARYLAND
Samuel Chase
William Paca
Thomas Stone
Charles Carroll of Carrollton

VIRGINIA
George Wythe
Richard Henry Lee
Thomas Jefferson
Benjamin Harrison
Thomas Nelson, Jr.
Francis Lightfoot Lee
Carter Braxton

NEW YORK
William Floyd
Philip Livingston
Francis Lewis
Lewis Morris

PENNSYLVANIA
Robert Morris
Benjamin Rush
Benjamin Franklin
John Morton
George Clymer
James Smith
George Taylor
James Wilson
George Ross

DELAWARE
Caesar Rodney
George Read
Thomas M'Kean

NORTH CAROLINA
William Hooper
Joseph Hewes
John Penn

SOUTH CAROLINA
Edward Rutledge
Thomas Heyward, Jr.
Thomas Lynch, Jr.
Arthur Middleton

NEW JERSEY
Richard Stockton
John Witherspoon
Francis Hopkins
John Hart
Abraham Clark

Mapping the Text

1. This document is often discussed as a revolutionary document. Go through the text and pull out words and phrases that constitute evidence for this point of view.
2. Read the Declaration again, closely and critically. Choose one passage from this document that you find meaningful. Write an essay in which you explain at least two points: the context in which the passage is meaningful; the meaning that you see and why.

Writing to Inquire

1. Review the list of statesmen who signed the Declaration. Choose two of them to research. Based on your search, write a profile of these men and their accomplishments.
2. Using the Declaration of Independence as the lens or the point of view, define who is an American. To what extent has this (implied) definition been a problem or issue?

1848 Declaration of Sentiments

ELIZABETH CADY STANTON WITH LUCRETIA MOTT

Elizabeth Cady Stanton (1815–1902) drafted the Seneca Falls Convention's Declaration of Sentiments with her colleague, Lucretia Mott. The well-attended convention, held in Seneca Falls, New York, in 1848, marked the beginning of the nineteenth-century women's movement. Stanton, along with Mott and others (for example, their close friend Susan B. Anthony) were leaders of the movement. The Declaration of Sentiments was arguably the most important document of this movement. It uses the Declaration of Independence as a textual model, arguing that women, too, have been wronged grievously by the American men who would keep them disfranchised.

Lucretia Mott (1793–1880) was reared in the Quaker faith, which encouraged the equality of women even in the nineteenth century. Mott was an abolitionist as well as an advocate for the women's movement, and she was one of several American delegates to the 1840 World's Anti-Slavery Convention in London, where women were denied seats. Mott coauthored the Declaration of Sentiments with Elizabeth Cady Stanton at the Seneca Falls convention.

When in the course of human events, it becomes necessary for one portion of the family of man to assume among the people of the earth a position different from that which they have hither to occupied, but one to which the laws of nature and of nature's God entitle them, a decent respect to the opinions of mankind requires that they should declare the causes that impel them to such a course.

We hold these truths to be self-evident: that all men and women are created equal; that they are endowed by their creator with certain inalienable rights; among these are life, liberty, and the pursuit of happiness; that to secure these rights governments are instituted, deriving their just powers from the consent of the governed.

Whenever any form of government becomes destructive of these ends, it is the right of those who suffer from it to refuse allegiance to it, and to insist upon the institution of a new government, laying its foundation on such principles, and organizing its powers in such form, as to them shall seem most likely to effect their safety and happiness.

Prudence, indeed, will dictate that governments long established should not be changed for light and transient causes; and accordingly all experience hath shown that mankind are more disposed to suffer, while evils are sufferable, than to right themselves by abolishing the forms to which they were accustomed. But when a long train of abuses and usurpations, pursuing invariably the same object evinces a design to reduce them under absolute despotism, it is their duty to throw off such government, and to provide new guards for their future security. Such has been the patient sufferance of the women under this government and such is now the necessity which constrains them to demand the equal station to which they are entitled.

5 The history of mankind is a history of repeated injuries and usurpations on the part of man toward woman, having in direct object the establishment of an absolute tyranny over her. To prove this, let facts be submitted to a candid world.

- He has never permitted her to exercise her inalienable right to the elective franchise.
- He has compelled her to submit to laws, in the formation of which she had no voice.
- He has withheld from her rights which are given to the most ignorant and degraded men—both natives and foreigners. Having deprived her of this first right of a citizen, the elective franchise, thereby leaving her without representation in the halls of legislation, he has oppressed her on all sides.
- He has made her, if married, in the eye of the law, civilly dead.
- He has taken from her all right in property, even to the wages she earns.
- He has made her, morally, an irresponsible being, as she can commit many crimes with impunity, provided they be done in the presence of her husband. In the covenant of marriage, she is compelled to promise obedience to her husband, he becoming, to all intents and purposes, her master—the law giving him power to deprive her of her liberty and to administer chastisement.

- He has so framed the laws of divorce, as to what shall be the proper causes, and in case of separation, to whom the guardianship of the children shall be given, as to be wholly regardless of the happiness of women—the law, in all cases, going upon a false supposition of the supremacy of man and giving all power into his hands.
- After depriving her of all rights as a married woman, if single, and the owner of property, he has taxed her to support a government which recognizes her only when her property can be made profitable to it.
- He has monopolized nearly all the profitable employments, and from those she is permitted to follow, she receives but a scanty remuneration.
- He closes against her all the avenues to wealth and distinction which he considers most honorable to himself. As a teacher of theology, medicine, or law, she is not known.
- He has denied her the facilities for obtaining a thorough education, all colleges being closed against her.
- He allows her in Church, as well as State, but a subordinate position, claiming Apostolic authority for her exclusion from the ministry, and, with some exceptions, from any public participation in the affairs of the Church.
- He has created a false public sentiment by giving to the world a different code of morals for men and women, by which moral delinquencies which exclude women from society, are not only tolerated, but deemed of little account in man.
- He has usurped the prerogative of Jehovah himself, claiming it as his right to assign for her a sphere of action, when that belongs to her conscience and to her God.
- He has endeavored, in every way that he could, to destroy her confidence in her own powers, to lessen her self-respect, and to make her willing to lead a dependent and abject life.

Now in view of this entire disfranchisement of one-half the people of this country, their social and religious degradation—in view of the unjust laws above mentioned, and because women do feel themselves aggrieved, oppressed, and fraudulently deprived of their most sacred rights, we insist that they have immediate admission to all the rights and privileges which belong to them as citizens of the United States.

In entering upon the great work before us, we anticipate no small amount of misconception, misrepresentation, and ridicule; but we shall use every instrumentality without our power to effect our object.

We shall employ agents, circulate tracts, petition the State and National legislatures, and endeavor to enlist the pulpit and the press on our behalf. We hope this Convention will be followed by a series of Conventions embracing every part of the country.

Mapping the Text

1. Make a list of the issues raised either directly or indirectly by Stanton and Mott. Which of the issues are time-bound, a function of a specific time and place? Which are longstanding and continue as challenges today, though perhaps in different ways or different terms?
2. Read the Declaration of Sentiments in light of the Declaration of Independence. Compare words, phrases, and issues. To what extent do Stanton and Mott take advantage of the structure and content of their model? What difference in effect does the shift in subject make?

Writing to Inquire

1. Search the resources of the library to gather information about the lives and conditions of different groups of nineteenth-century women—for example, middle- and upperclass white women, immigrant women, Southern women, African-American women, Native American women, and Asian-American women. Consider laws and public policies, education, the labor force, health care, social norms, and so on. Who is included in the Declaration of Sentiments?
2. Using the Declaration of Sentiments as the lens, the point of view, define who is an American. In what ways does this view extend the scope and values of the United States as a nation?

The Port Huron Statement

TOM HAYDEN—STUDENTS FOR A DEMOCRATIC SOCIETY

Tom Hayden (1939–) is perhaps best known as one of the Chicago Seven, a group of activists who were arrested in the summer of 1968 for inciting a riot at the Democratic National Convention. Hayden became a member of the California Assembly in 1982 and served as State Senator from 1992 to 2000. In 1962, however, while he was a student at the University of Wisconsin, he drafted a manifesto that became the founding document of Students for a Democratic Society (SDS). This group held a national convention in Port Huron, Michigan, June 11–15, 1962, and the manifesto evolved into the Port Huron Statement. This statement, which includes the excerpt below, stands as an official document of this organization. Even though the organization is no longer active, the group considered the statement a living document, capable of changing with the times and experiences. It raises concerns about the United States not responding adequately to global and national problems, and it asserts the view that students must understand the world, take direct action, and become involved in making history rather than just reading about it. The full statement is available online at <http://coursea.matrix.msu.edu/~hst306/documents/huron.html>.

Students for a Democratic Society (SDS), a radical student organization established in the United States in 1959, developed out of the youth branch of an older socialist educational organization, the League for Industrial Democracy. Robert Alan Haber was elected president of the new organization at its first organizational meeting in 1960 held in Ann Arbor, Michigan. The more than 60 founding members believed passionately that a nonviolent youth movement could transform U.S. society into a model political system in which the people, rather than just the social elite, would control social policy. By the end of 1966, there were more than 300 SDS chapters on college and university campuses across the country, and the group had become known primarily for its leading role in the New Left student movement and in campus activism against the Vietnam War. They orchestrated massive demonstrations against the War and were identified with popular slogans, such as: "Make Love, Not War" and "Hell No, We Won't Go." By the mid 1970s, with the decline of United States involvement in Vietnam, SDS lost much of its national strength as its members shifted their energies to other social causes.

For more information on this group, see <http://ma.essortment.com/ sdsstudentsfo rmsx.htm> and <http://www.bartleby.com/65/st/Students.html>

Introduction: Agenda for a Generation

We are people of this generation, bred in at least modest comfort, housed now in universities, looking uncomfortably to the world we inherit.

When we were kids the United States was the wealthiest and strongest country in the world: the only one with the atom bomb, the least scarred by modern war, an initiator of the United Nations that we thought would distribute Western influence throughout the world. Freedom and equality for each individual, government of, by, and for the people—these American values we found good, principles by which we could live as men. Many of us began maturing in complacency.

As we grew, however, our comfort was penetrated by events too troubling to dismiss. First, the permeating and victimizing fact of human degradation, symbolized by the Southern struggle against racial bigotry, compelled most of us from silence to activism. Second, the enclosing fact of the Cold War, symbolized by the presence of the Bomb, brought awareness that we ourselves, and our friends, and millions of abstract "others" we knew more directly because of our common peril, might die at any time. We might deliberately ignore, or avoid, or fail to feel all other human problems, but not these two, for these were too immediate and crushing in their impact, too challenging in the demand that we as individuals take the responsibility for encounter and resolution.

While these and other problems either directly oppressed us or rankled our consciences and became our own subjective concerns, we began to see complicated and disturbing paradoxes in our surrounding America. The declaration "all men are created equal" rang hollow before the facts of Negro life in the South and the big cities of the North. The proclaimed peaceful intentions of the United States contradicted its economic and military investments in the Cold War status quo.

We witnessed, and continue to witness, other paradoxes. With nuclear energy whole cities can easily be powered, yet the dominant nationstates seem more likely to unleash destruction greater than that incurred in all wars of human history. Although our own technology is destroying old and creating new forms of social organization, men still tolerate meaningless work and idleness. While two-thirds of mankind suffers undernourishment, our own upper classes revel amidst superfluous abundance. Although world population is expected to double in forty years, the nations still tolerate anarchy as a major principle of international conduct and uncontrolled exploitation governs the sapping of the earth's physical resources. Although mankind desperately needs revolutionary leadership, America rests in national stalemate, its goals ambiguous and tradition-bound instead of informed and clear, its democratic system apathetic and manipulated rather than "of, by, and for the people."

Not only did tarnish appear on our image of American virtue, not only did disillusion occur when the hypocrisy of American ideals was discovered, but we began to sense that what we had originally seen as the American Golden Age was actually the decline of an era. The worldwide outbreak of revolution against colonialism and imperialism, the entrenchment of totalitarian states, the menace of war, overpopulation, international disorder, supertechnology—these trends were testing the tenacity of our own commitment to democracy and freedom and our abilities to visualize their application to a world in upheaval.

Our work is guided by the sense that we may be the last generation in the experiment with living. But we are a minority—the vast majority of our people regard the temporary equilibriums of our society and world as eternally functional parts. In this is perhaps the outstanding paradox: we ourselves are imbued with urgency, yet the message of our society is that there is no viable alternative to the present. Beneath the reassuring tones of the politicians, beneath the common opinion that America will "muddle through," beneath the stagnation of those who have closed their minds to the future, is the pervading feeling that there simply are no alternatives, that our times have witnessed the exhaustion not only of Utopias, but of any new departures as well. Feeling the press of complexity upon the emptiness of life, people are fearful of the thought that at any moment things might thrust out of control. They fear change itself, since change might smash whatever invisible framework seems to hold back chaos for them now. For most Americans, all crusades are suspect, threatening. The fact that each individual sees apathy in his fellows perpetuates the common reluctance to organize for change. The dominant institutions are complex enough to blunt the minds of their potential critics, and entrenched enough to swiftly dissipate or entirely repel the energies of protest and reform, thus limiting human expectancies. Then, too, we are a materially improved society, and by our own improvements we seem to have weakened the case for further change.

Some would have us believe that Americans feel contentment amidst prosperity—but might it not better be called a glaze above deeply felt anxieties about their role in the new world? And if these anxieties produce a developed indifference to human affairs, do they not as well produce a yearning to believe there is an alternative to the present, that something can be done to change circumstances in the school, the workplaces, the bureaucracies, the government? It is to this latter yearning, at once the spark and engine of change, that we direct our present appeal. The search for truly democratic alternatives to the present, and a commitment to social experimentation with them, is a worthy and fulfilling human enterprise, one which moves us and, we hope, others today. On such a basis do we offer this document of our convictions and analysis: as an effort in understanding and changing the conditions of humanity in the late twentieth century, an effort rooted in the ancient, still unfulfilled conception of man attaining determining influence over his circumstances of life.

Values

Making values explicit—an initial task in establishing alternatives—

- is an activity that has been devalued and corrupted. The conventional moral terms of the age, the politician's moralities—"free world," "people's democracies"—reflect realities poorly, if at all, and seem to function more as ruling myths than as descriptive principles. But neither has our experience in the universities brought as moral enlightenment. Our professors and administrators sacrifice controversy to public relations; their curriculums change more slowly than the living events of the world; their skills and silence are purchased by investors in the arms race; passion is called unscholastic. The questions we might want raised—what is really important? can we live in a different and better way? if we wanted to change society, how would we do it?—are not thought to be questions of a "fruitful, empirical nature," and thus are brushed aside.

Unlike youth in other countries we are used to moral leadership being exercised and moral dimensions being clarified by our elders. But today, for us, not even the liberal and socialist preachments of the past seem adequate to the forms of the present. Consider the old slogans; Capitalism Cannot Reform Itself. United Front Against Fascism, General Strike, All Out on May Day. Or, more recently, No Cooperation with Commies and Fellow Travellers, Ideologies Are Exhausted, Bipartisanship, No Utopias. These are incomplete, and there are few new prophets. It has been said that our liberal and socialist predecessors were plagued by vision without program, while our own generation is plagued by program without vision. All around us there is astute grasp of method, technique—the committee, the ad hoc group, the lobbyist, that hard and soft sell, the make, the projected image—but, if pressed critically, such expertise is incompetent to explain its implicit ideals. It is highly fashionable to identify oneself by old categories, or by naming a respected political figure, or by explaining "how we would vote" on various issues.

Theoretic chaos has replaced the idealistic thinking of old—and, unable to reconstitute theoretic order, men have condemned idealism itself. Doubt has replaced hopefulness—and men act out a defeatism that is labeled realistic. The decline of utopia and hope is in fact one of the defining features of social life today. The reasons are various: the dreams of the older left were perverted by Stalinism and never recreated; the congressional stalemate makes men narrow their view of the possible; the specialization of human activity leaves little room for sweeping thought; the horrors of the twentieth century, symbolized in the gas-ovens and concentration camps and atom bombs, have blasted hopefulness. To be idealistic is to be considered apocalyptic, deluded. To have no serious aspirations, on the contrary, is to be "toughminded."

In suggesting social goals and values, therefore, we are aware of entering a sphere of some disrepute. Perhaps matured by the past, we have no sure formulas, no closed theories—but that does not mean values are beyond discussion and tentative determination. A first task of any social movement is to convenience people that the search for orienting theories and the creation of human values is complex but worthwhile. We are aware that to avoid platitudes we must analyze the concrete conditions of social order. But to direct such an analysis we must use the guideposts of basic principles. Our own social values involve conceptions of human beings, human relationships, and social systems.

We regard men as infinitely precious and possessed of unfulfilled capacities for reason, freedom, and love. In affirming these principles we are aware of countering perhaps the dominant conceptions of man in the twentieth century: that he is a thing to be manipulated, and that he is inherently incapable of directing his own affairs. We oppose the depersonalization that reduces human beings to the status of things—if anything, the brutalities of the twentieth century teach that means and ends are intimately related, that vague appeals to "posterity" cannot justify the mutilations of the present. We oppose, too, the doctrine of human incompetence because it rests essentially on the modern fact that men have been "competently" manipulated into incompetence—we see little reason why men cannot meet with increasing skill the complexities and responsibilities of their situation, if society is organized not for minority, but for majority, participation in decision-making.

Men have unrealized potential for self-cultivation, self-direction, self-understanding, and creativity. It is this potential that we regard as crucial and to which we appeal, not to the human potentiality for violence, unreason, and submission to authority. The goal of man and society should be human independence: a concern not with image of popularity but with finding a meaning in life that is personally authentic: a quality of mind not compulsively driven by a sense of powerlessness, nor one which unthinkingly adopts status values, nor one which represses all threats to its habits, but one which has full, spontaneous access to present and past experiences, one which easily unites the fragmented parts of personal history, one which openly faces problems which are troubling and unresolved: one with an intuitive awareness of possibilities, an active sense of curiosity, an ability and willingness to learn.

This kind of independence does not mean egoistic individualism—the object is not to have one's way so much as it is to have a way that is one's own. Nor do we deify man—we merely have faith in his potential.

Human relationships should involve fraternity and honesty. Human interdependence is contemporary fact; human brotherhood must be willed however, as a condition of future survival and as the most appropriate form of social relations. Personal links between man and man are needed, especially to go beyond the partial and fragmentary bonds of function that bind men only as worker to worker, employer to employee, teacher to student, American to Russian.

Loneliness, estrangement, isolation describe the vast distance between man and man today. These dominant tendencies cannot be overcome by better personnel management, nor by improved gadgets, but only when a love of man overcomes the idolatrous worship of things by man.

As the individualism we affirm is not egoism, the selflessness we affirm is not self-elimination. On the contrary, we believe in generosity of a kind that imprints one's unique individual qualities in the relation to other men, and to all human activity. Further, to dislike isolation is not to favor the abolition of privacy; the latter differs from isolation in that it occurs or is abolished according to individual will. Finally, we would replace power and personal uniqueness rooted in possession, privilege, or circumstance by power and uniqueness rooted in love, reflectiveness, reason, and creativity.

As a social system we seek the establishment of a democracy of individual participation, governed by two central aims: that the individual share in those social decisions determining the quality and direction of his life; that society be organized to encourage independence in men and provide the media for their common participation.

In a participatory democracy, the political life would be based in several root principles:

- that decision-making of basic social consequence be carried on by public groupings;

- that politics be seen positively, as the art of collectively creating an acceptable pattern of social relations;
- that politics has the function of bringing people out of isolation and into community, thus being a necessary, though not sufficient, means of finding meaning in personal life;
- that the political order should serve to clarify problems in a way instrumental to their solution; it should provide outlets for the expression of personal grievance and aspiration; opposing views should be organized so as to illuminate choices and facilitate the attainment of goals; channels should be commonly available relating men to knowledge and to power so that private problems—from bad recreation facilities to personal alienation—are formulated as general issues.

20 The economic sphere would have as its basis the principles:

- that work should involve incentives worthier than money or survival. It should be educative, not stultifying; creative, not mechanical; selfdirect, not manipulated, encouraging independence; a respect for others, a sense of dignity and a willingness to accept social responsibility, since it is this experience that has crucia! influence on habits, perceptions and individual ethics;
- that the economic experience is so personally decisive that the individual must share in its full determination;
- that the economy itself is of such social importance that its major resources and means of production should be open to democratic participation and subject to democratic social regulation.

Like the political and economic ones, major social institutions—cultural, education, rehabilitative, and others—should be generally organized with the well-being and dignity of man as the essential measure of success.

In social change or interchange, we find violence to be abhorrent because it requires generally the transformation of the target, be it a human being or a community of people, into a depersonalized object of hate. It is imperative that the means of violence be abolished and the institutions—local, national, international—that encourage nonviolence as a condition of conflict be developed.

These are our central values, in skeletal form. It remains vital to understand their denial or attainment in the context of the modern world.

The Students

In the last few years, thousands of American students demonstrated that they at least felt the urgency of the times. They moved actively and directly against racial injustices, the threat of war, violations of individual rights of conscience and, less frequently, against economic manipulation. They succeeded in restoring a small measure of controversy to the campuses after the stillness of the McCarthy period. They succeeded, too, in gaining some concessions from the people and institutions they opposed, especially in the fight against racial bigotry.

25 The significance of these scattered movements lies not in their success or failure in gaining objectives—at least not yet. Nor does the significance lie in the intellectual "competence" or "maturity" of the students involved—as some pedantic elders allege. The significance is in the fact the students are breaking the crust of apathy and overcoming the inner alienation that remain the defining characteristics of American college life.

If student movements for change are rarities still on the campus scene, what is commonplace there? The real campus, the familiar campus, is a place of private people, engaged in their notorious "inner emigration." It is a place of commitment to business-as-usual, getting ahead, playing it cool. It is a place of mass affirmation of the Twist, but mass reluctance toward the controversial public stance. Rules are accepted as "inevitable," bureaucracy as "just circumstances," irrelevance as "scholarship," selflessness as "martyrdom," politics as "just another way to make people, and an unprofitable one, too."

Almost no students value activity as a citizen. Passive in public, they are hardly more idealistic in arranging their private lives: Gallup concludes they will settle for "low success, and won't risk high failure." There is not much willingness to take risks (not even in business), no setting of dangerous goals, no real conception of personal identity except one manufactured in the image of others, no real urge for personal fulfillment except to be almost as successful as the very successful people. Attention is being paid to social status (the quality of shirt collars, meeting people, getting wives or husbands, making solid contacts for later on): much too, is paid to academic status (grades, honors, the med school rat-race). But neglected generally is real intellectual status, the personal cultivation of the mind.

"Students don't even give a damn about the apathy," one has said. Apathy toward apathy begets a privately constructed universe, a place of systematic study schedules, two nights each week for beer, a girl or two, and early marriage; a framework infused with personality, warmth, and under control, no matter how unsatisfying otherwise.

Under these conditions university life loses all relevance to some. Four hundred thousand of our classmates leave college every year.

30 But apathy is not simply an attitude; it is a product of social institutions, and of the structure and organization of higher education itself. The extracurricular life is ordered according to in loco parentis theory, which ratifies the Administration as the moral guardian of the young. The accompanying "let's pretend" theory of student extracurricular affairs validates student government as a training center for those who want to spend their lives in political pretense, and discourages initiative from more articulate, honest, and sensitive students. The bounds and style of controversy are

delimited before controversy begins. The university "prepares" the student for "citizenship" through perpetual rehearsals and, usually, through emasculation of what creative spirit there is in the individual.

The academic life contains reinforcing counterparts to the way in which extracurricular life is organized. The academic world is founded in a teacher-student relation analogous to the parent-child relation which characterizes in loco parentis. Further, academia includes a radical separation of student from the material of study. That which is studied, the social reality, is "objectified" to sterility, dividing the student from life—just as he is restrained in active involvement by the deans controlling student government. The specialization of function and knowledge, admittedly necessary to our complex technological and social structure, has produced and exaggerated compartmentalization of study and understanding. This has contributed to: an overly parochial view, by faculty, of the role of its research and scholarship; a discontinuous and truncated understanding, by students, of the surrounding social order; a loss of personal attachment, by nearly all, to the worth of study as a humanistic enterprise.

There is, finally, the cumbersome academic bureaucracy extending throughout the academic as well as extracurricular structures, contributing to the sense of outer complexity and inner powerlessness that transforms so many students from honest searching to ratification of convention and, worse, to a numbness of present and future catastrophes. The size and financing systems of the university enhance the permanent trusteeship of the administrative bureaucracy, their power leading to a shift to the value standards of business and administrative mentality within the university. Huge foundations and other private financial interests shape under-financed colleges and universities, not only making them more commercial, but less disposed to diagnose society critically, less open to dissent. Many social and physical scientists, neglecting the liberating heritage of higher learning, develop "human relations" or morale-producing" techniques for the corporate economy, while others exercise their intellectual skills to accelerate the arms race.

Tragically, the university could serve as a significant source of social criticism and an initiator of new modes and molders of attitudes. But the actual intellectual effect of the college experience is hardly distinguishable from that of any other communications channel—say, a television set—passing on the stock truths of the day. Students leave college somewhat more "tolerant" than when they arrived, but basically unchallenged in their values and political orientations. With administrators ordering the institutions, and faculty the curriculum, the student learns by his isolation to accept elite rule within the university, which prepares him to accept later forms of minority control. The real function of the educational system—as opposed to its more rhetorical function of "searching for truth"—is to impart the key information and styles that will help the student get by, modestly but comfortably, in the big society beyond.

. . .

These contemporary social movements—for peace, civil rights, civil liberties labor—have in common certain values and goals. The fight for peace is one for a stable and racially integrated world; for an end to the inherently volatile exploitation of most of mankind by irresponsible elites; and for freedom of economic, political and cultural organization. The fight for civil rights is also one for social welfare for all Americans; for free speech and the right to protest; for the shield of economic independence and bargaining power; for a reduction of the arms race which takes national attention and resources away from the problems of domestic injustice. Labor's fight for jobs and wages is also one labor; for the right to petition and strike; for world industrialization; for the stability of a peacetime economy instead of the insecurity of the war economy; for expansion of the Welfare State. The fight for a liberal Congress is a fight for a platform from which these concerns can issue. And the fight for students, for internal democracy in the university, is a fight to gain a forum for the issues.

But these scattered movements have more in common: a need for their concerns to be expressed by a political party responsible to their interests. That they have no political expression, no political channels, can be traced in large measure to the existence of a Democratic Party which tolerates the perverse unity of liberalism and racism, prevents the social change wanted by Negroes, peace protesters, labor unions, students, reform Democrats, and other liberals. Worse, the party stalemate prevents even the raising of controversy—a full Congressional assault on racial discrimination, disengagement in Central Europe, sweeping urban reform, disarmament and inspection, public regulation of major industries; these and other issues are never heard in the body that is supposed to represent the best thoughts and interests of all Americans.

An imperative task for these publicly disinherited groups, then, is to demand a Democratic Party responsible to their interests. They must support Southern voter registration and Negro political candidates and demand that Democratic Party liberals do the same (in the last Congress, Dixiecrats split with Northern Democrats on 119 of 300 roll-calls, mostly on civil rights, area redevelopment, and foreign aid bills; and breach was much larger than in the previous several sessions). Labor should begin a major drive in the South. In the North, reform clubs (either independent or Democratic) should be formed to run against big city regimes on such issues as peace, civil rights, and urban needs. Demonstrations should be held at every Congressional or convention seating of Dixiecrats. A massive research and publicity campaign should be initiated, showing to every housewife, doctor, professor, and worker the damage done to their interests every day a racist occupies a place in the Democratic Party. Where possible, the peace movement should challenge the "peace credentials" of the otherwise-liberals by threatening or actually running candidates against them.

The University and Social Change

There is perhaps little reason to be optimistic about the above analysis. True, the Dixiecrat-GOP coalition is the weakest point in the dominating complex of corporate, military and political power. But the civil rights and peace and student movements are too poor and socially slighted, and the labor movement too quiescent, to be counted with enthusiasm. From where else can power and vision be summoned? We believe that the universities are an overlooked seat of influence.

First, the university is located in a permanent position of social influence. Its educational function makes it indispensable and automatically makes it a crucial institution in the formation of social attitudes. Second, in an unbelievably complicated world, it is the central institution for organizing, evaluating, and transmitting knowledge. Third, the extent to which academic resources presently is used to buttress immoral social practice is revealed first, by the extent to which defense contracts make the universities engineers of the arms race. Too, the use of modern social science as a manipulative tool reveals itself in the "human relations" consultants to the modern corporation, who introduce trivial sops to give laborers feelings of "participation" or "belonging," while actually deluding them in order to further exploit their labor. And, of course, the use of motivational research is already infamous as a manipulative aspect of American politics. But these social uses of the universities' resources also demonstrate the unchangeable reliance by men of power on the men and storehouses of knowledge: this makes the university functionally tied to society in new ways, revealing new potentialities, new levers for change. Fourth, the university is the only mainstream institution that is open to participation by individuals of nearly any viewpoint.

These, at least, are facts, no matter how dull the teaching, how paternalistic the rules, how irrelevant the research that goes on. Social relevance, the accessibility to knowledge, and internal openness

- these together make the university a potential base and agency in a movement of social change.

  1. Any new left in America must be, in large measure, a left with real intellectual skills, committed to deliberativeness, honesty, reflection as working tools. The university permits the political life to be an adjunct to the academic one, and action to be informed by reason.
  2. A new left must be distributed in significant social roles throughout the country. The universities are distributed in such a manner.
  3. A new left must consist of younger people who matured in the post-war world, and partially be directed to the recruitment of younger people. The university is an obvious beginning point.

4. A new left must include liberals and socialists, the former for their relevance, the latter for their sense of thoroughgoing reforms in the system. The university is a more sensible place than a political party for these two traditions to begin to discuss their differences and look for political synthesis.
5. A new left must start controversy across the land, if national policies and national apathy are to be reversed. The ideal university is a community of controversy, within itself and in its effects on communities beyond.
6. A new left must transform modern complexity into issues that can be understood and felt close-up by every human being. It must give form to the feelings of helplessness and indifference, so that people may see the political, social and economic sources of their private troubles and organize to change society. In a time of supposed prosperity, moral complacency and political manipulation, a new left cannot rely on only aching stomachs to be the engine force of social reform. The case for change, for alternatives that will involve uncomfortable personal efforts, must be argued as never before. The university is a relevant place for all of these activities.

40 But we need not indulge in allusions; the university system cannot complete a movement of ordinary people making demands for a better life. From its schools and colleges across the nation, a militant left might awaken its allies, and by beginning the process towards peace, civil rights, and labor struggles, reinsert theory and idealism where too often reign confusion and political barter. The power of students and faculty united is not only potential; it has shown its actuality in the South, and in the reform movements of the North.

The bridge to political power, though, will be built through genuine cooperation, locally, nationally, and internationally, between a new left of young people, and an awakening community of allies. In each community we must look within the university and act with confidence that we can be powerful, but we must look outwards to the less exotic but more lasting struggles for justice.

To turn these possibilities into realities will involve national efforts at university reform by an alliance of students and faculty. They must wrest control of the educational process from the administrative bureaucracy. They must make fraternal and functional contact with allies in labor, civil rights, and other liberal forces outside the campus. They must import major public issues into the curriculum—research and teaching on problems of war and peace is an outstanding example. They must make debate and controversy, not dull pedantic cant, the common style for educational life. They must consciously build a base for their assault upon the loci of power.

Mapping the Text

1. Create an outline of the excerpt. Examine the evidence and arguments used for each section. Given this analysis, on what basis do you determine that the statement is effective and persuasive or not?
2. The Port Huron Statement, like the Declaration of Independence, the Declaration of Sentiments, and the next selection, A Black Feminist Statement, is a *manifesto.* Define this term and explain this genre of expression using examples from this chapter.

Writing to Inquire

1. Search your library resources for information on the participation of students in rebellions and revolutions. Choose one of these historical moments to explore. What role(s) did students play? In looking around you at the context in which you live, are there circumstances and conditions that might similarly inspire contemporary students to rebel or revolt? What might be the springboard(s)? What values or practices might form the basis of concern?
2. Consider the era of the 1960s and 1970s. What was happening during this time that seems to have been the inspiration for the Port Huron Statement?

A Black Feminist Statement

COMBAHEE RIVER COLLECTIVE

The Combahee River Collective began in 1974 as the Boston chapter of the National Black Feminist Organization (founded in 1973). The name was taken from a river in South Carolina where Harriet Tubman led a campaign during the Civil War to free 750 slaves. The Collective started *Azalea: A Magazine by Third World Lesbians* (1978) and Kitchen Table: Women of Color Press (1981). Three members of the Collective—Barbara Smith, Beverly Smith, and Demita Frazier—wrote a statement documenting the activities of the collective that included the philosophical position below. This manifesto embraced the women's liberation movement as important for African-American women during an era in which this movement was much criticized by many of them. It emphasized the importance of liberation for African-American women within black liberation, and it appealed for the eradication of homophobia in both struggles as it documented the evolution of contemporary black feminism.

We are a collective of black feminists who have been meeting together since 1974.[1] During that time we have been involved in the process of defining and clarifying our politics, while at the same time doing political work within our own group and in coalition with other progressive organizations and movements. The most general statement of our politics at the present time would be that we are actively committed to struggling against racial, sexual, heterosexual, and class oppression and see as our particular task the development of integrated analysis and practice based upon the fact that the major systems of oppression are interlocking. The synthesis of these oppressions creates the conditions of our lives. As black women we see black feminism as the logical political movement to combat the manifold and simultaneous oppressions that all women of color face.

We will discuss four major topics in the paper that follows; (1) The genesis of contemporary black feminism; (2) what we believe, i.e., the specific province of our politics; (3) the problems in organizing black feminists, including a brief herstory of our collective; and (4) black feminist issues and practice.

1. The Genesis of Contemporary Black Feminism

Before looking at the recent development of black feminism, we would like to affirm that we find our origins in the historical reality of Afro-American women's continuous life-and-death struggle for survival and liberation. Black women's extremely negative relationship to the American political system (a system of white male rule) has always been determined by our membership in two oppressed racial and sexual castes. As Angela Davis points out in "Reflections on the Black Woman's Role in the Community of Slaves," black women have always embodied, if only in their physical manifestation, an adversary stance to white male rule and have actively resisted its inroads upon them and their communities in both dramatic and subtle ways. There have always been black women activists—some known, like Sojourner Truth, Harriet Tubman, Frances E. W. Harper, Ida B. Wells-Barnett, and Mary Church Terrell, and thousands upon thousands unknown—who had a shared awareness of how their sexual identity combined with their racial identity to make their whole life situation and the focus of their political struggles unique. Contemporary black feminism is the outgrowth of countless generations of personal sacrifice, militancy, and work by our mothers and sisters.

A black feminist presence has evolved most obviously in connection with the second wave of the American women's movement beginning in the late 1960s. Black, other Third World, and working women have been involved in the feminist movement from its start, but both outside reactionary forces and racism and elitism within the movement itself have served to obscure our participation. In 1973 black feminists, primarily located in New York, felt the necessity of forming a separate black feminist group. This became the National Black Feminist Organization (NBFO).

5 Black feminist politics also have an obvious connection to movements for black liberation, particularly those of the 1960s and 1970s. Many of us were active in those movements (civil rights, black nationalism, the Black

Panthers), and all of our lives were greatly affected and changed by their ideology, their goals, and the tactics used to achieve their goals. It was our experience and disillusionment within these liberation movements, as well as experience on the periphery of the white male left, that led to the need to develop a politics that was antiracist, unlike those of white women, and antisexist, unlike those of black and white men.

There is also undeniably a personal genesis for black feminism, that is the political realization that comes from the seemingly personal experiences of individual black women's lives. Black feminists and many more black women who do not define themselves as feminists have all experienced sexual oppression as a constant factor in our day-to-day existence.

Black feminists often talk about their feelings of craziness before becoming conscious of the concepts of sexual politics, patriarchal rule, and, most importantly, feminism, the political analysis and practice that we women use to struggle against our oppression. The fact that racial politics and indeed racism are pervasive factors in our lives did not allow us, and still does not allow most black women, to look more deeply into our own experiences and define those things that make our lives what they are and our oppression specific to us. In the process of consciousness-raising, actually life-sharing, we began to recognize the commonality of our experiences and, from that sharing and growing consciousness, to build a politics that will change our lives and inevitably end our oppression.

Our development also must be tied to the contemporary economic and political position of black people. The post–World War II generation of black youth was the first to be able to minimally partake of certain educational and employment options, previously closed completely to black people. Although our economic position is still at the very bottom of the American capitalist economy, a handful of us have been able to gain certain tools as a result of tokenism in education and employment that potentially enable us to more effectively fight our oppression.

A combined antiracist and antisexist position drew us together initially, and as we developed politically we addressed ourselves to heterosexism and economic oppression under capitalism.

2. What We Believe

10 Above all else, our politics initially sprang from the shared belief that black women are inherently valuable, that our liberation is a necessity not as an adjunct to somebody else's but because of our need as human persons for autonomy. This may seem so obvious as to sound simplistic, but it is apparent that no other ostensibly progressive movement has ever considered our specific oppression a priority or worked seriously for the ending of that oppression. Merely naming the pejorative stereotypes attributed to black women (e.g., mammy, matriarch, Sapphire, whore, bulldagger), let alone

cataloguing the cruel, often murderous, treatment we receive, indicates how little value has been placed upon our lives during four centuries of bondage in the Western hemisphere. We realize that the only people who care enough about us to work consistently for our liberation is us. Our politics evolve from a healthy love for ourselves, our sisters, and our community, which allows us to continue our struggle and work.

This focusing upon our own oppression is embodied in the concept of identity politics. We believe that the most profound and potentially the most radical politics come directly out of our own identity, as opposed to working to end somebody else's oppression. In the case of black women this is a particularly repugnant, dangerous, threatening, and therefore revolutionary concept because it is obvious from looking at all the political movements that have preceded us that anyone is more worthy of liberation than ourselves. We reject pedestals, queenhood, and walking ten paces behind. To be recognized as human, levelly human, is enough.

We believe that sexual politics under patriarchy is as pervasive in black women's lives as are the politics of class and race. We also often find it difficult to separate race from class from sex oppression because in our lives they are most often experienced simultaneously. We know that there is such a thing as racial-sexual oppression that is neither solely racial nor solely sexual, e.g., the history of rape of black women by white men as a weapon of political repression.

Although we are feminists and lesbians, we feel solidarity with progressive black men and do not advocate the fractionalization that white women who are separatists demand. Our situation as black people necessitates that we have solidarity around the fact of race, which white women of course do not need to have with white men, unless it is their negative solidarity as racial oppressors. We struggle together with black men against racism, while we also struggle with black men about sexism.

We realize that the liberation of all oppressed peoples necessitates the destruction of the political-economic systems of capitalism and imperialism as well as patriarchy. We are socialists because we believe the work must be organized for the collective benefit of those who do the work and create the products and not for the profit of the bosses. Material resources must be equally distributed among those who create these resources. We are not convinced, however, that a socialist revolution that is not also a feminist and antiracist revolution will guarantee our liberation. We have arrived at the necessity for developing an understanding of class relationships that takes into account the specific class position of black women who are generally marginal in the labor force, while at this particular time some of us are temporarily viewed as doubly desirable tokens at white-collar and professional levels. We need to articulate the real class situation of persons who are not merely raceless, sexless workers, but for whom racial and sexual oppression are significant determinants in their working/economic lives. Although we are in essential agreement with Marx's theory as it applied to the very specific economic relationships he analyzed, we know that this analysis must be extended further in order for us to understand our specific economic situation as black women.

A political contribution that we feel we have already made is the expansion of the feminist principle that the personal is political. In our consciousness-raising sessions, for example, we have in many ways gone beyond white women's revelations because we are dealing with the implications of race and class as well as sex. Even our black women's style of talking/testifying in black language about what we have experienced has a resonance that is both cultural and political. We have spent a great deal of energy delving into the cultural and experiential nature of our oppression out of necessity because none of these matters have ever been looked at before. No one before has ever examined the multilayered texture of black women's lives.

As we have already stated, we reject the stance of lesbian separatism because it is not a viable political analysis or strategy for us. It leaves out far too much and far too many people, particularly black men, women, and children. We have a great deal of criticism and loathing for what men have been socialized to be in this society; what they support, how they act, and how they oppress. But we do not have the misguided notion that it is their maleness, per se—i.e., their biological maleness—that makes them what they are. As black women we find any type of biological determinism a particularly dangerous and reactionary basis upon which to build a politic. We must also question whether lesbian separatism is an adequate and progressive political analysis and strategy, even for those who practice it, since it so completely denies any but the sexual sources of women's oppression, negating the facts of class and race.

3. Problems in Organizing Black Feminists

During our years together as a black feminist collective we have experienced success and defeat, joy and pain, victory and failure. We have found that it is very difficult to organize around black feminist issues, difficult even to announce in certain contexts that we are black feminists. We have tried to think about the reasons for our difficulties, particularly since the white women's movement continues to be strong and to grow in many directions. In this section we will discuss some of the general reasons for the organizing problems we face and also talk specifically about the stages in organizing our own collective.

The major source of difficulty in our political work is that we are not just trying to fight oppression on one front or even two, but instead to address a whole range of oppressions. We do not have racial, sexual, heterosexual, or class privilege to rely upon, nor do we have even the minimal access to resources and power that groups who possess any one of these types of privilege have.

The psychological toll of being a black woman and the difficulties this presents in reaching political consciousness and doing political work can never be underestimated. There is a very low value placed upon black women's psyches in this society, which is both racist and sexist. As an early group member once said, "We are all damaged people merely by virtue of being black women." We are dispossessed psychologically and on every other level, and yet we feel the necessity to struggle to change our condition and the condition of all black women. In "A Black Feminist's Search for Sisterhood," Michele Wallace arrives at this conclusion:

> We exist as women who are black who are feminists, each stranded for the moment, working independently because there is not yet an environment in this society remotely congenial to our struggle—because, being on the bottom, we would have to do what no one else has done: we would have to fight the world.[2]

20 Wallace is not pessimistic but realistic in her assessment of black feminists' position, particularly in her allusion to the nearly classic isolation most of us face. We might use our position at the bottom, however, to make a clear leap into revolutionary action. If black women were free, it would mean that everyone else would have to be free since our freedom would necessitate the destruction of all the systems of oppression.

Feminism is, nevertheless, very threatening to the majority of black people because it calls into question some of the most basic assumptions about our existence, i.e., that gender should be a determinant of power relationships. Here is the way male and female roles were defined in a black nationalist pamphlet from the early 1970s.

> We understand that it is and has been traditional that the man is the head of the house. He is the leader of the house/nation because his knowledge of the world is broader, his awareness is greater, his understanding is fuller and his application of this information is wiser .... After all, it is only reasonable that the man be the head of the house because he is able to defend and protect the development of his home .... Women cannot do the same things as men—they are made by nature to function differently. Equality of men and women is something that cannot happen even in the abstract world. Men are not equal to other men, i.e., ability, experience, or even understanding. The value of men and women can be seen as in the value of gold and silver—they are not equal but both have great value. We must realize that men and women are a complement to each other because there is no house/family without a man and his wife. Both are essential to the development of any life.[3]

The material conditions of most black women would hardly lead them to upset both economic and sexual arrangements that seem to represent some stability in their lives. Many black women have a good understanding of both sexism and racism, but because of the everyday constrictions of their lives cannot risk struggling against them both.

The reaction of black men to feminism has been notoriously negative. They are, of course, even more threatened than black women by the possibility that black feminists might organize around our own needs. They realize that they might not only lose valuable and hard-working allies in their struggles, but that they might also be forced to change their habitually sexist ways of interacting with and oppressing black women. Accusations that black feminism divides the black struggle are powerful deterrents to the growth of an autonomous black women's movement.

Still, hundreds of women have been active at different times during the three-year existence of our group. And every black woman who came, came out of a strongly felt need for some level of possibility that did not previously exist in her life.

When we first started meeting early in 1974 after the NBFO first eastern regional conference, we did not have a strategy for organizing, or even a focus. We just wanted to see what we had. After a period of months of not meeting. We began to meet again late in the year and started doing an intense variety of consciousness-raising. The overwhelming feeling that we had is that after years and years we had finally found each other. Although we were not doing political work as a group, individuals continued their involvement in lesbian politics, sterilization abuse, and abortion rights work, Third World Women's International Women's Day activities, and support activity for the trials of Dr. Kenneth Edelin, Joan Little, and Inez Garcia. During our first summer, when membership had dropped off considerably, those of us remaining devoted serious discussion to the possibility of opening a refuge for battered women in a black community. (There was no refuge in Boston at that time.) We also decided around that time to become an independent collective since we had serious disagreements with NBFO's bourgeois-feminist stance and their lack of a clear political focus.

We also were contacted at that time by socialist feminists, with whom we had worked on abortion rights activities, who wanted to encourage us to attend the National Socialist Feminist Conference in Yellow Springs. One of our members did attend and despite the narrowness of the ideology that was promoted at that particular conference, we became more aware of the need for us to understand our own economic situation and to make our own economic analysis.

In the fall, when some members returned, we experienced several months of comparative inactivity and internal disagreements which were first conceptualized as a lesbian-straight split but which were also the result of class and political differences. During the summer those of us who were still meeting had determined the need to do political work and to move beyond consciousness-raising and serving exclusively as an emotional support group. At the beginning of 1976, when some of the women who had not wanted to do political work and who also had voiced disagreements stopped attending of their own accord, we again looked for a focus. We decided at that time, with the addition of new members, to become a study group. We had always shared our reading with each other, and some of us had written papers on black feminism for group discussion a few months before this decision was made. We began functioning as a study group and also began discussing the possibility of starting a black feminist publication. We had a retreat in the late spring, which provided a time for both political discussion and working out interpersonal issues. Currently we are planning to gather together a collection of black feminist writing. We feel that it is absolutely essential to demonstrate the reality of our politics to other black women and believe that we can do this through writing and distributing our work. The fact that individual black feminists are living in isolation all over the country, that our own numbers are small, and that we have some skills in writing, printing, and publishing makes us want to carry out these kinds of projects as a means of organizing black feminists as we continue to do political work in coalition with other groups.

4. Black Feminist Issues and Practice

During our time together we have identified and worked on many issues of particular relevance to black women. The inclusiveness of our politics makes us concerned with any situation that impinges upon the lives of women, Third World, and working people. We are of course particularly committed to working on those struggles in which race, sex, and class are simultaneous factors in oppression. We might, for example, become involved in workplace organizing at a factory that employs Third World women or picket a hospital that is cutting back on already inadequate health care to a Third World community, or set up a rape crisis center in a black neighborhood. Organizing around welfare or day-care concerns might also be a focus. The work to be done and the countless issues that this work represents merely reflect the pervasiveness of our oppression.

Issues and projects that collective members have actually worked on are sterilization abuse, abortion rights, battered women, rape, and health care. We have also done many workshops and educationals on black feminism on college campuses, at women's conferences, and most recently for high school women.

30 One issue that is of major concern to us and that we have begun to publicly address is racism in the white women's movement. As black feminists we are made constantly and painfully aware of how little effort white women have made to understand and combat their racism, which requires among other things that they have a more than superficial comprehension of race, color, and black history and culture. Eliminating racism in the white women's movement is by definition work for white women to do, but we will continue to speak to and demand accountability on this issue.

In the practice of our politics we do not believe that the end always justifies the means. Many reactionary and destructive acts have been done in the name of achieving "correct" political goals. As feminists we do not want to mess over people in the name of politics. We believe in collective process and a nonhierarchical distribution of power within our own group and in our vision of a revolutionary society. We are committed to a continual examination of our politics as they develop through criticism and self-criticism as an essential aspect of our practice. As black feminists and lesbians we know that we have a very definite revolutionary task to perform, and we are ready for the lifetime of work and struggle before us.

Notes

[1]This statement is dated April 1977.

[2]Michele Wallace. "A Black Feminist's Search for Sisterhood," *Village Voice,* 28 July 1975, 6–7.

[3]Mumininas of Committee for Unified Newark, *Mwanamke Mwananchi (The Nationalist Woman),* Newark, NJ, c. 1971, 4–5.

Mapping the Text

1. Describe in as much detail as you can and using the adjectives used in the statement itself the women for whom this group is voicing concern.
2. What does this group seek to accomplish in making this statement? What message(s) do you think the group seeks to convey? What issues do they identify as significant? To what extent do you think this group of issues continues the debates that gave rise to the Declaration of Independence, the Declaration of Sentiments, or the Port Huron Statement?

Writing to Inquire

1. In naming their collective the Combahee River Collective, how do you think this group of women seems to be linking itself to this historical place and image?
2. Assuming that you agree with the idea of having a democratic society, write an essay in which you argue for your view of what democracy means as a particularly American phenomenon.

I Hear America Singing

Walt Whitman

Walt Whitman (1819–1892) began his writing career as a journalist in New York, starting as a printer and eventually working as writer, contributing writer, and editor of various New York newspapers and literary magazines. During this time he also demonstrated his interests in politics in becoming active with the Democratic Party, writing political essays and publishing stories in the *Democratic Review,* the foremost magazine of the party. While Whitman wrote fiction and essays throughout his life, he is best known and appreciated as a poet. His most famous collection, *Leaves of Grass,* was first published in 1855, with many revised editions published over the remainder of his life. The preface to the collection, which was perhaps Whitman's response to Ralph Waldo Emerson's essay on American poetry, asserted his view of what an American poet needed to be like. The poems reflected his critical attention to his art, his love of people and nation, and his desire to be open and explicit about sexuality. The poem below is included in this collection.

I hear America singing, the varied carols I hear,
Those of mechanics, each one singing his as it should be blithe and strong,
The carpenter singing his as he measures his plank or beam,
The mason singing his as he makes ready for work, or leaves off work,
The boatman singing what belongs to him in his boat, the deckhand singing on the steamboat deck,
The shoemaker singing as he sits on his bench, the hatter singing as he stands,
The wood-cutter's song, the ploughboy's on his way in the morning, or at noon intermission or at sundown,
The delicious singing of the mother, or of the young wife at work, or of the girl sewing or washing.
Each singing what belongs to him or her and to none else,
The day what belongs to the day—at night the party of young fellows, robust, friendly,
Singing with open mouths their strong melodious songs.

Mapping the Text

1. Review the scenes of America that Whitman presents in his poem. Make your own list of scenes. How are your scenes like or different from Whitman's?
2. Who are the Americans in Whitman's poem? How does Whitman view them and feel about them?

Writing to Inquire

1. Make a list of all the patriotic songs that you can identify or find. In the spirit of Whitman's poem, which of these songs do you literally hear America singing today, and what dimension of American-ness do you think that the song symbolizes?
2. Search through your personal photograph collection, or magazines, or other sources of visual images for what you consider images of an America that you would like to celebrate, or perhaps question. Using a form other than an essay (e.g., a poem, song, letter, journal entry, narrative, etc.), express the point of view that you would like to convey.

I, Too, Sing America

LANGSTON HUGHES

Langston Hughes (1902–1967) is one of the best-known poets of the Harlem Renaissance as well as a prolific writer of prose. Deemed by many in his day the Poet Laureate of the Negro Race, Hughes published his first volume of poetry, *The Weary Blues,* in 1926. Other collections of poems include *Shakespeare in Harlem* (1942); *Montage of a Dream Deferred* (1951); *Ask Your Mama: Twelve Moods for Jazz* (1961); and *Collected Poems* (1994). His prose works include *The Big Sea* (1940); *Simple Speaks His Mind* (1950); *Simple Takes a Wife* (1953); *Simple's Uncle Sam* (1965); and *Good Morning, Revolution: Uncollected Social Protest Writings* (1973). Hughes's poetry is particularly distinctive in its incorporation of African-American jazz rhythms and imagery.

I, too, sing America.

I am the darker brother.
They send me to eat in the kitchen
When company comes,
But I laugh,
And eat well,
And grow strong.

Tomorrow,
I'll be at the table
When company comes.
Nobody'll dare
Say to me,
"Eat in the kitchen,"
Then.

Besides,
They'll see how beautiful I am
And be ashamed—

I, too, am America.

Mapping the Text

1. In "I, Too, Sing America," Langston Hughes seems to be in conversation with Walt Whitman. Examine both poems and account for the dialog. With what in Whitman's statement can Hughes be perceived as linking? What is his counterpoint? How does he question and extend Whitman's view?

2. What is the tone of voice in Hughes's poem? Is he joyful and celebratory? How would you describe the speaker in the poem? What words or phrases help create this impression?
3. To what audience(s) is Hughes speaking?

Writing to Inquire

1. What differences in history and experience help define and shape Hughes's point of view and its differences from your own?

America

CLAUDE MCKAY

Claude McKay (1889–1948) was born in Jamaica and educated by his older brother. His works include poetry and prose: *Songs of Jamaica* (1912); *A Long Way from Home* (1937); *Harlem: Negro Metropolis* (1940); and *The Negroes in America* (1979). McKay traveled extensively, visiting Russia and France and studying communism. He used the sonnet form to write about social injustice in the United States, and he wrote often of his life in Jamaica as well.

Although she feeds me bread of bitterness,
And sinks into my throat her tiger's tooth,
Stealing my breath of life, I will confess
I love this cultured hell that tests my youth!
Her vigor flows like tides into my blood,
Giving me strength against her hate.
Her bigness sweeps my being like a flood.
Yet as a rebel fronts a king in state,
I stand within her walls with not a shred
Of terror, malice, not a word of jeer.
Darkly I gaze into the days ahead,
And see her might and granite wonders there,
Beneath the touch of Time's unerring hand,
Like priceless treasures sinking in the sand.

Mapping the Text

1. In his poem "America," Claude McKay seems to be presenting an instance of ambivalence. Whose ambivalence is it? What is it? What words and images help set up the polarities?
2. Define *patriotism*. Do you consider this poem patriotic? What view, if any, of patriotism does it present?

Writing to Inquire

1. Many writers have chosen poetry as a form to express their sentiments about national values and identities. Consider the ways in which this genre seems to accommodate this type of expressiveness and speculate why this may be so.

My Name Is. . .

ARLENE MESTAS

Arlene Mestas (1940–) teaches English in Bernadillo, New Mexico. She states, "This poem comes from being called Maria, after I was introduced as Arlene; when someone confused me with Roseanne when I asked a question and Roseanne was given the answer. It is a poem about seeing a short brown woman, indistinguishable from others. Roseanne, Dianna [another friend], and I are Las tres Marias—the three Marias whose laughter is tinged with sorrow."

The only thing you saw
of note when we met
was the brown of my skin.
You could not hear me
through your blinders
Nor could I make myself
heard through the narrow
tunnel vision embedded
in you.

Though my roots
In northern New Mexico
are 400 years deep
on one side and
10,000 years on the other,
(I was here before America).
Your mentality tells me
I should be grateful
for the crumbs of equality
you've tossed aside.

And you wonder at my anger
When I am made to feel
unequal, incompetent,
when you dismiss me
in terms that are generic
when you call me
. . . Maria.

Mapping the Text

1. What audience do you think that Mestas is seeking to reach? What evidence from the poem do you have to support your view?

Writing to Inquire

1. Read the Mestas poem. Write an essay in which you consider the connections between names and identity. Consider, for example, how misnaming functions in the poem and how Mestas is using an instance of misnaming to express an idea. What idea do you think Mestas is expressing?
2. Do a library search of the history of the Southwest to identify the groups who have settled there over the centuries. How does this history of settlement in these areas affect definitions and images of what is American?

Lakota Woman

MARY CROW DOG

Mary Crow Dog (1953–) is best known for her autobiography, *Lakota Woman,* which chronicles her journey from the Rosebud Sioux Indian Reservation in South Dakota, where she grew up, to her work as a Native American rights activist. While Crow Dog was raised on the Sioux Indian Reservation, her mother did not speak their native language to her daughter at home. *Lakota Woman,* from which the excerpt below was taken, considers, among other issues, the high price of cultural assimilation for Native Americans.

To start from the beginning, I am a Sioux from the Rosebud Reservation in South Dakota. I belong to the "Burned Thigh," the Brule Tribe, the Sicangu in our language. Long ago, so the legend goes, a small band of Sioux was surrounded by enemies who set fire to their tipis and the grass around them. They fought their way out of the trap but got their legs burned and in this way acquired their name. The Brules are part of the Seven Sacred Campfires, the seven tribes of the Western Sioux known collectively as Lakota. The Eastern Sioux are called Dakota. The difference between them is their language. It is the same except that where we Lakota pronounce an *L,* the Dakota pronounce a *D.* They cannot pronounce an *L* at all. In our tribe we have this joke: "What is a flat tire in Dakota?" Answer; "A b*d*owout."

The Brule, like all Sioux, were a horse people, fierce riders and raiders, great warriors. Between 1870 and 1880 all Sioux were driven into reservations, fenced in and forced to give up everything that had given meaning to their life—their horses, their hunting, their arms, everything. But under the long snows of despair the little spark of our ancient beliefs and pride kept glowing, just barely sometimes, waiting for a warm wind to blow that spark into a flame again.

My family was settled on the reservation in a small place called He-Dog, after a famous chief. There are still some He-Dogs living. One, an old lady I knew, lived to be over a hundred years old. Nobody knew when she had been born. She herself had no idea, except that when she came into the world there was no census yet, and Indians had not yet been given Christian first names. Her name was just He-Dog, nothing else. She always told me. "You should have seen me eighty years ago when I was pretty." I have never forgotten her face—nothing but deep cracks and gullies, but beautiful in its own way. At any rate very impressive.

On the Indian side my family was related to the Brave Birds and Fool Bulls. Old Grandpa Fool Bull was the last man to make flutes and play them, the old-style flutes in the shape of a bird's head which had the elk power, the power to lure a young girl into a man's blanket. Fool Bull lived a whole long century, dying in 1976, whittling his flutes almost until his last day. He took me to my first peyote meeting while I was still a kid.

5 He still remembered the first Wounded Knee, the massacre. He was a young boy at that time, traveling with his father, a well-known medicine man. They had gone to a place near Wounded Knee to take part in a Ghost Dance. They had on their painted ghost shirts which were supposed to make them bulletproof. When they got near Pine Ridge they were stopped by white soldiers, some of them from the Seventh Cavalry, George Custer's old regiment, who were hoping to kill themselves some Indians. The Fool Bull band had to give up their few old muzzle-loaders, bows, arrows, and even knives. They had to put up their tipis in a tight circle, all bunched up, with the wagons on the outside and the soldiers surrounding their camp, watching them closely. It was cold, so cold that the trees were crackling with a loud noise as the frost was splitting their trunks. The people made a fire the following morning to warm themselves and make some coffee and then they noticed a sound beyond the crackling of the trees; rifle fire, salvos making a noise like the ripping apart of a giant blanket; the boom of cannon and the rattling of quick-firing Hotchkiss guns. Fool Bull remembered the grown-ups bursting into tears, the women keening: "They are killing our people, they are butchering them!" It was only two miles or so from where Grandfather Fool Bull stood that almost three hundred Sioux men, women, and children were slaughtered. Later grandpa saw the bodies of the slain, all frozen in ghostly attitudes, thrown into a ditch like dogs. And he saw a tiny baby sucking at his dead mother's breast.

I wish I could tell about the big deeds of some ancestors of mine who fought at the Little Big Horn, or the Rosebud, counting coup during the Grattan or Fetterman battle, but little is known of my family's history before 1880. I hope some of my great-grandfathers counted coup on Custer's men, I like to imagine it, but I just do not know. Our Rosebud people did not play a big part in the battles against generals Crook or Custer. This was due to the policy of Spotted Tail, the all-powerful chief at the time.

Spotted Tail had earned his eagle feathers as a warrior, but had been taken East as a prisoner and put in jail. Coming back years later, he said that he had seen the cities of the whites and that a single one of them contained more people than could be found in all the Plains tribes put together, and that every one of the wasičuns' factories could turn out more rifles and bullets in one day than were owned by all the Indians in the country. It was useless, he said, to try to resist the wasičuns. During the critical year of 1876 he had his Indian police keep most of the young men on the reservation, preventing them from joining Sitting Bull, Gall, and Crazy Horse. Some of the young bucks, a few Brave Birds among them, managed to sneak out trying to get to Montana, but nothing much is known. After having been forced into reservations, it was not thought wise to recall such things. It might mean no rations, or worse. For the same reason many in my family turned Christian, letting themselves be "white-manized." It took many years to reverse this process.

My sister Barbara, who is four years older than me, says she remembers the day when I was born. It was late at night and raining hard amid thunder and lightning. We had no electricity then, just the old-style kerosene lamps with the big reflectors. No bathroom, no tap water, no car. Only a few white teachers had cars. There was one phone in He-Dog, at the trading post. This was not so very long ago, come to think of it. Like most Sioux at that time my mother was supposed to give birth at home, I think, but something went wrong, I was pointing the wrong way, feet first or stuck sideways. My mother was in great pain, laboring for hours, until finally somebody ran to the trading post and called the ambulance. They took her—us—to Rosebud, but the hospital there was not yet equipped to handle a complicated birth, I don't think they had surgery then, so they had to drive mother all the way to Pine Ridge, some ninety miles distant, because there the tribal hospital was bigger. So it happened that I was born among Crazy Horse's people. After my sister Sandra was born the doctors there performed a hysterectomy on my mother, in fact sterilizing her without her permission, which was common at the time, and up to just a few years ago, so that it is hardly worth mentioning. In the opinion of some people, the fewer Indians there are, the better. As Colonel Chivington said to his soldiers: "Kill 'em all, big and small, nits make lice!"

I don't know whether I am a louse under the white man's skin. I hope I am. At any rate I survived the long hours of my mother's labor, the stormy drive to Pine Ridge, and the neglect of the doctors. I am an iyeska, a breed, that's what the white kids used to call me. When I grew bigger they stopped calling me that, because it would get them a bloody nose. I am a small woman, not much over five feet tall, but I can hold my own in a fight, and in a free-for-all with honkies I can become rather ornery and do real damage. I have white blood in me. Often I have wished to be able to purge it out of me. As a young girl I used to look at myself in the mirror, trying to find a clue as to who and what I was. My face is very Indian, and so are my eyes and my hair, but my skin is very light. Always I waited for the summer, for the prairie sun, the Badlands sun, to tan me and make me into a real skin.

The Crow Dogs, the members of my husband's family, have no such problems of identity. They don't need the sun to tan them, they are full-bloods—the Sioux of the Sioux. Some Crow Dog men have faces which make the portrait on the buffalo Indian nickel look like a washed-out white man. They have no shortage of legends. Every Crow Dog seems to be a legend in himself, including the women. They became outcasts in their stronghold at Grass Mountain rather than being whitemanized. They could not be tamed, made to wear a necktie or go to a Christian church. All during the long years when practicing Indian beliefs was forbidden and could be punished with jail, they went right on having their ceremonies, their sweat baths and sacred dances. Whenever a Crow Dog got together with some relatives, such as those equally untamed, unregenerated Iron Shells, Good Lances, Two Strikes, Picket Pins, or Hollow Horn Bears, then you could hear the sound of the can gleska, the drum, telling all the world that a Sioux ceremony was in the making. It took courage and suffering to keep the flame alive, the little spark under the snow.

10 The first Crow Dog was a well-known chief. On his shield was the design of two circles and two arrowheads for wounds received in battle—two white man's bullets and two Pawnee arrow points. When this first Crow Dog was lying wounded in the snow, a coyote came to warm him and a crow flew ahead of him to show him the way home. His name should be Crow Coyote, but the white interpreter misunderstood it and so they became Crow Dogs. This Crow Dog of old became famous for killing a rival chief, the result of a feud over tribal politics, then driving voluntarily over a hundred miles to get himself hanged at Deadwood, his wife sitting beside him in his buggy; famous also for finding on his arrival that the Supreme Court had ordered him to be freed because the federal government had no jurisdiction over Indian reservations and also because it was no crime for one Indian to kill another. Later, Crow Dog became a leader of the Ghost Dancers, holding out for months in the frozen caves and ravines of the Badlands. So, if my own family lacks history, that of my husband more than makes up for it.

Our land itself is a legend, especially the area around Grass Mountain where I am living now. The fight for our land is at the core of our existence, as it has been for the last two hundred years. Once the land is gone, then we are gone too. The Sioux used to keep winter counts, picture writings on buffalo skin, which told our people's story from year to year. Well, the whole country is one vast winter count. You can't walk a mile without coming to some family's sacred vision hill, to an ancient Sun Dance circle, an old battleground, a place where something worth remembering happened.

Mostly a death, a proud death or a drunken death. We are a great people for dying. "It's a good day to die!" that's our old battle cry. But the land with its tar paper shacks and outdoor privies, not one of them straight, but all leaning this way or that way, is also a land to live on, a land for good times and telling jokes and talking of great deeds done in the past. But you can't live forever off the deeds of Sitting Bull or Crazy Horse. You can't wear their eagle feathers, freeload off their legends. You have to make your own legends now. It isn't easy.

Mapping the Text

1. The writer of this personal narrative is a Native American woman. What social and political position does she create for herself, as a Native American woman, in her narrative?
2. Read the Crow Dog story carefully. What is the issue that Crow Dog is raising for thought and questioning?

Writing to Inquire

1. What is your reaction to the Crow Dog story? If you had to respond to her, what would you say?
2. Crow Dog refers to the Little Big Horn and Wounded Knee as significant events in her history. What were these events? What do they suggest to you about American-ness or American values?

CALLS TO ACTION AND RESPONSE

A Polyglot Nation

DIEGO CASTELLANOS

Diego Castellanos produces and hosts *Puerto Rican Panorama,* a television show filmed in Philadelphia. Born in Puerto Rico, Castellanos earned his Ph.D. at Farleigh Dickinson University, and he served as New Jersey's state director of bilingual education programs throughout most of the 1970s. Castellanos has worked extensively as a reporter, editor, and columnist, writing for publications in both Spanish and English. "A Polyglot Nation" is excerpted from his book *The Best of Two Worlds; Bilingual-Bicultural Education in the U.S.* (1983).

In the beginning the Western Hemisphere offered its bounty to the brave, the strong, the curious, and the lucky, whatever their national origin, social status, or motivation for coming here. Willing pioneers came from Spain, France, England, and other countries of the world. Scholars believe that the first Americans simply wandered in from Asia, crossing the Bering Strait from Siberia to Alaska. Although these prehistoric nomads preceded the Europeans by thousands of years, they—the ancestors of the "native" Americans—were migrants nonetheless. It is believed that at the time of the first European arrivals, there were more than a million natives living in what is today the contiguous United States. Spreading out over their new continent, they formed new nations. The Apache and Navajo would eventually settle in the southwestern deserts; the Kickapoo in the central prairies; the Cheyenne, Pawnee, and Crow in the northern plains; the Comanche in the southern plains; the Washo in the Great Basin; the Natchez and Arawak along the Gulf Coast; the Taino and Carib in the Caribbean Basin; the Chickasaw, Choctaw, Cherokee, Creek, and Shawnee in the southeastern woodlands; the Lenni Lenape along the mideastern seaboard; the Mohegan, Ottawa, Cayuga, Mohawk, Delaware, and Seneca in the northeastern woodlands; and others—all having their own peculiar rituals, culture, and language or dialect. Prior to the arrival of the Europeans, more than five hundred languages were spoken in North America.[1]

The first part of (what is today) the United States to be settled by the Europeans was Puerto Rico. The island was colonized by Juan Ponce de León in 1508, fifteen years after it had been visited by Christopher Columbus. After serving as Puerto Rico's first governor, Ponce de León migrated

[1] Gay Lawrence, "Indian Education: Why Bilingual-Bicultural?" *Education and Urban Society* 10, no. 3 (May 1978): 314.

toward the North American continent, reaching its southern peninsula in 1513. He explored the area, named it Florida, resettled there, and became its first governor. The lands discovered by Ponce de León and Juan de Garay were given in 1527 to Pánfilo de Narváez by the king of Spain. Ponce de León was followed by Alonso de Pineda, who reached the mouth of the Mississippi River in 1519. The Spanish established a colony (which did not survive) in the Carolinas in 1526, sixty years before Sir Walter Raleigh made a similar unsuccessful attempt. Around 1529, when he was governor of Florida, Narváez visited Louisiana with Alvar Núñez Cabeza de Vaca. In 1536 Hernando Cortés visited California and Cabeza de Vaca explored Texas. In 1539 Hernando de Soto visited Georgia and Tennessee, García López de Cárdenas discovered the Grand Canyon of Colorado, General Francisco Vásquez de Coronado explored New Mexico and Kansas, and Hernando Alarcón discovered the Colorado River. In 1541 de Soto discovered the Mississippi River near Memphis. The following year, twenty years before French colonizers reached the New World, Juan Rodríguez Cabrillo, a Portuguese, became the first European to set foot on the Pacific Coast, by the San Diego harbor.

The first permanent European settlement on this continent was Spanish-speaking St. Augustine, established in 1565 by Pedro Menéndez de Aviles (later governor of Florida) on a site where French Huguenots had failed two years earlier. The colony remained Spanish for more than two and a half centuries. In 1566 the colony of Santa Elena was founded at the site of today's Parris Island marine base in South Carolina. The settlement, which lasted twenty-one years, had sixty houses and reached a population of four hundred. It served as the capital of Spanish Florida. In 1573 Pedro Márquez discovered the Chesapeake Bay, and in 1582—five years before the first attempt to establish an English colony there (which failed)—Antonio de Espejo explored and named New Mexico. Sixteen years later Juan de Oñate led four hundred soldiers and their cattle into New Mexico and settled in the territory.

Spaniards held a virtual monopoly over the southern half of this country for one entire century before the arrival of other Europeans. They conducted extensive explorations, discovering and naming many of our national landmarks and spreading the gospel among the natives. Jesuits accompanying these pioneers used the autochthonous dialects of Florida, as well as Spanish, to teach Christianity to the natives. A similar bilingual approach was used by Franciscan missionaries in the Southwest, by Dominicans elsewhere. Spain's domain in the Western Hemisphere between the early sixteenth and nineteenth centuries extended southward to include Mexico, all of Central and South America except Brazil, and most of the Caribbean Islands. It seemed possible during the sixteenth century that Spanish would become not only the language of the Western Hemisphere, but of the entire world. That possibility was terminated by the defeat of the Spanish Armada by the British in 1588, as well as by further Spanish defeats by the French, who in the mid-seventeenth century became the leading power in Europe.

The French came to the New World in 1534, and by the end of the sixteenth century, France had established colonies in the St. Lawrence Valley, the region around Lake Superior, and the northern part of the Ohio Valley. In 1605 they settled Arcadia, off the coast of Canada. Not until 1607, 115 years after Columbus's first voyage, did the first permanent English colony in the New World appear, in Jamestown, Virginia. A dozen years later West Africans were brought to Jamestown as indentured servants. In 1620 another permanent colony was founded in Plymouth, Massachusetts, by a group of Pilgrims.

The first group of permanent Dutch settlers came to New Netherland (New York State) in 1624, when their country was still under Spanish rule. Two years later Peter Minuit purchased Manhattan from the natives. Spanish-Portuguese Jews, the Sephardim, arrived around the mid-seventeenth century. Meanwhile, Huguenots were settling in Charleston, South Carolina. Minuit brought a shipload of Finns and Swedes to the Delaware River Valley in 1638. William Penn, a Quaker, came to this area in 1682, and in October of the following year, the ship *Concord* brought thirteen Quaker and Mennonite families from the German town of Krefeld to Philadelphia. Led by Fritz Daniel Pastorius, a thirty-year-old lawyer from Franconia, they founded the community of Germantown.

It became obvious very early that the British would be the dominant nationality and that English would be the predominant language in the central portion of North America. Because of the many nationalities represented in Anglo-America, along with the many Indian nations that existed here, knowledge of two or more languages became a decided advantage for trading, scouting, teaching, and spreading the gospel, as well as for diplomacy. Anthony Sadowski, a Pole who came to America in the first decade of the eighteenth century, became one of many interpreters of Latin languages. Linguists performed other essential functions as some schools, churches, and other institutions offered bilingual services. The Protestant missionary schools established by these northwestern European settlers to "introduce Indians to civilization and Christianity" were—of necessity—also bilingual. While the efforts of missionaries to maintain the native tongues of the aborigines were not encouraged, they were tolerated by the powers that be.

Settlers from almost every northern and western European nation continued to arrive in the Americas during the seventeenth century. The immigration traffic was so diverse that eighteen different languages were being spoken by people of twenty different nationalities in New Amsterdam (Manhattan Island) in 1664 when it was captured from the Dutch by the English.[2]

[2] John F. Kennedy, *A Nation of Immigrants* (New York: Harper & Row, 1964), p. 11; and Clarence Senior, *Strangers—Then Neighbors: From Pilgrims to Puerto Ricans* (New York: Freedom Books, 1971), p. 1.

By 1763 England had succeeded in gaining total control over Franco-America, thus ending a hundred years of French sovereignty in that area. This conquest began the process of Anglicizing the land that was to become Canada, as British expansion extended Anglo-America to include the northern as well as the central regions of North America. In the mid-eighteenth century the British rulers of Nova Scotia expelled four thousand Acadians when they refused to pledge their loyalty to the British Empire. The outcasts ended up years later among other French speakers in Louisiana, where their descendants became known as the Cajuns. They settled in the bayou country of the Mississippi Delta and retained French as their primary language.

Around 1719 Scotch-Irish constituted one-fourth of the population of New York, New Jersey, and Pennsylvania. In 1736 Moravians, a German sect, arrived in Georgia and eventually migrated on to Pennsylvania. A great deal of conflict—having little to do with linguistic differences—was generated among the various nationalities of the New World. For example, in Pennsylvania the Scotch-Irish, who seemed more inclined toward belligerence, and the Quakers, who were devoted to nonviolence, disagreed on such issues as Indian relations.

It was around this time that the Germans, the most important group in the early history of bilingual education, were coming to Anglo-America. From Pennsylvania they followed the mountain valleys leading southward into the back country of Maryland, Virginia, and the Carolinas. By the mid-eighteenth century they had moved north into the Mohawk Valley of New York and east into New England. Settling in relatively unpopulated frontier areas, the Germans were often unnoticed, even when they were in the majority. In these farming districts the Germans initially had no teachers at their disposal who were familiar with English. In reality, there was little need for a command of English either for communicating with each other, raising their livestock, or harvesting their crops. The Germans' strong desire to perpetuate their culture in the new land and the relative unimportance of English in their early settlements—combined with the fact that they were unimpressed with Anglo-American schooling—led the Germans to establish their own private parochial schools to inculcate their ethnic traditions and to preserve their language.[3]

In 1753 Benjamin Franklin voiced the fear that the Germans "will soon so out number us that all the advantages we have will not, in My Opinion, be able to preserve our language." With Franklin's help a systematic attempt to introduce English schools into the German-speaking areas of Pennsylvania was made by the London-based Society for the Propagation

---

[3] Arnold B. Faust, *The German Element in the United States* (Salem, N.H.: Arno Press, 1969), p. 204; George S. Clark, "The Germans," in *The New Jersey Ethnic Experience,* ed. Barbara Cunningham (Union City, N.J.: William H. Wise, 1977), p. 224; and Gerald D. Kanoon, "The Four Phases of Bilingual Education in the United States," *TESOL Newsletter* 12 (Apr. 1978), p. 1.

of Christian Knowledge. The effort failed when Pennsylvania Germans became aware that the plan was ethnolingual in its aims, and not religious, as the name of the society implied.[4] A quarter of a million strong, Germans constituted the largest non-English-background group during the Revolutionary period. Although they were distributed more uniformly throughout Anglo-America than most other immigrant groups, one-third of the German population resided in Pennsylvania. There were smaller but significant German enclaves in each of the other twelve colonies, as well as along the Mississippi River and in the Northwest Territory.

Some of the other ethnic minorities in the United States at the time of its independence included large settlements of Scotch-Irish on the frontier (Virginia, Pennsylvania, and the Carolinas); Irish below the Mason-Dixon line; Scottish in North Carolina, New York, and Georgia; Dutch in Manhattan, Staten Island, and Long Island, as well as along the Hudson River and on the coastlines of New Jersey and Connecticut; French in Maine and Charleston; Huguenots in Manhattan; French Catholics in Louisiana; Swedes in the Delaware Valley; Jews in Manhattan and Rhode Island; Danes in New York; and Welsh in New England and Pennsylvania. The demographic registers circa 1776 officially listed the country's white population as 61 percent English, 10 percent Irish (mostly from Ulster), 9 percent German, 8 percent Scottish, 3 percent Dutch, 2 percent French, 1 percent Swedish, and 6 percent other.[5]

Twenty percent of the total population of Anglo-America was believed to be black, most of whom lived in the South. Although these Africans brought scores of languages with them, slave traders' practice of dispersing speakers of the same tongue, and the resulting development of pidgins and creoles, prevented any West African languages from surviving in North America.

15 Just months after the Revolution was won, in 1782, French-American writer Hector St. John de Crèvecoeur said of his adopted land: "Individuals of all nations are melted into a new race of men."[6] In line with this melting pot ideal, English came to assume a greater importance, although non-English-language instruction continued in many schools founded by immigrants. In some schools English was taught as the main language, while the native language was offered as a school subject and used for part of the instruction. The languages most frequently taught were German, Dutch, Polish, and French. Spanish was used exclusively in the Southwest, of course, but that area was not yet part of the United States.

[4] Heinz Kloss, *American Bilingual Tradition* (Rowley, Mass.: Newbury House, 1977). p. 148.

[5] *Reports of the Committee on Linguistic and National Stocks in the Population of the United States* (Washington, D.C.: American Council of Learned Societies, 1932).

[6] *Letters from an American Farmer;* for excerpts, see Oscar Handlin, ed., *This Was America: As Recorded by European Travelers in the Eighteenth, Nineteenth, and Twentieth Centuries* (New York: Harper Torchbooks, 1964), pp. 36–59.

During the eighteenth century, the German Lutheran and Reformed churches built a comprehensive private elementary school system, which at times received public funds. By the beginning of the Revolutionary War, 78 Reformed and 40 Lutheran parochial schools were thriving, and the total number (in both denominations) increased to 254 by 1800.[7] As the number of Germans increased, public schools began to adjust their programs to the needs of these children. Instruction in several districts in Pennsylvania, Maryland, Virginia, the Carolinas, and later Wisconsin was given in German—often to the exclusion of English. It is quite obvious that this nation was born multilingual and multicultural, despite the indisputable fact that English became accepted as a lingua franca.

Mapping the Text

1. Diego Castellanos offers an account of the settlement of the United States that does not begin with Plymouth Rock or the Pilgrims. What is the effect of his choosing this approach? At the end of his essay, Castellanos states that English rose to prominence as the language of the "melting pot," a lingua franca, but amid other languages that continued to exist. What issues are raised by the ways in which Castellanos views the United States historically through its languages?

Writing to Inquire

1. With each new wave of immigration, language use continues to be an important part of the process of making a new home. Through library research, determine how many significant waves of immigration the United States has experienced. What countries constituted major sites of origin during each wave? What were the languages of the people? Were there issues that emerged distinctively in each era? Do issues seem to be consistent across different groups and across time?

Why No Official Tongue?

SHIRLEY BRICE HEATH

Shirley Brice Heath is Professor of English and Linguistics at Stanford University. Her research blends cultural anthropology with linguistics and literacy studies. In her ethnographic fieldwork, she observes people as they engage in many activities over long periods of time; interviews them; considers the characteristics of their environment; and collects various artifacts associated with their uses of language, especially written language. She has studied the literacy prac-

[7] Kloss, *American Bilingual Tradition,* p. 147.

tices of adults and children, and she has traveled extensively throughout the United States and the world in order to pursue her studies across multiple communities and cultures. Her books include *Ways with Words: Language, Life and Work in Communities and Classrooms* (1983); *Identity and Inner-City Youth: Beyond Ethnicity and Gender* (1993); and (with Shelby Wolf) *The Braid of Literature: Children's Worlds of Reading* (1992).

The United States of America was born among speakers of many dialects and languages, and until well past its "critical age," the new nation had neither institutions nor processes designed to choose or promote a single linguistic norm as appropriate for identification with the national character. The colonial legacy of the United States did not include official selection of a specific language to be encouraged among the indigenous or a linguistic standard to be maintained among the settlers. The absence of a designation of official status for the English language within the colonies reflected both the notions of language which the peculiar historical events of the sixteenth and seventeenth centuries shaped for England and the diversity of settlement motivations which drew widely differing social, linguistic, and ethnic groups to America.

Unlike other colonial powers, which attempted to determine both language choice and processes of change for group unification and cultural assimilation, England's policy makers did not consider language problems in their determination of policies for their New World colonies. Moreover, most settlers of the colonies came to pursue their own interests, not to transplant either Christianization to indigenous peoples or to extend Old World political systems to the New. Therefore, they brought with them neither the institutional sponsorship nor the techniques of linguistic unification and change which were so prominent among French and Castilian colonizers.[1] Hence, at the founding of the United States, there were no colonial language policies or programs to build upon.

At the political decision-making level of the new nation, focus on political theory was all-pervasive and crucial. Acutely self-conscious about their role in adjusting and adapting European political theories to a newly independent nation, the founders of early U.S. national policy first considered issues in the context of particular systems or theories with which these topics had formerly been associated. Often, political decision-makers faced with suggestions related to language choice and standardization identified supranational language decisions with monarchies. The language academies of Spain and France, well known

[1] See Shirley Brice Heath, *Telling Tongues: Language Policy in Mexico, Colony to Nation* (New York: Teachers College Press, 1972), and "Colonial Language Status Achievement: Mexico, Peru, and the United States," in *Language in Sociology*, ed. Albert Verdoodt and Rolf Kjolseth (Louvain, Belgium: Editions Peeters, 1976).

to many U.S. leaders, provoked images of crowned heads and royal courts dictating cultural norms. Antimonarchical forces in the United States, therefore, viewed negatively any national polity–sponsored manipulation of language.

From 1770 to 1820, when policies related to either language choice or standardization were proposed, they were debated for their potential to meet pragmatic and universal aims consonant with those of the American political system. When political leaders recognized language as a problem, they did so most consistently in the institutional contexts of law and learning, and here they saw language as a pragmatic tool—not as an ideal or as an ideological symbol.[2] Recognition of the potential of a standard language of wide communication as an instrument of access to codes of law, institutions, and written sources of learning (particularly in science and literature) was common among the nation's elite. In addition, the political leaders of the new nation yearned for universal extension of American achievements in government and science. Extension had to be preceded by, or at least coordinate with, both standardization of the code and legitimatization through a national literature. The results of France's standardization program and that nation's coordinate rise to fame in literature and science in the eighteenth century particularly underscored this need to many political leaders in the United States. However, the ideals of the political system supported by many of these same men could not include a centralized agency designed to designate and control language choices. What alternatives existed?

5 During the early national period, those most frequently labeled "the founding fathers" discussed language problems in various contexts and proposed diverse solutions. However, the choice of a single language as the official communication mode was never made.[3] Multiple languages played critical roles in the political and social life of the nation during this period. Cultural and ethnic pluralities abounded both in the clusters of representatives of different nationalities which had come during the colonial period and in the sequences of diverse groups which entered the new nation during the years 1770–1820.[4] German and French armed forces played important roles during the Revolution; many of those who remained after the War became economically, politically, and socially prominent, while retaining their native tongues. Refugees from the French Revolution arrived in large numbers between 1790 and 1800, and these

[2] See, e.g., Thomas Jefferson's recommendations on language and law and his margin notes to the Declaration of Independence, cited in Saul K. Padover, *The Complete Jefferson* (New York: Duell, Sloan & Pearce, 1943), p. 856.

[3] Editor's note: Nevertheless, there have been various rumors about alternatives to English being considered. *See* Dennis Baron, "Federal English," pp 36–40.

[4] Marcus Lee Hansen, *The Atlantic Migration, 1607–1860,* ed. Arthur M. Schlesinger (Cambridge, Mass.: Harvard University Press, 1940), chap: 3.

émigrés were allowed to assume positions of power and support in business and politics. Even their establishment of little colonies within the United States and their support of land companies went undisturbed, an indication that English speakers held no great fears of their using different languages to build separate power bases or promote animosities.[5]

Many churches offered services in different languages. Acceptance of and support for separate schools, newspapers, and societies for French and German speakers occurred in both northern and southern cities. Benevolent societies of French and German speakers, which held as a prerequisite for membership the speaking of French or German, provided libraries, and either sponsored schools or provided tutors for both their own children and English speakers'. These societies provided not only cultural and social security to immigrants, but of their own volition, these institutions often became havens for the learning of English, as well.[6]

In the main, the use of languages other than English was encouraged and looked upon with favor by national leaders, because of both practical advantages and opportunities for the expansion of knowledge that different languages offered. Thomas Jefferson advised his daughters and young correspondents to learn French and Spanish—French not only for its obvious importance in diplomatic affairs, but also for the access it provided to publications presenting recent advancements in science. He recommended Spanish because of the increasing diplomatic importance Spain would presumably hold in U.S. foreign relations. Jefferson admitted that modern languages were not well taught in the United States, and he encouraged the importation of modern language professors from abroad and recommended that French be learned in Canada.

Benjamin Rush, a member of the Continental Congress and a signer of the Declaration of Independence, urged that German and French be taught in America's "English Schools." A strong proponent of the retention and spread of modern languages in the United States, Rush expressed his concern that "narrow-minded people," fearful of retention of the German language among Pennsylvania's citizens, would not recognize the benefits a German college might provide the nation. The spread of learning among citizens, no matter what their native tongues, was crucial to the cause of the government. Rush noted:

---

[5] Frances Sergeant Childs, *French Refugee Life in the United States, 1790–1800: An American Chapter of the French Revolution* (Baltimore: Johns Hopkins University Press, 1940).

[6] Representative of those who advocated the acceptance of diverse languages was Benjamin Rush, whose "Information to Europeans Who Are Disposed to Migrate to the United States" was published in Philadelphia in 1790. Rush saw the maintenance of various languages and institutions which promoted the assemblages of former fellow countrymen as an appeal to potential European immigrants; L. H. Butterfield, ed., *Letters of Benjamin Rush* (Princeton, N.J.: Princeton University Press, 1951) 1:549–62. See also Arthur Henry Hirsch, *The Huguenots of South Carolina* (Hamden, Ct.: Archon Books, 1962), pp. 259ff.

> What Pennsylvanian of British or Irish extraction would not prefer [German speakers] as fellow citizens learned in the arts and sciences than in a state of ignorance of them all? A man who is learned in the dialect of a Mohawk Indian is more fit for a legislator than a man who is ignorant even in the language of the learned Greeks. The German language has existed for fifty years in Pennsylvania. It never can be lost while German churches and schools exist in it. A German college will serve to preserve it, but it will preserve it, not in its present state, but in its original force and purity.[7]

Members of the Continental Congress also agreed that any and all languages could be used as instruments for spreading communication necessary to legitimate the political system within the new nation. The Congress issued critical documents in French and German in local areas where members recognized a need for spreading information to promote loyalty to the cause of Independence.[8] The use of multiple languages, moreover, would help preserve the fragile democracy. Rush summed up the view of many of his contemporaries: "Wherever learning is confined to *one* society, or to a *few* men, the government of that country will always be an *aristocracy,* whether the prevailing party be composed of rich or poor. It is by diffusing learning that we shall destroy aristocratic juntos of all parties, and establish a true commonwealth."[9]

Leaders throughout the nation repeatedly pleaded for recognition—not restriction or promotion—of local, regional, or special interests. The same theory applied to linguistic minorities; if a national government should legally pressure groups to abandon their native languages, the repression of these tongues and separate unities could provoke resistance. Instead, if leaders recognized the potential of plural languages to spread the ideas of the new government, the citizens would become capable of helping legitimate the new government. Recognizing that forces which cause one to change his language or add to it must be internally motivated, leaders reasoned that linguistic minorities would not become separate and distinct peoples within the nation so long as no legal force proscribed the use of their languages. Moreover, wider use of the majority language would come without coercion. On behalf of a German College, Rush pointed out: "It will open the eyes of the Germans to a sense of the importance, and utility of the English language and become perhaps *the only possible means,* consistent with their liberty, of spreading a knowledge of the English language among them."[10]

---

[7] *Letters of Benjamin Rush,* 1:365–66.

[8] The printed *Journals of the Continental Congress* note publications in both German and French. For example, "Extracts from Votes and Proceedings of the Congress" (1774), "Declaration of Articles Setting Forth Causes of Taking up Arms" (1775), and "Resolves of Congress" (1776) were printed in German; the Articles of Confederation (1777) and various memorials were printed in French.

[9] *Letters of Benjamin Rush,* 1:368; italics in original.

[10] Ibid., 1:366; italics in original.

Coexisting with the ideological climate favoring linguistic diversity in the new nation was the view that some type of standard English might be necessary. Two different standards were, however, urged: speakers of the English tongue should *either* retain the purity of their speech according to the standard of England *or* define and refine a new speech—an American version of English. Just as Rush had advocated that the Germans of Pennsylvania use their college to preserve German "in its original force and purity," so others would argue that native English speakers should have a national institution to do the same for their tongue. Some believed the English tongue to be the only legacy from British rule which should be held by citizens of the new nation.[11] Others argued that a politically independent nation needed and deserved to add its own features and its own processes of change to English. A uniquely standardized English could spread with news of the political system and national achievements of the United States. English in America should therefore be "improved and perfected" for its native speakers as well as for those speakers of other tongues who wished to acquire English.[12]

In nations such as Italy, France, and Spain, academies prepared an official dictionary, grammars, and regulated literary works which served as authorities for other institutions and for national elites. Academy members believed that their own national languages were superior to others and were necessary as national symbols. They appealed to traditions of civilizations and well-established national literatures. Associated with classical traditions of maintaining stability in language, these institutions linked language use primarily with literary forms rather than with spoken varieties. Leaders of the academies were elites in nations with highly stratified societies, and the position of intellectuals gave them particular responsibilities for preserving not so much a model in language and behavior for all classes as a standard by which elites could measure themselves or toward which aspiring elites could set their goals.

The first proposal for an academy of standardization in the American colonies represented a rejection of European models, not in form, but in purpose and practice. In addition, this proposal foreshadowed the two major themes in language policy of the early national years—pragmatism and universalism. In 1774 an anonymous contributor to the *Royal American Magazine* provided two basic reasons for an American Society of Language: the advantages to science and the example which the establishment of such an institution in a "*land* of light and freedom" would provide the rest of the world. To be sure, the institution would "correct, enrich, and refine" the language, but in so doing, the members would promote new

[11] See, e.g., Samuel Lorenzo Knapp, *Lectures on American Literature, with Remarks on Some Passages of American History* (New York, 1829).

[12] In Enquiry into the Utility of the Greek and Latin Languages," *The American Museum or Repository* 5 (1789):532. American Periodical Series, Reel 4.

ideas in science while "perfecting" and extending the English language as Great Britain had not been able to do.[13]

This proposal showed a recognition of the pragmatic value of English as a tool and the universal appeal of English propagated by the United States. American scientists recognized the value of using the English language to spread their scientific findings abroad to learned societies and individuals eager for knowledge from the New World. Furthermore, as the scientific accomplishments of the United States were extended, so would be news of its political system, which many believed also had universal appeal. By 1774 many intellectuals were self-assured about the contribution of the American colonies to the world of science. The United States could capitalize on the curiosity of Old World intellectuals about the New World to spread its language. French and Latin had dominated the world of science in the period prior to the founding of the United States; the English of America now had a chance to move into prominence.

15 John Adams, strongly influenced by his recognition of the power of language as a pragmatic tool and by a desire to promote the universal thrust of the new nation's achievements, urged that America extend English and help elevate it as a world language. In 1780 Adams proposed to the Continental Congress the establishment of a "public institution for refining, correcting, improving, and ascertaining the English language." He viewed the promotion of the language as an opening for the dissemination of American views of "liberty, prosperity, and glory." Citing Athens and Rome as examples, Adams argued that furtherance of English models of eloquent speech throughout the United States and around the world through "universal connection and correspondence with all nations" would contribute to a reputable status for the American nation. An heir of Puritan forefathers who had come to Massachusetts to establish "a city upon a hill" whose citizens would set examples "with the eyes of all people upon us,"[14] Adams carried a commitment to extend the influence of the United States in as many spheres as possible; language was not to be an exception.

Fresh from the Continental Congress's struggles to draft the Articles of Confederation, Adams had gone to Europe in 1778 on a diplomatic mission. Convictions drawn from his experiences among foreign tongues in foreign lands (by a man who confessed to great difficulties in learning French) lay behind Adams's proposal for an American academy of language. His diary reveals a fascination with the multilingualism of Euro-

---

[13]The writer has most frequently been identified as John Adams; see Daniel J. Boorstin, *The Americans: The Colonial Experience* (New York: Random House, 1958), p. 282. However, this is unlikely, since Adams's diaries and personal letters indicate little interest in language standardization until after his trip abroad in 1778.

[14]Page Smith, *As a City upon a Hill; The Town in American History* (New York: Alfred A. Knopf, 1966).

peans and the diplomatic and political implications for those nations which chose not only to preserve but also to promote their national tongues. While in Amsterdam attempting to negotiate a loan from Holland, Adams had dinner on the evening of August 28, 1780, with a Dutch minister and a lawyer, both of whom seemed favorable to the advancement of the United States. The lawyer observed that the United States would be responsible for expanding English in the nineteenth century, enabling it to take the place that Latin had held in the seventeenth century and French had assumed in the eighteenth.[15] Within a few weeks Adams developed the idea of an academy of language for the United States. He wrote the Contintental Congress and proposed both the organization of an academy and the establishment of a library containing writings concerning "languages of every Sort, ancient and modern."

In Adams's plan, language was an instrument, a tool of communication available for and in need of manipulation by the State for propagating ideals embedded within the nation itself. Political rules of a nation should be laid out clearly for use and adoption by its citizens and for consideration by other nations. In service within public institutions, language became a public institution; as such it should be determined, promoted, and put forward as an indication of the "unconquerability" of the nation. Adams carried the conviction of many of his European contemporaries that "tongues, like governments, have a natural tendency to degeneration."[16] Therefore, Adams saw the need for American language *and* government to be codified for presentation and expansion to other nations at the elemental point of creation.

Apparently sensing that some members of the Continental Congress would think he was proposing that the academy establish a new language, Adams reasserted his allegiance to the English tongue. "We have not made war against the English Language, any more than against the old English character. An Academy instituted by the Authority of Congress, for correcting, improving, and fixing the English language would strike all the World with Admiration and great Britain with Envy."[17] Aware that England had failed to establish a language academy, Adams insisted that if the

[15] L. H. Butterfield, ed., *Diary and Bibliography of John Adams* (Cambridge, Mass.: Harvard University Press, 1961), 2:446–48.

[16] This view, cited by Samuel Johnson in the preface to his 1755 *Dictionary,* was common among eighteenth-century intellectuals. Nevertheless, Johnson himself opposed a language academy as contrary to "the spirit of English liberty." Moreover, he rejected as futile the idea of "embalming" a language and suggested that neither academies nor lexicographers could prescribe or prevent linguistic change. Still, Johnson felt that a dictionary based on etymological studies and guided in usage by authors whose works represented "the wells of English undefiled" might slow down the tendency of languages to "degeneration" and help conserve "constancy and stability."

[17] Adams to Huntington, *Papers of the Continental Congress,* Sept. 25, 1780, item 84.

United States did so, the new nation could then have the responsibility for expanding English as a world tongue. In addition, while America promoted the English language, it could assert its own views and cultural confidence as well: "England will never have any more honor, excepting now and then that of imitating the Americans."[18]

However, as Adams had feared, the Continental Congress was not convinced of the importance of the academy to American goals; the proposal was sent to committee, from which it never emerged. With the temporary resolution of the European crisis and the acquisition of a loan from Holland, members of Congress did not consider Adams's arguments that the academy of language could help solve current problems. Furthermore, nationally sponsored cultural institutions faced severe obstacles during the early years of the Republic. Adams himself was often termed a monarchist, and his proposal for a centralized language academy must have seemed to many republicans further "proof" of his monarchical leanings. Adams's view of language as an instrument critical to a particular task—and the consequent need for the national government to shape, mend, and maintain that tool—could not overcome the ideological blocks of other early leaders to an American academy of language and the hints of monarchialism it carried.

In no plan for the elevation and extension of a standard English could there be a program for coercing speakers. Benjamin Rush's concern with means "consistent with liberty" applied not only to extension of the English language, but also to its elevation or standardization among native speakers. Furthermore, the United States could appeal neither to established traditions and literary pursuits nor to maintenance of class structure and elite norms—ever-present associations with academies in the minds of republicans. For liberals of the early nation, both the goals and the processes of state-imposed uniformity through standardized cultural norms seemed far too elitist for a democracy founded on the promise of equality of opportunities for all citizens.

Haunted by the assumption that great nations past and present had produced widely recognized national literatures, many in the United States felt the nation's claim to international acceptance depended on the spread of a national literature which would promote "moral and political research" within and beyond the nation.[19] Some leaders suggested the establishment of a university or union of learned societies under national patronage to further a literature which would provide written models of standards of usage for American English. However, all such plans failed

[18] Adams to Jennings, Sept. 23, 1780, in *Life and Works of John Adams* (Boston: Little, Brown, 1856), 9:510.

[19] Joel Barlow, *Prospectus of a National Institution to Be Established in the United States* (Washington City, 1806).

to meet Congress's approval. Samuel Mitchill, a congressman from New York who supported proposals for a national university, wrote Noah Webster that without federal promotion of literature, "individuals must continue to labour on as well as they can under all the disadvantages of solitary efforts."[20]

Solitary efforts and the resulting disadvantages were not unfamiliar to Webster or to other individuals who had in the past two decades proposed alternatives to a national institution of language standardization. Webster, whose name is synonymous with standardization in the modern period, had begun peddling his *Grammatical Institute of the English Language,* which included a speller, grammar, and readers, as early as 1783. Prior to 1800 individual contributors to periodicals frequently argued for instruction of English grammar in "English schools" in the United States. Skills in writing and speaking the mother tongue were emphasized as necessary to the improvement of individuals and the nation. Webster capitalized on this often-expressed ideal. He urged linguistic independence for the United States and proposed that this be accomplished through dissemination of written materials on the language which could be taken up by individuals independently choosing to further their education and to advance their social position. However, individual efforts toward standardization of the language were comparatively unsuccessful at that time in American history. Webster's *American Dictionary of the English Language,* published in 1828, sold only 2,500 copies. He was forced to mortgage his home to bring out a second edition. Neither this work nor others previously published on language provided enough support to prevent Webster from being almost constantly in debt, and his work drew relatively little praise during his lifetime.[21]

Nevertheless, in practical consequences if not in philosophy, Webster's work came to substitute for a national language academy. Along with the continuing insistence on the absence of national restraints on cultural habits, the nation's literate population increasingly stressed the "*naturalness*" of language learning, but the *need for training* in the skills of oratory and writing. The young learned language from their associates in the earliest years; until age eight a young student learned through hearing correct models and reading books "written in a simple and correct style."[22]

In the preface to his 1828 dictionary, Webster insisted that language was the pragmatic instrument of the people, and as such, would be molded by them in accordance with their choice for adoption and adaptation of grammars, spellers, dictionaries, or the emulation of models in public usage.

---

[20] Jan. 7, 1807, Noah Webster Manuscripts Collection, New York Public Library.

[21] Henry R. Warfel, *Noah Webster: Schoolmaster to America* (New York: Macmillan, 1936).

[22] "Plan of a Liberal English Education." *The American Museum* 5:533.

Webster admitted that there could be no nationally designated final authority in language. Written sources of standardization fit the democratic scheme of the early Republic; learning and achievement of "correctness in language" could thus be available to a wide spectrum of society. Dictionaries, grammars, and written handbooks representing different scholars' views provided a wider access among the population to language choice and change than did academies' approaches. Furthermore, there was an increasing recognition that a standard in usage had to be sought not just in literary works, but in the speech of the public—speech that would continue to change and could never be stabilized. Webster's philosophy held that flexibility and effectiveness, particularly with regard to science, technology, and new-found geographic and cultural items, had to be primary characteristics of a living, changing language in a young, growing Republic.

Language choice was considered an individual matter in the new nation, as were the direction and advancement of literature. Individuals were free to choose guidance through available written authorities or alliance with particular societies, which directed standardization in language according to their special interests; literary, scientific, religious, or business. The American ambiguity about whether limits upon government derived from the written text of constitutions or from an antecedent body of unwritten natural law applied also to language. Americans sought authorities, some in an academy, others in written sources or public models; yet others felt too that language was somehow "natural" in the Rousseauian sense and was governed by its own internal rules. A national language academy had proved too monarchical, too rigid for citizens whose colonial experiences had convinced them that language and other cultural items should not be matters of national dictate.

Moreover, language was not yet a national ideological symbol, although it could serve such goals as the stimulation of European applause for things American. Language was, indeed, a pragmatic instrument. The effectiveness of language as a tool had ultimately to be determined by those individuals or groups using the tool. Motivations for language choice, change, and use had to derive from estimations of local group identity, special-interest allegiance, or personal advancement. National intervention in choosing one form of English over an alternate form had the potential to eradicate familiar distinctions, regional, social, and ethnic, which made the daily world comprehensible to unlike-minded men in a fluctuating, developing, plural society.

Some have maintained that an American language standard is part of the heritage of the founding fathers and is somehow mystically bound up with patriotism and nationalism. Such folk notions have blocked or deflected efforts to provide for bilingual-bicultural individuals and groups through educational programs and legal decisions. Yet during the founding period of 1780–1820, the national elite recognized the plural nature of American society, as well as the need to strike a balance between the absence of restraint on the number and kind of languages to be spoken and the need and ability of the citizenry to belong to a common entity. During this period leaders rejected national institutions designed to determine either a uniform process of Anglicization or a consistent pattern of Americanization in language and culture. Diversification in language choice, change, and use not only prevailed, but was purposefully left unrestrained by leaders' repeated failure to provide a national language academy.

Mapping the Text

1. What, according to Heath, is the problem? What are the issues? What are the concerns?

Writing to Inquire

1. Heath's essay raises the issue of an "official" language for the United States, despite its history as a multilingual nation. Do you think that the United States should have an official language? What do you see to be the advantages and disadvantages?
2. Heath credits Noah Webster with insisting that "language was the pragmatic instrument of the people." Think about how she uses this view in her essay. Using examples from contemporary language use, illustrate how you see that this idea is true or not true. In other words, to what extent do contemporary uses of language show that language is indeed an instrument of the people?

The Confusing State of Minority Language Rights

BILL PIATT

Bill Piatt is dean of St. Mary's University School of Law. The selection below is excerpted from an essay titled "Toward Domestic Recognition of a Human Right to Language," published in the *Houston Law Review* in 1986. His books include *Only English? Law and Language Policy in the United States* (1990) and *Black and Brown in America* (1997). His research considers the implications of language issues, human rights issues, and workplace practices.

To what extent do we have the right in this country to express ourselves or receive communications in a language other than English? While there are threads of authority running through our law that appear to provide some answers to this question in several contexts, there is no clearly defined "right to language" in the United States. It is as though the threads have not been woven into the fabric of the law, but rather surface as bothersome loose ends to be plucked when convenient.

The notion that there is a constitutionally protected right to express oneself or receive communications in a language other than English is supported by federal court decisions in several contexts. In *Meyer v. Nebraska,* the U.S. Supreme Court reversed a conviction of Nebraska schoolteacher who had been convicted of violating a state statute which prohibited the teaching of any language other than English in any school to a child who had not passed the eighth grade. The court determined that the right to teach a language and the right of parents to engage a teacher to so instruct their children are among the liberties protected against infringement by the due process clause of the Fourteenth Amendment. On the same day, and relying upon the *Meyer* decision, the Supreme Court struck down similar statutes in Ohio and Iowa.[1]

Three years later the court again relied upon *Meyer* in declaring unconstitutional a Philippine territorial statute which required Chinese merchants to keep their books in English, Spanish, or in a local dialect, thereby prohibiting them from utilizing the only language they understood. The court found the law invalid "because it deprives Chinese persons—situated as they are, with their extensive and important business long established—of their liberty and property without due process of law, and denies them the equal protection of the laws."[2]

In 1970 it was determined that the Sixth Amendment's confrontation clause, made applicable to the states through the Fourteenth Amendment, requires that non-English-speaking defendants be informed of their right to simultaneous interpretation of proceedings at the government's expense. The 2d U.S. Circuit Court of Appeals determined that otherwise the trial would be a "babble of voices," with the defendant unable to understand the precise nature of the testimony against him and hampering the capacity of his counsel to conduct effective cross-examination. The court noted:

> Not only for the sake of effective cross-examination, however, but as a matter of simple humaneness, Negrón [the defendant] deserved more than to sit in total incomprehension as the trial proceeded. Particularly inappropriate in this nation where many languages are spoken is a callousness to the crippling language handicap of a newcomer to its shores, whose life and freedom the state by its criminal processes chooses to put in jeopardy. [*U.S.* ex rel. *Negrón v. New York.*]

5 At least one federal district court has recognized a constitutional right to bilingual education. In the case of *Serna v. Portales Municipal Schools,* the plaintiffs were Spanish-surnamed minors represented by their parents.

---

[1] *Bartels v. Iowa,* 262 U.S. 404, 409 (1923); the case was consolidated with *Bolming v. Ohio* and *Pohl v. Ohio.*

[2] *Yu Cong Eng v. Trinidad,* 271 U.S. 500, 524–25, 528 (1926).

They claimed that unlawful discrimination against them resulted from the defendant's educational program tailored to educate a middle-class child from an English-speaking family without regard for the educational needs of the child from an environment where Spanish is the predominant language. The trial court found that the school district had violated the equal protection rights of these children and ordered, among other remedies, that it provide bilingual instruction and seek funding under the federal and state bilingual education acts for that instructional program.[3] The 10th U.S. Circuit Court of Appeals found that the district court had reached the correct result and affirmed the remedial steps ordered, but it did not reach the constitutional issue of equal protection. Rather, the court chose to follow the approach adopted by the Supreme Court in *Lau v. Nichols.*

In the *Lau* case, Chinese-speaking plaintiffs alleged that the San Francisco public schools had denied them an education because the only classes offered were in the English language. The *Lau* decision found a deprivation of statutory rights under Title VI of the Civil Rights Act of 1964 and the guidelines of the U.S. Department of Health, Education, and Welfare that required school systems to take remedial steps to rectify language deficiency problems.[4] In *Serna* the 10th Circuit adopted the *Lau* approach and affirmed the court-ordered bilingual education plan on statutory grounds, noting the damage suffered by children whose language rights were not respected. This damage included feelings of inadequacy and lowered self-esteem which developed when Spanish-surnamed children came to school and found that their language and culture were totally rejected and that only English was acceptable. The child who goes to a school where he finds no evidence of his language, culture, and ethnic group withdraws and does not participate. Such children often demonstrate both academic and emotional disorders, feel frustrated, and express their frustration through lack of attendance or lack of school involvement. Their frustrations are further reflected in hostile behavior, discipline problems, and eventually dropping out of school.[5]

A tavern's policy against the speaking of "foreign" languages at the bar was held to be unlawful racial discrimination against Mexican Americans in *Hernández v. Erlenbusch.* In disposing of the argument that the English-only rule was justified because non-Spanish-speaking customers were "irritated" by the speaking of the Spanish language, the court stated:

---

[3] 351 F.Supp. 1279 (D. N.M. 1972), *aff'd,* 499 F.2d 1147 (10th Cir. 1974).

[4] 42 U.S.C. §2000d; Office for Civil Rights notice, 35 Fed. Reg. 11595, stating that "where inability to speak and understand the English language excludes national origin minority group children from effective participation in the educational program offered by a school district, the district must take affirmative steps to rectity the language deficiency in order to open its instructional program to these students."

[5] 499 F.2d 1150. Teaching the Spanish-speaking child exclusively in English communicates a powerful message to the child that he or she is a second-class citizen; see *U.S. v. Texas.* 506 F.Supp. 405 (E.D. Tex. 1981). *rev'd on other grounds.* 680 F.2d 356, 372 (5th Cir. 1982).

> Just as the Constitution forbids banishing blacks to the back of the bus so as not to arouse the racial animosity of the preferred white passengers, it also forbids ordering Spanish-speaking patrons to the "back booth or out" to avoid antagonizing English-speaking beer drinkers. The lame justification that a discriminatory policy helps preserve the peace is as unacceptable in barrooms as it was in buses. Catering to prejudice out of fear of provoking greater prejudice only perpetuates racism. Courts faithful to the Fourteenth Amendment will not permit, either by camouflage or cavalier treatment, equal protection to be so profaned.[6]

In addition to the recognition of a constitutional "right to language" in the contexts noted above, there may be a First Amendment right to receive broadcast programming in languages other than English.[7] Federal statutes (and accompanying regulations) also provide a guarantee of the exercise of language rights in a number of contexts, including education, court interpreters, employment, and voting rights. Various state constitutional provisions and statutes also afford recognition of language rights. State courts have invalidated default judgments taken against non-English-speaking litigants and have declared contract provisions unconscionable where a person's lack of English fluency precluded equality of bargaining power.[8]

While the reader at this point might conclude that the contours of a generic "language right" emerge from the authorities cited to this point, it is important to recognize contradicting lines of authority and the elusiveness of this right to language in a number of contexts where litigants have sought to assert it. One such area is the "right" of a bilingual worker to speak a language other than English on the job.

10 First, let us consider a bit of background. The federal Equal Employment Opportunity Act prohibits employment discrimination on the basis of race, color, religion, sex, or national origin. Early decisions by the U.S. Equal Employment Opportunity Commission protected language rights at the workplace under the "national origin" pigeonhole, and courts agreed that this category affords such protection.[9] Early violations, for example, involved situations where an employer fired a Spanish-surnamed employee for supposedly poor work attributed to language difficulties and for violating company rules prohibiting Spanish-language communications among employees. Courts accepted and continue to accept the proposition

[6] 368 F.Supp. 752, 755–56 (D. Ore. 1973).

[7] See Bill Piatt, "Linguistic Diversity on the Airwaves: Spanish Language Broadcasting and the F.C.C.," *La Raza Law Journal* 2 (1984): 101.

[8] See, e.g., *Cota v. Southern Arizona Bank & Trust Co.*, 17 Ariz. App. 326, 497 P.2d 833 (1972); *Frostifresh Corp. v. Reynoso*, 52 Misc. 2d 26, 274 N.Y.S. 2d 964 (Dist. Ct. 1966), *rev'd as to damages*, 54 Misc. 2d 119, 281, N.Y.S. 2d 964 (N.Y. App. Term 1967).

[9] See 29 C.F.R. §1606 (1985); *Jones v. United Gas Imp. Corp.*, 68 F.R.D. 1 (E.D. Pa. 1975).

that employment discrimination based upon language or accent is unlawful discrimination based upon national origin.[10]

However, the scope of the right to language on the job is questionable after the decision in *García v. Gloor,* a case involving a lumber store in Brownsville, Texas. More than three-fourths of the population in the business area was Hispanic, and many of the store's customers expressed the desire to be waited on by Spanish-speaking salespeople. García was hired in 1975 precisely because he was bilingual. He was instructed to use English with English-speaking customers and Spanish with Spanish-speaking customers. However, the owner imposed another language rule on García: even though three-fourths of the store's workers and customers spoke Spanish, employees were forbidden from speaking Spanish on the job unless communicating with a Spanish-speaking customer. Among the reasons given by the owner for this rule was that the English-speaking customers objected to the Spanish-speaking employees communicating in a language which they did not understand. One day García was asked a question by another Spanish-speaking clerk about an item requested by a customer, and he responded, in Spanish, that the article was not available. The owner overheard this exchange and fired García. In rejecting García's claim for relief under the Equal Employment Opportunity Act, the district court found there were "valid business reasons" for the rule. The 5th U.S. Circuit Court upheld this decision, refusing to examine critically either the validity of the "business reasons" offered or whether the business needs could be met in a less restrictive manner than the imposition of an English-only rule. The court found García's conduct to have been a deliberate violation of the rule, concluding that a language which a bilingual person elects to speak at a particular time is a matter of choice.[11]

The "right to language" has proved illusory in other areas as well. Courts have concluded that the refusal to appoint an interpreter in a civil proceeding does not violate due process, and that Spanish-speaking welfare recipients have no constitutional right to be notified in Spanish of the termination or reduction of their benefits.[12]

The confusing state of our domestic law regarding the right to language might well be illustrated by considering the curious results which follow

---

[10] *Saucedo v. Brothers Well Serv. Inc.* 464 F.Supp. 919 (S.D. Tex. 1979); *Carino v. University of Okla. Bd. of Regents,* 750 F.2d 815 (10th Cir. 1984).

[11] 618 F.2d 264 (5th Cir. 1980), *cert. denied,* 449 U.S. 1113 (1981). Editor's note: The 9th Circuit has since taken a contrary view, striking down an English-only workplace rule in *Gutiérrez v. Municipal Court,* 838 F.2d 1031 (9th Cir. 1988). The U.S. Supreme Court has yet to resolve the conflict.

[12] *Jara v. Municipal Ct.,* 21 C.3d 181, 578 P.2d 94, 145 Cal. Rptr. 847 (1978), *cert. denied,* 439 U.S. 1067 (1979); *Guerrero v. Carleson,* 9 C.3d 808, 512 P.2d 833, 109 Cal. Rptr. 201 (1973), *cert. denied,* 414 U.S. 1137 (1974).

from applying the principles elicited so far to the situation of a hypothetical Ms. Martínez, Ms. Martínez is a U.S. citizen. She works part-time and also receives public assistance for her children. She is bilingual, but her primary language, and that of her school-aged children, is Spanish. Ms. Martínez is fired from her job one day because some customers complain to her boss that she spoke Spanish to a coworker in their presence, contrary to the store's English-only rule. On the way home she stops in the tavern to drink a beer. The same customers who complained to her boss are seated in the bar. When Ms. Martínez begins to tell another patron of her problems, in Spanish, the customers object, this time to the tavern manager, who orders Ms. Martínez from the bar.

As it turns out, this has just not been her day. At home she learns of the status of two lawsuits filed against her several months previously by different department stores for failure to pay debts allegedly owed to them. In the first suit, Ms. Martínez had not fully understood the complaint and summons because of her language situation and had thrown them away. Now the store notifies her that it has taken a default judgment against her for failing to appear in court. Ms. Martínez did not really understand the second complaint and summons either, but tried to answer. Now, she finds, it has been set for trial in a few days. She is very worried because she knows her English is not good enough for her to understand what is going on in court and to explain her side of the story to the judge.

Poor Ms. Martínez's troubles are not finished. Her children tell her they have been thrown out of school because their English is so bad they are flunking all their subjects. The day's mail also brings word that the welfare assistance she receives for them has been terminated because she failed to provide information required last month by the welfare agency. Ms. Martínez understood neither the request nor the termination notice because they were written in English.

Consider the curious results which obtain from an application of our domestic laws to Ms. Martínez's situation. She would have a cause of action against the bar owner and its customers, and yet her employment termination for exactly the same conduct would be upheld. Is the right to speak Spanish more sacred in a bar than on the job? Regarding her consumer problems, it may be better for her to have ignored the summons and complaint rather than try to answer and appear to defend herself. Courts have set aside default judgments for a language barrier, but may not afford her an interpreter at the trial if she attempts to defend herself. Ms. Martínez would find, considering her children's situation, that the state could not deny her children an education based upon their language situation. It could, however, because of the language barrier, effectively deny them the food, shelter, and medical care necessary to sustain their lives while they try to study.

These are admittedly dramatic, oversimplified applications. They illustrate, however, that we have not thought through whether, why, and to what extent we might choose to respect language differences in this country.

Mapping the Text

1. Piatt connects language, identity, and authority. What is his basic point of view? What does he offer as evidence that his perspective is reasonable?

Writing to Inquire

1. Piatt raises the question of language and rights. Do you think that individuals have a right to their own language? What would such a right mean in the context of schooling or public institutions? What would be the rights and responsibilities of the individual? What would be the obligations of the nation and national institutions (i.e., publicly supported institutions) to the individual?
2. Piatt identifies several laws related to language. Choose one of these laws to explore further. Find library resources that help clarify either the history or the implementation of the law. Discuss the impact of the law on a particular group of citizens. What did the law enable? What did it prevent? Who benefited from it? What were those benefits?

INQUIRY: HOW DOES A NATION SHAPED BY DIVERSE HISTORIES AND CULTURES FORGE A SENSE OF ITSELF AS A PEOPLE?

1. Two images often emerge as significant to many Americans. One is a strong sense of individualism. Another is a sense of adventure. Think about these terms: *individualist* (someone who goes her or his own way); *adventurer* (someone who is pioneering, courageous, bold, daring). Choose an example from your life, or the life of whomever you choose to write about, that demonstrates a sense of individualism or adventure. Explain how this person either fits and/or defies your own view of what it means to be American.
2. Consider the various points of view of the writers in this chapter. What does this range of viewpoints suggest to you about what a citizen is and what that person's rights, obligations, and privileges are about? How are race, class, gender, culture, or other personal identities important in this discussion? What challenges do such identities raise? What opportunities for positive response or change do they offer?
3. Personal identity is presented in specific ways in each of the selections in this chapter. At what point in each case does a personal identity shift

At what point does personal identity become a matter of public concern? How is citizenship created and maintained by language? What does it mean to take an oath? To recite a pledge?

to a social dilemma or a public concern? Consider these three dimensions as you identify a specific writer and cast the particular issue from a personal, social, and public perspective.

4. How does the time period affect the issues identified in this chapter? For example, how does the issue of the right to vote and participate in public policy making shift as you move from Thomas Jefferson to Frederick Douglass to Stanton and Mott to Claude McKay to people who are bilingual?
5. Many of the writers also raise questions about respect, visibility, and the ability to act in one's own interest. What are the implications of such questions for interactions across various social and cultural boundaries?
6. The selections in this chapter are poems, or essays, or narratives. What difference does genre make in the expression of these ideas?
7. Choose a genre that seems appropriate to the expression of your own views of national identity. Using this form, you might choose to bring in in some meaningful way your experiences and observations, your own community values, a touchstone piece that serves as a model or an exemplar who functions instructively to illustrate your view. Then write a reflective essay in which you explain your choice.
8. Write a paper in which you identify what strikes you as the central challenges that emerge from our multivariant society. How do you think that the nation might face and overcome these challenges? What do you see that suggests strategies for action—for example, approaches that work that we might use more systematically?

CHAPTER 4

Migration, Immigration, Nation

The United States is almost entirely a nation of immigrants. Beginning with the earliest colonists in the seventeenth century, the population of the land has been defined by overlapping waves of immigration, a pattern of global and national migration that continues into the present. From 1990 to 2000, the U.S. population grew in both overall size and ethnic and racial diversity. One key marker of this history is language; according to the 2000 U.S. census, 17.6 percent of the nation's population speaks a language other than English at home. In California, New Mexico, and Texas, fully one-third or more of the population speaks a language other than English at home. The economic, political, and cultural forces that propel population changes and migrations—wars, technology, agriculture, slavery, ethnic persecution, weather, political and religious conflict—have continued, if not accelerated, into the early years of the new century. Both within its borders, and from without, the United States continues to be a nation in flux, a mobile and multiple society constituted by conflict and difference as much as by unity.

Where Chapter 3 looked at the idea of American identity, Chapter 4 looks at the boundaries of that identity and how they are changing. As the readings demonstrate, we often create both literal and imaginary boundaries to help define and understand our sense of nation. At the same time, these boundaries are repeatedly challenged and contested by demographic and social change that comes from both internal and external movements of many people and groups. The Constitution of the United States guarantees to citizens the rights, responsibilities, and privileges of citizenship. The selections in Chapter 4 focus on the question of *who* exactly the citizens of the nation are. These selections shift the inquiry toward the spirit within the nation and among the people. They examine what *nation* means, what it invokes, what it inspires. They focus more precisely on the experiences and values that have formed historically the fabric of who we are and who we continue to be as nations within a nation, as communities within a community. They raise difficult questions about symbols and images of American-ness, about policies and practices, about tensions and challenges, and they also describe critical moments of joy, appreciation, and celebration. The writers bring color and texture to being American and suggest by their example that the stories that we share have power and potential—the explanatory power of how people, in the spirit that they bring to the task, one by one by one, actually make the nation.

With these selections, you have the opportunity to think about your own residence in the United States, what your stories are, and how they contribute to the master narrative of *America.* You can think critically and creatively about the challenge of finding ways to balance notions of self, community, and nation, and do so with an eye toward how these concepts (self, community, nation) are becoming more meaningful on a global scale. The United States functions increasingly within a global network of achievements and problems. We live in a highly technological world where contact, relationships, interaction, and even patriotism are acquiring new definitions. The question is whether or not being a well-informed and productive citizen of a nation must inevitably mean being also a well-informed and productive citizen of the world. Can individuals envision themselves as holding multiple residences, and thereby multiple alliances, within national boundaries and across them? Can there be, in a meaningful way, a spirit of community, nation, and Earth?

FRAMING THE TOPIC

The Changing Face of America

BARBARA VOBEJDA

Barbara Vobejda is a staff writer for the *Washington Post.* The article below was first published September 23–29, 1991, and was republished as an exemplary selection for *Race and Ethnic Relations—93/94,* 3rd edition, edited by John A. Kromkowski (Guilford, Connecticut: The Dushkin Publishing Group, 1993). This volume, as well as the others in The Annual Editions Series, is designed to recognize the role played by the periodical press in providing educational information on social and political issues.

Garden City, Kan.—Every weekday morning, the booths at the Grant Avenue Diner fill with aging white men, most equipped with hearing aids and hard opinions. For years they have kept this ritual, leaning back against the padded seats, their fingers clasped around their coffee cups, chewing through the gossip and politics and crop prices that affect their lives.

The Formica table tops and vinyl benches form a kind of enclave, an elite circle of the powerful and formerly powerful in town. Little about that has changed, even as the community around them has moved through an extraordinary ethnic metamorphosis.

On the dusty streets outside the diner, their town has a new look and feel: Tornado warnings are posted in three languages, Vietnamese, Spanish and English. The police department is under pressure to hire Hispanics, and farmers look forward to the Asian dragon dance at the Cinco de Mayo parade.

The old-timers can't pronounce the name of the new Vietnamese restaurant, Pho-Hoa, but they know they like No. 38 (barbecue pork and noodles).

5 And on Thursdays, when the paychecks arrive, Juan Andrade's variety store, El Remedio, is crowded with shoppers. He stocks Mexican products from pottery to piñatas, and on that day, fresh tortillas from California.

Garden City has always had a larger share of Hispanics than many neighboring towns. "Now," Andrade says, "it's like you're in Mexico."

But you're not in Mexico. You're in Kansas, square in the middle of the American heartland. A giant beef-packing plant opened here one day in 1980, and the town swelled virtually overnight with newcomers eager for work, many of them immigrants from Mexico and Southeast Asia.

Garden City today is something new, a striking example of the extraordinary racial and ethnic changes that are transforming both U.S. coasts and pushing across the hinterland. This Great Plains town of 24,097, settled a century ago by cattle ranchers and farmers, reflects the newest face of America.

The nation's face is strikingly different from 10 or 20 years ago. Immigrants have arrived in near-record numbers. Black, Asian and Hispanic populations have grown at rates several times that of whites. Minorities have appeared in many communities that, until recently, were homogeneous and white.

10 America is still an overwhelmingly white country, and minority groups continue to concentrate in a handful of coastal states. But the white majority is slipping: Non-Hispanic whites made up 76 percent of the population in 1990, down from about 80 percent in 1980.

And the expansion of minorities into cities, suburbs and towns away from the traditional ports-of-entry has created an altogether new cultural map. The result is a nation more diverse than at any time in history.

A Washington Post analysis of 1990 census figures underscores the extent of that change: The proportion of whites declined in 72 percent of the nation's 3,137 counties. Although the changes appear minor in many places, more and more communities are becoming home to what academics call a "threshold" population of minorities, sufficient numbers to support businesses and activities. In other words, these new groups change the cultural feel of a place.

Nationally, the proportion of Asians increased in 80 percent of the nation's counties and the proportion of Hispanics increased in 64 percent of the counties over the past decade, the Post analysis showed. Blacks made up a larger share of the population in 60 percent of the counties, while the proportion of American Indians increased in nearly nine of 10—87 percent—of the counties.

Although the black population grew about three times faster than the non-Hispanic white population, it was the rapid growth among Asians and Hispanics that most altered the nation's ethnic makeup. For the black population, the most dramatic changes were geographic, with increased movement to the South and West and entry into metropolitan areas where relatively few blacks have lived in the past.

15 Behind the migration of minority groups into new communities is a web of economic and human factors: job opportunities, social networks pulling immigrants to new areas, refugee resettlement programs and suburbanization of minorities. Together, these forces are moving many cities away from the traditional white-black polarity to a racial mix that erases any dominant majority. They are also stirring new and more complex competition among groups.

In Santa Clara County, Calif., Asians and Hispanics grew from a quarter of the population to nearly 40 percent, boosted by thousands of newly arrived Asian immigrants settling in with families and friends.

In Texas, home to nine of the 23 counties where minorities became the majority in the past decade, the addition of 1.4 million Hispanics has set up a new political clash: Hispanics are challenging a redistricting plan in Dallas drawn by black state legislators.

Persons of Hispanic Origin for the United States: 1990

	1990 Census	
Hispanic Origin	*Number*	*Percent*
Total population	248,709,873	
Hispanic origin	21,900,089	100.0
Mexican	13,393,208	61.2
Puerto Rican	2,651,815	12.1
Cuban	1,053,197	4.8
Other Hispanic origin	4,801,869	21.9
Dominican Republic	520,151	2.4
Central American	1,323,830	6.0
Costa Rican	57,223	0.3
Guatemalan	268,779	1.2
Honduran	131,066	0.6
Nicaraguan	202,658	0.9
Panamanian	92,013	0.4
Salvadoran	565,081	2.6
Other Central American	7,010	0.0
South American	1,035,602	4.7
Argentinean	100,921	0.5
Bolivian	38,073	0.2
Chilean	68,799	0.3
Colombian	378,726	1.7
Ecuadorian	191,198	0.9
Paraguayan	6,662	0.0
Peruvian	175,035	0.8
Uruguayan	21,996	0.1
Venezuelan	47,997	0.2
Other South American	6,195	0.0
Spaniard	519,136	2.4
Spanish	444,896	2.0
Spanish American	93,320	0.4
All other Hispanic origin	864,934	3.9
Not of Hispanic origin	226,809,784	

Persons of Hispanic origin may be of any race. These data are based on a sample, they may differ from comparable figures shown in 100-percent tabulations, and they are subject to sampling variability and nonsampling error such as coverage error and processing error. The official 1990 census counts for total Hispanic, Mexican, Puerto Rican, Cuban, and other Hispanic, based on 100-percent tabulations, were released earlier in CB91-215.

Source: U.S. Department of Commerce, Bureau of the Census, Ethnic and Hispanic Branch, 1990 Census Special Tabulations.

The Foreign-Born Population by Place of Birth for the United States: 1990

Place of Birth	1990 Census Number	1990 Census Percent
Foreign-born persons	21,631,601	100.0
Europe	4,812,117	22.2
Austria	94,398	0.4
Belgium	41,111	0.2
Czechoslovakia	90,042	0.4
Denmark	37,657	0.2
Estonia	9,251	0.0
Finland	23,547	0.1
France	162,934	0.8
Germany	1,163,004	5.4
Greece	189,267	0.9
Hungary	112,419	0.5
Ireland	177,420	0.8
Italy	639,518	3.0
Latvia	26,380	0.1
Lithuania	30,344	0.1
Netherlands	104,216	0.5
Norway	46,240	0.2
Poland	397,014	1.8
Portugal	218,525	1.0
Romania	92,627	0.4
Spain	103,518	0.5
Sweden	57,166	0.3
Switzerland	43,991	0.2
United Kingdom	764,627	3.5
Yugoslavia	144,563	0.7
Other Europe	42,338	0.2
Soviet Union	336,889	1.6
Asia	5,412,127	25.0
Afghanistan	28,988	0.1
Burma	20,441	0.1
Cambodia	119,581	0.6
China	543,208	2.5
Hong Kong	152,263	0.7
India	463,132	2.1
Indonesia	50,388	0.2
Iran	216,963	1.0
Iraq	45,936	0.2
Israel	97,006	0.4
Japan	421,921	2.0
Jordan	33,019	0.2
Korea	663,465	3.1
Laos	172,925	0.8
Lebanon	91,037	0.4
Malaysia	34,906	0.2
Pakistan	93,663	0.4
Philippines	997,745	4.6
Saudi Arabia	17,312	0.1
Syria	37,654	0.2
Taiwan	253,719	1.2
Thailand	119,862	0.6
Turkey	65,244	0.3
Vietnam	556,311	2.6
Other Asia	115,438	0.5
North America	8,524,594	39.4
Canada	870,850	4.0
Caribbean	1,986,835	9.2
Antigua-Barbuda	12,452	0.1
Bahamas	24,341	0.1
Barbados	44,311	0.2
Cuba	750,609	3.5
Dominican Republic	356,971	1.7
Grenada	18,183	0.1
Haiti	229,108	1.1
Jamaica	343,458	1.6
Trinidad/Tobago	119,221	0.6
Other Caribbean	88,181	0.4

The Foreign-Born Population by Place of Birth for the United States: 1990 *(Cont'd)*

	1990 Census			*1990 Census*	
Place of Birth	*Number*	*Percent*	*Place of Birth*	*Number*	*Percent*
Central America	5,650,374	26.1	Other South America	20,853	0.1
Belize	31,222	0.1	Africa	400,691	1.9
Costa Rica	48,264	0.2			
El Salvador	472,885	2.2	Cape Verde	14,821	0.1
Guatemala	232,977	1.1	Egypt	68,662	0.3
Honduras	114,603	0.5	Ethiopia	37,422	0.2
Mexico	4,447,439	20.6	Ghana	21,714	0.1
Nicaragua	171,950	0.8	Kenya	15,871	0.1
Panama	124,695	0.6	Morocco	21,529	0.1
Other Central America	6,339	0.0	Nigeria	58,052	0.3
Other North America	16,535	0.1	Senegal	2,369	0.0
South America	1,107,000	5.1	South Africa	38,163	0.2
			Other Africa	122,088	0.6
Argentina	97,422	0.5	Oceania	122,137	0.6
Bolivia	33,637	0.2			
Brazil	94,023	0.4	Australia	52,469	0.2
Chile	61,212	0.3	Fiji	16,269	0.1
Colombia	303,918	1.4	New Zealand	18,039	0.1
Ecuador	147,867	0.7	Tonga	11,040	0.1
Guyana	122,554	0.6	Western Samoa	12,638	0.1
Peru	152,315	0.7	Other Oceania	11,682	0.1
Uruguay	21,628	0.1	Not reported	916,046	4.2
Venezuela	51,571	0.2			

Note: The foreign-born population includes 1,864,285 persons who were born abroad of American parents. Data for foreign-born persons by place of birth, citizenship and year of entry is planned for 1993. The former Soviet Union is now referred to as the following geopolitical entities: Armenia, Azerbaijan, Byelarus, Georgia, Kazakhstan, Kyrgyzstan, Moldova, Russia, Tajikistan, Turkmenistan, Ukraine, and Uzbekistan.

Source: U.S. Department of Commerce, Bureau of the Census, Ethnic and Hispanic Branch, 1990 Census Special Tabulations.

And in Finney County, Kan., where Garden City is located, the white share of the population fell faster than in all but five other counties. The changes that descended here in the 1980s were rooted as far back as the '50s, when new irrigation techniques made it more profitable to raise feed grain, which spurred an expansion of feedlots and drew the giants of the meatpacking industry.

Ancestry of the Population in the United States: 1990

Ancestry group	1990 Census Number	1990 Census Percent
Total population	248,709,873	100.0
EUROPEAN (excluding Hispanic groups)		
Alsatian	16,465	0.0
Austrian	870,531	0.4
Basque	47,956	0.0
Belgian	394,655	0.2
British	1,119,154	0.4
Cypriot	4,897	0.0
Celtic	29,652	0.0
Danish	1,634,669	0.7
Dutch	6,227,089	2.5
English	32,655,779	13.1
Finnish	658,870	0.3
French	10,320,935	4.1
German	57,985,595	23.3
Greek	1,110,373	0.4
Icelander	40,529	0.0
Irish	38,739,548	15.6
Italian	14,714,939	5.9
Luxemburger	49,061	0.0
Maltese	39,600	0.0
Manx	6,317	0.0
Norwegian	3,869,395	1.6
Portuguese	1,153,351	0.5
Scandinavian	678,880	0.3
Scotch-Irish	5,617,773	2.3
Scottish	5,393,581	2.2
Swedish	4,680,863	1.9
Swiss	1,045,495	0.4
Welsh	2,033,893	0.8
Albanian	47,710	0.0
Bulgarian	29,595	0.0
Carpath Russian	7,602	0.0
Croatian	544,270	0.2
Czech	1,300,192	0.5
Czechoslovakian	315,285	0.1
Estonian	26,762	0.0
European	466,718	0.2
German Russian	10,153	0.0
Hungarian	1,582,302	0.6
Latvian	100,331	0.0
Lithuanian	811,865	0.3
Macedonian	20,365	0.0
Polish	9,366,106	3.8
Rom	5,693	0.0
Romanian	365,544	0.1
Russian	2,952,987	1.2
Serbian	116,795	0.0
Slavic	76,931	0.0
Slovak	1,882,897	0.8
Slovene	124,437	0.1
Soviet Union	7,729	0.0
Ukrainian	740,803	0.3
Yugoslavian	257,994	0.1
Other European, n.e.c.	259,585	0.1
WEST INDIAN (excluding Hispanic groups)		
Bahamian	21,081	0.0
Barbadian	35,455	0.0
Belizean	22,922	0.0
Bermudan	4,941	0.0
British West Indies	37,819	0.0
Dutch West Indies	61,530	0.0
Haitian	289,521	0.1
Jamaican	435,024	0.2
Trinidad & Tobagoan	76,270	0.0
U.S. Virgin Islander	7,621	0.0
West Indian	159,167	0.1
Other West Indian, n.e.c.	4,139	0.0
CENTRAL AND SOUTH AMERICA (excluding Hispanic groups)		
Brazilian	65,875	0.0

Ancestry of the Population in the United States: 1990 *(Continued)*

	1990 Census	
Ancestry group	*Number*	*Percent*
Guyanese	81,665	0.0
Other Cen. & S. America, n.e.c.	1,217	0.0
NORTH AFRICA AND SOUTHWEST ASIA		
Algerian	3,215	0.0
Arab	127,364	0.1
Armenian	308,096	0.1
Assyrian	51,765	0.0
Egyptian	78,574	0.0
Iranian	235,521	0.1
Iraqi	23,212	0.0
Israeli	81,677	0.0
Jordanian	20,656	0.0
Lebanese	394,180	0.2
Middle Eastern	7,656	0.0
Moroccan	19,089	0.0
Palestinian	48,019	0.0
Saudi Arabian	4,486	0.0
Syrian	129,606	0.1
Turkish	83,850	0.0
Yemeni	4,011	0.0
Other North African and Southwest Asian, n.e.c.	10,670	0.0
SUBSAHARAN AFRICA		
African	245,845	0.1
Cape Verdean	50,772	0.0
Ethiopian	34,851	0.0
Ghanian	20,066	0.0
Kenyan	4,639	0.0
Liberian	8,797	0.0
Nigerian	91,688	0.0
Sierra Leon	4,627	0.0
South African	17,992	0.0
Sudanese	3,623	0.0
Ugandan	2,681	0.0
African, n.e.c.	20,607	0.0
PACIFIC		
Australian	52,133	0.0
New Zealander	7,742	0.0
NORTH AMERICA		
Acadian	668,271	0.3
American	12,396,057	5.0
Canadian	560,891	0.2
French Canadian	2,167,127	0.9
Pennsylvania German	305,841	0.1
United States	643,602	0.3
Other North American, n.e.c.	12,927	0.0
OTHER GROUPS OR UNCLASSIFIED		
Other groups, n.e.c.	63,562,346	25.6
Unclassified or not reported	26,101,616	10.5

n.e.c. represents "not elsewhere classified"

Note: Data are based on a sample and are subject to sampling variability. Data for "Other Groups" include groups identified separately in the Race and Hispanic origin items. Since persons who reported multiple ancestries were included in more than one group, the sum of the persons reporting the ancestry group is greater than the total; for example, a person reporting "English-French" was tabulated in both the "English" and "French" categories.

Source: U.S. Department of Commerce, Bureau of the Census, Ethnic and Hispanic Branch, 1990 Census Special Tabulations.

When IBP Inc. opened its plant and a second big company, Monfort, expanded its packing operation, the word went out that there were thousands of jobs that could not be filled by the local work force. The result was a wave of new arrivals to town, many of them without skills, many unable to speak English, all of them desperate for work.

20 Gene Rudd, the former owner of a local savings and loan, offers this shorthand for the town's new demography: "There are the old-timers, the Texicans and the wetbacks."

The "Texicans," he says, are longtime Mexican-American residents who moved to Garden City before the recent immigration wave. The "wetbacks" are undocumented immigrants from Mexico, a term he and his coffee mates use routinely but not, he insists, pejoratively.

"It's a name," he says, over coffee at the Grant Avenue Diner. "I ask my tenants, 'Do you have a green card or are you wet?' They say, 'I'm wet.'"

He does not mention the influx of Southeast Asians, but laughs that, out at the trailer parks, which are occupied heavily by Asians, "I think there's just three televisions out there, and they just keep stealing them" from each other.

The talk at the diner is a reminder of a time in Garden City when Hispanics were barred from the swimming pool and relegated to the movie theater balcony.

There is racial tension still, although Rudd's friends around the table and others in the coffee shop acknowledge that the packing plants and the thousands of workers they have drawn have brought a new economic vitality to the community.

25 Jim Fishback, a clothing salesman, argues that the Vietnamese children in local schools have "shown the American kids it can be done. They are good students."

"There's only one good thing about the good old days," says Tony Geier, 83, who has lived here since 1925. "You could trust people. You could leave your doors unlocked." Today, he says, "you can't trust anybody."

Geier is not the only old-timer to mention increased crime. Local police statistics show that the number of serious crimes—including murder, rape and major thefts—increased 51 percent from 1983 to 1990.

Some in town blame the increase in crime on the new transient population, others assign it to poverty among minorities.

Only a handful of blacks has ever lived in Finney County and Garden City, although Hispanics have been part of the community for as much as a century, drawn by railroad and farm jobs plentiful when the town was known for its sugar beet production.

30 But during the 1980s, the country's Hispanic population more than doubled, from 3,459 to 8,353. The Asian population rose even more dramatically, from just 100 in 1980 to 1,203 in 1990. And the county's population overall grew by half, to 33,070.

But the figures do not reflect the true ferment in the community, wrought by turnover rates at the plants ranging from 75 percent to 96 percent annually. The town has become accustomed to a stream of families coming and going; a third of the students in the local school district move in or out during the course of each year.

Despite the social problems associated with the rapid change—high dropout rates in the high school, poverty and language barriers—many in town say the newcomers have made their community a more interesting place to live.

"It feels very different, but I like the difference," says Mary Warren, who was raised in Garden City and now runs the county historical society. "To me, it's very stimulating."

University of Kansas anthropologist Don Stull, who conducted research and lived in Garden City for 16 months as part of a Ford Foundation study, concludes that despite some problems, the community has adjusted very well to the influx of minorities.

He attributes that to the small size of the community, a shared ethic honoring hard work and the lack of competition for jobs.

"Yes, there were some problems, but the community was really trying to respond. . . to accommodate the newcomers. It has a small-town mentality in the good sense of the word," he says.

Not everyone shares that assessment. Hispanics argue that the local police are much more likely to crack down on drinkers outside their bars than on those at the mostly white country club. And Hispanic parents say their children are reprimanded for speaking Spanish at school.

"When the kids get in fights, the ones who get suspended the most are the Mexicans," says Maria Zapata, a cook at the Grant Avenue Diner.

Southeast Asian immigrants are less likely to complain, local residents say. Dieu Vo, who arrived with his wife and three children last December, tells of the friendly welcome his family received, including a party held by other Vietnamese in the trailer park. The women prepared traditional Asian dishes, he says, and the men drank plenty of American beer. The other families donated $200 so Vo could buy a 1976 Chevrolet.

Vo, who had been a major in the South Vietnamese Army and a political prisoner for nine years, and his wife, Thuy Huynh, a former teacher, had never heard of Kansas before their refugee resettlement program brought them here. Now, they concede, they have little interaction with town residents, other than with the Vietnamese families who live nearby.

Both are employed at the IBP plant for $6.60 an hour. Vo trims the fat from hunks of beef moving along a conveyor belt; Thuy Huynh seals the meat in plastic, then hoists it into a bin.

For $300 a month the couple rents a sparse trailer, situated with scores of similar drab units on a treeless, windy plain outside town. The family spends money only on the basics, no restaurants or new furniture. They save between $500 and $600 a month, Vo says, which they will use for their children's education.

"My life is over," he says through an interpreter. "I cannot join the army. I cannot be a major any more. My future is nothing right now. I'm just only trying to establish the future for my children."

45 At the same time, Vo, who is 48, says he appreciates the benefits of American freedom. "If you don't violate the law, you're a free man," he says.

On a recent weekday, the family sat around their metal kitchen table, sharing a meal of vegetables and noodles.

Thuy Huynh asked if she might show off for her visitors a traditional Vietnamese dress, then modeled it with a child's pride, walking through the small trailer, shy and beaming. A few minutes later, she had to travel to the packing plant, cover her head with a hardhat, strap on a protective belt, pull on steel-toed boots and go to work on the bloody production floor.

Roger Vilaysing, a Laotian immigrant who runs a social service agency in Garden City, makes repeated trips to visit California on recruiting journeys. Using contacts through a Laotian Air Force veterans association, he gathers a group of welfare-dependent immigrants in a community hall in Fresno. Vilaysing, who is financed by a federal grant, says he speaks in his native Lao, telling the audience of the benefits of Kansas. He brings along a videotape on Garden City and its meat packing industry, borrowed from the Chamber of Commerce.

Then he promotes the nobility of self-sufficiency: You can get off welfare, he promises, if you are willing to take a job at the packing plants.

50 Since last fall, eight families have taken up his offer. Vilaysing packed their belongings in a rented moving truck and drove 1,640 miles to Garden City. A caravan of families followed in their cars, a modern-day wagon train.

Upon their arrival, the newcomers moved into trailers arranged by Vilaysing, rested for a few days, then started to work in the plants. For 45 days, their expenses were paid, enough time to put several paychecks in the bank.

But once on their own, Vilaysing argues, they would do well to save their money and move on.

"They are very glad they got the job," he says. But he most admires those who have saved $100,000 in five years, enabling them to buy a business or a fishing boat in Louisiana or Texas. "This," he says of Garden City, "is not a good place for living for five, 10 years. . . . The packing house is not a good place to live for the rest of their lives."

Still, Vilaysing says, he will retrace the route back to California as often as necessary, hoping to bring 18 families this year, 50 next, on this unlikely passage to middle America.

Mapping the Text

1. Vobejda chooses the unlikely town of Garden City, Kansas, to make her point about the changing face of America. What is the effect of this

choice, rather than a more obvious one, like a major port city such as San Francisco, New York, or Miami?

2. Think about the types of arguments that Vobejda makes, how she uses information to be convincing to a reader. In trying to be convincing, does she appeal to logical thinking (*logos*), to the emotions (*pathos*), to particular values, principles, and beliefs (*ethos*)? Choose one of her appeals and track her use of information in this way through the essay. For example, if you determine that she is appealing occasionally to the emotions, find examples of where she is doing that, cite the examples, and explain them.

Writing to Inquire

1. Read through Barbara Vobejda's essay and create an outline for each area of life that she asserts is affected by the changing face of America. Think about the list and choose what you consider the top three challenges to the society. Write an essay in which you explain your choices, citing the evidence that Vobejda provides and including other evidence as necessary to make your point.
2. What do you think Vobejda's purpose is in writing this essay? Why would she consider it meaningful in 1991 to write such an essay? What was happening during this period that would make such an essay make sense? To what extent is the face of America still changing? What are the implications of this change or lack of change as you see it?
3. Visit the website for the 2000 U.S. Census <http://www.census.gov/main/www/cen2000.html> and do some research to compare 2000 data with the 1990 census data used by Vobejda in her essay. How do the census data reinforce the general patterns of change she identified? How does it challenge or contradict what she is saying? Look closely at the census data for your local area. How do they compare to national patterns? In what way is your community changing? Write an essay based on your census research to offer a portrait of your town or city; think of it as an answer to Vobedja's portrait of Garden City.

The Laws

MAXINE HONG KINGSTON

Maxine Hong Kingston (1940–) is the author of several books, including *The Woman Warrior: Memoirs of a Girlhood Among Ghosts* (1976); *Hawaii One Summer* (1987); and *Tripmaster Monkey: His Fake Book* (1989). Born in Stockton, California, Kingston is the daughter of Chinese immigrant parents, and she writes often about themes of assimilation and acculturation. Kingston's work challenges traditional notions of form and genre, blending autobiography, fiction, and myth. "The Laws" is excerpted from her 1980 novel, *China Men.* This selection highlights the long history of legal persecution of Chinese immigrants in the United States.

> *The United States of America and the Emperor of China cordially recognize the inherent and inalienable right of man to change his home and allegiance, and also the mutual advantage of the free migration and emigration of their citizens and subjects respectively from the one country to the other for purposes of curiosity, of trade, or as permanent residents.*
> *ARTICLE V OF THE BURLINGAME TREATY, SIGNED IN WASHINGTON, D. C., JULY 28, 1868, AND IN PEKING, NOVEMBER 23, 1869*

The First Years: 1868, the year of the Burlingame Treaty, was the year 40,000 miners of Chinese ancestry were Driven Out. The Fourteenth Amendment, adopted in that same year, said that naturalized Americans have the same rights as native-born Americans, but in 1870 the Nationality Act specified that only "free whites" and "African aliens" were allowed to apply for naturalization. Chinese were not white; this had been established legally in 1854 when Chan Young unsuccessfully applied for citizenship in Federal District Court in San Francisco and was turned down on grounds of race. (He would have been illegal one way or another anyway; the Emperor of China did not give permission for any of his subjects to leave China until 1859.) Debating the Nationality Act, Congressmen declared that America would be a nation of "Nordic fiber."

1878: California held a Constitutional Convention to settle "the Chinese problem." Of the 152 delegates, 35 were not American citizens but Europeans. The resulting constitution, voted into existence by a majority party of Working Men and Grangers, prohibited Chinese from entering California. New state laws empowered cities and counties to confine them within specified areas or to throw them out completely. Shipowners and captains were to be fined and jailed for hiring or transporting them. (This provision was so little respected that the American merchant marine relied heavily on Chinese seamen from the Civil War years to World War I.) "Mongolians, Indians, and Negroes" were barred from attending public schools. The only California fishermen forced to pay fishing and shellfish taxes were the Chinese, who had brought shrimp nets from China and started the shrimp, abalone, and lobster industries. (The taxes were payable monthly.) Those Chinese over eighteen who were not already paying a miner's tax had to pay a "police tax," to cover the extra policing their presence required. Though the Chinese were filling and leveeing the San Joaquin Delta for thirteen cents a square yard, building the richest agricultural land in the world, they were prohibited from owning land or real estate. They could not apply for business licenses. Employers could be fined and jailed for hiring them. No Chinese could be hired by state, county, or municipal governments for public works. No "Chinese or Mongolian or Indian" could testify in court "either for or against a white man."

At this time San Francisco supplemented the anti-Chinese state laws with some of its own: a queue tax, a "cubic air ordinance" requiring that every residence have so many cubic feet of air per inhabitant, a pole law prohibiting the use of carrying baskets on poles, cigar taxes, shoe taxes, and laundry taxes.

Federal courts declared some of the state and city laws unconstitutional, and occasionally citizens of a county or city repealed an especially punitive ordinance on the grounds that it was wrong to invite the Chinese to come to the United States and then deny them a livelihood. The repealed laws were often reenacted in another form.

5 *1880:* The Burlingame Treaty was modified. Instead of being free, the immigration of Chinese laborers to the United States would be "reasonably limited." In return (so as not to bring about limits on American entry into China), the American government promised to protect Chinese from lynchings.

1881: The Burlingame Treaty was suspended for a period of twenty years. (Since 1881 there has been no freedom of travel between China and the United States.) In protest against this suspension and against the refusal to admit Chinese boys to U. S. Army and Naval academies. China ordered scholars studying in the United States to return home. The act suspending the treaty did have two favorable provisions: all Chinese already resident in the United States in 1882 could stay; and they were permitted to leave and reenter with a Certificate of Return.

1882: Encouraged by fanatical lobbying from California, the U.S. Congress passed the first Chinese Exclusion Act. It banned the entrance of Chinese laborers, both skilled and unskilled, for ten years. Anyone unqualified for citizenship could not come in—and by the terms of the Nationality Act of 1870, Chinese were not qualified for citizenship. Some merchants and scholars were granted temporary visas.

1884: Congress refined the Exclusion Act with An Act to Amend an Act. This raised fines and sentences and further defined "merchants" to exclude "hucksters, peddlers, or those engaged in taking, draying, or otherwise preserving shell or other fish for home consumption or exportation."

1888: The Scott Act, passed by Congress, again forbade the entry of Chinese laborers. It also declared that Certificates of Return were void. Twenty thousand Chinese were trapped outside the United States with now-useless re-entry permits. Six hundred returning travelers were turned back at American ports. A Chinese ambassador, humiliated by immigration officers, killed himself. The law decreed that Certificates of Residence had to be shown on demand; any Chinese caught without one was deported.

10 *1889:* Chinese pooled money to fight the various Exclusion Acts in the courts. They rarely won. In *Chae Chan Ping v. The United States,* Chae Chan Ping argued for the validity of his Certificate of Return. The Supreme Court ruled against him, saying that "regard less of the existence of a prior treaty," a race "that will not assimilate with us" could be excluded when deemed "dangerous to. . . peace and security. . . . It matters not in what form aggression and encroachment come, whether from the foreign nation acting in its national character or from vast hordes of its people crowding in

upon us," Moreover, said the Court, "sojourners" should not "claim surprise" that any Certificates of Return obtained prior to 1882 were "held at the will of the government, revocable at am time, at its pleasure."

1892: The Geary Act extended the 1882 Exclusion Act for another ten years. It also decreed that Chinese caught illegally in the United States be deported after one year of hard labor.

Chinese Americans formed the Equal Rights League and the Native Sons of the Golden State in order to fight disenfranchisement bills. Chinese Americans demanded the right to have their citizenship confirmed before traveling abroad.

1893: In *Yue Ting v. The United States,* the U. S. Supreme Court ruled that Congress had the right to expel members of a race who "continue to be aliens, having taken no steps toward becoming citizens, and incapable of becoming such under the naturalization laws." This applied only to Chinese; no other race or nationality was excluded from applying for citizenship.

1896: A victory. In *Yick Wo v. Hopkins,* the U. S. Supreme Court overturned San Francisco safety ordinances, saying that they were indeed designed to harass laundrymen of Chinese ancestry.

1898: Another victory. The Supreme Court decision in *The United States v. Wong Kim Ark* stated that a person born in the United States to Chinese parents is an American. This decision has never been reversed or changed, and it is the law on which most Americans of Chinese ancestry base their citizenship today.

1900: Deciding *The United States v. Mrs. Cue Lim,* the Supreme Court ruled that wives and children of treaty merchants—citizens of China, aliens traveling on visas—were allowed to come to the United States.

1904: The Chinese Exclusion Acts were extended indefinitely, and made to cover Hawai'i and the Philippines as well as the continental United States. The question of exclusion was not debated in Congress; instead, the measure passed as a rider on a routine appropriations bill. China boycotted American goods in protest.

1906: The San Francisco Board of Education ordered that all Chinese, Japanese, and Korean children be segregated in an Oriental school. President Roosevelt, responding to a protest from the Japanese government, persuaded the Board of Education to allow Japanese to attend white schools.

1917: Congress voted that immigrants over sixteen years of age be required to pass an English reading test.

1924: An Immigration Act passed by Congress specifically excluded "Chinese women, wives, and prostitutes." Any American who married a Chinese woman lost his citizenship; any Chinese man who married an American woman caused her to lose her citizenship. Many states had also instituted antimiscegenation laws. A Supreme Court case called *Chang Chan et al. v. John D. Nagle* tested the law against wives; Chang Chan et al. lost. For the first time, the 1924 Immigration Act distinguished between two kinds of "aliens": "immigrants" were admitted as permanent residents with the opportunity to become citizens eventually; the rest—scholars, merchants, ministers, and tourists—were admitted on a temporary basis and were not eligible for citizenship. The number of persons allowed in the category of immigrant was set by law at one-sixth of one percent of the total population of that ancestry in the United States as of the 1920 census. The 1920 census had the lowest count of ethnic Chinese in this country since 1860. As a result, only 105 Chinese immigrants were permitted each year.

In *Cheuno Sumchee v. Nagle,* the Supreme Court once again confirmed the right of treaty merchants to bring their wives to the United States. This was a right that continued to be denied to Chinese Americans.

1938: A Presidential proclamation lifted restriction on immigration for Chinese and nationals of a few other Asian countries. The Chinese were still ineligible for citizenship, and the quota was "100."

1943: The United States and China signed a treaty of alliance against the Japanese, and Congress repealed the Exclusion Act of 1882. Immigration continued to be limited to the 1924 quota of 105, however, and the Immigration and Nationalization Service claimed to be unable to find even that many qualified Chinese. A "Chinese" was defined as anyone with more than 30 percent Chinese blood, regardless of citizenship or country of residence. At this time Japanese invaders were killing Chinese civilians in vast numbers; it is estimated that more than 10 million died. Chinese immigration into the United States did not rise.

1946: Congress passed the War Bride Act, enabling soldiers to bring Japanese and European wives home, then enacted a separate law allowing the wives and children of Chinese Americans to apply for entry as "non-quota immigrants." Only now did the ethnic Chinese population in the United States begin to approach the level of seventy years previous. (When the first Exclusion Act was passed in 1882, there were some 107,000 Chinese here: the Acts and the Driving Out steadily reduced the number to fewer than 70,000 in the 1920s.)

25 *1948:* The Refugee Act passed by Congress this year applied only to Europeans. A separate Displaced Persons Act provided that for a limited time—1948 to 1954—ethnic Chinese already living in the United States could apply for citizenship. During the post-war period, about 10,000 Chinese were permitted to enter the country under individual private bills passed by Congress. Confidence men, like the Citizenship Judges of old, defrauded hopeful Chinese by promising to acquire one of these bills for $1,500.

1950: After the Chinese Communist government took over in 1949, the United States passed a series of Refugee Relief Acts and a Refugee Escapee Act expanding the number of "non-quota immigrants" allowed in. As a condition of entry, the Internal Security Act provided that these refugees swear they were not Communists. (Several hundred "subversives or anarchists" of various races were subsequently deported; some were naturalized citizens who were "denaturalized" beforehand.)

1952: The Immigration and Nationality Act denied admission to "subversive and undesirable aliens" and made it simpler to deport "those already in the country." Another provision of this act was that for the first time Chinese women were allowed to immigrate under the same conditions as men.

1954: Ruling on *Mao v. Brownell,* the Supreme Court upheld laws forbidding Chinese Americans to send money to relatives in China. Before the Communist Revolution, there were no such restrictions in effect; Chinese Americans sent $70 million during World War II. Nor could they send money or gifts through CARE, UNESCO, or church organizations, which provided only for non-Communist countries.

1957: The Refugee Relief Act of 1953 expired in 1956 and was followed by the Act of 1957, which provided for the distribution of 18,000 visas that had remained unused.

30 *1959:* Close relatives, including parents, were allowed to enter.

1960: A "Fair Share Refugee Act" allowed certain refugees from Communist and Middle Eastern countries to enter. Close to 20,000 people who were "persecuted because of race, religion, or political beliefs" immigrated before this act was repealed in 1965, when a new act allowed the conditional entry of 10,200 refugees annually.

1962: A Presidential directive allowed several thousand "parolees" to enter the United States from Hong Kong. Relatives of citizens and resident aliens were eligible. President Kennedy gave Congress a special message on immigration, saying, "It is time to correct the mistakes of the past."

1965: A new Immigration and Nationality Act changed the old quota system so that "national origin" no longer means "race" but "country of birth." Instead of being based on a percentage of existing ethnic populations in the United States, quotas were reallocated to countries—20,000 each. But this did not mean that 20,000 Chinese immediately could or did come to the United States. Most prospective immigrants were in Hong Kong, a British colony. Colonies received 1 percent of the mother country's allotment: only 200. "Immediate relatives," the children, spouses, and parents of citizens, however, could enter without numerical limitations. Also not reckoned within the quota limitations were legal residents returning from a visit abroad.

1968: Amendments to the Immigration and Nationality Act provided that immigrants not be allocated by race or nation but by hemispheres, with 120,000 permitted to enter from the Western Hemisphere and 170,000 from the Eastern Hemisphere. This act limits immigration from the Western Hemisphere for the first time in history. The 20,000-per-country quota remained in effect for the Eastern Hemisphere, no per-country limitation for the Western Hemisphere.

35 *1976:* The Immigration and Nationality Act Amendments, also called the Western Hemisphere Bill, equalized the provisions of law regulating immigration from the two hemispheres. The House Committee on the Judiciary in its report on this legislation stated, "This constitutes an essential first step in a projected long term reform of U. S. Immigration law." The

20,000-per-country limit was extended to the Western Hemisphere. The limitation on colonies was raised from 200 to 600.

1978: The separate quotas for the two hemispheres were replaced by a worldwide numerical limitation on immigration of 290,000 annually. On the basis of the "immediate relatives" clause, about 22,000 Chinese enter legally each year, and the rate is increasing. There are also special quotas in effect for Southeast Asian refugees, most of whom are of Chinese ancestry. In the last decade, the ethnic Chinese population of the United States has doubled. The 1980 census may show a million or more.

Mapping the Text

1. Kingston opens this selection with a quotation from a treaty signed by the United States and China in 1869. Do you agree or disagree with the sentiments of this statement? Does an individual have the right to change his or her home and allegiance, a right to free migration and immigration? What complicates this issue?
2. This selection contains vocabulary, particularly legal vocabulary, that helps create an impression. What is the vocabulary that accomplishes this task? What is the impression? Do other features help create this impression?
3. Kingston is a writer who typically uses narrative forms (e.g., fiction and autobiography) when she writes. This selection is different. How so? Why do you think Kingston chose this form of expression rather than the forms that she typically chooses?

Writing to Inquire

1. Consider the effect that might be created if you made different choices than Kingston to express these same ideas. What would happen to the account if the context for thinking about the laws was Chinese women rather than men? How would the account shift if the form were a short story or a poem? Try expressing these same details in a different genre. What decisions do you need to make as the writer to change from this detailed chronicle of immigration laws to a short story, a poem, or an essay? What is the difference in effect from genre to genre?

For My American Family: A Belated Tribute to a Legacy of Gifted Intelligence and Guts

JUNE JORDAN

June Jordan (1936–2002) was Professor of African Studies and Director of Poetry for the People at the University of California at Berkeley. Born to Jamaican immigrants in Harlem, Jordan grew up in Brooklyn, New York. She was a prolific poet and essayist as well as an author of children's books. Her works include *His Own Where* (1971), which was nominated for the National Book Award; *Fannie Lou Hamer* (1972); *Some Changes* (1981); *Civil Wars: Observations from the Front Lines of America* (1981); *On Call: Political Essays* (1985); *Lyrical Campaigns* (1989); *Technical Difficulties: African American Notes on the State of the Union* (1992); *Poetry for the People: Finding a Voice Through Verse* (1996); and *Affirmative Acts: Political Essays* (1998). The essay below, taken from *Technical Difficulties,* highlights Jordan's use of personal experience to examine critically various problems and issues of American life.

I would love to see pictures of the Statue of Liberty taken by my father. They would tell me so much about him that I wish I knew. He couldn't very well ask that lady to "hold that smile" or "put on a little something with red to brighten it up." He'd have to take her "as is," using a choice of angles or focus or distance as the means to his statement. And I imagine that my father would choose a long-shot, soft-focus, wide-angle lens: that would place Miss Liberty in her full formal setting, and yet suggest the tears that easily spilled from his eyes whenever he spoke about "this great country of ours: America."

A camera buff, not averse to wandering around the city with both a Rolleiflex and a Rolleicord at the ready, my father thought nothing of a two or three hours' "setup" for a couple of shots of anything he found beautiful. I remember one Saturday, late morning, when I watched my father push the "best" table in the house under the dining-room windows, fidget the venetian blinds in order to gain the most interesting, slatted light, and then bring the antique Chinese vase downstairs from the parlor, fill that with fresh roses from the backyard, and then run out to the corner store for several pieces of fruit to complete his still-life composition.

All of this took place in the 1940s. We lived in the Bedford-Stuyvesant neighborhood of Brooklyn, one of the largest urban Black communities in the world. Besides the fruit and the flowers of my father's aesthetic preoccupation, and just beyond those narrow brownstone dining-room windows, there was a burly mix of unpredictable street life that he could not control, despite incessant telephone calls, for example, to the Department of Sanitation: "Hello. This is a man by the name of Granville Ivanhoe Jordan, and I'm calling about garbage collection. What happened? Did you forget?!"

The unlikely elements of my father's name may summarize his history and character rather well. Jordan is a fairly common surname on the island of Jamaica where he was born, one of perhaps twelve or thirteen children who foraged for food, and who never forgot, or forgave, the ridicule his ragged clothing provoked in school. Leaving the classroom long before the normal conclusion to an elementary education, my father later taught himself to read and, after that, he never stopped reading and reading everything he could find, from Burpee seed catalogues to Shakespeare to the *National Geographic* magazines to "Negro" poetry to liner notes for the record albums of classical music that he devoured. But he was also "the little bull"—someone who loved a good rough fight and who even volunteered to teach boxing to other young "Negroes" at the Harlem YMCA, where he frequently participated in political and militant "uplifting-the-race" meetings, on West 135th Street.

5 Except for weekends, my father pursued all of his studies in the long early hours of the night, 3 or 4 A.M., after eight hours' standing up at the post office where he speed-sorted mail quite without the assistance of computers and zip codes which, of course, had yet to be invented. Exceptionally handsome and exceptionally vain, Mr. G. I. Jordan, immaculate in one of his innumerable, rooster-elegant suits, would readily back open a coconut with a machete, or slice a grapefruit in half, throw his head back, and squeeze the juice into his mouth—carefully held a tricky foot away—all to my mother's head-shaking dismay: "Why now you have to act up like a monkey chaser, eh?"

It is a sad thing to consider that this country has given its least to those who have loved it the most. I am the daughter of West Indian immigrants. And perhaps there are other Americans as believing and as grateful and as loyal, but I doubt it. In general, the very word *immigrant* connotes somebody white, while *alien* denotes everybody else. But hundreds and hundreds of thousands of Americans are hardworking, naturalized Black citizens whose trust in the democratic promise of the mainland has never been reckoned with fully, or truly reciprocated. For instance, I know that my parents would have wanted to say, "Thanks, America!" if only there had been some way, some public recognition and welcome of their presence, here, and then some really big shot to whom their gratitude might matter.

I have seen family snapshots of my mother pushing me in a baby carriage decorated with the single decal F.D.R., and I have listened to endless tall stories about what I did or didn't do when my father placed me in the lap of New York's mayor, Fiorello La Guardia, and, on top of the ornate wallpaper of our parlor floor there was a large color photograph of the archbishop of the Episcopal diocese of Long Island; my parents lived in America, full of faith.

When I visited the birthplace of my mother, twelve years ago, I was embarrassed by the shiny rented car that brought me there: even in 1974, there were no paved roads in Clonmel, a delicate dot of a mountain village in Jamaica. And despite the breathtaking altitude, you could not poke or peer yourself into a decent position for "a view": the vegetation was that dense, that lush, and that chaotic. On or close to the site of my mother's childhood home, I found a neat wood cabin, still without windowpanes or screens, a dirt floor, and a barefoot family of seven, quietly bustling about.

I was stunned. There was neither electricity nor running water. How did my parents even hear about America, more than a half century ago? In the middle of the Roaring Twenties, these eager Black immigrants came, by boat. Did they have to borrow shoes for the journey?

10 I know that my aunt and my mother buckled into domestic work, once they arrived, barely into their teens. I'm not sure how my father managed to feed himself before that fantastic 1933 afternoon when he simply ran all the way from midtown Manhattan up to our Harlem apartment, shouting out the news: A job! He had found a job!

And throughout my childhood I cannot recall even one utterance of disappointment, or bitterness with America. In fact, my parents hid away any newspaper or magazine article that dealt with "jim crow" or "lynchings" or "discrimination." These were terms of taboo status neither to be spoken nor explained to me. Instead I was given a child's biography of Abraham Lincoln and the Bible stories of Daniel and David, and, from my father, I learned about Marcus Garvey and George Washington Carver and Mary McLeod Bethune. The focus was relentlessly upbeat. Or, as Jimmy Cliff used to sing it, "You can make it if you really try."

My mother's emphasis was more religious, and more consistently race-conscious, and she was equally affirmative: God would take care of me. And, besides, there was ("C'mon, Joe! C'mon!") the Brown Bomber, Joe Louis, and then, incredibly, Jackie Robinson who, by himself, elevated the Brooklyn Dodgers into a sacred cult worshipped by apparently dauntless Black baseball fans.

We had a pretty rich life. Towards the end of the 1960s I was often amazed by facile references to Black communities as "breeding grounds of despair" or "culturally deprived" or "ghettos." That was not the truth. There are grounds for despair in the suburbs, evidently, and I more than suspect greater cultural deprivation in economically and racially and socially homogeneous Long Island commuter towns than anything I ever had to overcome!

In Bedford-Stuyvesant, I learned all about white history and white literature, but I lived and learned about my own, as well. My father marched me to the American Museum of Natural History and to the Planetarium, at least twice a month, while my mother picked up "the slack" by riding me, by trolley car, to public libraries progressively farther and farther away from our house. In the meantime, on our own block of Hancock Street, between Reid and Patchen avenues, we had rice and peas and curried lamb or, upstairs, in my aunt and uncle's apartment, pigs' feet and greens. On the piano in the parlor there was boogie-woogie, blues, and Chopin. Across the street, there were cold-water flats that included the Gumbs family or, more precisely, Donnie Gumbs, whom I saw as the inarguable paragon of masculine cute. There were "American Negroes," and "West Indians." Some rented their housing, and some were buying their homes. There were Baptists, Holy Rollers, and Episcopalians, side by side.

15 On that same one block, Father Coleman, the minister of our church, lived and worked as the first Black man on New York's Board of Higher Education. There was Mrs. Taylor, whose music studio was actually a torture chamber into which many of us were forced for piano lessons. And a Black policeman. And a mail carrier. And a doctor. And my beloved Uncle

Teddy, with a Doctor of Law degree from Fordham University. And the tiny, exquisite arrow of my aunt, who became one of the first Black principals in the entire New York City public school system. And my mother, who had been president of the first Black class to graduate from the Lincoln School of Nursing, and my father, who earned the traditional gold watch as a retiring civil servant, and Nat King Cole and calypso and boyfriends and Sunday School and confirmation and choir and stickball and roller skates and handmade wooden scooters and marbles and make-believe tea parties and I cannot recall feeling underprivileged, or bored, in that "ghetto."

And from such "breeding grounds of despair," Negro men volunteered, in droves, for active duty in an army that did not want or honor them. And from such "limited" communities, Negro women, such as my mother, left their homes in every kind of weather, and at any hour, to tend to the ailing and heal the sick, regardless of their color, or ethnicity. And in such a "culturally deprived" house as that modest home created by my parents, I became an American poet.

And in the name of my mother and my father, I want to say thanks to America. And I want something more:

My aunt has survived the deaths of her husband and my parents in typical, if I may say so, West Indian fashion. Now in her seventies, and no longer principal of a New York City public school, she rises at 5 A.M., every morning, to prepare for another day of complicated duties as the volunteer principal of a small Black private academy. In the front yard of her home in the Crown Heights section of Brooklyn, the tulips and buttercups have begun to bloom already. Soon every passerby will see her azaleas and jonquils and irises blossoming under the Japanese maple tree and around the base of the Colorado blue spruce.

She is in her seventies, and she tells me:

> I love the United States and I always will uphold it as a place of opportunity. This is not to say that you won't meet prejudice along the way but it's up to you to overcome it. And it can be overcome!

20 Well, I think back to Clonmel, Jamaica, and I visualize my aunt skipping along the goat tracks, fast as she can, before the darkness under the banana tree leaves becomes too scary for a nine-year-old. Or I think about her, struggling to fetch water from the river, in a pail. And I jump-cut to Orange High School, New Jersey, U.S.A., where my aunt maintained a 95 average, despite her extracurricular activities as a domestic, and where she was denied the valedictory because, as the English teacher declared, "You have an accent that the parents will not understand." And I stay quiet as my aunt explains, "I could have let that bother me, but I said, 'Naw, I'm not gone let this keep me down!'"

And what I want is to uphold this America, this beckoning and this shelter provided by my parents and my aunt. I want to say thank you to them, my faithful American family.

Mapping the Text

1. Consider the subtitle of June Jordan's essay, "A Belated Tribute to a Legacy of Gifted Intelligence and Guts." What do you think Jordan intends to suggest about family legacies by her choice of these words? What seems to be her purpose? What images of her family does she embed here? What evidence do you see that in drawing on such images Jordan is doing more than simply talking about her own family? What do you think Jordan is trying to accomplish?
2. Jordan is recognized as a poet. Can you find any evidence that she is "poetic" in style even though, in this case, she has written an essay? Consider words, phrases, length of sentences or paragraphs, for example; images and the way(s) she seems to use them; rhythm, sound, and pattern. How would you describe Jordan as a writer? On what basis does this description seem to you fair and accurate?
3. Go through Jordan's essay and find examples of the kind(s) of appeal she makes. What evidence do you see that Jordan is talking to our heads, hearts, backbones (our sense of ethics, what seems right and wrong, or good and evil, or just and unjust), or to our stomachs (in trying to help us understand what is distasteful or perhaps in poor taste)?
4. Who do you think Jordan imagines her readers to be in this essay? What readers do you think will be most moved by what she says? Why? Are there readers you suspect might feel surprised or uncomfortable with what she says? If so, what do you think will surprise them or make them uncomfortable?

Writing to Inquire

1. Given what Jordan says about her father and mother, how would you describe her family as an American family? What sense of themselves as Americans do you think her parents held based on the details that Jordan provides? What, if anything, is Jordan questioning or not questioning about people like her parents and perhaps even the ways in which they were able to define themselves as Americans? Why does Jordan say at the end of the essay, "And what I want is to uphold this America, this beckoning and this shelter provided by my parents and my aunt. I want to say thank you to them, my faithful American family"? What do you think she means? Why, for example, do you think Jordan chose to say "uphold this America" (What view of America is she talking about here?) or "my faithful American family" (Why "faithful"? What does the combination of "faithful" and "American" suggest?)?
2. Do you get the idea in this essay that Jordan feels about the United States the way she suggests that her parents felt? What are the similarities? What are the differences? What is she celebrating? What does she seem not to be celebrating? What do you see as Jordan's point of view? What is her attitude toward national identity? What do you think Jordan is saying in this essay? What is her message? Do you think her message has merit? Does her view complement yours? How? How not?

READINGS FOR INQUIRY AND EXPLORATION

The New Colossus

EMMA LAZARUS

Emma Lazarus (1849–1887) was a Jewish poet, essayist, and activist who worked for Zionist and Marxist causes. Born to wealthy parents in New York, Lazarus was a member of an elite family who traced their roots to the earliest Jewish settlers in the United States. Lazarus wrote in a range of genres, including poetry, novels, plays, and essays, and she translated poetry from German to English. Her 1883 sonnet, "The New Colossus," was engraved at the base of the Statue of Liberty, where it symbolizes the American welcome to immigrants from around the world.

Not like the brazen giant of Greek fame,
With conquering limbs astride from land to land;
Here at our sea-washed, sunset gates shall stand
A mighty woman with a torch, whose flame
Is the imprisoned lightning, and her name
Mother of Exiles. From her beacon-hand
Glows world-wide welcome; her mild eyes command
The air-bridged harbor that twin cities frame.
"Keep ancient lands, your storied pomp!" cries she
With silent lips. "Give me your tired, your poor,
Your huddled masses yearning to breathe free,
The wretched refuse of your teeming shore.
Send these, the homeless, tempest-tost to me,
I lift my lamp beside the golden door!"

Mapping the Text

1. Emma Lazarus's words, "Give me your tired, your poor / Your huddled masses yearning to breathe free," are inscribed on the Statue of Liberty. The poem, like the statue itself, represents something about the United States. What do you think this poem says about the nature of the country or the spirit of the people?

Writing to Inquire

1. The Statue of Liberty is a statue of a woman. How does gender help shape the meaning of this symbol? How might the symbol be perceived or function differently in the imagination of Americans if the statue were of a man? What might such a statue look like? What meaning do you think it would represent?

2. The Statue of Liberty is a dominant symbol of freedom for the United States. Does your own community offer symbols of freedom (statues, buildings, memorials, parks, or other types of natural areas or public gathering places)? What do they symbolize? Are their stories widely known in your community? Who celebrates them, and how? Are the celebrations solemn or high-spirited? Do you attend them?

The Unguarded Gates

THOMAS BAILEY ALDRICH

Thomas Bailey Aldrich (1836–1907) was a writer, journalist, and editor. He served as editor of *Every Saturday* from 1866 to 1874 and the *Atlantic Monthly* from 1881 to 1890. He also wrote poetry and fiction. His most famous work, *Story of a Bad Boy* (1870), was based on his boyhood experiences in Portsmouth, New Hampshire. His other works include *Prudence Palfrey* (1874); *Queen of Sheba* (1877); and *Stillwater Tragedy* (1880).

Wide open and unguarded stand our gates.
And through them press a wild, a motley throng—
Men from the Volga and the Tartar steppes,
Featureless figures of the Hoang Ho,
Malayan, Seythian, Teuton, Kelt, and Slav,
Flying the Old World's poverty and scorn;
These bringing with them unknown gods and rites,
Those tiger passions, here to stretch their claws.
In street and alley what strange tongues are these.
Accents of menace alien to our air,
Voices that once the tower of Babel knew!
O, Liberty, white goddess, is it well
To leave the gate unguarded? On thy breast
Fold sorrow's children, soothe the hurts of fate,
Lift the downtrodden, but with the hand of steel
Stay those who to thy sacred portals come
To waste the fight of freedom. Have a care
Lest from thy brow the clustered stars be torn
And trampled in the dust. For so of old
The thronging Goth and Vandal trampled Rome,
And where the temples of the Caesars stood
The lean wolf unmolested made her lair.

Mapping the Text

1. The view of immigrants in Thomas Aldrich's poem is not the view we typically associate with the Statue of Liberty. Explain his view and indicate the words and phrases from the poem that seem to validate your explanation.
2. Aldrich's attitudes toward immigration could be described as conservative. What about his viewpoint makes that label seem accurate? If Aldrich's view is a conservative one, what might constitute a liberal view, or a radical view?

Writing to Inquire

1. How do you see Aldrich's sentiments alive and well in the contemporary world? Choose a specific instance and compare the views associated with the contemporary situation to the views represented in Aldrich's poem.
2. Aldrich alludes to several periods of history he apparently feels help make his point about "unguarded gates." Make a list of these historical moments. Choose one of them to explore through library resources. What connections between his time and the historical moment is Aldrich making? What is your view of "unguarded gates"? What evidence do you think helps make your case?

Ellis Island Interview: Germany

FRIEDRICH LEIPZIG

Friedrich Leipzig, as suggested by the interview below, was among over 12 million people who entered the United States through Ellis Island. This portal began operating in 1892 as one of the first federal immigration stations, and it ceased operations in 1954. In 1965, by the authority of President Lyndon B. Johnson, Ellis Island became part of the Statue of Liberty National Monument, and in 1990, after major renovation, the main building of the station was reopened as the Ellis Island Immigration Museum in tribute to the millions of people who used this portal as the doorway to a new life in the United States. According to Peter Morton Coan in *Ellis Island Interviews: In Their Own Words* (1977), Leipzig was born in 1919 and raised in a middle-class Jewish family. In 1941, at the age of 22, he immigrated from Heidelberg, Germany, to escape the oppression of Adolph Hitler's regime. His father was beaten to death by the Nazis in the Dachau prison camp. His mother escaped to Palestine. His brother and sister also immigrated to New York. Leipzig, like so many immigrants of his era, made a new life for himself in a new land.

I had a wonderful childhood. I lived in Heidelberg until I was fifteen. I had a brother and a sister in a house where we had just about everything you could hope for, all material wants. I was the youngest. It was a good-sized house, about nineteen, twenty rooms. And there were servants. I never really appreciated it until it was all gone, and it was too late. My father ran a tobacco factory on the outskirts of Heidelberg that he inherited from his father, and my mother ran the household. I had a nanny who I loved as much as my mother.

My father's business, M & F Leipzig, made cigars, smoke tobacco, pipe tobacco. I remember in the main square in Heidelberg there was, much to my embarrassment as a little boy, a sign that said in German, "Every Smoker With Good Taste Smokes Only Leipzig's Pipe Tobacco." [Laughs.] I didn't like to see my name on a neon sign. I thought it was tacky.

The tobacco was grown in Turkey and America. Once in a while I was allowed to go out to the factory and there were bales of tobacco my brother and I climbed over and the best ones smelled just wonderful, and those were usually the Virginia tobacco. [Laughs.] My mother never smoked. My father smoked a lot. My mother's family came from Bruchsal, a town about fifteen miles from Heidelberg. Her father was also in the tobacco business, curing tobacco, and their marriage was arranged between the two fathers.

My father was strict and hard to get close with. My mother was always ready for a good joke or a good laugh. Full of wild ideas and unexpected things. My mother's family was less conventional. My mother's mother lived with us for a while after my grandfather died. My mother would pull tricks on my father. She would change her voice and call him up. Say my father just came back from a night out with the boys. She would call him at work the next day and say, "I'm so glad I found out where you are. Don't you remember the wonderful night we had together." My father didn't know a thing about it. She made it up. But he was embarrassed, so he went along with it, and she just teased him along and said, "Can I come visit you?" And he said, "All right." And she went over to visit him, and he knew, of course, that the whole thing was a joke. Those things went on quite a good deal.

5 By 1939, the atmosphere in Heidelberg had gotten pretty bad for Jews. People were paranoid. When they walked down the street, they looked over their shoulders to see who was following behind. And when the grownups discussed whether or not we should leave the country, they took a bed pillow and covered the telephone because they thought the telephone was bugged. People were just getting paranoid. Everything was suspect. Not even your best friend was trustworthy anymore. Everybody was turned in, and you heard nothing but horror stories; especially about the famous *Krystallnacht*. That day, my father was rounded up and taken to Dachau, the concentration camp. When they let him out, my mother took him to a Catholic hospital. That was the only hospital that would take him. He was literally beaten, beaten in many different ways. He had broken

bones. He had pneumonia. He was bruised all over his body to the extent his body was not able to sustain life anymore. And he died two days later.

My mother called me in Switzerland to tell me. I was at a boarding school at the time. I had been in Switzerland many times before as a child for different health reasons. I was a sickish child, and I was sent to a children's home in Otaboden once every year for a few weeks. But I was ultimately transferred to a Swiss boarding school because it was the only secure place I could be. It was a decision made by my parents. I enjoyed it tremendously. It was a school with students from all over the world. Their families had sent them there to be safe. You could hear almost any language you could think of. It's the only time I ever heard Spaniards and Italians talk to each other in their own language. When they don't understand each other they just raise their voices, and then they understand each other. [Laughs.] Most importantly, it was a place where my self-confidence was built up, and they knew how to do it. They challenged me. They gave me opportunities to prove myself. It's not that they praised me so much as they were very good at handling children. The lady who was in charge of the place gave me a large amount of money one day and said, "Take it down to the post office and deposit it." She gave me instructions, and I thought it was a very difficult task. I was very young. I must have been about seven. I loved it there.

While this was going on, the SS came to our house and took everything from my mother. Furniture, jewelry, naturally. They even pulled the wedding ring off her finger, which bothered me very much. I didn't care if they took the furniture.

Another day, an SS man visited my mother and said, "Mrs. Leipzig, I'm not here to take anything away from you, but I have to tell you you must leave the country. I remember you from long ago. I know your family, and I want to do you a favor. You have to leave the country."

And she said, "I do?"

10 "Yes," he said. "You have to leave today." And she didn't know what she should do.

"I have a taxi," he said. "The driver will take you wherever you tell him, but you have to go."

So she packed a suitcase, as much as she could. And by that time my mother's mother was in Holland. She told the driver to drive to the Dutch border. The moment she crossed the border she heard Hitler give a speech over the car radio that Germany was invading Poland, that the war had officially started, and that all borders were sealed. So that man knew this was the last chance to get out. He had done a good deed.

My mother had no permission to stay in Holland. So she went to Palestine. She went there in a small boat. And she eventually died there. She wrote me detailed letters of what had happened. She wrote me letters from Holland, and she wrote me letters from Palestine, which later became

Israel. I still have some of the letters, and I reread them occasionally. I'm now translating them for my kids to read.

After graduating [from] boarding school, I tried to get an immigration permit to come to America. My brother and my sister were already here. My brother came first, my sister a year later. I always wanted to come to the United States. The United States to me was a country full of miracles, and wonderful things that I had read in books that were really exciting and nice, and high-rise buildings. I read about the Pennsylvania Turnpike, a road that was dedicated for only automobiles without intersections. And things of that sort really impressed me, and I thought, that's a country where you can do almost anything you want to. While I was in Switzerland my brother and sister were writing me and telling me these things.

But I had a difficult time getting my immigration permit from the American consulate. There were too many people trying to come to the United States, more people than the quota permitted. If I had the money, I could have bribed my way; I would have been able to slip the right amount of money to the right person at the right moment and gotten my permit. But I was a young kid and I didn't have any money, so I was too naive to do that. And after a while the Swiss were trying to get rid of foreigners, Jews, anyway. They were a burden to them. I was taken to a labor camp for close to a year. It was a hard life. We were given shoes with wooden soles, which were very handy because we were draining a swamp area. And the wooden soles insulated us from the cold ground. I learned to work with my hands. We had to dig out stumps of trees so that the land could be used for agriculture. Switzerland suffered from a great lack of food. They were surrounded by Nazi-controlled countries. Hitler allowed as much food into Switzerland as he felt like. Switzerland was actually manufacturing weapons for Germany, and that gave them a bargaining point, so they did get some food in.

After I got out, I worked illegally in Switzerland. Only Swiss natives were allowed to work. But I had to get some money somehow, so I worked for an architectural photographer in a darkroom, until the police found out and I quit. I asked the photographer what I should do, and he said, "Disappear." I remembered a farmer who had a hut high up in the mountains. So I stayed alone there for a couple of weeks. I rented it for one franc, or twenty cents a day. It was very primitive. The farmers used to drive their cows up there in summer, high into the mountains, tend them, and come down in fall.

My immigration permit finally came through. My brother had helped. Apparently he knew someone who knew someone on the House Foreign Affairs Committee. The committee inquired about my case by writing a letter to the consulate, and that's all it took.

Then came the real problem. How do I get out of Switzerland? It was surrounded by Nazi-occupied countries, except France, which was divided into occupied France and Vichy France. The Swiss government started negotiating with the German government to let trains go through occupied

France into Vichy France, so they could get rid of some of the foreigners living in Switzerland. I went to Geneva and got on a guarded, sealed train. I was very uneasy about leaving Switzerland because I still felt secure there. But as we went through France the guards slowly disappeared. There were only a few guards left by the time we got to Spain. The train went along the Mediterranean at the foot of the Pyrenees, and there it stopped suddenly. No tracks. Spain was still suffering greatly from its civil war and had not been rebuilt at all. We took a bus from there through Barcelona to Sevilla, and from Sevilla to Cadiz, but there was no ship at Cadiz, and we waited. I ran out of money, and it was desperate. I was staying in a hotel I couldn't really afford, but I stayed there anyway. Ernest Hemingway had been there a few days before. I stayed in his room.

I stayed in Cadiz about a month until we got news that the ship was coming to Sevilla. They provided transportation from Cadiz to Sevilla. And I rode the bus to Sevilla along a river, up and inland to the north. I spent my last night in Spain in a hotel. It was wonderful. I blew the last peso I had. I did not like Cadiz. But I enjoyed Sevilla, perhaps because I knew my ship was there, the *Navemar.* It had a black hull. And we left the next day downriver.

I was appalled how many people were waiting to get on board that ship. It was a freighter converted to handle a few passengers. But it had booked thirteen hundred. So accommodations were poor. We had triple decker bunks in the various holds. There were three freight holds for the thirteen hundred passengers. Not very good. The holds were left open for air, which was all right, except when it rained, then people got wet. But I didn't sleep down there. I slept in a lifeboat. I pulled back the tarp slightly and I sneaked in every night. That was much better. There were about eight kids all told who slept in that lifeboat.

I knew it was uncomfortable, and I didn't care. It was going to America! I couldn't understand why some people felt so bad about it. Some just couldn't stand it. Some people jumped overboard as time went on, and some became sick and died. It was a pretty horrible situation. We finally had to form our own ship's police to maintain order. I became a member. We could only eat in shifts because we were too many people to eat, and we had two meals a day. We had to take great care that people would eat just their two meals. There were some people who ate first shift, second shift, and third shift. And then the other people couldn't get any meals at all, so that had to be regulated, and the ship's crew was unable to regulate that, so we succeeded in doing that. I also succeeded in meeting a very attractive girl from France with whom I got along very well. She wanted me to speak French, but my French wasn't that good. And she didn't want to speak English. So she spoke French and I answered her in English.

The trip took forty-seven days. It was a slow boat. [Laughs.] We went from Sevilla to Lisbon, where we stayed a whole week in the outer harbor. We had to take on food and some live cattle that were put on deck. We had waited so long, all of our American immigration permits had run out. So one day we were taken into Lisbon, also in shifts, one busload at a time, to the American consulate. The American officials in Lisbon were wonderful compared to those in Geneva. They were friendly and helpful, and I returned with a care package full of good food including canned sardines and a bottle of brandy, which was just heaven. In the end, I shared everything with the eight kids in the lifeboat.

We went on to Bermuda, because we were intercepted in the mid-Atlantic by a British frigate. In Bermuda all the women and children were taken off by the British and fed. We were allowed to take a bath, which was heaven. We only had cold, saltwater showers. From Bermuda, we went down to Havana, Cuba, and from there, up to New York.

We came to the outer harbor, and it was very exciting. Everybody rushed out on deck with the cattle to see the skyline of New York, and the Statue of Liberty. And then we stopped, dropped anchor. We were very disappointed. Somebody observed that we had raised the yellow flag, which meant we were being quarantined. The Public Health Service came on board in a launch and examined everybody. Alongside the launch was a press ship, and I noticed they were taking pictures with flash bulbs, and I couldn't understand why anyone would shoot flash in the middle of the day. I remember that clearly. This was September 1941.

25 My brother, who was in the U.S. Army, greeted me in uniform. He could come to the front of the dock because he was military. I was up on the top deck. I hadn't seen my brother in years and it felt good. I yelled down to him that I was running a fever. And that they told me to go to the hospital on Ellis Island. They wanted to find out why I was running a fever. I left my brother at the dock. That was very disappointing. I was taken in a launch to Ellis Island, and the hospital. There were a dozen others besides me, and a nurse checked off our names. She was sitting downstairs by the door. We were separated by sex. I was the only male.

Then we were sent upstairs [to] what looked like real beds. I hadn't seen a real bed for so long. And we were told we could take a shower, which was absolutely unbelievable, with real soap and warm water, unsalty. I was beginning to get in a much better mood already. We came out of our showers and we were sitting around the ward and suddenly somebody asked us, "Have you guys eaten yet?" And we said, "No." Even if we had eaten, we would have said no. We were starved. We were taken to a cafeteria. The concept of a cafeteria was new to me. I had seen something like it in movies, but never in reality. We were given stainless steel trays that had partitions in it, and we had to go from one station to the other, and they dished the food in. The women and I had ham, mashed potatoes, green peas. For dessert I had a pink strawberry ice cream bar that was unbelievably good. And so we sat and talked and ate all the food, and we didn't want to go away. Somebody from the cafeteria said. "Have you had enough, or would you like more?"

"Can we have more?" we asked.

"Sure, you can have as much as you want."

So we ate more. I went through the line five times. The doctor saw this and said to the cafeteria worker, "You're going to make these people sick. Don't give them any more food." Then we went to the wards, and I slept just heavenly.

The next morning we had breakfast, a very important event. [Laughs.] And then a man came by and said, "You may leave." I only had one suitcase plus a used piece of soap I stuck in my pocket, and a piece of sugar I swiped from the cafeteria. I went from the hospital and walked a long distance across this grassy area to the main building. There were three tables with immigration officials. I was told to wait until they called me.

It was my turn. They wanted to see my immigration permit, which thank God had been fixed properly in Lisbon. But my passport had run out. It was no longer valid. "If you want to renew your passport," they said, "you have to go back to Germany." Which I wasn't about to do. He stamped the permit and said, "You may go."

It was wonderful. I stepped outside. It was a warm, breezy, summer day. I could see Manhattan. The high-rise buildings. The water was blue. Just heaven. I was taken by ferry to the mainland where my brother was waiting with a car and we drove at high speed up the West Side Highway to Yonkers.

One of the things that was hard understanding was the coins. In Europe, all coins have numbers that show what they're worth, but in America no coin has a number on it. Show me where a quarter says twenty-five, or where a dime says ten, or where a nickel says five. Nowhere. The other problem was language. I knew some English—British English, and not very much.

About five months after I entered the United States I was drafted into the army. I was in basic training, and my drill sergeant yelled, "About face!" I had no idea what it meant. I knew "about" and "face," and I had no idea what he wanted me to do about my face. I looked right and left and I saw everybody turned around. . . But that's how I learned.

Mapping the Text

1. This selection is a written version of an oral interview. What characteristics do you notice about the way Leipzig tells his story? How does he create a sense of humor? drama? excitement? Is his story representative of others you have heard or read? Do you think "immigrant story" might be a kind of literary genre? Based on this example, what are some of the key characteristics of such a genre?
2. Search for other immigrant stories. Read stories that were written by men and others written by women. What were the similarities and differences in their experiences, or in the ways in which they render these experiences? Are they all the same? Do they vary in any way?

Writing to Inquire

1. Find out more about Ellis Island as a waystation for immigrants. What were the other portals through which immigrants entered the country? Were they similar to or different than Ellis Island?
2. Friedrich Leipzig immigrated to the United States from Germany to escape tyranny. Search library sources to find out about other waves of immigration. What reasons other than tyranny have brought immigrants to the United States?
3. Many European immigrants coming into the United States during the period Leipzig entered settled in urban areas. What was life like in American cities for immigrants during the 1930s and 1940s? What work was available? What sorts of tensions arose between and among groups of immigrants? What was educational opportunity like? What were their living conditions? How did these conditions vary? On what bases did they vary?

Kazuko Itoi: A Nisei Daughter's Story, 1925–1942

MONICA (ITOI) SONE

Monica Sone (1919–) was born Monica Kazuko Itoi in Seattle, Washington. In 1941, she was a student at the University of Washington. After Pearl Harbor, however, she and her family were taken to an internment camp in Topaz, Idaho. Sone tells her story of this experience in *Nisei Daughter* (1953), using her first name and married name. In this memoir, she writes of the disruption to lives, the reality of imprisonment, and the efforts of Japanese-Americans to maintain their lives, cultural values, and dignity in spite of the nation's disregard of the rights and privileges of their citizenship. The selection below is excerpted from this memoir.

A Shocking Fact of Life

The first five years of my life I lived in amoebic bliss, not knowing whether I was plant or animal, at the old Carrollton Hotel on the waterfront of Seattle. One day when I was a happy six-year-old, I made the shocking discovery that I had Japanese blood. I was a Japanese.

Mother announced this fact of life to us in a quiet, deliberate manner one Sunday afternoon as we gathered around for dinner in the small kitchen, converted from one of our hotel rooms. Our kitchen was cozily comfortable for all six of us as long as everyone remained in his place around the oblong table covered with an indestructible shiny black oilcloth; but if more than Mother stood up and fussed around, there was a serious traffic jam—soy sauce splattered on the floor and elbows jabbed into the pot of rice. So Father sat at the head of the table, Kenji, Henry, and I lined up on one side along the wall, while Mother and baby Sumiko occupied the other side, near the kitchen stove.

Now we watched as Mother lifted from a kettle of boiling water a straw basket of steaming slippery noodles. She directed her information at Henry and me, and I felt uneasy. Father paid strict attention to his noodles, dipping them into a bowl of fragrant pork broth and then sprinkling finely chopped raw green onion over them.

"Japanese blood—how is it I have that, Mama?" I asked, surreptitiously pouring hot tea over my bowl of rice. Mother said it was bad manners to wash rice down with tea, but rice was delicious with *obancha.*[1]

5 "Your father and I have Japanese blood and so do you, too. And the same with Henry, Ken-chan, and Sumi-chan."

"Oh." I felt nothing unusual stirring inside me. I took a long cool sip of milk and then with my short red chopsticks I stabbed at a piece of pickled crisp white radish.

"So, Mama?" Henry looked up at her, trying to bring under control with his chopsticks the noodles swinging from his mouth like a pendulum.

"So, Papa and I have decided that you and Ka-chan will attend Japanese school after grammar school every day." She beamed at us.

I choked on my rice.

10 Terrible, terrible, terrible! So that's what it meant to be a Japanese—to lose my afternoon play hours! I fiercely resented this sudden intrusion of my blood into my affairs.

"But, Mama!" I shrieked. "I go to Bailey Gatzert School already. I don't want to go to another!"

Henry kicked the table leg and grumbled, "Aw gee, Mama, Dunks and Jiro don't have to—why do I!"

"They'll be going, too. Their mothers told me so."

My face grew hot with anger. I shouted, "I won't, I won't!"

15 Father and Mother painted glowing pictures for me. Just think you'll grow up to be a well-educated young lady, knowing two languages. One of these days you'll thank us for giving you this opportunity.

But they could not convince me. Until this shattering moment. I had thought life was sweet and reasonable. But not any more. Why did Father and Mother make such a fuss just because we had Japanese blood? Why did we have to go to Japanese school? I refused to eat and sat sobbing, letting great big tears splash down into my bowl of rice and tea.

Henry, who was smarter and adjusted more quickly to fate, continued his meal, looking gloomy, but with his appetite unimpaired.

Up to that moment, I had never thought of Father and Mother as Japanese. True, they had almond eyes and they spoke Japanese to us, but I never felt that it was strange. It was like one person's being red-haired and another black.

---

[1]*Obancha*: coarse tea.

Father had often told us stories about his early life. He had come from a small village in the prefecture of Tochigi-ken.[2] A third son from among five brothers and one sister, Father had gone to Tokyo to study law, and he practiced law for a few years before he succumbed to the fever which sent many young men streaming across the Pacific to a fabulous new country rich with promise and opportunities.

In 1904 Father sailed for the United States, an ambitious young man of twenty-five, determined to continue his law studies at Ann Arbor, Michigan. Landing in Seattle, he plunged into sundry odd jobs with the hope of saving enough money to finance his studies. Father worked with the railroad gang, laying ties on virgin soil, he toiled stubbornly in the heat of the potato fields of Yakima, he cooked his way back and forth between Alaska and Seattle on ships of all sizes and shapes, but fortune eluded him. Then one day he bought a small cleaning and pressing shop on Tenth and Jackson Street, a wagon and a gentle white dobbin, "Charlie." The years flew by fast, but his savings did not reflect his frenzied labor. With each passing year, his dream of Ann Arbor grew dimmer.

At last Father's thoughts turned toward marriage. About this time the Reverend Yohachi Nagashima—our grandfather—brought his family to America. Grandfather Nagashima was a minister of a Congregational church in Sanomachi, about twenty miles north of Tokyo in Tochigi-ken prefecture. He had visited the United States twice before on preaching missions among the Japanese. Grandfather had been impressed with the freedom and educational opportunities in America. He arrived in Seattle, with his wife, Yuki, three daughters, Yasuko, my mother Benko, and Kikue, twenty-two, seventeen and sixteen years of age respectively, and two little round-eyed sons, Shinichi and Yoshio, six and four years. . . .

Father heard of the Nagashimas' arrival. He immediately called to pay his respects. Seeing three marriageable daughters. Father kept going back. Eventually he sent a mutual friend to act as go-between to ask for the hand of the first daughter, Yasuko, but the friend reported that Mr. Nagashima had already arranged for Yasuko's marriage to a Mr. Tani. Undaunted, Father sent his friend back to ask for the second daughter, Benko. Mother said that when her father called her into his study and told her that a Mr. Itoi wanted to marry her, she was so shocked she fled to her room, dived under her bed and cried in protest. "I can't, Otoh-san, I can't. I don't even know him!"

Her father had got down on his hands and knees and peered at her under the bed, reprimanding her sternly. "Stop acting like a child, Benko. I advise you to start getting acquainted with Mr. Itoi at once."

---

[2] Tochigi-ken: Japan is divided into administrative districts known as prefectures. Tochigi is located north of Tokyo on the main island of Honshu. Most emigrants from Japan between 1890 and 1924 came from the southern Honshu prefectures of Hiroshima and Wakayama.

And that was that. Finally Mother gave her consent to the marriage, and the wedding ceremony was performed at the Japanese mission branch of the Methodist Episcopal Church on Fourteenth and Washington Street. Years later, when Henry and I came upon their wedding picture in our family album, we went into hysterics over Mother's face which had been plastered white and immobile with rice powder, according to Japanese fashion. . . .

In January, 1918, their first child was born. Henry Seiichi—son of truth. Shortly after, Father sold his little shop and bought the Carrollton Hotel on Main Street and Occidental Avenue, just a stone's throw from the bustling waterfront and the noisy railroad tracks. . . .

When Father took over the hotel in 1918, the building fairly burst with war workers and servicemen. They came at all hours of the day, begging to sleep even in the chairs in the lobby. Extra cots had to be set up in the hallways.

Father and Mother loved to tell us how they had practically rejuvenated the battered, flea-ridden Carrollton by themselves. Father had said firmly. "If I have to manage a flophouse, it'll be the cleanest and quietest place around here." With patience and care, they began to patch the aches and pains of the old hotel. The tobacco-stained stairways were scrubbed, painted and lighted up. Father varnished the floors while Mother painted the woodwork. New green runners were laid out in the corridors. They repapered the sixty rooms, one by one. Every day after the routine room-servicing had been finished. Mother cooked up a bucket of flour and water and brushed the paste on fresh new wallpaper laid out on a long makeshift work table in the hall. . . .

Shortly after the Armistice of World War I was signed, I was born and appropriately named Kazuko Monica, the Japanese name meaning "peace." (Mother chose Monica from her reading about Saint Augustine and his mother, Saint Monica.) Two years later Kenji William arrived, his name meaning "Healthy in body and spirit." Mother added "William" because she thought it sounded poetic. And two years after that, Sumiko, "the clear one," was born.

For our family quarters, Mother chose three outside rooms looking south on Main Street, across an old and graying five-story warehouse, and as the family increased, a fourth room was added. Father and Mother's small bedroom was crowded with a yellow brass bed that took up one wall. Mother's dainty white-painted dresser and a small square writing table piled with her books and papers occupied another wall. Father's brown dresser stood off in another corner, its only ornament a round, maroon-lacquered collar box. A treadle sewing machine squatted efficiently in front of the window where Mother sat in the evenings, mending torn sheets and pillowcases. Their closet was a pole slung against the fourth wall, covered with a green, floral-print curtain.

30 The living room was large, light and cheerful-looking, with a shiny mahogany-finished upright piano in one corner. Right above it hung a somber picture of Christ's face which looked down upon me each time I sat in front of the piano. Depending on my previous behavior, I felt restless and guilty under those brooding eyes or smugly content with myself. Against another wall, next to the piano, stood an elegant-looking, glass-cased secretary filled with Father's Japanese books, thick hotel account books, a set of untouched, glossy-paged encyclopedias, and the back numbers of the *National Geographic.* In the corner, near the window, was a small square table, displaying a monstrous, iridescent half of an abalone shell and a glass ball paperweight filled with water, depicting an underwater scene with tiny corals and sea shells lying on the ocean bottom. In front of the other two windows was a long, brown leather davenport with a small gas heater nearby. A round dining table in the center of the room was surrounded by three plain chairs. . . .

At first glance, there was little about these simple, sparse furnishings to indicate that a Japanese family occupied the rooms. But there were telltale signs like the *zori* or straw slippers placed neatly on the floor underneath the beds. On Mother's bed lay a beautiful red silk comforter patterned with turquoise, apple-green, yellow and purple Japanese parasols. And on the table beside the local daily paper were copies of the *North American Times.* Seattle's Japanese-community paper, its printing resembling rows of black multiple-legged insects. Then there was the Oriental abacus board which Father used once a month to keep his books.

Our kitchen was a separate room far down the hall. The kitchen window opened into an alley, right above the Ace Café. An outdoor icebox, born of an old apple crate, was nailed firmly to our kitchen window sill.

Father had put in a gas stove next to the small sink. The huge stove took up nearly all the floor space. He had nailed five layers of shelves against the opposite wall almost up to the ceiling, and next to this, he installed a towering china cabinet with delicate, frosted glass windows. A large, oblong table was wedged into the only space left, in a corner near the door. Here in the kitchen were unmistakable Oriental traces and odors. A glass tumbler holding six pairs of red and yellow lacquered chopsticks, and a bottle of soy sauce stood companionably among the imitation cut-glass sugar bowl and the green glass salt and pepper shakers at the end of the table. The tall china cabinet bulged with bright hand-painted rice bowls, red lacquered soup bowls, and Mother's precious *somayaki* tea set.

The tea set was stunningly beautiful with the uneven surface of the gray clay dusted with black and gold flecks. There was a wisp of soft green around the rim of the tiny cups, as if someone had plucked off grass from the clay and the green stain had remained there. At the bottom of each teacup was the figure of a galloping golden horse. When the cup was filled with tea, the golden horse seemed to rise to the surface and become animated. But the tea set was only for special occasions and holidays, and most of the time we used a set of dinner ware Americana purchased at the local hardware store and a drawerful of silver-plated tableware.

In the pantry, the sack of rice and gallon jug of *shoyu*[3] stood lined up next to the ivory-painted canisters of flour, sugar, tea and coffer. From a corner near the kitchen window, a peculiar, pungent odor emanated from a five-gallon crock which Mother kept filled with encumbers, *nappa* (Chinese cabbage) *daikon* (large Japanese radishes), immersed in a pickling mixture of *nuka,* consisting of rice polishings, salt, rice and raisins. The fermented products were sublimely refreshing, delicious, raw vegetables, a perfect side dish to a rice and tea mixture at the end of a meal.

Among the usual pots and pans stood a dark red stone mixing bowl inside of which were cut rows and rows of minute grooves as on a record disc. The bowl was used to grind poppy seeds and *miso* (soybeans) into soft paste for soups and for flavoring Japanese dishes. I spent many hours bent over this bowl, grinding the beans into a smooth, fine paste with a heavy wooden club. For all the work that went into making *miso shiru,* soybean soup, I thought it tasted like sawdust boiled in sea brine. Mother told me nothing could be more nutritious, but I could never take more than a few shuddering sips of it.

In our family we ate both Western and Oriental dishes. Mother had come to America just fresh out of high school and had had little training in Japanese culinary art. In the beginning, Father taught Mother to cook all the dishes he knew. Father had a robust, mass-cooking style which he had learned in the galleys of Alaska-bound ships and he leaned heavily toward ham and eggs, steak and potatoes, apple and pumpkin pies. Later Mother picked up the technique of authentic Japanese cooking herself and she even learned to cook superb Chinese dishes. Although we acquired tastes for different types of food, we adhered mostly to a simple American menu.

So we lived in the old Carrollton. Every day, amidst the bedlam created by four black-eyed, jet-propelled children, Father and Mother took care of the hotel. Every morning they went from room to room, making beds and cleaning up. To help speed up the chores, we ran up and down the corridors, pounding on doors. We brutally woke the late sleepers, hammering with our fists and yelling. "Wake up, you sleepy head! Wake up, make bed!" Then someone would think of pushing the linen cart for Father and the rest of us would rush to do the same. We usually ended up in a violent tussle. . . .

I thought the whole world consisted of two or three old hotels on every block. And that its population consisted of families like mine who lived in a corner of the hotels. And its other inhabitants were customers—fading, balding, watery-eyed men, rough-tough bearded men, and good men like Sam, Joe, Peter and Montana who worked for Father, all of whom lived in these hotels.

---

[3]*Shoyu:* soy sauce.

It was a very exciting world in which I lived. . . . And when I finally started grammar school, I found still another enchanting world. Every morning I hurried to Adams Hotel, climbed its dark flight of stairs, and called for Matsuko. Together we made the long and fascinating journey—from First Avenue to Twelfth Avenue—to Bailey Gatzert School. We always walked over the bridge on Fourth Avenue where we hung over the iron rails, waiting until a train roared past under us, enveloping us completely in its hissing, billowing cloud of white, warm steam. We meandered through the international section of town, past the small Japanese shops and stores, already bustling in the early morning hour, past the cafés and barber shops filled with Filipino men, and through Chinatown. Then finally we went up a gentle sloping hill to the handsome low-slung, red-brick building with its velvet green lawn and huge play yard. I felt like a princess walking through its bright, sunny corridors on smooth, shiny floors. I was mystified by a few of the little boys and girls. There were some pale-looking children who spoke a strange dialect of English, rapidly like gunfire. Matsuko told me they were *"hagu-jins,"* white people. Then there were children who looked very much like me with their black hair and black eyes, but they spoke in high, musical singing voices. Matsuko whispered to me that they were Chinese.

And now Mother was telling us we were Japanese. I had always thought I was a Yankee, because after all I had been born on Occidental and Main Street. Montana, a wall-shaking mountain of a man who lived at our hotel, called me a Yankee. I didn't see how I could be a Yankee and Japanese at the same time. It was like being born with two heads. It sounded freakish and a lot of trouble. Above everything. I didn't want to go to Japanese school.

The Stubborn Twig

The inevitable, dreaded first day at Nihon Gakko arrived. Henry and I were dumped into a taxicab, screaming and kicking against the injustice of it all. When the cab stopped in front of a large, square gray-frame building. Mother pried us loose, though we clung to the cab door like barnacles. She half carried us up the hill. We kept up our horrendous shrieking and wailing, right to the school entrance. Then a man burst out of the door. His face seemed to have been carved out of granite and with turned-down mouth and nostrils flaring with disapproval, his black marble eyes crushed us into a quivering silence. This was Mr. Ohashi, the school principal, who had come out to investigate the abominable, un-Japanesey noise on the school premises.

Mother bowed deeply and murmured, "I place them in your hands."

He bowed stiffly to Mother, then fastened his eyes on Henry and me and again bowed slowly and deliberately. In our haste to return the bow, we nodded our heads. With icy disdain, he snapped, "That is not an *ojigi.*" He bent forward with well-oiled precision. "Bow from the waist, like this."

45 I wondered, if Mr. Ohashi had the nerve to criticize us in front of Mother, what more would he do in her absence.

School was already in session and the hallway was empty and cold. Mr. Ohashi walked briskly ahead, opened a door, and Henry was whisked inside with Mother. I caught a glimpse of little boys and girls sitting erect, their books held upright on their desks. . . .

I was ushered into a brightly lighted room which seemed ten times as brilliant with the dazzling battery of shining black eyes turned in my direction. I was introduced to Yasuda-sensei, a full-faced woman with a large, ballooning figure. She wore a long, shapeless cotton print smock with streaks of chalk powder down the front. She spoke kindly to me, but with a kindness that one usually reserves for a dull-witted child. She enunciated slowly and loudly. "What is your name?"

I whispered, "Kazuko," hoping she would lower her voice. I felt that our conversation should not be carried on in such a blatant manner.

"Kazuko-san desuka?" she repeated loudly. "You may sit over there." She pointed to an empty seat in the rear and I walked down an endless aisle between rows of piercing black eyes.

50 "Kazuko-san, why don't you remove your hat and coat and hang them up behind you?"

A wave of tittering broke out. With burning face, I rose from my seat and struggled out of my coat.

When Mother followed Mr. Ohashi out of the room, my throat began to tighten and tears flooded up again. I did not notice that Yasuda-sensei was standing beside me. Ignoring my snuffling, she handed me a book, opened to the first page. I saw a blurred drawing of one huge, staring eye. Right above it was a black squiggly mark, resembling the arabic figure one with a bar across the middle. Yasuda-sensei was up in front again, reading aloud, *"Meh!"* That was "eye." As we turned the pages, there were pictures of a long, austere nose, its print reading *"hana,"* an ear was called *"mi-mi,"* and a wide anemic-looking mouth. *"ku-chi."* Soon I was chanting at the top of my voice with the rest of the class. *"Meh! Hana! Mi-Mi! Ku-chi!"*

Gradually I yielded to my double dose of schooling. Nihon Gakko was so different from grammar school I found myself switching my personality back and forth daily like a chameleon. At Bailey Gatzert School I was a jumping, screaming, roustabout Yankee, but at the stroke of three when the school bell range and doors burst open everywhere, spewing out pupils like jelly beans from a broken bag, I suddenly became a modest, faltering, earnest little Japanese girl with a small, timid voice. I trudged down a steep hill and climbed up another steep hill to Nihon Gakko with other black-haired boys and girls. On the playground, we behaved cautiously. Whenever we spied a teacher within bowing distance, we hissed at each other to stop the game, put our feet neatly together, slid our hands down to our knees and bowed slowly and sanctimoniously. In just the proper, moderate tone, putting in every ounce of respect, we chanted, *"Konichi-wa, sensei.* Good day."

For an hour and a half each day, we were put through our paces. At the beginning of each class hour, Yasuda-seusei punched a little bell on her desk; We stood up by our seats, at strict attention. Another "ping!" We all bowed to her in unison while she returned the bow solemnly. With the third "ping!" we sat down together.

55 There was *yomi-kata* time when individual students were called upon to read the day's lesson, clear and loud. The first time I recited I stood and read with swelling pride the lesson which I had prepared the night before. I mouthed each word carefully and paused for the proper length of time at the end of each sentence. Suddenly Yasuda-sensei stopped me.

"Kazuko-san!"

I look up at her confused, wondering what mistakes I had made.

"You are holding your book in one hand," she accused me. Indeed, I was. I did not see the need of using two hands to support a thin book I could balance with two fingers.

"Use both hands!" she commanded me.

60 Then she peered at me. "And are you leaning against your desk?" Yes, I was, slightly. "Stand up straight!"

"*Hai!* Yes, ma'am!". . .

As time went on, I began to suspect that there was much more to Nihon Gakko than learning the Japanese language. There was a driving spirit of strict discipline behind it all which reached out and weighed heavily upon each pupil's consciousness. That force emanated from the principal's office.

Before Mr. Ohashi came to America, he had been a zealous student of the Ogasawara Shiko Saho, a form of social conduct dreamed up by a Mr. Ogasawara. Mr. Ohashi himself had written a book on etiquette in Japan. He was the Oriental male counterpart of Emily Post. Thus Mr. Ohashi arrived in America with the perfect bow tucked under his waist and a facial expression cemented into perfect samurai control. He came with a smoldering ambition to pass on this knowledge to the tender Japanese saplings born on foreign soil. The school-teachers caught fire, too, and dedicated themselves to us with a vengeance. It was not enough to learn the language. We must talk and walk and sit and bow in the best Japanese tradition.

As far as I was concerned, Mr. Ohashi's superior standard boiled down to one thing. The model child is one with deep *rigor mortis*. . . no noise, no trouble, no back talk.

65 We understood too well what Mr. Ohashi wanted of us. He yearned and wished more than anything else that somehow he could mold all of us into Genji Yamadas. Genji was a classmate whom we detested thoroughly. He was born in Seattle, but his parents had sent him to Japan at an early age for a period of good, old-fashioned education. He returned home a stranger among us with stiff mannerisms and an arrogant attitude. . . .

. . .Every time Mr. Ohashi came into our room for a surprise visit to see if we were under control, he would stop at Genji's desk for a brief chat. Mr. Ohashi's eyes betrayed a glow of pride as he spoke to Genji, who sat up erect, eyes staring respectfully ahead. All we could make out of the conversation was Genji's sharp staccato barks, *"Hai! . . . Hai! . . . Hai!"*

This was the response sublime to Mr. Ohashi. It was real man to man talk. Whenever Mr. Ohashi approached us, we froze in our seats. Instead of snapping into attention like Genji, we wilted and sagged. Mr. Ohashi said we were more like *"konyaku,"* a colorless, gelatinous Japanese food. If a boy fidgeted too nervously under Mr. Ohashi's stare, a vivid red stain rose from the back of Mr. Ohashi's neck until it reached his temple and then there was a sharp explosion like the crack of a whip. *"Keo-tsuke!* Attention!" It made us all leap in our seats, each one of us feeling terribly guilty for being such an inadequate Japanese.

I asked Mother, "Why is Mr. Ohashi so angry all the time? He always looks as if he had just bitten into a green persimmon. I've never seen him smile."

Mother said, "I guess Mr. Ohashi is the old-fashioned schoolmaster. I know he's strict, but he means well. Your father and I received harsher discipline than that in Japan. . . not only from schoolteachers, but from our own parents."

70 "Yes, I know. Mama." I leaned against her knees as she sat on the old leather davenport, mending our clothes. I thought Father and Mother were still wonderful, even if they had packed me off to Nihon Gakko. "Mrs. Matsui is so strict with her children, too. She thinks you spoil us." I giggled, and reassured her quickly, "But I don't think you spoil us at all."

Mrs. Matsui was ten years older than Mother, and had known Mother's father in Japan. Therefore she felt it was her duty to look after Mother's progress in this foreign country. . . .

Mrs. Matsui thought Mother's relationship with her children was chaotic. She clucked sympathetically at Mother. "Do they still call you, 'Mama' and 'Papa'?"

"Oh, yes," Mother smiled to hide her annoyance. "You know how it is. That's all they've ever heard around here. In fact, my husband and I have been corrupted, too. We call each other 'Mama' and 'Papa.' It just seems natural in our environment."

Mrs. Matsui drew herself up stiffly. "I taught my young ones to say *'Otoh-san'* and *'Okoh-san'* from the very beginning."

75 "That's wonderful, Mrs. Matsui, but I'm afraid it's too late for us."

"Such a pity! You really ought to be more firm with them, too. Itoi-san. When I say 'no,' my children know I mean it. Whenever I feel they're getting out of hand, my husband and I take steps."

Mother looked interested.

"We give *'okyu'* quite often." Mrs. Matsui folded her hands neatly together. *Okyu* was an old-country method of discipline, a painful and lasting punishment of applying a burning punk on a child's bare back. "Believe me, after *okyu,* we don't have trouble for a long, long time."

Henry, Kenji, Sumiko and I eyed each other nervously. We wished Mrs. Matsui would stop talking about such things to Mother.

80 Mr. Ohashi and Mrs. Matsui thought they could work on me and gradually mold me into an ideal Japanese *ojoh-san,* a refined young maiden who is quiet, pure in thought, polite, serene, and self-controlled. They made little headway, for I was too much the child of Skidrow. As far as I was concerned, Nihon Gakko was a total loss. I could not use my Japanese on the people at the hotel. Bowing was practical only at Nihon Gakko. If I were to bow to the hotel patrons, they would have laughed in my face. Therefore promptly at five-thirty every day, I shed Nihon Gakko and returned with relief to an environment which was the only real one to me. Life was too urgent, too exciting, too colorful for me to be sitting quietly in the parlor and contemplating a spray of chrysanthemums in a bowl as a cousin of mine might be doing in Osaka. . . .

We Are Outcasts

A gray gloom settled down over our family. Sumiko was ill. Always during the winter she had asthmatic attacks, but this particular winter was the worst. The little black kitten, Asthma, which Mrs. Matsui had given her because, she said, black cats could cure asthma, mewed all day long and rubbed its back against the bed. Almost every day Dr. Moon climbed the long flight of stairs and walked through the hotel without a glance at our rough-looking hotel guests who stared rudely at him. . . .

That evening Dr. Stimson came. We stood, gray-lipped, quietly waiting to hear the verdict. Dr. Stimson's eyes twinkled as he told us that Sumiko did not have tuberculosis. We cried with relief as we hugged Sumiko, swathed in a heavy flannel nightgown and smelling of camphor oil. Like a thin little sparrow burrowed deep in its nest, Sumiko cocked her Dutch-bobbed head at us and spoke carefully so as not to wheeze or cough. "I'm glad I don't have to go on that vacation!"

Dr. Stimson said Sumiko must have plenty of milk, rest and sunshine. So Father and Mother decided to rent a cottage by the sea for the summer. Father said, "Yes, we must do it this summer. We'll start looking right away for a suitable place near Alki Beach."

Early one day, Mother and I set out to Alki to find a cottage near the beach where we always picnicked. We found a gray house with a FOR RENT sign on its window, just a block from the beach. One side of the house was quilted with wild rambler roses and the sprawling green lawn was trim behind a white-painted picket fence. When I pressed the doorbell, musical chimes rang softly through the house. A middle-aged woman wearing a stiffly starched apron opened the door. "Yes, what can I do for you?" she asked, looking us over.

85 Mother smiled and said in her halting English, "You have nice house. We like to rent this summer," Mother paused, but the woman said nothing. Mother went on, "How much do you want for month?"

The woman wiped her hands deliberately on her white apron before she spoke, "Well, I'm asking fifty dollars, but I'm afraid you're a little too late. I just promised this place to another party."

"Oh," Mother said, disappointed. "That's too bad. I'm sorry. We like it so much."

I swallowed hard and pointed to the sign on the window. "You still have the sign up. We thought the house was still open."

"I just rented it this morning. I forgot to remove it. Sorry, I can't do anything for you," she said sharply.

90 Mother smiled at her, "Thank you just the same. Good-by." As we walked away. Mother said comfortingly to me, "Maybe we'll find something even nicer, Ka-chan. We have a lot of looking to do yet."

But we scoured the neighborhood with no success. Every time it was the same story. Either the rent was too much or the house was already taken. We had even inquired at a beautiful new brick apartment facing the beach boulevard, where several VACANCY signs had been propped against empty windows, but the caretaker told us unsmilingly that these apartments were all taken.

That night I went to bed with burning feet. From my darkened bedroom, I heard Mother talking to Father in the living room. "Yes, there were some nice places, but I don't think they wanted to rent to Japanese."

I sat bolt upright. That had not occurred to me. Surely Mother was mistaken. Why would it make any difference? I knew that Father and Mother were not Americans, as we were, because they were not born here, and that there was a law which said they could not become naturalized American citizens because they were Orientals. But being Oriental had never been an urgent problem to us, living in Skidrow.

A few days later, we went to Alki again. This time I carried in my purse a list of houses and apartments for rent which I had cut out from the newspaper. My hands trembled with a nervousness which had nothing to do with the pure excitement of house-hunting. I wished that I had not overheard Mother's remark to Father.

95 We walked briskly up to a quaint, white Cape Cod house. The door had a shiny brass knocker in the shape of a leaping dolphin. A carefully marcelled, blue-eyed woman, wearing a pince-nez on her sharp nose, hurried out. The woman blinked nervously and tapped her finger on the wall as she listened to Mother's words. She said dryly, "I'm sorry, but we don't want Japs around here," and closed the door. My face stiffened. It was like a sharp, stinging slap. Blunt as it was, I had wanted to hear the truth to wipe out the doubt in my mind. Mother took my hand and led me quickly away, looking straight ahead of her. After a while, she said quietly, "Ka-chan, there are people like that in this world. We have to bear it, just like all the other unpleasant facts of life. This is the first time for you, and I know how deeply it hurts; but when you are older, it won't hurt quite as much. You'll be stronger."

Trying to stop the flow of tears, I swallowed hard and blurted out, "But, Mama, is it so terrible to be a Japanese?"

"Hush, child, you mustn't talk like that." Mother spoke slowly and earnestly. "I want you, Henry, and Sumi-chan to learn to respect yourselves. Not because you're white, black or yellow, but because you're a human being. Never forget that. No matter what anyone may call you, to God you are still his child. Mah, it's getting warm. I think we had better stop here and get some refreshment before we go on."

I wiped my eyes and blew my nose hastily before I followed Mother into a small drugstore. There I ordered a towering special de luxe banana split, and promptly felt better.

The rest of the day we plodded doggedly through the list without any luck. They all turned us down politely. On our way home, Mother sat silent, while I brooded in the corner of the seat. All day I had been torn apart between feeling defiant and then apologetic about my Japanese blood. But when I recalled the woman's stinging words, I felt raw angry fire flash through my veins, and I simmered.

100 We found Sumiko sitting up in bed, waiting for us with an expectant smile. Mother swung her up into the air and said gaily, "We didn't find a thing we liked today. The houses were either too big or too small or too far from the beach, but we'll find our summer home yet! It takes time." I set my teeth and wondered if I would ever learn to be as cheerful as Mother.

Later in the evening, Mr. Kato dropped in. Father told him that we were looking for a cottage out at Alki and that so far we had had no luck. Mr. Kato scratched his head, "Yahhh, it's too bad your wife went to all that trouble. That district has been restricted for years. They've never rented or sold houses to Orientals and I doubt if they ever will."

My face burned with shame. Mother and I had walked from house to house, practically asking to be rebuffed. Our foolish summer dream was over.

Somehow word got around among our friends that we were still looking for a place for the summer. One evening, a Mrs. Saito called on the phone. She lived at the Camden Apartments. She said, "My landlady, Mrs. Olsen, says there is a small apartment in our building for rent. She is a wonderful person and has been kind to us all in the apartments, and we're practically all Japanese. You'd like it here."

Mother said to me afterwards, "See, Ka-chan, I told you, there are all kinds of people. Here is a woman who doesn't object to Orientals."

105 The Camden Apartments was a modest, clean building in a quiet residential district uptown, quite far from Alki. . . .

The modest apartment on the top fourth floor was just large enough to accommodate Mother and Sumiko in the one bedroom while I occupied the sofa in the living room. Father and Henry, we decided, would stay at the hotel, but join us every evening for dinner. Marta assured us that by winter we would all be together in a larger apartment which would be vacated.

Of course, we were grateful for even this temporary arrangement, especially when we found the Olsens to be such warm, friendly folks. Marta and her husband were a middle-aged childless couple; but they apparently looked upon all the children living in the apartments as their own. . . .

That summer Sumiko and I pretended we were living in the turret of a castle tower. We made daily swimming trips to Lake Washington, surrounded by cool green trees and beautiful homes. But deep in our hearts we were still attached to Alki Beach. We kept comparing the mud-bottom lake and its mosquitoes to the sparkling salt water of Puget Sound, its clean, hot sands and its fiery sunsets. . . .

Pearl Harbor Echoes in Seattle

On a peaceful Sunday morning, December 7, 1941, Henry, Sumi and I were at choir rehearsal singing ourselves hoarse in preparation for the annual Christmas recital of Handel's "Messiah." Suddenly Chuck Mizuno, a young University of Washington student, burst into the chapel, gasping as if he had sprinted all the way up the stairs.

110 "Listen, everybody!" he shouted. "Japan just bombed Pearl Harbor. . . in Hawaii! It's war!". . .

A shocked silence followed. Henry came for Sumi and me. "Come on, let's go home," he said.

We ran trembling to our car. Usually Henry was a careful driver, but that morning he bore down savagely on the accelerator, Boiling angry, he shot us up Twelfth Avenue, rammed through the busy Jackson Street intersection, and rocketed up the Beacon Hill bridge. We swung violently around to the left of the Marine Hospital and swooped to the top of the hill. Then Henry slammed on the brakes and we rushed helter-skelter up to the house. . . .

Mother was sitting limp in the huge armchair as if she had collapsed there, listening dazedly to the turbulent radio. Her face was frozen still, and the only words she could utter were, "*Komatta neh, komatta neh.* How dreadful, how dreadful."

Henry put his arms around her. She told him she first heard about the attack on Pearl Harbor when one of her friends phoned her and told her to turn on the radio. . . .

115 Father rushed home from the hotel. He was deceptively calm as he joined us in the living room. Father was a born skeptic, and he believed nothing unless he could see, feel and smell it. He regarded all newspapers and radio news with deep suspicion. He shook his head doubtfully, "It must be propaganda. With the way things are going now between America and Japan, we should expect the most fantastic rumors, and this is one of the wildest I've heard yet." But we noticed that he was firmly glued to the radio. It seemed as if the regular Sunday programs, sounding off relentlessly hour after hour on schedule, were trying to blunt the catastrophe of the morning. . . .

Late that night Father got a shortwave broadcast from Japan. Static sputtered, then we caught a faint voice, speaking rapidly in Japanese. Father sat unmoving as a rock, his head cocked. The man was talking about the war between Japan and America. Father bit his lips and Mother whispered to him anxiously, "It's true then, isn't it, Papa? It's true?"

Father was muttering to himself, "So they really did it!" Now having heard the news in their native tongue, the war had become a reality to Father and Mother. . . .

Next morning the newspapers fairly exploded in our faces with stories about the Japanese raids on the chain of Pacific islands. We were shocked to read Attorney General Biddle's announcement that 736 Japanese had been picked up in the United States and Hawaii.[4] Then Mrs. Tanabe called Mother about her husband's arrest, and she said at least a hundred others had been taken from our community. Messrs. Okayama, Higashi, Sughira, Mori, Okada—we knew them all.

"But why were they arrested, Papa? They weren't spies, were they?"

Father replied almost curtly. "Of course not! They were probably taken for questioning."

The pressure of war moved in on our little community. The Chinese consul announced that all the Chinese would carry identification cards and wear "China" badges to distinguish them from the Japanese. Then I really felt left standing out in the cold. The government ordered the bank funds of all Japanese nationals frozen. Father could no longer handle financial transactions through his bank accounts, but Henry, fortunately, was of legal age so that business could be negotiated in his name. . . .

It made me positively hivey the way the FBI agents continued their raids into Japanese homes and business places and marched the Issei men away into the old red brick immigration building, systematically and efficiently, as if they were stocking a cellarful of choice bottles of wine. At first we noted that the men arrested were those who had been prominent in community affairs, like Mr. Kato, many times president of the Seattle Japanese Chamber of Commerce, and Mr. Ohashi, the principal of our Japanese language school, or individuals whose business was directly connected with firms in Japan; but as time went on, it became less and less apparent why the others were included in these raids.

We wondered when Father's time would come. We expected momentarily to hear strange footsteps on the porch and the sudden demanding ring of the front doorbell. Our ears became attuned like the sensitive antennas of moths, translating every soft swish of passing cars into the arrival of the FBI squad.

---

[4] In all, the FBI arrested and detained about 1,500 Japanese as "enemy aliens" in the aftermath of Pearl Harbor. See Roger Daniels. *Concentration Camps USA: Japanese Americans and World War II* (Hinsdale, Ill.: Dryden Press, 1971), p. 34.

. . .Mrs. Matsui became an expert on the FBI, and she stood by us, rallying and coaching us on how to deal with them. She said to Mother, "You must destroy everything and anything Japanese which may incriminate your husband. It doesn't matter what it is, if it's printed or made in Japan, destroy it because the FBI always carries off those items for evidence."

In fact all the women whose husbands had been spirited away said the same thing. Gradually we became uncomfortable with our Japanese books, magazines, wall scrolls, and knickknacks. When Father's hotel friends, Messrs. Sakaguchi, Horiuchi, Nishibue and a few others vanished, and their wives called Mother weeping and warning her again about having too many Japanese objects around the house, we finally decided to get rid of some of ours. We knew it was impossible to destroy everything. The FBI would certainly think it strange if they found us sitting in a bare house, totally purged of things Japanese. But it was as if we could no longer stand the tension of waiting, and we just had to do something against the black day. We worked all night, feverishly combing through bookshelves, closets, drawers, and furtively creeping down to the basement furnace for the burning. I gathered together my well-worn Japanese language schoolbooks which I had been saving over a period of ten years with the thought that they might come in handy when I wanted to teach Japanese to my own children. I threw them into the fire and watched them flame and shrivel into black ashes. But when I came face to face with my Japanese doll which Grandmother Nagashima had sent me from Japan, I rebelled. It was a gorgeously costumed Miyazukai figure, typical of the lady in waiting who lived in the royal palace during the feudal era. The doll was gowned in an elegant purple silk kimono with the long, sweeping hemline of its period and sashed with rich-embroidered gold and silver brocade. With its black, shining coiffed head bent a little to one side, its delicate pink-tipped ivory hand holding a red lacquer message box, the doll had an appealing, almost human charm. I decided to ask Chris if she would keep it for me. Chris loved and appreciated beauty in every form and shape, and I knew that in her hands, the doll would be safe and enjoyed.

Henry pulled down from his bedroom wall the toy samurai sword he had brought from Japan and tossed it into the flames. Sumi's contributions to the furnace were books of fairy tales and magazines sent to her by her young cousins in Japan. We sorted out Japanese classic and popular music from a stack of records, shattered them over our knees and fed the pieces to the furnace. Father piled up his translated Japanese volumes of philosophy and religion and carted them reluctantly to the basement. Mother had the most to eliminate, with her scrapbooks of poems cut out from newspapers and magazines, and her private collection of old Japanese classic literature.

It was past midnight when we finally climbed upstairs to bed. Wearily we closed our eyes, filled with an indescribable sense of guilt for having destroyed the things we loved. This night of ravage was to haunt us for years. As I lay struggling to fall asleep, I realized that we hadn't freed ourselves at all from fear. We still lay stiff in our beds, waiting. . . .

Then a new menace appeared on the scene. Cries began to sound up and down the coast that everyone of Japanese ancestry should be taken into custody. For years the professional guardians of the Golden West had wanted to rid their land of the Yellow Peril, and the war provided an opportunity for them to push their program through. As the chain of Pacific islands fell to the Japanese, patriots shrieked for protection from us. A Californian sounded the alarm: "The Japanese are dangerous and they must leave. Remember the destruction and the sabotage perpetrated at Pearl Harbor. Notice how they have infiltrated into the harbor towns and taken our best land."...

In February, Executive Order No. 9066 came out, authorizing the War Department to remove the Japanese from such military areas as it saw fit, aliens and citizens alike. Even if a person had a fraction of Japanese blood in him, he must leave on demand.

A pall of gloom settled upon our home. We couldn't believe that the government meant that the Japanese-Americans must go, too. We had heard the clamoring of superpatriots who insisted loudly, "Throw the whole kaboodle out. A Jap's a Jap, no matter how you slice him. You can't make an American out of little Jap Junior just by handing him an American birth certificate." But we had dismissed these remarks as just hot blasts of air from an overheated patriot. We were quite sure that our rights as American citizens would not be violated, and we would not be marched out of our homes on the same basis as enemy aliens.

In anger, Henry and I read and reread the Executive Order. Henry crumpled the newspaper in his hand and threw it against the wall. "Doesn't my citizenship mean a single blessed thing to anyone? Why doesn't somebody make up my mind for me. First they want me in the army. Now they're going to slap an alien 4-C on me because of my ancestry. What the hell!"[5]

Once more I felt like a despised, pathetic two-headed freak, a Japanese and an American, neither of which seemed to be doing me any good....

Life in Camp Harmony

General DeWitt kept reminding us that E day, evacuation day, was drawing near. "E day will be announced in the very near future. If you have not wound up your affairs by now, it will soon be too late."

Father negotiated with Bentley Agent and Company to hire some one to manage his business. Years ago Father had signed a long-term lease with the owner of the building and the agent had no other alternative than to let Father keep control of his business until his time ran out. He was one of the fortunate few who would keep their businesses intact for the duration.

---

[5] Henry is referring to a nondraftable classification with the U.S. Selective Service here. Eventually Japanese American young men (native-born who were American citizens) were permitted to volunteer for an all-Japanese-American combat unit that fought in Europe. Later the draft was extended to Japanese Americans. Daniels. *Concentration Camps USA*, pp. 123–29.

135 And Mother collected crates and cartons. She stayed up night after night, sorting, and re-sorting a lifetime's accumulation of garments, toys and household goods. Those were pleasant evenings when we rummaged around in old trunks and suitcases, reminiscing about the good old days, and almost forgetting why we were knee-deep in them. . . .

Henry went to the Control Station to register the family. He came home with twenty tags, all numbered "10710," tags to be attached to each piece of baggage, and one to hang from our coat lapels. From then on, we were known as Family #10710. . . .

The front doorbell rang. It was Dunks Oshima, who had offered to take us down to Eighth and Lane in a borrowed pickup truck. Hurriedly the menfolk loaded the truck with the last few boxes of house hold goods which Dunks was going to take down to the hotel. He held up a gallon can of soy sauce, puzzled, "Where does this go, to the hotel, too?"

Nobody seemed to know where it had come from or where it was going, until Mother finally spoke up guiltily. "Er, it's going with me. I didn't think we'd have shoyu where we're going."

Henry looked as if he were going to explode. "But Mama, you're not supposed to have more than one seabag and two suitcases. And of all things, you want to take with you—shoyu!"

140 I felt mortified. "Mama, people will laugh at us. We're not going on a picnic!"

But Mother stood her ground. "Nonsense. No one will ever notice this little thing. It isn't as if I were bringing liquor!". . .

We climbed into the truck, chattering about the plucky little swallow. As we coasted down Beacon Hill bridge for the last time, we fell silent, and stared out at the delicately flushed morning sky of Puget Sound. We drove through bustling Chinatown, and in a few minutes arrived on the corner of Eighth and Lane. This area was ordinarily lonely and deserted but now it was gradually filling up with silent, labeled Japanese, standing self-consciously among their seabags and suitcases. . . .

Newspaper photographers with flash-bulb cameras pushed busily through the crowd. One of them rushed up to our bus, and asked a young couple and their little boy to step out and stand by the door for a shot. They were reluctant, but the photographers were persistent and at length they got out of the bus and posed, grinning widely to cover their embarrassment. We saw the picture in the newspaper shortly after and the caption underneath it read, "Japs good-natured about evacuation."

Our bus quickly filled to capacity. All eyes were fixed up front, waiting. The guard stepped inside, sat by the door, and nodded curtly to the gray-uniformed bus driver. The door closed with a low hiss. We were now the Wartime Civil Control Administration's babies.[6]. . .

---

[6] This was the agency formed within the army to handle evacuation and resettlement of West Coast Japanese and Japanese Americans.

145 About noon we crept into a small town. Someone said, "Looks like Puyallup, all right."[7] Parents of small children babbled excitedly, "Stand up quickly and look over there. See all the chick-chicks and fat little piggies?" One little city boy stared hard at the hogs and said tersely, "They're *bachi*—dirty!"

Our bus idled a moment at the traffic signal and we noticed at the left of us an entire block filled with neat rows of low shacks, resembling chicken houses. Someone commented on it with awe, "Just look at those chicken houses. They sure go in for poultry in a big way here." Slowly the bus made a left turn, drove through a wire-fenced gate, and to our dismay, we were inside the oversized chicken farm. The bus driver opened the door; the guard stepped out and stationed himself at the door again. Jim, the young man who had shepherded us into the buses, popped his head inside and sang out, "Okay, folks, all off at Yokohama, Puyallup."

We stumbled out, stunned, dragging our bundles after us. It must have rained hard the night before in Puyallup, for we sank ankle deep into gray, gluttinous mud. The receptionist, a white man, instructed us courteously, "Now, folks, please stay together as family units and line up. You'll be assigned your apartment."

We were standing in Area A, the mammoth parking lot of the state fairgrounds. There were three other separate areas, B, C and D, all built on the fair grounds proper, near the baseball field and the race tracks. This camp of army barracks was hopefully called Camp Harmony.

We were assigned to apartment 2-1-A, right across from the bachelor quarters. The apartments resembled elongated, low stables about two blocks long. Our home was one room, about 18 by 20 feet, the size of a living room. There was one small window in the wall opposite the one door. It was bare except for a small, tiny wood-burning stove crouching in the center. The flooring consisted of two by fours laid directly on the earth, and dandelions were already pushing their way up through the cracks. Mother was delighted when she saw their shaggy yellow heads. "Don't anyone pick them. I'm going to cultivate them.". . .

150 Mother and Father wandered out to see what the other folks were doing and they found people wandering in the mud, wondering what other folks were doing. Mother returned shortly, her face lit up in an ecstatic smile, "We're in luck. The latrine is right nearby. We won't have to walk blocks."

We laughed, marveling at Mother who could be so poetic and yet so practical. Father came back, bent double like a woodcutter in a fairy tale, with stacks of scrap lumber over his shoulder. His coat and trouser pockets bulged with nails. Father dumped his loot in a corner and explained.

---

[7] Puyallup was one of a number of West Coast assembly centers established at former fairgrounds or race tracks to accommodate Japanese and Japanese Americans until more permanent inland facilities were constructed. For a detailed description of another family's experience at a similar assembly center, see John Modell, ed., *The Kikuchi Diary: Chronicle from an American Concentration Camp* (Urbana: University of Illinois Press, 1973).

"There was a pile of wood left by the carpenters and hundreds of nails scattered loose. Everybody was picking them up, and I hustled right in with them. Now maybe we can live in style with tables and chairs.". . .

We felt fortunate to be assigned to a room at the end of the barracks because we had just one neighbor to worry about. The partition wall separating the rooms was only seven feet high with an opening of four feet at the top, so at night. Mrs. Funai next door could tell when Sumi was still sitting up in bed in the dark, putting her hair up. *"Mah, Sumi-chan,"* Mrs. Funai would say through the plank wall, "are you curling your hair tonight again? Do you put it up every night?" Sumi would put her hands on her hips and glare defiantly at the wall. . . .

All through the night I heard people getting up, dragging cots around. I stared at our little window, unable to sleep. I was glad Mother had put up a makeshift curtain on the window for I noticed a powerful beam of light sweeping across it every few seconds. The lights came from high towers placed around the camp where guards with Tommy guns kept a twenty-four hour vigil. I remembered the wire fence encircling us, and a knot of anger tightened in my breast. What was I doing behind a fence like a criminal? If there were accusations to be made, why hadn't I been given a fair trial? Maybe I wasn't considered an American anymore. My citizenship wasn't real, after all. Then what was I? I was certainly not a citizen of Japan as my parents were. On second thought, even Father and Mother were more alien residents of the United States than Japanese nationals for they had little tie with their mother country. In their twenty-five years in America, they had worked and paid their taxes to their adopted government as any other citizen.

Of one thing I was sure. The wire fence was real. I no longer had the right to walk out of it. It was because I had Japanese ancestors. It was also because some people had little faith in the ideas and ideals of democracy. They said that after all these were but words and could not possibly insure loyalty. New laws and camps were surer devices. I finally buried my face in my pillow to wipe out burning thoughts and snatch what sleep I could.

Mapping the Text

1. In her autobiography, Sone brings to light differences between the Issei generation and the Nisei generation in Japanese culture. What are some of these differences? In what ways were differences evident during the Japanese internment?
2. This selection is a narrative told in the first person, using the pronoun "I." What is the effect created by this choice, as compared, for example, with the same story being told in the third person, using the pronouns, "she," "he," or "they"?
3. Reread the final paragraph in the this story. In this paragraph, Sone says, "some people had little faith in the ideas and ideals of democracy." What in her story suggests that this point of view is a possibility?

Writing to Inquire

1. Choose a scene from Sone's story that stands out for you in some way, perhaps as one that is interesting, or provocative, or disturbing, etc. Write an essay in which you identify the passage and explain your response to it.

Migrations

ABENA BUSIA

Abena Busia is an associate professor of English at Rutgers University. A poet, literary critic, and former president of the African Literature Association, Busia was born in Accra, Ghana, and spent her childhood years in Ghana, Holland, and Mexico before her family settled in Oxford, England. Her work has appeared in multiple journals and anthologies, and she is author of a collection of poems, *Testimonies of Exile* (1990), from which the poem below is taken.

for homi, because I changed his words—

We have lived that moment of the scattering of the people—
    Immigrant, Migrant, Emigrant, Exile,
    Where do the birds gather?
That in other nations, other lives, other places has become:

The gathering of last warriors on lost frontiers,
The gathering of lost refugees on lasting border-camps,
The gathering of the indentured on the side-walks of strange cities,
The gathering of émigrés on the margins of foreign cultures.

    Immigrate, Migrate, Emigrate, Exile,
    Where do the birds fly?

In the half-life, half-light of alien tongues,
In the uncanny fluency of the other's language,
We relive the past in rituals of revival,
Unravelling memories in slow time; gathering the present.

    Immigrant, Migrant, Emigrant, Exile,
        After the last sky, Where do the birds fly?

Mapping the Text

1. Using the evidence of lines in Busia's poem, draw inferences about her attitudes toward migration and immigration.
2. When people immigrate and migrate, they take some things with them and leave others behind. Identify specific legacies you feel are important

for people to take with them and legacies that might better be left behind. How might this process of leaving and taking be similar to what Busia refers to when she says, "Unravelling memories in slow time; gathering the present"?

Writing to Inquire

1. Abena Busia immigrated to the United States from Africa in the twentieth century; she is not the descendant of Africans who were enslaved in the United States between the seventeenth and mid-nineteenth centuries. Search library sources for information on twentieth-century immigration from Africa. Were there peaks during the twentieth century in African immigration? From which countries did the immigrants come? What conditions and circumstances brought them to the United States? Was there a pattern to their settlement?
2. Busia speaks in "Migrations" about "the scattering of the people." One term for such a scattering is *diaspora.* It can be applied to several cultural groups, including people of African descent. Choose a group for which the term is meaningful and define it in the context of their immigration and/or migration experiences.

Melting into Canaan

SAMANTHA DUNAWAY

Samantha Dunaway (1971–) teaches at Nome-Beltz High School in Alaska. When she is not teaching or studying, she writes. She has published poems in various small magazines, including the *Louisville Review, Blue Violin, Frogpond, and English Journal.* Her favorite poet is Emily Dickinson. She wrote the poem below in tribute to her grandmother.

Grandmother Lena,
first born in the new land,
you hated Germans
with the zeal of any other American
during the Great War,
even your parents, yourself.
Assimilated, Americanized,
you became a new woman,
with a new name, new faith, new language,
shedding your past like a used skin,
never looking back.
Still, they hated you—
immigrant daughter—

throwing schoolyard insults
(Dirty Kraut) like rocks.
But you, too proud
to cry over words,
even those that cut,
saved them, instead,
to hurl them at others.
The promises
your father followed eluded him,
but you won the American dream:
a house and garden,
children,
a husband
with a soft voice and touch,
and an American name,
generations old.

I, the daughter of your daughter's daughter,
I am so American
that I don't remember
when we were
Dutch
German
English
Irish
Scots.
I check "white"
on colorless government forms and go on,
with only a muted sense of loss.
My ancestry is only a list of countries
and no one among your grandchildren knows
the color of the sky
or the smell of the sea
on the shores of our origins.
We were the best kind of immigrants—
the kind America loves—
whose pale skin melts/blends into the neutral background
in only a few generations,
whose round eyes only see what is shown—
who gave up what we used to be,
pretending (pretending) to be something else
until we believed/became our lies.

I am still immigrating.
So many years after you forgot/denied your home,

I am leaving one shore for another,
looking for my inevitable place:
the one where the air smells familiar
and the rain sinks into my skin
and nourishes my bones.
But this, too, is not my shore,
though its rains have soaked me through.
Hundreds of years before my mothers and fathers
stepped onto the ships that brought them
to the new land, this Greatland—this Alaska—fed
the hungry of cultures too old
to remember another land.
Now, this land belongs to no one,
and no one belongs to it.

Maybe I should go back instead of forward,
east instead of west,
back to a nameless village
on an unknown shore,
where a grandmother I do not remember knowing
said yes to a boy she could barely remember loving
when he raised his bright eyes and asked her
to come with him to the new land (milk and honey)—she
who kept a handful of sand
until the shore of her birth disappeared
into the fog closing behind them,
only then letting the grains scatter to the winds.
Another grandmother talks of the way
she used to sit, smelling the palms of her hands,
eyes closed to enjoy a forgotten breeze.
But she never spoke of home
except as the land before
    before I knew your grandfather
    before you were born
    before we lived here.

But we are American now,
Grandmother Lena,
and have learned to speak like Americans,
soft sounds for an easy life,
to eat like Americans,
identical meals in wrapping paper,
like gifts,
to sing like Americans,
songs of youth in English

played on drums and electric guitars,
words that glide into one another
with the lazy mumble of youth,
to believe like Americans,
faith in government over god,
in self over others—
our young country, so young
it thinks history is for the old,
that the present is all that matters,
where you are going
ouweighs where you have been,
and tomorrow is more significant than yesterday.

Mapping the Text

1. Samantha Dunaway's poem speaks to the idea of memory and how it might be passed from generation to generation. What does Dunaway indicate is being passed along and not passed along in her own family? How does she take the reader from her Grandmother Lena and her grandmother's parents to her mother to herself? What thread(s) does she weave between them? What does this strategy help her convey about immigration?
2. Reread Dunaway's second stanza. What does Dunaway indicate that being white means to her? To what extent do you think Dunaway's attitude toward whiteness is typical?
3. Discuss how the remainder of Dunaway's poem speaks to migration and immigration as an ongoing phenomenon. What issues does she raise? How does she address them? What message do you think she seeks to convey?

Writing to Inquire

1. Think about your own mobility or immobility throughout your life. Write a narrative in which you tell the story of a move you made, whether it was across the street, across town, to another state, or around the world. What happened? What was most difficult about the process? What was easiest? What had the most lasting effect on you? Or, if you have not moved around much, write a narrative in which you tell a story about being in or from the same place your family has lived for many generations and what that means to you. What does it mean not to move? What is most positive? What may not be so positive? Would you have preferred that anything about your family's staying or leaving had been different?

The Melting Pot

DUDLEY RANDALL

Dudley Randall (1914–2000) built a professional career as a reference librarian while creating a distinctive record as a creative writer, editor, and publisher. His poems and other writings have been published in journals and literary magazines; his poems are frequently anthologized. His collections include *Ballad of Birmingham* (1963); *Dressed All in Pink* (1965); *Cities Burning* (1968); *Green Apples* (1972); *Broadside Memories: Poets I Have Known* (1975); *A Litany of Friends: New and Selected Poems* (1981); and *For Vivian* (1983). One of Randall's most striking achievements, however, is as an editor and publisher. In 1965, he created the Broadside Press in Detroit, Michigan, in order to publish his own poetry and to produce reasonably priced, high-quality broadsides and books. This press, which he sold in 1985, was a critical outlet for African-American writers during the Black Arts Movement, and Randall is often credited with being "the father of the Black poetry movement" of this era. In addition to publishing individual collections, he also edited several volumes, including *For Malcolm: Poems on the Life and Death of Malcolm X* (1967, with Margaret Burroughs); *Black Poetry: A Supplement to Anthologies Which Exclude Black Poets* (1969); *Homage to Hoyt Fuller* (1984); *and Selected Poems* (1981).

The Melting Pot

There is a magic melting pot
where any girl or man
can step in Czech or Greek or Scot,
step out American.

Johann and Jan and Jean and Juan,
Giovanni and Ivan
step in and then step out again
all freshly christened John.

Sam, watching, said, "Why, I was here
even before they came,"
and stepped in too, but was tossed out
before he passed the brim.

And every time Sam tried that pot
they threw him out again.

"Keep out. This is our private pot
We don't want your black stain."

At last, thrown out a thousand times,
Sam said, "I don't give a damn.
Shove your old pot. You can like it or not,
but I'll be just what I am."

Mapping the Text

1. Think about the character Sam in Randall's poem. What impression of Sam do you get? What words and phrases in the poem help convey this impression?
2. Randall's poem suggests longstanding tensions between the ideal of America and its realities. Consider the contemporary scene. To what extent is there evidence that such tensions still exist?

Writing to Inquire

1. As Randall suggests in the first stanza of his poem, one view of the heritage of Americans is having the opportunity not only to move about freely in geographical space, in terms of migration and immigration, but also through identities, in being able to make themselves anew, to have another chance to be better or different. Write a short essay in which you discuss how Randall uses this view to make a contrasting point. What is his message?
2. In the world today, migration and immigration—that is, moving from one place to another—is not at all unusual. In fact, the distance between where a person is born and where he or she ends up living can be considerable. How is contemporary migration or immigration still like or unlike such movements in earlier times?

Overland Diary, 1847

ELIZABETH SMITH DIXON GEER

Elizabeth Smith Dixon Geer, who made the trip to Oregon between 1847 and 1850, kept a diary from which the entry below comes. Because of women like Geer who recorded their day-to-day experiences, we now have a clearer sense of what the migration West was like for women.

JAN. 31.—Rain all day. If I could tell you how we suffer you would not believe it. Our house, or rather a shed joined to a house, leaks all over. The roof descends in such a manner as to make the rain run right down into the fire. I have dipped as much as six pails of water off of our dirt hearth in one night. Here I sit up, night after night, with my poor sick husband, all alone, and expecting him every day to die. I neglected to tell you that Welch and all the rest moved off and left us. Mr. Smith has not been moved off his bed for six weeks only by lifting him by each corner of the sheet, and I had hard work to get help enough for that, let alone getting watchers. I have not undressed to lie down for six weeks. Besides all our sickness, I had a cross little babe to take care of. Indeed, I cannot tell you half.

Feb. 1.—Rain all day. This day my dear husband, my last remaining friend, died.

Feb. 2.—Today we buried my earthly companion. Now I know what none but widows know; that is, how comfortless is that of a widow's life, especially when left in a strange land, without money or friends, and the care of seven children. Cloudy.

Feb. 3.—Clear and warm.

Feb. 4.—Clear and warm.

Feb. 5.—Clear and warm.

Feb. 6.—Clear and cool.

Feb. 7.—Clear and warm.

Feb. 8.—Cloudy. Some rain.

Feb. 9.—Clear and cool. Perhaps you will want to know how cool. I will tell you. We have lived all winter in a shed constructed by setting up studs 5 feet high on the lowest side. The other side joins a cabin. It is boarded up with clapboards and several of them are torn off in places, and there is no shutter to our door, and if it was not for the rain putting out our fire and leaking down all over the house, we would be comfortable.

Feb. 10.—Clear and warm.

Feb. 11.—Clear and warm.

Feb. 12.—Cool and cloudy.

Feb. 13.—Rainy.

Feb. 14.—Cloudy. Rain in the afternoon.

Feb. 15.—Cool. Rain all day.

Feb. 16.—Rain and snow all day.

Feb. 17.—Rain all day.

Feb. 18.—Rain all day.

Feb. 19.—Rain all day.

Feb. 20.—Rain and hail all day.

Feb. 21.—Clear and cool. You will think it strange that we do not leave this starved place. The reason is this—the road from here to the country is impassable in the winter, the distance being 12 miles, and because our cattle are yet very weak.

Feb. 22.—Clear and cool.

Feb. 23.—Clear and cool.

Feb. 24.—Clear and warm. Today we left Portland at sunrise. Having no one to assist us, we had to leave one wagon and part of our things for the want of teams. We traveled 4 or 5 miles, all the way up hill and through the thickest woods I ever saw—all fir from 2 to 6 feet through, with now and then a scattering cedar, and an intolerably bad road. We all had to walk. Sometimes I had to place my babe on the ground and help to keep the wagon from turning over. When we got to the top of the mountain we descended through mud up to the wagon hubs and over logs two feet through, and log bridges torn to pieces in the mud. Sometimes I would be behind out of sight of the wagons, carrying and tugging my little ones along. Sometimes the boys would stop the teams and come back after us. Made 9 miles. Encamped in thick woods. Found some grass. Unhitched the oxen; let them feed two hours, then chained them to trees. These woods are infested with wild cats, panthers, bears and wolves. A man told me that he had killed 7 tigers; but they are a species of wolves. We made us a fire and made a bed down on the wet ground, and laid down as happy as circumstances would admit. Glad to think we had escaped from Portland—such a game place.

Butteville, Oregon Ty., Yamhill County, Sept. 2, 1850.

Dear and Estimable Friends, Mrs. Paulina Foster and Mrs. Cynthia Ames:

I promised when I saw you last to write to you when I got to Oregon, and I done it faithfully, but as I never have received an answer, I do not know whether you got my letter and diary or not, consequently I do not know what to write now. I wrote four sheets full and sent it to you, but now I have not time to write. I write now to know whether you got my letter; and I will try to state a few things again. My husband was taken sick before we got to any settlement, and never was able to walk afterwards. He died at Portland, on the Willamette River, after an illness of two months. I will not attempt to describe my troubles since I saw you. Suffice it to say that I was left a widow with the care of seven children in a foreign land, without one solitary friend, as one might say, in the land of the living; but this time I will only endeavor to hold up the bright side of the picture. I lived a widow one year and four months. My three boys started for the gold mines, and it was doubtful to me whether I ever saw them again. Perhaps you will think it strange that I let such young boys go; but I was willing and helped them off in as good style as I could. They packed through by land. Russell Welch went by water. The boys never saw Russell in the mines. Well, after the boys were gone, it is true I had plenty of cows and hogs and plenty of wheat to feed them on and to make my bread. Indeed, I was well off if I had only known it; but I lived in a remote place where my strength was of little use to me. I could get nothing to do, and you know I could not live without work. I employed myself in teaching my children: yet that did not fully occupy my mind. I became as poor as a snake, yet I was in good health, and never was so nimble since I was a child. I could run a half a mile without stopping to breathe. Well, I thought perhaps I had better try my fortune again; so on the 24th of June, 1849, I was married to a Mr. Joseph Geer, a man 14 years older than myself, though young enough for me. He is the father of ten children. They are all married, but two boys and two girls. He is a Yankee from Connecticut and he is a Yankee in every sense of the word, as I told you he would be if it ever proved my lot to marry again. I did not marry rich, but my husband is very industrious, and is as kind to me as I can ask. Indeed, he sometimes provokes me for trying to humor me so much. He is a stout, healthy man for one of his age.

The boys made out poorly at the mines. They started in April and returned in September, I think. They were sick part of the time and happened to be in poor diggings all the while. They only got home with two hundred dollars apiece. They suffered very much while they were gone. When they came home they had less than when they started. Perley did not get there. He started with a man in partnership. The man was to provide for and bring him back, and he was to give the man half he dug; but when they got as far as the Umpqua River, they heard it was so very sickly there that the man turned back; but Perley would not come back. There were two white men keeping ferry on the Umpqua, so Perley stayed with them all summer and in the fall he rigged out on his own hook and started again; but on his way he met his brothers coming home, and they advised him for his life not to go, and so he came back with them.

At this time we are all well but Perley. I cannot answer for him; he has gone to the Umpqua for some money due him. The other two are working for four dollars a day. The two oldest boys have got three town lots in quite a stirring place called Lafayette in Yamhill County. Perley has four horses. A good Indian horse is worth one hundred dollars. A good American cow is worth sixty dollars. My boys live about 25 miles from me, so that I cannot act in the capacity of a mother to them; so you will guess it is not all sunshine with me, for you know my boys are not old enough to do without a mother. Russell Welch done very well in the mines. He made about twenty hundred dollars. He lives 30 miles below me in a little town called Portland on the Willamette River. Sarah has got her third son. It has been one year since I saw her. Adam Polk's two youngest boys live about wherever they see fit. The oldest, if he is alive, is in California. There is some ague in this country this season, but neither I nor my children, except those that went to California, have had a day's sickness since we came to Oregon.

I believe I will say no more until I hear from you. Write as soon as possible and tell me everything. My husband will close this epistle.

ELIZABETH GEER.

Mapping the Text

1. Elizabeth Smith Dixon Geer traveled overland in 1847 to what is now the northwest of the United States, to Oregon. She was one among numbers of people who chose to make this arduous trek. What was the pull to go West? What did the travelers hope to find? What does Geer's selection suggest that some of them found?
2. In reviewing Geer's account of her life during this migration, are there details that make it a woman's tale?

Writing to Inquire

1. Both Geer's diary entries and her letters named their audience, her two friends back home. How is such a specific audience revealed in the selections? Choose another form of expression (a story, a poem, an essay, a play) and rewrite Geer's story for a different audience and purpose.
2. Having read both the diary entries and the letters, what impression of Geer do you have? Develop a profile of her based on the details that you draw from the selections.

Letter to Her Daughter

MARY JANE MEGQUIER

Mary Jane Megquier (1813–1899) and her husband, a physician, left their children with relatives in Maine in 1849 to migrate to San Francisco during the days of the gold rush. They traveled by ship down the Atlantic Coast to Panama, where, according to Lillian Schlissel and Catherine Lavender (*The Western Women's Reader* [New York: Harper Perennial, 2000]), they crossed the isthmus by mule-drawn carriage to settle on the Pacific Coast. In San Francisco, Megquier recognized the many opportunities for income that were available to women and determined to earn money herself. She and her husband opened a hotel, at which point she wrote the letter below to her daughter.

Dear Daughter:

I should like to give you an account of my work if I could do it justice. We have a store the size of the one we had in Winthrop, in the morning the boy gets up and makes a fire by seven o'clock when I get up and make the coffee, then I make the biscuit, then I fry the potatoes then broil three pounds of steak, and as much liver, while the woman is sweeping, and setting the table, at eight the bell rings and they are eating until nine. I do not sit until they are nearly all done. I try to keep the food warm and in shape as we put it on in small quantities after breakfast I bake six loaves of bread (not very big) then four pies, or a pudding then we have lamb, for which we have paid nine dollars a quarter, beef, and pork, baked, turnips, beets, potatoes, radishes, sallad, and that everlasting soup, every day, dine at two, for tea we have hash, cold meat bread and butter sauce and some kind of cake and I have cooked every mouthful that has been eaten excepting one day and a half that we were on a steamboat excursion. I make six beds every day and do the washing and ironing you must think that I am very busy and when I dance all night I am obliged to trot all day and if I had not the constitution of six horses I should [have] been dead long ago but I am going to give up in the fall whether or no, as I am sick and tired of work. . . . The woman washes the dishes and carpets which have to be washed every day and then the house looks like a pig pen it is so dusty. . . . Write. Write. Write.

Mapping the Text

1. Mary Jane Megquier was the wife of a physician. What evidence of her social and economic class is evident in her letter? To what extent do you think that this status affects her experiences as a woman who migrated West?

Writing to Inquire

1. Use library resources to find out more about San Francisco during the last half of the nineteenth century. Who were the women who lived there? What were their origins? What work did they typically do? How typical or unusual was Megquier's work?
2. Consider Megquier's daughter and what her point of view might have been. Take on the daughter's character as you think that she might have been and respond to Megquier. Then write an essay in which you explain the choices you made.
3. During the nineteenth century, letter writing (epistolary) was a common way of communicating with others. Today, e-mail is a popular form. Think about e-mail as an epistolary genre. How are e-mails similar to and different from more traditional forms of letter writing? Do you send more e-mails or written letters? Why?

The Later Journeys, 1856–1867

LILLIAN SCHLISSEL

Lillian Schlissel earned a Ph.D. in American Civilization from Yale University in 1957 and served as director (1974–1988) of the American Studies Program at Brooklyn College, City University of New York. Currently, she is Professor Emerita of English and American Studies at Brooklyn College. She has authored and coauthored several books, including *The World of Randolph Bourne* (1965); *Conscience in America* (1970); *Women's Diaries of the Westward Journey* (1982); *The Diary of Amelia Stewart Knight* (1992); *Black Frontiers* (1994); and (with Catherine Lavender) *The Western Women's Reader: The Remarkable Writings of Women Who Shaped the American West, Spanning 300 Years* (2000). The excerpt below is taken from the latter publication.

During the years of the Civil War, able-bodied men were called upon to fight, and the westward emigration dwindled. The garrisons along the overland route were emptied of soldiers, and volunteers took over guard duties. The North released Confederate prisoners to fight the Indians and frontiersmen called them "galvanized Yankees." Yet the emigrants pressed on, six thousand of them. Ignorance of the road had not stopped them in the 1840s; cholera had not stopped them in the 1850s, and neither Civil War nor Indians would stop them now.

The diaries of the women who went overland in the 1860s show how remarkably little had changed in the life of the road. Louisa Rahm wrote that she "washed and baked and had a hail storm." For most emigrants, life and death still hung in a precarious balance. Ada Millington was twelve when her family set out for California. It was a large family; her father, who had five children by his first marriage, was traveling with his second wife and their six children. The youngest was a year and a half old. In addition, there were five young hired hands. And there were Mrs. Millington's sister and brother-in-law, their children, and their hired hands. And there was the brother-in-law's sister, stepfather and mother. The party seemed large and secure. The families were well provided. "We have a nice large tent and a good sheet iron stove. Six cows, three calves and two loose horses." By June, Ada had learned to drive the four-mule team by herself.

Although telegraph and stagecoach had made the route more secure, a common ailment on this particular journey produced disaster. Dysentery, which affected almost everyone at some time or other on the overland journey, wracked the baby's body, and not any of Mrs. Millingtons' knowledge of herbal teas could halt the wasting illness. "The doctor they called says our George had flux and mountain fever and if we had been at home he needn't have died."

The prospect of having to leave their youngest in a grave along the roadside was intolerable. Ada's diary, because it is the diary of a child not yet given to reserve and stoicism, opens the family's pain to our eyes. "We couldn't bear the thought of leaving his little body among the sands of this wilderness surrounded by Indians and wolves. . . . we used spirits of camphor very freely on George's clothes and think we will try to take his body on at least another day. Isaac. . . cut the letters [of his name] on the coffin lid so that it will be easier to identify [when we come back]." The prospect of burial on the road was the most painful burden the emigrants had to bear.

5 One's natural instinct was to mark a gravesite so as to find the resting place of a loved one again. But no adequate grave could be dug on the road. The sun had baked the ground until digging was like breaking through concrete. Then the rains would come and wash away the shallow graves. No matter what marker one might devise—a pile of rocks, a piece of wood, a shred of cloth—no emblem would survive the weather or the passage of time.

On the other hand, there was also the urgent need to obliterate a grave. The Indians made a common practice of digging up the dead for clothing, spreading cholera among themselves even as they gathered up their trophies. The emigrants came to believe that the greatest service they could do the deceased was to *hide* the gravesite. Some companies dug beneath the road itself so that the ox teams would trample over all evidence of a grave:

> One of the emigrants in our party was named Crowley. He had lost several members of his family by death while crossing the plains, and at one of our camps. . . a daughter. Martha Leland Crowley, died. . . . They buried her beneath a big plane tree on the banks of a small stream which they christened Grave Creek. . . . The oxen were corralled over her grave so that Indians would not dig her up and get her clothing.

But even if a grave escaped the notice of Indians, it was not likely that it would escape the prowling wolves and coyotes. "Col. Nesmith saw the grave in 1848 and said it had been opened [and] that a number of human bones were scattered about." The child's bones had to be reinterred and the grave filled.

There was no time to care for the sick and the dying. Fear of Indians forced families to hurry along. The cattle needed water and grass. The provisions might give out if one lingered. Always, delay for the dying threatened the life of the living.

Popular songs of the 1850s depicted the "happy death" of a good Christian as something that occurred in the bosom of the family. Pioneer family and friends gathered beside the deathbed in order to comfort the dying (Ada Millington wrote of her baby brother's death, "we all gathered around his little bed in the tent to see him die.") Portraits and photographs of dead family members, particularly infants and young children, became cherished mementos of families, a way of holding on to a life too soon snuffed out. Death along the road was a palpable wound, and it scarred the lives of emigrants who had dared to break so completely with home. Baptism seemed a lesser concern. It might be a required sacrament under stable life conditions, but the emigrants set such practices aside on the journey. Too many other problems seemed more pressing.

On the day of their fourteenth wedding anniversary, the Millingtons discussed where to bury their child. Near the road were three graves on a hill. Ada wrote of how they debated "whether or not to bury George here with other graves where it doesn't seem so lonesome, but if we could get him to Carson City we might be able to send for him from California later. His body is still well preserved so we are taking it on." Finally they reached Carson City:

> Pa, ma and we children went to see George's grave about a mile from town and nearly in the corner of yard next to town. Desolate enough but we are better satisfied than to have left him on Dry Creek. . . . Pa cut 20 notches on each rail near the head of the grave for his age—20 months, and cut some letters and emblems on the board at the head and foot of the grave. Then we went away hoping in a year or so to have him sent to California. . . . Seth who is four cannot take the baby's place.

Years later, faithful to the memory of the dead infant, one member of the family returned to Carson City to bring the coffin for reburial in California, but the cemetery had been obliterated, and no trace was ever found of the grave the father had so lovingly and carefully marked.

Three days after the baby's burial, Ada's mother managed to bake ginger cakes to celebrate the birthday of her six-year-old. Life for the emigrants went on.

By 1863 there were new ways to travel the overland route. Hallie Riley Hodder and her sister rode to Atchison, Kansas, on a "steam car," and from there went on seven hundred miles to Denver, Colorado, by stagecoach. "We changed horses every ten miles at the little stations on the way, and riding nights as well as days we made 100 miles in twenty-four hours and reached Denver on the evening of the seventh day." Hallie spent a year and a half in Colorado and then returned East. "Before leaving Denver, my cousin had provided me with a small revolver, and had taught me how to use it. It was loaded and I had taken it from the holster at my belt, so I presume I was ready to use it on myself if we were captured." Hallie apparently saw suicide as the ladylike alternative to killing Indians.

Catherine Wever Collins also traveled West by train. "I left Cincinnati, Ohio, in the Express train last evening. . . and arrived (in St. Louis) about 11 a.m." She left at 4 in the morning and "after due shrieks from the engine [we] launched into the darkness. . . ." Passengers were ferried across the Missouri River and then scrambled as best they could up the banks to the waiting train on the other side. Even travel by train required a certain agility. Catherine reached Atchison, Kansas, at half past one in the morning, and from there for sixty dollars she found a place on the stagecoach. Eleven hectic days after her journey had begun in Ohio, she reached Fort Laramie, Wyoming.

But not all emigrants had changed their mode of travel. Wagons were still the mainstay of travelers. Mary Eliza Warner was fifteen and just the right age to travel The journey was a lark. Early on a May morning, she wrote in her diary: "I drove four horses nearly all day," and on Sunday I saw the most magnificent scenery I ever saw." After finishing their work the young people "had a good time singing." When the weather was fine, she and "Aunt Celia," a married lady scarcely out of her teens herself, rode horseback for the sheer fun of it. Surely this was a delicious way to spend the summer months.

Katherine Dunlap was older and she marked the dangers more carefully. "A little girl was jostled out of a wagon run over and killed." Perhaps because she traveled with a small child of her own, she noticed a pine board at the head of a grave with the inscription: "Two children, killed by a stampede." And on July 16, she came upon the grave of an infant. "Oh, what a lonely, dark and desolate place to bury a sweet infant—We read the following inscription on the headboard of the death-sleeping infant: 'Morlena Elizabeth Martess, died Aug. 9th, 1863, born July 7th, 1862. Friends nor physician could save her from the grave." The gravestone carried a plea to all emigrants who might pass to repair the grave, and Katherine noted in her diary: "It *was repaired* and a pen of logs built around it."

Deep in the hills of Idaho and Colorado were two other women whose journeys had brought them to the camps where men were digging for gold and for silver. Each determined to get herself a share of that wealth. Mrs. Theodore Schultz was the "first white woman in [the mining camp]." She started a boarding house and "charged $3.00 per meal and on Sunday [I] often got 200 extra [men]. I worked 18 hours a day lots of times. We had little provisions but bushels of gold dust. I had gold dust everywhere in everything. . . . I threw it in the wood box. . . and under beds." Mrs. Fowler ran a boarding house in Pueblo, Colorado. She charged a dollar a meal, and had all the men she could cook for. Space was so much at a premium that men paid for the privilege of sleeping on the ground *outside* the boarding house. For women who provided a semblance of home—a warm meal and a clean bed—there were fortunes to be made in the mining camps.

Some of the women who worked in the mining camps had come as slaves, like the seventeen-year-old boy sold by his father to Helen Carpenter and her husband. Sometimes whole families had come with their masters, traveling in their own wagons at the end of the long trains, secretly hoping to find a way to freedom in the territories.

Oregon was less hospitable to blacks than many of them had hoped. The territorial legislature passed laws prohibiting admission to black settlers, even though exceptions were made on individual petition. When Oregon was admitted to the union in 1857, a Free Negro Admission Article was proposed for the state's constitution, but it was defeated, and the small number of blacks who had made their way to Oregon lived uneasily until the Emancipation Proclamation of 1863.

California, on the other hand, outlawed slavery within its boundaries in 1830 because miners feared the appearance of slave labor. The mines soon became places where an exotic mixture of races and nationalities shouldered one another in the feverish search for wealth. Mary Ballou wrote home that she lived in a mining camp called "Negro Bar," where "French and Duch and Scoth and Jews and Italians and Sweeds and Chineese and Indians" were all panning for gold. Even before the discovery of gold, California had been settled by men and women of Mexican, Indian, and African descent. Eighteen percent of the population, according to a Spanish census of 1790, were of other than Anglo-American origin. By 1849, San Francisco blacks had formed a "mutual Benefit and Relief Society" of then own. By 1854, that city had three black churches, and within the next decade there were black newspapers and as many black churches.

Some of the black women who came to western lands we cannot name. Margaret Frink wrote in her journal that somewhere in the Humboldt Sink she saw a Negro woman tramping along through the heat and dust, carrying a cast iron bake stove on her head, with her provisions and a blanket piled on top. . . bravely pushing on for California."

Some of the black women we do know about. Mary Ellen Pleasants came to San Francisco in 1849. Born a slave in Georgia, she was married to a free black in Boston and came to the West Coast with a sizable fortune. In 1858 she traveled all the way back to eastern Canada, in order to deliver thirty thousand dollars personally into the hands of John Brown, to help him in his crusade to free her people. When she came back to California, she was put off a San Francisco streetcar, and she filed a suit, along with other black women, and eventually compelled the streetcar lines to allow Negroes to ride. "Mammy" Pleasants, as she had come to be called, was a formidable citizen.

Another black emigrant was Clara Brown, who took in washing at the western roads. At the end of the Civil War, twenty-five thousand emigrants made the overland crossing. They were among the last Americans to make the journey by wagon. Cora Wilson Agatz and her family were prosperous Iowa farm people. They had five span of matched mules, a team of horses, a saddle pony and four wagons to carry beds and tables, linen, silver, china, carpets, books, and pictures. They took "canned goods, bacons, hams, bologna sausage, flour, barrels of both white and brown sugar, great cakes of maple sugar. . . ." They had a sheet iron camp stove and an oven and a wagon filled with clothing. Also "a maiden lady devoid of hearing and eyelashes who begged passage for the avowed purpose of finding a life mate out west, which she did very shortly after her arrival." Cora described the "gymnasium costumes" worn by some of the women. "Short gray wool skirts, full bloomer pants of the same, fastened at the knee, high laced boots, and. . . white stockings which were changed often enough to be kept spotless. Large straw hats finished these picturesque and sensible costumes. When compared with the long, slovenly, soiled calico gowns worn by the other women of the train, these simple costumes elicited many commendatory remarks." What a wonderful picture: these ladies kept their stockings washed, their high boots laced and their large straw hats in good order through the long journey! Surely they were a far cry from poor Rebecca Ketcham in her one dress, and from Martha Morrison's mother wading through the swamps.

But lest one come to believe the road had become a place of fashion and ease, the diary of Barsina French, the last diary of this collection, reminds us that in 1867, traveling through Apache country along the southern route, the mothers had to take their turns standing guard against the Indians at night. And in the morning, the women cooked what they called "red mud" for coffee at breakfast.

Migration dwindled after 1868. The railroad began to replace the wagon and settlers also began to look to the lands of the middle mountain regions rather than to the coast. It was a time for consolidation and for a different kind of building, not log houses this time, but the fabric of social life—

schools and churches and the reweaving of families separated and broken by the migration. It was time for the women to build.

Mapping the Text

1. In this account, Schlissel shares information about several women. Which account stands out most in your thinking? Why?
2. Given Schlissel's account of pioneer women from 1856 to 1867, what images and experiences do you think help make clearer who these pioneering women were and what their lives were like?

Writing to Inquire

1. Consider the women who did *not* migrate during this era. Choose a particular place as the focal point and discuss the lives and conditions of these women. Consider in discussion their differences in race, social class, and occupation or roles. How like or unlike were their lives and those of the pioneering women who moved West?
2. At the end of this selection, Schlissel writes:

   > Migration dwindled after 1868. The railroad began to replace the wagon and settlers also began to look to the lands of the middle mountain regions rather than to the coast. It was a time for consolidation and for a different kind of building, not log houses this time, but the fabric of social life—schools and churches and the reweaving of families separated and broken by the migration. It was time for the women to build.

   Search library sources to find out more about the late nineteenth century and the participation of women in those societies. What roles did women play in these communities? What work did they do in the public sphere (political or work environments) or the private sphere (home, family, local community)? How did technology affect women's lives and work in building communities and making lives for themselves, whether in new homes or long standing ones?

CALLS TO ACTION AND RESPONSE

My Education

CARLOS BULOSAN

Carlos Bulosan (1911–1956), who completed only three years of formal schooling in the Philippines, taught himself to write stories and poetry by studying books in the children's section of the Los Angeles public library. He emigrated to the United States in 1930, but he never became an American citizen. A writer of poetry and prose, his works include *The Laughter of My Father* (1944); *America Is in the Heart* (1946); *Sound of Falling Light* (1960); and *The Cry and the Dedication* (1995). In "My Education," Bulosan reflects on the painful process of coming to understand America's shortcomings as well as its promise.

I came to America sixteen years ago from the village where I was born in the Philippines. In reality it was only the beginning of a tortuous search for roots in a new world. I hated absentee-landlordism, not only because it had driven my family from our home and scattered us, but also because it had shattered the life and future of my generation. This system had originated in Spanish times when most of the arable lands and navigable waters were controlled by the church and powerful men in the government. It came down our history, and threatened the security of the peasantry till it became a blight in our national life.

But now that I was in America I felt a vague desire to see what I had not seen in my country. I did not know how I would approach America. I only knew that there must be a common denominator which every immigrant or native American should look for in order to understand her, and be of service to her people. I felt like Columbus embarking upon a long and treacherous voyage. I felt like Icarus escaping from prison to freedom. I did not know that I was coming closer to American *reality.*

I worked for three months in an apple orchard in Sunnyside, in the state of Washington. The labor movement was under persecution and the minorities became the national scapegoat. Toward the end I was disappointed. I had worked on a farm all my life in the Philippines, and now I was working on a farm again. I could not compromise my picture of America with the filthy bunkhouses in which we lived and the falling wooden houses in which the natives lived. This was not the America I wanted to see, but it was the first great lesson in my life.

I moved to another town and found work on a farm again. Then again I moved to another farm town. I followed the crops and the seasons, from Washington to Oregon to California, until I had worked in every town on the Pacific Coast. In the end I was sick with despair. Wherever I went I found the same honor, the same anguish and fear.

5 I began to ask if this was the real America—and if it was, why did I come? I was sad and confused. But I believed in the other men before me who came and stayed to discover America. I knew they came because there was something in America which needed them and which they needed. Yet slowly I began to doubt the *promise* that was America.

If it took me almost a decade to dispel this doubt, it was because it took me that long to catch a glimpse of the *real* America. The nebulous and dynamic qualities of the dream took hold of me immensely. It became the periscope of my search for roots in America. I was driven back to history. But going back to history was actually a return to the early beginnings of America.

I had picked hops with some Indians under the towering shadow of Mt. Rainier. I had pruned apples with the dispossessed Americans in the rich deltas of the Columbia River. I had cut and packed asparagus in California. I had weeded peas with Japanese in Arizona. I had picked tomatoes with Negroes in Utah. Yet I felt that I did not belong to America. My departure from the Philippines was actually the breaking of my ground, the tearing up of my roots. As I stayed longer and searched farther, this feeling of not belonging became more acute, until it distorted my early vision of America. I did not know what part of America was mine, and my awareness of not belonging made me desperate and terribly lonely.

The next two years were like a nightmare. There were sixteen million unemployed. I joined those disinherited Americans. Again I saw the rich fields and wide flat lands. I saw them from the top of a passing freight train. Sometimes I saw them from the back of a truck. I became more confused and rootless.

I was sick with despair. I was paralyzed with fear. Everywhere I went I saw the shadow of this country falling. I saw it in the anguish of girls that cried at night. I saw it in the abstract stares of unemployed workers. I saw it in the hollow eyes of children. I saw it in the abuses suffered by immigrants. I saw it in the persecution of the minorities. *I heard some men say that this was America—the dream betrayed. They told me that America was done for—dead. I fought against believing them. Yet, when I was socially strangled. I almost believed what they said about America—that she was dead.*

10 I do not recall how I actually started to identify myself with America. The men and women around me were just as rootless as I was in those years. I spent the next two years reading in public libraries. How well I remember those long cold nights of winter and the months of unemployment. Perhaps the gambling houses that opened only at night with one free meal for everybody—perhaps reading at the libraries in the daytime and waiting for the dark to hide my dirty clothes in the streets—perhaps all these terrible humiliations gave me the courage to fight through it all, until

the months passed into years of hope and the *will* to proceed became obdurate and illumined with a sincere affinity for America. Finally, I realized that the great men who contributed something positive to the growth of America also suffered and were lonely.

I read more books, and became convinced that it was the duty of the artist to trace the origin of the disease that was festering in American life. I was beginning to be aware of the dynamic social ideas that were disturbing the minds of leading artists and writers in America. I felt angry with those who fled away from her. I hated the expatriates in Paris and Madrid. I studied Whitman with naive anticipations, hoping to find in him an affirmation of my growing faith in America. For a while I was inclined to believe that Whitman was the key to my search for roots. And I found that he also was terribly lonely, and he wrote of an America that would be.

I began to wonder about those who stayed in America and suffered the narrowness of the society in which they lived. I read Melville and Poe, who chose to live and work in a narrow world. I became intimate with their humiliations and defeats, their hopes and high moments of success. Then I began to hate the crass materialism of our age and the powerful chains and combines that strangled human life and made the world a horrible place to live in. Slowly, I was beginning to feel that I had found a place in America. The fight to hold on to this feeling convinced me that I was becoming a growing part of living America.

It was now toward the end of 1935, and the trade union movement was in turmoil. The old American Federation of Labor was losing power and a new union was being born. I started to write my own impressions of America. Now I was beginning to give meaning to my life. It was a discovery of America and myself. Being able to write, now, was a personal triumph and a definite identification with a living tradition. I began to recognize the forces that had driven many Americans to other countries and had made those who stayed at home homeless. *Those who went away never escaped from themselves; those who stayed at home never found themselves.*

I determined to find out why the artist took flight or revolted against his heritage. Then it was that, doing organization work among agricultural workers, I fell sick with a disease caused by the years of hunger and congested living. I was forced to lie in a hospital for more than two years. Now, all that I had won seemed irrelevant to my life. Here I was dying—six years after my arrival in America. What was wrong? Was America so dislocated that she had no more place for the immigrant?

15 I could not believe that the resources of this country were exhausted. I almost died in the hospital. I survived death because I was determined to convince those who had lost faith in America. I knew that in convincing them I would be convincing myself that America was not dead.

The Civil War in Spain was going on, it was another factor that gave coherence to the turmoil and confusion [in] my life. The ruthless bombings of churches and hospitals by German and Italian planes clarified some of my beliefs. I believe that this intellectual and spiritual participation in the Spanish conflict fired in me a new vision of life.

It was at this period that the Congress of Industrial Organizations came to power in industry. At last its militant stand in labor disputes reinvigorated me. Some of my democratic beliefs were confirmed. I felt that I had found the mainsprings of American democracy. In this feeling I found some coherence and direction and the impulse to create became more ardent and necessary.

America's most articulate artists were stirring. They refused to follow the example of those who went into voluntary exile and those who stayed at home and were angry with America. They knew that they could truly work if they stayed near their roots and walked proudly in familiar streets. They no longer created alone. They framed a program broad enough to cover the different aspects of their needs and abilities. It was not a vow to write for art's sake.

I found a new release. I reacted to it as a sensitive artist of my generation without losing my firm belief that America was happy and alive if her artists were happy and alive. But Spain was lost and a grand dream was lost with her. The equilibrium of the world was dislocated, and the writers were greatly affected by the setback of democratic forces.

20 I tried in the next two years to work with the progressive forces. But some of the organizations dribbled into personal quarrels and selfish motives. There were individuals who were saturated with the false values of capitalism and the insidiousness of their bourgeois prejudices poisoned their whole thinking. I became convinced that they could not liberate America from decay. And I became doubly convinced, as Hitler seized one country after another, that their prejudices must be challenged by a stronger faith in America.

We were now moving toward the end of another decade. Writing was not sufficient. Labor demanded the active collaboration of writers. In the course of eight years I had relived the whole course of American history. I drew inspiration from my active participation in the workers' movement. *The most decisive move that the writer could make was to take his stand with the workers.*

I had a preliminary knowledge of American history to guide me. What could I do? I had read *Gone with the Wind,* and saw the extent of the lie that corrupted the American dream. I read Dreiser, Anderson, Lewis, and their younger contemporaries: Faulkner, Hemingway, Caldwell, Steinbeck. I had hoped to find in these writers a weapon strong enough to blast the walls that imprisoned the American soul. But they were merely describing the disease—they did not reveal any evidence that they knew how to eradicate it.

Hemingway was too preoccupied with himself, and consequently he wrote of himself and his frustrations. I was also disappointed with Faulkner. Why did he give form to decay? And Caldwell, Steinbeck—why did they write in costume? And Odets, why *only* middle class disintegration? Am I not an immigrant like Louis Adamic? Perhaps I could not understand America like Richard Wright, but I felt that I would be ineffectual if I did not return to my own people. I believed that my work would be more vital and useful if I dedicated it to the cause of my own people.

It was now almost ten years since I had landed in America. But as we moved rapidly toward the war with Japan, I realized how foolish it was to believe that I could define roots in terms of places and persons. I knew, then, that I would be as rootless in the Philippines as I was in America, because these roots are not physical things but the quality of faith deeply left and clearly understood and integrated in one's life. The roots I was looking for were not physical but intellectual and spiritual things. In fact, I was looking for a common faith to believe in and of which I could be a growing part.

Now I knew that I was living in the collective era. Where was I to begin? I read Marxist literature. Russia was then much in the minds of the contemporaries. In the Soviet system we seemed to have found a workable system and a common belief that bound races and peoples together for a creative purpose. I studied Russian history as I had studied American history. I tried to explain the incoherence of my life on the ground that I was living in a decaying capitalist society.

Then we felt that something was bound to happen in America. Socialist thinking was spreading among the workers, professionals and intellectuals. Labor demanded immediate political action. For the first time a collective faith seemed to have appeared. To most of us it was a revelation—and a new morning in America. Here was a collective faith dynamic enough to release the creative spirit that was long thwarted in America. My personal predicaments seemed to vanish and for the first time I could feel myself growing and becoming a living part of America.

It was now the middle of 1941. The dark clouds of war were approaching our shores. Then December 7 came to awaken a decadent world. Japan offered us a powerful collective faith that was pervasive enough to sweep away our fears and doubts of America. Suddenly I began to see the dark forces that had uprooted me from my native land, and had driven me to a narrow corner of life in America. At last the full significance of my search for roots came to me, because the war with Japan and against Fascism revealed the whole meaning of the fears that had driven me as a young writer into hunger and disease and despair.

I wrote in my diary: "It is well that we in America take nourishment from a common spring. The Four Freedoms may not be realized in our times but if the war against Fascism ends, we may be sure that we have been motivated by a native force dynamic enough to give form to the creative spirit in America. Now I believe that all of us in America must be bound together by a common faith and work toward our goal. . . ."

Mapping the Text

1. What seems to be Carlos Bulosan's motivation in writing this narrative?
2. What stands out most for you in Bulosan's narrative? Why? How does what you notice relate to the general message(s) that Bulosan is trying to convey?
3. What impression do you get of Bulosan from reading his narrative? Develop a profile of him using details from the narrative that support your point of view.

Writing to Inquire

1. Bulosan is writing about his youth. What specific issues does he raise about coming to America? Do these issues still exist for immigrants? What options were available to Bulosan? What options are available to immigrants today?
2. Bulosan immigrated to the United States through a western portal rather than Ellis Island. Find out more about the different ports of entry. Discuss how Bulosan's experience might have varied from that of European immigrants. Compare, for example, points of origin, the geographical features of the ports, and the conditions the immigrants found on their arrival.

The Homeland, Aztlán

GLORIA ANZALDUA

Gloria Anzaldua (1942–) describes herself as a "chicana dyke-feminist, tejana patlache poet, writer, and cultural theorist." The daughter of sharecroppers, she was born in the Rio Grande Valley of South Texas and raised in a family of migrant workers who traveled the Southwest during her childhood. Educational opportunity made a difference for her in offering another career path; it also provided many occasions for her to reflect on the experience of multiple heritages and multiple identities. As a writer, Anzaldua is best known for *Borderlands/La Frontera: The New Mestiza* (1987). However, she has also edited several essay collections, including *Making Face, Making Soul/Haciendo Caras: Creative and Critical Perspectives by Feminists of Color* (1990), and she has written children's books, including *Friends from the Other Side/Amigos del Otro Lado: A Bilingual Children's Picture Book* (1993). She has received numerous awards, including the Before Columbus Foundation Book Award, a National Endowment for the Arts Fiction Award, the Sappho Award of Distinction, and the Lambda Literary Best Small Book Press Award. In "The Homeland, Aztlán," which is taken from *Borderlands,* she explores, as she often does in her writing, the relationships between language and identity, demonstrating the distinctive ways in which she blends languages and genres.

El otro México

El otro México que acá hemos construido
el espacio es lo que ha sido
territorio nacional.
Esté el esfuerzo de todos nuestros hermanos
y latinoamericanos que han sabido
progressar.

—Los Tigres del Norte[1]

"The *Aztecas del norte*. . . compose the largest single tribe or nation of Anishinabeg (Indians) found in the United States today. . . . Some call themselves Chicanos and see themselves as people whose true homeland is Aztlán [the U.S. Southwest].[2]

Wind tugging at my sleeve
feet sinking into the sand
I stand at the edge where earth touches ocean
where the two overlap
a gentle coming together
at other times and places a violent clash.

Across the border in Mexico
stark silhouette of houses gutted by waves,
cliffs crumbling into the sea,
silver waves marbled with spume
gashing a hole under the border fence.
Miro el mar atacar
la cerca en Border Field Park
con sus buchones de agua,
an Easter Sunday resurrection
of the brown blood in my veins.

Oigo el llorido del mar, el respiro del aire,
my heart surges to the beat of the sea.
In the gray haze of the sun
the gulls' shrill cry of hunger,
the tangy smell of the sea seeping into me.

I walk through the hole in the fence to the other side.
Under my fingers I feel the gritty wire
rusted by 139 years
of the salty breath of the sea.

Beneath the iron sky
Mexican children kick their soccer ball across,
run after it, entering the U.S.

I press my hand to the steel curtain—
chainlink fence crowned with rolled barbed wire—
rippling from the sea where Tijuana touches San Diego
unrolling over mountains
and plains
and deserts,
this "Tortilla Curtain" turning into *el río Grande*
flowing down to the flatlands
of the Magic Valley of South Texas
its mouth emptying into the Gulf.

1,950 mile-long open wound
dividing a *pueblo,* a culture,
running down the length of my body,
staking fence rods in my flesh,
splits me splits me
me raja me raja
This is my home
this thin edge of
barbwire.

But the skin of the earth is seamless.
The sea cannot be fenced,
el mar does not stop at borders.
To show the white man what she thought of his arrogance,
Yemaya blew that wire fence down.

This land was Mexican once,
was Indian always
and is.
And will be again.

Yo soy un puente tendido
del mundo gabacho al del mojado,
lo pasado me estirá pa' 'trás
y lo presente pa' 'delante.
Que la Virgen de Guadalupe me cuide
Ay ay ay, soy mexicana de este lado.

The U.S.-Mexican border *es una herida abierta* where the Third World grates against the first and bleeds. And before a scab forms it hemorrhages again, the lifeblood of two worlds merging to form a third country—a border culture. Borders are set up to define the places that are safe and unsafe, to distinguish *us* from *them.* A border is a dividing line, a narrow strip along a steep edge. A borderland is a vague and undetermined place created by the emotional residue of an unnatural boundary. It is in a constant state of transition. The prohibited and forbidden are its inhabitants. *Los atravesados* live here: the squint-eyed, the perverse, the queer, the troublesome, the mongrel, the mulato, the half-breed, the half dead; in short, those who cross over, pass over, or go through the confines of the "normal." Gringos in the U.S. Southwest consider the inhabitants of the borderlands transgressors, aliens—whether they possess documents or not, whether they're Chicanos, Indians or Blacks. Do not enter, trespassers will be raped, maimed, strangled, gassed, shot. The only "legitimate" inhabitants are those in power, the whites and those who align themselves with whites. Tension grips the inhabitants of the borderlands like a virus. Ambivalence and unrest reside there and death is no stranger.

> In the fields, *la migra.* My aunt saying, "*No corran,* don't run. They'll think you're *del otro lao.*" In the confusion, Pedro ran, terrified of being caught. He couldn't speak English, couldn't tell them he was fifth generation American. *Sin papeles*—he did not carry his birth certificate to work in the fields. *La migra* took him away while we watched. *Se lo llevaron.* He tried to smile when he looked back at us, to raise his fist. But I saw the shame pushing his head down, I saw the terrible weight of shame hunch his shoulders. They deported him to Guadalajara by plane. The furthest he'd ever been to Mexico was Reynosa, a small border town opposite Hidalgo, Texas, not far from McAllen. Pedro walked all the way to the Valley. *Se lo llevaron sin un centavo al pobre. Se vino andando desde Guadalajara.*

During the original peopling of the Americas, the first inhabitants migrated across the Bering Straits and walked south across the continent. The oldest evidence of humankind in the U.S.—the Chicanos' ancient Indian ancestors—was found in Texas and has been dated to 35000 B.C.[3] In the Southwest United States archeologists have found 20,000-year-old campsites of the Indians who migrated through, or permanently occupied, the Southwest, Aztlán—land of the herons, land of whiteness, the Edenic place of origin of the Azteca.

In 1000 B.C., descendants of the original Cochise people migrated into what is now Mexico and Central America and became the direct ancestors of many of the Mexican people. (The Cochise culture of the Southwest is the parent culture of the Aztecs. The Uto-Aztecan languages stemmed from the language of the Cochise people.)[4] The Aztecs (the Nahuatl word for people of Aztlán) left the Southwest in 1168 A.D.

Now let us go.
  Tihueque, tihueque,
Vámonos, vámonos.
  Un pájaro cantó.
Con sus ocho tribus salieron
  de la "cueva del origen."
los aztecas siguieron al dios
    Huitzilopochtli.

5 *Huitzilopochtli,* the God of War, guided them to the place (that later became Mexico City) where an eagle with a writhing serpent in its beak perched on a cactus. The eagle symbolizes the spirit (as the sun, the father); the serpent symbolizes the soul (as the earth, the mother). Together, they symbolize the struggle between the spiritual/celestial/male and the underworld/earth/feminine. The symbolic sacrifice of the serpent to the "higher" masculine powers indicates that the patriarchal order had already vanquished the feminine and matriarchal order in pre-Columbian America.

At the beginning of the 16th century, the Spaniards and Hernán Cortés invaded Mexico and, with the help of tribes that the Aztecs had subjugated, conquered it. Before the Conquest, there were twenty-five million Indian people in Mexico and the Yucatán. Immediately after the Conquest, the Indian population had been reduced to under seven million. By 1650, only one-and-a-half-million pure-blooded Indians remained. The *mestizos* who were genetically equipped to survive small pox, measles, and typhus (Old World diseases to which the natives had no immunity), founded a new hybrid race and inherited Central and South America.[5] *En 1521 nacío una nueva raza, el mestizo, el mexicano* (people of mixed Indian and Spanish blood), a race that had never existed before. Chicanos, Mexican-Americans, are the offspring of those first matings.

Our Spanish, Indian, and *mestizo* ancestors explored and settled parts of the U.S. Southwest as early as the 16th century. For every gold-hungry *conquistador* and soul hungry missionary who came north from Mexico, ten to twenty Indians and *mestizos* went along as porters or in other capacities.[6] For the Indians, this constituted a return to the place of origin, Aztlán, thus making Chicanos originally and secondarily indigenous to the Southwest. Indians and *mestizos* from central Mexico intermarried with North American Indians. The continual intermarriage between Mexican and American Indians and Spaniards formed an even greater *mestizaje.*

El destierro/The Lost Land

Entonces corré la sangre
no sabe el indio que hacer,
le van a quitar su tierra,
la tiene que defender,
el indio se cae muerto,
y el afuerino de pie.
Levántate, Manquilef.

Arauco tiene una pena
más negra que su chamal,
ya no son los españoles
los que les hacen llorar,

hoy son los propios chilenos
los que les quitan su pan.
Levántate, Pailahuan.
—Violeta Parra, "*Arauco tiene una pena*"[7]

In the 1800s, Anglos migrated illegally into Texas, which was then part of Mexico, in greater and greater numbers and gradually drove the *tejanos* (native Texans of Mexican descent) from their lands, committing all manner of atrocities against them. Their illegal invasion forced Mexico to fight a war to keep its Texas territory. The Battle of the Alamo, in which the Mexican forces vanquished the whites, became, for the whites, the symbol for the cowardly and villainous character of the Mexicans. It became (and still is) a symbol that legitimized the white imperialist takeover. With the capture of Santa Anna later in 1836, Texas became a republic. *Tejanos* lost their land and, overnight, became the foreigners.

Ya la mitad del terreno
les vendió el traidor Santa Anna,
con lo que se ha hecho muy rica
la nación americana.

¿Qué acaso no se conforman
con el oro de las minas?
Ustedes muy elegantes
y aquí nosotros en ruinas.
—from the Mexican corrido, "*Del peligro de la Intervención*"[8]

In 1846, the U.S. incited Mexico to war. U.S. troops invaded and occupied Mexico, forcing her to give up almost half of her nation, what is now Texas, New Mexico, Arizona, Colorado and California.

With the victory of the U.S. forces over the Mexican in the U.S.-Mexican War, *los norteamericanos* pushed the Texas border down 100 miles, from *el río Nueces* to *el río Grande.* South Texas ceased to be part of the Mexican state of Tamaulipas. Separated from Mexico, the Native Mexican-Texan no longer looked toward Mexico as home; the Southwest became our homeland once more. The border fence that divides the Mexican people was born on February 2, 1848 with the signing of the Treaty of Guadalupe-Hidalgo. It left 100,000 Mexican citizens on this side, annexed by conquest along with the land. The land established by the treaty as belonging to Mexicans was soon swindled away from its owners. The treaty was never honored and restitution, to this day, has never been made.

The justice and benevolence of God
will forbid that. . . Texas should again
become a howling wilderness
trod only by savages, or. . . benighted

by the ignorance and superstition,
the anarchy and rapine of Mexican misrule.
The Anglo-American race are destined
to be forever the proprietors of
this land of promise and fulfillment.
Their laws will govern it,
their learning will enlighten it,
their enterprise will improve it.
Their flocks range its boundless pastures,
for them its fertile lands will yield. . .
luxuriant harvests. . .
The wilderness of Texas has been redeemed
by Anglo-American blood & enterprise.

—William H. Wharton[9]

The Gringo, locked into the fiction of white superiority, seized complete political power, stripping Indians and Mexicans of their land while their feet were still rooted in it. *Con el destierro y el exilo fuimos desuñados, destroncados, destripados*—we were jerked out by the roots, truncated, disemboweled, dispossessed, and separated from our identity and our history. Many, under the threat of Anglo terrorism, abandoned homes and ranches and went to Mexico. Some stayed and protested. But as the courts, law enforcement officials, and government officials not only ignored their pleas but penalized them for their efforts, *tejanos* had no other recourse but armed retaliation.

After Mexican-American resisters robbed a train in Brownsville, Texas, on October 18, 1915, Anglo vigilante groups began lynching Chicanos. Texas Rangers would take them into the brush and shoot them. One hundred Chicanos were killed in a matter of months, whole families lynched. Seven thousand fled to Mexico, leaving their small ranches and farms. The Anglos, afraid that the *mexicanos*[10] would seek independence from the U.S., brought in 20,000 army troops to put an end to the social protest movement in South Texas. Race hatred had finally fomented into an all-out war.[11]

My grandmother lost all her cattle,
  they stole her land.

"Drought hit South Texas," my mother tells me. "*La tierra se puso bien seca y los animales comenzaron a morrirse de se'. Mi papá se murío de un* heart attack *dejando a mamá* pregnant *y con ocho huercos,* with eight kids and one on the way. *Yo fuí la mayor, tenía diez años.* The next year the drought continued *y el ganado* got hoof and mouth. *Se calleron* in droves *en las pastas y el* brushland, *pansas blancas* ballooning to the skies. *El siguiente año* still no rain. *Mi pobre madre viuda perdió* two-thirds of her *ganado.* A smart *gabacho* lawyer took the land away *mamá* hadn't paid taxes. *No hablaba inglés,* she didn't know how to ask for time to raise the money." My father's mother, Mama Locha, also lost her *terreno.* For a while we got $12.50 a year for the "mineral rights" of six acres of cemetery, all that was left of the ancestral lands. Mama Locha had asked that we bury her there beside her husband. *El cemeterio estaba cercado.* But there was a fence around the cemetery, chained and padlocked by the ranch owners of the surrounding land. We couldn't even get in to visit the graves, much less bury her there. Today, it is still padlocked. The sign reads: "Keep out. Trespassers will be shot."

In the 1930s, after Anglo agribusiness corporations cheated the small Chicano landowners of their land, the corporations hired gangs of *mexicanos* to pull out the brush, chaparral and cactus and to irrigate the desert. The land they toiled over had once belonged to many of them, or had been used communally by them. Later the Anglos brought in huge machines and root plows and had the Mexicans scrape the land clean of natural vegetation. In my childhood I saw the end of dryland farming. I witnessed the land cleared; saw the huge pipes connected to underwater sources sticking up in the air. As children, we'd go fishing in some of those canals when they were full and hunt for snakes in them when they were dry. In the 1950s I saw the land, cut up into thousands of neat rectangles and squares, constantly being irrigated. In the 340-day growth season, the seeds of any kind of fruit or vegetable had only to be stuck in the ground in order to grow. More big land corporations came in and bought up the remaining land.

15 To make a living my father became a sharecropper. Rio Farms Incorporated loaned him seed money and living expenses. At harvest time, my father repaid the loan and forked over 40% of the earnings. Sometimes we earned less than we owed, but always the corporations fared well. Some had major holdings in vegetable trucking, livestock auctions and cotton gins. Altogether we lived on three successive Rio farms; the second was adjacent to the King Ranch and included a dairy farm; the third was a chicken farm. I remember the white feathers of three thousand Leghorn chickens blanketing the land for acres around. My sister, mother and I cleaned, weighed and packaged eggs. (For years afterwards I couldn't stomach the sight of an egg.) I remember my mother attending some of the meetings sponsored by well-meaning whites from Rio Farms. They talked about good nutrition, health, and held huge barbeques. The only thing salvaged for my family from those years are modern techniques of food canning and a food-stained book they printed made up of recipes from Rio Farms' Mexican women. How proud my mother was to have her recipe for *enchiladas coloradas* in a book.

El cruzar del mojado/Illegal Crossing

> *"Ahora si ya tengo una tumba para llorar,"*
> *dice Conchita,* upon being reunited with
> her unknown mother just before the mother dies
> —from Ismael Rodriguez' film,
> *Nosotros los pobres*[12]

La crisis. Los gringos had not stopped at the border. By the end of the nineteenth century, powerful landowners in Mexico, in partnership with

U.S. colonizing companies, had dispossessed millions of Indians of their lands. Currently, Mexico and her eighty million citizens are almost completely dependent on the U.S. market. The Mexican government and wealthy growers are in partnership with such American conglomerates as American Motors, IT&T and Du Pont which own factories called *maquiladoras.* One-fourth of all Mexicans work at *maquiladoras;* most are young women. Next to oil, *maquiladoras* are Mexico's second greatest source of U.S. dollars. Working eight to twelve hours a day to wire in backup lights of U.S. autos or solder miniscule wires in TV sets is not the Mexican way. While the women are in the *maquiladoras,* the children are left on their own. Many roam the street, become part of *cholo* gangs. The infusion of the values of the white culture, coupled with the exploitation by that culture, is changing the Mexican way of life.

The devaluation of the *peso* and Mexico's dependency on the U.S. have brought on what the Mexicans call *la crisis. No hay trabajo.* Half of the Mexican people are unemployed. In the U.S. a man or woman can make eight times what they can in Mexico. By March, 1987, 1,088 pesos were worth one U.S. dollar. I remember when I was growing up in Texas how we'd cross the border at Reynosa or Progreso to buy sugar or medicines when the dollar was worth eight *pesos* and fifty *centavos.*

La travesía. For many *mexicanos del otro lado,* the choice is to stay in Mexico and starve or move north and live. *Dicen que cada mexicano siempre sueña de la conquista en los brazos de cuatro gringas rubias, la conquista del país poderoso del norte, los Estados Unidos. En cada Chicano y mexicano vive el mito del tesoro territorial perdido.* North Americans call this return to the homeland the silent invasion.

> *"A la cueva volverán"*
> —El Puma *en la cancion "Amalia"*

South of the border, called North America's rubbish dump by Chicanos, *mexicanos* congregate in the plazas to talk about the best way to cross. Smugglers, *coyotes, pasadores, enganchadores* approach these people or are sought out by them. *"¿Qué dicen muchachos a echársela de mojado?"*

> "Now among the alien gods with
> weapons of magic am I."
> —Navajo protection song,
> sung when going into battle.[13]

We have a tradition of migration, a tradition of long walks. Today we are witnessing *la migración de los pueblos mexicanos,* the return odyssey to the historical/mythological Aztlán. This time, the traffic is from south to north.

El retorno to the promised land first began with the Indians from the interior of Mexico and the *mestizos* that came with the *conquistadores* in the 1500s. Immigration continued in the next three centuries, and, in this century, it continued with the *braceros* who helped to build our railroads and who picked our fruit. Today thousands of Mexicans are crossing the border legally and illegally; ten million people without documents have returned to the Southwest.

Faceless, nameless, invisible, taunted with "Hey cucaracho" (cockroach). Trembling with fear, yet filled with courage, a courage born of desperation. Barefoot and uneducated, Mexicans with hands like boot soles gather at night by the river where two worlds merge creating what Reagan calls a frontline, a war zone. The convergence has created a shock culture, a border culture, a third country, a closed country.

Without benefit of bridges, the *"mojados"* (wetbacks) float on inflatable rafts across *el río Grande,* or wade or swim across naked, clutching their clothes over their heads. Holding onto the grass, they pull themselves along the banks with a prayer to *Virgen de Guadalupe* on their lips: *Ay virgencita morena, mi madrecita, dame tu bendición.*

The Border Patrol hides behind the local McDonalds on the outskirts of Brownsville, Texas or some other border town. They set traps around the river beds beneath the bridge.[14] Hunters in army-green uniforms stalk and track these economic refugees by the powerful nightvision of electronic sensing devices planted in the ground or mounted on Border Patrol vans. Cornered by flashlights, frisked while their arms stretch over their heads, *los mojados* are handcuffed, locked in jeeps, and then kicked back across the border.

One out of every three is caught. Some return to enact their rite of passage as many as three times a day. Some of those who make it across undetected fall prey to Mexican robbers such as those in Smugglers' Canyon on the American side of the border near Tijuana. As refugees in a homeland that does not want them, many find a welcome hand holding out only suffering, pain, and ignoble death.

25 Those who make it past the checking points of the Border Patrol find themselves in the midst of 150 years of racism in Chicano *barrios* in the Southwest and in big northern cities. Living in a no-man's-borderland, caught between being treated as criminals and being able to eat, between resistance and deportation, the illegal refugees are some of the poorest and the most exploited of any people in the U.S. It is illegal for Mexicans to work without green cards. But big farming combines, farm bosses and smugglers who bring them in make money off the "wetbacks"' labor—they don't have to pay federal minimum wages, or ensure adequate housing or sanitary conditions.

The Mexican woman is especially at risk. Often the *coyote* (smuggler) doesn't feed her for days or let her go to the bathroom. Often he rapes her or sells her into prostitution. She cannot call on county or state health or economic resources because she doesn't know English and she fears deportation. American employers are quick to take advantage of her helplessness. She can't go home. She's sold her house, her furniture, borrowed from friends in order to pay the *coyote* who charges her four or five thousand dollars to smuggle her to Chicago. She may work as a live-in maid for white, Chicano or Latino households for as little as $15 a week. Or work in the garment industry, do hotel work. Isolated and worried about her family back home, afraid of getting caught and deported, living with as many as fifteen people in one room, the *mexicana* suffers serious health problems. *Se enferma de los nervios, de alta presión.*[15]

La mojada, la mujer indocumentada, is doubly threatened in this country. Not only does she have to contend with sexual violence, but like all women, she is prey to a sense of physical helplessness. As a refugee, she leaves the familiar and safe homeground to venture into unknown and possibly dangerous terrain.

This is her home
  this thin edge of
    barbwire.

Notes

[1]Los Tigres del Norte is a *conjunto* band.

[2]Jack D. Forbes, *Aztecas del Norte: The Chicanos of Aztlán.* (Greenwich, CT: Fawcett Publications, Premier Books, 1973). 13, 183; Eric R. Wolf, *Sons of Shaking Earth* (Chicago, IL: University of Chicago Press, Phoenix Books, 1959), 32.

[3]John R. Chávez, *The Lost Land: The Chicano Images of the Southwest* (Albuquerque, NM: University of New Mexico Press, 1984), 9.

[4]Chávez, 9. Besides the Aztecs, the Ute. Gabriiiino of California, Pima of Arizona, some Pueblo of New Mexico, Comanche of Texas, Opata of Sonora, Tarahumara of Sinaloa and Durango, and the Huichol of Jalisco speak Uto-Aztecan languages and are descended from the Cochise people.

[5]Reay Tannahill, *Sex In History* (Briarcliff Manor, NY: Stein and Day/Publishers/Scarborough House, 1980), 308.

[6]Chávez, 21.

[7]Isabel Parra, *El Libro Mayor de Violeta Parra* (Madrid, España: Ediciones Michay. S.A., 1985), 156–7.

[8]From the Mexican *corrido, "Del peligro de la Intervención"* Vicente T. Mendoza, *El Corrido Mexicano* (México. D.F.: Fondo De Cultura Económica, 1954), 42.

[9]Arnoldo De León. *They Called Them Greasers: Anglo Attitudes Toward Mexicans in Texas, 1821–1900* (Austin, TX: University of Texas Press, 1983), 2–3.

[10]The Plan of San Diego, Texas, drawn up on January 6, 1915, called for the independence and segregation of the states bordering Mexico: Texas, New Mexico, Arizona, Colorado, and California. Indians would get their land back, Blacks would get six states from the south and form their own independent republic. Chávez, 79.

[11]Jesús Mena, "Violence in the Rio Grande Valley," *Nuestro* (Jan/Feb. 1983), 41–42.

[12]*Nosotros los pobres* was the first Mexican film that was truly Mexican and not an imitation European film. It stressed the devotion and love that children should have for their mother and how its lack would lead to the dissipation of their character. This film spawned a generation of mother-devotion/ungrateful-sons films.

[13]From the Navajo "Protection Song" (to be sung upon going into battle). George W. Gronyn, ed., *American Indian Poetry: The Standard Anthology of Songs and Chants* (New York. NY: Liveright, 1934), 97.

[14]Grace Halsell, *Los ilegales,* trans. Mayo Antonio Sánchez (Editorial Diana Mexica, 1979).
[15]Margarita B. Melville, "Mexican Women Adapt to Migration," *International Migration Review,* 1978.

Mapping the Text

1. In the second prose paragraph of her essay, Anzaldua raises the question of *legitimacy.* She writes:

> A borderland is a vague and undetermined place created by the emotional residue of an unnatural boundary. It is in a constant state of transition. The prohibited and forbidden are its inhabitants. . . . Gringos in the U.S. Southwest consider the inhabitants of the borderlands transgressors, aliens—whether they possess documents or not, whether they're Chicanos, Indians or Blacks. . . . The only "legitimate" inhabitants are those in power, the whites and those who align themselves with whites. Tension grips the inhabitants of the borderlands like a virus. Ambivalence and unrest reside there and death is no stranger.

   On what basis does Anzaldua seem to be asserting that the people whom she names (Gringos, Chicanos, Indians, Blacks) are legitimate or illegitimate occupants of U.S. Southwest borderlands? What makes the difference, given her point of view, between the two categories? On what basis is she questioning these categories? State what you think her point of view is given what she writes in this essay. List specific sentences that suggest to you that your assessment of her viewpoint is accurate.
2. Anzaldua mixes forms of expression (in terms of both genre and language) in this piece of writing. She writes mostly in the form of an essay, but she also includes poetry. She writes mostly in English, but she also includes Spanish. Who do you think she imagines her audience to be, and what effect do you think she creates for this audience by mixing genres and languages? How would you describe your emotions as you read this essay? Include in your description any changes in the way that your body reacts as you read from beginning to end. For example, do you feel anger in one part and revulsion in another? Do you feel surprised in one part and uncomfortable in another? Do you feel excited or captivated or impatient from part to part?
3. Anzaldua uses her own family story to support her point of view. Through what way(s) of reasoning is she appealing to the reader by sharing these personal experiences? Consider whether she is directing her appeals toward the head (what is logical based on facts), the heart (what stirs the emotions), the backbone (what is right and good), or the stomach (what is sickening, absolutely distasteful, and horrifying). Find other examples in this text of appeals. Do you find Anzaldua's reasoning convincing? What is most appealing/convincing to you? What is least appealing/convincing?

Writing to Inquire

1. What effect is created when Anzaldua speaks in the first paragraph about Aztlán as the "true homeland" of "the largest single tribe or nation of Anishinabeg (Indians) found in the United States today"? What questions can you raise about the impact of conquest on a people, when they must become citizens of a new country simply because their homelands were lost in war? How does having citizens who are part of the country through conquest affect our general sense of "nation"? What complications are likely to emerge in the creation of a sense of national identity? What is the evidence in Anzaldua's essay of such complications? How do you account for the existence of such complications 150 years after the conquest? What does this viewpoint suggest to you about the spirit of a people and/or the making of a nation?
2. As in Anzaldua's selection, in contemporary society, when we think of migration and labor, images of agriculture and seasonal labor as a focus of such work often come to mind. However, there are other types of seasonal labor as well, such as that performed by student populations during the academic year (especially on campuses that are not urban) and student laborers who work at summer camps or resort areas or theme parks. How do these waves of workers affect local areas? How is this type of migrant labor force like or unlike migrant laborers who work in agricultural jobs? What significance do you see for race, class, gender, and ethnicity? How would you describe the differences in impact on individuals, families, or groups?

INQUIRY: WHAT ARE THE BOUNDARIES OF OUR NATION? WHAT PATTERNS OF MIGRATION AND IMMIGRATION HAVE REDRAWN THEM?

1. We do not typically consider ourselves a nation with colonies or as a nation of conquerors or imperialists who have taken what belongs to someone else and arbitrarily laid claim to it. Instead, we tend to think of the United States as the champion of the weak and downtrodden, the protector of freedom and justice. Write an essay in which you explain the ways in which Anzuldua and Bulosan offer challenges to these dominant images.
2. How many major waves of immigration have we experienced since the first Europeans and Africans arrived in 1619? What circumstances brought each group to the country? Which borders of the United States were the point of entry for which groups of people? Who came across the eastern, western, southern, and northern borders? Which borders have caused controversy? What problems and concerns seem centered at which borders? How can we account for these problems or concerns in social, economic, political, or cultural terms, and so forth?

How is history commemorated by public monuments like the Ellis Island Wall of Honor? Are Ellis Island immigrants pictured differently than contemporary immigrants? How do time and history create the boundaries of our nation?

3. Look for the immigration patterns of your own state. When did your state become a state? During the prestatehood era, who occupied the land, and when? How much do we know now about the earliest of these people? When did the earliest European settlers come into your state's territory? From which European countries did they come, and when? Were there waves of immigration from the same country(ies) at different points? What interests brought the European settlers to this area? What, primarily, did they do when they got there? What were their sources of work and survival?
4. What, historically, are the languages of your state? What languages are spoken by students who attend your college or university? Can you determine how to calculate the home languages of the students, faculty, and staff who currently live and/or work there?
5. Look at the current population of your city or state. Who lives there? Do language groups tend to live in recognizable communities? What historical circumstances seem to account for patterns of migration, immigration, and/or current residence?
6. Consider your own family photographs or photographs that you imagine might be representative of your family. What do the photographs look like? Who is pictured? What is happening? What do the photographs suggest about the sense that your family has of being American?
7. What, given the global context in which we live, is *patriotism?*
8. In light of the likelihood in the contemporary world of an individual embracing multiple heritages and multiple identities, how does a person develop a sense of good citizenship—in a nation, in the world?
9. Viewing the United States primarily as a nation of immigrants, early policymakers are perceived in popular belief to have invented a new, more liberal sense of what a citizen is and what the rights and privileges of citizenship are. What was new and different about citizenship in the United States? Which government documents served to write this point of view into law? At what points were specific rights guaranteed? For example, what is guaranteed in the Constitution, in the Bill of Rights, in other constitutional amendments, and so forth?
10. Looking at the national scene in terms of migration and immigration, what are the contemporary problems? With the globalization of business and industry, for example, or the internationalization of various other enterprises (banking, technology, scientific research), or the sophistication of new technologies (such as transportation and communication), how is the sense of national identity, migration, or immigration changing? Who are the new immigrants? How might concepts such as *transnational* or *multinational* apply these days to people rather than just corporations? Did such categories of migrancy always exist,

or are we experiencing an extension of definitions? How can we discuss the issues in ways that take into account traditional images of migrants and immigrants and more contemporary images of migrants and immigrants? For whom along this range of definitions are current immigrant laws set? In other words, who benefits? Who is brought into question in terms of national or transnational mobility?

CHAPTER 5

Education Matters

Education is the process by which we inculcate ideas, formally and informally, and train people to do the work whereby the community and the nation survive and thrive. Given this combination of formal and informal education, learning is revealed as a lifelong activity that continuously enables individuals to accomplish what we generally recognize as life goals. One goal of education is to enable individuals to provide for themselves and their loved ones food, clothing, shelter, and meaning for their existence. A second goal is to enable them to contribute positively and productively to the maintenance, growth, and prosperity of the world(s) around them.

Even though the process and goals of education sound simple, their actual implementation is complex. In a nation, like the United States, where the citizens are diverse in their histories, beliefs, and practices, education inevitably means a negotiation that turns on the intersections of rights, privileges, and responsibilities. Some negotiations involve issues that seem mostly personal. How does an individual develop his or her talents and abilities? What options and resources are available (or not) for educating oneself? What does it mean to make a meaningful life? Other negotiations involve issues that suggest social implications. What does the nation need, and how should our educational system respond to these needs? What should be taught in the interest of both the individual and the nation? How? By whom? When? In what context? With which goals in mind? To whose benefit? Other negotiations center on public issues. Who pays? For what? Who is entitled to participate? What constitutes fair and equal access? What constitutes fair and equal implementation? What can a citizen expect as a right? What can a citizen expect as a responsibility? By what systems and processes do we negotiate competing interests? How do we measure success and credit achievement?

Chapter 5 examines such issues from personal, social, and institutional perspectives. The selections in the "Framing the Topic" section focus on what constitutes education and how a particular view relates to images of selfhood, community values, and American-ness. The selections in "Readings for Inquiry and Exploration" offer various other perspectives that extend and enrich your view and understanding of personal challenges and address deeply rooted national problems. The "Calls to Action and Response" selections invite you to think about issues related to difference in the context of educational processes and to consider the troublesome question of whether it is possible for education to be a viable opportunity for everyone.

FRAMING THE TOPIC

The American Scholar

RALPH WALDO EMERSON

Ralph Waldo Emerson (1803–1882) was one of the best-known spiritual leaders and the most highly respected essayist of his day. He was ordained as a minister in 1829, becoming pastor of Boston's Second Church, a profession that appealed, according to his biographers, more to his desire to use his rhetorical abilities in public service than to his commitment to a ministerial life. With the death of his first wife, Emerson received an inheritance that permitted him financial independence and removed the necessity of his needing to hold a steady job. From then on he preached occasionally, lectured widely, and published many essays. Having settled in Concord, Massachusetts, Emerson remarried and started a family. In this setting, he was instrumental in the formation of the Transcendental Club, an organization whose members included the ministers Theodore Parker and Orestes A. Brownson, the educator Bronson Alcott, and writers Margaret Fuller and Henry David Thoreau. Over the course of his life, Emerson wrote many essays and editorials, some of which were published in the Transcendentalist magazine, *The Dial*. His book publications include *Nature* (1836); *Essays* (1841); *Essays: Second Series* (1844); *Representative Men* (1849), and *Conduct of Life* (1860). The essay below, "The American Scholar," was a lecture he delivered before the Phi Beta Kappa Society at Harvard University (his alma mater) in 1837. In it Emerson advocates the development of an American literature independent of European definitions.

MR. PRESIDENT AND GENTLEMEN:

I greet you on the recommencement of our literary year. Our anniversary is one of hope, and, perhaps, not enough of labor. We do not meet for games of strength or skill, for the recitation of histories, tragedies, and odes, like the ancient Greeks; for parliaments of love and poesy, like the Troubadours; nor for the advancement of science, like our contemporaries in the British and European capitals. Thus far, our holiday has been simply a friendly sign of the survival of the love of letters amongst a people too busy to give to letters any more. As such it is precious as the sign of an indestructible instinct. Perhaps the time is already come when it ought to be, and will be, something else; when the sluggard intellect of this continent will look from under its iron lids and fill the postponed expectation of the world with something better than the exertions of mechanical skill. Our day of dependence, our long apprenticeship to the learning of other lands, draws to a close. The millions that around us are rushing into life, cannot always be fed on the sere remains of foreign harvests. Events, actions arise, that must be sung, that will sing themselves. Who can doubt that poetry will revive and lead in a new age, as the star in the constellation Harp, which now flames in our zenith, astronomers announce, shall one day be the polestar for a thousand years?

In this hope I accept the topic which not only usage but the nature of our association seem to prescribe to this day,—the AMERICAN SCHOLAR. Year by year we come up hither to read one more chapter of his biography. Let us inquire what light new days and events have thrown on his character and his hopes.

It is one of those fables which out of an unknown antiquity convey an unlooked-for wisdom, that the gods, in the beginning, divided Man into men, that he might be more helpful to himself; just as the hand was divided into fingers, the better to answer its end.

The old fable covers a doctrine ever new and sublime; that there is One Man,—present to all particular men only partially, or through one faculty; and that you must take the whole society to find the whole man. Man is not a farmer, or a professor, or an engineer, but he is all. Man is priest, and scholar, and statesman, and producer, and soldier. In the *divided* or social state these functions are parcelled out to individuals, each of whom aims to do his stint of the joint work, whilst each other performs his. The fable implies that the individual, to possess himself, must sometimes return from his own labor to embrace all the other laborers. But, unfortunately, this original unit, this fountain of power, has been so distributed to multitudes, has been so minutely subdivided and peddled out, that it is spilled into drops, and cannot be gathered. The state of society is one in which the members have suffered amputation from the trunk, and strut about so many walking monsters,—a good finger, a neck, a stomach, an elbow, but never a man.

5 Man is thus metamorphosed into a thing, into many things. The planter, who is Man sent out into the field to gather food, is seldom cheered by any idea of the true dignity of his ministry. He sees his bushel and his cart, and nothing beyond, and sinks into the farmer, instead of Man on the farm. The tradesman scarcely ever gives an ideal worth to his work, but is ridden by the routine of his craft, and the soul is subject to dollars. The priest becomes a form; the attorney a statute-book; the mechanic a machine; the sailor a rope of the ship.

In this distribution of functions the scholar is the delegated intellect. In the right state he is *Man Thinking*. In the degenerate state, when the victim of society, he tends to become a mere thinker, or still worse, the parrot of other men's thinking.

In this view of him, as Man Thinking, the theory of his office is contained. Him Nature solicits with all her placid, all her monitory pictures; him the past instructs; him the future invites. Is not indeed every man a student, and do not all things exist for the student's behoof? And, finally, is not the true scholar the only true master? But the old oracle said, "All things have two handles: beware of the wrong one." In life, too often, the scholar errs with mankind and forfeits his privilege. Let us see him in his school, and consider him in reference to the main influences he receives.

I. The first in time and the first in importance of the influences upon the mind is that of nature. Every day, the sun; and, after sunset, Night and her stars. Ever the winds blow; ever the grass grows. Every day, men and women, conversing—beholding and beholden. The scholar is he of all men whom this spectacle most engages. He must settle its value in his mind. What is nature to him? There is never a beginning, there is never an end, to the inexplicable continuity of this web of God, but always circular power returning into itself. Therein it resembles his own spirit, whose beginning, whose ending, he never can find,—so entire, so boundless. Far too as her splendors shine, system on system shooting like rays, upward, downward, without center, without circumference,—in the mass and in the particle, Nature hastens to render account of herself to the mind. Classification begins. To the young mind every thing is individual, stands by itself. By and by, it finds how to join two things and see in them one nature; then three, then three thousand; and so, tyrannized over by its own unifying instinct, it goes on tying things together, diminishing anomalies, discovering roots running under ground whereby contrary and remote things cohere and flower out from one stem. It presently learns that since the dawn of history there has been a constant accumulation and classifying of facts. But what is classification but the perceiving that these objects are not chaotic, and are not foreign, but have a law which is also a law of the human mind? The astronomer discovers that geometry, a pure abstraction of the human mind, is the measure of planetary motion. The chemist finds proportions and intelligible method throughout matter; and science is nothing but the finding of analogy, identity, in the most remote parts. The ambitious soul sits down before each refractory fact; one after another reduces all strange constitutions, all new powers, to their class and their law, and goes on forever to animate the last fiber of organization, the outskirts of nature, by insight.

Thus to him, to this schoolboy under the bending dome of day, is suggested that he and it proceed from one root; one is leaf and one is flower; relation, sympathy, stirring in every vein. And what is that root? Is not that the soul of his soul? A thought too bold; a dream too wild. Yet when this spiritual light shall have revealed the law of more earthly natures,—when he has learned to worship the soul, and to see that the natural philosophy that now is, is only the first gropings of its gigantic hand, he shall look forward to an ever expanding knowledge as to a becoming creator. He shall see that nature is the opposite of the soul, answering to it part for part. One is seal and one is print. Its beauty is the beauty of his own mind. Its laws are the laws of his own mind. Nature then becomes to him the measure of his attainments. So much of nature as he is ignorant of, so much of his own mind does he not yet possess. And, in fine, the ancient precept, "Know thyself," and the modern precept, "Study nature," become at last one maxim.

II. The next great influence into the spirit of the scholar is the mind of the Past,—in whatever form, whether of literature, of art, of institutions, that mind is inscribed. Books are the best type of the influence of the past, and perhaps we shall get at the truth,—learn the amount of this influence more conveniently,—by considering their value alone.

The theory of books is noble. The scholar of the first age received into him the world around; brooded thereon; gave it the new arrangement of his own mind, and uttered it again. It came into him life; it went out from him truth. It came to him short-lived actions; it went out from him immortal thoughts. It came to him business; it went from him poetry. It was dead fact; now, it is quick thought. It can stand, and it can go. It now endures, it now flies, it now inspires. Precisely in proportion to the depth of mind from which it issued, so high does it soar, so long does it sing.

Or, I might say, it depends on how far the process had gone, of transmuting life into truth. In proportion to the completeness of the distillation, so will the purity and imperishableness of the product be. But none is quite perfect. As no air-pump can by any means make a perfect vacuum, so neither can any artist entirely exclude the conventional, the local, the perishable from his book, or write a book of pure thought, that shall be as efficient, in all respects, to a remote posterity, as to contemporaries, or rather to the second age. Each age, it is found, must write its own books; or rather, each generation for the next succeeding. The books of an older period will not fit this.

Yet hence arises a grave mischief. The sacredness which attaches to the act of creation, the act of thought, is transferred to the record. The poet chanting was felt to be a divine man: henceforth the chant is divine also. The writer was a just and wise spirit: henceforward it is settled the book is perfect; as love of the hero corrupts into worship of his statue. Instantly the book becomes noxious: the guide is a tyrant. The sluggish and perverted mind of the multitude, slow to open to the incursions of Reason, having once so opened, having once received this book, stands upon it, and makes an outcry if it is disparaged. Colleges are built on it. Books are written on it by thinkers, not by Man Thinking; by men of talent, that is, who start wrong, who set out from accepted dogmas, not from their own sight of principles. Meek young men grow up in libraries, believing it their duty to accept the views which Cicero, which Locke, which Bacon, have given; forgetful that Cicero, Locke, and Bacon were only young men in libraries when they wrote these books.

Hence, instead of Man Thinking, we have the bookworm. Hence the book-learned class, who value books, as such; not as related to nature and the human constitution, but as making a sort of Third Estate[1] with the

[1]The medieval parliament was divided into three "estates"—nobility, clergy, and commons.

world and the soul. Hence the restorers of readings, the emendators, the bibliomaniacs of all degrees.

Books are the best of things, well used; abused, among the worst. What is the right use? What is the one end which all means go to effect? They are for nothing but to inspire. I had better never see a book than to be warped by its attraction clean out of my own orbit, and made a satellite instead of a system. The one thing in the world, of value, is the active soul. This every man is entitled to; this every man contains within him, although in almost all men obstructed and as yet unborn. The soul active sees absolute truth and utters truth, or creates. In this action it is genius; not the privilege of here and there a favorite, but the sound estate of every man. In its essence it is progressive. The book, the college, the school of art, the institution of any kind, stop with some past utterance of genius. This is good, say they,—let us hold by this. They pin me down. They look backward and not forward. But genius looks forward: the eyes of man are set in his forehead, not in his hindhead: man hopes: genius creates. Whatever talents may be, if the man create not, the pure efflux of the Deity is not his;—cinders and smoke there may be, but not yet flame. There are creative manners, there are creative actions, and creative words; manners, actions, words, that is, indicative of no custom or authority, but springing spontaneous from the mind's own sense of good and fair.

On the other part, instead of being its own seer, let it receive from another mind its truth, though it were in torrents of light, without periods of solitude, inquest, and self-recovery, and a fatal disservice is done. Genius is always sufficiently the enemy of genius by over-influence. The literature of every nation bears me witness. The English dramatic poets have Shakespearized now for two hundred years.

Undoubtedly there is a right way of reading, so it be sternly subordinated. Man Thinking must not be subdued by his instruments. Books are for the scholars' idle times. When he can read God directly, the hour is too precious to be wasted in other men's transcripts of their readings. But when the intervals of darkness come, as come they must,—when the sun is hid and the stars withdraw their shining,—we repair to the lamps which were kindled by their ray, to guide our steps to the East again, where the dawn is. We hear, that we may speak. The Arabian proverb says, "A fig tree, looking on a fig tree, becometh fruitful."

It is remarkable, the character of the pleasure we derive from the best books. They impress us with the conviction that one nature wrote and the same reads. We read the verses of one of the great English poets, of Chaucer, of Marvell, of Dryden, with the most modern joy,—with a pleasure, I mean, which is in great part caused by the abstraction of all *time* from their verses. There is some awe mixed with the joy of our surprise, when this poet, who lived in some past world, two or three hundred years ago, says that which lies close to my own soul, that which I also had well-nigh thought and said. But for the evidence thence afforded to the philosophical doctrine of the identity of all minds, we should suppose some preëstablished harmony, some foresight of souls that were to be, and some preparation of stores for their future wants, like the fact observed in insects, who lay up food before death for the young grub they shall never see.

I would not be hurried by any love of system, by any exaggeration of instincts, to underrate the Book. We all know, that as the human body can be nourished on any food, though it were boiled grass and the broth of shoes, so the human mind can be fed by any knowledge. And great and heroic men have existed who had almost no other information than by the printed page. I only would say that it needs a strong head to bear that diet. One must be an inventor to read well. As the proverb says, "He that would bring home the wealth of the Indies, must carry out the wealth of the Indies." There is then creative reading as well as creative writing. When the mind is braced by labor and invention, the page of whatever book we read becomes luminous with manifold allusion. Every sentence is doubly significant, and the sense of our author is as broad as the world. We then see, what is always true, that as the seer's hour of vision is short and rare among heavy days and months, so is its record, perchance, the least part of his volume. The discerning will read, in his Plato or Shakespeare, only that least part,—only the authentic utterances of the oracle;—all the rest he rejects, were it never so many times Plato's and Shakespeare's.

Of course there is a portion of reading quite indispensable to a wise man. History and exact science he must learn by laborious reading. Colleges, in like manner, have their indispensable office,—to teach elements. But they can only highly serve us when they aim not to drill, but to create; when they gather from far every ray of various genius to their hospitable halls, and by the concentrated fires, set the hearts of their youth on flame. Thought and knowledge are natures in which apparatus and pretension avail nothing. Gowns and pecuniary foundations, though of towns of gold, can never countervail the least sentence or syllable of wit. Forget this, and our American colleges will recede in their public importance, whilst they grow richer every year.

III. There goes in the world a notion that the scholar should be a recluse, a valetudinarian,—as unfit for any handiwork or public labor as a penknife for an axe. The so-called "practical men" sneer at speculative men, as if, because they speculate or *see,* they could do nothing. I have heard it said that the clergy,—who are always, more universally than any other class, the scholars of their day,—are addressed as women; that the rough, spontaneous conversation of men they do not hear, but only a mincing and diluted speech. They are often virtually disfranchised; and indeed there are advocates for their celibacy. As far as this is true of the studious classes, it is not just and wise. Action is with the scholar subordinate, but it is essential. Without it he is not yet man. Without it thought can never ripen into truth. Whilst the world hangs before the eye as a cloud of beauty, we cannot even see its beauty. Inaction is cowardice, but there can be no scholar without the heroic mind. The preamble of thought, the transition through which it passes from the unconscious to the conscious, is action. Only so much do I know, as I have lived. Instantly we know whose words are loaded with life, and whose not.

The world,—this shadow of the soul, or *other me,*—lies wide around. Its attractions are the keys which unlock my thoughts and make me acquainted with myself. I run eagerly into this resounding tumult. I grasp the hands of those next me, and take my place in the ring to suffer and to work, taught by an instinct that so shall the dumb abyss be vocal with speech. I pierce its order; I dissipate its fear; I dispose of it within the circuit of my expanding life. So much only of life as I know by experience, so much of the wilderness have I vanquished and planted, or so far have I extended my being, my dominion. I do not see how any man can afford, for the sake of his nerves and his nap, to spare any action in which he can partake. It is pearls and rubies to his discourse. Drudgery, calamity, exasperation, want, are instructors in eloquence and wisdom. The true scholar grudges every opportunity of action past by, as a loss of power. It is the raw material out of which the intellect molds her splendid products. A strange process too, this by which experience is converted into thought, as a mulberry leaf is converted into satin. The manufacture goes forward at all hours.

The actions and events of our childhood and youth are now matters of calmest observation. They lie like fair pictures in the air. Not so with our recent actions,—with the business which we now have in hand. On this we are quite unable to speculate. Our affections as yet circulate through it. We no more feel or know it than we feel the feet, or the hand, or the brain of our body. The new deed is yet a part of life,—remains for a time immersed in our unconscious life. In some contemplative hour it detaches itself from the life like a ripe fruit, to become a thought of the mind. Instantly it is raised, transfigured; the corruptible has put on incorruption. Henceforth it is an object of beauty, however base its origin and neighborhood. Observe too the impossibility of antedating this act. In its grub state, it cannot fly, it cannot shine, it is a dull grub. But suddenly, without observation, the selfsame thing unfurls beautiful wings, and is an angel of wisdom. So is there no fact, no event, in our private history, which shall not, sooner or later, lose its adhesive, inert form, and astonish us by soaring from our body into the empyrean. Cradle and infancy, school and playground, the fear of boys, and dogs, and ferules, the love of little maids and berries, and many another fact that once filled the whole sky, are gone already; friend and relative, profession and party, town and country, nation and world, must also soar and sing.

Of course, he who has put forth his total strength in fit actions has the richest return of wisdom. I will not shut myself out of this globe of action, and transplant an oak into a flower-pot, there to hunger and pine; nor trust the revenue of some single faculty, and exhaust one vein of thought, much like those Savoyards, who, getting their livelihood by carving shepherds, shepherdesses, and smoking Dutchmen, for all Europe, went out one day to the mountain to find stock, and discovered that they had whittled up the last of their pine trees. Authors we have, in numbers, who have written out their vein, and who, moved by a commendable prudence, sail for Greece or Palestine, follow the trapper into the prairie, or ramble round Algiers, to replenish their merchantable stock.

If it were only for a vocabulary, the scholar would be covetous of action. Life is our dictionary. Years are well spent in country labors; in town; in the insight into trades and manufactures; in frank intercourse with many men and women; in science; in art; to the one end of mastering in all their facts a language by which to illustrate and embody our perceptions. I learn immediately from any speaker how much he has already lived, through the poverty or the splendor of his speech. Life lies behind us as the quarry from whence we get tiles and copestones for the masonry of today. This is the way to learn grammar. Colleges and books only copy the language which the field and the work-yard made.

But the final value of action, like that of books, and better than books, is that it is a resource. That great principle of Undulation in nature, that shows itself in the inspiring and expiring of the breath; in desire and satiety; in the ebb and flow of the sea; in day and night; in heat and cold; and, as yet more deeply ingrained in every atom and every fluid, is known to us under the name of Polarity,—these "fits of easy transmission and reflection," as Newton called them, arc the law of nature because they are the law of spirit.

The mind now thinks, now acts, and each fit reproduces the other. When the artist has exhausted his materials, when the fancy no longer paints, when thoughts are no longer apprehended and books are a weariness,—he has always the resource *to live.* Character is higher than intellect. Thinking is the function. Living is the functionary. The stream retreats to its source. A great soul will be strong to live, as well as strong to think. Does he lack organ or medium to impart his truths? He can still fall back on this elemental force of living them. This is a total act. Thinking is a partial act. Let the grandeur of justice shine in his affairs. Let the beauty of affection cheer his lowly roof. Those "far from fame," who dwell and act with him, will feel the force of his constitution in the doings and passages of the day better than it can be measured by any public and designed display. Time shall teach him that the scholar loses no hour which the man lives. Herein he unfolds the sacred germ of his instinct, screened from influence. What is lost in seemliness is gained in strength. Not out of those on whom systems of education have exhausted their culture, comes the helpful giant to destroy the old or to build the new, but out of unhandselled savage nature; out of terrible Druids and Berserkers come at last Alfred and Shakespeare.

I hear therefore with joy whatever is beginning to be said of the dignity and necessity of labor to every citizen. There is virtue yet in the hoe and the spade, for learned as well as for unlearned hands. And labor is everywhere welcome; always we are invited to work; only be this limitation observed, that a man shall not for the sake of wider activity sacrifice any opinion to the popular judgments and modes of action.

I have now spoken of the education of the scholar by nature, by books, and by action. It remains to say somewhat of his duties.

They are such as become Man Thinking. They may all be comprised in self-trust. The office of the scholar is to cheer, to raise, and to guide men by showing them facts amidst appearances. He plies the slow, unhonored, and unpaid task of observation. Flamsteed and Herschel, in their glazed observatories, may catalogue the stars with the praise of all men, and the results being splendid and useful, honor is sure. But he, in his private observatory, cataloguing obscure and nebulous stars of the human mind, which as yet no man has thought of as such,—watching days and months sometimes for a few facts; correcting still his old records;—must relinquish display and immediate fame. In the long period of his preparation he must betray often an ignorance and shiftlessness in popular arts, incurring the disdain of the able who shoulder him aside. Long he must stammer in his speech; often forego the living for the dead. Worse yet, he must accept—how often!—poverty and solitude. For the case and pleasure of treading the old road, accepting the fashions, the education, the religion of society, he takes the cross of making his own, and, of course, the self-accusation, the faint heart, the frequent uncertainty and loss of time, which are the nettles and tangling vines in the way of the self-relying and self-directed; and the state of virtual hostility in which he seems to stand to society, and especially to educated society. For all this loss and scorn, what offset? He is to find consolation in exercising the highest functions of human nature. He is one who raises himself from private considerations and breathes and lives on public and illustrious thoughts. He is the world's eye. He is the world's heart. He is to resist the vulgar prosperity that retrogrades ever to barbarism, by preserving and communicating heroic sentiments, noble biographies, melodious verse, and the conclusions of history. Whatsoever oracles the human heart, in all emergencies, in all solemn hours, has uttered as its commentary on the world of actions,—these he shall receive and impart. And whatsoever new verdict Reason from her inviolable seat pronounces on the passing men and events of today,—this he shall hear and promulgate.

These being his functions, it becomes him to feel all confidence in himself, and to defer never to the popular cry. He and he only knows the world.

The world of any moment is the merest appearance. Some great decorum,[2] some fetish of a government, some ephemeral trade, or war, or man, is cried up by half mankind and cried down by the other half, as if all depended on this particular up or down. The odds are that the whole question is not worth the poorest thought which the scholar has lost in listening to the controversy. Let him not quit his belief that a popgun is a popgun, though the ancient and honorable of the earth affirm it to be the crack of doom. In silence, in steadiness, in severe abstraction, let him hold by himself; add observation to observation, patient of neglect, patient of reproach, and bide his own time,—happy enough if he can satisfy himself alone that this day he has seen something truly. Success treads on every right step. For the instinct is sure, that prompts him to tell his brother what he thinks. He then learns that in going down into the secrets of his own mind he has descended into the secrets of all minds. He learns that he who has mastered any law in his private thoughts, is master to that extent of all men whose language he speaks, and of all into whose language his own can be translated. The poet, in utter solitude remembering his spontaneous thoughts and recording them, is found to have recorded that which men in crowded cities find true for them also. The orator distrusts at first the fitness of his frank confessions, his want of knowledge of the persons he addresses, until he finds that he is the complement of his hearers;—that they drink his words because he fulfils for them their own nature; the deeper he dives into his privatest, secretest presentiment, to his wonder he finds this is the most acceptable, most public, and universally true. The people delight in it; the better part of every man feels, This is my music; this is myself.

In self-trust all the virtues are comprehended. Free should the scholar be,—free and brave. Free even to the definition of freedom, "without any hindrance that does not arise out of his own constitution." Brave; for fear is a thing which a scholar by his very function puts behind him. Fear always springs from ignorance. It is a shame to him if his tranquillity, amid dangerous times, arise from the presumption that like children and women his is a protected class; or if he seek a temporary peace by the diversion of his thoughts from politics or vexed questions, hiding his head like an ostrich in the flowering bushes, peeping into microscopes, and turning rhymes, as a boy whistles to keep his courage up. So is the danger a danger still; so is the fear worse. Manlike let him turn and face it. Let him look into its eye and search its nature, inspect its origin,—see the whelping of this lion,—which lies no great way back; he will then find in himself a perfect comprehension of its nature and extent; he will have made his hands meet on the other side, and can henceforth defy it and pass on superior. The world is his who can see through its pretension. What deafness, what stone-blind custom, what overgrown error you behold is there only by sufferance,—by your sufferance. See it to be a lie, and you have already dealt it its mortal blow.

[2]Code of propriety.

Yes, we are the cowed,—we the trustless. It is a mischievous notion that we are come late into nature; that the world was finished a long time ago. As the world was plastic and fluid in the hands of God, so it is ever to so much of his attributes as we bring to it. To ignorance and sin, it is flint. They adapt themselves to it as they may; but in proportion as a man has any thing in him divine, the firmament flows before him and takes his signet and form. Not he is great who can alter matter, but he who can alter my state of mind. They are the kings of the world who give the color of their present thought to all nature and all art, and persuade men by the cheerful serenity of their carrying the matter, that this thing which they do is the apple which the ages have desired to pluck, now at last ripe, and inviting nations to the harvest. The great man makes the great thing. Wherever Macdonald[3] sits, there is the head of the table. Linnacus makes botany the most alluring of studies, and wins it from the farmer and the herb-woman; Davy, chemistry; Cuvier, fossils. The day is always his who works in it with serenity and great aims. The unstable estimates of men crowd to him whose mind is filled with a truth, as the heaped waves of the Atlantic follow the moon.

For this self-trust, the reason is deeper than can be fathomed,—darker than can be enlightened. I might not carry with me the feeling of my audience in stating my own belief. But I have already shown the ground of my hope, in adverting to the doctrine that man is one. I believe man has been wronged; he has wronged himself. He has almost lost the light that can lead him back to his prerogatives. Men are become of no account. Men in history, men in the world of today, are bugs, are spawn, and are called "the mass" and "the herd." In a century, in a millennium, one or two men; that is to say, one or two approximations to the right state of every man. All the rest behold, in the hero or the poet their own green and crude being,—ripened; yes, and are content to be less, so *that* may attain to its full stature. What a testimony, full of grandeur, full of pity, is borne to the demands of his own nature, by the poor clansman, the poor partisan, who rejoices in the glory of his chief. The poor and the low find some amends to their immense moral capacity, for their acquiescence in a political and social inferiority. They are content to be brushed like flies from the path of a great person, so that justice shall be done by him to that common nature which it is the dearest desire of all to see enlarged and glorified. They sun themselves in the great man's light, and feel it to be their own element. They cast the dignity of man from their downtrod selves upon the shoulders of a hero, and will perish to add one drop of blood to make that great heart beat, those giant sinews combat and conquer. He lives for us, and we live in him.

Men, such as they are, very naturally seek money or power; and power because it is as good as money,—the "spoils," so called, "of office." And why not? for they aspire to the highest, and this, in their sleep-walking, they dream is highest. Wake them and they shall quit the false good and leap to

[3]I.e., the head of the clan.

the true, and leave governments to clerks and desks. This revolution is to be wrought by the gradual domestication of the idea of Culture. The main enterprise of the world for splendor, for extent, is the upbuilding of a man. Here are the materials strewn along the ground. The private life of one man shall be a more illustrious monarchy, more formidable to its enemy, more sweet and serene in its influence to its friend, than any kingdom in history. For a man, rightly viewed, comprehendeth the particular natures of all men. Each philosopher, each bard, each actor has only done for me, as by a delegate, what one day I can do for myself. The books which once we valued more than the apple of the eye, we have quite exhausted. What is that but saying that we have come up with the point of view which the universal mind took through the eyes of one scribe; we have been that man, and have passed on. First, one, then another, we drain all cisterns, and waxing greater by all these supplies, we crave a better and more abundant food. The man has never lived that can feed us ever. The human mind cannot be enshrined in a person who shall set a barrier on any one side to this unbounded, unboundable empire. It is one central fire, which, flaming now out of the lips of Etna, lightens the capes of Sicily, and now out of the throat of Vesuvius, illuminates the towers and vineyards of Naples. It is one light which beams out of a thousand stars. It is one soul which animates all men.

But I have dwelt perhaps tediously upon this abstraction of the Scholar. I ought not to delay longer to add what I have to say of nearer reference to the time and to this country.

Historically, there is thought to be a difference in the ideas which predominate over successive epochs, and there are data for marking the genius of the Classic, of the Romantic, and now of the Reflective or Philosophical age. With the views I have intimated of the oneness or the identity of the mind through all individuals, I do not much dwell on these differences. In fact, I believe each individual passes through all three. The boy is a Greek; the youth, romantic; the adult, reflective. I deny not, however, that a revolution in the leading idea may be distinctly enough traced.

Our age is bewailed as the age of Introversion. Must that needs be evil? We, it seems, are critical; we are embarrassed with second thoughts; we cannot enjoy any thing for hankering to know whereof the pleasure consists; we are lined with eyes; we see with our feet; the time is infected with Hamlet's unhappiness,—

> "Sicklied o'er with the pale cast of thought."

It is so bad then? Sight is the last thing to be pitied. Would we be blind? Do we fear lest we should outsee nature and God, and drink truth dry? I look upon the discontent of the literary class as a mere announcement of the fact that they find themselves not in the state of mind of their fathers, and regret the coming state as untried; as a boy dreads the water before he has learned that he can swim. If there is any period one would desire to be born in, is it not the age of Revolution; when the old and the new stand side by side and admit of being compared; when the energies of all men are searched by fear and by hope; when the historic glories of the old can be compensated by the rich possibilities of the new era? This time, like all times, is a very good one, if we but know what to do with it.

I read with some joy of the auspicious signs of the coming days, as they glimmer already through poetry and art, through philosophy and science, through church and state.

One of these signs is the fact that the same movement which effected the elevation of what was called the lowest class in the state, assumed in literature a very marked and as benign an aspect. Instead of the sublime and beautiful, the near, the low, the common, was explored and poetized. That which had been negligently trodden under foot by those who were harnessing and provisioning themselves for long journeys into far countries, is suddenly found to be richer than all foreign parts. The literature of the poor, the feelings of the child, the philosophy of the street, the meaning of household life, are the topics of the time. It is a great stride. It is a sign—is it not?—of new vigor when the extremities are made active, when currents of warm life run into the hands and the feet. I ask not for the great, the remote, the romantic; what is doing in Italy or Arabia; what is Greek art, or Provençal minstrelsy; I embrace the common, I explore and sit at the feet of the familiar, the low. Give me insight into today, and you may have the antique and future worlds. What would we really know the meaning of? The meal in the firkin; the milk in the pan; the ballad in the street; the news of the boat; the glance of the eye; the form and the gait of the body;—show me the ultimate reason of these matters; show me the sublime presence of the highest spiritual cause lurking, as always it does lurk, in these suburbs and extremities of nature; let me see every trifle bristling with the polarity that ranges it instantly on an eternal law; and the shop, the plough, and the ledger referred to the like cause by which light undulates and poets sing;—and the world lies no longer a dull miscellany and lumber-room, but has form and order; there is no trifle, there is no puzzle, but one design unites and animates the farthest pinnacle and the lowest trench.

This idea has inspired the genius of Goldsmith, Burns, Cowper, and, in a newer time, of Goethe, Wordsworth and Carlyle. This idea they have differently followed and with various success. In contrast with their writing, the style of Pope, of Johnson, of Gibbon, looks cold and pedantic. This writing is blood-warm. Man is surprised to find that things near are not less beautiful and wondrous than things remote. The near explains the far. The drop is a small ocean. A man is related to all nature. This perception of the worth of the vulgar is fruitful in discoveries. Goethe, in this very thing the most modern of the moderns, has shown us, as none ever did, the genius of the ancients.

There is one man of genius who has done much for this philosophy of life, whose literary value has never yet been rightly estimated;—I mean Emanuel Swedenborg. The most imaginative of men, yet writing with the precision of a mathematician, he endeavored to engraft a purely philosophical Ethics on the popular Christianity of his time. Such an attempt of course must have difficulty which no genius could surmount. But he saw and showed the connection between nature and the affections of the soul. He pierced the emblematic or spiritual character of the visible, audible, tangible world. Especially did his shade-loving muse hover over and interpret the lower parts of nature; he showed the mysterious bond that allies moral evil to the foul material forms, and has given in epical parables a theory of insanity, of beasts, of unclean and fearful things.

Another sign of our times, also marked by an analogous political movement, is the new importance given to the single person. Every thing that tends to insulate the individual,—to surround him with barriers of natural respect, so that each man shall feel the world is his, and man shall treat with man as a sovereign state with a sovereign state,—tends to true union as well as greatness. "I learned," said the melancholy Pestalozzi, "that no man in God's wide earth is either willing or able to help any other man." Help must come from the bosom alone. The scholar is that man who must take up into himself all the ability of the time, all the contributions of the past, all the hopes of the future. He must be an university of knowledges. If there be one lesson more than another which should pierce his car, it is, The world is nothing, the man is all; in yourself is the law of all nature, and you know not yet how a globule of sap ascends; in yourself slumbers the whole of Reason; it is for you to know all; it is for you to dare all. Mr. President and Gentlemen, this confidence in the unsearched might of man belongs, by all motives, by all prophecy, by all preparation, to the American Scholar. We have listened too long to the courtly muses of Europe. The spirit of the American freeman is already suspected to be timid, imitative, tame. Public and private avarice make the air we breathe thick and fat. The scholar is decent, indolent, complaisant. See already the tragic consequence. The mind of this country, taught to aim at low objects, eats upon itself. There is no work for any but the decorous and the complaisant. Young men of the fairest promise, who begin life upon our shores, inflated by the mountain winds, shined upon by all the stars of God, find the earth below not in unison with these, but are hindered from action by the disgust which the principles on which business is managed inspire, and turn drudges, or die of disgust, some of them suicides. What is the remedy? They did not yet see, and thousands of young men as hopeful now crowding to the barriers for the career do not yet see, that if the single man plant himself indomitably on his instincts, and there abide, the huge world will come round to him. Patience,—patience; with the shades of all the good and great for company; and for solace the perspective of your own infinite life; and for work the study and the communication of principles, the making those instincts prevalent, the conversion of the world. Is it not the chief disgrace in the world, not to be an unit;—not to be reckoned one character;—not to yield that peculiar fruit which each man was created to bear, but to be reckoned in the gross, in the hundred, or the thousand, of the party, the section, to which we belong; and our opinion predicted geographically, as the north, or the south? Not so, brothers and friends—please God, ours shall not be so. We will walk on our own feet; we will work with our own hands; we will speak our own minds. The study of letters shall be no longer a name for pity, for doubt, and for sensual indulgence. The dread of man and the love of man shall be a wall of defence and a wreath of joy around all. A nation of men will for the first time exist, because each believes himself inspired by the Divine Soul which also inspires all men.

Mapping the Text

1. The title of this essay is "The American Scholar." What does the essay indicate is the occasion for this address? Describe the audience. Identify sentences in the essay that indicate the author's purpose and basic message.
2. Ralph Waldo Emerson is credited in literary circles with being a master essayist. Reread this essay carefully. Think about Emerson's basic rhetorical choices in terms of question #1 (occasion, audience, purpose, and message). Think also about other rhetorical concepts, such as who he presents himself to be in the essay; how he establishes his credibility and authority to speak; what seem to be the conditions and circumstances that encouraged him to speak out; how he uses appeals (logos, ethos, pathos). Write an essay in which you agree or disagree with his categorization as a master essayist using the evidence from your rhetorical analysis.
3. Choose a passage in Emerson's essay that stands out in some way for you. Write an essay in which you explain the passage and how it fits in with the rest of the essay. Explain also what appeals to you about the passage and perhaps the extent to which it still has significance over one hundred years later.

Writing to Inquire

1. Make two lists. In the first, jot down features of the world in which Emerson was writing. What was his world like, the United States, the eastern United States like in 1837? Include features that are evident from what Emerson actually says in the essay as well as other characteristics that you know to be true about this era. In your second list, jot down features of the contemporary world, focusing particularly on what has and has not changed since Emerson's day. Consider the two lists and write an essay in which you speculate about the likely topic of an essay that Emerson might want to write today. Be sure to use the evidence of your two lists to argue your point of view.

2. Given your understanding of what he is talking about in this essay, what view of education does Emerson convey? What does *education* mean? What kind of learning does it entail? Is this type of education a democratic view? Do you consider it, for example, a model of learning for all?

Fishing Among the Learned

NIKKY FINNEY

Nikky Finney (1957–), a poet who reads her poetry and lectures widely, is a founding member of a group known as the Affrilachian Poets, a group of writers in Kentucky who combine the heritage of their African descent with their experience of living in the Appalachian Mountains. Although Finney was not born and raised in Kentucky, she is an alumna of the University of Kentucky and was a visiting professor there in the creative writing program. Finney's poems have appeared in many anthologies and literary magazines, and she has also published her own volumes of poetry, *On Wings Made of Gauze* (1985) and *Rice* (1995), and an anthology, *Blood Root* (1998).

On the banks of her butterfly pond
Grandmother would stand
as fluid as a waterfall, teaching
with a Five and Dime pole in her hand,

Be still, and listen to that
She could be heard to say.

She would make more good decisions
lose more control, gain, relinquish power
care about more people, recycle more energy
discern more foolishness
in an afternoon of Fishing
than Congress ever could
be they all Democrat, all Republican

My first semesters ever were spent
staring up at this Human University,
shifting my weight from bamboo leg
to trout flat foot waving first cow fly
then firefly from off her apron dress,
listening to the sounds swelling
around us, there was noise, there
was instruction, there was a difference in the two

This kind of standing stare at still water;
Fresh Water Philosophy, this speaking on

the depths of a true life lived full; Saturday
Sociology, footprints baked into the soft
bank; Advanced Lucy Geography. These
outdoor lessons could go on for days and
as long as there was sun and bait there
was learning

To educate means to lead out
she whispered to me on the snakish road
home. I had no idea what she was saying
or why now.
of country bugs I'd wonder why she'd stood
me there, that pole in my hand gripped tight
as teeth full born to a jaw insisting, Girl,
Pond water is as good as any book

A good teacher can do more than talk about it
She'd already said to me in dreams *A good*
teacher can do more than talk about it, she
can see it beyond the convincing skinny pages
of any flattened tree.

There on that bank preparing me for giant
whales when she knew full well Bream
and Mullet were all we had tugging our lines

You don't fish just to catch, you fish so you
can keep, so you can put something back
the fisherwoman taught. *It has less to do*
with the fish and more to do with your line
staying in the water, with your hand on the
pole, with discerning rituals, sniffing out the
weather, with what you can figure out about
yourself that early in the quiet morning in
between the iridescent help of sun or moon,
in between the magnificent bites

Know what you will not let corrupt you, that
you cannot be bought or sold, assume another
will come after you have gone, their own pole
tight in hand as well hoping to catch something.
put something back whenever you can. *Then She'd*
untie the hook from its mouth, lay it back
in the soft velvet water, her fingers already
asking forgiveness

Now that is something to keep

(2)

I cast out among the learned and teach
to alter sleeping states. I stand before the
university pond and fish for the living who
send air bubbles up to the learned who know
real life bestows no terminal degrees.

I have come to know that we all dangle here;
grub and silk worms alike casting out our
many different lines. The well baited and the
barely hooked while the new recruits watch,
the old sentry's look out silently. We push away
from shore annually, calling our rolls like salmon
pole vaulting, determined to remember the old
ways to wisdom, do or die
Fishing is the key to everything that moves

A poet needs to fly fish in the middle of the
bluest grass in order to catch glimpses of
the privileged information; that there are too
many meetings and not enough conversations
going on. A poet needs to stand girded before the
listening eyes of those who pay their hard earned
money wondering, *Will I teach them anything that*
the world will later ask of them
to be sure and know

I must.

Inside the polished granite of Academe
A poet must hope beyond hope that we will
all keep fishing at the bank and one day forego
the carnivorous weigh-in, the comparison of
scales, and instead throw our prime catch back
while keeping the feeling of casting out close

A poet invited to the marble table must cast out
a cat gut cord, a thousand pound live wire,
with hook enough for all and reel in everything
she sees and speak of the good with the bad
and hope for the best, do or die

And cocoon along with the rest spinning for
silk, for sheepskin, for sanity, for something
higher, more enduring that sweet tenure
or paper trails, for the high and honored art

of teaching, of returning something real to the
mental food chain; to transform one single life

I stand I cast I feel I fish for something
that lives here in these waters, something
some of us have hooked but most have never
pulled all the way to the surface, something
it is something we have hooked but not yet pulled to surface, something
we'll eternally feel nibbling our lines but never
lay our eyes free and flat upon if we do not
study the scholarship of fishing.

(3)

In the spirit of the old blind ones, those who
would take their chances in a heartbeat, pull
up safe anchor, all their eggs trembling in one
basket, throw your line out a little farther
tomorrow, Remember their commandment;
"If you do what you've always done,
you're gonna get what you've always got."

Don't pull your line in too fast,
Grandmother would say out of the corner of her eye,
Keep your hook in the water all the way to the edge
that's where the great tadpoles swim.

There are possibilities all the way to the end
whatever you do, take fishing with you.

The sound of air bubbles
and that of lips pursed
just below the surface of an idea
ready to bite, the bobber being pulled
down into the luminous murky world
of the imagination. Once airborne and
arcing the tiny mullet changing into the
giant Orca right before our very eyes,

Now that is something to keep.

Mapping the Text

1. Go through "Fishing Among the Learned" and list all the words and phrases that mention teaching, learning, education, or what is being taught. Read over your list. How do you categorize the type of education that Finney is talking about? What does it entail? What are its goals?

2. Reread the last stanza of Finney's poem. What message does it convey? Find lines in the poem that you think suggest that Finney might actually have been expressing this message as an argument. If this were true, what lines from the poem would constitute the parts of this argument? How does she present and build her point of view? To what extent do you think she presents this idea convincingly?
3. In this poem, Finney uses the image of fishing to represent her point of view. Go through the poem and find three or four ways in which she uses this image. Discuss the images you identified and how you think Finney uses them to make her point.

Writing to Inquire

1. A writer has the option of choosing from among a variety of literary and nonliterary forms of expression or *genres*. Literary genres, for example, include fiction (novels, short stories), nonfiction (narratives, essays), poetry, drama. In addition to the literary forms are others we typically do not think of as literary as such—for example, letters, journals, diaries, reports. Think about your own life and experiences. Make a list of lessons you live by based on these experiences. Place yourself in Nikky Finney's position. You want to write convincingly about your lesson(s) as valuable to take with you. Finney chose to write a poem. What genre of expression would you choose? Why?

READINGS FOR INQUIRY AND EXPLORATION

Analogy As the Core of Cognition

DOUGLAS R. HOFSTADTER

Douglas R. Hofstadter, Professor of Computer science and Cognitive science, is director of the Center for Research on Concepts and Cognition and adjunct professor of philosophy, psychology, comparative literature, and the history and philosophy of science at Indiana University. His books include *Gödel, Escher, Bach: An Eternal Golden Braid* (1979), for which he won the Pulitzer Prize, and *Metamagical Themas* (1985). He has written numerous articles that address subjects ranging from artificial intelligence to human error-making. In "Analogy As the Core of Cognition," Hofstadter examines the intricate links between language and understanding.

Grand Prelude and Mild Disclaimer

Once upon a time, I was invited to speak at an analogy workshop in the legendary city of Sofia in the far-off land of Bulgaria. Having accepted but wavering as to what to say, I finally chose to eschew technicalities and instead to convey a personal perspective on the importance and centrality of analogy-making in cognition. One way I could suggest this perspective is to re-chant a refrain that I've chanted quite oft in the past, to wit:

> One should not think of analogy-making as a special variety of *reasoning* (as in the dull and uninspiring phrase "analogical reasoning and problem-solving," a long-standing cliché in the cognitive-science world), for that is to do analogy a terrible disservice. After all, reasoning and problem-solving have (at least I dearly hope!) been at long last recognized as lying far indeed from the core of human thought. If analogy were merely a special variety of something that in itself lies way out on the peripheries, then it would be but an itty-bitty blip in the broad blue sky of cognition. To me, however, analogy is anything but a bitty blip—rather, it's the very blue that fills the whole sky of cognition—analogy is *everything,* or very nearly so, in my view.

End of oft-chanted refrain. If you don't like it, you won't like what follows.

The thrust of my article is to persuade readers of this unorthodox viewpoint, or failing that, at least to give them a strong whiff of it. In that sense, then, my article shares with Richard Dawkins' eye-opening book *The Selfish Gene* [Dawkins 1976] the quality of trying to make a scientific contribution mostly by suggesting to readers a shift of viewpoint—a new take on familiar phenomena. For Dawkins, the shift was to turn causality on its head, so that the old quip "a chicken is an egg's way of making another egg" might be taken not as a joke but quite seriously. In my case, the shift is to suggest that every concept we have is essentially nothing but a tightly packaged bundle of analogies, and to suggest that all we do when we think is to move fluidly from concept to concept—in other words, to leap from one analogy-bundle to another—and to suggest, lastly, that such concept-to-concept leaps are themselves made via analogical connection, to boot.

This viewpoint may be overly ambitious, and may even—horrors—be somewhat wrong, but I have observed that many good ideas start out by claiming too much territory for themselves, and eventually, when they have received their fair share of attention and respect, the air clears and it emerges that, though still grand, they are not quite so grand and all-encompassing as their proponents first thought. But that's all right. As for me, I just hope that my view finds a few sympathetic readers. That would be a fine start.

Two Riddles

We begin with a couple of simple queries about familiar phenomena: "Why do babies not remember events that happen to them?" and "Why does each new year seem to pass faster than the one before?"

I wouldn't swear that I have the final answer to either one of these queries, but I do have a hunch, and I will here speculate on the basis of that hunch. And thus: the answer to both is basically the same, I would argue, and it has to do with the relentless, lifelong process of *chunking*—taking "small" concepts and putting them together into bigger and bigger ones, thus recursively building up a giant repertoire of concepts in the mind.

How, then, might chunking provide the clue to these riddles? Well, babies' concepts are simply *too small.* They have no way of framing entire events whatsoever in terms of their novice concepts. It is as if babies were looking at life through a randomly drifting keyhole, and at each moment could make out only the most local aspects of scenes before them. It would be hopeless to try to figure out how a whole room is organized, for instance, given just a keyhole view, even a randomly drifting keyhole view.

Or, to trot out another analogy, life is like a chess game, and babies are like beginners looking at a complex scene on a board, not having the faintest idea how to organize it into higher-level structures. As has been well known for decades, experienced chess players chunk the setup of pieces on the board nearly instantaneously into small dynamic groupings defined by their strategic meanings, and thanks to this automatic, intuitive chunking, they can make good moves nearly instantaneously and also can remember complex chess situations for very long times. Much the same holds for bridge players, who effortlessly remember every bid and every play in a game, and months later can still recite entire games at the drop of a hat.

All of this is due to chunking, and I speculate that babies are to life as novice players are to the games they are learning—they simply lack the experience that allows understanding (or even perceiving) of large structures, and so nothing above a rather low level of abstraction gets perceived at all, let alone remembered in later years. As one grows older, however, one's chunks grow in size and in number, and consequently one automatically starts to perceive and to frame ever larger events and constellations of events; by the time one is nearing one's teen years, complex fragments from life's stream are routinely stored as high-level wholes—and chunks just keep on accreting and becoming more numerous as one lives. Events that a baby or young child could not have possibly perceived as such—events that stretch out over many minutes, hours, days, or even weeks—are effortlessly perceived and stored away as single structures with much internal detail (varying amounts of which can be pulled up and contemplated in retrospect, depending on context). Babies do not have large chunks and simply cannot put things together coherently. Claims by some people that they remember complex events from when they were but a few months old (some even claim to remember being born!) strike me as nothing more than highly deluded wishful thinking.

So much for question number one. As for number two, the answer, or so I would claim, is very similar. The more we live, the larger our repertoire of concepts becomes, which allows us to gobble up ever larger coherent stretches of life in single mental chunks. As we start seeing life's pattern's on higher and higher levels, the lower levels nearly vanish from our perception. This effectively means that seconds, once so salient to our baby selves, nearly vanish from sight, and then minutes go the way of seconds, and soon so do hours, and then days, and then weeks. . .

10 "Boy, this year sure went by fast!" is so tempting to say because each year is perceived in terms of chunks at a higher, grander, larger level than any year preceding it, and therefore *each passing year contains fewer top-level chunks* than any year preceding it, and so, psychologically, each year seems sparser than any of its predecessors. One might, somewhat facetiously, symbolize the ever-rapider passage of time by citing the famous harmonic series:

$$1 + 1/2 + 1/3 + 1/4 + 1/5 + 1/6 + 1/7 + 1/8 \ldots$$

by which I mean to suggest that one's nth year feels subjectively n times as short as one's first year, or $n/5$ times as short as one's fifth year, and so on. Thus when one is an adult, the years seem to go by about at roughly a constant rate, because—for instance—(1/35)/(1/36) is very nearly 1. Nonetheless, according to this theory, year 70 would still shoot by twice as fast as year 35 did, and seven times as fast as year 10 did.

But the exact numerical values shown above are not what matter; I just put them in for entertainment value. The more central and more serious idea is simply that relentless mental chunking makes life seem to pass ever faster as one ages, and there is nothing one can do about it. So much for our two riddles.

Analogy, Abstract Categories, and High-level Perception

Before I go any further, I would like to relate all this to analogy, for to some, the connection may seem tenuous, if not nonexistent. And yet to me, by contrast, analogy does not just lurk darkly here, but is right up there, front and center. I begin with the mundane observation that vision takes an input of millions of retinal dots and gives an output of concepts—often words or phrases, such as "duck," "Victorian house," "funky chair," "Joyce Carol Oates hairdo," or "looks sort of like President Eisenhower." The (visual) perceptual process, in other words, can be thought of as the triggering of mental categories—often standard lexical items—by scenes. Of course high-level perception can take place through other sensory modalities: we can hear a low rumbling noise and say "helicopter," can sniff something and remark "doctor's office," can taste something and find the words "okra curry" jumping to our tongue, and so on.

In fact, I should stress that the upper echelons of high-level perception totally transcend the normal flavor of the word "perception," for at the highest levels, input modality plays essentially no role. Let me explain. Suppose I read a newspaper article about the violent expulsion of one group of people by another group from some geographical region, and the phrase "ethnic cleansing," nowhere present in the article, pops into my head. What has happened here is a quintessential example of high-level perception—but what was the input medium? Someone might say it was *vision,* since I used my eyes to read the newspaper. But really, was I perceiving ethnic cleansing *visually?* Hardly. Indeed, I might have heard the newspaper article read aloud to me and had the same exact thought pop to mind. Would that mean that I had *aurally* perceived ethnic cleansing? Or else I might be blind and have read the article in braille—in other words, with my fingertips, not my eyes or ears. Would that mean that I had *tactilely* perceived ethnic cleansing? The suggestion is absurd.

The sensory input modality of a complex story is totally irrelevant; all that matters is how it jointly activates a host of interrelated concepts, in such a way that further concepts (e.g., "ethnic cleansing") are automatically accessed and brought up to center stage. Thus "high-level perception" is a kind of misnomer when it reaches the most abstract levels, but I don't know what else to call it, because I see no sharp line separating it from cases of recognizing "French impressionism" in a piece of music heard on the radio or thinking "Art Deco" when looking at a typeface in an advertisement.

The triggering of prior mental categories by some kind of input—whether sensory or more abstract—is, I insist, an act of analogy-making.

Why is this? Because whenever a set of incoming stimuli activates one or more mental categories, some amount of slippage must occur (no instance of a category ever being precisely identical to a prior instance). Categories are quintessentially fluid entities; they adapt to a set of incoming stimuli and try to align themselves with it. The process of inexact matching between prior categories and new things being perceived (whether those "things" are physical objects or bite-size events or grand sagas) is analogy-making *par excellence.* How could anyone deny this? After all, it is the mental mapping onto each other of two entities—one old and sound asleep in the recesses of long-term memory, the other new and gaily dancing on the mind's center stage—that in fact differ from each other in a myriad of ways.

The Mental Lexicon: A Vast Storehouse of Triggerable Analogies

We humans begin life as rather austere analogy-makers—our set of categories is terribly sparse, and each category itself is hardly well-honed. Categories grow sharper and sharper and ever more flexible and subtle as we age, and of course fantastically more numerous. Many of our categories, though by no means all, are named by words or standard phrases shared with other people, and for the time being I will concentrate on those categories—categories that are named by so-called "lexical items." The public labels of such categories—the lexical items themselves—come in many grades, ranging more or less as follows:

- simple words: *chair, clock, cork, cannon, crash, clown, clue, cloak, climber. . .*
- compound words: *armchair, alarm clock, corkscrew, cannonball, skyscraper, station wagon, sexpot, salad dressing, schoolbus, jukebox, picket line, horror movie, wheeler-dealer. . .*
- short phrases: *musical chairs, out of order, Christmas tree ornament, nonprofit organization, business hours, foregone conclusion, rush-hour traffic, country-Western music, welcome home, tell me about it, give me a break, and his lovely wife, second rate, swallow your pride. . .*
- longer phrases: *stranded on a desert island; damned if you do, damned if you don't; praise the Lord and pass the ammunition; not in the foreseeable future; to the best of my knowledge; and they lived happily ever after; if it were up to me; haven't seen her since she was knee-high to a grasshopper; you could have knocked me over with a feather; thank you for not smoking; handed to him on a silver platter. . .*

Such lists go on and on virtually forever, and yet the amazing fact is that few people have any inkling of the vastness of their mental lexicons (I owe a major debt here to Joe Becker—see [Becker 1975]). To be sure, most adults use their vast mental lexicons with great virtuosity, but they have stunningly little explicit awareness of what they are doing.

It was Roger Schank, I believe, who pointed out that we often use *proverbs* as what I would call "situation labels," by which I mean that when we perceive a situation, what often springs to mind, totally unbidden, is some proverb tucked away in our unconscious, and if we are talking to someone, we will quote that proverb, and our listener will in all likelihood understand very clearly how the proverb "fits" the situation—in other words, will effortlessly make the mapping (the *analogy,* to stress what it is that we are talking about here) between the phrase's meaning and the situation. Thus the following kinds of phrases can easily be used as situation labels:

That's the pot calling the kettle black if *I* ever saw it!
It just went in one ear and out the other. . .
Speak of the devil!
When the cat's away the mice will play!

The Common Core Behind a Lexical Item

I now make an observation that, though banal and obvious, needs to be made explicitly nonetheless—namely, things "out there" (objects, situations, whatever) that are labeled by the same lexical item have something, some core, in common; also whatever it is that those things "out there" share is shared with the abstract mental structure that lurks behind the label used for them. Getting to the core of things is, after all, what categories are for. In fact, I would go somewhat further and claim that getting to the core of things is what thinking itself is for—thus once again placing high-level perception front and center in the definition of cognition.

The noun "shadow" offers a good example of the complexity and subtlety of structure that lurks behind not just *some* lexical items, but behind every single one. Note, first of all, the subtle difference between "shadow" and "shade": we do not speak of cattle seeking *shadow* on a hot day, but *shade.* Many languages do not make this distinction, and thus they offer their native speakers a set of categories that is tuned slightly differently.

In many parts of the world, there are arid zones that lie just to the east of mountain ranges (e.g., the desert in Oregon just to the east of the Cascade mountains); these regions are standardly referred to as the mountain chain's "rain shadow."

What does one call the roughly circular patch of green seen underneath a tree after a snowfall? It could clearly be called a "snow shadow"—the region where snow failed to fall, having been blocked by an object.

A young woman who aspires to join her high-school swimming team, but whose mother was an Olympic swimmer, can be said to be "in the shadow of her mother." In fact, if she joins the team and competes, she might even be said to be "swimming in the shadow of her mother." And if she performs less well than her mother did, she will be said to be "overshadowed" by her mother.

One might say about a man who has had a bout with cancer but has recovered and is now feeling more secure about his health, "He is finally feeling more or less out of the shadow of his cancer." Along similar lines, many countries in Europe have recovered, to a large extent, from the ravages of World War II, but some might still be said to lie "in the shadow of World War II."

Another type of shadow cast by World War II (or by any war) lies in the skewed population distribution of any decimated group; that is, one imagines the human population as constituting a kind of flow of myriad tiny entities (individual people) down through the years (like that of photons or snowflakes through space), but long after the war's end, there are certain "regions" of humanity (e.g., certain ethnic groups) where the flow of births has been greatly reduced, much as if by an "obstacle" (namely, the millions of deaths in prior generations, whose effect continues to reverberate for many decades before gradually fading away, as a group's population replenishes itself).

There is of course no sharp line between cases where a world like "shadow" is used conventionally and cases where it is used in a novel manner; although "rain shadow" is something of a standard phrase, "snow shadow" (even though it is far easier to see) is less common. And notions like that of "population shadow" mentioned at the end are probably novel to most readers of this article, even though a closely related notion like "in the shadow of the war" is probably not new.

In short, the domain of the word "shadow" is a blurry region in semantic space, as is any human category, and—here I hark back to my initial refrain—that blur is due to the subtleties of mapping situations onto other situations—due, in other words, to the human facility of making analogies. The point is, a concept is a package of analogies.

Complex Lexical Items as Names of Complex Categories

Over the next few pages I will present a potpourri of mental categories (via proxies—namely, their English-language lexical-item representations); I invite you to think, as you consider each item, just what it is that very different exemplars of the category in question tend to have in common. Thus:

- dog
- backlog
- probably
- probab-*lee!*

I interrupt the list momentarily to comment on the last two entries above, which of course are not nouns. (Who says nouns are the only mental categories? Obviously, verbs represent categories as well—but the same holds true, no less, for adjectives, adverbs, and so forth.) Some situations call forth the word "probably"; most do not. To some situations, the concept behind the word "probably" simply *fits,* while to most, it does not fit. We learn how to use the word "probably" over the course of years in childhood, until it becomes so ingrained that it never crosses our mind that "probably" is the name that English speakers give to a certain category of situations; it simply is *evoked* effortlessly and rapidly by those situations, and it is uttered without any conscious thought as to how it applies. It just "seems right" or "sounds right."

What, then about the word below it: "probab-*lee*"? This, too, is a lexical item in the minds of most native speakers of contemporary American English—perhaps not often used, perhaps more commonly heard than uttered by readers of this article, but nonetheless, we native speakers of American English all relate to hearing the word "probably" accented on its final rather than its initial syllable, and we all somehow realize the connotations hidden therein, though they may be terribly hard to articulate. I won't try to articulate them myself, but I would merely point out that this phonetic variant of the word "probably" fits only certain situations and not others (where the "situation" includes, needless to say, not just what is being talked about but also the mood of the speaker, *and* the speaker's assessment of the mood of the listener as well). Example: "Are our stupid leaders ever going to learn their lesson?" "Who knows? Maybe they're doomed to keep on repeating the mistakes of the past." "Mmm. . . Probab-*lee*. . ."

My point, with all the phrases cited above, is to bring to your conscious awareness the fact that there are certain situations that one could call "*probab*-lee! situations," no less than there are certain situations that are "*musical chairs* situations" or "*speak of the devil* situations." In short, lexical items can be very abstract categories evoked by special classes of situations and not by others. This applies to adjectives, adverbs, prepositions, interjections, short and long phrases, and so on. Thus let me continue my list.

- Come *on!*
- Go for it!
- It's about time!
- Well, excuuuuuuuuuse me!
- Let's not stand on ceremony!
- without batting an eyelash
- ain't

Lest the lowest item above seem puzzling, let me point out that the notorious contraction "ain't," although it is in a certain sense ungrammatical and improper, is nonetheless used very precisely, like pinpoint bombing, by politicians, reporters, university presidents, and the like, who carefully and deliberately insert it into their speech at well-limed moments when they know their audience almost expects it—it fits the context perfectly. For example, a general trying to justify a bombing raid might say, in describing the series of deadly skirmishes that provoked it, "I'm sorry, but a Sunday picnic it just *ain't*." This is just one of many types of "ain't" situations. We native speakers know them when we hear them, and we likewise have a keen ear for *improper* uses of the word "ain't" by educated people, even if we ain't capable of putting our finger on what makes them inappropriate. (Curiously enough, shortly after drafting this paragraph, I came across an article in the *New York Times* about the failure of a test missile to hit its target, and a perfectly straight photo caption started out, "Two out of four goals ain't bad. . . ." As I said above, even the most highly placed sources will use this "ungrammatical" word without batting an eyelash.)

. . .

Winding Up: On Associationism and the Cartesian Theater

The crux of this essay is the claim that thinking (at least when isolated from external influences) is a series of leaps involving high-level perception, activation of concepts in long-term memory, transfer to short-term memory, partial and context-dependent unpacking of chunks, and then further high-level perception, and so forth.

This may sound like no more than the age-old idea of associationism—that we think by jumping associatively from one thing to another. If that's all it came down to, my thesis would certainly be a sterile and vapid non-contribution to cognitive science. But the mechanisms I posit are more specific, and in particular they depend on the the transfer of tightly packed mental chunks from the dormant area of long-term memory into the active area of short-term memory, and on their being unpacked on arrival, and then scrutinized. Both transfer and perception are crucial, and in that respect, my thesis departs significantly from associationism.

Some readers, such as the author of *Consciousness Explained* [Dennett 1991], might feel they detect in this theory of thinking an insidious residue of the so-called "Cartesian theater"—a hypothetical theater in which an "inner eye" watches as various images go parading by on a "mental screen," and becomes "aware" or "conscious" of such imagery. Such a notion of thinking leads very easily down the slippery slope of nested homunculi, and thus to an infinite regress concerning the site of consciousness.

I would gladly plead guilty to the accusation of positing a "screen" upon which are "projected" certain representations dredged up from long-term memory, and I would also plead guilty to the accusation of positing an "inner eye" that scans that screen and upon it posts further representational structures, which trigger a descent via analogy into the dormant depths of long-term memory. I would insist, however, that the label "perception," as applied to what the "inner eye" does, be sharply distinguished from visual or any other kind of sensory perception, since in general it involves no sensory modality in any normal sense of the term (recall the perception of "ethnic cleansing" in a newspaper story). The nature of such abstract or high-level perceptual processing has been sketched out in work done by my students and myself over the years (see [Hofstadter & FARG, 1995]), and I will not attempt to describe it here. Clearly, since it has been implemented as a computer program (at least to a first approximation), such a model does not succumb to snagging on the fatal hook of infinite regress.

To those who would scoff at the very notion of any "inner screen" involved in cognition, I would point to the large body of work of perceptual psychologist Anne Treisman [e.g., Treisman 1988], which in my view establishes beyond any doubt the existence of temporary perceptual structures created on the fly in working memory (she calls them "object files")—a stark contrast to the connectionist-style thesis that all cognition takes place in long-term memory, and that it consists merely of simultaneous *conceptual activations* (possibly with attached temporal phases, so as to handle the "binding problem") without any type of transfer to, or structure-building in, a distinct working area. Although this more distributed view of the essence of cognition might appeal to opponents of the Cartesian theater, it does not seem to me that it comes anywhere close to allowing the richness of thought that back-and-forth flow between long-term and short-term memory would allow.

I hope that my speculative portrayal of analogy as the lifeblood, so to speak, of human thinking, despite being highly ambitious and perhaps somewhat overreaching, strikes a resonant chord in those who study cognition. My most optimistic vision would be that the whole field of cognitive science suddenly woke up to the centrality of analogy, that all sides suddenly saw eye to eye on topics that had formerly divided them most bitterly, and naturally—indeed, it goes without saying—that they lived happily ever after. Whatever.

Bibliography

Barnstone, Willis (1993). *The Poetics of Translation: History, Theory, Practice.* New Haven: Yale University Press.

Becker, Joseph (1975). "The Phrasal Lexicon," in R. Schank and B. Nash-Webber, eds., *Theoretical Issues in Natural Language Processing.* Cambridge, MA: Bolt, Beranek and Newman.

Blackmore, Susan (1999). *The Meme Machine.* New York: Oxford University Press.

Dawkins, Richard (1976). *The Selfish Gene.* New York: Oxford University Press.

Dennett, Daniel C. (1991). *Consciousness Explained.* Boston: Little, Brown, and Company.

Hofstadter, Douglas R. (1997). *Le Ton beau de Marot.* New York: Basic Books.

Hofstadter, Douglas R., and David J. Moser (1989). "To Err Is Human: To Study Error-making Is Cognitive Science." *Michigan Quarterly Review,* vol. 28, no. 2, pp. 185–215.

Hofstadter, Douglas R., and the Fluid Analogies Research Group (1995). *Fluid Concepts and Creative Analogies.* New York: Basic Books.

Kanerva, Pentti (1988). *Sparse Distributed Memory.* Cambridge, Massachusetts: MIT Press (Bradford Books).

Schank, Roger (1982). *Dynamic Memory.* New York: Cambridge University Press.

Treisman, Anne (1988). "Features and Objects: The Fourteenth Bartlett Memorial Lecture." *Quarterly Journal of Experimental Psychology,* vol. 40A, pp. 201–237.

Mapping the Text

1. In the opening paragraph of Douglas R. Hofstadter's essay "Analogy As the Core of Cognition," he states that he chose not to do a technical analysis of the centrality of analogy-making in cognition but to convey instead a personal perspective. Create an outline of the essay. To what extent do you think Hofstadter has succeeded in achieving this distinction between technical and personal? On what basis is he justified in making this claim? Use your analysis to explain how this essay can be categorized as personal and how it might be categorized in other ways.
2. Find definitions of the words *cognition, analogy, and reasoning.* Explain how you think Hofstadter views these terms and the relationships between them. Do you find his view helpful to your own thinking about the ways that the human mind works, how learning happens, or what good thinking means?
3. Reread Hofstadter's essay and focus on the person you envision behind these words. How would you characterize the person thinking and the person speaking? What is your impression of this person? What personal characteristics seem to show through? Write a profile of this writer based on your impressions.

Writing to Inquire

1. Near the end of his essay, Hofstadter extends an invitation to the reader to think about possible connections among a specific list of words and where those connections might take a person's thinking. Take the invitation. Generate a list of five or six words. Exchange your list with that of someone else in the class. Read your classmate's list and jot down the connections you make. What memories or experiences do you bring to each of the words? How do you make connections? Consider the idea that Hofstadter's view of how we think may also be connected to how we learn; write a paper in which you discuss how you think and learn. Consider in your discussion whether Hofstadter's terms are useful in understanding and articulating your own view. To what extent do cognition, analogy, reason, language, experience matter?

Indian Education

SHERMAN ALEXIE

Sherman Alexie (1966–)—an author of poetry, fiction, and screenplays—is a Native American writer known for his offbeat, often painfully humorous accounts of reservation life. Alexie, a Spokane/Coeur d'Alene Indian, was raised on the Spokane Indian Reservation in Washington state, a setting that features prominently in his work. Aware of the educational inequities of the reservation school system, Alexie attended public high school and became valedictorian of his class. He later earned his B.A. at Washington State University in Pullman. In 1992, he published his first collection of poetry and stories, titled *The Business of Fancydancing,* which earned a nod from the *New York Times Book Review* as a "1992 Notable Book of the Year." Alexie also received the National Endowment for the Arts Poetry Fellowship in 1992. His works include *The Lone Ranger and Tonto Fistfight in Heaven (1994)* and *Reservation Blues* (1995). His first screenplay, *Smoke Signals,* based on *The Lone Ranger and Tonto Fistfight in Heaven,* was made into the first feature film produced, written, and directed by American Indians. It won the 1998 Sundance Film Festival's Audience Award and Filmmakers Trophy. The short piece below, "Indian Education," excerpted from *The Lone Ranger and Tonto Fistfight in Heaven,* highlights Alexie's signature fiction writing style, which often involves the kind of conciseness we normally associate with poetry.

First Grade

My hair was too short and my U.S. Government glasses were horn-rimmed, ugly, and all that first winter in school, the other Indian boys chased me from one corner of the playground to the other. They pushed me down, buried me in the snow until I couldn't breathe, thought I'd never breathe again.

They stole my glasses and threw them over my head, around my outstretched hands, just beyond my reach, until someone tripped me and sent me falling again, facedown in the snow.

I was always falling down; my Indian name was Junior Falls Down. Sometimes it was Bloody Nose or Steal-His-Lunch. Once, it was Cries-Like-a-White-Boy, even though none of us had seen a white boy cry.

Then it was a Friday morning recess and Frenchy SiJohn threw snowballs at me while the rest of the Indian boys tortured some other *top-yogh-yaught* kid, another weakling. But Frenchy was confident enough to torment me all by himself, and most days I would have let him.

5 But the little warrior in me roared to life that day and knocked Frenchy to the ground, held his head against the snow, and punched him so hard that my knuckles and the snow made symmetrical bruises on his face. He almost looked like he was wearing war paint.

But he wasn't the warrior. I was. And I chanted *It's a good day to die, it's a good day to die,* all the way down to the principal's office.

Second Grade

Betty Towle, missionary teacher, redheaded and so ugly that no one ever had a puppy crush on her, made me stay in for recess fourteen days straight.

"Tell me you're sorry," she said.

"Sorry for what?" I asked.

10 "Everything," she said and made me stand straight for fifteen minutes, eagle-armed with books in each hand. One was a math book; the other was English. But all I learned was that gravity can be painful.

For Halloween I drew a picture of her riding a broom with a scrawny cat on the back. She said that her God would never forgive me for that.

Once, she gave the class a spelling test but set me aside and gave me a test designed for junior high students. When I spelled all the words right, she crumpled up the paper and made me eat it.

"You'll learn respect," she said.

She sent a letter home with me that told my parents to either cut my braids or keep me home from class. My parents came in the next day and dragged their braids across Betty Towle's desk.

15 "Indians, indians, indians." She said it without capitalization. She called me "indian, indian, indian."

And I said, *Yes, I am. I am Indian. Indian, I am.*

Third Grade

My traditional Native American art career began and ended with my very first portrait: *Stick Indian Taking a Piss in My Backyard.*

As I circulated the original print around the classroom, Mrs. Schluter intercepted and confiscated my art.

Censorship, I might cry now. *Freedom of expression,* I would write in editorials to the tribal newspaper.

20 In third grade, though, I stood alone in the corner, faced the wall, and waited for the punishment to end.

I'm still waiting.

Fourth Grade

"You should be a doctor when you grow up," Mr. Schluter told me, even though his wife, the third grade teacher, thought I was crazy beyond my years. My eyes always looked like I had just hit-and-run someone.

"Guilty," she said. "You always look guilty."

"Why should I be a doctor?" I asked Mr. Schluter.

25 "So you can come back and help the tribe. So you can heal people."

That was the year my father drank a gallon of vodka a day and the same year that my mother started two hundred different quilts but never finished any. They sat in separate, dark places in our HUD house and wept savagely.

I ran home after school, heard their Indian tears, and looked in the mirror. *Doctor Victor,* I called myself, invented an education, talked to my reflection. *Doctor Victor to the emergency room.*

Fifth Grade

I picked up a basketball for the first time and made my first shot. No. I missed my first shot, missed the basket completely, and the ball landed in the dirt and sawdust, sat there just like I had sat there only minutes before.

But it felt good, that ball in my hands, all those possibilities and angles. It was mathematics, geometry. It was beautiful.

30 At that same moment, my cousin Steven Ford sniffed rubber cement from a paper bag and leaned back on the merry-go-round. His ears rang, his mouth was dry, and everyone seemed so far away.

But it felt good, that buzz in his head, all those colors and noises. It was chemistry, biology. It was beautiful.

Oh, do you remember those sweet, almost innocent choices that the Indian boys were forced to make?

Sixth Grade

Randy, the new Indian kid from the white town of Springdale, got into a fight an hour after he first walked into the reservation school.

Stevie Flett called him out, called him a squawman, called him a pussy, and called him a punk.

35 Randy and Stevie, and the rest of the Indian boys, walked out into the playground.

"Throw the first punch," Stevie said as they squared off.

"No," Randy said.

"Throw the first punch," Stevie said again.

"No," Randy said again.

40 "Throw the first punch!" Stevie said for the third time, and Randy reared back and pitched a knuckle fastball that broke Stevie's nose.

We all stood there in silence, in awe.

That was Randy, my soon-to-be first and best friend, who taught me the most valuable lesson about living in the white world: *Always throw the first punch.*

Seventh Grade

I leaned through the basement window of the HUD house and kissed the white girl who would later be raped by her foster-parent father, who was also white. They both lived on the reservation, though, and when the headlines and stories filled the papers later, not one word was made of their color.

Just Indians being Indians, someone must have said somewhere and they were wrong.

But on the day I leaned through the basement window of the HUD house and kissed the white girl, I felt the good-byes I was saying to my entire tribe. I held my lips tight against her lips, a dry, clumsy, and ultimately stupid kiss.

But I was saying good-bye to my tribe, to all the Indian girls and women I might have loved, to all the Indian men who might have called me cousin, even brother.

I kissed that white girl and when I opened my eyes, she was gone from the reservation, and when I opened my eyes, I was gone from the reservation, living in a farm town where a beautiful white girl asked my name.

"Junior Polatkin," I said, and she laughed.

After that, no one spoke to me for another five hundred years.

Eighth Grade

At the farm town junior high, in the boys' bathroom, I could hear voices from the girls' bathroom, nervous whispers of anorexia and bulimia. I could hear the white girls' forced vomiting, a sound so familiar and natural to me after years of listening to my father's hangovers.

"Give me your lunch if you're just going to throw it up," I said to one of those girls once.

I sat back and watched them grow skinny from self-pity.

Back on the reservation, my mother stood in line to get us commodities. We carried them home, happy to have food, and opened the canned beef that even the dogs wouldn't eat.

But we ate it day after day and grew skinny from self-pity.

There is more than one way to starve.

Ninth Grade

At the farm town high school dance, after a basketball game in an overheated gym where I had scored twenty-seven points and pulled down thirteen rebounds, I passed out during a slow song.

As my white friends revived me and prepared to take me to the emergency room where doctors would later diagnose my diabetes, the Chicano teacher ran up to us.

"Hey," he said. "What's that boy been drinking? I know all about these Indian kids. They start drinking real young."

Sharing dark skin doesn't necessarily make two men brothers.

Tenth Grade

60 I passed the written test easily and nearly flunked the driving, but still received my Washington State driver's license on the same day that Wally Jim killed himself by driving his car into a pine tree.

No traces of alcohol in his blood, good job, wife and two kids.

"Why'd he do it?" asked a white Washington State trooper.

All the Indians shrugged their shoulders, looked down at the ground.

"Don't know," we all said, but when we look in the mirror, see the history of our tribe in our eyes, taste failure in the tap water, and shake with old tears, we understand completely.

65 Believe me, everything looks like a noose if you stare at it long enough.

Eleventh Grade

Last night I missed two free throws which would have won the game against the best team in the state. The farm town high school I play for is nicknamed the "Indians," and I'm probably the only actual Indian ever to play for a team with such a mascot.

This morning I pick up the sports page and read the headline: INDIANS LOSE AGAIN.

Go ahead and tell me none of this is supposed to hurt me very much.

Twelfth Grade

I walk down the aisle, valedictorian of this farm town high school, and my cap doesn't fit because I've grown my hair longer than it's ever been. Later, I stand as the school board chairman recites my awards, accomplishments, and scholarships.

70 I try to remain stoic for the photographers as I look toward the future.

Back home on the reservation, my former classmates graduate: a few can't read, one or two are just given attendance diplomas, most look forward to the parties. The bright students are shaken, frightened, because they don't know what comes next.

They smile for the photographer as they look back toward tradition.

The tribal newspaper runs my photograph and the photograph of my former classmates side by side.

Postscript: Class Reunion

Victor said, "Why should we organize a reservation high school reunion? My graduating class has a reunion every weekend at the Powwow Tavern."

Mapping the Text

1. Alexie utilizes a *structure* that moves readers through an extended chronological period of time in relatively few pages. What might such a structure suggest about Alexie's ways of thinking about Indian education? If Alexie offers readers a series of lessons here, what do they teach us?
2. Alexie's work often conveys both bitterness and humor at the same time. Cite some examples of this *rhetorical technique*—the juxtaposition of scathing critique with humor or self-parody—in the text. What is the overall effect of this technique? How does it shape your reading of his narrative?
3. "Indian Education" features a first-person *narrative perspective*. How is that perspective complicated/enriched/extended by what we might call a *cultural perspective* within the piece? Where do we see Alexie's voice echo or channel other voices of American Indians, voices that we may associate with American Indian history or culture? To what effect?

Writing to Inquire

1. Who do you assume is Alexie's audience for this piece? Do you see yourself as an intended member of that audience? Why/why not? What evidence from the text might you cite in order to support your response?
2. Alexie's prose often exhibits characteristics that we normally associate with poetry: conciseness, startling or unusual images, parallel phrasing or imagery, and so on. Select one section of "Indian Education" and rewrite or recast that section as a poem. Make decisions about stanza lengths, line breaks, and punctuation. What happens when Alexie's work becomes poetry? What is gained or lost by making this shift in genre?
3. In many ways, Alexie's story might be read as a coming-of-age narrative, a story of one person's growth, development, and identity formation over time. Using Alexie's work as a model, draft your own educational coming-of-age narrative, choosing carefully a series of events to highlight or emphasize. Then, write a short analytical statement to accompany your narrative. In that statement, explore your reasons for making particular choices. Why did you select specific events to highlight? What makes them significant to the development of your identity as an educated person?

Learning in the Shadow of Race and Class

BELL HOOKS

bell hooks is Distinguished Professor of English at City College in New York. Her long list of books includes *Ain't I a Woman: Black Women and Feminism; Feminist Theory: From Margin to Center* (1984); *Talking Back: Thinking Feminist, Thinking Black* (1989); *Yearning: Race, Class and Cultural Politics* (1990); *Art on*

My Mind: Visual Politics (1995); and *Remembered Rapture: The Writer at Work* (1999). Born in Hopkinsville, Kentucky, as Gloria Watkins, hooks writes often about the need for critical consciousness in a racist, sexist, and classist society. In "Learning in the Shadow of Race and Class," hooks considers the ways identity issues shape the educational process in the United States.

As a child, I often wanted things money could buy that my parents could not afford and would not get. Rather than tell us we did not get some material thing because money was lacking, mama would frequently manipulate us in an effort to make the desire go away. Sometimes she would belittle and shame us about the object of our desire. That's what I remember most. That lovely yellow dress I wanted would become in her storytelling mouth a really ugly mammy-made thing that no girl who cared about her looks would desire. My desires were often made to seem worthless and stupid. I learned to mistrust and silence them. I learned that the more clearly I named my desires, the more unlikely those desires would ever be fulfilled.

I learned that my inner life was more peaceful if I did not think about money, or allow myself to indulge in any fantasy of desire. I learned the art of sublimation and repression. I learned it was better to make do with acceptable material desires than to articulate the unacceptable. Before I knew money mattered, I had often chosen objects to desire that were costly, things a girl of my class would not ordinarily desire. But then I was still a girl who was unaware of class, who did not think my desires were stupid and wrong. And when I found they were, I let them go. I concentrated on survival, on making do.

When I was choosing a college to attend, the issue of money surfaced and had to be talked about. While I would seek loans and scholarships, even if everything related to school was paid for, there would still be transportation to pay for, books, and a host of other hidden costs. Letting me know that there was no extra money to be had, mama urged me to attend any college nearby that would offer financial aid. My first year of college, I went to a school close to home. A plain-looking white woman recruiter had sat in our living room and explained to my parents that everything would be taken care of, that I would be awarded a full academic scholarship, that they would have to pay nothing. They knew better. Still they found this school acceptable.

After my parents dropped me at the predominately white women's college, I saw the terror in my roommate's face that she was going to be housed with someone black, and I requested a change. She had no doubt also voiced her concern. I was given a tiny single room by the stairs—a room usually denied a first-year student—but I was a first-year black student, a scholarship girl who could never in a million years have afforded to pay her way or absorb the cost of a single room. My fellow students kept their distance from me. I ate in the cafeteria and did not have to worry about who would pay for pizza and drinks in the world outside. I kept my desires to myself, my lacks, and my loneliness; I made do.

5 I rarely shopped. Boxes came from home, with brand-new clothes mama had purchased. Even though it was never spoken, she did not want me to feel ashamed among privileged white girls. I was the only black girl in my dorm. There was no room in me for shame. I felt contempt and disinterest. With their giggles and their obsession to marry, the white girls at the women's college were aliens. We did not reside on the same planet. I lived in the world of books. The one white woman who became my close friend found me there reading. I was hiding under the shadows of a tree with huge branches, the kinds of trees that just seemed to grow effortlessly on well-to-do college campuses. I sat on the "perfect" grass reading poetry, wondering how the grass around me could be so lovely, and yet, when daddy had tried to grow grass in the front yard of Mr. Porter's house, it always turned yellow or brown and then died. Endlessly, the yard defeated him, until finally he gave up. The outside of the house looked good, but the yard always hinted at the possibility of endless neglect. The yard looked poor.

Foliage and trees on the college grounds flourished. Greens were lush and deep. From my place in the shadows, I saw a fellow student sitting alone weeping. Her sadness had to do with all the trivia that haunted our day's classwork, the fear of not being smart enough, of losing financial aid (like me she had loans and scholarships, though her family paid some), and boys. Coming from an Illinois family of Czechoslovakian immigrants, she understood class.

When she talked about the other girls who flaunted their wealth and family background, there was a hard edge of contempt, anger, and envy in her voice. Envy was always something I pushed away from my psyche. Kept too close for comfort, envy could lead to infatuation and on to desire. I desired nothing that they had. She desired everything, speaking her desires openly, without shame. Growing up in the kind of community where there was constant competition to see who could buy the bigger better whatever, in a world of organized labor, of unions and strikes, she understood a world of bosses and workers, of haves and have-nots.

White friends I had known in high school wore their class privilege modestly. Raised, like myself, in church traditions that taught us to identify only with the poor, we knew that there was evil in excess. We knew rich people were rarely allowed into heaven. God had given them a paradise of bounty on earth, and they had not shared. The rare ones, the rich people who shared, were the only ones able to meet the divine in paradise, and even then it was harder for them to find their way. According to the high-school friends we knew, flaunting wealth was frowned upon in our world, frowned upon by God and community.

The few women I befriended my first year in college were not wealthy. They were the ones who shared with me stories of the other girls flaunting the fact that they could buy anything expensive—clothes, food, vacations. There were not many of us from working-class backgrounds; we knew who we were. Most girls from poor backgrounds tried to blend in, or fought back by triumphing over wealth with beauty or style or some combination of the above. Being black made me an automatic outsider. Holding their world in contempt pushed me further to the edge. One of the fun things the "in" girls did was choose someone and trash their room. Like so much else deemed cute by insiders, I dreaded the thought of strangers entering my space and going through my things. Being outside the in crowd made me an unlikely target. Being contemptuous made me first on the list. I did not understand. And when my room was trashed, it unleashed my rage and deep grief over not being able to protect my space from violation and invasion. I hated the girls who had so much, took so much for granted, never considered that those of us who did not have mad money would not be able to replace broken things, perfume poured out, or talcum powder spread everywhere—that we did not know everything could be taken care of at the dry cleaner's, because we never took our clothes there. My rage fueled by contempt was deep, strong, and long-lasting. Daily it stood as a challenge to their fun, to their habits of being.

10 Nothing they did to win me over worked. It came as a great surprise. They had always believed black girls wanted to be white girls, wanted to possess their world. My stony gaze, silence, and absolute refusal to cross the threshold of their world was total mystery; it was for them a violation they needed to avenge. After trashing my room, they tried to win me over with apologies and urges to talk and understand. There was nothing about me I wanted them to understand. Everything about their world was over-exposed, on the surface.

One of my English professors had attended Stanford University. She felt that was the place for me to go—a place where intellect was valued over foolish fun and games and dress-up, and finding a husband did not overshadow academic work. I had never thought about the state of California. Getting my parents to agree to my leaving Kentucky to attend a college in a nearby state had been hard enough. They had accepted a college they could reach by car, but a college thousands of miles away was beyond their imagination. Even I had difficulty grasping going that far away from home. The lure for me was the promise of journeying and arriving at a destination where I would be accepted and understood.

All the barely articulated understandings of class privilege that I had learned my first year of college had not hipped me to the reality of class shame. It still had not dawned on me that my parents, especially mama, resolutely refused to acknowledge any difficulties with money because her sense of shame around class was deep and intense. And when this shame was coupled with her need to feel that she had risen above the low-class backwoods culture of her family, it was impossible for her to talk in a straightforward manner about the strains it would put on the family for me to attend Stanford.

All I knew then was that, as with all my desires, I was told that this desire was impossible to fulfill. At first, it was not talked about in relation to money, it was talked about in relation to sin. California was an evil place, a modern-day Babylon where souls were easily seduced away from the path of righteousness. It was not a place for an innocent young girl to go on her own. Mama brought the message back that my father had absolutely refused to give permission.

I expressed my disappointment through ongoing unrelenting grief. I explained to mama that other parents wanted their children to go to good schools. It still had not dawned on me that my parents knew nothing about "good" schools. Even though I knew mama had not graduated from high school, I still held her in awe.

15 When my parents refused to permit me to attend Stanford, I accepted the verdict for awhile. Overwhelmed by grief, I could barely speak for weeks. Mama intervened and tried to change my father's mind, as folks she respected in the outside world told her what a privilege it was for me to have this opportunity, that Stanford University was a good school for a smart girl. Without their permission, I decided I would go. And even though she did not give her approval, mama was willing to help.

My decision made conversations about money necessary. Mama explained that California was too far away, that it would always "cost" to get there, that if something went wrong, they would not be able to come and rescue me, that I would not be able to come home for holidays. I heard all this, but its meaning did not sink in. I was just relieved I would not be returning to the women's college, to the place where I had truly been an outsider.

There were other black students at Stanford. There was even a dormitory where many black students lived. I did not know I could choose to live there. I went where I was assigned. Going to Stanford was the first time I flew somewhere. Only mama stood and waved farewell as I left to take the bus to the airport. I left with a heavy heart, feeling both excitement and dread. I knew nothing about the world I was journeying to. Not knowing made me afraid, but my fear of staying in place was greater.

I had no idea what was ahead of me. In small ways, I was ignorant. I had never been on an escalator, a city bus, an airplane, or a subway. I arrived in San Francisco with no understanding that Palo Alto was a long drive away—that it would take money to find transportation there. I decided to take the city bus. With all my cheap overpacked bags, I must have seemed like just another innocent immigrant when I struggled to board the bus.

This was a city bus with no racks for luggage. It was filled with immigrants. English was not spoken. I felt lost and afraid. Without words the strangers surrounding me understood the universal language of need and distress. They reached for my bags, holding and helping. In return, I told them my story—that I had left my village in the South to come to Stanford University and that, like them, my family were workers.

On arriving, I called home. Before I could speak, I began to weep as I heard the faraway sound of mama's voice. I tried to find the words, to slow down, to tell her how it felt to be a stranger, to speak my uncertainty and longing. She told me this is the lot I had chosen. I must live with it. After her words, there was only silence. She had hung up on me—let me go into this world where I am a stranger still.

Stanford University was a place where one could learn about class from the ground up. Built by a man who believed in hard work, it was to have been a place where students of all classes would come, women and men, to work together and learn. It was to be a place of equality and communalism. His vision was seen by many as almost communist. The fact that he was rich made it all less threatening. Perhaps no one really believed the vision could be realized. The university was named after his son, who had died young, a son who had carried his name but who had no future money could buy. No amount of money can keep death away. But it could keep memory alive.

Everything in the landscape of my new world fascinated me, the plants brought from a rich man's travels all over the world back to this place of water and clay. At Stanford University, adobe buildings blend with Japanese plum trees and leaves of kumquat. On my way to study medieval literature, I ate my first kumquat. Surrounded by flowering cactus and a South American shrub bougainvillea of such trailing beauty it took my breath away, I was in a landscape of dreams, full of hope and possibility. If nothing else would hold me, I would not remain a stranger to the earth. The ground I stood on would know me.

Class was talked about behind the scenes. The sons and daughters from rich, famous, or notorious families were identified. The grown-ups in charge of us were always looking out for a family who might give their millions to the college. At Stanford, my classmates wanted to know me, thought it hip, cute, and downright exciting to have a black friend. They invited me on the expensive vacations and ski trips I could not afford. They offered to pay. I never went. Along with other students who were not from privileged families, I searched for places to go during the holiday times when the dormitory was closed. We got together and talked about the assumption that everyone had money to travel and would necessarily be leaving. The staff would be on holiday as well, so all students had to leave. Now and then the staff did not leave, and we were allowed to stick around. Once, I went home with one of the women who cleaned for the college.

Now and then, when she wanted to make extra money, mama would work as a maid. Her decision to work outside the home was seen as an act of treason by our father. At Stanford, I was stunned to find that there were maids who came by regularly to vacuum and tidy our rooms. No one had ever cleaned up behind me, and I did not want them to. At first I roomed with another girl from a working-class background—a beautiful white girl from Orange County who looked like pictures I had seen on the cover of *Seventeen* magazine. Her mother had died of cancer during her high-school years, and she had since been raised by her father. She had been asked by the college officials if she would find it problematic to have a black roommate. A scholarship student like myself, she knew her preferences did not matter and, as she kept telling me, she did not really care.

25 Like my friend during freshman year, she shared the understanding of what it was like to be a have-not in a world of haves. But unlike me, she was determined to become one of them. If it meant she had to steal nice clothes to look the same as they did, she had no problem taking these risks. If it meant having a privileged boyfriend who left bruises on her body now and then, it was worth the risk. Cheating was worth it. She believed the world the privileged had created was all unfair—all one big cheat; to get ahead, one had to play the game. To her, I was truly an innocent, a lamb being led to the slaughter. It did not surprise her one bit when I began to crack under the pressure of contradictory values and longings.

Like all students who did not have seniority, I had to see the school psychiatrists to be given permission to live off campus. Unaccustomed to being around strangers, especially strangers who did not share or understand my values, I found the experience of living in the dorms difficult. Indeed, almost everyone around me believed working-class folks had no values. At the university where the founder, Leland Stanford, had imagined different classes meeting on common ground, I learned how deeply individuals with class privilege feared and hated the working classes. Hearing classmates express contempt and hatred toward people who did not come from the right backgrounds shocked me.

To survive in this new world of divided classes, this world where I was also encountering for the first time a black bourgeois elite that was as contemptuous of working people as their white counterparts were, I had to take a stand, to get clear my own class affiliations. This was the most difficult truth to face. Having been taught all my life to believe that black people were inextricably bound in solidarity by our struggles to end racism, I did not know how to respond to elitist black people who were full of contempt for anyone who did not share their class, their way of life.

At Stanford, I encountered for the first time a black diaspora. Of the few black professors present, the vast majority were from African or Caribbean backgrounds. Elites themselves, they were only interested in teaching other elites. Poor folks like myself, with no background to speak of, were invisible. We were not seen by them or anyone else. Initially, I went to all meetings welcoming black students, but when I found no one to connect with, I retreated. In the shadows, I had time and books to teach me about the nature of class—about the ways black people were divided from themselves.

Despite this rude awakening, my disappointment at finding myself estranged from the group of students I thought would understand, I still looked for connections. I met an older black male graduate student who also came from a working-class background. Even though he had gone to the right high school, a California school for gifted students, and then to Princeton as an undergraduate, he understood intimately the intersections of race and class. Good in sports and in the classroom, he had been slotted early on to go far, to go where other black males had not gone. He understood the system. Academically, he fit. Had he wanted to, he could have been among the elite, but he chose to be on the margins, to hang with an intellectual artistic avant-garde. He wanted to live in a world of the mind where there was no race or class. He wanted to worship at the throne of art and knowledge. He became my mentor, comrade, and companion.

Slowly, I began to understand fully that there was no place in academe for folks from working-class backgrounds who did not wish to leave the past behind. That was the price of the ticket. Poor students would be welcome at the best institutions of higher learning only if they were willing to surrender memory, to forget the past and claim the assimilated present as the only worthwhile and meaningful reality.

Students from nonprivileged backgrounds who did not want to forget often had nervous breakdowns. They could not bear the weight of all the contradictions they had to confront. They were crushed. More often than not, they dropped out with no trace of their inner anguish recorded, no institutional record of the myriad ways their take on the world was assaulted by an elite vision of class and privilege. The records merely indicated that, even after receiving financial aid and other support, these students simply could not make it, simply were not good enough.

At no time in my years as a student did I march in a graduation ceremony. I was not proud to hold degrees from institutions where I had been constantly scorned and shamed. I wanted to forget these experiences, to erase them from my consciousness. Like a prisoner set free, I did not want to remember my years on the inside. When I finished my doctorate, I felt too much uncertainty about who I had become. Uncertain about whether I had managed to make it through without giving up the best of myself, the best of the values I had been raised to believe in—hard work, honesty, and respect for everyone no matter their class—I finished my education with my allegiance to the working class intact. Even so, I had planted my feet on the path leading in the direction of class privilege. There would always be contradictions to face. There would always be confrontations around the issue of class. I would always have to reexamine where I stand.

Mapping the Text

1. What message do you think bell hooks intends to convey in this essay? What do you think she means in entitling her essay "Learning in the Shadow of Race and Class"? What is the shadow? How is this shadow defined by race? How is it defined by class? What are the implications for learning?
2. What sorts of appeals (logos, ethos, pathos) does hooks use in presenting her point of view?

Writing to Inquire

1. Hooks says, "Slowly, I began to understand fully that there was no place in academe for folks from working-class backgrounds who did not wish to leave the past behind." Do you agree or disagree with this statement? On what evidence do you base your point of view?

Battling Bigotry on Campus

KENNETH S. STERN

Kenneth S. Stern (1953–) is a lawyer and writer whose activist work relates to some of the most politically charged movements in society. He was a law student volunteer for the defense attorneys and later lead counsel before the United States Supreme Count in the case of *United States v. Loud Hawk*, a prominent case, connected with the American Indian movement, that arose from the armed conflicts at Wounded Knee in South Dakota in 1973. He is a leading expert on the militia movement, having tracked hate groups for over a decade. For several years, he has also worked as a program specialist with the American Jewish Committee in New York. His books include *Loud Hawk: The United States Versus the American Indian Movement* (1994); *A Force Upon the Plain: The American Militia Movement and the Politics of Hate* (1997); and *Holocaust Denial* (1993). In the essay below, written in 1992, Stern was an early voice in suggesting the probability that race, religion, sexism, homophobia, and ethnocentricity have the potential, as we have seen repeatedly since then, to disrupt campus life violently.

Swastikas. Cross burnings. Date rape. Assaults motivated by racial hatred. T-shirts with homophobic slurs. Shouts of "JAP! . . . JAP! . . . JAP!" from a crowd as a Jewish student walked to her seat at a sporting event. Whispers of "nigger" by a member of the board of trustees. KKK literature. Campus security checking African-American male, but not white male, identification at a school dance. A faculty member using the term "Jap test" to describe a surprise exam. A note with the word "Spic!" slid under a student's door. Hate mail: "Custer should have finished off your entire degenerate race." A picture in a school newspaper showing African-American students at a concert, with the caption "Music soothes the savage beast." Palestinian students displaying a poster of a kaffiyeh-clad woman protruding through the center of a yellow Star of David, her legs spread, her sandals untied, blood dripping from her thighs. The Black Student Union inviting Minister Louis Farrakhan to speak. A professor asking Ku Klux Klan members to address his class. Incidents like these are charged with racial, religious, sexist, homophobic, and ethnic tension. They tear at the tranquility of academic institutions.

Incidents of bigotry are becoming commonplace on college campuses. According to the National Institute Against Prejudice and Violence, more than 250 of the nation's 3,300 colleges and universities have reported acts of ethnoviolence since 1986. Many more have gone unreported.

Campus officials say they don't know what to do. Incidents vary in origin and burst on the scene unpredictably. Some are very complex, as, for example, when a faculty member says something that some people interpret as bigoted, while others do not; or when pressures from the outside community come into play, dividing the campus along previously unobserved seams, all under the watchful eyes of the media. Incidents also raise different institutional concerns and passions, frequently challenging the university's self image, pitting academic freedom against the need for a campus free from ethnic and racial hostility.

Why is this happening? What should officials do when such an incident occurs? More importantly, what should they do *before* an incident occurs? How effective are the codes against bigoted behavior? These, and other related questions, are difficult to answer. What if the professor who invited KKK members wanted to teach his students how to sharpen their interview skills so they could expose bigots? If a student can be expelled for engraving a swastika on a Jewish student's door in the dead of night (this is vandalism), what about the student who distributes a swastika-covered leaflet to Jewish students (First Amendment right)? What should the university do if the perpetrator is never found? Or if found, how does the perpetrator's due process rights limit the administration's response?

5 What is the underlying, everyday level of bigotry on campus, and how does this relate to the explosions? Even if there are no explosions, what could campuses be doing to help students enjoy healthy intergroup relations? What should universities be doing to prepare students for life in an increasingly diverse society?

Bigotry always has been on campus. Whereas some of today's university administrators may be insensitive to problems of intergroup hatred, their predecessors practiced it. Jews were tolerated, but only in small numbers. African-Americans—and, on many campuses, women—weren't welcome at all. This institutionalized discrimination almost has disappeared.

Certainly, it is better that an African-American or Hispanic or Asian or Jew or woman be called an offensive name than not be allowed into the university at all.

Years ago, slurs were confined to scribblings on bathroom walls. Today's graffiti have overflowed the bounds of propriety and, at many institutions, become part of campus life. They appear in classrooms and dorms, at sporting events, and in casual conversation.

This trend is disturbing because campuses mirror society. In the 1950s, when so many school policies discriminated against African-Americans, it was not coincidental that some states had poll taxes and literacy tests and *de jure* segregation. Today's campus bigotry reflects the larger society as well, with all its injustices and racial, ethnic, sexist, religious, homophobic, and class tensions. Overtly hateful incidents, groups, and individuals in power, while still a minor phenomenon, are on the rise.

Colleges attract our brightest youngsters. If our young people finish their educations without learning to respect each other's differences and cherish their own backgrounds, the future will be a troubled one. Our leaders-to-be will be bigots or, perhaps more disturbing, people who tolerate a bigoted society.

10 Some students will come to campus with bigoted or intolerant attitudes. Knowing this, the universities must strive to make every student feel welcome. They need an environment free from the abrasive disruption of bigotry in which to study. Colleges must adopt programs and plans to make their community as bias-free as possible. As leaders in the educational field, they should direct changes in high and elementary school programs, so that their future students are better prepared to live peaceable with each other.

Responding to Incidents

Many universities assume they never will have to respond to an act of bigotry. An incident occurs, then administration officials wonder what they should do. It is a rare *ad hoc* response that is effective. Most make a difficult situation worse.

Assume, as has happened, that a professor called a student a "black bitch." Students are angry and want action. Yet, which administration member has prime responsibility to act? That may not be certain. A decision takes time. What happened may not be clear. Facts need to be found. Conflicting accounts must be weighed and reconciled where possible. People's reputations can be destroyed. The alleged bigot may be a colleague or friend. The tension grows.

The administration official put in charge wants any response to be completely accurate and fair. Two days pass. The students don't understand the deliberative process. All they know is that some bigoted sexist called one of his students a "black bitch," and the administration hasn't said a word. The university apparently doesn't care. It never did anything about the everyday low-visibility bigotry that students endure.

"Look at how few minority faculty members there are," students will point out, "how few blacks are incorporated into the curriculum, as if no black person ever contributed to art or literature or science. . . ." A wide range of unredressed ills will be thrown onto the stage, not as something important to be discussed rationally and planned with a long-term perspective, but as demands in the midst of a tension-filled, media-monitored eruption. Two words from one mouth have paralyzed an entire campus.

15 To avoid this chaos, universities must have two types of plan. First, they need a response plan. Basic decisions about what to do, and who should do it, should be made before a crisis erupts. Once an incident occurs, the response will be quicker and more effective. Second, they must have a plan to reduce the level of bigotry on campus, not only so there will be fewer and less explosive incidents, but also because students deserve an environment that makes them feel welcome.

As any administration official who has had to do it can attest, responding to an incident is a complex affair. Passions are high, and each incident has a new wrinkle not previously thought through. The institution's view of itself and its commitment to free speech are challenged.

Yet, much can be distilled from the hundreds of distinct incidents that have occurred. Some principles are specific to types of incidents—*e.g.*, graffiti, slurs, speakers, assaults—but the most important lessons apply regardless of the particular circumstances.

The most important rule is the simplest to effectuate. When an incident occurs, the university, at its highest level, must respond immediately and strongly. Presidents must make themselves as public as possible and say—in the most powerful words—that bigotry has no place on campus. Failure to act quickly with a clear statement will create an escalating crisis. Wishy-washy, delayed, or low-level pronouncements indicate that bigotry is not a serious problem, that the hurt students feel is somehow invalid. That invites further, and longer-lasting, explosions.

Sometimes the facts are known, and action can be taken quickly—for example, when a student assaults someone while yelling ethnic slurs. If that student can be suspended immediately, before a hearing, he or she should be. Even if disciplinary codes do not provide for pre-hearing suspensions, the facts justifying such action are not apparent, or the perpetrator is unknown or beyond the scope of the disciplinary code (*e.g.*, faculty, staff, or from outside the campus family), immediate, visible, clear action by the head of the institution is still possible, and necessary. The president's statement should be transcribed and disseminated throughout the community and, where appropriate, mailed to parents and alumni as well.

20 Second, a predesignated, well-rehearsed "bigotry team" should meet immediately. This should include the university president, appropriate deans, campus security, and representatives from students and faculty.

The group can assess the incident better and plan appropriate action. For example, if a culprit has not been found, the team can mobilize the campus. The president can announce an award for information resulting in apprehension.

Other responses can be pre-planned as well. Regardless of the nature of the incident, rumors abound. A hotline should be in place, so that there is one central controlled source of information. (Hotlines also allow people to know where to report incidents and encourage reporting of incidents that, but for an easily understood reporting mechanism, would be suffered in silence).

If the incident is serious, students are likely to protest. The university president should call a rally, before the students do. The entire community should be invited. A presidentially instigated rally will diffuse anger and make students perceive a real commitment to their security.

Other prepared responses can be crafted for the particular community, given its size, location, population, and history. The purpose is always to remind the victimized students that they truly are wanted and that bigotry has no place on campus.

To make these actions work, however, they have to be sincere. Public statements have risks. When presidents of universities speak, newspaper articles follow. The school's reputation for harmony may be tarnished. Minority students, whom the university are trying to attract, may be less inclined to attend if they know that KKK literature was distributed or an African-American student was beaten up and called "nigger."

25 Yet, the short-term risks from drawing attention to incidents will pay off in the long run. The university will benefit from strong stances which end the crisis quicker. Prospective students will know that the administration really cares.

A university's commitment to free speech complicates the desire to discipline students who engage in bigotry. Universities work best when students and faculty feel free to say whatever they think. Whereas students should be aware that their words can hurt others, they should not be forced to weigh their thoughts against the administration-imposed limits of political correctness. Higher education is at its best when the clash between ideas is heated, not chilled. Yet, bigotry many times manifests itself through a sanctionable act. Free speech issues diminish, and acts can be punished promptly and forcefully.

If a student commits an assault, burglary, arson, or other serious offense and the disciplinary code allows for summary suspension, and the known facts warrant it, he or she should be suspended immediately, pending a hearing. If there are questions about what happened or who did what, summary suspension should not be used, regardless of any pressure to do so. The response to critics who call for immediate suspension is to have a realistic "fast track" disciplinary hearing procedure established, so that a full due process hearing can be held quickly.

While the university can not punish bigoted thoughts or words, it can do so for bigoted behavior. As in the larger society, acts which are already circumscribed by law can and should be punished more severely if committed with a bigoted motive.

Punishment must be fair. When there are many students involved, each should be disciplined according to the seriousness of his or her act and prior history. Other factors that can inflame a campus—such as treating the star athlete differently from others—should be rejected, despite institutional pressure.

30 Schools have a real interest in separating people who commit violent acts from their community, especially when such an act is against gays, women, Jews, African-Americans, Asians, Indians, or anyone else just because of who they are. Swift clear action can be a deterrent and reaffirm the school's commitment to make the victimized group truly welcome.

However, that is only half the task. Regardless of what the administration does, the student who has been traumatized still hurts. The effects of any bias assault—whether physical or verbal—are devastating. Fear is engendered "far beyond what the average person would imagine," according to Joan Weiss, executive director of the National Institute Against Prejudice and Violence.

The trauma is long-lasting and frequently affects family, friends, the entire campus, and sometimes the community beyond. Some victims even abandon their college plans and leave. Others are too afraid to report incidents, fearing a backlash that could jeopardize their education.

Universities must help victims recover. A specially trained victims' advocate should be available to counsel students and direct them to therapists and lawyers where appropriate. The advocate also can help shape the university's plans and institutions to meet the needs of bias victims. Otherwise, they feel increasingly isolated, bouncing from one unprepared campus service to another without receiving any help.

Disciplinary Codes

Acts of bigotry, even when not physically violent, are psychologically distressing. Ethnic slurs, whether yelled, painted on a sign, or printed in a leaflet, are emotional assaults. People have their identity and self-worth shattered. Bigotry injures. Everyone wants justice. Someone should be punished.

35 Some universities seem to think that all their bigotry problems can be solved through strong disciplinary codes. In theory, offenders are punished and would-be offenders are deterred. However, institutions that see codes as "magic cures" are deceiving themselves.

First, many bigots are not caught. As one Berkeley student said, "If I call you a name to your face or do damage to your person or your property, then it's easy to pursue someone. But if in the dark of night I throw a stone through your window and vanish, then how do you pursue the culprit?"

Second, even if found, the person may be beyond the disciplinary code. Faculty members and university officials are subject to different standards. Outsiders, like Ku Klux Klan members who paint swastikas and Skinheads who beat up gay students, are also beyond the code's jurisdiction.

Third, rules that punish assault, arson, vandalism, burglary, harassment, threats, or intimidation are effective on their own. Codes need not be changed to punish bigots who hit, burn, burgle, or harass.

When universities speak of codes against bigotry, they mean regulations to proscribe students from what is, essentially, verbal or symbolic expression. The arguments in favor of such codes are attractive at first blush. What better way to demonstrate that the institution will not tolerate bigotry? If the school can punish a person who spray paints the word "nigger" on the wall of a predominately African-American dorm in the middle of the night (that is vandalism), why shouldn't it be able to punish another student who, in broad daylight, walks up to a particular African-American student and yells, "I hate niggers!" Certainly, the hurt caused by a personally directed scream exceeds that from the written slur.

One suggested rationalization for punishing the vandal, but not the screamer is that the school has an interest in knowing who its bigots are. This rationale fails when the comparison is between a spray painted swastika and one drawn on paper and taped to the dorm wall. The harm is practically the same, but the former, as destruction of property, can result in expulsion; the latter may be protected speech.

That result seems, and is, unsatisfactory. Yet, it is better to draw the line here—between action that is punishable regardless of its bigoted character and action that is not punishable precisely because it has no character beyond being an expression of bigotry.

Justice can not always be found in laws. Laws are imperfect. Results may be unsatisfactory, but it is nonetheless true that attempts to punish the expression of words simply don't work. Codes designed to outlaw bigotry—such as the University of Michigan's and the University of Connecticut's—have been found violative of the First Amendment. No lawyer can draft language precise enough to punish the person who says "nigger" only when he or she *really* means it.

Attempts at broad codes have backfired. Students at the University of Michigan—which adopted different standards of speech for the classroom, dorm, etc.—had a grand time making fun of the entire effort with "free speech zones" written in broad chalk strokes around the campus. What is the deterrent effect of that ridiculed rule or any code when acts of bigotry are likely to be spontaneous, frequently committed under the influence of alcohol? No drunk about to yell "nigger!" at a passing African-American student weighs his words against the finely drawn limits of a disciplinary code.

Egregious use of hateful words can be punished under most existing codes that proscribe harassment, intimidation, or threats of violence. Codes that would punish a student who repeatedly calls another at 3:00 a.m. and says, "I hate your mother" also would punish a student whose harassing phone calls are racist. Codes that prohibit one student from threatening and intimidating another (*e.g.*, "You go out with Peggy Sue again and I'll slash your face") also apply when the student warned to stay away from Peggy Sue is called a racial epithet.

45 Even narrowly drawn anti-bigotry codes tarnish the schools' reputation for academic freedom and open inquiry. Punishing a student for using bigoted words or printing bigoted articles drapes the bigot, instead of the school, in the First Amendment. The bigot becomes the victim, even a martyr, as the real victim disappears, a casualty of a fight that has become one for free speech instead of against bigotry.

The practical limits of codes are difficult to accept. Some people who should be disciplined will not be. Nevertheless, the university will benefit from a narrow code. A student's suspension for writing "Gays should die of AIDS," or "I kill Jews, therefore I am," or "Puerto Ricans are scum" can not outweigh the damage of months of disruption, legal proceedings, and constitutional debate that continue to open wounds. There are other ways to respond to such cases.

While no perfect definitional line can be drawn, a functional code that punishes action and not words is preferable to an unacceptably fuzzy one that tries to legislate morality. If the campus develops a real commitment to fighting bigotry, community ostracism will be punishment enough.

Controversial Speakers

Outside speakers with reputations for bigotry who come to campus, and then leave, often create traumatic moments that take years to undo. The problem is not as much what the speaker says (usually the address is tamer than people expect), but the tension that precedes and follows the event.

Universities are places for open inquiry. No idea should be barred. On most campuses, student groups and faculty members have the absolute right to invite anyone they want. However, what happens when someone invites a member of the Ku Klux Klan; or Louis Farrakhan, who peppers his words of African-American political action with gross anti-Semitism (Judaism is a "gutter religion"); or the late Meir Kahane, whose views on Arabs were akin to Farrakhan's on Jews or the KKK's on African-Americans?

50 The students who are the targets of the speaker's hatred feel insecure, misunderstood, and powerless. The protestation that "we want to hear about the good things [the speaker] has done," or "everyone has a right to speak—ask him questions and expose him, if you can" are wholly inadequate. "Why should our student fees be used to bring someone here who would kill us if he could?" some ask.

The greatest pain for the students who feel unfairly maligned may be that their fellow classmates can not—or will not—understand why they feel so hurt. Lines are drawn, and victimized students react angrily—in protest if they are strong enough numerically; in silence if they are too few.

The inviting group also feels misunderstood. African-American students who invite Farrakhan can't comprehend why Jewish groups are so upset. He speaks strongly for empowering African-Americans. "Can it be that the Jewish students are afraid of such a strong leader?" they may ask themselves. "So what if Farrakhan said some nasty things. That's not important. His message of power for African-American people is. Who are they to tell us we can't listen to him, anyway?"

Administration officials—committed to free speech—are caught in the middle between two polarized campus groups that desire punishment, even victory. It is not easy to hold the community together as the conflict heats up. Sometimes the cost of additional security is prohibitive and the speaker does not come, but usually he or she does, and the campus is paralyzed in anticipation of what may happen.

The group opposed to the speaker may protest and seek faculty and community support for their own exercise of First Amendment rights. Officials may fear hecklers. Many times, speakers can not be heard over screams. Infringing on other students' free speech rights may violate disciplinary rules.

55 The administration's priorities in the weeks before and after the crisis peaks should be twofold. The commitment to free speech must be ironclad, and so must be the commitment to intergroup sensitivity. While the tension between these two principles can not be eliminated, it can be reduced with planning.

On campuses where the polarization is not extreme, the administration might invite student groups to submit the names of contemplated speakers to each other before an invitation is extended. Such a procedure would be voluntary and, regardless of any opposition, the right to invite speakers would remain inviolate.

A voluntary pre-invitation notice to other groups would allow discussion and decision before "saving face" issues, such as how to uninvite an invited speaker, come into play. Jewish students, for example, could let African-American students know why having Farrakhan on campus is hurtful. The point might be made at a meeting (coordinated by an intergroup professional) with role plays, transposing Farrakhan's words, substituting the words "African-American" for "Jew," so that the African-American students can understand the hurt better. Jewish students, meanwhile, could begin to understand the isolation African-Americans feel on a white campus with white values and why an African-American speaker who talks of power is important to them.

Even with the implementation of procedures to make people more sensitive to others' feelings, controversial speakers still will come to campus—as they should. The administration must ensure that students pro and con can exercise their First Amendment rights with minimal interference. Hecklers should not be allowed, but protests should be accommodated. Innovative protests that show respect for fellow students should be encouraged. At Oberlin College, for example, Jewish students protested an anti-Semitic African-American speaker silently. They attended the speech, sitting patiently in their white T-shirts with the Star of David on the back. At the speaker's first anti-Semitic words, they stood and turned their backs to the stage. Their silent protest was dramatic and effective. Other people in the audience stood and joined them in sympathy.

Campus Police Bias

Campus police forces frequently are a source of tension on campus. Sometimes they instigate incidents. Frequently, they exacerbate them. In many universities, male minority students complain that campus police officials are more likely to stop and question them than they do whites or women. Sometimes, campus police use racial slurs, and false detention cases (*e.g.*, presuming the African-American student in an interracial brawl is the culprit) have resulted in lawsuits.

60 One problem is that many low-paid guards bring with them bigoted attitudes exacerbated by economic resentment. Administrators, or the agencies with whom they contract, should try to weed out bigots before they are hired. Guidelines for relating to and detaining students should be clear, and the color-blindness of the rules reasserted. They can be screened and educated to act more sensitively. They should know that swastikas and racial and sexual assaults are not pranks, be able to ensure that no evidence is destroyed, and make sure that the victim is treated with sympathy.

Larger universities should have one better-trained and higher-paid special campus security team on duty, or on call, at all times. This group should be trained to respond to every type of bias incident. It can soothe the victims and help prevent incidents from turning into riots. Also, the presence of a better-paid anti-bias group provides the regular security guards with an option for advancement. If they want this better job, they know they have to be sensitive to all students to get it.

During and after an explosion of bigotry, the campus is in turmoil. Emotions and anger run high. Rational thought is sometimes difficult.

Students forced to confront ethnic conflict and other potentially divisive issues can react defensively and lash out, or withdraw. There are practitioners in the field of intergroup relations who go to campuses and cultivate ethnic pride and understanding. They also help the university community develop structures and procedures for managing diversity. The American Jewish Committee's Institute for American Pluralism and the National Coalition Building Institute are but two of many. These groups provide valuable assistance to schools even in calm times. Certainly, they should be contacted before, and invited to campus after, any incident of bigotry.

Specialists also train faculty members to deal with the difficult situations in their classrooms that nothing in their education has prepared them for. Even faculty members who know what to do when a student utters a blatantly prejudiced remark may have no idea what to do when student A says something from which student B infers a hidden prejudiced agenda.

65 The university president must encourage students and faculty to develop their own anti-bigotry institutions. Anti-bias student groups can distribute anti-racist literature and buttons (such as one with a slash through the encircled word "bias"), organize rallies, empower victims, initiate discussion, and form coalitions with the students on other campuses. The more involved students are in developing their own programs, the better they will succeed.

Faculty groups can lend intellectual credibility to the fight against bias. Professors can teach about bigotry both in their classes and at specially designed forums, including freshman orientation. They also can pre-plan ways to exploit incidents for their educational value.

There is much that can be planned before the onset of the unpredictable, but inevitable, crisis. The suggestions given here are certainly not all the possible responses. Experience, experimentation, and changing personnel and circumstances will dictate the details of any particular response plan.

Hotlines, response teams, training, a "fast track" for disciplinary cases, improving campus security, and many other practical things can be done so that the administration doesn't grope or give the impression of negligence or insensitivity.

The most important thing is that university presidents articulate a commitment to creating a campus community with zero tolerance for bigotry. This should be communicated not only after an incident, but also at calmer times. It must be demonstrated with actions that build structures so the campus community can manage conflict better. The commitment must include plans not only for responding to bigotry, but for reducing it.

70 Change is a long process, best achieved when people are persuaded by example rather than fiat. A faculty member may see a suggestion to include James Baldwin in his literature class as an invasion of academic freedom. If others he or she respects are seen changing their courses and the faculty member allowed the time and access to outside help to make similar curriculum modifications, he or she may do so enthusiastically.

While some changes take time, others can be made while the university studies itself and encourages change gently. First, every way it can, the school must make students, faculty, staff, and alumni know that it is committed to eradicating bigotry while upholding academic freedom and free speech. The president has to lead, but others must follow.

All members of the incoming freshman class should undergo intergroup training workshops as part of their orientation. Faculty, administration, and other staff—including janitors, telephone operators, and secretaries—should receive this training as well. Everyone should be encouraged and empowered to take a stand when they encounter bigotry.

Since it will take years to integrate examples of the contribution of all groups into the everyday curriculum, ethnic studies courses should be offered and promoted. Students and faculty alike should learn that people interpret their own realities differently, that there is no one perspective that necessarily defines truth.

Teaching diversity should be an educational mission that saturates the campus. Programs that help different student groups achieve a healthy group identity and feel that they can have a real role in campus life should be encouraged, as long as they are not myopic. Others should be developed that draw students from different backgrounds together to work on common goals.

Our universities must teach our students how to live in the America that will be. That nation will be multiethnic and multicultural, and will demand citizens who understand, appreciate, and respect pluralism. The institutional changes needed to meet this future must have the support of an enthusiastic and forward-looking board of trustees.

The entire institution must be energized. It is not enough that faculty and students survey themselves or begin to recognize bigotry as an issue. That is only the first step. Chaplains, deans of students, staff, administration, faculty, and students must become involved in the process of change. They all have to be encouraged through forums, presidential statements, and campus debate to remold the institution into one that will be stimulating, relevant, and comfortable for all its members.

Mapping the Text

1. Having read Kenneth S. Stern's essay, how would you define *bigotry?*
2. What is Stern's view on campus bigotry? What sorts of evidence does he present in conveying this point of view? Do you find his evidence and arguments convincing? Why or why not?

Writing to Inquire

1. Stern offers several examples of bigotry on college campuses. Go to the library or search online in periodicals for other examples. Given these data, do you believe that bigotry is a problem on contemporary college campuses?
2. Check your own campus policies and procedures. Is there a code of conduct or ethics that guards against campus bigotry? Are there initiatives in the recruiting and retention of students, in the recruiting and retention of faculty and staff, in the course curricula, in other campus operations that support a tolerance of difference? Do you think that these measures, if they exist, are working well? How do you think your campus community might respond to an incident of bigotry?

Affirmative Action and Stigma: The Education of a Professor

JUDY SCALES-TRENT

Judy Scales-Trent teaches at the State University of New York, Buffalo School of Law. Before becoming a professor of law, she served as a civil rights attorney in Washington, D.C. She has published articles in several venues, including legal journals and anthologies of African-American women writers. In her book *Notes of a White Black Woman: Race, Color, Community* (1995), Scales-Trent considers ways in which race and color are conflated and vividly shares her experiences as a white-skinned African-American woman as she develops a theory of the social construction of race. In the essay below, which is taken from this book, Scales-Trent focuses on education.

At the age of forty-four, I changed careers and communities when I left the civil rights community in Washington, D.C., for the academic world in western New York. The move was hard. It was not only the career change, the geographic dislocation, the social disruption that were difficult. It was also the move from a black city—and a community of civil rights lawyers within that city—to the white world of academia. Instead of working in tandem with black and white attorneys on a civil rights agenda, I was teaching civil rights law in a white workplace that had its own unknown agenda. I was teaching in a workplace with twelve black faculty on tenure track out of a total of 1,200 faculty members. I would be the second black woman out of that group.

Here in the academic world I have been forced to think hard thoughts about my entitlement to be a part of this community. I have also had to think about the entitlement of latino and black students to belong. Here in the academic world I have learned hard lessons about affirmative action and stigma.

The reason my education as a professor has been so profound has to do, I think, with numbers. The white community in Washington, D.C., although powerful, is a numerical minority in a black city. It is therefore not very forthright when speaking about its privilege. It has learned to curb its tongue, to speak in nonracist ways to black listeners. In academia, the white community has not learned that lesson. As an overwhelming numerical majority, it has not had to. It has thus taught me better—better than I had expected, better than I had wanted. It is those lessons that I write about now, in an effort to understand them and to diminish their control over my life.

Let me start out by stating that I agree with Jesse Jackson: There is nothing new about affirmative action. In this country there has been affirmative action for white men for more than three hundred years. All we are trying to do now is balance things out by changing the beneficiaries of affirmative action for a while. Thus, when we talk about affirmative action, we are not talking about special treatment for people of color or for white women. We are talking about equal treatment—three hundred years for them, three hundred years for us. White men got good jobs and good pay for three hundred years because of their race and sex. Now it is our turn to get access to those same benefits, also because of our race and sex.

5 But somehow, in the transposition, things get murky and muddy. Somehow the clear, clean concept of "turnabout is fair play" gets lost. All of a sudden, there is talk of who is qualified and who is not. All of a sudden, there is stigma.

Although this is something I recognized for years, I relearned it in an overt and dramatic way from my students. I remember in particular one session in a course on employment discrimination law, when I was introducing the concept of affirmative action. The case we were discussing was the *Weber* case, where Kaiser Aluminum and the steel workers' union had jointly created a craft training program to remedy the historic exclusion of blacks from craft positions. They would admit black and white workers, one for one, until the training program was full. I had planned to use that class time to discuss how the Supreme Court had reached the conclusion that creating such a program did not violate Title VII of the 1964 Civil Rights Act, which prohibits basing employment decisions on the race of the worker. Oddly enough, we never got to that discussion. The entire hour was spent on the concerns of white students about the lack of qualifications of the black workers. And what is really remarkable about their concerns is that in *Weber* no one was qualified and no one was expected to be qualified to do the job: that is precisely the point of a training program.

Now it is true that Brian Weber, the white worker who filed suit because he was not allowed into the program, did have more seniority than some of the black workers who were selected, but this only speaks to the fact that Kaiser had undoubtedly discriminated with respect to hiring—of course black workers would have less seniority overall than white workers. Even then, relative seniority does not speak to the basic question of qualifications—that is, to the question of who can do the job. And it certainly does not speak to the question of who can be trained for the job. But somehow the white students in the class could not let go of that issue. "Affirmative action" meant "unqualified." The notion of qualifications had such a hold on them that the facts of the case became irrelevant.

I remember, in another course, discussing the affirmative action hiring and promotion order entered by the federal district court in Buffalo, New York, with respect to long-standing discrimination by the Buffalo police and fire departments. Because the hiring and promotion exams were shown to have an adverse impact on the hire and promotion of black, hispanic, and white female candidates, and because the city was unable to show that the exams were related to the jobs in question, the court ordered a one-for-one hiring quota of black and white candidates who had passed the exam, but without regard to their scores on those exams. Again, the white students were outraged. "Unqualified!" they cried. But how could the question of qualifications even be addressed, I argued, if the city could not show any connection between the exam and doing the job? Again, the fact that there was no validation of the exam was irrelevant to them.

Let me tell you one more story about affirmative action and qualifications and stigma. It is a true story, about a conversation that took place on my arrival in academia. As I began to learn about the nature of the tenure struggle, a colleague (a white male colleague) was denied tenure. He came into my office soon afterward to offer advice about tenure, to share lessons learned from his loss. "The pace of publishing is important," he said. "I waited too long to publish my first piece, and they lost confidence in me as a scholar. Be sure to publish early." "What a gift," I thought. "How kind of him to reach out through his pain to help a novice." He gave more suggestions, then concluded: "But really, you don't need to worry, because you're black. You will get tenure anyhow." His statement hit me like a smack across the face. How dare he try to invalidate all my past and future work so easily! I stammered a response: "If that is so, why have none of the black law professors who came here before me been granted tenure?" But once again, the facts seemed irrelevant, a feeble answer to his charge—a charge that my work would not be judged on merit, a charge that the only reason he did not get tenure was because he was white (because, surely, his credentials were impeccable), a charge that the only reason that I might get tenure was because I was black. Irrefutable charges, both. Perhaps he was right. And how would I ever know? Or was it ultimately impossible to know?

10 This is the connection between affirmative action and stigma: "You were only allowed in this job because you are black. You will only get tenure because you are black. You would never get anything otherwise, because you are not otherwise qualified." And this is a good example, because it shows the dynamics of that interaction. It shows that it is a tool used by those who feel threatened and weak to attack those who are vulnerable. It shows that it is a convenient, ever-present tool that can be used against a convenient, ever-present victim. It is new language, but it is an old dynamic, an old victim, and an old story. The story used to go like this:

> "You *can't* get the job *because* you are not qualified. Everybody knows that black people are stupid."

Now the story has a new beat. Now it sounds like this:

> "You *can* get the job *even though* you are not qualified. Everybody knows that black people are stupid."

Stigma does not grow out of affirmative action. Affirmative action redefined as special help for the unqualified is merely a new way of reinforcing stigma. A tool to remedy social injustice becomes a tool to reinforce that same injustice. And we are reminded that those who create the stigma turn every event, every action, to that end, even the proposed remedy.

In this dynamic, then, it becomes clear that there are two possibilities if one wants a particular job (or tenure, or admission to college, or a promotion). Either one gets the job because one is also a member of a stigmatized group, or one does not get the job, again because one is a member of a stigmatized group. Stigma is constant. The only question, then, is this: "Do you want the job or not?" Some say "no," and opt out. Like Richard Rodriguez, who was appalled that he received so many teaching offers

> ("After all, not many schools are going to pass up the chance to get a Chicano with a Ph.D. in Renaissance literature.")

while his fellow graduate students received none, some decide the game is not worth the candle and try to live outside the labeling:

> "My decision was final. No, I would say to them all. Finally, simply, no."

But what then of the rest of us? What if you decide that you *do* want the job? It is one thing to be willing to use the people who are using you—they want to hire people of color, or white women, for whatever reason. Does it then follow that you were hired only because of your status and not because of your qualifications? And once you have started down that line of "reasoning," the problem becomes one of self-validation. And then the problem becomes one of getting your work done. When the stigma so affects one's sense of self—the very source of ideas and creativity and energy—it is easy to see the problem of getting one's work done. In fact, it is a wonder that any work gets done at all. Perhaps this is what Countee Cullen was alluding to when he wondered what God could have been thinking of

> "To make a poet black, and bid him sing!"

How can one live inside the stigma, and yet remain enough untouched by it to do one's work? How can we live inside the stigma and still "sing"? How can we fight against the stigma, fight against the belief that we are "unqualified," and still retain enough energy and belief in ourselves to enable us to get our work done? This is hard, but clearly it can be done. Black poets *do* sing.

One way to survive at living and working within stigma is to keep in close contact with others who wear that stigma, to try to see each other honestly, and to give each other the encouragement and honest assessment of our work that we all need. Many minority and white women law professors do this for each other. I have also found it helpful to read about the lives of those who have retained a strong sense of self and found the energy to "sing." How could one read about the Grimké sisters, Anna Julia Cooper, Malcolm X, or Mary Church Terrell without being inspired to keep on with our work. And literature also helps. The words of writers like James Baldwin, Lucille Clifton, and Sandra Cisheros can bring wonder, understanding, and nourishment into our lives.

There is a danger, however, in being successful at this. The oppressor groups expend enormous energy creating and maintaining the purity of these categories and definitions. If society has stigmatized you and you act as if you are not stigmatized, you are violating some serious social norms Stigma is used for a reason—for social structure and for social control. It tells you what your place is, and it tells you to stay in your place. And there is dislocation, there is confusion, there is rage if you act in inappropriate ways. There is a sense in which you are "out of control" (out of *its* control, that is). And society does not tolerate well those who are out of control.

15 I have seen this dynamic manifest itself in academia through white colleagues' insistence on stigma, both for minority students and faculty. I offer two examples. The first incident took place during my first year in academia, when, like most newcomers, I often floundered and erred. A university administrator told me that when she asked a white colleague if he would help me, he explained he could not because he didn't know how to talk to me: I was "not from the street." My sameness was thus raised as a barrier: Only if I were more clearly different, operating within the stigma (that is, "under control"), would I receive support.

Students are harmed the same way. I once saw white colleagues consider denying a benefit to a latino student precisely because of his impressive background (graduate degree, professional experience, board memberships), when white students with similar backgrounds were found acceptable. When I protested, one admitted that I was right: white faculty members did prefer minority students who seemed "different" (weaker, lesser), even though that was not fair. And he reminded me that I should not forget to start from the presumption that all white people are racists. I have not forgotten his lesson. You will be punished for failing to operate by the rules of control, for failing to act within the stigma.

You will also be punished by the members of the stigmatized group who have become used to the stigma and accept it as a part of their own identity. For shifting the definition of self is too hard, and seeing others make the shift becomes too painful a reflection of who one has become. I remember arguing with other black members of the law school admissions committee, in favor of admitting a black applicant with a B average from a top-ranked college who had taken a lot of courses in the history and literature of black Americans. "Her B average doesn't mean much," they insisted. "Look at the meaningless, easy courses she has taken." "Since when are history and literature courses 'easy' courses?" I asked. The answer was that "everyone knew" there is nothing to these courses. Well, in a sense they were right. Everyone in a racist society is supposed to know that anything the oppressed group has accomplished is of little merit. And many in the oppressed group have so internalized that "knowledge" that they will take it on themselves to punish those who refuse to "know" that truth.

So here is the dilemma: You are punished if you are controlled by the stigma, for then you cannot get your work done. And you are punished if you transcend the stigma, for then you *can* get your work done. Society has created a "lose-lose" situation for us. What we have to do is turn that situation around and see it for the free-ing gift that it is. The best way I can think of to describe that freedom is to describe Merle, a friend and former colleague. A white woman raised in a professional family in the south, Merle lived what I viewed as a very free life. While practicing law full-time in Washington, D.C., she also lived by herself on a farm in Virginia, a two-hour drive away, where she raised chickens and vegetables, repaired old farm buildings, and kept her Dobermans in line, with toughness and grit. Once, when I asked her how she got so free to choose her own life, she explained that in the world of white Southerners the boundaries are very narrow and very precise. Once you step over those boundaries, you are *completely* outside. You might as well be a mile away from the line, as a foot. It makes no difference—out is out. And once she became a civil rights lawyer, she was definitely on the other side of the line. There was no way she would ever get back inside. It didn't even matter if she stood close to that line. She was thus "free" to go as far as she wanted.

So I think about Merle, who found a path to personal freedom by being stigmatized and locked out. And I think that maybe there is something helpful in that for us. We can let the stigma eat us alive. Or we can look at it, walk away from it, and sing.

Mapping the Text

1. How would you characterize the view of affirmative action Judy Scales-Trent presents in this essay? What features of her experience justify her thinking of it as related to affirmative action?
2. What is the stigma Scales-Trent sees? What evidence do you see that this sense of stigma is accurate or inaccurate?
3. What responses or solutions to this dilemma does Scales-Trent offer? What other responses or solutions might be available?

Writing to Inquire

1. Through library sources, review opinions about the issue of affirmative action over the last 20 years. What does affirmative action mean? What do the data show about who has benefited from affirmative action measures? What sorts of initiatives have been typical in school environments? What are some of the initiatives that have been employed in other arenas (for example, business, industry, or government)?

Blinded by the White: Crime, Race, and Denial in America

TIM WISE

Tim Wise is a social critic who lectures nationally and internationally. He is the founder of the Association for White Anti-Racist Education (AWARE), an organization dedicated to educating white people about the social and economic costs of institutionalized racism and to encouraging them to combat racial inequity. As a political activist, he has served as assistant director of the Louisiana Coalition Against Racism and Nazism; as a member of the Leadership Council of the Southern Anti-Racism Network; and as an advisory board member of the Fisk University Race Relations Institute in Nashville, Tennessee, and of the Institute for Democratic Education and Culture in Oakland. Currently, he is the executive director of the Tennessee Coalition to Abolish State Killing, a group dedicated to eliminating the death penalty and the development of alternative responses to crime and violence. Wise is the author of *Little White Lies: The Truth About Affirmative Action and "Reverse Discrimination"* (1995) and many essays and articles, such as the one below, in which he speaks out provocatively on contentious contemporary issues and problems.

Imagine if you will the following: The place is a quiet, suburban community. The kind commonly referred to by its residents as a "nice place to live and raise children." It's a community known for civic pride, affluent families, and schools where the students score well above the national average on aptitude tests. It's also 93 percent white.

Now imagine that at this community's high school, a handful of black students who say they feel like outcasts begin talking openly about how they hate everyone. They start dressing alike—perhaps wearing the same colors, or leather jackets, or black berets—and referring to themselves as the "dashiki posse."

Furthermore, they show off their gun collection in a video, which they produce for a class project. In this video, they act out the murders of dozens of their fellow students and teachers.

In addition to all this, the students are known to operate a website which espouses hatred and violence, and on this website they have been known to post what amounts to hit lists—letting everyone know who they hate most, and intend to kill first. One of the targets of their hatred discovers the list, tells his father, and the two of them inform police of the thinly veiled threat.

5 Let's imagine these black students are fond of a particularly "violent" form of music—say, gangsta' rap—and are known to paint viciously anti-white slogans and symbols on their clothing, and sing the praises of a particular black mass murderer—say, Colin Ferguson.

Now, let us answer the following question: How long would it take, based on the above information, for school officials, teachers, and parents to make sure these kids were expelled from school and perhaps prosecuted? How long would it take for their families to be run out of town on a rail? Does anyone believe this scenario would have been met with apathy, cautious indifference, or even amusement?

Of course not. But that's exactly what happened in the real world when at this same school, in this same community, two white students from "good families" began dressing alike, saying they hated everyone, calling themselves the "Trenchcoat Mafia," listening to "shock-rock" and the sometimes violent lyrics of white musical artists, showing off their guns and murder fantasies on film, operating a website which praised Hitler and advocated violence, painting swastikas on their clothes, and naming the people they wanted to kill over the Internet. Still seen as "basically normal kids" by their families, friends, and teachers, these two would be ignored. Ignored that is until last week, when they would go on a killing rampage reminiscent of the previous seven that have occurred at schools around the country in the past two years.

"No one really thought they'd do anything," said some of their classmates. "We thought it was all talk," said others. Of course. These were white kids, with BMW's, whose families make six figures or more. These are the beautiful people. They never do anything wrong.

"We moved from the city to get away from things like this." The statement rings in my ears with a burning familiarity. It's the same thing heard after Paducah, Pearl, Fayetteville, Jonesboro, Edinboro, Springfield, and now Littleton. Some people never get it. Some people are so caught up in their race and class stereotypes about what "danger" looks like, they still insist "things like this just don't happen here."

10 Oh yeah? Well, where do they happen? I have yet to hear of one black or Latino kid in even one inner-city high school plotting, let alone carrying out mass murder. Just where does an urban-dweller go to build 30 bombs anyway? Where can they sit around sawing off shotguns without someone noticing? Christ, if these kids had been black they would have been followed around the hardware store for so long that they would never have been able to buy any pipes, let alone the other ingredients needed for the kind of explosives Klebold and Harris concocted.

So in light of what's happened, not only in Littleton, but in other "nice, quiet" suburbs all around the country lately, one must ask: just what were these folks trying to get away from in the cities? Must not have been violence. Must have been black and brown people (except, of course, for the handful that can afford to live among them in style), and poor folks generally. How sad. Once again, the racialization of crime and deviance has allowed us to let down our guard to the greatest threats to our safety: not people of color (if we're white), but our own white children, white parents, white neighbors, white husbands, white lovers, and white friends.

We have been so conditioned to see deviant and destructive behavior as a byproduct of melanin or "defective" black culture, that commentators can, without any sense of irony continue to remark about how, well, remarkable it is when things like this happen.

It reminds me of something James Baldwin once said about the Holocaust—a much bigger paroxysm of white violence no doubt, but which nonetheless resonates here—" They did not know that they could act that way. But I doubt very much whether black people were astounded."

The white American myth of innocence, decency, morality, and the cowboys who never fired on an "injun" unless it was self-defense, have all been laid bare for those willing to see. That people of color always knew the myths to be bullshit, while the dominant majority refused to listen and look at themselves only makes the situation more tragic. But not a damn bit more shocking. Of course, that the mass killers in the schoolyards have all been white as of late has gone without mention in the media. Oh sure, we hear about the similarities between the Columbine High tragedy and the others—well, at least some of the similarities: all the shooters were boys; all the shooters used guns; all the shooters talked openly about violence; all the shooters played violent video games; all the shooters ate Cheerios at some point in the last ten years—you get the picture. In other words, the racial similarities between all these gun-lovin', trash-talking, dark-clothes wearing, "Doom"-playin', Cheerios-eatin', Marilyn Manson–listenin' bundles of testosterone are irrelevant. While we can rest assured these kids would have been "raced" had they come from black "ghetto matriarchs" in the 'hood, it seems as though no one can see the most obvious common characteristic among them: namely, their white skin. This, I guess, is what folks mean when they say they're color-blind: they can see color all right, it's white they have a problem with.

15 Typical, typical, typical. White folks go off, killing wholesale like there's a frickin' closeout on semi-automatic ammunition, and we get fifty "explanations" from the so-called experts who are called in by the media to make sense of it all. People of color do something horrific or commit random acts of retail violence and the whole world lines up to blame one of three things: their black families (particularly their black single mommas); their black DNA (as in the rantings of *The Bell Curve*); or their "defective" black culture and inverted value system. Whatever the case, their blackness never, and I mean never, gets overlooked.

Gang violence in the cities heats up and we've got *U.S. News and World Report* running a cover story entitled: "A Shocking Look at Blacks and Crime," and every nighttime news program running stories asking "what's wrong with the black family (as if there's only one); what's wrong with these people in the "ghetto underclass." But when Charles Manson, John Wayne Gacy, Ted Bundy, and Jeffrey Dahmer go out and do their thing, no one thinks to ask what it is about white folks that makes them cut babies out of their mothers' wombs, torture young men and bury them under the house, kill two dozen or more women for the hell of it, or consume human flesh. White deviants are afforded the privilege of individualization—"that's just crazy Charlie, ignore him, he's a potted plant"—while those of color get to represent the whole community and become exhibit A in David Duke and Charles Murray's eugenic fantasy. You say 90 percent of modern serial killers have been white? Well, isn't that puzzling. Next question.

You'll never even hear the term "white crime" uttered in polite conversation. White collar crime, maybe; but to suggest that the collar might not be the only thing lacking color, would be dogma non grata in mainstream discussion. "White-on-white violence?" What the hell is that? Never heard of it. Even in the wake of these massacres. Even as white folks are killing other white folks in Kosovo (and still other white folks are bombing them to get them to stop).

The media and politicians have done such a fine job making sure everyone knows who to fear (namely the dark and poor) that we forget how whites are disproportionately likely to engage in all kinds of destructive behavior, from drunk driving, to drug use as teenagers, to animal mutilation, to fratricide, to cutting corners on occupational safety standards and pollution control, which then result in the deaths of twice as many people as are murdered each year.

We forget that when it comes to violent crime, whites are four times more likely to be victimized by another white person than by a person of color, and that only sixteen-thousandths of 1 percent of the white community will be killed by a black person in a given year.

20 It all leads one to wonder: how many of the white families with kids at Columbine would have moved away, or at least taken their kids out of the school if, say, 50 or 100 black families had moved in and enrolled their children there? If other suburban communities and other white folks are any indication, the answer is quite a few. Study after study for 25 years has found that whites begin to leave an area and disenroll their kids from the local schools when the community becomes as little as 8 percent black. As the numbers get higher, the slow trickle becomes a mass exodus. Why? Well, to get away from crime, of course. I'm pretty sure this is the textbook definition of irony.

Even more hilarious is the tendency to act as if young white people were ever innocent, upstanding citizens compared to the rest of the country. Even as far back as 1966, a national survey of 15- to 17-year-old whites found that "virtually all" had committed numerous criminal offenses, from breaking and entering, to minor property destruction, to armed robbery.

I've decided that's why all those shows like "Leave it To Beaver," "Father Knows Best," and "The Brady Bunch" were so popular: not because many people actually lived like that, but because they didn't, and could escape into this unreal fantasy life via the television. After all, why watch a program that looks just like your daily routine? That would be boring. So just as with westerns that allowed (mostly white) kids to fantasize about a more exciting life, these wholesome family programs allowed (and still allow in syndication) mostly white viewers to ignore the dysfunction which is really all around them, and always has been, long before the first black kid set foot in their schools, and long before the "Godless" humanists bounced prayer from homeroom.

Unfortunately, I have no doubt this kind of thing will happen again. In fact, had it not been for a few folks informing on plots they knew about, we would already have added a Milwaukee suburb to the list of white teen angst killing fields, and a week after Columbine would have gotten a look at what kind of explosives Caucasians in Texas are capable of putting together. And still, according to my morning paper, less than half of all teens and their parents (mostly white if modern survey techniques are any guide) think their schools are at risk for this kind of violence.

Yeah, well, just keep telling yourself that. Keep watching "COPS" and "Real Stories of the Highway Patrol," and "America's Most Wanted," where most of the bad guys fit the more comfortable profile to which we've grown accustomed. I can hear the dialogue now: "Why look at how menacing the large Negro is, honey! My, oh, my, we sure are glad we moved out here to Pleasantville. Me, my lovely wife, and our son. Speaking of whom, honey, where is Waldo anyway? I don't think I've seen him all week. Is he on that computer of his again? That scamp. Such a hard worker. Oh, and honey, what was that sawing sound coming from the garage last night?"

Mapping the Text

1. Tim Wise's essay, "Blinded by the White," is a response to recent incidents of violence perpetrated by students in high schools. What point is Wise making? What is he implying about issues of race, class, or other differences?
2. Who is the audience for Wise's essay? On what evidence do you draw your conclusion?
3. Describe the voice and tone you hear when you read Wise's essay. What impression they convey? How they help (or not help) Wise to share his point of view and to be convincing (or not)?

Writing to Inquire

1. In this essay, Wise discusses gang violence. Use library resources to examine the extent to which gang violence is or is not a contemporary problem. Write a position paper in which you argue for the extent to which gang violence is a real problem in today's educational settings.

Not Enough Girls

JOHN GEHRING

John Gehring is a journalist who writes about school reform efforts. Having been a staff writer for several newspapers, he currently writes for *Education Week,* a national newspaper based in Bethesda, Maryland, that covers education issues. In the article below, published in *Education Week,* (10 May 2001), Gehring raises issues about gender and technology.

Ashley Weagraff doesn't worry about the boys anymore. She is the exception.

One of the few girls taking technology-related classes at G. Ray Bodley High School in Fulton, N.Y., the 15-year-old fought back her initial anxiety and now works well with male students in a computer-enhanced technical drawing, design, and production class.

But she still knows well the fear that keeps many girls from taking similar courses that feature a heavy dose of technology. "A lot of the time, girls steer clear of technology classes because they are intimidated by the majority of males in the classes," she says.

The gender divide in technology classes at Weagraff's school is not an anomaly. Across the country, the vast majority of girls shy away from technology-related classes. Last year, for instance, only 15 percent of those taking the Advanced Placement exam for computer science were girls, according to the College Board, which sponsors the exams.

5 Results from a national survey released in January by the University of California, Los Angeles, in conjunction with the American Council on Education, showed that male college students were twice as likely as their female peers to rate their computer skills as above average, and five times more likely to pursue careers in computer programming.

The U.S. Department of Education reports that in 1998 women received 27 percent of undergraduate degrees in computer science, down from a high of 37 percent in 1984—a gender divide in technology education that is contributing to an already acute shortage of skilled technology workers.

While overt discrimination against girls in schools appears to be rare, students, teachers, and advocacy groups say that work remains to be done in lifting the subtle barriers that still limit young women from having the information and opportunities to explore technology-rich classes.

Those roadblocks range from teachers who grew up in an era when careers were often starkly delineated along gender lines to outdated school counseling material. Experts also suggest that because most school districts are occupied with the demands of standards-based reform and high-stakes testing, trying to get schools to think more critically about gender stereotyping and increasing the number of girls in technology-related courses can be difficult.

Donna Matteson, a teacher in the technology department at Bodley High, says the challenge of attracting more girls to classes that involve the use of technology is not unique to her school or state.

10 "This is an issue for people who I have talked to all over the country," she says. "It is one of those constant struggles to make sure you produce a program that is gender-fair. You are battling so many societal issues."

Fifteen years ago, Matteson was among only a handful of women enrolled as technology education majors at the State University of New York at Oswego. "It wasn't much better when my daughter graduated three years ago," Matteson says. "Things haven't improved a whole lot."

Marcia Greenberger, a co-president of the National Women's Law Center, a Washington-based advocacy organization, says that school systems have lagged behind the business world when it comes to creating an equal-opportunity environment. The law center, which works to advance girls in school and women in the workplace, has started a public-information campaign that takes aim at gender stereotyping and discrimination in career and technical programs.

"Women and girls are not getting the education they need to prepare them for high-wage careers in areas such as computers and engineering," Greenberger contends. "Even with all the advancements for women, many job-training and career programs are still segregated by sex, with female students in classes such as cosmetology and typing, that lead to traditionally female, low-wage careers."

Subtle Biases

Other groups are pushing a high-tech agenda for girls, too.

15 Last year, the Washington-based American Association of University Women released a report, "TechSavvy: Educating Girls in the New Computer Age," that says schools need to do a better job of teaching and applying information technology, particularly as it relates to girls.

"Girls are an untapped source of talent to lead the high-tech economy and culture," the report argues. Teachers and those who write curricula, it continues, "need to cultivate girls' interest by infusing technology concepts and uses into subject areas ranging from music to history to the sciences in order to interest a broader array of learners."

And women's groups say efforts need to be made to get girls interested in technical careers while they're in high school.

The Cisco Networking Academy Program—which teaches students to design, build, and maintain computer systems and is taught in schools across the country—has made recruiting and retaining women for its program a high priority. Among other projects, Cisco has asked the Institute for Women in Trades, Technology, and Science, an organization that works to encourage women to enter fields such as technology, to review Cisco programs to find better ways to attract girls and women into technology.

An informal survey conducted by Cisco officials found a ratio of roughly 5 to 1 of males to females in its academy programs.

20 "We believe there is a real need to encourage young women," says Erin Walsh, the manager for international strategies and partnerships at Cisco. "Technology is a terrific career choice."

Gender Equity Loses Steam

A 1998 update of the federal law that helps pay for state vocational education programs eliminated a separate funding source that the initial law had earmarked for nontraditional populations and efforts to eliminate sex bias and stereotypes in vocational education, the curriculum umbrella that covers many school technology classes. Under the old version of the law, states were required to have gender-equity coordinators to make sure relatively equal numbers of girls and boys were benefiting from such classes.

But today, although states still have the option of funding such positions, they are not required to do so. Congress also set a cap on how much set-aside money states can spend on programs for special populations, such as clubs for girls interested in technology.

"This is a touchy issue, and a lot of states don't want to deal with it," says Mimi Lufkin, the executive director of the Cochranville, Pa–based National Alliance for Partnerships in Equity, Inc., or NAPE, which promotes gender equity in education. "Teachers can be defensive if someone comes in and says, 'You are not doing this right.'"

Training teachers and guidance counselors to be sensitive to gender issues, Lufkin argues, is critical in improving the environment for vocational and technology education programs. Currently, only four states out of 36 that responded to a NAPE survey reported that they had a full-time employee devoted to gender equity.

Different Preferences

25 Other experts, meanwhile, question the premises of much of the discussion of girls and technology.

Judith S. Kleinfeld, a professor of psychology at the University of Alaska, Fairbanks, argues that what many advocates and teachers see as a disturbing "gender gap" in technology is really a natural process of students choosing to pursue different interests.

In general, she says, research shows that women prefer activities that involve working with other people, and men have more of an interest in working with "things"—including computers. Talking about a gender gap, she says, makes it seem that girls somehow aren't doing as well as boys.

Encouraging girls to pursue courses oriented toward technology can be positive, but pressuring girls into technology-related careers when their interest lies with teaching or nursing, she cautions, is wrong and makes young women feel that such careers are less worthy.

"As long as we have a society in which males and females are free to make choices, they are going to make choices," Kleinfeld says. "Males and females have different preferences."

Mapping the Text

1. What is Gehring's message and purpose in writing this essay?
2. How does Gehring account for the absence of girls in technology courses? Does he propose solutions that seem reasonable?

Writing to Inquire

1. Gehring asserts in "Not Enough Girls" that girls often stay away from technology courses. Use library sources or evidence from data collected on your campus about technology courses to determine the extent to which his view is true for your local site.
2. Gehring is concerned about gender gaps and technology. Do you see other issues of gender in education that are similarly problematic? Does gender matter in education or educational opportunity?

CALLS TO ACTION AND RESPONSE

Transforming the Federal Role in Education So That No Child Is Left Behind

GEORGE W. BUSH

George W. Bush (1946–) forty-third president of the United States of America, was elected to this office in 2000 amid controversy over election proceedings. Before entering politics, his career included working in the energy industry and owning the Texas Rangers baseball franchise. He was elected governor of Texas in 1994, a position that he held until becoming president. The defining moment of Bush's presidency may well prove his handling of the terrorist attacks on New York City and Washington, D.C., on September 11, 2001. Before these attacks, however, he had identified education as one of the major priorities of his administration. The executive summary below, presented in a speech to the nation on January 28, 2001, outlines Bush's educational philosophy and agenda.

"If a nation expects to be ignorant and free, in a state of civilization, it expects what never was and never will be."

—THOMAS JEFFERSON, 1816

As America enters the 21st Century full of hope and promise, too many of our neediest students are being left behind.

Today, nearly 70 percent of inner city fourth graders are unable to read at a basic level on national reading tests. Our high school seniors trail students in Cyprus and South Africa on international math tests. And nearly a third of our college freshmen find they must take a remedial course before they are able to even begin regular college level courses.

Although education is primarily a state and local responsibility, the federal government is partly at fault for tolerating these abysmal results. The federal government currently does not do enough to reward success and sanction failure in our education system.

Since 1965, when the federal government embarked on its first major elementary-secondary education initiative, federal policy has strongly influenced America's schools. Over the years Congress has created hundreds of programs intended to address problems in education without asking whether or not the programs produce results or knowing their impact on local needs. This "program for every problem" solution has begun to add up—so much so that there are hundreds of education programs spread across 39 federal agencies at a cost of $120 billion a year. Yet, after spending billions of dollars on education, we have fallen short in meeting our goals for educational excellence. The academic achievement gap between rich and poor, Anglo and minority is not only wide, but in some cases is growing wider still.

In reaction to these disappointing results, some have decided that there should be no federal involvement in education. Others suggest we merely add new programs into the old system. Surely, there must be another way—a way that points to a more effective federal role. The priorities that follow are based on the fundamental notion that an enterprise works best when responsibility is placed closest to the most important activity of the enterprise, when those responsible are given greatest latitude and support, and when those responsible are held accountable for producing results. This education blueprint will:

- **Increase Accountability for Student Performance:** States, districts and schools that improve achievement will be rewarded. Failure will be sanctioned. Parents will know how well their child is learning, and that schools are held accountable for their effectiveness with annual state reading and math assessments in grades 3–8.
- **Focus on What Works:** Federal dollars will be spent on effective, research based programs and practices. Funds will be targeted to improve schools and enhance teacher quality.
- **Reduce Bureaucracy and Increase Flexibility:** Additional flexibility will be provided to states and school districts, and flexible funding will be increased at the local level.
- **Empower Parents:** Parents will have more information about the quality of their child's school. Students in persistently low-performing schools will be given choice.

Though these priorities do not address reforms in every federal education program, they do address a general vision for reforming the Elementary and Secondary Education Act (ESEA) and linking federal dollars to specific performance goals to ensure improved results. Details about other programs and priorities will be provided at a later date.* (NOTE: These proposals—highlighted with*—are presented within a new legislative framework. There are programs and policies in the current Elementary and Secondary Education Act that are not addressed in these proposals. The proposals that are starred in this document will be considered separately from the ESEA reauthorization.)

Our priorities in this blueprint consist of seven performance-based titles:

I. Improving the academic performance of disadvantaged students

II. Boosting teacher quality

III. Moving limited English proficient students to English fluency

IV. Promoting informed parental choice and innovative programs

V. Encouraging safe schools for the 21st Century

VI. Increasing funding for Impact Aid

VII. Encouraging freedom and accountability

There will be additional funds targeted to needy schools and districts. States and school districts will have the flexibility to produce results, and may lose funds if performance goals are not met.

In America, no child should be left behind. Every child should be educated to his or her full potential. This proposal sets forth the President's proposed framework to accomplish that goal. This Administration will work with Congress to ensure that this happens quickly, and in a bipartisan manner.

The Policy

The Administration's education reform agenda is comprised of the following key components, many of which would be implemented during the re-authorization of the Elementary and Secondary Education Act (ESEA):

Closing the Achievement Gap:

- **Accountability and High Standards.** States, school districts, and schools must be accountable for ensuring that all students, including disadvantaged students, meet high academic standards. States must develop a system of sanctions and rewards to hold districts and schools accountable for improving academic achievement.
- **Annual Academic Assessments.** Annual reading and math assessments will provide parents with the information they need to know how well their child is doing in school, and how well the school is educating their child. Further, annual data is a vital diagnostic tool for schools to achieve continuous improvement. With adequate time for planning and implementation, each state may select and design assessments of their choosing. In addition, a sample of students in each state will be assessed annually with the National Assessment of Educational Progress (NAEP) 4th and 8th grade assessment in reading and math.
- **Consequences for Schools That Fail to Educate Disadvantaged Students.** Schools that fail to make adequate yearly progress for disadvantaged students will first receive assistance, and then come under corrective action if they still fail to make progress. If schools fail to make adequate yearly progress for three consecutive years, disadvantaged students may use Title I funds to transfer to a higher-performing public or private school, or receive supplemental educational services from a provider of choice.

Improving Literacy by Putting Reading First:

- **Focus on Reading in Early Grades.** States that establish a comprehensive reading program anchored in scientific research from kindergarten to second grade will be eligible for grants under a new Reading First initiative.
- **Early Childhood Reading Instruction.** States participating in the Reading First program will have the option to receive funding from a new "Early Reading First" program to implement research-based pre-reading methods in pre-school programs, including Head Start centers.

Expanding Flexibility, Reducing Bureaucracy:

- **Title I Flexibility.** More schools will be able to operate Title I schoolwide programs and combine federal funds with local and state funds to improve the quality of the entire school.
- **Increased Funds to Schools for Technology.** E-rate funds and technology grant funds will be consolidated and distributed to schools through states and local districts based on need. This will also ensure that schools no longer have to submit multiple grant applications and incur the associated administrative burdens to obtain education technology funding.
- **Reduction in Bureaucracy.** Overlapping and duplicative categorical grant programs will be consolidated and sent to states and school districts.
- **New State and Local Flexibility Options.** A charter option for states and districts committed to accountability and reform will be created. Under this program, charter states and districts would be freed from categorical program requirements in return for submitting a five-year performance agreement to the Secretary of Education and being subject to especially rigorous standards of accountability.

Rewarding Success and Sanctioning Failure:

- **Rewards for Closing the Achievement Gap.** High performing states that narrow the achievement gap and improve overall student achievement will be rewarded.
- **Accountability Bonus for States.** Each state will be offered a one-time bonus if it meets accountability requirements, including establishing annual assessments in grades 3–8, within two years of enacting this plan.
- **"No Child Left Behind" School Rewards.** Successful schools that have made the greatest progress in improving the achievement of disadvantaged students will be recognized and rewarded with "No Child Left Behind" bonuses.

- **Consequences for Failure.** The Secretary of Education will be authorized to reduce federal funds available to a state for administrative expenses if a state fails to meet their performance objectives and demonstrate results in academic achievement.

Promoting Informed Parental Choice:

- **School Reports to Parents.** Parents will be enabled to make informed choices about schools for their children by being given access to school-by-school report cards on student achievement for all groups of students.
- **Charter Schools.** Funding will be provided to assist charter schools with start-up costs, facilities, and other needs associated with creating high-quality schools.
- **Innovative School Choice Programs and Research.** The Secretary of Education will award grants for innovative efforts to expand parental choice, as well as to conduct research on the effects of school choice.

Improving Teacher Quality:

- **All Students Taught by Quality Teachers.** States and localities will be given flexibility in the use of federal funds so that they may focus more on improving teacher quality. States will be expected to ensure that all children are taught by effective teachers.
- **Funding What Works.** High standards for professional development will be set to ensure that federal funds promote research-based, effective practice in the classroom.
- **Strengthening Math and Science Education.** K–12 math and science education will be strengthened through math and science partnerships for states to work with institutions of higher education to improve instruction and curriculum.

Making Schools Safer for the 21st Century:

- **Teacher Protection.** Teachers will be empowered to remove violent or persistently disruptive students from the classroom.
- **Promoting School Safety.** Funding for schools will be increased to promote safety and drug prevention during and after school. States will be allowed to give consideration to religious organizations on the same basis as other nongovernmental organizations when awarding grants for after-school programs.
- **Rescuing Students from Unsafe Schools.** Victims of school-based crimes or students trapped in persistently dangerous schools will be provided with a safe alternative. States must report to parents and the public whether a school is safe.
- **Supporting Character Education.** Additional funds will be provided for Character Education grants to states and districts to train teachers

in methods of incorporating character-building lessons and activities into the classroom.

Mapping the Text

1. The executive summary of Bush's speech begins with a quotation from Thomas Jefferson. What is the effect of this choice on the speech? How does the quotation relate to what Bush is actually saying in the speech?
2. Who is the audience for this speech? What sorts of appeals (logos, ethos, pathos) does Bush use in conveying his view to this audience?

Writing to Inquire

1. Bush is defining education as a "national crisis." On what evidence is he making this assertion? Make a list of the problems and solutions he poses. Do you agree or disagree with his perspective? with his solutions?
2. Given the way Bush presents this view, what counterargument(s) might be raised? From your perspective, does he leave out any important issue or fail to address a dimension of the problem that might need to be addressed?

Other People's Children: North Lawndale and the South Side of Chicago

JONATHAN KOZOL

Noted activist and author Jonathan Kozol (1936–) currently lives in Byfield, Massachusetts. A graduate of Harvard University and a former Rhodes Scholar at Oxford, Kozol has contributed to the continuing fight for higher-quality public schools for disadvantaged American children since the early 1960s. Kozol was born into a middle-class Jewish family in Boston. He began his teaching career working with inner-city children in Roxbury, Massachusetts, in the 1960s, but was quickly fired after he taught selections of poetry that were not on the school system's approved curriculum list. That experience led to the publication of his first book of nonfiction, *Death at an Early Age: The Destruction of the Hearts and Minds of Negro Children in the Boston Public Schools* (1968), for which he won the National Book Award. Other works include *Rachel and Her Children: Homeless Families in America* (1988); *Savage Inequalities: Children in America's Schools* (1991); *Amazing Grace: The Lives of Children and the Conscience of a Nation* (1993); and *Will Standards Save Public Education?* (2000). In the following excerpt from *Savage Inequalities,* Kozol describes the realities of poverty and hopelessness as factors shaping the public schools of the South Side of Chicago.

Almost anyone who visits in the schools of East St. Louis, even for a short time, comes away profoundly shaken. These are innocent children, after all. They have done nothing wrong. They have committed no crime. They are too young to have offended us in any way at all. One searches for some way to understand why a society as rich and, frequently, as generous as ours would leave these children in their penury and squalor for so long—and with so little public indignation. Is this just a strange mistake of history? Is it unusual? Is it an American anomaly? Even if the destitution and the racial segregation and the toxic dangers of the air, and soil cannot be immediately addressed, why is it that we can't at least pour vast amounts of money, ingenuity and talent into public education for these children?

Admittedly, the soil cannot be de-leaded overnight, and the ruined spirits of the men who camp out in the mud and shacks close to the wire fencing of Monsanto can't be instantly restored to life, nor can the many illnesses these children suffer suddenly be cured, nor can their asthma be immediately relieved. Why not, at least, give children in this city something so spectacular, so wonderful and special in their public schools that hundreds of them, maybe thousands, might be able somehow to soar up above the hopelessness, the clouds of smoke and sense of degradation all around them?

Every child, every mother, in this city is, to a degree, in the position of a supplicant for someone else's help. The city turns repeatedly to outside agencies—the federal Department of Housing and Urban Development, the federal and Illinois EPA, the U.S. Congress, the Illinois State Board of Education, religious charities, health organizations, medical schools and educational foundations—soliciting help in much the way that African and Latin American nations beg for grants from agencies like AID. And yet we stop to tell ourselves: *These are Americans.* Why do we reduce them to this beggary—and why, particularly, in public education? Why not spend on children here at least what we would be investing in their education if they lived within a wealthy district like Winnetka, Illinois, or Cherry Hill, New Jersey, or Manhasset, Rye, or Great Neck in New York? Wouldn't this be natural behavior in an affluent society that seems to value fairness in so many other areas of life? Is fairness less important to Americans today than in some earlier times? Is it viewed as slightly tiresome and incompatible with hard-nosed values? What do Americans believe about equality?

"Drive west on the Eisenhower Expressway," writes the *Chicago Tribune,* "out past the hospital complex, and look south." Before your eyes are block after block of old, abandoned, gaping factories. "The overwhelming sensation is emptiness. . . . What's left is, literally, nothing."

5 This emptiness—"an industrial slum without the industry," a local resident calls it—is North Lawndale. The neighborhood, according to the *Tribune,* "has one bank, one supermarket, 48 state lottery agents. . . and 99 licensed bars and liquor stores." With only a single supermarket, food is of poor quality and overpriced. Martin Luther King, who lived in this neighborhood in 1966, said there was a 10- to 20-percent "color tax" on produce,

an estimate that still holds true today. With only a single bank, there are few loans available for home repair; private housing therefore has deteriorated quickly.

According to the 1980 census, 58 percent of men and women 17 and older in North Lawndale had no jobs. The 1990 census is expected to show no improvement. Between 1960 and 1970, as the last white families left the neighborhood, North Lawndale lost three quarters of its businesses, one quarter of its jobs. In the next ten years, 80 percent of the remaining jobs in manufacturing were lost.

"People carry a lot of crosses here," says Reverend Jim Wolff, who directs a mission church not far from one of the deserted factories. "God's beautiful people live here in the midst of hell."

As the factories have moved out, he says, the street gangs have moved in. Driving with me past a sprawling red-brick complex that was once the world headquarters of Sears, Roebuck, he speaks of the increasing economic isolation of the neighborhood: "Sears is gone. International Harvester is gone. Sunbeam is gone. Western Electric has moved out. The Vice Lords, the Disciples and the Latin Kings have, in a sense, replaced them.

"With the arrival of the gangs there is, of course, more violence and death. I buried a young man 21 years old a week ago. Most of the people that I bury are between the ages of 18 and 30."

10 He stops the car next to a weed-choked lot close to the corner of Sixteenth and Hamlin. "Dr. King," he says, "lived on this corner." There is no memorial. The city, I later learn, flattened the building after Dr. King moved out. A broken truck now occupies the place where Dr. King resided. From an open side door of the truck, a very old man is selling pizza slices. Next door is a store called Jumbo Liquors. A menacing group of teen-age boys is standing on the corner of the lot where Dr. King lived with his family. "Kids like these will kill each other over nothing—for a warm-up jacket," says the pastor.

"There are good people in this neighborhood," he says, "determined and persistent and strong-minded people who have character and virtues you do not see everywhere. You say to yourself, 'There's something here that's being purified by pain.' All the veneers, all the façades, are burnt away and you see something genuine and beautiful that isn't often found among the affluent. I see it in children—in the youngest children sometimes. Beautiful sweet natures. It's as if they are refined by their adversity. But you cannot sentimentalize. The odds they face are hellish and, for many, many people that I know, life here is simply unendurable.

"Dr. King once said that he had met his match here in Chicago. He said that he faced more bigotry and hatred here than anywhere he'd been in the Deep South. Now he's gone. The weeds have overgrown his memory. I sometimes wonder if the kids who spend their lives out on that corner would be shocked, or even interested, to know that he had lived there once. If you told them, I suspect you'd get a shrug at most. . . ."

On a clear October day in 1990, the voices of children in the first-floor hallway of the Mary McLeod Bethune School in North Lawndale are as bright and optimistic as the voices of small children anywhere. The school, whose students are among the poorest in the city, serves one of the neighborhoods in which the infant death rate is particularly high. Nearly 1,000 infants die within these very poor Chicago neighborhoods each year. An additional 3,000 infants are delivered with brain damage or with other forms of neurological impairment. But, entering a kindergarten classroom on this autumn morning, one would have no sense that anything was wrong. Kindergarten classes almost anywhere are cheerful places, and whatever damage may already have been done to children here is not initially apparent to a visitor.

When the children lie down on the floor to have their naps, I sit and watch their movements and their breathing. A few of them fall asleep at once, but others are restless and three little boys keep poking one another when the teacher looks away. Many tiny coughs and whispers interrupt the silence for a while.

15 The teacher is not particularly gentle. She snaps at the ones who squirm around—"Relax!" and "Sleep!"—and forces down their arms and knees.

A little boy lying with his head close to my feet looks up, with his eyes wide open, at the ceiling. Another, lying on his stomach, squints at me with one eye while the other remains closed. Two little girls, one in blue jeans, one in purple tights, are sound asleep.

The room is sparse: a large and clean but rather cheerless space. There are very few of those manipulable objects and bright-colored shelves and boxes that adorn suburban kindergarten classrooms. The only decorations on the walls are posters supplied by companies that market school materials: "Winter," "Spring," "Summer," "Autumn," "Zoo Animals," "Community Helpers." Nothing the children or teacher made themselves.

As the minutes pass, most of the children seem to sleep, some of them with their arms flung out above their heads, others with their hands beneath their cheeks, though four or five are wide awake and stare with boredom at the ceiling.

On the door is a classroom chart ("Watch us grow!" it says) that measures every child's size and weight. Nakisha, according to the chart, is 38 inches tall and weighs 40 pounds. Lashonda, is 42 inches and weighs 45. Seneca is only 36 inches tall. He weighs only 38.

20 After 30 minutes pass, the teacher tells the children to sit up. Five of the boys who were most restless suddenly are sound asleep. The others sit up. The teacher tells them, "Folded hands!" They fold their hands. "Wiggle your toes!" They wiggle their toes. "Touch your nose!" They touch their noses.

The teacher questions them about a trip they made the week before. "Where did we go?" The children answer, "Farm!" "What did we see?" The children answer, "Sheep!" "What did we feed them?" A child yells out,

"Soup!" The teacher reproves him: "You weren't there! What is the right answer?" The other children answer, "Corn!"

In a somewhat mechanical way, the teacher lifts a picture book of Mother Goose and flips the pages as the children sit before her on the rug.

"Mary had a little lamb, its fleece was white as snow. . . . Old Mother Hubbard went to the cupboard to fetch her poor dog a bone. . . . Jack and Jill went up the hill. . . . This little piggy went to market. . . ."

The children recite the verses with her as she turns the pages of the book. She's not very warm or animated as she does it, but the children are obedient and seem to like the fun of showing that they know the words. The book looks worn and old, as if the teacher's used it many, many years, and it shows no signs of adaptation to the race of the black children in the school. Mary is white. Old Mother Hubbard is white. Jack is white. Jill is white. Little Jack Horner is white. Mother Goose is white. Only Mother Hubbard's dog is black.

"Baa, baa, black sheep," the teacher reads, "have you any wool?" The children answer: "Yessir, yessir, three bags full. One for my master. . . ." The master is white. The sheep are black.

Four little boys are still asleep on the green rug an hour later when I leave the room. I stand at the door and look at the children, most of whom are sitting at a table now to have their milk. Nine years from now, most of these children will go on to Manley High School, an enormous, ugly building just a block away that has a graduation rate of only 38 percent. Twelve years from now, by junior year of high school, if the neighborhood statistics hold true for these children, 14 of these 23 boys and girls will have dropped out of school. Fourteen years from now, four of these kids, at most, will go to college. Eighteen years from now, one of those four may graduate from college, but three of the 12 boys in this kindergarten will already have spent time in prison.

If one stands here in this kindergarten room and does not know these things, the moment seems auspicious. But if one knows the future that awaits them, it is terrible to see their eyes look up at you with friendliness and trust—to see this and to know what is in store for them.

In a fifth grade classroom on the third floor of the school, the American flag is coated with chalk and bunched around a pole above a blackboard with no writing on it. There are a couple of pictures of leaves against the windowpanes but nothing like the richness and the novelty and fullness of expression of the children's creativity that one would see in better schools where principals insist that teachers fill their rooms with art and writing by the children. The teacher is an elderly white woman with a solid bun of sensible gray hair and a depleted grayish mood about her. Among the 30 children in the room, the teacher says that several, all of whom are black, are classified "learning disabled."

The children are doing a handwriting lesson when I enter. On a board at the back of the room the teacher has written a line of letters in the standard cursive script. The children sit at their desks and fill entire pages with these letters. It is the kind of lesson that is generally done in second grade in a suburban school. The teacher seems bored by the lesson, and the children seem to feel this and compound her boredom with their own. Next she does a social studies lesson on the Bering Strait and spends some time in getting the class to give a definition of a "strait." About half of the children pay attention. The others don't talk or interrupt or fidget. They are well enough behaved but seem sedated by the teacher's voice.

30 Another fifth grade teacher stops me in the corridor to ask me what I'm doing in the building. He's 50 years old, he tells me, and grew up here in North Lawndale when it was a middle-class white neighborhood but now lives in the suburbs. "I have a low fifth grade," he says without enthusiasm, then—although he scarcely knows me—launches into an attack upon the principal, the neighborhood and the school.

"It's all a game," he says. "Keep them in class for seven years and give them a diploma if they make it to eighth grade. They can't read, but give them the diploma. The parents don't know what's going on. They're satisfied."

When I ask him if the lack of money and resources is a problem in the school, he looks amused by this. "Money would be helpful but it's not the major factor," he replies. "The parents are the problem."

The principal, Warren Franczyk, later tells me this: "Teachers are being dumped from high school jobs because of low enrollment. But if they've got tenure they cannot be fired so we get them here. I've got two of them as subs right now and one as a permanent teacher. He's not used to children of this age and can't control them. But I have no choice."

The city runs a parallel system of selective schools—some of which are known as "magnet" schools—and these schools, the principal tells me, do not have the staffing problems that he faces. "They can select their teachers and their pupils. So it represents a drain on us. They attract the more sophisticated families, and it leaves us with less motivated children."

35 Chicago, he tells me, does not have a junior high school system. Students begin Bethune in kindergarten and remain here through eighth grade. Eighth grade graduation, here as elsewhere in Chicago, is regarded as a time for celebration, much as twelfth grade graduation would be celebrated in the suburbs. So there are parties, ball gowns and tuxedos, everything that other kids would have at high school graduation. "For more than half our children," says the principal, "this is the last thing they will have to celebrate."

Even in the most unhappy schools there are certain classes that stand out like little islands of excitement, energy and hope. One of these classes is a combination fifth and sixth grade at Bethune, taught by a woman, maybe 40 years of age, named Corla Hawkins.

The classroom is full of lively voices when I enter. The children are at work, surrounded by a clutter of big dictionaries, picture books and gadgets, science games and plants and colorful milk cartons, which the teacher purchased out of her own salary. An oversized Van Gogh collection, open to a print of a sunflower, is balanced on a table-ledge next to a fish tank and a turtle tank. Next to the table is a rocking chair. Handwritten signs are on all sides: "Getting to know you," "Keeping you safe," and, over a wall that holds some artwork by the children, "Mrs. Hawkins's Academy of Fine Arts." Near the windows, the oversized leaves of several wild-looking plants partially cover rows of novels, math books, and a new World Book Encyclopedia. In the opposite corner is a "Science Learning Board" that holds small packets which contain bulb sockets, bulbs and wires, lenses, magnets, balance scales and pliers. In front of the learning board is a microscope. Several rugs are thrown around the floor. On another table are a dozen soda bottles sealed with glue and lying sideways, filled with colored water.

The room looks like a cheerful circus tent. In the center of it all, within the rocking chair, and cradling a newborn in her arms, is Mrs. Hawkins.

The 30 children in the class are seated in groups of six at five of what she calls "departments." Each department is composed of six desks pushed together to create a table. One of the groups is doing math, another something that they call "math strategy." A third is doing reading. Of the other two groups, one is doing something they describe as "mathematics art"—painting composites of geometric shapes—and the other is studying "careers," which on this morning is a writing exercise about successful business leaders who began their lives in poverty. Near the science learning board a young-looking woman is preparing a new lesson that involves a lot of gadgets she has taken from a closet.

"This woman," Mrs. Hawkins tells me, "is a parent. She wanted to help me. So I told her, 'If you don't have somebody to keep your baby, bring the baby here. I'll be the mother. I can do it.'"

As we talk, a boy who wears big glasses brings his book to her and asks her what the word *salvation* means. She shows him how to sound it out, then tells him, "Use your dictionary if you don't know what it means." When a boy at the reading table argues with the boy beside him, she yells out, "You ought to be ashamed. You woke my baby."

After 15 minutes she calls out that it is time to change their tables. The children get up and move to new departments. As each group gets up to move to the next table, one child stays behind to introduce the next group to the lesson.

"This is the point of it," she says. "I'm teaching them three things. Number one: self-motivation. Number two: self-esteem. Number three: you help your sister and your brother. I tell them they're responsible for one another.

I give no grades in the first marking period because I do not want them to be too competitive. Second marking period, you get your grade on what you've taught your neighbors at your table. Third marking period, I team them two-and-two. You get the same grade as your partner. Fourth marking period, I tell them, 'Every fish swims on its own.' But I wait a while for that. The most important thing for me is that they teach each other. . . ."

"All this stuff"—she gestures at the clutter in the room—"I bought myself because it never works to order things through the school system. I bought the VCR. I bought the rocking chair at a flea market. I got these books here for ten cents apiece at a flea market. I bought that encyclopedia—" she points at the row of World Books—"so that they can do their research right here in this room."

45 I ask her if the class reads well enough to handle these materials. "Most of them can read some of these books. What they cannot read, another child can read to them," she says.

"I tell the parents, 'Any time your child says, "I don't have no homework," call me up. Call me at home.' Because I give them homework every night and weekends too. Holidays I give them extra. Every child in this classroom has my phone."

Cradling the infant in her lap, she says, "I got to buy a playpen."

The bottles of colored water, she explains, are called "wave bottles." The children make them out of plastic soda bottles which they clean and fill with water and food coloring and seal with glue. She takes one in her hand and rolls it slowly to and fro. "It shows them how waves form," she says. "I let them keep them at their desks. Some of them hold them in their hands while they're at work. It seems to calm them: seeing the water cloud up like a storm and then grow clear. . . .

"I take them outside every day during my teacher-break. On Saturdays we go to places like the art museum. Tuesdays, after school, I coach the drill team. Friday afternoons I tutor parents for their GED [high school equivalency exam]. If you're here this afternoon, I do the gospel choir."

50 When I ask about her own upbringing, she replies, "I went to school here in Chicago. My mother believed I was a 'gifted' child, but the system did not challenge me and I was bored at school. Fortunately one of my mother's neighbors was a teacher and she used to talk to me and help me after school. If it were not for her I doubt that I'd have thought that I could go to college. I promised myself I would return that favor."

At the end of class I go downstairs to see the principal, and then return to a second-floor room to see the gospel choir in rehearsal. When I arrive, they've already begun. Thirty-five children, ten of whom are boys, are standing in rows before a piano player. Next to the piano, Mrs. Hawkins stands and leads them through the words. The children range in age from sixth and seventh graders to three second graders and three tiny children, one of whom is Mrs. Hawkins's daughter, who are kindergarten pupils in the school.

They sing a number of gospel songs with Mrs. Hawkins pointing to each group—soprano, alto, bass—when it is their turn to join in. When they sing, "I love you, Lord," their voices lack the energy she wants. She interrupts and shouts at them, "Do you love Him? Do you?" They sing louder. The children look as if they're riveted to her directions.

"This next song," she says, "I dreamed about this. This song is my favorite."

The piano begins. The children start to clap their hands. When she gives the signal they begin to sing:

Clap your hands!
Stamp your feet!
Get on up
Out of your seats!
Help me
Lift 'em up, Lord!
Help me
Lift 'em up!

55 When a child she calls "Reverend Joe" does not come in at the right note, Mrs. Hawkins stops and says to him: "I thought you told me you were saved!"

The children smile. The boy called "Reverend Joe" stands up a little straighter. Then the piano starts again. The sound of children clapping and then stamping with the music fills the room. Mrs. Hawkins waves her arms. Then, as the children start, she also starts to sing.

Help me lift 'em up, Lord!
Help me lift 'em up!

There are wonderful teachers such as Corla Hawkins almost everywhere in urban schools, and sometimes a number of such teachers in a single school. It is tempting to focus on these teachers and, by doing this, to paint a hopeful portrait of the good things that go on under adverse conditions. There is, indeed, a growing body of such writing; and these books are sometimes very popular, because they are consoling.

The rationale behind much of this writing is that pedagogic problems in our cities are not chiefly matters of injustice, inequality or segregation, but of insufficient information about teaching strategies: If we could simply learn "what works" in Corla Hawkins's room, we'd then be in a position to repeat this all over Chicago and in every other system.

But what is unique in Mrs. Hawkins's classroom is not what she does but who she is. Warmth and humor and contagious energy cannot be replicated and cannot be written into any standardized curriculum. If they could, it would have happened long ago; for wonderful teachers have been heroized in books and movies for at least three decades. And the problems of Chicago are, in any case, not those of insufficient information. If Mrs. Hawkins's fellow fifth grade teachers simply needed information, they could get it easily by walking 20 steps across the hall and visiting her room. The problems are systemic: The number of teachers over 60 years of age in the Chicago system is twice that of the teachers under 30. The salary scale, too low to keep exciting, youthful teachers in the system, leads the city to rely on low-paid subs, who represent more than a quarter of Chicago's teaching force. "We have teachers," Mrs. Hawkins says, "who only bother to come in three days a week. One of these teachers comes in usually around nine-thirty. You ask her how she can expect the kids to care about their education if the teacher doesn't even come until nine-thirty. She answers you, 'It makes no difference. Kids like these aren't going anywhere.' The school board thinks it's saving money on the subs. I tell them, 'Pay now or pay later.'"

60 But even substitute teachers in Chicago are quite frequently in short supply. On an average morning in Chicago, 5,700 children in 190 classrooms come to school to find they have no teacher. The number of children who have no teachers on a given morning in Chicago's public schools is nearly twice the student population of New Trier High School in nearby Winnetka.

"We have been in this class a whole semester," says a 15-year-old at Du Sable High, one of Chicago's poorest secondary schools, "and they still can't find us a teacher."

A student in auto mechanics at Du Sable says he'd been in class for 16 weeks before he learned to change a tire. His first teacher quit at the beginning of the year. Another teacher slept through most of the semester. He would come in, the student says, and tell the students, "You can talk. Just keep it down." Soon he would be asleep.

"Let's be real," the student says. "Most of us ain't going to college. . . . We could have used a class like this."

The shortage of teachers finds its parallel in a shortage of supplies. A chemistry teacher at the school reports that he does not have beakers, water, bunsen burners. He uses a popcorn popper as a substitute for a bunsen burner, and he cuts down plastic soda bottles to make laboratory dishes.

65 Many of these schools make little effort to instruct their failing students. "If a kid comes in not reading," says an English teacher at Chicago's South Shore High, "he goes out not reading."

Another teacher at the school, where only 170 of 800 freshmen graduate with their class, indicates that the dropout rate makes teaching easier. "We lose all the dregs by the second year," he says.

"We're a general high school," says the head of counseling at Chicago's Calumet High School. "We have second- and third-grade readers. . . . We hope to do better, but we won't die if we don't."

At Bowen High School, on the South Side of Chicago, students have two or three "study halls" a day, in part to save the cost of teachers. "Not much studying goes on in study hall," a supervising teacher says. "I let the students play cards. . . . I figure they might get some math skills out of it."

At the Lathrop Elementary School, a short walk from the corner lot where Dr. King resided in North Lawndale, there are no hoops on the basketball court and no swings in the playground. For 21 years, according to the *Chicago Tribune*, the school has been without a library. Library books, which have been piled and abandoned in the lunch room of the school, have "sprouted mold," the paper says. Some years ago the school received the standard reading textbooks out of sequence: The second workbook in the reading program came to the school before the first. The principal, uncertain what to do with the wrong workbook, was told by school officials it was "all right to work backwards. . . ."

70 This degree of equanimity in failure, critics note, has led most affluent parents in Chicago to avoid the public system altogether. The school board president in 1989, although a teacher and administrator in the system for three decades, did not send his children to the public schools. Nor does Mayor Richard Daley, Jr., nor did any of the previous four mayors who had school-age children.

"Nobody in his right mind," says one of the city's aldermen, "would send [his] kids to public school."

Many suburban legislators representing affluent school districts use terms such as "sinkhole" when opposing funding for Chicago's children. "We can't keep throwing money," said Governor Thompson in 1988, "into a black hole."

The *Chicago Tribune* notes that, when this phrase is used, people hasten to explain that it is not intended as a slur against the race of many of Chicago's children. "But race," says the *Tribune*, "never is far from the surface."

. . .

City and state business associations, in Chicago as in many other cities, have lobbied for years against tax increments to finance education of low-income children. "You don't dump a lot of money into guys who haven't done well with the money they've got in the past," says the chief executive officer of Citicorps Savings of Illinois. "You don't rearrange deck chairs on the *Titanic*."

75 In recent years, however, some of the corporate leaders in Chicago who opposed additional school funding and historically resisted efforts at desegregation have nonetheless attempted to portray themselves as allies to poor children—or, as they sometimes call themselves, "school partners"—and they even offer certain kinds of help. Some of the help they give is certainly of use, although it is effectively the substitution of a form of charity, which can be withheld at any time, for the more permanent assurances of justice; but much of what the corporations do is simply superficial and its worth absurdly overstated by the press.

Celebrities are sometimes hired, for example, by the corporations to come into the Chicago schools and organize a rally to sell children on the wisdom of not dropping out of school. A local counterpart to Jesse Jackson often gives a motivational address. He tells the kids, "You are somebody." They are asked to chant it in response. But the fact that they are in this school, and doomed to be here for no reason other than their race and class, gives them a different message: "In the eyes of this society, you are not much at all." This is the message they get every day when no celebrities are there and when their business partners have departed for their homes in the white suburbs.

Business leaders seem to have great faith in exhortation of this kind—a faith that comes perhaps from marketing traditions. Exhortation has its role. But hope cannot be marketed as easily as blue jeans. Human liberation doesn't often come this way—from mass hypnosis. Certain realities—race and class and caste—are there, and they remain.

Not surprisingly, the notion that such private-sector boosterism offers a solution to the miseries of education for poor children is not readily accepted by some parents in Chicago who have seen what private-sector forces have achieved in housing, in employment and in medical provision for their children. "The same bank presidents who offer gifts to help our segregated schools," a mother in Chicago said, "are the ones who have assured their segregation by redlining neighborhoods like these for 30 years, and they are the ones who send their kids to good schools in Winnetka and who vote against the equalizing plans to give our public schools more money. Why should we trust their motives? They may like to train our children to be good employees. That would make their businesses more profitable. Do they want to see our children taking corporate positions from their children? If they gave our kids what their kids have, we might earn enough to move into their neighborhoods."

The phrasing "private-sector partner" is employed somewhat disarmingly in corporate pronouncements, but the language does not always strike responsive chords among sophisticated leaders of the poor. "These people aren't my children's friends," said the woman I have quoted in Chicago. "What have things come to in America when I am told they are the people that I have to trust? If they want to be my 'partner,' let them open up their public schools and bring my children out into their neighborhoods to go to school beside their children. Let them use their money to buy buses, not to hold expensive conferences in big hotels. If they think that busing is too tiring for poor black children—I do find it interesting that they show so much concern for poor black children—I don't mind if they would like to go for limousines. But do not lock us in a place where you don't need to live beside us and then say you want to be my 'partner.' I don't accept that kind of 'partner.' No one would—unless he was a fool or had no choice."

80 But that is the bitter part of it. The same political figures who extol the role of business have made certain that these poor black people would have no real choice. Cutting back the role of government and then suggesting that the poor can turn to businessmen who lobbied for such cuts is cynical

indeed. But many black principals in urban schools know very well that they have no alternative; so they learn to swallow their pride, subdue their recognitions and their dignity, and frame their language carefully to win the backing of potential "business partners." At length they are even willing to adjust their schools and their curricula to serve the corporate will: as the woman in Chicago said, to train the ghetto children to be good employees. This is an accomplished fact today. A new generation of black urban school officials has been groomed to settle for a better version of unequal segregated education.

Mapping the Text

1. Kozol spends a great deal of time sharing what anthropologists call *thick description*—details (often sensory) that help readers experience a moment-by-moment introduction to a particular place or group of people. How does Kozol focus his thick description of the schools of North Lawndale? What do you learn from that description? What assumptions about *audience* influence his choices?
2. Kozol's *descriptive technique* gives way to a specific *argument* in this excerpt. What, exactly, is his argument? Is it *stated directly* or *implied?* What textual moments, specifically, communicate the argument most clearly?
3. Earlier in this text, the following *rhetorical appeals* were discussed: logos, ethos, and pathos. Which appeals seem to be used most frequently by Kozol? Why? Do you see places where Kozol uses multiple rhetorical appeals at once? To what effect?

Writing to Inquire

1. In this excerpt from *Savage Inequalities,* Kozol describes the classroom of Corla Hawkins, who teaches a combined fifth- and sixth-grade class. His depiction of Hawkins, her classroom, and her students serves multiple purposes and might be viewed as a powerful persuasive tool. Write an essay in which you analyze Kozol's use of Hawkins in the chapter. What images of Hawkins does this description convey? What does he emphasize about her character? What does he suggest by other descriptions of people or places? To what effect? What messages about "good teaching" does he offer? What does Kozol highlight about cultural values through these descriptions? Considering the overall effects of the excerpt, what educational practices does Kozol seem to prefer or value?
2. Toward the end of this excerpt, Kozol quotes the CEO of Citicorps Savings of Illinois, a businessman who has argued against increasing taxes to help support education for low-income children. According to this executive, "You don't rearrange deck chairs on the *Titanic.*" Using your own educational experiences as well as Kozol's excerpt, as evidence, draft a short response paper in which you support or refute the executive's statement.

3. Is the vision of public education for low-income children offered within Kozol's excerpt a hopeful one or a hopeless one? Why? Support your response with evidence from the text. Be sure to think not only about the facts and the reasoning presented by Kozol but also about other features of his text that seem to help the excerpt to be persuasive (for example, the tone, the register of the language, or other features that contribute to Kozol's writing style).

INQUIRY: HOW DOES A NATION MAKE EDUCATIONAL OPPORTUNITY A CONCRETE POSSIBILITY FOR ALL?

1. Consult library resources to determine when a national commitment to public education began. Examine your own state's records to determine what early laws, policies, and procedures it sought to put in place for citizens. Given what you find, write an essay in which you explore the nature of public education and what its rights, privileges, and responsibilities should entail.
2. Check with the local and/or state department of education, state teachers' organizations, and the popular press to determine how they articulate the contemporary challenges of public education and why. Write a paper in which you analyze these views, then present your own list of pressing issues for public education.
3. Make a list of the purposes of education from several points of view (for example, with respect to race, class, gender, or culture; with respect to personal benefits, social benefits, or public benefits). What should

What concept of education is pictured here? What kind of learning process is taking place? What assumptions about the purpose of education are reinforced by such images? How do you picture learning?

the agenda of public education be? How should society determine its agenda for public education in light of competing interests?

4. Use library resources to explore the ways in which public education is funded in the United States. How do you account for differences in funding levels from school system to school system? What are the implications of these differences?
5. Alternatives to public education exist. What are the advantages and disadvantages of the various educational choices?
6. Focus on just one educational issue and explore what the issue is, how it came to be the issue that it is, what strategies have been employed to address the problems, what the successes and failures have been, what the contemporary challenges seem to be.
7. Choose a particular type of school site (urban, suburban, rural). How do students, teachers, school administrators, legislators, parents, and community members articulate educational problems in these areas? Are any of the problems unique to the particular type of site? What problems transcend these types of boundaries?
8. Educational opportunity is considered a basic American value, a democratic ideal. How do you assess the nation's ability to make this ideal a reality?
9. Think back over your own educational experiences. Write a personal narrative about one of your most memorable learning moments. Was the experience positive or negative? What made it so? What implications do you see in your story that might be related to race, gender, class, culture, or that might be a function of social expectations? How might your story be different if one of these conditions were changed (for example, your geographical location, gender, race, or religious beliefs)?

CHAPTER 6

Our Bodies, Our Selves

When most people think of living a good life, a vital part of the image is good health. These days, in fact, we are surrounded by calls for wellness and healthy lifestyles. We are told to eat right, to exercise vigorously, and to eliminate unhealthy behaviors such as smoking, drugs, and alcohol. We are encouraged to buy ergonomic furniture and to use good lighting. Media campaigns announce the benefits of wearing sunscreen and drinking bottled water. If you look critically at our media and popular culture—television, movies, magazines, newspapers—it is easy to come away with the view that this society is obsessed with health. So, too, Americans seem obsessed with disease and illness (the inverse of wellness), as there seem to be just as many calls for frequent trips to the doctor, the dentist, and the therapist, and just as much concern about wounded hearts, souls, and spirits.

How do we cope, as individuals and as a society, with a lack of perfection in our physical lives? How does illness, and especially devastating disease, influence or shape how we think of ourselves and others? How does it affect our personal choices? How does it affect our view of social responsibility? The selections in Chapter 6 focus attention on issues related to health, providing you with an opportunity to consider your own views of illness, health, and well-being, and to consider also the roles that language plays in shaping attitudes and directing personal, social, and public choices.

The reading selections in Chapter 6 make clear that questions of health, disease, and medicine are complex; they cannot be approached and evaluated in a vacuum. New discoveries in medical science may produce unintended consequences around the globe. Medical technologies exist, in fact, in a global economy, and their effects are as much cultural and political as they are scientific. Through the converging interests of science and culture, we have begun to understand the vital interconnectedness of life on Earth and to see how the individual human body is more like a busy urban center than a quiet grove in the woods. History, politics, economics, science, and technology play key roles in how we understand and care for our bodies and our selves. These merging viewpoints also help us understand that personal decision making is often affected by social and cultural conditions and that such decisions are likely to have their own effects and consequences within the communities in which we live (in terms of education about disease and illness, the cost of medical care, the cost of medical research, public accommodations for medical needs, and so forth). How, then, do we make distinctions between private decisions and public policies? between individual choice and social responsibility? Keep these questions in mind as a focus of inquiry as you read the selections here.

FRAMING THE TOPIC

What Are the Leading Health Indicators?

U.S. DEPARTMENT OF HEALTH AND HUMAN SERVICES

The United States Department of Health and Human Services (HHS) officially came into being on May 4, 1980, replacing (along with the newly authorized Department of Education) the cabinet-level Department of Health, Education and Welfare. The origins of HHS, however, go back to the earliest days of the nation with the creation of the first hospital, established in 1798 for the health care of sailors. Since those early days, health care, health-related research, and a broad range of human services have been delivered to citizens through a variety of federal programs and offices. HHS drew the list of leading health indicators below from a much larger report entitled "Healthy People 2010." This report set a ten-year agenda for the nation in challenging all sectors of our society to take specific action to ensure good health and long life for all. The ten indicators identify specific focal points and steps that individuals, communities, and health care professionals can take to maintain and improve health and the quality of life, and they will be used during the ten-year period to measure the health of the nation. For more information, go to <http://www.health.gov/healthypeople/LHI/Resources.htm>.

The Leading Health Indicators will be used to measure the health of the Nation over the next 10 years. Each of the 10 Leading Health Indicators has one or more objectives from Healthy People 2010 associated with it. As a group, the Leading Health Indicators reflect the major health concerns in the United States at the beginning of the 21st century. The Leading Health Indicators were selected on the basis of their ability to motivate action, the availability of data to measure progress, and their importance as public health issues.

The Leading Health Indicators are—

1. Physical Activity
2. Overweight and Obesity
3. Tobacco Use
4. Substance Abuse
5. Responsible Sexual Behavior
6. Mental Health
7. Injury and Violence
8. Environmental Quality
9. Immunization
10. Access to Health Care

Mapping the Text

1. Review the list of HHS health indicators. Organize the list based on what you think is most critical to address. Jot down your thoughts about each item in terms of the extent to which it is a personal concern, a social issue, or a public issue. Compare your list with those of two or three other classmates and discuss with them what you collectively know about the problems and concerns and how they are being or might be systematically addressed. Based on your discussion, choose one indicator to explore further. Write an essay in which you report on your findings.

Writing to Inquire

1. Go to the HHS web page to take a more careful look at "Healthy People 2010" and to explore the wide range of problems, concerns, and initiatives related to this area. Based on your exploration, write an essay in which you discuss the role(s) of the federal government in health care and present your view of the advantages and disadvantages of our current system.
2. Think about your own sources of information and your knowledge of various health-related issues and concerns. How is information about devastating disease disseminated to the general public? What kinds of mechanisms are employed by the disseminators of information to signal attention or urgency without signaling panic or alarm? To what extent is the medium by which information is conveyed important? For example, what is the difference in effect when the medium is a commercial film, a documentary film, or a newspaper or magazine article? What difference does the source of information make? For example, what is the difference in effect when information is shaped, defined, and presented by the HHS, or the Centers for Disease Control (CDC), or another governmental health agency; by the FBI or some other nonhealth governmental agency; by a local community organization, physicians, schools, or churches?

READINGS FOR INQUIRY AND EXPLORATION

The Alchemists

LINDA HOGAN

Linda Hogan (1947–) is a Native American (Chickasaw) poet, novelist, playwright, essayist, and political activist. Her works include *Calling Myself Home* (1978); *Daughters, I Love You* (1981); *Eclipse* (1983); *Seeing through the Sun* (1985); *Savings: Poems* (1988); *Mean Spirit* (1990); *Book of Medicines* (1993); *Dwellings: A Spiritual History of the Living World* (1995); *Power* (1998); and *The Sweet Breathing of Plants: Women and the Green World* (2000). "The Alchemists" is taken from the *Book of Medicines*. Many of the poems in this collection function as prayers and incantations, exploring relationships between individual health and environmental healing. In the poem below, Hogan focuses on an intersection between science and mysticism as her father confronts illness.

By day
they bent over lead's
heavy spirit of illness,
asking it to be gold,
the lord from humble beginnings.

And the mad soul of mercury
fell through their hands
through settled floors
and came to rest
silver and deadly
in a hidden corner
where it would grow.

Gold was the property
that could take sickness out
from lead.
It was fire
held still.
At night
they lifted the glass
of black grapes
and sugar to their lips

and drank the flaked gold
suspended in wine
like sparks of fire,
then watched it fall
like fool's gold
to the bottom of a pond.

Yesterday, my father behind a curtain
in the sick ward
heard a doctor
tell a man where the knife
would cut flesh.

Listen, my father said,
that man is saying a poem.
No, he's telling a story.
No, I believe
he is reading from a magical book.

But he was only a man
talking to iron,
willing it to be gold.

If it had worked
we would kneel down before it
and live forever,
all base metals
in ceremonial fire.

Mapping the Text

1. Look up the word *alchemist*. What does Linda Hogan's use of this word suggest about the theme of the poem? How do these allusions relate to the meaning(s) that Hogan actually conveys? What other words and images in the poem help sustain these relationships?
2. What attitude toward medicine and medical science does Hogan convey in the poem? What words, phrases, and images help project this attitude?
3. In the fourth stanza of the poem, Hogan indicates that she is concerned about her father. What is her concern? What is the effect of her expressing this concern in a poem rather than a narrative or an essay?

Writing to Inquire

1. Think about your own attitude toward medicine and medical science. Do you support Hogan's view? Why or why not?
2. Many "truths" once founded in scientific research are now considered quaint superstitions or misperceptions. Today we know the Earth is round

and revolves around the sun (rather than the other way around), for example. Choose a particular "revolution" in recent scientific history and research the ways in which science has changed its views on a foundational issue. Do some exploratory research, and write a brief essay to report your findings. Are any projects currently underway in scientific research that might reveal current "truths" to be, in fact, myths or superstitions?

Race and Health Care in the United States

DAVID BARTON SMITH

David Barton Smith is a professor and chair of the Department of Health Administration at Temple University. He has also worked in the Office of Research and Policy of the Health Care Financing Administration. Smith has been honored for his research on the racial segregation of health care. His works include *The White Labyrinth: Understanding the Organization of Health Care* (with A. Kaluzny, 1975); *Long Term Care in Transition: The Regulation of Nursing Homes* (1981); and *Health Care Divided: Race and the Uncompleted Journey to Heal a Health System and a Nation* (1998). The excerpt below is taken from *Health Care Divided.*

Race

Discussions about race are always awkward. Race is not a scientifically defensible biological or genetic classification scheme.[1] There is more variability within than between racial categories on any characteristic that should matter in shaping life chances. Race should not predict morbidity, mortality, or occupational success. Nor is it a classification scheme that defines distinctive cultural subgroups, despite the current wave of interest in "cultural diversity" training. There are as many cultural and class differences within racial categories as there are between them. Race does not fit the conventional American "melting pot" theories that predict the acculturation and intergenerational upward mobility of immigrant populations. Nuances aside, African Americans and white Americans share the same language, root for the same professional sports teams, enjoy most of the same popular music, and watch most of the same soaps. African Americans can trace their roots in the United States back much further than most white Americans can.

What makes race difficult to talk about is that it deals with resources and power. It has served as America's version of a caste system, while racism has been the ideology that justified it. The attributed cultural and genetic differences between the races have been used to justify slavery, Jim Crow laws, and differences in life chances in a world where the "Whites Only" signs have been removed. Race remains the "American dilemma," as Swedish economist Gunnar Myrdal observed more than half a century ago.

On the one hand, Americans value equality of opportunity. On the other hand, race continues to limit the equality of opportunity. It is one thing to make the visible symbols of Jim Crow disappear in order to embrace the rhetoric of equal opportunity. It has proved far more difficult to make the real differences in life chances disappear. That involves reallocating goods and power and effecting real change within institutions. However necessary, that is a much more difficult change to bring about.

The solution that we seem to have drifted into is not to talk about race, and particularly, not to talk about the racial separation that assures unequal access to resources. As one group of researchers recently observed, we have done a good job of that: "During the 1970s and 1980s a word disappeared from the American vocabulary,"[2] they write. The word is *segregation.* The word was not a part of the vocabulary of politicians, private foundations, government officials, journalists, academicians, or business executives in their discussion of the nation's social problems. Current health care reform proposals that express the desire to assure universal access and an end to a tiered system of care do not mention it. In no area has the silence been as complete as in health care. We compile statisties on segregation in housing, schools, and employment. No such information has ever been systematically collected on health care. Title VI of the Civil Rights Act of 1964 specifically prohibits the use of federal financial assistance for any activity or program that denies benefits or excludes participation based on race, color, or national origin. Yet, more than thirty years after the passage of Medicare and Medicaid, which made the federal government the dominant source of funds, this information void continues. Far more federal dollars flow into health care than into housing, schools, and employment. Far more federal dollars flow into collecting data about health and health care than into data about education and housing. Yet no one reports information on segregation in health care. We have done a good job of making the word disappear, but the problem remains. It is what Philip Slater in *The Pursuit of Loneliness* described as the "toilet assumption," the

> notion that unwanted matter, unwanted difficulties, unwanted complexities and obstacles will disappear if they are removed from our immediate field of vision. . . . when these discarded problems rise to the surface again as a riot, a protest, an exposé in the mass media we react as if a sewer had backed up. We are shocked, disgusted and angered and immediately call for the emergency plumber (the special commission, the crash program) to insure that the problem is once again removed from consciousness.[3]

It is time to take a harder look at the plumbing.

. . .

Health Care

Health care is a perfect place to start looking at that plumbing. . . . Health care is more than just a peculiar struggle over who gets what kind of care and who gets stuck with the bill. As the preceding discussion suggests, health care is an *ethical and moral matter.* Lack of access to adequate health care can restrict an individual's normal range of opportunities and raises basic issues of fairness and social justice.[4] Health care and the way we organize public health services has a profound effect on people's well-being and opportunities. Health care can provide the information we need to plan our lives in the face of illness, prevent premature death, alleviate pain, and restore function. As a culture we profess a moral commitment to equality of opportunity. Access to health care often has a more immediate impact on opportunities than access to the ballot, education, housing, and jobs.

5 Health care, in summary, serves as (1) a mechanism of social control, (2) a public economic good, and (3) an ethical and moral touchstone. These three characteristics distinguish it from other goods and services. The tensions created by these three distinctive characteristics have shaped the development of health services in the United States, as they have in other countries. In the United States, however, they were shaped through the filter of race.

Health Care Divided: Race and the Development of Health Care in the United States

> My father's family came from Georgia, where they owned a farm. The story goes that in the 1930s a neighboring white plantation owner wanted the land, but my granddad refused to sell it. I guess the plantation owner got angry, and the Klan came the next night, grabbed two of my grandmother's brothers, and lynched them. My grandfather returned, killed the plantation owner, and escaped. My grandmom and her kids had to escape also to avoid retaliation. They ended up in Greenville, South Carolina, and my grandmom took in washing. She never saw her husband again, but they never caught him either. He ended up in the Winston-Salem area living under an assumed name. Every once in a while she'd get word passed along about him. There was an underground thing; an understanding that you helped other blacks who had got in trouble. That's how my grandmother was able to move to Greenville.
>
> I grew up on a farm outside Greenville. There was a thing about going to town on Saturdays. We'd all walk three miles to town. In Walgreen's or Woolworth's we'd see something different. There were "white" and "colored" water fountains. I wanted to see what the white water tasted like. You'd get there and one of the other kids was always daring you. One day I got up enough nerve to dip my head down and squirted it up. Got in a lot trouble for that. My parents didn't want any trouble.
>
> When I was growing up, Dr. Bailey on Main Street in Greenville was the family physician. There was a separate waiting room for blacks, and you had to wait till all the white patients had been seen before he'd see the blacks. As long as the white patients kept coming in, you kept being pushed further and further back. Later, when a black physician set up practice in Greenville, blacks flocked to him. I got a bad virus when I was a little kid and was admitted to

> the hospital. I got a private room on a white floor. My aunt did washing for a white physician, and that gave me special pull. I felt extra special. I remember when I was a teen I had to help my grandmom go for care at Greenville General. She had cancer. We had to wait in a horrible small room for black patients in the basement. We'd get there at 9:00, and we often didn't return until 5:30. The local mortician provided the transportation to the hospital. The understanding was that the transportation was free, but he would get the body. It wasn't a bad experience. It was the way it was.[5]

"The way it was," the underlying caste divisions in American society shaped the institutions that developed to care for the health needs, patient expectations, and the very purposes of the services provided. It also shaped outcomes. A research memorandum prepared as a part of the Carnegie Foundation–supported study that would produce Myrdal's watershed book, *The American Dilemma,* concluded that if black death rates in 1930 were made equivalent to white death rates, 70 percent of the black deaths would have been eliminated.[6] That same memorandum concluded,

> The economic problem of providing medical facilities for Negroes is complicated by racial discrimination. Color restricts the Negro's access to many medical facilities even when he is able to pay for the services rendered. Negro physicians are admitted to some hospitals operated by white persons but the more usual situation is to bar them entirely.[7]

Segregated systems of care that developed in slavery were perpetuated in the post-Reconstruction period. The underlying assumptions of scientific medicine and the mechanisms developed for financing health services helped reinforce these divisions. Thus, the transformation of medicine in the twentieth century heightened both racial segregation and inequalities.

Antebellum Health Care

Medical care in the United States before the Civil War was limited and unorganized. The country was largely rural, populated by farmers and independent craftspersons. There was no standing army, and there were few large employers. Medical care, except for a few institutions established for the destitute by local governments and philanthropists in the larger cities, was provided by independent, fee-for-service practitioners. They took diverse, sometimes conflicting approaches to disease and applied treatments that were often ineffectual or even harmful. Many were part-time practitioners whose practice income was not sufficient for a livelihood. With the mix of altruism and self-interest that is always present among professionals, local groups of physicians began to organize. Physicians in a New Jersey medical society, for example, as early as 1786 established a fee schedule that "shall be deemed the general rule of charging by the members of the Society and so far binding that in no instance [shall a member] exceed it and further, the Society will deem it highly dishonorable in any member to make a different charge with a view to injure a neighboring practitioner who is also a member."[8] In effect, discount fee competition among physicians was stifled by local medical societies until the recent emergence of managed care.

The only instances of organized medical services comparable to current managed-care plans were found on the plantations and directed toward slaves. Plantation owners were the only group of large employers before the Civil War. They were also the only employers that had a direct financial interest in protecting the health of their employees. In 1860 the estimated four million slaves in the United States were valued at more than two billion dollars.[9] Slaves sometimes received better health care than poor southern whites or northern laborers. Every major plantation had a hospital of some kind, and some were well equipped by the standards of the day. An older black woman was typically placed in charge. Some of these black attendants were considered so knowledgeable that whites consulted them. Occasionally, white physicians sought to prevent such competition. Courts in Tennessee, for example, ruled that slaves could not practice medicine. In the larger towns of the south, such as New Orleans, Savannah, and Montgomery, private physicians organized hospitals for slaves. Natchez, Mississippi, had several slave hospitals, including a two-story building next to the slave market known as the Mississippi State Hospital and the Homeopathic Infirmary for Slaves. The infirmary provided care for one dollar a day. Several hospitals in New Orleans provided separate wards for slaves. Alternatively, plantation owners sometimes arranged for physicians to care for slaves on an annual retainer. Those arrangements with health care facilities served as the first form of employer-based health insurance in this country, and those contracts between the plantation owners and physicians for overseeing the care of slaves represented the first forms of managed care.

Post-Reconstruction Health Care

10 The plantation system of medical care ended with emancipation. Massive dislocation and migration to southern urban centers began to take place. The federal government established the Freedmen's Bureau to help the emancipated slaves. Its medical department set up more than ninety hospitals and dispensaries in the South but closed all except one by 1868. Only Freedmen's Hospital (Howard University Medical Center) survived. Whose responsibility would black health care be now? Blacks were mostly excluded from existing health and social-service organizations. Orphanages, private charitable hospitals, local almshouses, and state facilities, with rare exceptions, served only whites. Local municipalities reluctantly began to develop segregated services for blacks, largely in response to pressures from local black populations exercised through the ballot. Some private hospitals in the larger northern cities provided care in segregated services

for blacks. They tended to be less exclusionary, but the bulk of the black population remained concentrated in the South. As another method of providing care, local municipalities and states in the nineteenth century instituted lump-sum payments to municipal and some private hospitals to subsidize the care of the indigent, which included segregated services for the poor. (That approach is now being reinvented. In order to control escalating costs, most state Medical Assistance programs have adopted regional capitation approaches.)

An implicit division of labor emerged between public and voluntary hospitals in cities and towns large enough to accommodate both types of facilities. Both types of nineteenth-century hospitals had been asylums or refuges for the destitute who lacked housing or the means to pay for private nursing and physicians in their home. The voluntary hospitals, however, created through the donations of local community members and philanthropists as private charities, defined their mission in more narrow, moralistic terms. They saw their role as providing care to the "deserving poor," not as a service to all people in the community. It was the role of governments, not voluntary hospitals, to provide for the "undeserving." Government hospitals should provide the shelter and basic services to the unworthy, impoverished social failures, as well as the chronically ill whom charitable hospitals were not prepared to admit.[10] Being a "socially worthy" impoverished patient meant being morally respectable and suitably deferential. Those whose need for care resulted from alcohol or drug abuse or sexual indiscretions were not deserving of such charity. Being a member of the right racial, ethnic, or religious group also helped. Board members of voluntary hospitals often personally participated in admission decisions. Both the public and voluntary hospitals served to police and control individual behavior. The voluntary hospitals supported the socially worthy, and public hospitals controlled those who were not. This meant that blacks were mostly relegated to the use of public institutions. Blacks, nevertheless, were increasingly able to exercise influence over those public institutions and the care they provided through their growing political influence in local elections.

Toward the end of the nineteenth century, however, both the public and voluntary hospitals were becoming more important to medicine. Asepsis, anesthesia, and other surgical advances were transforming these institutions into workshops essential to the practice of medicine. Increasingly, middle- and upper-class patients would receive and pay for care in these facilities. Some voluntary charitable hospitals felt uncomfortable with that shift. The board of one Philadelphia hospital for a decade debated the appropriateness of accepting paying patients, before acquiescing to an experiment with six private rooms in 1899.[11] The shift of private medical practice to hospital settings spread quickly; correspondingly, effective control of the institutions shifted from their boards and charitable benefactors to the hospitals' medical staff.[12]

The Social Transformation of American Medicine

The transformation of medicine at the turn of the century coincided with the failure of Reconstruction and the passage of Jim Crow laws by states across the South. Until the last decade of the nineteenth century, the divisions between the races had been more fluid. While there was informal segregation, as there is today, little had been prescribed by state laws.[13] The climate hardened in the 1890s. The *Plessy v. Ferguson* Supreme Court decision in 1896 ruled that a Louisiana state law segregating railroad passenger cars did not violate the Fourteenth Amendment guarantee of equal protection. Modern medicine and the organization of health services in the United States were a particularly bitter part of the harvest of the seeds sown by *Plessy v. Ferguson.* The subsequent wave of Jim Crow legislation solidified a caste system that most whites and blacks seemed either to endorse or dare not to defy. The modern U.S. health care system was constructed according to those blueprints restricting the opportunities available to blacks, shaping the physical design of facilities and even influencing the nature of scientific inquiry.

Much of the care provided in increasingly segregated black communities was provided by black physicians. For those practitioners and the communities they served, the social transformation they experienced was traumatic. The net impact was to (1) restrict the supply of black physicians, (2) limit the ability of black communities to control the hospitals that served them, and (3) exclude black physicians from hospital practice.

. . .

Scientific Medicine's Reinforcement of the Racial Divide

15 Meanwhile, the mainstream of medical science and medical care marched onward. Medical science, however, did not take place in a social vacuum. It was heavily influenced by attitudes about race, morality, and the politics of segregation.

Race was routinely defined as both a behavioral and a biological risk factor. The view at least of many southern white physicians writing before the turn of the century was that emancipation had increased the death rates of blacks. This, they felt, proved both the value of slavery and the incapacity of blacks to take care of themselves. They believed that blacks' inferior constitution, natural tendencies toward sexual promiscuity, drug and alcohol abuse, and lack of personal hygiene would, in Darwinian fashion, solve the race problem through extinction.[14] Medical discourse blended naturally into racist diatribes on miscegenation. A commentary on a paper on the prevalence of high TB rates among blacks presented at the Tennessee State Medical Association meetings in 1907 reflects this mixture of attitudes.

> It is principally the yellow Negro that shows the enormous death-rate from tuberculosis today. In all cases, wherever we find a hybrid race, we find a race which has not the stamina, physical, moral or mental, of either of the races

in the mixture. Then, again, we must remember that in the hybridization, as a rule, we add a vicious tendency to what might be expressed as the lowest strata of the upper race, mixed with the vicious tendency of the lower race. That carries with it to begin with a poor hereditary foundation, one lacking in natural resistant qualities. Again, we are in the attitude in regard to the Negro question of attempting to force in one or two generations a civilization upon an inferior race which it has taken the Caucasian race centuries to attain. He staggers under the burden and falls, as you would naturally expect, even though you had no data on which to base your judgement. Then, his other vices add to the list of predisposing causes. Syphilis is almost universal among Negroes in cities, so that in our dispensary work we do not say, "Have you got syphilis?" but say to them, "When did you get it?" (Laughter.) We take it for granted that he has got it just the same in most cases. That helps to lay the foundation for Tuberculosis.

Again, in the antebellum days the Negro got a drink now and then, when it was good for him possibly. Now, he gets a drink every time he gets paid off, and in between if he can. As has been said by one of the French writers, alcoholism makes a bed for tuberculosis. You gentlemen, who are familiar with the conditions in the larger cities know to what extent addiction to drugs, especially cocaine has reached among Negroes. Besides that, you also know the extent to which abortion is practiced among Negro women. These things in the older days were not known, and yet every one of the factors I have mentioned is of stupendous moment as a predisposing cause in any infectious disease. Possibly no one cause mentioned would of itself suffice to insure contracting of the disease, but taken collectively they leave an outlook for the race which is hopeless, if help from without is not forthcoming.[15]

Gradually, however, the pessimistic view that the poor health of blacks would lead to extinction gave way to acknowledgment that it was a problem. Often, this was defined not so much as a problem for blacks but as a problem for whites.

I feel that not only is the Negro mortality of the Southern city increased by these diseases from the lack of preventive measures amongst this people, but that the white mortality and morbidity is raised by these same causes, through their prevalence in the other race. To quote from another paper on this subject: "These Negro citizens among whom we find such an undue prevalence of diarrheal diseases, tuberculosis and venereal infections, who live under the worst of sanitary conditions, through circumstances, racial inferiority or our neglect, mingle with us in a hundred intimate ways, in our stores and factories, our kitchens and nurseries. They kneed our bread and rock our babies to sleep in their arms, dress them, fondle them and kiss them; can anyone doubt that we may not escape close exposure? The missed and carrier cases of typhoid and other intestinal diseases that wait upon our tables must exact their toll nor is this lessened by any habits of personal cleanliness discernable."[16]

Black physicians did not take kindly to this new genre in the medical literature that defined blacks simply as vectors of disease, "[l]ike the fly, the mosquito, the rats, and mice, an arch-carrier of disease to white people."[17] Yet, black hospitals were not averse to using such racial fears to raise funds in the white community. When the oldest black-controlled hospital in the country, Provident Hospital in Chicago, began a fund drive in 1929 to raise funds for black medical education at the hospital, the slogan was "Germs Have No Color Line." This reminded potential white donors of their own self-interest in providing support.[18]

The discovery of the sickle-cell trait in 1910 in blacks illustrates the peculiar way that medical knowledge blended with ideologies about race. Sickle cell became quickly defined as a genetic marker of "Negro blood." Those with the trait who denied any such heritage were suspected of lying out of shame or guilt. The spread of this trait into an apparently white person was twisted to provide proof of the dangers of race mixing or miscegenation. One physician in 1943 went so far as to declare it a national health problem. He argued that intermarriage between Negroes and whites directly endangered the white race by transmission of the sickling trait and that such intermarriage should be prohibited by federal law. Similar ideas in less strident terms found their way into an editorial in the *Journal of the American Medical Association* in 1947. Another physician used the "Negro blood" theory to argue that it suggested a more general physical inferiority and that blacks should not be inducted into the armed services in World War I.[19]

The Use of Blacks in Teaching and Research

Medicine's most troubling legacy has been the use of blacks as clinical material in teaching and research. That legacy has produced a schizophrenic political marriage of convenience between medical schools and teaching hospitals and state and municipal financing of indigent care. On the one hand, teaching hospitals have complained about the paucity of indigent care payments, while, on the other hand, their medical chiefs have worried periodically during the ebb and flow of indigent care financing that individual patient payments might be too high, thus encouraging competition with private-practice physicians and the erosion of the numbers they need to accredit residency programs. Reflecting on his experiences, Aubre Maynard, one of the surgeons who successfully challenged racial exclusion in making staff appointments at Harlem Hospital in 1926, observed,

> As the helpless slave, as the impoverished freedman following emancipation, as the indigent ghetto resident of today, the share-cropper or dirt farmer of the South, the Negro has always been appropriated as choice "clinical material" by the medical profession. In the mind of the unregenerate racist, who,

> unfortunately, has always been represented in the profession, the Negro was always next in line beyond the experimental animal. Without option in the peculiar situation, he has contributed to the training of generations of surgeons, his fate subject to the quality of their skill, and the integrity of their character. He has sometimes benefited from their efforts, but he has also occupied the role of victim and expendable guinea pig.[20]

20 Such fears about being used in experiments and as teaching material are well embedded in the concerns many blacks have with medical encounters even today. They reflect a troubling history. In the antebellum period slaves were sometimes used to test experimental surgical procedures.[21]

The "teaching material" of northern white medical schools and urban hospitals became increasingly African American after World War I, coincident with the great migration from the South to northern cities. That migration had been preceded by the shipment of southern Negro corpses concealed in the barrels labeled "turpentine" to northern medical schools for teaching and anatomical research that began after the Civil War. A survey of such practices in 1933 showed that for years most southern medical schools had taught their students fundamentals of human anatomy on African American cadavers. Reflecting on this practice, Howard University professor of anatomy and editor of the *Journal of the National Medical Association,* W. Montague Cobb, was struck by the irony that such acknowledged physical equality of the races was restricted only to corpses.[22]

The Tuskegee syphilis experiment, which involved following the natural course of syphilis over a thirty-year period in 399 black males, is the most commonly cited example of such abuses. It was the longest experiment in withholding treatment from human subjects in medical history, lasting from 1932 to 1972. The health professionals involved in the project clung to three assumptions that vividly illustrate the powerful hold of the racial legacy on judgment. These assumptions still exert a powerful hold on the organization of services and on treatment decisions. Today, however, they exist in more subtle forms.

1. *The disease affected blacks differently than whites and thus was a legitimate focus of research.* While such ideas did not square well with the bulk of the medical evidence even at the time the study began in 1932, it continued to serve as the justification for a black-only study of the withdrawal of treatment.
2. *Since the subjects had no access to medical care, whatever was provided was better than what they would have received without the project.* The subjects were "uncontaminated" by any form of treatment and thus more useful from a research perspective. They posed no ethical dilemma, at least from the perspective of the researchers, since they were not withholding something the subjects would have received in the absence

of the experiment. When the project began, few of the subjects had ever seen a physician. Rural blacks in Alabama did not go to physicians. Thus, whatever care was provided to them, project directors argued, was better than what they would have received without participating in the project. (Through various public-health programs and eventually through the passage of Medicare and Medicaid, the availability of medical care for these subjects changed dramatically over the lifetime of the project.)

3. *The subjects were poorly educated, poorly motivated, and the course of treatment was too demanding and complicated to assure the compliance necessary for success.* The treatment became less difficult and problematic with the introduction of antibiotics after World War II. Educational levels of the subjects and their families probably also increased. Yet, the assumption that these rural Alabama black males were not good patients or good risks for treatment persisted.

Most remarkable, however, is how pervasive and well entrenched were the basic assumptions that permitted the study.[23] It was not a secret experiment conducted by rogue researchers. Outside professionals regularly reviewed the project's protocols. More than a dozen publications were generated by the project and were widely read. Active participants included the Milbank Memorial Fund, the Rosenwald Fund, the United States Public Health Service, state and county public-health officials, and members of the local white medical society. It also used the facilities and had the full support of the Tuskegee Institute, the proud creation of Booker T. Washington's efforts to assure self-sufficiency for blacks. Even after integration had taken place and the county medical society had become a predominantly black body in the late 1960s, the project continued to receive full support, including the referral of patients to the project's control group, which was not supposed to receive treatment for syphilis. Much of the more progressive, liberal wing of medicine and public health during this period was involved in the project.[24]

The Tuskegee syphilis project, the legacy of a divided health care system, continued with a life of its own. No one, black or white, questioned it for forty years. A faculty member at Howard's medical school reflected,

> I have thought about it many times and have asked myself how in the hell I knew about it and I thought it was perfectly all right to do this experiment. I remember reviewing an article in *Public Health Reports* in the early 1950s, and I said, "This is interesting." I have asked myself many times why I didn't raise that ethical point. I didn't, and nobody else did either.[25]

25 The Tuskegee study and the myths surrounding it continue to resonate in black low-income neighborhoods. The distrust of medical providers reflects an historical legacy of which the Tuskegee study is but a small

part.[26] That distrust has undermined many outreach efforts of health care providers, including childhood immunization drives, flu vaccinations for seniors, and AIDS education projects. For example, a federal pilot study of the prevalence of AIDS in the District of Columbia had to be scrapped in 1988. Many local people accused the project of using Washington's black community as a "guinea pig" in a study that would stigmatize the city and minority communities.[27]

The assumptions that served as the justification for the Tuskegee study remain in evidence among those providing health services to this population. They appear to be reflected in substantial differences in rates of use of many more complex medical procedures. Blacks have lower rates of use of kidney transplants, coronary bypass surgery, and many other procedures, even where no differences in insurance or the ability to pay exist.

The assumptions were embedded in the training of physicians. The larger public hospitals in the United States persisted as the premier training centers up until the 1960s as well as the almost exclusive source of care for a growing urban black population. A physician reflected on his experience as an intern at Cook County Hospital in Chicago in the late 1940s.

> On the medical side it was a premier training place. I got there just after World War II, and it was still riding on its prewar reputation as a training center. It was a very sought-after site. Yet the patient loads were ridiculous, you had limited support, and your training came largely from the resident and by the seat of your pants. I think it trained a lot of people very well, but at what cost, one wonders.
>
> The place had a battle mentality. It was not a place for liberals. At County you either had a very conservative right-wing view that the people you were seeing were getting their just rewards for their substance abuse, fornication, and that this was God's will, or you would see it more as the congealed oppression and the end product of lousy housing, poor education, poverty, and ignorance. The group was divided up that way because doctors tend to come from conservative origins, but the County could make you pretty radical. Much as you'd like to think that the good doctors were the bleeding hearts and the bad doctors were the reactionaries, it wasn't so. You were judged by your colleagues on how well your patients did, and your attitude didn't matter. But some were pretty terrible people who I'd have huge shouting matches about their racism. They could justify their attitudes. They'd see the pregnant woman who was shooting up, but how do you interpret the experience that she has had? Is she violating God's law or is she a victim of capitalist oppression? Which? Both! God's a capitalist.[28]

The view of the more conservative public-hospital-trained physicians and the underlying assumptions that sustained the Tuskegee study prevailed in the development of health insurance in this country.

Race and the Soul of Insurance

As medicine developed into something that could make a difference in people's lives, a parallel struggle took place over how to pay for it. It has been, in essence, "a struggle for the soul of insurance.[29] It has also been a struggle over the national soul. Should medical care be provided based on need rather than the ability to pay? Should one pay only for the medical services one receives, or should one also pay a share of the excess expenses of others? In other words, should the logic of the market and actuarial forecasts be substituted for the logic of solidarity? The logic of solidarity dictates, just as the early black fraternal orders recognized, the social importance of protecting all members of the community and spreading the costs equitably. The answer in the United States, unlike any other developed country that has embraced the logic of solidarity through some form of universal health insurance, is, "It depends." Race has played a role in shaping that answer.

Just as in other countries, insurance started in the nineteenth century as a way for groups that shared a common bond to care for the misfortunes faced by their members. The black benevolent societies created by freed slaves after the Civil War were an impressive example of such efforts. Other mutual-aid societies were formed by guilds, craft unions, and churches. All these groups, the precursors of modern forms of health insurance, valued group solidarity. Many helped to cover the costs of illness among their members. One way that such mutual-aid societies helped their members was through arrangements negotiated with a local physician. They would typically negotiate an annual fee per member with the physician. Such "lodge practice of medicine," an early form of managed care, was fought by local medical societies.[30] The ability of medical staffs to exclude physicians involved in such lodge practices from hospital staffs eventually discouraged such practices.

In other developed countries such arrangements naturally evolved into universal-entitlement programs for health care, covering the entire population. In part because of race, that evolution never took place in the United States. Insurance, as it developed in the United States, was divided along racial lines. Accepting the conventional wisdom of medical practitioners at the turn of the century, most life insurance companies would not write insurance policies for blacks. Uninsurable risks for one life insurance company in 1930 included "Negroes, Chinese, Japanese, Mexicans and more than one-fourth blood Indians.[31] Enterprising blacks in Durham, Atlanta, and elsewhere created their own life insurance companies, and some became the first black millionaires. They took advantage of the niche offered by these racial exclusions, building on the strong tradition of black benevolent societies.

Many groups in the United States resisted the expansion of the idea of the mutual-benefit societies to the whole population. Divisions similar to those that had existed between the roles of private voluntary hospitals and public hospitals emerged in the financing of health care. Public programs were for blacks; private ones for whites. The Committee on the Cost of Medical Care, whose comprehensive pathbreaking research efforts in the 1930s set the direction of the financing of health care for the rest of the century, even excluded blacks from their survey of nine thousand households used to estimate patterns of expenditure and use of health services. They concluded that "the procedure adopted could not procure satisfactory information from Negro families."[32] Trade unions resisted efforts during World War I to expand coverage through public health insurance programs. They saw such programs as threats to their own influence and control, preferring to negotiate their own arrangements directly through the workplace. Organized medicine and the emerging voluntary hospital system preferred the development of voluntary insurance programs, thus assuring greater influence and control for themselves. The consequence was a sharp division along racial lines between those dependent on the public system and those whose employment offered benefits or who could afford private care in the voluntary system. The self-interests of labor unions, physicians, and hospitals against such national comprehensive plans was not that different from those in other developed countries where such comprehensive plans were enacted. What were different were the racial divisions that made more universal approaches less attractive to the white majority.

The voluntary health insurance system developed as a defense against public or government-run programs that would also be more racially integrated. Rufus Rorem, a key staff member of the Committee on the Cost of Medical Care, was the chief architect and advocate of the Blue Cross voluntary hospital insurance system. In 1938 he predicted that "voluntary hospital care insurance may post one indefinitely the need for nationwide compulsory health insurance.[33] Many early practices of the voluntary hospital insurance plans were modeled after those of the benevolent societies. Some of these early Blue Cross hospital insurance plans relied on volunteers to collect monthly premiums, just as the benevolent societies had of their members. They also were firmly committed to something called "community rating." That is, all members of the plan would pay the same rate, and that rate would be based on the average hospital cost per member. Just as in the early benevolent societies, each member took on responsibility for a fair share of the misfortunes of other members. This romanticized ideology was the trump card in defeating national health insurance in the 1940s. The "community" in "community rating" excluded a large portion of the population. Coverage privately found through employment also insulated such programs from the political power of blacks to affect change.

The early racial divisions between publicly financed and privately financed health programs propelled further divisions and fragmentation. Community rating was an alien notion to commercial life insurance, which could not resist the lure of the rapidly expanding market for employer-based health insurance after World War II. Their version of fairness was quite different and based on actuarial calculations. Each person's premium should be based on their own estimated risk, rather than the sharing and pooling of risks across all community members. In reality, the underwriting process took on moral tones, similar to the idea of the "deserving poor" found in nineteenth-century voluntary hospitals. The moral tones adopted in the underwriting of life insurance were eventually applied to health insurance. One simply separated out the "good risks" and resigned others to the purgatory of the uninsured. According to the commercial insurance companies, "there were only two classes of people in the world: one entitled to all the privileges and benefits of life insurance and the other entitled to nothing."[34] The same principles of underwriting were applied eventually to health care through experience rating of groups.

35 What then, is the ethic that should govern health care? Who are we, and what are we responsible for? What is the "soul of insurance?" In small homogenous societies and communities with shared values people are willing, as the black benevolent societies were, to give whatever limited pooled resources are available to the most needy. In a large racially divided community, no one wants to put much in the common pool. People's willingness to contribute is guided by their calculation of the payback for themselves and their immediate families. Perhaps the most that can be hoped for is a contribution to a floor of basic needs we are unwilling to see others fall below. We do not want to see children die on the streets from asthma attacks because hospitals refuse to admit them.

The legacy of racial segregation and the caste structure of American society is one we are yet to free ourselves from. It is a legacy that divides the world of private insurance from the world of public responsibilities. Ultimately the story of the civil rights struggle and the struggle to assure a decent level of basic health and health care were essentially the same.

That viewpoint was expressed by Dr. Louis T. Wright, the black physician who had integrated Harlem Hospital's medical staff in the 1920s, when he spoke out at a hearing on national health insurance in 1938.

> It is hoped at this time that the American people will begin to realize that the health of the American Negro is not a separate racial problem to be met by separate segregated set ups or dealt with on a dual standard basis, but that it is an American problem that should be adequately and equitably handled by the identical agencies and met with identical methods as the health of the remainder of the population.[35]

Unfortunately, his advice was not followed. Yet a small but growing group of physicians, nurses, and kindred spirits had begun to speak out for the racial integration of health services.

Notes

[1]For a useful review see David R. Williams, Risa Lavizzo-Mourey, and Rueben Warren, "The Concept of Race and Health Status in America," *Public Health Reports* 109, no. 1 (1994): 26–41. In addition, see the issue of *Health Services Research* devoted to "The Role of Race and Ethnicity in Health Services Research," *Health Services Research* 30, no. 1, pt. 2 (1995): 145–273.
[2]Douglas S. Massey and Nancy A. Denton, *American Apartheid: Segregation and the Making of the Underclass* (Cambridge: Harvard University Press, 1993), 1.
[3]Philip Slater, *The Pursuit of Loneliness* (Boston: Beacon Press, 1970), 15.
[4]See, for example, Norman Daniels, *Just Health Care* (New York: Cambridge University Press, 1985).
[5]Confidential interview by the author, tape recording, April 17, 1996.
[6]Harold F. Dorn, "The Health of the Negro, a Research Memorandum," Carnegie-Myrdal Study, Schomburg Center for Research in Black Culture, New York, 1940.
[7]Ibid., 125.
[8]Fred B. Rogers and A. Reasoner Sayre, *The Healing Art: A History of the Medical Society of New Jersey* (Trenton: Medical Society of New Jersey, 1966), 51.
[9]Mitchell F. Rice and Woodrow Jones Jr., *Public Policy and the Black Hospital: From Slavery to Segregation to Integration* (Westport, Conn: Greenwood Press, 1994), 1.
[10]See Rosemary Stevens, *In Sickness and in Wealth: American Hospitals in the Twentieth Century* (New York: Basic Books, 1989), 18–51.
[11]Mark Lloyd, *A History of Caring for the Sick since 1863* (Philadelphia: Germantown Hospital and Medical Center, 1981).
[12]See, for example, Charles Perrow, "Goals and Power Structures: A Historical Case Study," in *The Hospital in Modern Society*, ed. E. Freidson (New York: Free Press of Glencoe, 1963), 112–46.
[13]For origins of the still-debated argument over the degree of segregation after the Civil War, see C. Vann Woodward, *The Strange Career of Jim Crow* (New York: Oxford University Press, 1955).
[14]John S. Haller, Jr. "The Physician versus the Negro," in *Outcasts from Evolution: Scientific Attitudes of Racial Inferiority*, 1859–1900 (Urbana: University of Illinois Press, 1971), 40–68.
[15]Discussion on the paper of Dr. Jones, *Transactions of the Tennessee State Medical Association*, 1907, 180, as reproduced in Gamble, *Germs*, 25.
[16]C. E. Terry, "The Negro, a Public Health Problem," *Southern Medical Journal* 5 (1915): 462–63, as reproduced in Gamble, *Germs*, 49–58.
[17]E. Mayfield Boyle, "A Comparative Physical Study of the Negro," *Journal of the National Medical Association* 4 (1912): 344–48, as cited in Gamble, *Germs*, "Introduction," 3.
[18]Gamble, *Germs*, "Introduction," 1.
[19]Keith Wailoo, *Drawing Blood: Technology and Disease Identity in Twentieth-Century America* (Baltimore: Johns Hopkins University Press, 1997).
[20]Aubre L. Maynard, *Surgeons to the Poor: The Harlem Hospital Story* (New York: Appleton-Century-Crofts, 1978), 3.

[21]Clovis E. Semmes, *Racism, Health, and Post-industrialism: A Theory of African-American Health* (Westport, Conn: Praeger 1996), 110–11.
[22]W. Montague Cobb, "Surgery and the Negro Physician: Some Parallels in Background," *Journal of the National Medical Association* 43 (1951): 148.
[23]James H. Jones, *Bad Blood: The Tuskeegee Syphilis Experiment* (New York: Free Press, 1981).
[24]No one directly involved in the project has ever acknowledged that anything about it was unethical. All became ensnared in the web of deceit, not only of the subjects of the experiment, but of themselves. In May 1997 at a White House ceremony, President Clinton apologized on behalf of the nation to the remaining survivors and their relatives. Five of the eight remaining survivors, all over ninety years of age, attended the ceremony (Allison Mitchell, "Clinton Regrets 'Clearly Racist' U.S. Study," *New York Times,* May 17, 1997, A1).
[25]Paul Cornely, interview by the author, tape recording, July 8, 1990.
[26]See, for example: Vanessa N. Gamble, "Under the Shadow of Tuskegee: African Americans and Health Care," *American Journal of Public Health* 87, no. 11 (1997): 1773–78.
[27]Philip M. Boffey, "U.S. Drops AIDS Study in Community Protests," *New York Times,* August 17, 1988, A14.
[28]Quentin Young, interview by the author, tape recording, June 14, 1997.
[29]Deborah Stone, "The Struggle for the Soul of Insurance," *Journal of Health Policy Politics and Law* 18, no. 2 (1993): 287–318.
[30]David T. Beito, "The Lodge Practice Evil Reconsidered: Medical Care Through the Fraternal Societies 1900–1930," *Journal of Urban History* 23 (1987): 569–600.
[31]Stone, "Struggle for Soul," 296.
[32]Isadore Sydney Falk, Margaret Klem, and Nathan Sinai, *The Incidence of Illness and the Receipt and Costs of Medical Care among Representative Families,* Committee on the Cost of Medical Care Report No. 27 (Chicago: University of Chicago Press, 1933), 5.
[33]Rufus Rorem, "Scope and Significance of Hospital Care Insurance," summary of remarks at luncheon meeting, Palmer House, April 18, 1938, for announcement of hospital care insurance plans approved by the American Hospital Association and for presentation of approval certificate to Plan for Hospital Care, Chicago, in *Claude A. Barnett Papers: Associated Negro Press, 1918–1967.* Microfilmed from holdings of Chicago Historical Society (Fredrick, Md.: University Publications of America), part 3, series E, 9.
[34]L. Abbott, *The Story of NYLIC: A History of the Origin and Development of New York Life Insurance Company 1845 to 1929* (New York: New York Life Insurance Company) 279, as quoted in Stone "Struggle the Soul," 299.
[35]Interdepartmental Committee to Coordinate Health and Welfare Activities, *Proceedings of the National Health Conference, July 18–20, 1938,* 87.

Mapping the Text

1. Make a list of the issues that David Barton Smith identifies in this essay. What seem to be his goals or purposes in raising these issues? What do you think he wishes to accomplish?
2. Go through the essay and identify the types of appeals Smith uses and the types of details he uses to make these appeals. Assess the extent to which you think Smith is persuasive in presenting his point of view.

3. History seems to be an important part of Smith's presentation. How is he using these details? In other words, how do historical details function in the essay?

Writing to Inquire

1. At the end of this essay, Smith asks these questions: What is the ethic that should govern health care? Who are we, and what are we responsible for? Do insurance companies have social obligations, or is it perhaps reasonable to assume that profit is indeed their prime imperative? How do you respond to these questions? Write a brief persuasive essay offering your own definitions and claims for the "ethic of health care."
2. Do some exploratory research on one of the issues raised by Smith. In what ways does race continue to play a part in access to and quality of health care in the United States? How have things changed since the time covered by Smith in this essay? What still needs to change?

The Disease of Young Women

BRETT SILVERSTEIN AND DEBORAH PERLICK

Brett Silverstein and Deborah Perlick, authors of *The Cost of Competence: Why Inequality Causes Depression, Eating Disorders, and Illness in Women* (1995), use scientific research and biographies of notable historical women to argue that rather than treating illnesses such as anorexia, bulimia, and anxiety as separately occurring entities, we should begin to look at them collectively and politically as a product of women's experience over the centuries. *The Cost of Competence* combines data from over 2000 interviews with contemporary women with a historical account and analysis of depression, anxiety, anorexia, and bulimia. The selection below is excerpted from *The Cost of Comptence.*

During the 1970s, psychologists, psychiatrists, and the general public became increasingly aware of forms of disordered eating that appeared new. Obesity and overeating had been well known for many years, but not until the late 1960s, or so it seemed, did significant numbers of women exhibit the self-starvation of anorexia. A few more years had to pass before the syndrome of bingeing alternating with purgeing, referred to as bulimarexia, or bulimia for short, was recognized. Mental health professionals were intrigued—and perhaps even a little bit shocked—by what seemed to be the sudden increase in cases of what had been considered a "curiosity and a rarity."[1]

Modern industrial societies place a great deal of emphasis on novelty, newness, originality. This is particularly true of the United States, the center of much recent medical research, with its short history and its pride in not being tainted by the old-fashioned, feudal roots of Europe and Asia. To most of the general public, and to many professionals involved in studying or treating eating disorders, anorexia and bulimia were new phenomena. This is true despite the outbreak of self-starvation among young women that occurred during the 1920s, a period experienced by millions of Americans alive today. When we first became aware of this earlier outbreak, we were not only somewhat surprised that it had existed but also a bit chagrined at our short cultural memory. Realizing that the disorders are not new, we searched the medical literature of past centuries to determine when they first appeared.

Since the earliest large body of medical work available to modern researchers is comprised of texts of ancient Greece written by Hippocrates and several of his followers, we began our search there. One of these texts has been translated as "On the diseases of young women," sometimes as "On the diseases of virgins." Another is almost never referred to by modern researchers, perhaps because it has not yet been translated into English, but the French title, "De la Superfetation," has been translated as "On Overeating."[2] Together, these texts describe a syndrome afflicting females at adolescence that includes symptoms of disordered eating and depression, along with several other symptoms. Focusing on the amenorrhea that has been found to be associated with both depression and disordered eating, these texts attributed many symptoms to the lack of menstruation among pubescent females, including the wasting away of bodies, later termed "consumption" (referred to as phthisis), great hunger, vomiting, difficulty breathing, aches and pains, feeling "afraid and fearful," hearing voices ordering them to drown themselves, and loving death. The treatment of the disorder recommended in the Hippocratic texts focused on the connections with sexuality, and childbearing:

> My prescription is that when virgins experience this trouble, they should cohabit with a man as quickly as possible. If they become pregnant, they will be cured. If they don't do this, either they will succumb at the onset of puberty or a little later, unless they catch another disease. Among married women, those who are sterile are more likely to suffer what I have described.[3]

The linkage in the medical literature between disordered eating, amenorrhea, and consumption continued for many centuries after Hippocrates. In the fifteenth century, Antonio Benivieni, one of the founders of pathological anatomy, left records of several cases linking amenorrhea and disordered eating, including one in which a woman "whose monthly courses were held back for a whole year was reduced to complete emaciation" causing her to suffer from "wasting and consumption."[4]

5 In 1694, in his *Phtisiologia or a Treatise on Consumption,* Dr. Richard Morton described the case of Mr. Duke's daughter, a consumptive woman who in "the Eighteenth Year of her Age. . . fell into a total suppression of Her

Monthly Courses. . . from which time her appetite began to abate and her Digestion to be bad, her Flesh also began to be flaccid and loose." Eventually, the young woman was subject to fainting fits and came to look like "a Skeleton only clad with skin." She had "no fever. . . no cough or difficulty of breathing. . . . Only her appetite was diminished, and her Digestion was uneasy, with fainting fits."[5]

Morton went on to describe other cases of consumption in which young women stopped menstruating and became emaciated. In a chapter entitled "Of a Consumption proceeding from the Green Sickness, and a suppression of the Monthly Purgations in Women," he wrote: "This [i.e., amenorrhea] is most commonly the Original of Women's Consumptions and I have very seldom seen any Woman that was capable of the Monthly Purgations, either Virgin, married Woman or Widdow, who ever fell into a consumption without an Obstruction of these Purgations coming upon it."[6]

These descriptions contain several themes that we see repeated in later centuries. One is the emphasis on the cessation of menstruation. But many authorities would conclude that the authors of these earlier descriptions reversed the causal connection between amenorrhea and emaciation: Nowadays the amenorrhea is usually thought to result when females become too thin or when they become anxious and depressed. But to Morton, Benivieni, and Hippocrates the most striking symptom of the disorders was the cessation of the menses and its associated fertility problems.

"Consumption" (or phthisis) was the term of choice for Hippocrates, Morton, and Benivieni in describing the wasting away associated with this disorder. Several twentieth-century authorities related tuberculosis to the anorexia exhibited by many young women. These authorities used the term "tuberculosis" and were primarily discussing a lung disease. They believed that anorexia led to poor nutrition, which in turn increased susceptibility to tuberculosis.

Many people now consider consumption synonymous with tuberculosis. But note that, in the seventeenth century, Morton diagnosed consumption in the case of Mr. Duke's daughter, whose only symptoms were diminished appetite and amenorrhea. Like Morton, the ancient Greeks may have given the name consumption to the symptom of wasting away. It may be that, throughout history, the labels "phthisis" and "consumption" have been used to describe symptoms of the lung disease we now call "tuberculosis" as well as the syndrome discussed here that sometimes involves both wasting away and difficulty breathing. Other authors who have studied the medical literature of previous centuries provide additional evidence linking what was sometimes called "nervous consumption" to the disorder now thought of as anorexia.[7] Unfortunately, because modern methods for the collection of epidemiologic statistics were not used in previous centuries, we cannot estimate how many other cases of consumption, "the wasting disease," may really have been instances of the syndrome we discuss here.

Hysteria, Neurasthenia, and Chlorosis: The Disease of Young Women by Other Names?

10 The medical literature of the seventeenth, eighteenth, and nineteenth centuries continued to describe disorders that afflicted young, unmarried women at adolescence with depression, disordered eating, and several other physical and psychological symptoms. In 1796, Dr. Ebenezer Sibly wrote that the "sallow and inanimate female, by coition often becomes plump and robust."[8] Sibley's description, so reminiscent of Hippocrates' prescription that females suffering from the disease of young women should cohabit with a man, dealt with a disease known at the time as chlorosis. Chlorosis, the "green sickness" mentioned by Morton, was frequently diagnosed among adolescent women prior to the twentieth century. Common symptoms were depression, nervousness, amenorrhea, headaches, breathing difficulties, heart clicks and murmurs, and insomnia, as well as anorexia, bulimia, and vomiting.[9] In a 1901 description that sounds strikingly modern, Dr. Thomas C. Allbutt noted that "Chlorosis is a malady of puberty.... Many young women, as their frames develop fall into a panic fear of obesity and not only cut down their food but swallow... alleged antidotes to fatness." Chlorotic women also felt "gloom, despondency, ennui... giving up all for lost they indulge in depression and despair."[10]

Another name given to a disease of young women involving depression, disordered eating, and other somatic symptoms was "hysteria." Today, most people who could list the symptoms of hysteria would probably mention fits, fainting, or paralyzed limbs. As recently as 1953, however, psychiatrist Judd Marmor wrote that "vomiting, anorexia, and bulemia are by-words in the symptomatology of hysteria." In 1951, over 60 percent of a sample of hysteric women were found to exhibit anorexia, vomiting, variations in weight, nervousness, symptoms of depression, headaches, breathing difficulties, and sexual indifference.[11]

These results confirmed what had been reported by physicians for many years. In 1840, Dr. Thomas Laycock discussed the anorexia, bulimia, and vomiting of hysteric women, and Dr. Leonard Corning in 1888 noted that hysteria was frequently complicated with melancholia and attempted suicide.[12] Many of the hysteric female patients Freud treated as he first developed his principles of psychoanalysis exhibited symptoms of depression and disordered eating. In describing the case of Frau Emmy von N., the woman with whom he developed the technique of catharsis, Freud wrote:

> I called on her one day at lunch-time and surprised her in the act of throwing something wrapped up in paper into the garden, where it was caught by the children of the house-porter. In reply to my question, she admitted that it was her (dry) pudding, and that this went the same way every day. This led me to investigate what remained of the other courses and I found that there was more than half left on the plates. When I asked her why she ate so little she answered that she was not in the habit of eating more and that it would be bad for her if she did.... When on my next visit I ordered some alkaline water and forbade

> her usual way of dealing with her pudding, she showed considerable agitation. . . . Next day the nurse reported that she had eaten the whole of her helpings and had drunk a glass of the alkaline water. But I found Frau Emmy herself lying in a profoundly depressed state. . . . she said. . . "I've ruined my digestion, as always happens if I eat more or drink water, and I have to starve myself entirely for five days to a week before I can tolerate anything." . . .I assured her that. . . her pains were only due to the anxiety over eating.[13]

The famous Anna O., who was treated by Freud's colleague Breuer and helped to develop the "talking cure" on which psychoanalytic treatment is based, also suffered from depression and anorexia, accompanied by severe headaches. On the death of her beloved father, she stopped eating. She would go for days without nourishment and for long periods subsisting on a bit of fruit. Dora, the other well-known hysteric patient of Freud's, also appeared to be depressed as well as anorexic. In fact, in 1893, Breuer and Freud concluded that among the symptoms that were "idiopathic products of hysteria" were chronic vomiting and "anorexia, carried to the pitch of rejection of all nourishment."[14]

Neurasthenia was yet another late nineteenth-century disease characterized by symptoms of depressed mood and disordered eating. While the most widely discussed symptom of this ailment was nervous exhaustion, others included dyspepsia, insomnia, asthma, headaches, and emaciation. Physician George Savage described a typical case of neurasthenia as follows:

> A woman, generally single, or in some way not in a condition for performing her reproductive function. . . becomes bed-ridden, often refuses her food, or is capricious about it, taking strange things at odd times, or pretending to starve. . . . The body wastes, and the face has the thin, anxious look not unlike that represented by Rosetti in many of his pictures of women.[15]

15 As in other quotes already cited, the woman is described as "not in a condition for performing her reproductive function," and we return to this point later not only because it is central in this disorder but because it is salient to the doctors treating these women. Misogynists; perhaps, and clearly the conveyors of societal values.

In 1894, two physicians included nervous depression, headaches, insomnia, nausea, and vomiting in a list of common symptoms of neurasthenia in young women and noted that "the line of demarcation in this disease between hysteria on the one hand and melancholia on the other is indeed a fine one. Some would consider both as phases of it."[16] They pointed out that neurasthenia often afflicted young, unmarried, slender women.

Saints and Fasting Girls

Not all women who exhibited similar symptoms were diagnosed as ill. In a recent book, *Holy Anorexia,* Rudolph Bell concluded that over half the Italian women officially recognized by the Roman Catholic church from 1200 A.D. onward as saints, blesseds, venerables, or servants of God displayed clear signs of anorexia, including fasting, vomiting, bingeing, and amenorrhea. Many also felt "deeply depressed."[17]

The women Bell studied were treated as holy figures. But, as described by historian Joan Jacobs Brumberg, by the nineteenth century, young women who went for very long periods seemingly without eating were beginning to be viewed as curiosities and termed "fasting girls." One woman, Mollie Fancher of Brooklyn, New York, in 1864 refused to eat and began to waste away. In 1866, the *Brooklyn Daily Eagle* reported that she had gone for seven weeks without food and looked "more like parchment than flesh and blood."[18] Like the fasts of the holy women studied by Bell, Fancher's apparent ability to survive without food was treated by many people as a miracle. But, living during a period when the explanations offered by science had come to vie with those offered by religion, she was also labeled by many physicians as "hysteric."

Were All the Disorders Identical?

Thus, the Hippocratic "disease of young women," chlorosis, hysteria, and neurasthenia are all names given over the years to syndromes that were said to afflict women at adolescence and that involved depression, anxiety, disordered eating, headache, and several other symptoms we will discuss. We do not believe that all these disorders were identical. Further research is needed to determine whether individual differences between women in, for example, genetic predispositions, family constellations, societal influences, or the age at which they begin to experience problems may lead to different forms of this disorder. For now, we wish to emphasize that all these disorders were characterized by a wide range of symptoms, allowing physicians throughout history to use the diagnostic categories popular in their own day in describing women whom we believe suffered from one or another variant of what we call anxious somatic depression.

. . .

20 We will sometimes use the term "forgotten syndrome" as a convenient way to refer to the collection of symptoms on which we focus. We chose the term "syndrome" to emphasize that we are not simply referring to a single currently recognized disorder such as anorexia or depression, but to a combination of symptoms. We use the word "forgotten" to acknowledge that the idea that several of these symptoms often tend to coexist among particular individuals is not a new creation of ours, but is based on the writings of many authorities over the centuries.

. . .

Discontent with Traditional Gender Roles

Our historical research indicated that, over the centuries, women who suffered from the symptoms under the various names it was given were nontraditional females discontent with societal limitations placed on them.

For example, anthropologists and historians who have studied holy women, like those discussed by Bell, have noted that women who entered convents after growing up in the outside world tended to view females as weak and vulnerable, and that they saw joining a monastery as a way to rebel against social constraints placed on them and as a means of achieving autonomy and self-sufficiency. Historians have also found that many medieval holy women dressed as males. Several have offered the explanation that "because male was in Western culture superior to female, women had to take on symbolic maleness (or, at the very least, abandonment of femaleness) in order to signify spiritual advance."[19]

The most famous Italian holy woman described by Bell may have done just this. Saint Catherine of Sienna, copatron of Italy with Francis of Assisi, was born Catherine Benincasa around 1347. After the death of her father, she could not eat. According to the priest assigned by the Pope to be her confessor, "Not only did she not need food, but she could not even eat without pain. If she forced herself to eat, her body suffered greatly, she could not digest and she had to vomit."[20] She lost half of her body weight and bound an iron chain around her hips. She also suffered from depression.

Catherine's "symptoms" first started after her beloved sister died in childbirth. At this point, Catherine's mother began to prepare her for marriage, teaching her to put on makeup and how to dye and curl her hair. She rebelled, cutting her hair very short. Her angry mother reacted by forcing her to do additional housework and telling her she would be compelled to marry. Catherine's self-starvation eventually forced her family to relent, allowing her to remain unmarried and enter a convent. Her neighbors called her "Euphrosyne" because she idolized this character from a legend who, as a young girl, escaped an unwanted marriage by changing into men's attire and retiring to a monastery. Catherine escaped an unwanted marriage not only by shedding her female attire, but also her female physique.

25 Another famous holy woman also appeared to exhibit disordered eating. Several authorities have speculated that Joan of Arc, who led the army of France, tonsured and garbed as a male, was also anorexic.[21] Marina Warner based her conclusion on Joan's abstemious eating and frequent fasting, evidence that Joan did not menstruate, and descriptions of Joan vomiting when forced to eat.

. . .

Anxious Somatic Depression among America's First College Women

The argument that problems resulted from mental overstimulation among young women seeking higher education was common in the nineteenth century, a period of major advances in higher education for women. Prior to then, women received no formal education after high school. By the early part of the century, seminaries for females were established, offering training in some advanced topics, but it was not until 1839 that the first college for women, the Georgia Female College, opened its doors to students. Several other women's colleges began in the 1840s and 1850s, but these were, for the most part, small, financially troubled institutions, and few survived. By the time Vassar opened in 1861, however, the idea of higher education for at least some women was firmly established, and by 1875, when Smith and Wellesley opened, significant numbers of females aspired to become college graduates.[22]

But the idea of higher education for women engendered tremendous resistance. Intellectual arguments against educating women took two forms. The more straightforward attacks were based on social and psychological arguments regarding women's proper functions: Educated women would have smaller families, experience "a dropping out of maternal instincts," and become less feminine, "analogous to the sexless class of termites," or "eunuchs of Oriental civilization."[23]

In the words of one authority writing in the *Popular Science Monthly* in 1904:

> Not only does wifehood and motherhood not require an extraordinary development of brain but the latter is a decided barrier against the performance of these duties. Any family physician could give innumerable cases out of his experience of failures of marriage directly due to too great a cultivation of the female intellect, which results in the scorning to perform those duties which are cheerfully performed and even desired by the uneducated wife.[24]

Yet most arguments made against higher education for women were not so overtly self-interested. They were couched in concern for the women and usually based on medical reports regarding the effects of education on women's health. To choose only one example: "As for training young ladies through a long intellectual course, as we do young men, it can never be done. They will die in the process."[25] Too much education for women was said to be responsible for ailments ranging from headaches and insomnia to depression and indigestion.

30 Once again, we could ignore these arguments solely for their obvious biases and the offensive form they took. Doing so, however, leads us to overlook the reasons why these arguments took that particular form.

. . .

Perhaps the mistake of these physicians was not that, because of some bias, they imagined a connection between women going to college and the development of these symptoms, for they apparently found these symptoms in many patients, but that they misconstrued its cause. We believe that it was obviously not the expenditure of intellectual energy that damaged the health of so many first-generation college women, but instead the conflicting role aspirations and emotional turmoil experienced by ambitious women in the context of a society that discredited and placed obstacles in their paths toward achievement. This emotional turmoil was expressed in the symptoms described by the physicians.

Many physicians posited that the ill effects on women's health caused by too much learning resulted from damage done to the women's reproductive systems. These experts expressed particular concern about women expending energy on education just at a time when their complex reproductive systems were rapidly developing. The most obvious sign of this supposed misexpenditure of energy was the development of amenorrhea, the symptom Hippocrates, Benivieni, and Morton had focused so much attention on. As Dr. Meigs noted in 1859, "It is very common for me to find young women who have grown up admirably. . . to lose, in five or six weeks, the habit of menstruation, upon being brought to town and set on the school form and compelled to undergo the fatiguing labor of mental and educational discipline and culture."[26]

Mental Strain

The effect of too much education on the women was usually referred to as "mental strain," which was reputed to be implicated in the development of a wide range of problems, including chlorosis, neurasthenia, and hysteria.[27] In 1894, for example, physicians Henry B. Deale and S. S. Adams attributed the symptoms of neurasthenia to "the natural nervous tendency of a young girl or woman harassed by the ambitions of school life. . . or annoyed with household and family chores." Dr. S. W. Hammond of Rutland, Vermont, went so far as to cite neurasthenia as "a positive argument against higher education of women."[28]

. . .

Here again, we see the symptoms being blamed on the schooling. It was not mental strain that caused the hysteria, we contend, but the discontent of these women with the limitations they experienced as they sought avenues of higher education. For example, Anna O. was described by Breuer and Freud in the *Studies on Hysteria* as "markedly intelligent," and possessing a "powerful intellect." She resented that she was not allowed to attend college although she was brighter than her brother, who was sent to the University of Vienna, which was closed to women. Because she was female, she remained at home "engaged on her household duties." According to Breuer, "This girl, who was bubbling over with intellectual vitality, led an extremely monotonous existence in her puritanically-minded family." He noted: "She possessed a powerful intellect which would have been capable of digesting solid mental pabulum and which stood in need of it—though without receiving it after she had left school."[29]

35 Anna, whose real name was Bertha Pappenheim, went on to a distinguished career as an influential social worker and leader of the Jewish women's movement. She wrote a play entitled *Women's Rights* dealing with women's powerlessness and exploitation by men and translated Mary Wollstonecraft's *A Vindication of the Rights of Women,* which argued for equal educational opportunity. She believed that, to men, women were

mere "beasts of burden" and found her lack of formal education a "defective spiritual nourishment." One description of the characteristics of hysteric patients made by Breuer and Freud appears to suggest that parental belief in mental strain may have increased the barriers placed in the paths of bright women, perhaps bringing on the development of hysteria. They wrote: "Adolescents who are later to become hysterical are for the most part lively, gifted and full of intellectual interests before they fall ill. . . . They include girls who get out of bed at night so as secretly to carry on some study that their parents have forbidden from fear of their overworking." Freud even noted that intellectual effort not only did not cause neurasthenia, but was helpful in protecting against it.[30]

Thus, the observations of Breuer and Freud, viewed from a social roles perspective, lead us to conclude that the adolescent hysteric symptoms experienced by Anna O., including her depression, her anorexia, and her headaches, were rooted not in the overstimulation of her mind but in the opposite problem—understimulation, anger, and low self-esteem felt by very intelligent women like herself not allowed to exercise their abilities.

Historical Commonalities and Differences

It appears to us that for millennia, young women have been afflicted with a syndrome that involves not only the symptoms of disordered eating, but also depression, anxiety, headaches, breathing difficulties, and several other psychological and somatic symptoms. Although abundant evidence is scattered throughout recent research in psychology and psychiatry that a similar syndrome continues to afflict young women, possibly in very large numbers, science and society have lost sight of its existence.

. . .

Cross-cultural Comparisions

. . . The past is not the only blind spot of science in modern, industrialized nations. Most people living in nations like ours know very little about what goes on in developing countries. Except for some brief attention to sensationalized media treatments of famines or coups, events in those nations go unnoticed even by most social and behavioral scientists. The body of knowledge that we call the sciences of psychology and psychiatry is in some respects limited to an understanding of the behaviors and problems of people living in Western nations in the late twentieth century. Attention to whether these problems look the same in developing nations is generally kept isolated in the books and journals of anthropology and cross-cultural psychology and psychiatry, disciplines that specialize in studying other cultures. The literature of these disciplines contains many contemporary reports of women at adolescence beginning to exhibit afflictions involving depression in combination with disordered eating and other somatic symptoms. As we found in the literature and documents of earlier centuries, these afflictions go under a variety of names. Authorities writing about one form seldom refer to any others. And as we saw in the incarnations of these symptoms over the ages, under any name it takes among cultures throughout the world, this syndrome afflicts women who are experiencing rapid changes in gender roles and come to feel disadvantaged by their femininity.

Arab women in Qatar, for example, suffer from what has been called "culture-bound syndrome," which is characterized by nausea, poor appetite, breathing difficulties, palpitations, faintness, and fatigue. Like those with the Hippocratic "disease of young women," these modern women are likely to be unmarried or to have fertility problems. El Islam, who studied these Arab women, noted that the culture-bound syndrome is rooted in the notion that the value of women is based on their husbands and the children they have, which has become more problematic now that these women are receiving more education and are exposed to radio and television, which depict different male-female relationships of the more developed nations. Thus, women experiencing culture-bound syndrome are not successful as measured by traditional standards of their culture, but are still influenced by them, they have not yet been able to "trade in" traditional values for the newer values and role expectations of women they are being exposed to.[31]

Medieval Roman Catholics were not the only religious women whose rituals included behaviors associated with disordered eating. Zar cults, for example, in which people are possessed by spirits called "Zars," are common in North Africa and parts of Asia. In Northern Sudan, typical symptoms of Zar possession include anorexia, nausea, depression, anxiety, headaches, and fertility problems. Over 40 percent of women over the age of 15 in one region of Sudan said that they had been possessed at some time by Zar. Some scholars have argued that Zar possession is a strategy women use to redress gender inequality because they observed that women possessed by Zar are clearly those who have been subjected to unfair treatment as a result of being female.

. . .

Nerves

In many nations, this syndrome is simply called "nerves." Spiritualist healers in Mexico, for example, have been observed to diagnose nerves among women exhibiting amenorrhea, "emptiness" in the stomach, and nausea, as well as headaches, insomnia, and excessive crying. Symptoms of nerves reported by Setha M. Low in Guatemala include headache, despair, anxiety, stomach pain, insomnia, difficulty breathing, and nausea. As we might expect, nerves tends to be much more common among females than among males, and is often found to be particularly frequent among women exhibiting problems in reproduction.[32]

Several anthropologists have noted that nerves is likely to occur among women who are experiencing a transition from a traditional society to a modern one.[33] Once again, with changing gender roles, we see the symptoms of anxious somatic depression. Case histories of women afflicted with nerves exhibit the discontent with traditional female roles that we believe plays such a large part in the development of the syndrome. For example, Toula was a 19-year-old woman living in a village in Greece, which had recently experienced dramatic increases in women's rights and opportunities when the Socialists took over from the military dictatorship. Although she lived for several years in the United States, where she was exposed to less traditional views of women, Toula was not allowed to attend secondary school when her parents brought her back to Greece. Her twin brother, however, was able to pursue his education. Like Anna O., she was envious of the advantages accorded her brother simply because he was male. In what we interpret as a wish to be masculine in order to reap those advantages for herself, she said that when he died, she would take over her brother's spirit. Toula also had a poor body image clearly associated with her discomfort over her developing femininity. Although slim and attractive, she felt "fat and ugly," a term she applied to a neighbor, too, because of what she called the neighbor's "huge breasts."[34]

In many cultures, the syndrome may sometimes simply be called depression, which may manifest itself somewhat differently in non-Western nations. Researchers and clinicians in these nations observe less guilt and hopelessness than in the West, and find somatic symptoms predominating. Nigerian psychiatrist T. Adeoye Lambo observed much confusion in his country between the diagnosis of depression and that of neurasthenia because the typical depressed patient "is invariably preoccupied with vague somatic complaints." In one international survey, the primary symptoms of depression found in non-Western nations were "fatigue, anorexia, weight loss, and loss of libido."[35]

Just as when it is called culture-bound syndrome or nerves, when this constellation of symptoms is called depression it is often related to changing gender roles. For example, Helen E. Ullrich conducted interviews in a village in India in which women recently experienced a high rate of depression as well as dramatic increases in educational opportunities. Of the 23 women age 40 or older interviewed by Ullrich, none had attended high school. Of the 22 women less than 40 years old, 20 had graduated from high school and 7 of these had even more education. Like American women in the late nineteenth century, these Brahmin Indian women were pioneers in their culture in attempting to seek higher education. Several women expressed discontent with the traditional female roles of wife and homemaker and wanted more education than they were allowed. They became depressed when they realized the full extent of the disadvantages of being female.

45 For example, Vani, a 24-year-old woman, was married at age 20 but "wanted to continue her education and still regrets her parents' insistence on marriage." Ullrich adds: "Vani openly discusses the misfortunes of

being female." During her first year of marriage, she had a major depressive episode, "she ate little, had no appetite, lost weight, lost interest in everything, just sat in one position, refused to talk, cried a lot, and could not sleep." When her weight loss continued, a physician was consulted. "The depression resolved when she had a son." In Ullrich's words: "Vani . . . may have conflicts with the traditional female role and with parents' values that a woman should have primarily a domestic identity."[36]

Thus, like physicians of previous centuries, contemporary anthropologists have described a syndrome afflicting women at adolescence or early adulthood that involves depression, anxiety, disordered eating, and several other somatic symptoms. The one difference between the descriptions made by anthropologists in recent years and those made by physicians in past centuries is that the cross-cultural observations were made primarily by investigators quite knowledgeable about the workings of gender roles. As described in fascinating detail in the historical treatments of hysteria and neurasthenia written by such scholars as Carol Smith Rosenberg and Elaine Showalter, physicians of earlier centuries for the most part ignored the role played by gender inequality in the etiology of earlier versions of the syndrome.[37] In contrast, connections made by contemporary anthropologists between the changing status of women, particularly in the form of increased education, and the development of the depressive and somatic symptoms associated with nerves, Zar cults, culture-bound syndrome, and depression focus on gender roles, not mental strain. Most of the experts who study manifestations of this syndrome cross-culturally, however, seem unaware of the commonalities they exhibit with each other, with our culture, and with past cultures. As with the differences between hysteria, neurasthenia, and chlorosis, the factors leading to differences between these various forms of the syndrome found in contemporary developing nations need to be investigated further. But these differences should not be allowed to obscure the many commonalities.

During the past three decades, millions of women living in the United States and other industrialized nations have grown up in cultures that have socialized them to aspire to achievements historically reserved for men, and have confronted myriad barriers. The women of their mothers' generation did not, for the most part, achieve outside of the home. If such experiences lead to the development of the syndrome we have been discussing, we should be seeing evidence of this syndrome in high-school guidance offices, college infirmaries, mental health clinics, and hospitals throughout the developed world.

Notes

[1] Hill, O. W. (1977). Epidemiologic aspects of anorexia nervosa. *Advances in Psychosomatic Medicine, 9,* 48–62.

[2] Lefkowitz, M. R. & Fant, M. B. (1982). *Women's life in Greece and Rome.* Baltimore: Johns Hopkins, Ch. VII.
Littre, P. (1853). *Oeuvres completes d'Hippocrate.* Paris: J. B. Bailliere, p. 503.
[3] Lefkowitz et al., ibid., p. 96.
[4] Benivieni, A. (1954). *De abditis nonnullis ac mirandis morborum et sanationum causis.* (C. Singer, trans.) Springfield, Ill.: Charles C. Thomas, p. 95.
[5] Morton, R. (1694). *Phthisiologia or a treatise of consumption.* London: Smith & Walford, pp. 8, 9.
[6] Ibid., p. 258.
[7] Van Deth, R. & Vandereycken, W. (1991). Was nervous consumption a precursor of anorexia nervosa? *Journal of the History of Medicine and Allied Sciences, 46,* 3–19.
[8] Cited in Porter, R. (1986). Love, sex, and madness in eighteenthcentury England. *Social Research, 53,* 238.
[9] Allbutt, T. C. (1901). Chlorosis. In Allbutt, T. C. (ed.), *A system of medicine by many authors, Vol. V.* New York: Macmillan, pp. 481–518.
Loudon, I. (1984). The diseases called chlorosia. *Psychological Medicine, 4,* 27–36.
[10] Fear of obesity quote—Allbutt, ibid., p. 485. Depression and despair quote—Ashwell, cited in Loudon, op. cit., p. 29.
[11] Marmor, J. (1953). Orality in the hysterical personality. *Journal of the American Psychoanalytic Association, 1,* 656–671, quote p. 658.
Purtell, J. J., Robins, E., & Cohen, M. E. (1951). Observations on clinical aspects of hysteria. *Journal of the American Medical Association, 146,* 902–910.
[12] Laycock, T. (1840). *An essay on hysteria.* Philadelphia: Haswell, Barrington & Haswell.
Coming, L. (1888). *A treatise on hysteria and epilepsy.* Detroit: George S. Davis.
[13] Emmy von N quote—Breuer, J. & Freud, S. (1893–95). *Studies on hysteria.* New York: Basic, reprinted, pp. 80–81.
[14] Anna O.—ibid., pp. 21–47. Rejection of all nourishment quote—ibid., p. 4.
[15] Lutz, T. (1991). *American nervousness, 1903.* Ithaca, N.Y.: Comell University Press.
Savage, G. (1884). *Insanity and allied neuroses.* Philadelphia: Henry C. Lea, p. 90.
[16] Deale, H. B. & Adams, S. S. (1894). Neurasthenia in young women. *American Journal of Obstetrics, 29,* 190–195; quote p. 190.
[17] Bell, R. M. (1985). *Holy anorexia.* Chicago: University of Chicago; quote p. 56.
[18] Brumberg, J. J. (1988). *Fasting girls.* Cambridge, Mass.: Harvard University, p. 79.
[19] Magli cited in Bell, op. cit., p. 55.
Bynum, C. W. (1987). *Holy feast and holy fast.* Berkeley: University of California, pp. 27, 290.
[20] Bell, op. cit., p. 25.
[21] Bell, op. cit.
Warner, M. (1981). *Joan of Arc.* New York: Knopf.
[22] Woody, T. (1929). *A history of women's education in the United States. Vol 2.* New York: Science Press.
[23] Clarke, E. H. (1972). *Sex in education; or, a fair chance for the girls.* New York: Amo Press, p. 3.
[24] Woody, op. cit., p. 205.
[25] Ibid., p. 154.

[26] Meigs, ibid., p. 385.
[27] Allbutt, op. cit.
Simon, J. (1897). A study of chlorosis. *American Journal of Medical Science, 113,* 349–423.
Gosling, F. G. (1987). *Before Freud: Neurasthenia and the American medical community, 1870–1910.* Urbana: University of Illinois.
Preston, G. J. (1897). *Hysteria and certain allied conditions.* Philadelphia: P. Blakiston.
[28] Deale & Adams, op. cit., p. 191.
Hammond cited in Gosling, op. cit., p. 100.
[29] Breuer and Freud, op. cit., pp. 21, 22.
[30] Hunter, D. (1983). Hysteria, psychoanalysis, and feminism: The case of Anna O., *Feminist Studies, 9*(3), pp. 470, 478.
Freud, S. (1957). The sexual aetiology of the neuroses. In S. Freud, *Collected Papers Vol. I.* New York: Basic Books, pp. 220–248.
Breuer et al., op. cit., p. 240.
[31] El Islam, F. (1975). Culture bound neurosis in Qatari women. *Social Psychiatry, 10,* 25–29.
[32] Finkler, K. (1989). The universality of nerves. In D. L. Davis & S. M. Low (eds.), *Gender, health, and illness: The case of nerves.* New York: Hemisphere, pp. 79–87.
Cayleff, S. E. (1988). "Prisoners of their own feebleness": Women, nerves and Western medicine—A historical overview. *Social Science and Medicine, 26*(12), 1199–1208.
Nations, M. K., Camino, L. A., & Walker, F. B. (1988). "Nerves": Folk idiom for anxiety and depression? *Social Science and Medicine, 26*(12), 1245–1259.
Low, S. M. (1989). Gender, emotion, and nervios in urban Guatemala. In D. L. Davis & S. M. Low (eds.), op. cit., 23–48.
[33] Barnett, E. A. (1989). Notes on nervios: A disorder of menopause. In D. L. Davis & S. M. Low (eds.), op. cit., 67–78.
Finerman, R. (1989). The burden of responsibility: Duty, depression, and nervios in Andean Ecuador. In D. L. Davis & S. M. Low (eds.), op. cit., 49–66.
[34] Clark, M. H. (1989). Nevra in a Greek village: Idiom, metaphor, symptoms, or disorder? In D. L. Davis & S. M. Low (eds.), op. cit., 103–126.
As is evident in the citations above to several chapters in a single book, the disorder nerves has been studied throughout the world. The articles and chapters cited also discuss connections between nerves and other disorders such as neurasthenia and hysteria. This is the one case in which various forms taken by what we are calling "anxious somatic depression" have been related to one another.
[35] Lambo, T. A. (1960). Further neuropsychiatric observations in Nigeria. *British Medical Journal,* December 10, p. 1699.
Murphy, H. E. (1964). Cross-cultural inquiry into the symptomatology of depression. *Transcultural Psychiatric Research Review, 1,* 5–21.
[36] Ullrich, H. E. (1987). A study of change and depression among Havik Brahmin women in a South Indian village. *Culture, Medicine and Psychiatry, 11,* 276.
[37] Showalter, E. (1985). *The female malady: Women, madness, and English culture, 1830–1980.* New York: Pantheon.
Smith-Rosenberg, C. (1985). *Disorderly conduct: Visions of gender in Victorian America.* New York: Knopf.

Mapping the Text

1. Outline Silverstein and Perlick's point of view in "The Disease of Young Women." Identify their intended audience, purpose, and basic message. How does this essay add to the discussion of issues related to gender and health? What advice do you take from the essay for contemporary times?
2. Focus on the historical examples related to women and disease in this essay. If these views of women were the only source of information about women and their ailments over time, what image of women do you think would prevail?
3. What message(s) do you think Silverstein and Perlick are trying to convey? What do you think they are trying to assert? Do you agree or disagree with their point of view?

Writing to Inquire

1. Do you think the issues raised by Silverstein and Perlick continue in contemporary society? On the basis of what evidence do you hold this belief?
2. Interview some women in your class to assess the prevalence of issues and concerns raised by Silverstein and Perlick. Is "the disease of young women" an issue in your local community? Do you know any women who suffer from the types of ailments described in this essay? Write a persuasive essay, or a letter to your campus paper, to outline your own position on women's health issues and awareness on your campus.

Confessions of an Eater

KIM CHERNIN

Kim Chernin (1940–) has been described as "a poet, a mystic, and an interpreter of women's psychological experiences." She was born in the Bronx, New York, to parents who were committed leftists, and throughout her childhood she was exposed to her parents' life of political activism. In 1950, Chernin's parents moved to California; in 1951, her mother was arrested for "advocating the overthrow of the government" at the height of postwar anticommunist paranoia. Chernin later broke with her mother's revolutionary ideologies, and her renegotiation of her relationship to her mother figures prominently in many of her writings. Chernin is a psychotherapist in private practice, counseling patients with eating and identity disorders. Her prolific output as a writer includes poems, novels, and nonfiction works. *The Hungry Self: Women, Eating, and Identity* (1985) and *The Obsession: Reflections on the Tyranny of Slenderness* (1981) both address eating disorders and related health issues in the context of feminism and women's spirituality. The excerpt printed here is taken from *The Obsession.*

> *What a surprising effect food has on our organisms. Before I ate, I saw the sky, the trees, and the birds all yellow, but after I ate, everything was normal to my eyes. . . . I was able to work better. My body stopped weighing me down. . . . I started to smile as if I was witnessing a beautiful play. And will there ever be a drama more beautiful than that of eating? I felt that I was eating for the first time in my life.*
>
> —CAROLINA MARIA DE JESUS

> *She got up at once, went to get a magnificent apple, cut a piece and gave it to me, saying: "Now Mama is going to feed her little Renée. It is time to drink the good milk from Mama's apples." She put the piece in my mouth, and with my eyes closed, my head against her breast, I ate, or rather drank, my milk. A nameless felicity flowed into my heart. It was as though, suddenly, by magic, all my agony, the tempest which had shaken me a moment ago, had given place to a blissful calm. . . .*
>
> —RENÉE, *AUTOBIOGRAPHY OF A SCHIZOPHRENIC GIRL*

I remember the first time I ate compulsively. I was seventeen years old, not yet an introspective person. I had no language or vocabulary for what was happening to me. The issue of compulsive eating had not yet become a matter of public confession. Looking back I can say: "That was the day my neurosis began." But at the time, if I knew the word at all, I would not have known to apply it to myself.

I was in Berlin, sitting at the breakfast table with my American roommate and our German landlords. I remember the day vividly: the wind blows, the curtain lifts on the window, a beam of sunlight crosses the room and stops just at the spout of the teapot. A single, amber drop becomes luminous at the tip of the spout. I feel that I am about to remember something and then, unaccountably, I am moved to tears. But I do not cry. I say nothing, I look furtively around me, hoping this wave of strong feeling has not been observed. And then, I am eating. My hand is reaching out. And the movement, even in the first moments, seems driven and compulsive. I am not hungry. I had pushed away my plate moments before. But my hand is reaching and I know that I am reaching for something that has been lost. I hope for much from the food that is on the table before me but suddenly it seems to me that nothing will ever still this hunger—an immense implacable craving that I do not remember having felt before.

Suddenly, I realize that I am putting too much butter on my breakfast roll. I am convinced that everyone is looking at me. I put down the butter knife. I break off a piece of the roll and put it in my mouth. But it seems to me that I am wolfing it down. That I am devouring it.

I notice, with alarm, that Olga is beginning to clear the table. Unable to control myself, I lurch forward, reach out for another roll and pull the butter plate closer to myself. Everyone laughs and I am mortified. I am blushing the way I have not blushed since I was twelve or thirteen years old. I feel trapped and I want to go on eating. I *must* go on eating. And yet I feel an acute and terrible self-consciousness.

5 While Olga looks away and Rudi bends over to take something from the mouth of his child, I stuff the two rolls in my pocket, stand up from the table, and leave the room.

Once out of the house I begin running. And as I run I eat. I break the pieces of the roll without taking them from my pocket; I keep the broken portion covered with my hand. Making an apparently casual gesture I raise my hand to my mouth. Smoothly, as if I have practiced this many times, I drop the portion of bread into my mouth. And I continue to run.

Suddenly, as I fly by, I catch a glimpse of myself in the reflecting surface of a store window, looking for all the world as if a tempestuous spirit had been unleashed upon this quiet, bourgeois town. My hair is floating up in wisps, there is something frantic in my face. Perhaps it is a look of astonishment that the body I see there is so very slender when I imagine that it is terribly fat. And then I am violently parted from my own reflection as I race around the corner and stand still for a moment, staring down the street.

I see one of those stations where you can get a sausage, a paper plate, mustard, a white roll. You don't have to enter the restaurant, you can take the thing from an open window, carry it over to a table, stand outside, and dip the sausage in mustard, using your hands. No utensils, no formalities, no civilized behaviors. I slow down and walk up to the window, making every effort to appear at ease. But there is someone in line before me. Suddenly, a wave of tremendous anger and frustration comes over me. I think, if I do not control myself, I shall take this man by the shoulders and shove him aside.

I don't want to wait, I can't wait, I can't bear waiting. I must eat now, at this moment, without delay. I fumble in my pocket for another bit of roll. The pocket is empty. I am kicking at the ground, nudging a small stone about on the pavement. It seems to me, as I become aware of this gesture, that I am pawing the earth. I am terrified now that I will lose control completely—start swearing or muttering or even yelling at the man. I have seen such things before: people who sit speaking to themselves on subways, who burst out yelling for no apparent reason, while everyone laughs. I look down at my coat—it is covered with crumbs. My shoes look shabby. All at once I feel that I am filthy—a gross and alien creature at the edge of unbearable rage. I don't know what to do with myself, the man in front of me still talking to the woman behind the window, his sausage steaming on the counter before him and he does not reach out to take it in his hands. . . .

10 It is a cold day. I become aware of this as I stand, pawing the ground, watching the steam rise from the sausage. And I know exactly what I am doing when I suddenly dart forward, grab the plate and begin to run. I do not look back over my shoulder, I run with a sudden sense of release, as if I have finally cut the restraint that has been binding me. I hear the man's

voice call out. *"Verdammtes Mädel,"* it says. "You damn girl." And then he begins to laugh. I too am laughing as I dart around a corner and stand with my back pressed to a cement building, urgently dipping the sausage into the mustard, stuffing large chunks of it into my mouth. And then I am crying. . . .

And so I ran from bakery to bakery, from street stall to street stall, buying cones of roasted chestnuts, which made me frantic because I had to peel away the skins. I bought a pound of chocolate and ate it as I ran. I never went to the same place twice. I acquired a mesh bag and carried supplies with me, wrapped in torn pieces of newspaper. When I felt tired, I sat down on benches, spread out my food next to me, tried to move slowly, as if I were enjoying a picnic, felt constrained by this pretense, darted the food into my mouth, ran on. . . .

In a few weeks I was planning to return to America. The summer vacation, which had lasted for more than seven months, had finally come to an end. I was out of money; I was tired of traveling, I should have returned home to start college months before. But I knew that I could not go home fat. I looked down at parts of my body—at my wrists, at my ankles, at my calves. There was always something wrong with them, something that could be improved or perfected. How could I know then that the time would never come when I would regard myself as sufficiently slender? How indeed could I possibly imagine that one day I would weigh less than ninety pounds and still be ashamed to go out in a bathing suit? The future was completely dark. I had no idea that this episode of compulsive eating would become a typical event in my life over the next twenty years. It never occurred to me that a whole generation of women would become familiar with this unfortunate experience of their appetites and their bodies, or that I myself would one day weave their experience and my own into a book. At the time my thoughts were riveted upon the shame I felt. I considered going to the movies but I felt so self-conscious that I walked on down the street, feeling that I was a woman of perverse, almost criminal tendencies. I thought that in this obsession with food I was completely alone.

Twenty years later there is laughter. The event has become a story; I tell it to friends and we all smile knowingly. I write it down on the page and I marvel at that young woman running about the streets so frantically, that tempestuous gobbler with her wild eyes. But what has happened during the twenty years? What cycle, beginning that day in Berlin, has now almost accomplished itself, so that today I can sit at my typewriter and dare to look back? Or stand and look at myself in the mirror without considering how I might change this body I see? For it has happened during the last years (and from this I come by degree to believe in miracles) that I have been able to sit down at a meal without computing the calories involved, without warning my appetite about its excess, without fearing what might happen if I took pleasure from my plate. My body, my hunger and the food I give to myself, which have seemed like enemies to me, now have begun to look like friends. And this, it strikes me, is the way it should be; a natural relationship to oneself and the food that nourishes one. Yet, this natural way of being does not come easily to many women in our culture. Certainly it has not come easily to me.

Indeed, if I think back ten years or eight or nine, or to any period of my life, I find that I know exactly how much I weighed, whether I had recently gained or lost weight, exactly what clothes I was able to wear. These facts remain where so many other details have been forgotten. And of course, even in the act of recollection, I hasten to assure anyone who is listening that I was never really fat. Sometimes too slender, I would stand in front of a mirror, practically knocking against my own bones. At other times, when I had gained weight, I would grow attached to a particular pair of blue jeans and Chinese shirt. If an occasion required me to change out of these I felt extremely uncomfortable. These clothes, which I had grown accustomed to, seemed to hide me; anything else I might have changed into would be, I felt, a revelation of how fat I had become. Finally, I acquired a bright colored Mexican poncho; draped in this covering garment, I felt protected from judgments about my immense weight. But that was when I weighed 120 pounds. Surely even the weight charts consider that normal for a woman five feet four-and-a-half inches tall?

15 During those years my body and my appetite usually inspired me with a sense of profound uneasiness. True, for a week or two after losing weight I would feel that my body had become a celebration. I would rush out and buy new clothes for it, eager to have it testify to this triumph of my will. Inevitably, however, the weight would return. Mysteriously, the willpower would give way to desire. "An extra grape," I'd say, "and I've gained it all back again."

My hunger filled me with despair. It would always return, no matter how often I resolved to control it. Although I fasted for days, or went on a juice diet, or ate only vegetables, always, at the end of this fast, my hunger was back. The shock I would feel made me aware that my secret goal in dieting must have been the intention to kill off my appetite entirely.

When I write about this now it reminds me of the way people in the nineteenth century used to feel about sexuality and particularly about masturbation. I had these same feelings about masturbating when I was a little girl. Then, too, it seemed to me that a powerful force would rise up from my body and over-come my moral scruples and all my resistance. I would give in to it with a sense of voluptuous release, followed by terrible shame. Today, I begin to see that there is a parallel here. A woman obsessed with losing weight is also caught up in a terrible struggle against her sensual nature. She is trying to change and transform her body, she is attempting to govern, control, limit and sometimes even destroy her appetite. But her body and her hunger are, like sexual appetite, the expression of what is natural in herself; it is a futile, heartbreaking and dismal struggle to be so violently pitted against them. Indeed, this struggle against the natural self is one of the essential and hidden dramas of obsession.

Such an understanding did not come to me at all, however, when I was rushing about eating food, or going on diets, or swallowing diuretics, or staring at myself in the mirror, or pinching my waist, or using tape measures to measure the size of my wrists or ankles. For ten or eleven years after that episode in Berlin I felt that my obsession with food and weight was steadily growing more extreme. Finally, I was passing through a period when I found it very difficult to control my eating. Every day, when I woke up, my first thought was about food. Frequently, I could not make it even as far as lunch without eating a pound of candy. When I weighed myself I was filled with alarm by the needle creeping up the scale. "The scale is broken," I would say to myself. "It just wants to pay me back for kicking it," I would explain, not knowing whether or not I actually believed this nonsense. When I went past a mirror I would put my hands over my eyes, frightened of what I might behold there. I even hid from the toaster and the curved surface of a large spoon or the fender of a polished car. In that mood the world seemed filled with reminders that I was not as slender as the woman on the magazine cover, that I, in spite of all my will and effort, was not now able to make myself lean and gaunt.

One night, during this time, I woke around midnight, wondering how I could possibly be hungry, since I had eaten a great deal that day. I lay in bed, hoping I would not get up and go into the kitchen. But I was still hoping this as I made my way down the hallway, walking on tiptoe although I was alone in the house and there was no one to hear me. I opened the refrigerator; there had been a party at my house the day before and much of the food had remained behind. There were, I recall, neatly wrapped packages of feta and grape leaves, a basket of black figs, a few slices of green melon with prosciutto folded across the top, a carefully sliced piece of *boeuf* Wellington, and several chunks of halvah, rising up from a plate of sliced strudel that was flaking off bits of its dough. These were, without question, my most beloved foods and now as I looked at them I was suddenly faced with the necessity of choice. Which should I eat first? I went through several complex computations, persuading myself I would like the halvah better if I ate it after the feta, would not really want the *boeuf* Wellington if I had eaten the strudel first.

20 In truth, I really wasn't the least bit interested in these foods. Did I want to rush out then and find something in a late-night market? The donut shop perhaps? Or the ice cream store where you could get extra portions of butterscotch? But these foods too seemed to be lacking something. I went to the window of my bedroom and looked out into the garden, trying still to figure out what it was I wanted to eat. But now suddenly, for the first time in my life, I realized that what I was feeling was not hunger at all. I was rest-

less, that was true; I had awakened feeling lonely, I was sad at being alone in the house, and I was frightened: the creaking of stairs, the noise of wind blowing in the window sounded like footsteps to me or like a door opening. What I wanted from food was companionship, comfort, reassurance, a sense of warmth and well-being that was hard for me to find in my own life, even in my own home. And now that these emotions were coming to the surface, they could no longer be easily satisfied with food. I was hungering, it was true; but food apparently was not what I was hungering for.

Recently, I came across a poem which would have helped me greatly if I could have read it years ago. It is by June Jordan and it contains an astonishing insight into the relationship between feeling and hunger:

> Nothing fills me up at night
> I fall asleep for one or two hours then
> up again my gut
> alarms
> I must arise
> and wandering into the refrigerator
> think about evaporated milk homemade vanilla ice cream
> cherry pie hot from the oven with Something like Vermont
> Cheddar Cheese disintegrating luscious
> on the top while
> mildly
> I devour almonds and raisins mixed to mathematical
> criteria or celery or my very own sweet and sour snack
> composed of brie peanut butter honey and
> a minuscule slice of party size salami
> on a single whole wheat cracker *no salt added*. . .

The poem, as it continues, observes the complex social and personal reasons for anger, for loneliness, for the lack of self-love, those emotions which become hunger and rise up from the gut, driving us back to the refrigerator late at night. And it concludes:

> Maybe when I wake up in the middle of the night
> I should go downstairs
> dump the refrigerator contents on the floor
> and stand there in the middle of the spilled milk
> and the wasted butter spread beneath my dirty feet
> writing poems
> writing poems. . . [1]

This shift from literal to symbolic understanding is always overwhelming. The poet, distilling the learning of years, dumps out this food that cannot satisfy the complex hunger that is driving her, and stands there writing her poem. And so I learn from her: this hunger I feel, which drives me to eat more than I need, requires more than the most perfectly mixed handful of almonds and raisins. It requires, in whatever form is appropriate, the evolution and expression of self.

Not that this shift to the symbolic will change overnight the way anyone feels about her body or its food. Many times over these years I have continued to wake late at night and have gone back to the refrigerator. I did not dump out its contents. I stood plotting the perfect sequence of food, perplexed at the growing dissatisfaction I felt when I finally began to eat; guilty the next morning, of course, but increasingly driven to reflect upon my experience. For I had the first clue into the resolution of this problem of obsession. I could no longer take it literally. Now, whenever I began to hate my body, or feel fear about the size of my appetite, whenever I began to long for food, I would ask myself what these fears and longings meant.

This research into the meaning of hunger went on for many years, during which I began to talk seriously with other women about their problems with weight. Slowly, it began to occur to me that my understanding of our condition was producing material worthy to become a book. At times, I was excited by this prospect of presenting a careful and detailed analysis of the cultural and psychological meanings of our obsession; at other times I felt that I did not want to continue with this undertaking because its subject matter seemed so trivial to me.

Imagine, I said to myself, spending the next years of your life writing about a woman's problem with her weight. Imagine using all your intellect and all your skill to analyze the reasons for an obsession with food. The obsession had always seemed so petty to me that I could not at times bear the idea that my whole life had already been swallowed up by this preoccupation.

One day, returning from the library, I suddenly realized that this whole idea of triviality was itself revealing. I had been reading Cocteau's book about his addiction to opium and had felt in its writer a distinct sort of pride. "I am speaking of the real smokers," he had written in what seemed to me a remarkably revealing passage. "The amateurs feel nothing, they wait for dreams and risk being seasick; because the effectiveness of opium is the result of a pact. If we fall under its spell, we shall never be able to give it up."[2] I was aware that no woman with a weight problem would make this distinction between the real obsessive and the amateur, for she would see herself, not as a member of an elite fraternity ("the nurses only know the counterfeit smokers, the elegant smokers, those who combine opium, alcohol, drugs. . ."), but as a being afflicted with a dreadful problem she cannot transcend and cannot control. For her, there could be no pride in this, no feeling that her addiction to food exalted her. And yet, Cocteau was able to claim precisely this exaltation for the opium addict. "The addict," he wrote, "can become a masterpiece. A masterpiece which is above discussion. A perfect masterpiece, because it is fugitive, without form and without judges."[3] Opium, I understood, opened the doors to a higher imaginative life; whatever disadvantages the addiction held for the addict, the glamour of this surrender to the higher self placed the addict above the condition of the average mortal. But the woman who surrendered to her obsession with food—who would ever assert this on her behalf? And yet, I reasoned, there must be in this obsession of ours the same deep promptings, the same longings and dissatisfactions, which drove a man to become addicted to opium, to make this pact, to fall under its spell, and never be able to give it up. Our insistence—my own insistence—that our obsession was trivial, was no doubt merely a resistance to what these deeper promptings might reveal.

Some indication of the very great significance of eating can be found in the story of G. T. Fechner, which is told by James Hillman in *The Dream and the Underworld*.[4] Fechner, the founder of psychophysics, was highly regarded by Freud for his work on dreams. But after years of productive work, at the age of thirty-nine, Fechner began to experience a breakdown. His eyes failed and he finally went blind. He also "fell into melancholic isolation, lost control over his thoughts, hallucinated tortures, and his alimentary tract broke down." He remained in this unfortunate condition for three years. Twice, however, he was "miraculously healed: once when a woman friend dreamed of preparing him a meal of Bauerschinken, a heavily spiced raw ham cured in lemon juice and Rhine wine." When she took this dish to him he ate it, against his better judgment, and discovered that his appetite and digestion were both restored. And he was healed also on another occasion when suddenly one morning at dawn "he found that he was able to bear the light and even hungered for it." From this moment his recuperation began, his eyesight returned and he lived on, in good health, for another forty-four years.

As it happened, I was reading this story quite recently in a Berkeley coffee shop. When I looked up from my book I caught sight of several perfectly sliced pieces of Italian rum chocolate cake behind the glass counter next to the espresso machine. I found myself wondering whether I would be able to immerse myself again in the story of old Fechner and prove once more the power of my will to resist my appetite, when the significance of the tale I had just read came home to me. Suddenly, it seemed no accident that Hillman had spoken of Fechner's *hunger* for light. For Fechner, I thought, had been cured precisely by the return of his appetite, when his melancholic withdrawal from the world was superseded by desire. Thus, he begins to eat and his alimentary tract is cured. He begins to hunger for light and his vision is restored. Was it possible, I wondered, that Fechner had been suffering from a severe and controlling attitude towards sensual existence, like so many other intellectual men of the nineteenth century? If so, it made sense that he was healed by giving himself permission to eat, since this permission would have represented a profound reconciliation with instinctual life, a willingness to gratify rather than control desire.

This reflection came upon me as something distinctly new and it made me aware that our obsession had in it as much potential "exaltation" as the surrender to opium. It, too, might be seen as a quest for reconciliation within the self. Opium, perhaps, opened the doors to the higher, imaginative life; but I could now see that our obsession with food expressed a yearning for permission to enjoy the sensual aspects of the self.

This insight had an immediate impact upon my own relationship to food. For the first time in my conscious life I began to imagine appetite as a healthful, natural aspect of myself. I imagined standing up from my table, holding my head high, and walking across the room. In my fantasy I stood calmly in line, not swearing under my breath about the man taking too much time in front of me. Then, I requested the man who worked behind the counter to fill up a tray for me, with two pieces of Italian rum chocolate cake, a large cup of hot chocolate, with espresso and whipped cream. I intended to go sit by myself at a table near the door, letting everyone who passed by look in at me, peacefully eating, not devouring, taking my time, giving myself permission to gratify my appetite.

But now, before I could enact this fantasy, my eyes fell upon the oranges stacked up in an informal pyramid at the top of the counter. The light from the window must have been falling upon them, because they were burnished with a vivid and beautiful glow. I was so fascinated by them that I forgot my conflict about eating; I stared at the oranges, entranced by their roundness. And suddenly I was aware that I had seen them like this when I was a child, on my first trip to California. What a vision that had been as the train passed by the orchard and I shook my mother by the shoulder. "Mama, look," I cried out, waking the old lady drowsing on the seat in front of us, "in California the oranges grow on trees."

This early sense of wonder and delight came to me again now; I looked at the fruit as if it were the gift of a divine being or were itself divine. And now suddenly I realized that my hunger had vanished. I felt that I was being filled with my own joy in the beauty of the world. Everything I looked at now had this same quality of fullness and abundance that gleamed from the oranges stacked in their pyramid across the room. A friend stopped at my table, setting down her tray and bending over to kiss me on the cheek. "You're glowing," she said. "I could practically see you from the other side of the street." She offered me a brioche, which I accepted. But at the first bite I found that I was already satisfied. I took a sip of her coffee, sat back in my chair. "You look," she said, "as if you've swallowed the canary." "Yes," I replied, "I feel as if I'd just eaten the whole world."

For many weeks after that time I found that whenever I was in conflict about food what I needed was permission to eat. If I was in fact able to let myself eat for pleasure, the terrible conflict abated and with it the sense of an insatiable hunger. Frequently, as I observed this conflict over food, I noticed that the permission to eat was closely linked to a delight in life, a sense of joy and abundance, an awareness of some unexpected meaning or beauty. And frequently, too, there were memories of childhood. Occasionally, walking down the street with a salted pretzel from the street stand at the edge of the college campus, I would feel that I had little legs and hands, that I was walking in the Bronx with my mother, tasting everything for the first time. In this state of delight, it never took a great deal of food to satisfy my hunger. However plain or simple it was, to me it seemed exactly the pleasure and satisfaction I had been looking for. The moral to draw from this seemed clear. There was a state of mind and being in which food became a simple, uncomplicated sensual pleasure. But if I were lacking this state, if I simply could not give myself permission to eat, food would not satisfy me, no matter how excellent it was or how much of it I consumed in compulsive rebellion against my own prohibition.

35 The process of understanding, which over the years was gradually changing my relationship to food, had one last dramatic insight in store for me. This one occurred during a time in my life when I no longer ate compulsively, but would still experience periods of anxiety about my body, feeling that suddenly, overnight I had become fat. On this occasion I was lying in bed counting over the calories I'd eaten during the day. My attention was vaguely focused upon my body, which was filling me with a sense of extreme dissatisfaction. Now, I reverted to a fantasy about my body's transformation from this state of imperfection to a consummate loveliness, the flesh trimmed away, stomach flat, thighs like those of the adolescent runner on the back slopes of the fire trail, a boy of fifteen or sixteen, running along there one evening in a pair of red trunks, stripped to the waist, gleaming with sweat and suntan oil, his muscles stretching and relaxing, as if he'd been sent out there to model for me a vision of everything I was not and could never be. I don't know how many times this fantasy of transformation had occupied me before, but this time it ended with a sudden eruption of awareness, for I had observed the fact that the emotions which prompted it were a bitter contempt for the feminine nature of my own body. The sense of fullness and swelling, of curves and softness, the awareness of plenitude and abundance, which filled me with disgust and alarm, were actually the qualities of a woman's body.

With this knowledge I now got up and went to look at myself in the mirror. For the first time I was able to perceive the transparent film of expectation I placed over my image in the looking glass. I had never seen myself before. Until now, all I had been able to behold was my body's failure to conform to an ideal. Now, I realized that what I had called fat in myself, and considered gross, was this body of a woman. And it was beautiful. The thighs, too large for an adolescent boy, were appropriate to a woman's body. Hips rounding, belly curved, what had driven me to deny this evidence that I was a woman?

For a long moment I stood before my own image, coming to knowledge of myself. Suddenly, I saw all that I was supposed to be but was not—taller, more ethereal, more refined, less hungry, not so powerful, much less emotional, more subdued, not such a big talker; a more generous, loving, considerate, nurturant person; less selfish, less ambitious, and far less given to seeking pleasure for myself.

Now, however, all this came into question: Who, I wondered, had made up this ideal for women? Who had imposed it and why hadn't I seen through it before? Why, for that matter, did I imagine a slender body would bring me these attainments, even if I decided I actually wanted them for myself? And why, finally, wasn't I free simply to throw off this whole coercive system of expectation and be myself—eating, lusting, laughing, talking, taking?

It was a moment of clear vision and it would, I knew, organize the ideas and impressions I had been gathering around a central theme. For now I could no longer doubt that my alienation from my body was the key to understanding my troubled relationship to food, to my appetite, and to my very identity as a woman. I knew also that I would have to go further—to understand, for instance, why so many women of my generation could not tolerate their bodies. I would have to ask why our culture held up before us an ideal image that was appropriate only to an adolescent. I needed to understand whether this inappropriate ideal was part of a much larger coercion exercised against the full and natural development of women.

A book comes into being at that juncture where a personal problem, which has caused great distress, has begun to resolve itself, so that the deeper meanings and wider issues of the problem are apparent. Certainly, I was now beginning to experience a vivid transformation in my way of seeing and hearing. Now, listening to women talk about their problems of weight, I felt myself understanding on many levels at the same time. I went to the same places as before, I listened often to the same women talking, recorded again and again the power of this obsession over their lives, but now I was asking new questions, following different leads, translating everything into a new structure of meaning. And therefore, when a woman said to me one day, "I have rarely had a moment of peace about my body. All my life, no matter what else is going on, I have felt an uneasiness. A sense that something was about to get out of control. That I needed to keep watch. That something about me needed changing," I reached for my notebook and went out to gather evidence that might show how widespread was this uneasiness about the body and its urges. For this obsession, I felt, might well be considered one of the most serious forms of suffering affecting women in America today.

Notes

[1] June Jordan, *Passion,* Boston, 1980.

[2] Jean Cocteau, *Opium: The Diary of a Cure,* London, 1957.

[3] Ibid.

[4] James Hillman, *The Dream and the Underworld,* New York, 1979.

Mapping the Text

1. Chernin shares a very personal story about her relationship with food in this essay. Why would she choose to reveal such a personal story to a public audience? What purpose would sharing this story serve for a writer? a reader? How does Chernin build on her own experience to develop an argument or perspective on women, food, and cultural ideals about body size?
2. How does Chernin overcome her eating disorders? What is it that enables her to move from tragedy to laughter? How would you summarize the process of her transformation? What lessons or implications do you draw from this that might be applied to other young women, or even to yourself?
3. Chernin places eating disorders and body image in a broader context, "part of a larger coercion exercised against the full and natural development of women" in our culture. How does she build this argument? What types of evidence and reasoning does she use to support this argument? How convincing is her case? What counterarguments might you make in response?

Writing to Inquire

1. Write a personal narrative about your own history with food and eating. How is your story similar to and different than Chernin's? If you were going to share this story with your class or a public audience, what parts would you include? What parts would you choose not to make public? Why? What value does confessional writing of this sort serve in the context of public health issues and policy?
2. How well informed do you think the women on your campus are about issues of body size and eating disorders? What about the men? Write a proposal in which you outline a campaign you might direct on your campus to raise awareness about eating disorders. How would you present this information? in what form? How would you try to get the attention of your peers and others on campus?

Dear Dr. Menninger

KARL MENNINGER

Dr. Karl Menninger (1893–1990) was a psychiatrist in Topeka, Kansas, who founded with his father, Charles Frederick Menninger, The Menninger Clinic in 1920, as a collective of specialists in mental health. In 1941, The Menninger Foundation was established as a psychiatric center for research, training, and public education. From 1929 to 1942, Menninger published an advice column for troubled parents in a magazine called *Household.* Letters addressed topics ranging from homosexuality to divorce to depression. In 1930, the *Ladies'*

Home Journal invited Menninger to contribute a monthly column to their national publication. More than two thousand people wrote in response to Menninger's monthly column. Menninger's other publications include *The Vital Balance* (1963) and *Whatever Became of Sin?* (1973, 1988). *Dear Dr. Menninger: Women's Voices from the Thirties* (1997), edited by Howard J. Faulkner and Virginia D. Pruitt, is a collection of letters written to Menninger and his subsequent responses. The letters below are taken from this collection.

Portland, Ore.
May 8, 1931

Dear Sir:

Please advise me. I am so disgusted with myself and so miserable. Until recently I didn't know there was such a thing as homosexualism and now that seems to explain my past and present unhappiness. It is too hideous.

My mother died when I was three. During childhood my craving for motherlove found an outlet in worshipping different women. I would "play" I was the loved child of whichever charming woman held my fancy at the time.

This unnatural make-believe continued through high school, where I had "crushes" on my teachers. I no longer pretended to be their child, of course, but wanted their friendship, their attention, even their love, more than anything in the world and was naturally very unhappy over real and imagined slights.

In college my infatuation turned to upper classmen, and I knew periods of exaltation and despondency over these "cases." It was late in my college life before I began to feel the normal interest in men.

5 After graduation from college there was a blessed period of five years—blessed because it was free from what now seems so perverted an emotional life. I had the usual friendships with men, and married.

Now, after two years of comparatively happy married life the old curse is back. I have fought against it this time in view of my later knowledge of psychology. Yet, even while I tell myself how revolting it all is, my interest in this older, charming woman supplies me with a satisfaction I cannot explain. It seems the one absorbing thing in life. Infantile as it is, I carry on imaginary conversations with her, and she is constantly on my mind.

I feel my love for my husband disappearing. I am critical of him. Perhaps I should say that he is not passionate and we have had sexual intercourse only at rare intervals. I have told him this is not normal.

This is all revolting to me and I hate myself more every day. Is there something I can do to rid myself of this complex, or whatever it is? Am I going crazy? Sometimes I think so. Am I really that awful thing, a homosexualist? Be frank with me. I need it.

Sincerely yours,

Jun. 30, 1931

My dear Mrs.:

I have read with much interest your letter addressed to me in care of the *Ladies' Home Journal.*

I think you have probably made a correct diagnosis of yourself but I do not believe that you understand the diagnosis. Homosexuality is a phase of psychological development thru which all people go. In the normal person it is relinquished or at least submerged in favor of a preponderant degree of heterosexuality. Why this has not occurred in your case or why it has not occurred to a more satisfying degree, I cannot say. I am sure, however, that it is not something for you to reproach yourself about but rather something for you to attempt to get rid of in the interest of a happier union with your husband and a better motherhood.

I think the best way to get rid of it is by submitting oneself to psychoanalysis and I would recommend that you go to any length necessary to have a consultation with a psychoanalyst.... Take his advice and work out the reasons for your clinging to this infantile emotional attitude.

Sincerely yours,

Georgia
Sep. 28, 1931

Dear Dr. Menninger:

Perhaps this does not come under the head of *Mental Hygiene.* I hardly know where to turn since, under the conditions, a psychiatrist is out of the question. Properly speaking the problem is not mine, and yet it touches me nearly, so that I am giving you the part of the story with which I am familiar.

I met the girl I shall call W. two years ago. She was one of the younger children in a family where, figuratively speaking, "dementia scholastica" was apparently inherent. The parents were unusually strict: reading comic strips was forbidden on the grounds of vulgarity. Discipline was enforced by a leather belt. The child admired her big, handsome brothers above all others, and she competed with them for the parents' attention in vain. The father, who was a teacher, died just before W. entered college, leaving the family finances in a precarious condition. She secured a scholarship to a small, Southern teachers' college, took a degree in Manual Arts, and has the best job of any one of her class. As a high school girl she was in no sense a social success. As nearly as I can gather, her curiosity concerning the other sex earned her a punishment at the age of five that she never forgot; she was never curious again. As a freshman and sophomore she took quite an active part in campus life; president of her class, officer in her sorority and the glee club, and Art Editor of the annual. The next two years the glow wore off of being collegiate, she dropped out of everything pretty well and earned the name of being a little "queer." When she was a senior and I was a junior I knew her only by sight as a heavily-built, attractive looking girl, whom the voice instructor had discouraged because there are no songs written for women written low enough for W.'s voice. She was easily the brainiest girl in her class.

We were thrown together often and soon became very good friends. After a while I began to be aware that an unpleasant situation was shaping itself. We had a very definite physical attraction for each other. Neither of us is a simpleton; one doesn't live three years in a girls' school without a working knowledge of "crushes," besides a thorough grounding in psychology had showed us the reasons for such. I was quite confident of my own control and sense of humor, and counted on our approaching separation to clear the air. In January of the following year (we had not seen each other since May) she became ill and one of her friends wrote, asking me to come to see her in an effort to lift her depression. The intimacy of that three-weeks' visit proved too great a strain for our resistance; I am afraid things went much further than is generally the case. She was so upset when I left that I knew there must never, under any circumstances, be a repetition of that particular brand of idiocy. When W. came to see me in June I assumed the responsibility for our good behavior—and averaged one hour's sleep out of the twenty-four during those two weeks. The fact that I was not financially able kept me from a nervous breakdown.

15 Ours was only one of a series of similar affairs for her, beginning when she was thirteen. A year is about the average duration, and there is one every year. Before I left college, I went to one of the instructors in whose common sense I had much confidence and indirectly asked for her opinion of W. She said: "W. is one of our problems on the campus, a case of delayed adolescence." I happen to know that W. had asked for, but received no intelligent direction. This summer she took a course in psychoanalysis at the University of Illinois, and in desperation at the beginning of another affair with a woman, conducted an experiment with a man who had "biological doubts" concerning himself to see whether she had any attraction for the other sex. Though it was not consummated, she got the response. Consulting her family physician, W. was told that she had done a wise thing but the experience should have been completed and suggested that she do the completing. The man is kindly, reputable, middle-aged and married, but W. can not make up her mind even in the face of obvious attraction for him. Back in the small, university town, teaching school, she is tormented by a sort of super-susceptibility to obvious masculinity regardless of size, shape or previous condition. There is danger of her marrying the first man who inspires her with confidence.

Dr. Menninger, as nearly as I am able to judge, W. could no more make a go of a marriage than she could fly to Jericho. She is absolutely self-centered, though as unconsciously as a child. She has no conception of the give and take that makes for successful marriage, and [is] incapable of sustained interest in one person. Though she does not realize it [her] attitude of living is masculine rather than feminine, if such delineation is possible. Because of an unsympathetic mother and an uninterested older sister, she turns to me for advice, and I am getting distinctly out of my depth. Where does she go from here? Is she to waste so much of her time and brain fighting a recurrent homosexuality all her life? What do you think of marriage as a remedy? Any direction that you can give us as to where to find help and any suggestion you would be kind enough to give would be deeply appreciated.

Sincerely yours,

Jan. 3, 1932

My dear Miss:

I am very sorry to have been delayed in answering your letter of September 28.

I think you have analyzed the factors entering into your friend's case quite well.

My comments on your final paragraph would be these: I have the impression that you are still too anxious to control your friend. You seem to think it is up to you to decide what she should do and I get the impression that you are rather too much concerned as to whether or not she marries. Your logic may be correct but I do not see how one can make logic take any effect on a person who is so obviously driven by her emotions and her unconscious impulses.

Of course the girl needs help. Anyone who is struggling with homosexual tendencies needs help because society is constituted to favor only heterosexual investments. I do not think you are in a position to give her very much help because aside from your own personal difficulties which you frankly confess you cannot see the case clearly and dispassionately. Moreover, it is a technical job for which I presume you have had no training, and I can assure you it is very wise to turn such problems over to people who have had training.

Naturally one cannot withdraw interest from one's friends but I think you could do her the greatest favor if you would help her to see that she needs help from someone other than you, especially a psychiatrist and preferably a psychiatrist who is recognized as a competent psychoanalyst. Whatever it costs her in time, comfort, money, etc., must be measured against the happiness of her entire future.

Sincerely yours,

Mapping the Text

1. The exchange in this selection is through letters. What effect does this genre choice create in the expression of health-related concerns, as

compared with Dr. Menninger choosing to write a personal essay, or an article for a medical journal, or a feature article for a newspaper?

2. Read the letters written to Dr. Menninger carefully. What health concerns does each letter raise? Does the time period and context matter? Are these concerns still relevant today? Has anything changed?
3. What is your response to Dr. Menninger's advice? Given your own knowledge of the issues raised, do you consider his answers adequate and responsible? Why or why not? Are there issues that you would raise with Dr. Menninger?

Writing to Inquire

1. What issues of gender and sexuality do you see in these letters? How have these issues continued (or not) in our society? Is our contemporary world better able to address such concerns than the world in which Dr. Menninger and his correspondents lived?
2. What have been some of the effects of the treatment of homosexuality as medically "deviant"? Do some research to explore the history of cultural attitudes toward and treatment of lesbians and gay men. What role has medicine and science played in the history of cultural attitudes toward homosexuality? What role should medicine play today in educating the public? How successful has it been in playing this role?

Hands

OLIVER SACKS

Oliver Sacks (1933–) is Clinical Professor of Neurology at the Albert Einstein College of Medicine in New York. Born in England and educated at Oxford University, Sacks is considered a creative medical thinker who is noted for his concern with the psychological, moral, and spiritual dimensions of illness and treatment. Sacks is the author of seven books, including *The Man Who Mistook His Wife for a Hat* and *Awakenings* (1985), *An Anthropologist on Mars* (1995), and *The Island of the Colorblind* (1997). The majority of his books are actually case studies of patients, most of whom suffer from neurological dysfunctions. "Hands," the narrative below, is included in *The Man Who Mistook His Wife for a Hat.*

Madeleine J. was admitted to St. Benedict's Hospital near New York City in 1980, her sixtieth year, a congenitally blind woman with cerebral palsy, who had been looked after by her family at home throughout her life. Given this history, and her pathetic condition—with spasticity and athetosis, i.e., involuntary movements of both hands, to which was added a failure of the eyes to develop—I expected to find her both retarded and regressed.

She was neither. Quite the contrary: she spoke freely, indeed eloquently (her speech, mercifully, was scarcely affected by spasticity), revealing herself to be a high-spirited woman of exceptional intelligence and literacy.

'You've read a tremendous amount,' I said. 'You must be really at home with Braille.'

'No, I'm not,' she said. 'All my reading has been done for me—by talking-books or other people. I can't read Braille, not a single word. I can't do *anything* with my hands—they are completely useless.'

She held them up, derisively. 'Useless godforsaken lumps of dough—they don't even feel part of me.'

I found this very startling. The hands are not usually affected by cerebral palsy—at least, not essentially affected: they may be somewhat spastic, or weak, or deformed, but are generally of considerable use (unlike the legs, which may be completely paralysed—in that variant called Little's disease, or cerebral diplegia).

Miss J.'s hands were *mildly* spastic and athetotic, but her sensory capacities—as I now rapidly determined—were completely intact: she immediately and correctly identified light touch, pain, temperature, passive movement of the fingers. There was no impairment of elementary sensation, as such, but, in dramatic contrast, there was the profoundest impairment of perception. She could not recognise or identify anything whatever—I placed all sorts of objects in her hands, including one of my own hands. She could not identify—and she did not explore; there were no active 'interogatory' movements of her hands—they were, indeed, as inactive, as inert, as useless, as 'lumps of dough.'

This is very strange, I said to myself. How can one make sense of all this? There is no gross sensory 'deficit.' Her hands would seem to have the potential of being perfectly good hands—and yet they are not. Can it be that they are functionless—'useless'—because she had never used them? Had being 'protected,' 'looked after,' 'babied' since birth prevented her from the normal exploratory use of the hands which all infants learn in the first months of life? Had she been carried about, had everything done for her, in a manner that had prevented her from developing a normal pair of hands? And if this was the case—it seemed far-fetched, but was the only hypothesis I could think of—could she now, in her sixtieth year, acquire what she should have acquired in the first weeks and months of life?

Was there any precedent? Had anything like this ever been described—or tried? I did not know, but I immediately thought of a possible parallel—what was described by Leont'ev and Zaporozhets in their book *Rehabilitation of Hand Function* (Eng. tr. 1960). The condition they were describing was quite different in origin: they described a similar 'alienation' of the hands in some two hundred soldiers following massive injury and surgery—the injured hands felt 'foreign,' 'lifeless,' 'useless,' 'stuck on,' despite elementary neurological and sensory intactness. Leont'ev and Zaporozhets spoke of how the 'gnostic systems' that allow 'gnosis,' or perceptive use of the hands, to take place could be 'dissociated' in such cases as a consequence of injury, surgery and the weeks- or months-long hiatus in the use of the hands that followed. In Madeleine's case, although the phenomenon was identical—'uselessness,' 'lifelessness,' 'alienation'—it was lifelong. She did not need just to recover her hands, but to discover them—to acquire them, to achieve them—for the first time: not just to regain a dissociated gnostic system, but to construct a gnostic system she had never had in the first place. Was this possible?

The injured soldiers described by Leont'ev and Zaporozhets had normal hands before injury. All they had to do was to 'remember' what had been 'forgotten,' or 'dissociated,' or 'inactivated,' through severe injury. Madeleine, in contrast, had no repertoire of memory for she had never used her hands—and she felt she *had* no hands—or arms either. She had never fed herself, used the toilet by herself, or reached out to help herself, always leaving it for others to help her. She had behaved, for sixty years, as if she were a being without hands.

This then was the challenge that faced us: a patient with perfect elementary sensations in the hands, but, apparently, no power to integrate these sensations to the level of perceptions that were related to the world and to herself; no power to say, 'I perceive, I recognise, I will, I act,' so far as her 'useless' hands went. But somehow or other (as Leont'ev and Zaporozhets found with their patients), we had to get her to act and to use her hands actively, and, we hoped, in so doing, to achieve integration: 'The integration is in the action,' as Roy Campbell said.

Madeleine was agreeable to all this, indeed fascinated, but puzzled and not hopeful. 'How *can* I do anything with my hands,' she asked, 'when they are just lumps of putty?'

'In the beginning is the deed,' Goethe writes. This may be so when we face moral or existential dilemmas, but not where movement and perception have their origin. Yet here too there is always something sudden: a first step (or a first word, as when Helen Keller said 'water'), a first movement, a first perception, a first impulse—total, 'out of the blue,' where there was nothing, or nothing with sense before. 'In the beginning is the impulse.' Not a deed, not a reflex, but an 'impulse,' which is both more obvious and more mysterious than either. . . We could not say to Madeleine, 'Do it!' but we might hope for an impulse; we might hope for, we might solicit, we might even provoke one. . .

I thought of the infant as it reached for the breast. 'Leave Madeleine her food, as if by accident, slightly out of reach on occasion,' I suggested to her nurses. 'Don't starve her, don't tease her, but show less than your usual alacrity in feeding her.' And one day it happened—what had never happened before: impatient, hungry, instead of waiting passively and patiently, she reached out an arm, groped, found a bagel, and took it to her mouth. This was the first use of her hands, her first manual act, in sixty years, and it marked her birth as a 'motor individual' (Sherrington's term for the person who emerges through acts). It also marked her first manual perception, and thus her birth as a complete 'perceptual individual.' Her first perception, her first recognition, was of a bagel, or 'bagelhood'—as Helen Keller's first recognition, first utterance, was of water ('waterhood').

After this first act, this first perception, progress was extremely rapid. As she had reached out to explore or touch a bagel, so now, in her new hunger, she reached out to explore or touch the whole world. Eating led the way—the feeling, the exploring, of different foods, containers, implements, etc. 'Recognition' had somehow to be achieved by a curiously roundabout sort of inference or guesswork, for having been both blind and 'handless' since birth, she was lacking in the simplest internal images (whereas Helen Keller at least had tactile images). Had she not been of exceptional intelligence and literacy, with an imagination filled and sustained, so to speak, by the images of others, images conveyed by language, by the *word*, she might have remained almost as helpless as a baby.

A bagel was recognised as round bread, with a hole in it; a fork as an elongated flat object with several sharp tines. But then this preliminary analysis gave way to an immediate intuition, and objects were instantly recognised as themselves, as immediately familiar in character and 'physiognomy,' were immediately recognised as unique, as 'old friends.' And this sort of recognition, not analytic, but synthetic and immediate, went with a vivid delight, and a sense that she was discovering a world full of enchantment, mystery and beauty.

The commonest objects delighted her—delighted her and stimulated a desire to reproduce them. She asked for clay and started to make models: her first model, her first sculpture, was of a shoehorn, and even this was somehow imbued with a peculiar power and humour, with flowing, powerful, chunky curves reminiscent of an early Henry Moore.

And then—and this was within a month of her first recognitions—her attention, her appreciation, moved from objects to people. There were limits, after all, to the interest and expressive possibilities of things, even when transfigured by a sort of innocent, ingenuous and often comical genius. Now she needed to explore the human face and figure, at rest and in motion. To be 'felt' by Madeleine was a remarkable experience. Her hands, only such a little while ago inert, doughy, now seemed charged with a preternatural animation and sensibility. One was not merely being recognised, being scrutinised, in a way more intense and searching than any visual scrutiny, but being 'tasted' and appreciated meditatively, imaginatively and aesthetically, by a born (a newborn) artist. They were, one felt, not just the hands of a blind woman exploring, but of a blind artist, a meditative and creative mind, just opened to the full sensuous and spiritual reality of the world. These explorations too pressed for representation and reproduction as an external reality.

She started to model heads and figures, and within a year was locally famous as the Blind Sculptress of St. Benedict's. Her sculptures tended to be half or three-quarters life size, with simple but recognisable features, and with a remarkably expressive energy. For me, for her, for all of us, this was a deeply moving, an amazing, almost a miraculous, experience. Who would have dreamed that basic powers of perception, normally acquired in the first months of life, but failing to be acquired at this time, could be acquired in one's sixtieth year? What wonderful possibilities of late learning, and learning for the handicapped, this opened up. And who could have dreamed that in this blind, palsied woman, hidden away, inactivated, over-protected all her life, there lay the germ of an astonishing artistic sensibility (unsuspected by her, as by others) that would germinate and blossom into a rare and beautiful reality, after remaining dormant, blighted, for sixty years?

Postscript

The case of Madeleine J., however, as I was to find, was by no means unique. Within a year I had encountered another patient (Simon K.) who also had cerebral palsy combined with profound impairment of vision. While Mr K. had normal strength and sensation in his hands, he scarcely ever used them—and was extraordinarily inept at handling, exploring, or recognising anything. Now we had been alerted by Madeleine J., we wondered whether he too might not have a similar 'developmental agnosia'—and, as such, be 'treatable' in the same way. And, indeed, we soon found that what had been achieved with Madeleine could be achieved with Simon as well. Within a year he had become very 'handy' in all ways; and particularly enjoyed simple carpentry, shaping plywood and wooden blocks, and assembling them into simple wooden toys. He had no impulse to sculpt, to make reproductions—he was not a natural artist like Madeleine. But still, after a half-century spent virtually without hands, he enjoyed their use in all sorts of ways.

20 This is the more remarkable, perhaps, because he is mildly retarded, an amiable simpleton, in contrast to the passionate and highly gifted Madeleine J. It might be said that she is extraordinary, a Helen Keller, a woman in a million—but nothing like this could possibly be said of simple Simon. And yet the essential achievement—the achievement of hands—proved wholly as possible for him as for her. It seems clear that intelligence, as such, plays no part in the matter—that the sole and essential thing is *use.*

Such cases of developmental agnosia may be rare, but one commonly sees cases of acquired agnosia, which illustrate the same fundamental principle of use. Thus I frequently see patients with a severe 'glove-and-stocking' neuropathy, so-called, due to diabetes. If the neuropathy is sufficiently severe, patients go beyond feelings of numbness (the 'glove-and-stocking' feeling), to a feeling of complete nothingness or de-realisation. They may feel (as one patient put it) 'like a basket-case', with hands and feet completely 'missing.' Sometimes they feel their arms and legs end in stumps, with lumps of 'dough' or 'plaster' somehow 'stuck on.' Typically this feeling of de-realisation, if it occurs, is absolutely sudden. . . and the return of reality, if it occurs, is equally sudden. There is, as it were, a critical (functional and ontological) threshold. It is crucial to get such patients to *use* their hands and feet—even, if necessary, to 'trick' them into so doing. With this there is apt to occur a sudden re-realisation—a sudden leap back into subjective reality and 'life. . . provided there is sufficient physiological potential (if the neuropathy is total, if the distal parts of the nerves are quite dead, no such re-realisation is possible).

For patients with a severe but sub-total neuropathy, a modicum of use is literally vital, and makes all the difference between being a 'basket-case' and reasonably functional (with excessive use, there may be fatigue of the limited nerve function, and sudden derealisation again).

It should be added that these subjective feelings have precise objective correlates: one finds 'electrical silence,' locally, in the muscles of the hands and feet; and, on the sensory side, a complete absence of any 'evoked potentials,' at every level up to the sensory cortex. As soon as the hands and feet are re-realised, with use, there is a complete reversal of the physiological picture.

Mapping the Text

1. What goals do you think that Oliver Sacks has in his narrative "Hands"?
2. Sacks begins his narrative by pointing out the difference between his expectations and the realities of the woman about whom he is writing. How does this contrast set up the story? How does it establish a lens for seeing his point of view? What is his point of view? Do you find it convincing? Why or why not?

Writing to Inquire

1. Sacks marks the moment when Madeleine first used her hands as a pivotal one, as she went on from there to learn and to develop her talents. What does this situation illustrate about perceptions of disability and opportunities for people with disabilities in our society?
2. Does it matter in this narrative that Oliver Sacks is a medical doctor? Why?

From The Cancer Journals

AUDRE LORDE

Audre Lorde (1934–1992) described herself often with a litany of identities, Black, feminist, lesbian, poet, mother, warrior—and, later, person living with cancer. Her activist approach was to resist oppressions of whatever kind through the language she used. She began her professional career as a librarian and went on to become a nationally and internationally recognized poet and essayist. Her honors and awards include a National Endowment for the Arts Grant (1968); a Creative Arts Public Service Book Award for Poetry (1972); a nomination for a National Book Award; being named the Thomas Hunter Professor at Hunter College in New York (1987); being named the State Poet of New York (1991–1993). She published 18 books, including poetry volumes, essay collections, and a biography. Among these are *The First Cities* (1968); *Cables to Rage* (1970); *From a Land Where Other People Live* (1973); *Coal* (1976); *The Black Unicorn* (1978); *Zami: A New Spelling of My Name* (1982); *Sister Outsider: Essays and Speeches* (1984); and *A Burst of Light* (1988). The essay below is taken from *The Cancer Journals* (1980).

1

Each woman responds to the crisis that breast cancer brings to her life out of a whole pattern, which is the design of who she is and how her life has been lived. The weave of her every day existence is the training ground for how she handles crisis. Some women obscure their painful feelings surrounding mastectomy with a blanket of business-as-usual, thus keeping those feelings forever under cover, but expressed elsewhere. For some women, in a valiant effort not to be seen as merely victims, this means an insistence that no such feelings exist and that nothing much has occurred. For some women it means the warrior's painstaking examination of yet another weapon, unwanted but useful.

I am a post-mastectomy woman who believes our feelings need voice in order to be recognized, respected, and of use.

I do not wish my anger and pain and fear about cancer to fossilize into yet another silence, nor to rob me of whatever strength can lie at the core of this experience, openly acknowledged and examined. For other women of all ages, colors, and sexual identities who recognize that imposed silence about any area of our lives is a tool for separation and poweriessness, and for myself, I have tried to voice some of my feelings and thoughts about the travesty of prosthesis, the pain of amputation, the function of cancer in a profit economy, my confrontation with mortality, the strength of women loving, and the power and rewards of self-conscious living.

Breast cancer and mastectomy are not unique experiences, but ones shared by thousands of american women. Each of these women has a particular voice to be raised in what must become a female outcry against all preventable cancers, as well as against the secret fears that allow those cancers to flourish. May these words serve as encouragement for other women to speak and to act out of our experiences with cancer and with other threats of death, for silence has never brought us anything of worth. Most of all, may these words underline the possibilities of self-healing and the richness of living for all women.

5 There is a commonality of isolation and painful reassessment which is shared by all women with breast cancer, whether this commonality is recognized or not. It is not my intention to judge the woman who has chosen the path of prosthesis, of silence and invisibility, the woman who wishes to be 'the same as before.' She has survived on another kind of courage, and she is not alone. Each of us struggles daily with the pressures of conformity and the loneliness of difference from which those choices seem to offer escape. I only know that those choices do not work for me, nor for other women who, not without fear, have survived cancer by scrutinizing its meaning within our lives, and by attempting to integrate this crisis into useful strengths for change.

2

These selected journal entries, which begin 6 months after my modified radical mastectomy for breast cancer and extend beyond the completion of the essays in this book, exemplify the process of integrating this crisis into my life.

1/26/79
I'm not feeling very hopeful these days, about selfhood or anything else. I handle the outward motions of each day while pain fills me like a puspocket and every touch threatens to breech the taut membrane that keeps it from flowing through and poisoning my whole existence. Sometimes despair sweeps across my consciousness like luna winds across a barren moonscape. Ironshod horses rage back and forth over every nerve. Oh Seboulisa ma, help me remember what I have paid so much to learn. I could die of difference, or live—myriad selves.

2/5/79
The terrible thing is that nothing goes past me these days, nothing. Each horror remains like a steel vise in my flesh, another magnet to the flame. Buster has joined the rollcall of useless wasteful deaths of young Black people; in the gallery today everywhere ugly images of women offering up distorted bodies for whatever fantasy passes in the name of male art. Gargoyles of pleasure. Beautiful laughing Buster, shot down in a hallway for ninety cents. Shall I unlearn that tongue in which my curse is written?

3/1/79
It is such an effort to find decent food in this place, not to just give up and eat the old poison. But I must tend my body with at least as much care as I tend the compost,

particularly now when it seems so beside the point. Is this pain and despair that surround me a result of cancer, or has it just been released by cancer? I feel so unequal to what I always handled before, the abominations outside that echo the pain within. And yes I am completely self-referenced right now because it is the only translation I can trust, and I do believe not until every woman traces her weave back strand by bloody self-referenced strand, will we begin to alter the whole pattern.

4/16/79
The enormity of our task, to turn the world around. It feels like turning my life around, inside out. If I can look directly at my life and my death without flinching I know there is nothing they can ever do to me again. I must be content to see how really little I can do and still do it with an open heart. I can never accept this, like I can't accept that turning my life around is so hard, eating differently, sleeping differently, moving differently, being differently. Like Martha said, I want the old me, bad as before.

4/22/79
I must let this pain flow through me and pass on. If I resist or try to stop it, it will detonate inside me, shatter me, splatter my pieces against every wall and person that I touch.

5/1/79
Spring comes, and still I feel despair like a pale cloud waiting to consume me, engulf me like another cancer, swallow me into immobility, metabolize me into cells of itself; my body, a barometer. I need to remind myself of the joy, the lightness, the laughter so vital to my living and my health. Otherwise, the other will always be waiting to eat me up into despair again. And that means destruction. I don't know how, but it does.

9/79
There is no room around me in which to be still, to examine and explore what pain is mine alone—no device to separate my struggle within from my fury at the outside world's viciousness, the stupid brutal lack of consciousness or concern that passes for the way things are. The arrogant blindness of comfortable white women. What is this work all for? What does it matter whether I ever speak again or not? I try. The blood of black women sloshes from coast to coast and Daly says race is of no concern to women. So that means we are either immortal or born to die and no note taken, un-women.

10/3/79
I don't feel like being strong, but do I have a choice? It hurts when even my sisters look at me in the street with cold and silent eyes. I am defined as other in every group I'm a part of. The outsider, both strength and weakness. Yet without community there is certainly no liberation, no future, only the most vulnerable and temporary armistice between me and my oppression.

11/19/79

15 *I want to write rage but all that comes is sadness. We have been sad long enough to make this earth either weep or grow fertile. I am an anachronism, a sport, like the bee that was never meant to fly. Science said so. I am not supposed to exist. I carry death around in my body like a condemnation. But I do live. The bee flies. There must be some way to integrate death into living, neither ignoring it nor giving in to it.*

1/1/80

Faith is the last day of Kwanza, and the name of the war against despair, the battle I fight daily. I become better at it. I want to write about that battle, the skirmishes, the losses, the small yet so important victories that make the sweetness of my life.

1/20/80

The novel is finished at last. It has been a lifeline. I do not have to win in order to know my dreams are valid, I only have to believe in a process of which I am a part. My work kept me alive this past year, my work and the love of women. They are inseparable from each other. In the recognition of the existence of love lies the answer to despair. Work is that recognition given voice and name.

2/18/80

I am 46 years living today and very pleased to be alive, very glad and very happy. Fear and pain and despair do not disappear. They only become slowly less and less important. Although sometimes I still long for a simple orderly life with a hunger sharp as that sudden vegetarian hunger for meat.

4/6/80

Somedays, if bitterness were a whetstone, I could be sharp as grief.

5/30/80

20 *Last spring was another piece of the fall and winter before, a progression from all the pain and sadness of that time, ruminated over. But somehow this summer which is almost upon me feels like a part of my future. Like a brand new time, and I'm pleased to know it, wherever it leads. I feel like another woman, de-chrysalised and become a broader, stretched-out me, strong and excited, a muscle flexed and honed for action.*

6/20/80

I do not forget cancer for very long, ever. That keeps me armed and on my toes, but also with a slight background noise of fear. Carl Simonton's book, Getting Well Again, *has been really helpful to me, even though his smugness infuriates me sometimes. The visualizations and deep relaxing techniques that I learned from it help make me a less anxious person, which seems strange, because in other ways, I live with the constant fear of recurrence of another cancer. But fear and anxiety are not the same at all. One is an appropriate response to a real situation which I can accept and learn to work through just as I work through semi-blindness. But the other, anxiety, is an immobilizing yield to things that go bump in the night, a surrender to namelessness, formlessness, voicelessness, and silence.*

7/10/80
I dreamt I had begun training to change my life, with a teacher who is very shadowy. I was not attending classes, but I was going to learn how to change my whole life, live differently, do everything in a new and different way. I didn't really understand, but I trusted this shadowy teacher. Another young woman who was there told me she was taking a course in "language crazure," the opposite of discrazure (the cracking and wearing away of rock). I thought it would be very exciting to study the formation and crack and composure of words, so I told my teacher I wanted to take that course. My teacher said okay, but it wasn't going to help me any because I had to learn something else, and I wouldn't get anything new from that class. I replied maybe not, but even though I knew all about rocks, for instance, I still liked studying their composition, and giving a name to the different ingredients of which they were made. It's very exciting to think of me being all the people in this dream.

3

I have learned much in the 18 months since my mastectomy. My visions of a future I can create have been honed by the lessons of my limitations. Now I wish to give form with honesty and precision to the pain faith labor and loving which this period of my life has translated into strength for me.

Sometimes fear stalks me like another malignancy, sapping energy and power and attention from my work. A cold becomes sinister; a cough, lung cancer; a bruise, leukemia. Those fears are most powerful when they are not given voice, and close upon their heels comes the fury that I cannot shake them. I am learning to live beyond fear by living through it, and in the process learning to turn fury at my own limitations into some more creative energy. I realize that if I wait until I am no longer afraid to act, write, speak, be, I'll be sending messages on a ouija board, cryptic complaints from the other side. When I dare to be powerful, to use my strength in the service of my vision, then it becomes less important whether or not I am unafraid.

As women we were raised to fear. If I cannot banish fear completely, I can learn to count with it less. For then fear becomes not a tyrant against which I waste my energy fighting, but a companion, not particularly desirable, yet one whose knowledge can be useful.

I write so much here about fear because in shaping this introduction to *The Cancer Journals,* I found fear laid across my hands like a steel bar. When I tried to reexamine the 18 months since my mastectomy, some of what I touched was molten despair and waves of mourning—for my lost breast, for time, for the luxury of false power. Not only were these emotions difficult and painful to relive, but they were entwined with the terror that if I opened myself once again to scrutiny, to feeling the pain of loss, of despair, of victories too minor in my eyes to rejoice over, then I might also open myself again to disease. I had to remind myself that I had lived through it all, already. I had known the pain, and survived it. It only remained for me to give it voice, to share it for use, that the pain not be wasted.

Living a self-conscious life, under the pressure of time, I work with the consciousness of death at my shoulder, not constantly, but often enough to leave a mark upon all of my life's decisions and actions. And it does not matter whether this death comes next week or thirty years from now; this consciousness gives my life another breadth. It helps shape the words I speak, the ways I love, my politic of action, the strength of my vision and purpose, the depth of my appreciation of living.

I would lie if I did not also speak of loss. Any amputation is a physical and psychic reality that must be integrated into a new sense of self. The absence of my breast is a recurrent sadness, but certainly not one that dominates my life. I miss it, sometimes piercingly. When other one-breasted women hide behind the mask of prosthesis or the dangerous fantasy of reconstruction, I find little support in the broader female environment for my rejection of what feels like a cosmetic sham. But I believe that socially sanctioned prosthesis is merely another way of keeping women with breast cancer silent and separate from each other. For instance, what would happen if an army of one-breasted women descended upon Congress and demanded that the use of carcinogenic, fat-stored hormones in beef-feed be outlawed?

The lessons of the past 18 months have been many: How do I provide myself with the best physical and psychic nourishment to repair past, and minimize future damage to my body? How do I give voice to my quests so that other women can take what they need from my experiences? How do my experiences with cancer fit into the larger tapestry of my work as a Black woman, into the history of all women? And most of all, how do I fight the despair born of fear and anger and powerlessness which is my greatest internal enemy?

I have found that battling despair does not mean closing my eyes to the enormity of the tasks of effecting change, nor ignoring the strength and the barbarity of the forces aligned against us. It means teaching, surviving and fighting with the most important resource I have, myself, and taking joy in that battle. It means, for me, recognizing the enemy outside and the enemy within, and knowing that my work is part of a continuum of women's work, of reclaiming this earth and our power, and knowing that this work did not begin with my birth nor will it end with my death. And it means knowing that within this continuum, my life and my love and my work has particular power and meaning relative to others.

It means trout fishing on the Missisquoi River at dawn and tasting the green silence, and knowing that this beauty too is mine forever.

29 August 1980

Mapping the Text

1. Cancer is a disease about which historically this society has been silent. How does Audre Lorde counter this avoidance? On what basis does she make a case for speaking out?
2. Lorde chooses to speak by sharing her journal entries. What is the effect of her choosing this particular form? What does she accomplish by this means? What message does she convey by content and by form?
3. Who constitutes Lorde's audience? How might the message change if it were written for other audiences?

Writing to Inquire

1. Choose one of the journal entries in Lorde's selection as a springboard for expressing your own message. What form do you want your message to take? What idea do you want to convey? How does the form help or hinder your efforts?

The Clan of One-Breasted Women

TERRY TEMPEST WILLIAMS

Terry Tempest Williams (1955–) formerly naturalist-in-residence at the Utah Muslem of National History, lives in Castle Valley, Utah. She writes often of her intimate relationship with the natural world. She is the author of several books, including *Pieces of a White Shell: A Journey to Navajoland* (1984); *Coyote's Canyon* (1989); *Refuge: An Unnatural History of Place* (1991); *An Unspoken Hunger: Stories from the Field* (1994); and, most recently, *Desert Quarter: An Erotic Landscape* (1995); *Leap* (2000); and *Red: Passion and Patience in the Desert* (2001). In "The Clan of One-Breasted Women," Williams raises concerns about the impact of toxic environments on humans.

I belong to a Clan of One-Breasted Women. My mother, my grandmothers, and six aunts have all had mastectomies. Seven are dead. The two who survive have just completed rounds of chemotherapy and radiation.

I've had my own problems: two biopsies for breast cancer and a small tumor between my ribs diagnosed as a "borderline malignancy."

This is my family history.

Most statistics tell us breast cancer is genetic, hereditary, with rising percentages attached to fatty diets, childlessness, or becoming pregnant after thirty. What they don't say is living in Utah may be the greatest hazard of all.

5 We are a Mormon family with roots in Utah since 1847. The "word of wisdom" in my family aligned us with good foods—no coffee, no tea, tobacco, or alcohol. For the most part, our women were finished having their babies by the time they were thirty. And only one faced breast cancer prior to 1960. Traditionally, as a group of people, Mormons have a low rate of cancer.

Is our family a cultural anomaly? The truth is, we didn't think about it. Those who did, usually the men, simply said, "bad genes." The women's attitude was stoic. Cancer was part of life. On February 16, 1971, the eve of my mother's surgery, I accidently picked up the telephone and overheard her ask my grandmother what she could expect.

"Diane, it is one of the most spiritual experiences you will ever encounter."

I quietly put down the receiver.

Two days later, my father took my brothers and me to the hospital to visit her. She met us in the lobby in a wheelchair. No bandages were visible. I'll never forget her radiance, the way she held herself in a purple velvet robe, and how she gathered us around her.

10 "Children, I am fine. I want you to know I felt the arms of God around me."

We believed her. My father cried. Our mother, his wife, was thirty-eight years old.

A little over a year after Mother's death, Dad and I were having dinner together. He had just returned from St. George, where the Tempest Company was completing the gas lines that would service southern Utah. He spoke of his love for the country, the sandstoned landscape, bare-boned and beautiful. He had just finished hiking the Kolob trail in Zion National Park. We got caught up in reminiscing, recalling with fondness our walk up Angel's Landing on his fiftieth birthday and the years our family had vacationed there.

Over dessert, I shared a recurring dream of mine. I told my father that for years, as long as I could remember, I saw this flash of light in the night in the desert—that this image had so permeated my being that I could not venture south without seeing it again, on the horizon, illuminating buttes and mesas.

"You did see it," he said.

15 "Saw what?"

"The bomb. The cloud. We were driving home from Riverside, California. You were sitting on Diane's lap. She was pregnant. In fact, I remember the day, September 7, 1957. We had just gotten out of the Service. We were driving north, past Las Vegas. It was an hour or so before dawn, when this explosion went off. We not only heard it, but felt it. I thought the oil tanker in front of us had blown up. We pulled over and suddenly, rising from the desert floor, we saw it, clearly, this golden-stemmed cloud, the mushroom. The sky seemed to vibrate with an eerie pink glow. Within a few minutes, a light ash was raining on the car."

I stared at my father.

"I thought you knew that," he said. "It was a common occurrence in the fifties."

It was at this moment that I realized the deceit I had been living under. Children growing up in the American Southwest, drinking contaminated milk from contaminated cows, even from the contaminated breasts of their mothers, my mother—members, years later, of the Clan of One-Breasted Women.

20 It is a well-known story in the Desert West, "The Day We Bombed Utah," or more accurately, the years we bombed Utah: above ground atomic testing in Nevada took place from January 27, 1951, through July 11, 1962. Not only were the winds blowing north covering "low-use segments of the population" with fallout and leaving sheep dead in their tracks, but the climate was right. The United States of the 1950s was red, white, and blue. The Korean War was raging. McCarthyism was rampant. Ike was it, and the cold war was hot. If you were against nuclear testing, you were for a communist regime.

Much has been written about this "American nuclear tragedy." Public health was secondary to national security. The Atomic Energy Commissioner, Thomas Murray, said, "Gentlemen, we must not let anything interfere with this series of tests, nothing."

Again and again, the American public was told by its government, in spite of burns, blisters, and nausea, "It has been found that the tests may be conducted with adequate assurance of safety under conditions prevailing at the bombing reservations." Assuaging public fears was simply a matter of public relations. "Your best action," an Atomic Energy Commission booklet read, "is not to be worried about fallout." A news release typical of the times stated, "We find no basis for concluding that harm to any individual has resulted from radioactive fallout."

On August 30, 1979, during Jimmy Carter's presidency, a suit was filed, *Irene Allen v. The United States of America.* Mrs. Allen's case was the first on an alphabetical list of twenty-four test cases, representative of nearly twelve hundred plaintiffs seeking compensation from the United States government for cancers caused by nuclear testing in Nevada.

Irene Allen lived in Hurricane, Utah. She was the mother of five children and had been widowed twice. Her first husband, with their two oldest boys, had watched the tests from the roof of the local high school. He died of leukemia in 1956. Her second husband died of pancreatic cancer in 1978.

25 In a town meeting conducted by Utah Senator Orrin Hatch, shortly before the suit was filed, Mrs. Allen said, "I am not blaming the govern-

ment, I want you to know that, Senator Hatch. But I thought if my testimony could help in any way so this wouldn't happen again to any of the generations coming up after us. . . I am happy to be here this day to bear testimony of this."

God-fearing people. This is just one story in an anthology of thousands.

On May 10, 1984, Judge Bruce S. Jenkins handed down his opinion. Ten of the plaintiffs were awarded damages. It was the first time a federal court had determined that nuclear tests had been the cause of cancers. For the remaining fourteen test cases, the proof of causation was not sufficient. In spite of the split decision, it was considered a landmark ruling. It was not to remain so for long.

In April 1987, the Tenth Circuit Court of Appeals overturned Judge Jenkins's ruling on the ground that the United States was protected from suit by the legal doctrine of sovereign immunity, a centuries-old idea from England in the days of absolute monarchs.

In January 1988, the Supreme Court refused to review the Appeals Court decision. To our court system it does not matter whether the United States government was irresponsible, whether it lied to its citizens, or even that citizens died from the fallout of nuclear testing. What matters is that our government is immune: "The King can do no wrong."

30 In Mormon culture, authority is respected, obedience is revered, and independent thinking is not. I was taught as a young girl not to "make waves" or "rock the boat."

"Just let it go," Mother would say. "You know how you feel, that's what counts."

For many years, I have done just that—listened, observed, and quietly formed my own opinions, in a culture that rarely asks questions because it has all the answers. But one by one, I have watched the women in my family die common, heroic deaths. We sat in waiting rooms hoping for good news, but always receiving the bad. I cared for them, bathed their scarred bodies, and kept their secrets. I watched beautiful women become bald as Cytoxan, cisplatin, and Adriamycin were injected into their veins. I held their foreheads as they vomited green-black bile, and I shot them with morphine when the pain became inhuman. In the end, I witnessed their last peaceful breaths, becoming a midwife to the rebirth of their souls.

The price of obedience has become too high.

The fear and inability to question authority that ultimately killed rural communities in Utah during atmospheric testing of atomic weapons is the same fear I saw in my mother's body. Sheep. Dead sheep. The evidence is buried.

35 I cannot prove that my mother, Diane Dixon Tempest, or my grandmothers, Lettie Romney Dixon and Kathryn Blackett Tempest, along with my aunts developed cancer from nuclear fallout in Utah. But I can't prove they didn't.

My father's memory was correct. The September blast we drove through in 1957 was part of Operation Plumbbob, one of the most intensive series of bomb tests to be initiated. The flash of light in the night in the desert, which I had always thought was a dream, developed into a family nightmare. It took fourteen years, from 1957 to 1971, for cancer to manifest in my mother—the same time, Howard L. Andrews, an authority in radioactive fallout at the National Institutes of Health, says radiation cancer requires to become evident. The more I learn about what it means to be a "downwinder," the more questions I drown in.

What I do know, however, is that as a Mormon woman of the fifth generation of Latter-day Saints, I must question everything, even if it means losing my faith, even if it means becoming a member of a border tribe among my own people. Tolerating blind obedience in the name of patriotism or religion ultimately takes our lives.

When the Atomic Energy Commission described the country north of the Nevada Test Site as "virtually uninhabited desert terrain," my family and the birds at Great Salt Lake were some of the "virtual uninhabitants."

One night, I dreamed women from all over the world circled a blazing fire in the desert. They spoke of change, how they hold the moon in their bellies and wax and wane with its phases. They mocked the presumption of even-tempered beings and made promises that they would never fear the witch inside themselves. The women danced wildly as sparks broke away from the flames and entered the night sky as stars.

40 And they sang a song given to them by Shoshone grandmothers:

Ah ne nah, nah	Consider the rabbits
nin nah nah—	How gently they walk on the earth—
ah ne nah, nah	Consider the rabbits
nin nah nah—	How gently they walk on the earth—
Nyaga mutzi	We remember them
oh ne nay—	We can walk gently also—
Nyaga mutzi	We remember them
oh ne nay—	We can walk gently also—

The women danced and drummed and sang for weeks, preparing themselves for what was to come. They would reclaim the desert for the sake of their children, for the sake of the land.

A few miles downwind from the fire circle, bombs were being tested. Rabbits felt the tremors. Their soft leather pads on paws and feet recognized the shaking sands, while the roots of mesquite and sage were smoldering. Rocks were hot from the inside out and dust devils hummed unnaturally. And each time there was another nuclear test, ravens watched the desert heave. Stretch marks appeared. The land was losing its muscle.

The women couldn't bear it any longer. They were mothers. They had suffered labor pains but always under the promise of birth. The red hot pains beneath the desert promised death only, as each bomb became a stillborn. A contract had been made and broken between human beings and the land. A new contract was being drawn by the women, who understood the fate of the earth as their own.

Under the cover of darkness, ten women slipped under a barbed-wire fence and entered the contaminated country. They were trespassing. They walked toward the town of Mercury, in moonlight, taking their cues from coyote, kit fox, antelope squirrel, and quail. They moved quietly and deliberately through the maze of Joshua trees. When a hint of daylight appeared they rested, drinking tea and sharing their rations of food. The women closed their eyes. The time had come to protest with the heart, that to deny one's genealogy with the earth was to commit treason against one's soul.

At dawn, the women draped themselves in mylar, wrapping long streamers of silver plastic around their arms to blow in the breeze. They wore clear masks, that became the faces of humanity. And when they arrived at the edge of Mercury, they carried all the butterflies of a summer day in their wombs. They paused to allow their courage to settle.

45 The town that forbids pregnant women and children to enter because of radiation risks was asleep. The women moved through the streets as winged messengers, twirling around each other in slow motion, peeking inside homes and watching the easy sleep of men and women. They were astonished by such stillness and periodically would utter a shrill note or low cry just to verify life.

The residents finally awoke to these strange apparitions. Some simply stared. Others called authorities, and in time, the women were apprehended by wary soldiers dressed in desert fatigues. They were taken to a white, square building on the other edge of Mercury. When asked who they were and why they were there, the women replied, "We are mothers and we have come to reclaim the desert for our children."

The soldiers arrested them. As the ten women were blindfolded and handcuffed, they began singing:

You can't forbid us everything
You can't forbid us to think—
You can't forbid our tears to flow
And you can't stop the songs that we sing.

The women continued to sing louder and louder, until they heard the voices of their sisters moving across the mesa:

Ah ne nah, nah
nin nah nah—

Ah ne nah, nah
nin nah nah—
Nyaga mutzi
oh ne nay—
Nyaga mutzi
oh ne nay—

"Call for reinforcements," one soldier said.

"We have," interrupted one woman, "we have—and you have no idea of our numbers."

I crossed the line at the Nevada Test Site and was arrested with nine other Utahns for trespassing on military lands. They are still conducting nuclear tests in the desert. Ours was an act of civil disobedience. But as I walked toward the town of Mercury, it was more than a gesture of peace. It was a gesture on behalf of the Clan of One-Breasted Women.

50 As one officer cinched the handcuffs around my wrists, another frisked my body. She found a pen and a pad of paper tucked inside my left boot.

"And these?" she asked sternly.

"Weapons," I replied.

Our eyes met. I smiled. She pulled the leg of my trousers back over my boot.

"Step forward, please," she said as she took my arm.

55 We were booked under an afternoon sun and bused to Tonopah, Nevada. It was a two-hour ride. This was familiar country. The Joshua trees standing their ground had been named by my ancestors, who believed they looked like prophets pointing west to the Promised Land. These were the same trees that bloomed each spring, flowers appearing like white flames in the Mojave. And I recalled a full moon in May, when Mother and I had walked among them, flushing out mourning doves and owls.

The bus stopped short of town. We were released.

The officials thought it was a cruel joke to leave us stranded in the desert with no way to get home. What they didn't realize was that we were home, soul-centered and strong, women who recognized the sweet smell of sage as fuel for our spirits.

Mapping the Text

1. Terry Tempest Williams is often categorized as a "nature writer." What in this story supports this view? How is she using nature (or the environment) to convey the message of this story?
2. Many contemporary problems and concerns have ties to technology. What are the technological implications in "The Clan of One-Breasted Women"?

Writing to Inquire

1. Make a list of the issues Williams raises in this story. Discuss your list with others in the class. Write an essay in which you discuss the message of Williams's story and use quotations from the story to support your view of the response(s) she would like to elicit about the issues.

Facing AIDS

RAE LEWIS-THORNTON

Rae Lewis-Thornton (1962–), diagnosed with AIDS at the age of 23, is an AIDS educator and activist who draws on her own life and experiences to inform young people about AIDS and to emphasize to them that AIDS is a disease that does not discriminate. Lewis-Thornton has been active also in political arenas, serving as national youth director for Jesse Jackson's 1984 and 1988 presidential campaigns, as Illinois state youth coordinator for the 1988 Dukakis presidential campaign, and as Senator Carol Mosley Braun's 1992 senatorial campaign advance coordinator. Ms. Lewis-Thornton was the first African-American woman to tell her story to a national magazine. In addition to her continued efforts around HIV/AIDS, she is currently working on a Master's in Divinity at McCormick Theological Seminary in Chicago, Illinois. The narrative below is an example of the way in which Lewis-Thornton tells her own story as a person with AIDS and functions as a health activist.

The day I found out, I was so calm. The counselor noticed it, too.

"How am I supposed to be?" I asked her.

"I'm just used to people freaking out on me," she said. "It doesn't mean that you have AIDS. You may never get AIDS. It just means that you are HIV-positive. Do you understand?"

"I'm okay," I told her.

5 I walked out of the American Red Cross office and into the Washington, D.C., sunshine, flagged a cab and went back to work. I worked late that night.

It was 1986 and I was 24. I'd just been given a death sentence.

I am the quintessential Buppie: I'm young—32. Well educated. Professional. Attractive. Smart. I've been drug- and alcohol-free all my life. I'm a Christian. I've never been promiscuous. Never had a one-night stand. And I am dying of AIDS.

I've been living with the disease for nine years, and people still tell me that I am too pretty and intelligent to have AIDS. But I do. I discovered I was HIV-positive when I tried to give blood at the office. I have no idea who infected me or when it happened.

Still, there is one thing I am absolutely certain of: I am dying now because I had one sexual partner too many. And I'm here to tell you one is all it takes.

10 Make no mistake about it, AIDS is a horrible, sick, foul, filthy disease. I *look* great to everybody. But I don't feel great. My life is an endless round of doctors' visits, night sweats, chronic yeast infections, debilitating medications and body-numbing fatigue. I've had to give up a promising career as a political organizer. I may never live to finish graduate school. I can't get health insurance. I will never have children. Some days I am filled with rage and despair. Other days I am at peace. I am trying to peacefully coexist with a disease that eats away at my body each and every day. I am its host—and I don't have any choice in the matter.

I've always been this independent person, the life of the party. My mama locked me out when I was 17, and I've been steppin' ever since. I made a way out of no way. Stayed off the welfare rolls and managed never to get pregnant. I graduated magna cum laude from college. I've worked with and dated the best and the brightest. It's scary that eventually I will have to surrender my independence and my vibrancy to this disease.

But the day I found out my HIV status, I wasn't thinking of dying. I'd already overcome a lot, and I believed there was nothing I couldn't conquer. God never put an obstacle in my way that I couldn't get around. I *knew* I would be okay.

However, there was one little matter that sent me into a panic: telling the man I was dating. I knew I had to do it. But every time I thought about it, my stomach would twist into knots. We'd used condoms for the entire three or four months we'd been seeing, each other, so I was pretty sure he hadn't infected me—nor I him. He was a seminary student studying to be a minister; I was an activist working overtime to help my people. We'd enjoyed some good times—and some good sex. We weren't in love; we were in like.

That night, as I waited for my boyfriend. I did his laundry in the apartment where I lived alone. As I washed and folded his clothes, I tried to still the jitters in my belly.

15 I told him as soon as he walked in the door, schoolbooks in hand.

"You're *what?*" he said.

I took a deep breath and repeated my little bombshell.

"I'm HIV-positive. When I gave blood at the Red Cross, they told me I'm HIV-positive."

He chuckled as if he thought I was playing.

20 "No, I'm very serious," I told him. I immediately gave him the name and number of the place where he should be tested. Just in case.

Then he realized I was serious. "You bitch," he said. As he grabbed his laundry and walked out my door, he declared, "This is over." I never spoke to him again.

That's when the sorrow came. He left, and I was all alone. *Damn,* I thought, *I'm HIV-positive, and the man I was kicking it with just walked out of my life!*

The rest of the night. I called a couple of ex-boyfriends, informing them of what had happened and searching for clues as to who had infected me. I cried and cried, and prayed and prayed, and cried some more. The next day I repeated the process. No man admitted that he had infected me. Not one. No one came to the reseue. Not one. I realized that I was in this alone. There would be no man to take care of me or tell me that it was going to be okay.

Superwoman kicked in. I told myself that this was a small thing—I could overcome *anything* with the help of God. My childhood had been both dysfunctional and abusive, and very early in my life I believed that God was making me strong. I was sure that I would overcome HIV.

25 I was referred to the National Institutes of Health (NIH) in Bethesda, Maryland, where I began participating in a long-term study on blood and HIV. With the study I visited a doctor once every six months. There they'd draw my blood for tests and give me a physical exam.

Initially, outside of the study I had no medical treatment for my illness. For years I didn't tell my private physician about my HIV status. I was not sick: there were no symptoms. I pushed AIDS and HIV to the back of my mind. I did minimal reading on the subject. I ignored the television specials. I told only a small group of friends about my condition, and the only time we ever discussed it was after my semiannual NIH visit. My buddies were convinced I would never get AIDS. So was I.

In fact, during those first six years, the only two situations where HIV became real for me were during my doctors' visits and when I would meet a man I wanted to date. Then I would have to come clean.

The male problem became easier over time. I found that if a man really wanted to be with me sexually, he would. I didn't yet have AIDS. I looked healthy. Most men—if not all—were willing to go for it. To them HIV seemed to be a small problem easily managed with latex. And I was serupulous about using condoms; none of the men I dated ever tested positive for HIV.

Meanwhile, the specter of AIDS hovered in the background. Each time I went for my NIH checkup, I anxiously awaited the results. Had the virus progressed to AIDS? I would get my answer in writing, and each time the result was the same: My immune system was stable. The virus was not active. I found great comfort in this bit of news. It helped me to continue my life the same way I had before.

30 After four years I began taking AZT, a drug prescribed for HIV patients to delay the progression of the virus. I was told the medication was not a big deal; the side effects would be minimal and would last no longer than about three weeks. If only I had been so lucky: My body rejected the medicine for almost six months. I was constantly nauseated and had excruciating headaches that lasted for days, even weeks at a time. I gained 15 pounds and sneaked naps every available second. Still, I suffered in secret, finishing my undergraduate degree and senior honors thesis while working part-time. Superwoman returned. The AZT would keep AIDS at bay.

But it wasn't to last. By winter 1992 the worst was confirmed: I had AIDS. I *really* had AIDS. I sank into a deep depression.

So far I haven't been hospitalized. But there have been problems. When I visited Paris last year, my period started a week early. It continued for 22 days. Another time my period lasted for an hour. My doctor said, "It's dysfunctional uterine bleeding. Women with AIDS get that all the time." I'm getting used to the irregularities.

What's harder to get used to is the side effects of the nine to 14 pills that I swallow each day. One drug, ddI (an antiretroviral medication), gave me extreme diarrhea. It was horrible. I had no control.

Not so long ago, my doctor noticed that I'd lost weight. I didn't think much of it until the day I went shopping for a New Year's Eve dress. I grabbed a bunch of size 10's. I tried them all on. Then I went back and got some 8's. I eventually bought a size 4. Me, who'd always fluctuated between a 10 and a 12. I mean, I was built like a sistah! I had *meat* on my bones. But no more. That day I cried.

35 Through it all, my friends have been very supportive, very pushy. Because I'm not on the best of terms with either my birth mother or the woman who raised me, my friends are my family. One friend is always bugging me to come over for dinner. Another will drive across town to tempt me with food. They put a lot of pressure on me. "If you think healthy," they say, "you'll be healthy."

It's easy for them to say that because I still look well. But my friends don't see me when I'm in too much pain to get out of bed. They don't see the illness. And I feel like screaming, "Don't you get it? I'm *not* going to be okay. I have AIDS!"

But somewhere in the midst of my grief I slowly began to gain some control. I started seeing a therapist twice a week. Antidepressants reined in my emotions. I read everything I could find on AIDS and HIV.

Yet I was lonely, so lonely. I dreaded coming home to an empty house, with no one waiting for me. But home was my only refuge—the one place where I could hide from this ugly disease.

Dating meant rejection and false hope, though men were still attracted to me. When I met men, I didn't waste a lot of time. After several dates. I told them of my illness. Some were brave enough to spend time with me. But invariably, after several weeks or months, it would prove too much. They couldn't handle the magnitude of the illness: the depression, the pills, the diarrhea, the despair, and ultimately the fear of infection. One brother, a successful businessman, often called just to see if I still had AIDS. Eventually I told him to stop calling. It was just too painful.

40 I felt isolated. Damaged. My anger at God was profound, and I questioned Him often. What were the lessons in dying? Was He punishing me? Forsaking me? Hadn't I suffered enough as a child? I tried to live my life by the example that Christ set. What had I done wrong?

Superwoman was exhausted. Living with AIDS was too complex. Yes, I was tired, but my spirit wanted to go on. I understood that the person I used to be was gone. The new person had AIDS. Could there be a way to live in peace with my disease? I went within myself for the answers. I surrendered to God. I just let go.

It was then that I found answers. The first step in the healing process was to move beyond the shame and stigma of having AIDS. For six years I had hidden my secret from all but a handful of my closest friends. When I came out with my illness, it felt as if tons of bricks had been lifted off my body. I told people at work. I told all my friends. Gossip moved quickly, but the response was overwhelming. People reached out to me in a special way. My support base became strong and powerful. Last March I told the woman who raised me that I was sick. Telling Mama was the hardest thing I've had to do. She still won't accept that I'm dying. She tells me the doctors must be wrong. And I tell her again and again. "Mom, it's been nine years. I *know.*"

I buried Superwoman. And in doing so I found my strengths. One day I was asked to speak to some high-school students about my disease. The prospect frightened me. But as I stood in front of those kids, with nothing prepared and with no idea of where to begin. I asked God to simply use me. The words poured out. Some students cried. Others missed class to hear me speak again. One such student worked her way into my life. We talk often. I try to keep her out of trouble and on the right track.

More than a year and perhaps 70,000 high-school students later. I understand that my suffering is not in vain. I just have to tell the story—as a lesson for others. I talk to young people not just about AIDS but also about destructive sexual behavior, about taking control of their bodies before it is too late.

Surrendering myself to God is the smartest decision I have made in this odyssey. As I let go of the old person. God created a new one. This new Rae has a purpose. What I discovered was that God uses us in ways not of our own understanding. And once you let go and let God, He reveals the plan. When you accept it, blessings flow.

And my blessings are abundant. I have not worked in more than a year, but I've never done without. I recently married. Only when I defined my new life with AIDS did I open my mind and heart to a nice guy. And that's just what I got—a nice guy. I met Kenny through my minister early this year and knew right away he was my soul mate. God sent me a man grounded in Christianity and bursting with compassion, love—and fun.

Nonetheless, the disease continues to progress in my body. Managing AIDS is a full-time job. My immune system is impaired. At last count my T-cells were at an all-time low of 66. I often have night sweats. I spend days at a time in bed. Where it once was hidden, AIDS has now become a very real part of my life.

What I have clearly learned is that, unlike people, AIDS does not discriminate. My wish is that all women would realize this and take control of their lives and their bodies. To not use a condom in this day and age is *suicide.*

I can see the light at the end of the tunnel. Of course there are some bad times. I am sad some days. Other days I am scared, and I'm terrified of the destruction AIDS is causing to my body. Some nights I cry long and hard.

The difference now is that I have someone to hold me and wipe the tears. And most important, I don't wallow in the sadness. Kenny wipes the tears, and I keep going.

50 The misery, the despair, the hopelessness are gone. Of course I am dying. But I will live until I do!

Mapping the Text

1. Rae Lewis-Thornton is an activist. Consider the characteristics of activism and develop a definition that seems to capture adequately who activists are and what they do. Use this definition to analyze Lewis-Thornton's essay. What features, if any, suggest that it is indeed written by an activist?
2. Lewis-Thornton wrote this essay during an era in which one purpose of such writing was to place a human face on AIDS. To what extent is Lewis-Thornton fulfilling this purpose? How does the title of the essay function?

Writing to Inquire

1. Imagine yourself living in an era in which AIDS is not a global epidemic, but something else (for example, polio or tuberculosis) is a major disease and topic of concern. Write a narrative in which you assume the point of view of a specific person at a specific moment of public understanding about the disease. For example, think about what it would be like to be a 14-year-old boy in 1947 before the invention of the Salk vaccine. You know two people who have contracted polio. One is expected to die soon, as her respiratory system has become affected. The other has lost the use of his legs. There is no cure. The adults around you seem to know little about the disease, and doctors don't seem to know how to treat it. You and your parents are afraid. How, given this point of view, do you see things? What do you have to say? What do you think should be happening or not happening? After you have written your narrative, write a short essay in which you explain how you made your decisions as a writer of the narrative and why.

What I Did on My Summer Vacation

NELS P. HIGHBERG

Nels Highberg (1969–) is a doctoral student in language, literacy, and rhetoric in the Department of English at the University of Illinois at Chicago and holds masters degrees in women's studies and comparative studies from Ohio State University. He has served as production editor of the journal *Literature and Medicine* and has published essays in collections such as *Generation Q* (1996) Highberg's work as a scholar crosses boundaries between rhetoric and composition, queer theory, and comparative literature.

Summer is over. I am back in school. Summer was very, very busy. I did a lot. I got married in May. I loved a man. His name was Blane. Blane loved me. I am also a man. We decided to have a wedding ceremony even though it wouldn't count. My friends from high school came. My friends from work and college came. His friends came. He said he loved me and wanted to live with me in front of everybody. Then I said it. Then we all ate cake and drank Coke. It was fun. We were very tired. We went to our home. I slept very well. I had my arm around him all night.

I moved all of my stuff to our home. I bought a desk and a bookcase. I bought a washer and a dryer. Blane was still very tired. He sat in bed and watched television. He saw many game shows and soap operas. At night we watched television together. We ate dinner in bed. Then he would sleep. I would go downstairs to work.

My mother wanted us to go on vacation with her and my family. Blane wanted to go but he was still tired and wanted to stay in bed. He told her he couldn't go. He told me to go and I went. We went to Washington, D.C. I saw the Washington Monument. We went to the zoo and I saw monkeys and panda bears. I called Blane many times. I told him about the monkeys and panda bears. He was happy I called. I missed him very much.

He was in bed when I got home. He was more tired. He couldn't walk to the bathroom. He had to wear diapers. His mother and brother flew all the way from Philadelphia. His mother was very sad. They sat downstairs and talked about him. I sat with him and fed him and watched television when he slept. They took him away to Philadelphia.

5 My mother came to Houston to take me home. I had to move my desk and my bookcase. I put everything in my bedroom. I put my washer and dryer outside with a sign that said "For Sale." There was a lot of stuff in my room. I could not walk around. I tried to help my mother. I cut the grass. I put wet clothes on the line outside so that the wind would dry them. I fed our dog, Pugsley. He is very cute and very fat. He likes to run and jump. He was glad I was there. Every night he slept in my room with me. He slept on the floor.

It was July. It was very, very hot outside. Blane's brother called. Blane was dead. I walked around outside for a very long time. I could not go to the funeral. It was too much money. The airline said I was not family. I could buy a special ticket only for August. I sat at home. I watched television. I watched *The Price Is Right.* Klondike bars are $2.99. I watched *As the World Turns.* Evan slept with Emily. He told Courtney. She broke up with him. I watched *Where in the World Is Carmen Sandiego?* I know where Albania is. I sat in front of the air conditioner and watched television every day.

In August I flew to Philadelphia. I saw a pile of dirt covered with dead flowers. Some ribbons on the flowers said "Son." Some said "Brother." It was Blane's grave. I sat in front of it for a long time. I sat under a pine tree. The wind was blowing. Then I walked around Philadelphia. I saw Independence

Hall and Benjamin Franklin's grave. Then I rode a train to New York City. I liked the train. I walked down Broadway. I sat in Central Park. I watched the Hudson River. I sat at a table on a sidewalk and ate something called Middle Eastern. It was green. It was good.

I flew back to Texas. I packed all of my stuff into boxes again. I moved to an apartment. I said goodbye to my mother. I said goodbye to Pugsley. I went back to my job. I am back in school. Summer is over.

8 February 1993, 12:13 PM

Bill Clinton is president. Pugsley died. Mama said Eddie had gallstone surgery. I'm delivering a paper in Arkansas on women's video art in March. Pam had a baby, a boy. I still miss you. Gerrie's dating a guy named Eric. The sun is shining. Madonna has the number one song. I'm wearing your red shirt and hippo tie. Elisa moved to her own apartment. Garth Brooks and Reba McEntire are playing at the rodeo. I'm dating someone. He's taking me to Dallas in two weeks. Adele is in love. Malcolm is in lust. Dr. Yongue is lecturing on Emily Dickinson at two o'clock. I'm going to have pizza for lunch. Arthur Ashe died. Tria graduated last semester. Prince Charles and Lady Diana split. The bus was late this morning. My last test was negative. This guy behind me is talking about Jesus. You will never know any of this.

Mapping the Text

1. The title of this essay makes use of a classic writing assignment: Write about how you spent your summer vacation. How does Nels Highberg use the ordinariness of this assignment to say something that is not so ordinary? What effect does he create by using this approach?
2. What message do you think Highberg seeks to convey?
3. How would you describe the writing style Highberg uses in this selection? What stylistic and rhetorical strategies does he use? Why do you think he made some of these stylistic decisions? What are the effects of the voice, persona, and style of this essay on you as a reader?

Writing to Inquire

1. What do we know now about AIDS that we did not know in 1981, when the first cases were officially reported by the CDC?
2. Think about Highberg's point of view. Consider that there are several other possible points of view in this account. Choose someone in the essay other than Highberg and speculate about what this person's experience might have been. Write your own essay or narrative from this perspective.

How to Watch Your Brother Die

MICHAEL LASSELL

Michael Lassell (1947–) is a prolific writer and literary critic who writes both poetry and prose. He is the author of three books of poetry: *Poems for Lost and Un-Lost Boys* (1985); *Decade Dance* (1990); and *A Flame for the Touch that Matters* (1998). He has written a book of short stories, *Certain Ecstasies* (1999), and a collection of poetry, stories, and essays, *The Hard Way.* His critical work includes the following edited and coedited collections: *The Name of Love: Classic Gay Love Poems* (1995); *Eros in Boystown: Contemporary Gay Poems about Sex* and *Men Seeking Men: Adventures in Gay Personals* (1998); and *The World in Us: Lesbian and Gay Poetry of the Next Wave: An Anthology* (2001).

For Carl Morse

When the call comes, be calm.
Say to your wife, "My brother is dying. I have to fly
to California."
Try not to be shocked that he already looks like
a cadaver.
Say to the young man sitting by your brother's side,
"I'm his brother."
Try not to be shocked when the young man says,
"I'm his lover. Thanks for coming."

Listen to the doctor with a steel face on.
Sign the necessary forms.
Tell the doctor you will take care of everything.
Wonder why doctors are so remote.

Watch the lover's eyes as they stare into
your brother's eyes as they stare into
space.
Wonder what they see there.
Remember the time he was jealous and
opened your eyebrow with a sharp stick.
Forgive him out loud
even if he can't
understand you.
Realize the scar will be
all that's left of him.

Over coffee in the hospital cafeteria
say to the lover, "You're an extremely good-looking
young man."
Hear him say,

"I never thought I was good enough looking to
deserve your brother."

Watch the tears well up in his eyes. Say,
"I'm sorry. I don't know what it means to be
the lover of another man."
Hear him say,
"It's just like a wife, only the commitment is
deeper because the odds against you are so much
greater."
Say nothing, but
take his hand like a brother's.

Drive to Mexico for unproven drugs that might
help him live longer.
Explain what they are to the border guard.
Fill with rage when he informs you,
"You can't bring those across."
Begin to grow loud.
Feel the lover's hand on your arm
restraining you. See in the guard's eye
how much a man can hate another man.
Say to the lover, "How can you stand it?"
Hear him say, "You get used to it."
Think of one of your children getting used to
another man's hatred.

Call your wife on the telephone. Tell her,
"He hasn't much time.
I'll be home soon." Before you hang up say,
"How could anyone's commitment be deeper than
a husband and wife?" Hear her say,
"Please. I don't want to know all the details."

When he slips into an irrevocable coma,
hold-his lover in your arms while he sobs,
no longer strong. Wonder how much longer
you will be able to be strong.
Feel how it feels to hold a man in your arms
whose arms are used to holding men.
Offer God anything to bring your brother back.
Know you have nothing God could possibly want.
Curse God, but do not
abandon Him.

Stare at the face of the funeral director
when he tells you he will not

embalm the body for fear of
contamination. Let him see in your eyes
how much a man can hate another man.

Stand beside a casket covered in flowers,
white flowers. Say,
"Thank you for coming," to each of several hundred men
who file past in tears, some of them
holding hands. Know that your brother's life
was not what you imagined. Overhear two
mourners say, "I wonder who'll be next?" and
"I don't care anymore,
as long as it isn't you."

Arrange to take an early flight home.
His lover will drive you to the airport.
When your flight is announced say,
awkwardly, "If I can do anything, please
let me know." Do not flinch when he says,
"Forgive yourself for not wanting to know him
after he told you. He did."
Stop and let it soak in. Say,
"He forgave me, or he knew himself?"
"Both," the lover will say, not knowing what else
to do. Hold him like a brother while he
kisses you on the cheek. Think that
you haven't been kissed by a man since
your father died. Think,
"This is no moment not to be strong."

Fly first class and drink Scotch. Stroke
your split eyebrow with a finger and
think of your brother alive. Smile
at the memory and think
how your children will feel in your arms,
warm and friendly and without challenge.

Mapping the Text

1. Poetry is often considered a useful form for expressing intense feelings and critical human moments. How does Michael Lassell's poem show evidence of this view?
2. Reread Lassell's poem in order to make a list of personal, social, and public issues he suggests.
3. What meaning(s) do you think Lassell intends to convey through this poem?

Writing to Inquire

1. Write a personal essay in which you discuss when you first began to know about AIDS and how, and what your degree of understanding suggests about the issues and implications of AIDS awareness among your age group or among people in general.

AIDS and the Responsibility of the Writer

SARAH SCHULMAN

Sarah Schulman (1958–) is an activist, a journalist, and a writer. She has published plays as well as literary criticism, and her work is commonly studied in queer theory courses. Her works include novels, such as *Girls, Vision, and Everything: A Novel* (1986), *Rat Bohemia* (1995), and *Shimmer* (1998), as well as plays and essays. Schulman's work often focuses on the lives of lesbians within their own, often urban, communities.

First I want to talk about writing and then I want to talk about responsibility. I've just published a novel, *People in Trouble,* about the AIDS crisis. I spent three years working on it and in the process confronted a lot of questions relevant to AIDS fiction. When I began working there were very few books about AIDS. They were mostly about facing one's own illness or the death of a lover. I knew that I was not writing from either of these perspectives and so identified for myself the category of "witness fiction," so that I could understand the position of my words in this event.

To be writing about something of this enormity when it surrounds you leaves those of us who write about AIDS no possibility of objectivity. Nor can there be any conclusiveness since the crisis and our responses to it change radically and daily. So, I knew that I was committing to ideas and impressions that would already be history by the time the book actually reached readers.

In *People in Trouble* I imagined a small demonstration by AIDS activists outside Saint Patrick's Cathedral in New York City. Two-and-a-half years ago I imagined forty nervous men cautiously standing up to disrupt a religious service. By the time the book was published, there had been a real life demonstration of seven thousand angry men and women confronting the Cathedral. In this case, the community I was writing for and about made the boundaries of my imagination obsolete.

There is no existing vocabulary for discussing AIDS. To expect one would be unreasonable since this is an event that we will be spending generations trying to understand and define. In order to discuss it in novel form, I needed to identify a series of words that were generally resonant.

This is a challenging task in a culture that does not acknowledge truth and a community that is emotionally overwhelmed. I started out by making lists of hundreds of details pertaining to the crisis. Rock Hudson at the airport being whisked off to Paris. Watch alarms going off in public places reminding their bearers to take their AZT. Men with teddy bears. Friends spreading AL721 on their toast in the morning. People spending their life savings on Ampligen or Dextrane Sulfate. Finding out later that those drugs were worthless. Then I chose fifty that I felt would be meaningful symbols to large groups of people, symbols that might have lasting resonance. It was an attempt to identify a vocabulary while understanding that to establish this group of words is perhaps all that the first generation of AIDS writers can do in the hope that future writers can use this foundation to develop a comprehensive and challenging literature. I also had to reject words. Words that were being used to distort. Words that were lies. Words like *innocent victim.* Words like *general population.*

5 I also made a decision for myself personally that I was not writing a novel documenting the life and death of a single individual. Instead I wanted to use the examples of people's lives to express a precise political idea—namely, how personal homophobia becomes societal neglect. That there is a direct relationship between the two and that this nation needs to confront this configuration in order to adequately address this crisis.

In the past I've written novels about the interior lives of people in marginal communities, and this enabled me to have some approval from the straight press because my work could be read voyeuristically. This time I knew I wanted to accuse straight people—to bring them into the literature in a manner equal to the role they play in this crisis: one of apathy, neglect, and denial. For that reason I had to write a primary character who was a straight man. That's when I discovered that just as literature has distorted women into the virgin/whore dichotomy, straight men have been distorted into the hero/villain dichotomy—neither of which I find generally appropriate. So, when I committed to violating these conventions by describing someone unaware of how other people are living and unaware of how much power he wields, I found myself vulnerable to being dismissed with, "Oh, she's a lesbian, she hates men." There does not yet exist a way for lesbian and gay male writers to address the straight male character and his societal power without being subjected to this dismissal. The fact remains that marginal people know how they live and they know how the dominant culture lives. Dominant culture people only know how *they* live. And so the people with the most power have the least information. And to state this is still considered didactic or extreme.

I had more surprises when I began touring with the book. Since, except in New York and San Francisco, men do not generally come to my readings, or those of lesbian writers in general, my audiences are mostly women. In cities where AIDS is not as much in people's daily lives as it is for us in San

Francisco and New York, I found that people no longer wanted to talk about writing or books. They wanted to talk about AIDS. They asked me various questions about transmission in addition to expressing levels of discomfort with the politics of AIDS activism. One question that came up over and over again is. "If the shoe were on the other foot and this were happening to lesbians, don't you think the guys wouldn't help *us?*" And of course I had to answer *yes,* but, at the same time, not give in to the homophobic stereotype that gay men hate women and assert, instead, that this lack of reciprocity exists between all men and all women. Straight men are noticeably absent from the battle to win full abortion rights for straight women—and they're *married* to them. It's more about being raised male in this culture which insists that the male experience is the objective, neutral experience from which all other experiences can be generalized. This is why we see so little awareness or advocacy by gay men on women's behalf. Not only with regard to AIDS but also with regard to sexual assault, economic oppression, cancer, and abortion. However, I know at the same time that gay men have been allowed to die because they are *gay,* not because they are men. And I also know, from two years of involvement in ACT UP, New York, that there is a general understanding in that organization that sexism is not only wrong—it is politically inefficient.

On a human level, the fact of the gay community going co-ed is something that has certainly enriched my life personally and intellectually, although it has been a strange experience, in a country where women earn half of what men earn, to go from a movement of all women to a movement of men. I guess it is something akin to experiencing heterosexual privilege for the first time because we now have access to the money, power, visibility, and resources that men move with in this culture, and I hope we can use these resources to benefit all of us.

10 I'd like to say one more thing about responsibility. There are people in this room, many people, who would not be alive today if it weren't for ACT UP. There is no book that got any drug released, any drug trial opened, or any service provided. Reading a book may help someone decide to take action, but it is not the same thing as taking action. The responsibility of every writer is to take their place in the vibrant, activist movements along with everybody else. The image created by the male intellectual model of an enlightened elite who claim that its artwork is its political work is parasitic and useless for us. At the same time I don't think that any writer must write about any specific topic or in any specific way—writers have to be free of formal and political constraints in their work so that the community can grow in many directions. But, when they're finished with their work, they need to be at demonstrations, linking envelopes and putting their bodies on the line with everybody else. We live in the United States of Denial, a country where there is no justice. The way we get justice is by confronting the structures that oppress us in a manner that is most threatening to those structures. That means in person as well as in print.

Mapping the Text

1. Schulman raises interesting notions about the responsibilities of writers. Do you agree or disagree that writers have social or public responsibilities rather than just the personal privilege of expressing themselves?
2. What are the genre issues Schulman raises in her desire to write about AIDS? What are your thoughts about these issues?

Writing to Inquire

1. Consider how writers have presented the issue of AIDS over the last three decades. Use library or Internet sources to identify and explore in one type of publication (for example, a health magazine, a popular magazine, a news magazine, or a newspaper). Choose a snapshot view at three or four points (for example, 1981, 1991, and 2001). How did writers in this publication present AIDS-related issues? What words and images dominated? What images, details, and appeals were used? With each selection, identify the audience, message, purpose, etc. What conclusions do you draw from your analysis?
2. What inferences can you make, based on the data you find, about the relationships between class, age, geographical location, and lifestyle, and the prevalence of HIV and AIDS?

Visiting the Sick

ELLIOT N. DORFF

Elliot N. Dorff is a rabbi and professor of philosophy at the University of Judaism in Bel-Air, California, as well as vice president of the Jewish Family Services organization in Los Angeles. Born and raised in Milwaukee, Dorff's works include numerous articles as well as *Matters of Life and Death: A Jewish Approach to Matters of Modern Medical Ethics* (1998), and *Knowing God: Jewish Journeys to the Unknowable* (1992). Rabbi Dorff has written on subjects ranging from family violence to medical ethics. "Visiting the Sick" is excerpted from *Matters of Life and Death.*

The communal measures necessary to preserve or restore health are not limited to physical factors alone, for sick people are not simply physical organisms afflicted with a virus or bacterium; they are whole human beings. Thus even if medicine cannot cure a person, Jews have a collective duty to attend to his or her emotional, psychological, and social well-being. As the Zohar, a thirteenth-century work of Jewish mysticism, says, "If a physician cannot give his patient medicine for his body, he should [at least] make sure that medicine is given him for his soul."[1] Visiting the sick *(bikkur ḥolim)* is a requirement of every Jew (not just the rabbi, doctor, or nurse); and so at least as early as the fourteenth century and continuing today in many congregations of all denominations, synagogues have established Bikkur Ḥolim societies consisting of members who have taken it upon themselves to make sure that the sick people in their community are visited, whether they have family doing that or not.[2]

Visiting the sick is important not only to give emotional and social support to the ailing but for physical reasons as well. As some of the talmudic and medieval sources we will consider below point out, often physical illness is affected significantly by the state of the other parts of a person's being. Certainly, those who are visited often have much more motivation to fight to overcome their disease, for it is clear that others want them to survive. This makes the social setting in which people cope with their illness absolutely critical in their prognosis for recovery.

We meet most people in the active course of our working lives. Recreation with friends commonly involves going out somewhere to play ball, watch a movie, listen to a concert, or enjoy a meal together. Good friends and some family members visit each other at home, but everyone is aware that that is only one setting in which their relationship is played out, that they could choose at any time to leave home to do something somewhere else.

Illness changes all of that. The sick person must stay at home or in the hospital; she or he cannot leave to engage in normal work routines or to do something enjoyable with friends. This requires colleagues, family members, and friends to make time in their schedules to go to the sick person's home or hospital room and to interact with the person in strange circumstances. Visiting the sick is therefore both inconvenient and alien.

5 The encounter, in fact, is uncomfortable for both the sick person and the visitors. The ill feel not only the physical pains of their illness but also the loss of self-esteem associated with diminished capacity. They do not know how to handle themselves in these new, strange circumstances. This awkwardness is compounded by the additional embarrassment of having friends see them dressed in pajamas. Moreover, the ill often feel as if they are intruding on their friends' time and making them do something they really would prefer not to do.

Their suspicions are frequently accurate. Friends and family feel annoyed and put upon by this new duty. They may also feel ill at ease because they are not used to interacting with people in this diminished state and do not know what to say or do. This uneasiness is compounded by general discomfort with illness: seeing a sick person starkly reminds them of their own vulnerability.

For all these reasons, people commonly avoid visiting the sick as much as they can, thus isolating the ill and making their recovery all the harder. After all, if you were bedridden by illness, especially by a long-term one, and were seldom visited, you might well feel that nobody cared about you.

This would diminish your motivation to combat your illness or, when it could not be cured, to learn how to live life as fully as possible with it. In extreme cases, you might even think seriously about taking your life.

Conversely, if you were visited often, it would be hard to wallow in self-pity. After all, you would reason, one or more people care enough about me to see me often, and I cannot let them down. This would reinforce your will to live.

The Jewish tradition was keenly aware that recovery from illness involves the patients' minds and spirits as well as their bodies. The Talmud says this:

> Rabbi Abba son of Rabbi Ḥanina said: He who visits an invalid takes away a sixtieth of his pain [or, in another version, a sixtieth of his illness]. . . .
>
> When Rabbi Dimi came [from Palestine], he said: He who visits the sick causes him to live, while he who does not causes him to die. How does he cause this?. . . He who visits the sick prays that he may live, . . . [while] he who does not visit the sick prays neither that he may live nor die.[3]

The Talmud here is asserting two aspects of the spiritual elements of recovery. On a social plane, those who visit the sick help to shift the patient's focus from the pain and degradation of the illness to the joy of the company of friends and family. They thus take away a sixtieth of the pain of the illness. Visitors also reassure the patient that family and friends are keenly interested in their recovery, and they remind the patient of life outside the sickroom. They thereby reinforce the patient's determination to overcome the illness altogether, or at least as many of its effects as possible. Visitors are thus instrumental in motivating the patient to follow a medical regimen of healing, however tedious or painful it may be, and so, in the Talmud's alternative reading, they effectively take away a sixtieth of the patient's illness itself.

10 Visitors affect the patient on a more religious plane as well. By praying for the patient, and by indicating that prayers are being offered in the synagogue on his or her behalf, visitors invoke the aid of God, the ultimate Healer. Jewish prayer is traditionally done in community, in part because Jewish sources maintain that communal prayer persuades God to grant a request more effectively than private prayer does.[4] Visitors' prayers and those recited in the synagogue on behalf of the patient thus throw the weight of the entire community behind the patient's own plea to God for recovery.

The tradition links sickness with sin, and so the Talmud records this remark by Rabbi Alexandri in the name of Rabbi Hiyya bar Abba: "A sick person does not recover from illness until all his or her sins are forgiven, as [the juxtaposition in the following verse shows, for] it is written, 'God forgives all your sins, God heals all your diseases' (Psalms 103:3)."[5] Jewish confessional prayers, though, are expressed in the first person plural, for

Jewish sources maintain that requests for forgiveness are most effective when *we* recite them as part of a community rather than when I recite them by myself.[6] Praying for the sick may thus alleviate feelings of guilt connected with the disease, for now the entire community is asking for both forgiveness and healing.

Visitors must also pay attention to the physical needs of the sick. Thus the Talmud tells the following story:

> Rabbi Ḥelbo fell ill. Rabbi Kahana then went [to the house of study] and proclaimed, "Rabbi Ḥelbo is ill." Nobody, however, visited him. Rabbi Kahana rebuked them [the disciples], saying, "Did it ever happen that one of Rabbi Akiba's students fell ill, and the [rest of the] disciples did not visit him?" So Rabbi Akiba himself entered [Rabbi Ḥelbo's house] to visit him, and because they swept and sprinkled the ground before him [that is, cleaned the house and put it in order], Rabbi Ḥelbo recovered. Rabbi Akiba then went forth and lectured: He who does not visit the sick is like one who sheds blood.[7]

Taking physical care of the sick can include not only cleaning house but shopping for groceries, doing laundry, taking over carpool duties, and seeing to the other needs of the patient's family. Depending upon the circumstances, it can also include more direct physical interventions like taking the patient for a ride in a wheelchair (if medically permitted), feeding the patient (if necessary), and attending to the patient's other physical needs.

Mostly, though, visiting the sick involves talking with the patient, and that is often what causes the greatest degree of discomfort for the visitor. People often do not know what to say or do. Some would rather not hear about the patient's aches and pains, much less about a painful or dangerous procedure the patient has just endured or is facing, because such talk makes them sad and engenders thoughts about their own vulnerability. The food served at the facility and the weather quickly pall as topics of conversation. Since few of us are trained in effective visiting techniques, visitors soon feel frustrated in their desires to help and support the patient. All of these feelings deter people from visiting the sick any more than they feel they absolutely must.

The Jewish tradition has some practical advice for making such visits more pleasant and effective:[8]

1. *Identifying who should visit the sick.* The duty of visiting the sick is not confined to friends and family—or, for that matter, to rabbis; rather, everyone is obligated to visit the sick, regardless of the relative social station of the patient and the potential visitor.[9] Jews are obligated to visit not only ill Jews but non-Jews as well, as part of our duty to promote peace between Jews and non-Jews.[10] "Anyone who visits the sick has, as it were, taken away a part of the illness and made it easier to bear," says Maimonides, "and anyone who neglects to visit the sick has, as it were, shed blood."[11]

2. *Ensuring that a visit is welcome.* Through consultation with the patient's family or friends, potential visitors should make sure that a visit would be neither embarrassing nor physically detrimental to the patient.[12]
3. *Timing the day of one's visit.* "As a matter of good manners," according to the Jerusalem Talmud,[13] only family and close friends should visit during the first two days of an illness, and others should wait until the third day. That restriction does not apply, however, to patients with acute, life-threatening illnesses.
4. *Timing the hours of one's visit.* The hours of visitation must not interfere with the patient's medical treatment or unduly tax the patient's strength.[14] Hospitals have the right to restrict visiting hours to assure this. If the patient is helped by visits, though, they need not be limited to one per day.[15]
5. *Positioning oneself to make the patient feel comfortable.* Visitors who stand or sit higher than the patient's head accentuate the patient's incapacity in contrast to the visitor's able-bodied state. They also make the patient look up to them, thus further symbolizing a gap in status. To avoid these feelings, visitors should sit down to communicate equality and support.[16]
6. *Attending to the patient's needs.* As discussed above, part of the point of visiting the sick is to learn how one can help the patient or the family cope with the illness. Since patients and their close family members are often reticent in asking for help, visitors need to offer it. They should make one or two specific suggestions so that the patient or family members understand that the offer is serious and get a sense of the scope of what the visitor is willing to do.
7. *Praying for and with the patient.* Jewish sources state that one fulfills the commandment of visiting the sick only if one prays with and for the patient for healing.[17] Many Jews—patients as well as visitors—are unaccustomed to prayer, but illness is often an occasion for a felt need to pray. One can use the short, standard formula stated in the Talmud and codes—*ha-makom ye'raḥem 'aleikha be-tokh ḥolei yisrael* (May the All-Present have mercy on you among the sick of Israel)[18]—and then add whatever one thinks appropriate and meaningful, whether in Hebrew or in English.[19] Many prayer books include suggested texts, often from the Book of Psalms.
8. *Speaking with the patient.* Aside from praying for and with the patient, how do you fill the time? What do you talk about? Conversations normally flow out of joint activities, but patients cannot engage in the work or recreation that usually brings people together and gets them talking. Moreover, the illness itself and the strange setting of a sickbed, especially in a hospital, make visitors feel uncomfortable. How, then, can they overcome these obstacles to meaningful and helpful conversation?

> Some topics that should be raised are practical in nature. Specifically, if the patient has a life-threatening illness and has not previously filled out a will or a living will for health care, visitors can help the patient specify his or her desired disposition of property and preferred course of medical treatment.

15 Regardless of the seriousness of the illness, visitors can also help a patient complete an ethical will. Ethical wills are often read and reread (or heard and reheard) by descendants of their author. They can be a treasure trove of information about the author and the extended family, the kind of information we all want to know as part of learning about ourselves.

Ethical wills, though, are just as valuable to their authors, especially if they are bedridden for a long time. Patients who know that they have a task to accomplish in order to leave their children and (especially) grandchildren a record of their experiences, values, thoughts, dreams, and hopes will redouble their efforts to live as long as they can so that they can complete this important project.

Ethical wills are also a boon for visitors. In providing a program and goal for visits, helping a patient complete an ethical will can transform visits from boring and uncomfortable encounters to be avoided as much as possible to interesting and meaningful exchanges for all concerned.

Most time spent with the patient, though, does lend itself to discussion of specific decisions or projects. How, then, should visitors fill the time of their visit?

Jewish legal sources are silent about this, but Jewish theological concepts provide important clues. Every human being, according to the Torah, bears the dignity of being created in the image of God. The key to speaking with sick people, then, is to bolster that sense of worth.

20 Illness is inherently degrading: the person is not capable of engaging in normal activities. Visitors must be especially on guard, then, to avoid infantilizing the patient, for doing so reinforces his or her sense of loss of power and honor. Visitors should rather engage the patient in conversations on the level and subjects of the patient's normal interests.

Sometimes ill people can even stretch beyond the topics that normally occupy them. One of the most enlightening experiences of my early rabbinic career was giving a series of lectures on Jewish theology to residents of a Jewish nursing home. The group included former doctors, lawyers, teachers, and entrepreneurs. The residents themselves, all college graduates, had specifically asked for these classes, even though none of them had ever studied Jewish theology before, because they were sick of playing Bingo. They had been intellectually active at earlier stages of their lives, and their physical illnesses now had not significantly changed their intellectual interests or even their mental capacity—except that I had to speak just a little more slowly and loudly than I usually do. The social workers who arranged these lessons had also warned me not to be deterred by the fact that sometimes the students' eyes would close, for in older people closed eyes do not necessarily signal sleep. As the social workers predicted, some of the people who had their eyes closed through most of the class later asked me pointed questions about what I had said; they clearly were awake and listening. The students even read assignments in preparation for the class from specially prepared sheets with enlarged print. I wish my younger students were always as well prepared!

Visitors do not normally discuss Jewish theology, but this example will, I hope, make clear that conversations with patients should be challenging and should cover a wide variety of topics. The very normalcy of such discussions communicates that the illness has not diminished the visitor's respect for the patient's intelligence and humanity and that the remainder of even a very limited life can still be filled with meaningful conversation.

Finally, in the spirit of Nel Noddings's book *On Caring,*[20] I would like to pose some questions. Do male and female patients need different kinds of emotional caring? Do male and female visitors, as a rule, offer different forms of caring to patients, whether male or female? Put more broadly, are gender issues relevant to emotional caring?

Apart from the contemporary work of Noddings, Carol Gilligan, Deborah Tannen, and many others,[21] there is one hint in the Jewish tradition that gender does affect one's mode of caring and one's need for specific types of care. Traditionally, a Hebrew name comprises the person's given name(s) and then "son of," or "daughter of," that person's *father's* name, for it is the man who represented the family in the community. When a blessing is invoked in the synagogue to heal an ill person, however, that person is usually referred to as son or daughter of his or her *mother.* One common explanation for this custom in the folklore is that when one is ill, one needs the kind of caring that mothers are known to give.[22] In recognition of changing gender roles, and in greater fulfillment of the command to honor one's father *and mother,* contemporary Conservative and Reform congregations now often call people to the Torah using both their father's and mother's name; and blessings for those who are ill increasingly name both parents as well. Fathers, after all, can and should be involved in caring for their sick children just as much as mothers are. Nevertheless, it may be the case that in illness, as in other areas of life, fathers care for their children somewhat differently than mothers do, and sons may need somewhat different kinds of care than daughters do. The traditional practice at least hints in that direction, and it is a direction, I think, worth considering.

Notes

Key to Notes

The following abbreviations are used in the notes throughout this book:

M. = Mishnah (edited by Rabbi Judah ha-Nasi, president of the Sanhedrin ["Judah the Prince"] c. 200 C.E.)

T. = Tosefta (edited by Rabbi Hiyya and Rabbi Oshaiya c. 200 c.e.)
J. = Jerusalem (Palestinian) Talmud (editor unknown, but edited c. 400. c.e.)
B. = Babylonian Talmud (edited by Ravina and Rav Ashi c. 500 c.e.)
M.T. = Maimonides' *Mishneh Torah* (completed 1177 c.e.)
S.A. = *Shulḥan Arukh,* completed in 1565 c.e. by Joseph Caro, a Spanish (Sephardic) Jew, with glosses by Moses Isserles indicating differences in German and eastern European (Ashkenazic) Jewish practice
All modern books and articles are referred to in the notes solely by their author(s) or editor(s) and date. They are listed with full bibliographical information in the Bibliography.

[1] *Zohar,* I, 229b.
[2] Rabbi Nissim Gerondi (c. 1360) is the first to mention such societies, perhaps because in earlier times Jews lived in communities sufficiently small to ensure that everyone would be visited even without such a formal structure to make sure that that happened. See *Encyclopedia Judaica* 14:1498.
[3] B. *Nedarim* 39b–40a.
[4] B. *Berakhot* 6a; 7b–8a; J. *Berakhot* 5:1; cf. M.T. *Laws of Prayer* 8:1.
[5] B. *Nedarim* 41a.
[6] B. *Ta'anit* 8a; cf. M.T. *Laws of Prayer* 8:1.
[7] B. *Nedarim* 39b–40a.
[8] As the endnotes in the various paragraphs of this list will indicate, the primary places where the classical codes deal with this topic are in M.T. *Laws of Mourning,* chap. 14, and in S.A. *Yoreh De'ah* 335. Other sources in English on Jewish practices regarding visiting the sick include Klein (1979), pp. 271–272; Krauss (1988), esp. chaps. 16 and 17, pp. 123–139; Schur (1987), esp. chap. 6, pp. 66–69; Abraham (1980), chap. 35, pp. 135–138; and a new pamphlet, *Bikkur Holim* (1992), for all the Conservative congregations.
[9] B. *Shabbat* 127a; B. *Sotab* 14a; B. *Nedarim* 39–40b; B. *Bava Kamma* 100a; M.T. *Laws of Mourning* 14:4.
[10] B. *Gittin* 61a; M.T. *Laws of Mourning* 14:12; M.T. *Laws of Kings* 10:12; S.A. *Yoreh De'ah* 335:9.
[11] M. T. *Laws of Mourning* 14:4.
[12] Thus Maimonides (M.T. *Laws of Mourning* 14:5) says this: "We visit neither those with bowel disease nor those with eye disease nor those with headaches, for visits are hard on them," either because the patient will be embarrassed by the disease, as in bowel trouble, or because a visit will add to the patient's pain and impede recovery, as in the cases of patients with eye trouble or frequent headaches, for whom speaking with visitors is, according to talmudic medicine (B. *Nedarim* 41a), physically and psychologically burdensome.
[13] J. *Pe'ah* 3:9. Other sources (e.g., *Bayit Ḥadash* on *Tur* 335; M.T. *Laws of Mourning* 14:5; S.A. *Yoreh De'ah* 335:1 and *Turei Zahav* there) tie this to the talmudic story (B. *Nedarim* 40a) of Rava, who, when he fell sick, asked that on the first day of the illness his servants not make it known, "lest his fortune be impaired"—that is, lest people talk about it generally and thus attract evil spirits. Relatives and close friends who commonly came into the house to visit would not arouse such spirits.
[14] Thus Maimonides (M.T. *Laws of Mourning* 14:5) says: "We do not visit the sick in the first or last three hours of the day because at those times the caregivers are busy with the needs of the sick person." The Talmud (B. *Nedarim* 40a) and, following that,

the *Shulḥan Arukh* (*Yoreh De'ah* 335:4) give a less medical and more theological reason: During the first three hours of the day, the illness is generally less acute than it is later, and so visitors will not remember to offer prayers on behalf of the sick because they will not think it necessary. During the last three hours of the day, the illness may appear so serious that visitors will despair from offering prayers for the sick, thinking that prayer in such serious cases would inevitably be ineffective. This would be theologically spurious reasoning, for God, according to the tradition, is always open to hear prayer and may respond in even the direst of circumstances, but the *Shulḥan Arukh* is here reflecting what people may think anyway.

[15]M.T. *Laws of Mourning* 14:4: "People should visit many times during the day, and all who add to their visits are to be praised—as long as they do not burden the patient."

[16]M.T. *Laws of Mourning* 4:6; Tosafot on B. *Shabbat* 127a; S.A. *Yoreh De'ah* 35:3, gloss.

[17]Ramban (Naḥmanides), *Torat ha-Adam*, "Sha'ar ha-Mehush"; S.A. *Yoreh De'ah* 335:4, gloss.

[18]B. *Shabbat* 12b; S.A. *Yoreh De'ah* 335:6.

[19]S.A. *Yoreh De'ah* 335:5. Hebrew and/or the vernacular may be used in the presence of the patient; presumably the visitor should base the decision his or her own abilities and the knowledge and sensitivities of the patient. In the synagogue, though, Jewish law states that the prayer for healing should be done in Hebrew.

[20]Nel Noddings (1984). I raise these questions even though years before Noddings wrote her book claiming that women resolve moral questions on the basis of caring rather than the moral rules that men tend to use; a man, Milton Mayeroff, wrote a book with almost the exact same title claiming, "In the sense in which a man can ever be said to be at home in the world, he is at home not through dominating, or explaining, or appreciating, but through caring and being cared for." See Milton Mayeroff (1971).

[21]Carol Gilligan (1982). Deborah Tannen (1990).

[22]The custom of using the mother's name in a prayer for the sick (instead of the more usual custom of identifying the person as so-and-so, son or daughter of *the father*): Scherman (1986), pp. 144–145, 442–443. No explanation is given there, and the explanation I found in two published sources links it to the question the Zohar raises in interpreting Psalm 86:16, namely, why did David, the presumed author of the Psalm, identify himself as "the son of your maidservant" rather than "son of Yeshai," his father? From this the Zohar concludes that when asking for God's deliverance, individuals should identify themselves by the name of their mother, whose identity is beyond question. See also Psalms 116:16; J. D. Eisenstein (1938), p. 220; and Abraham Isaac Sperling (1957), p. 164, para. 353.

The rationale in the folklore, though, as told to me by my father, is that one uses one's mother's name when praying for healing since mothers generally take care of their sick children more than fathers do—or did! Moreover, the Hebrew term for mercy, *raḥamim,* is etymologically related to the word for womb, *reḥem,* and so mothers are associated linguistically in Hebrew with mercy, and that has an effect on the popular imagination. (Along these lines, though, it is interesting that Sperling [1957], in a note on p. 164, cites one source saying that to acquire God's mercy it would be better to identify the patient by his or her *father's* name. Although Sperling himself rejects that custom and quotes another source to reaffirm the custom of using the mother's name, the very existence of a source that suggests using the father's name specifically to induce God to be more merciful is a clear blow against sexual stereotypes!)

Mapping the Text

1. The title of this essay, "Visiting the Sick," brings in a different point of view of illness. What personal, social, and public responsibilities do you think individuals have with respect to visiting the sick? What are the benefits and consequences?
2. In this essay, Elliot Dorff connects visiting the sick to cultural and spiritual values. What message do you think he seeks to convey?
3. At the end of his essay, Dorff shares practical advice about making visits to people who are sick. Do you think this advice is useful?

Writing to Inquire

1. Write an essay in which you discuss whether people seem to have the same attitudes about "visiting the sick" they once had. If, in your view, anything has changed about these attitudes, how do you account for the changes? If, in your view, attitudes are pretty much the same, how do you account for this continuity?
2. Dorff suggests that modes of caring may be gendered. What evidence does he offer for this claim? Do you agree or disagree with this idea? How would you develop your responses to Dorff in an essay?

CALLS TO ACTION AND RESPONSE

Stem-Cell Speech

George W. Bush

George W. Bush (1946–), forty-third president of the United States of America, was elected to office in 2000 amid controversy over election proceedings. Before entering politics, his career included working in the energy industry and owning the Texas Rangers baseball franchise. He was elected governor of Texas in 1994, a position that he held until becoming president. The defining moment of Bush's presidency may well be the terrorist attacks on New York City and Washington, D.C., on September 11, 2001. However, before these attacks, stem-cell research already had arisen as an issue in which health, ethics, science, and government funding merged. The speech below was presented to the nation on August 9, 2001.

August 9, 2001
REMARKS BY THE PRESIDENT ON STEM CELL RESEARCH
The Bush Ranch
Crawford, Texas
8:01 P.M. CDT

Good evening. I appreciate you giving me a few minutes of your time tonight so I can discuss with you a complex and difficult issue, an issue that is one of the most profound of our time.

The issue of research involving stem cells derived from human embryos is increasingly the subject of a national debate and dinner table discussions. The issue is confronted every day in laboratories as scientists ponder the ethical ramifications of their work. It is agonized over by parents and many couples as they try to have children, or to save children already born.

The issue is debated within the church, with people of different faiths, even many of the same faith coming to different conclusions. Many people are finding that the more they know about stem cell research, the less certain they are about the right ethical and moral conclusions.

My administration must decide whether to allow federal funds, your tax dollars, to be used for scientific research on stem cells derived from human embryos. A large number of these embryos already exist. They are the product of a process called in vitro fertilization, which helps so many couples conceive children. When doctors match sperm and egg to create life outside the womb, they usually produce more embryos than are planted in the mother. Once a couple successfully has children, or if they are unsuccessful, the additional embryos remain frozen in laboratories.

5 Some will not survive during long storage; others are destroyed. A number have been donated to science and used to create privately funded stem cell lines. And a few have been implanted in an adoptive mother and born, and are today healthy children.

Based on preliminary work that has been privately funded, scientists believe further research using stem cells offers great promise that could help improve the lives of those who suffer from many terrible diseases—from juvenile diabetes to Alzheimer's, from Parkinson's to spinal cord injuries. And while scientists admit they are not yet certain, they believe stem cells derived from embryos have unique potential.

You should also know that stem cells can be derived from sources other than embryos—from adult cells, from umbilical cords that are discarded after babies are born, from human placenta. And many scientists feel research on these types of stem cells is also promising. Many patients suffering from a range of diseases are already being helped with treatments developed from adult stem cells.

However, most scientists, at least today, believe that research on embryonic stem cells offer the most promise because these cells have the potential to develop in all of the tissues in the body.

Scientists further believe that rapid progress in this research will come only with federal funds. Federal dollars help attract the best and brightest scientists. They ensure new discoveries are widely shared at the largest number of research facilities and that the research is directed toward the greatest public good.

10 The United States has a long and proud record of leading the world toward advances in science and medicine that improve human life. And the United States has a long and proud record of upholding the highest standards of ethics as we expand the limits of science and knowledge. Research on embryonic stem cells raises profound ethical questions, because extracting the stem cell destroys the embryo, and thus destroys its potential for life. Like a snowflake, each of these embryos is unique, with the unique genetic potential of an individual human being.

As I thought through this issue, I kept returning to two fundamental questions: First, are these frozen embryos human life, and therefore, something precious to be protected? And second, if they're going to be destroyed anyway, shouldn't they be used for a greater good, for research that has the potential to save and improve other lives?

I've asked those questions and others of scientists, scholars, bioethicists, religious leaders, doctors, researchers, members of Congress, my Cabinet, and my friends. I have read heartfelt letters from many Americans. I have given this issue a great deal of thought, prayer and considerable reflection. And I have found widespread disagreement.

On the first issue, are these embryos human life—well, one researcher told me he believes this five-day-old cluster of cells is not an embryo, not yet an individual, but a pre-embryo. He argued that it has the potential for life, but it is not a life because it cannot develop on its own.

An ethicist dismissed that as a callous attempt at rationalization. Make no mistake, he told me, that cluster of cells is the same way you and I, and all the rest of us, started our lives. One goes with a heavy heart if we use these, he said, because we are dealing with the seeds of the next generation.

15 And to the other crucial question, if these are going to be destroyed anyway, why not use them for good purpose—I also found different answers. Many argue these embryos are byproducts of a process that helps create life, and we should allow couples to donate them to science so they can be used for good purpose instead of wasting their potential. Others will argue there's no such thing as excess life, and the fact that a living being is going to die does not justify experimenting on it or exploiting it as a natural resource.

At its core, this issue forces us to confront fundamental questions about the beginnings of life and the ends of science. It lies at a difficult moral intersection, juxtaposing the need to protect life in all its phases with the prospect of saving and improving life in all its stages.

As the discoveries of modern science create tremendous hope, they also lay vast ethical mine fields. As the genius of science extends the horizons of what we can do, we increasingly confront complex questions about what we should do. We have arrived at that brave new world that seemed so distant in 1932, when Aldous Huxley wrote about human beings created in test tubes in what he called a "hatchery."

In recent weeks, we learned that scientists have created human embryos in test tubes solely to experiment on them. This is deeply troubling, and a warning sign that should prompt all of us to think through these issues very carefully.

Embryonic stem cell research is at the leading edge of a series of moral hazards. The initial stem cell researcher was at first reluctant to begin his research, fearing it might be used for human cloning. Scientists have already cloned a sheep. Researchers are telling us the next step could be to clone human beings to create individual designer stem cells, essentially to grow another you, to be available in case you need another heart or lung or liver.

20 I strongly oppose human cloning, as do most Americans. We recoil at the idea of growing human beings for spare body parts, or creating life for our convenience. And while we must devote enormous energy to conquering disease, it is equally important that we pay attention to the moral concerns raised by the new frontier of human embryo stem cell research. Even the most noble ends do not justify any means.

My position on these issues is shaped by deeply held beliefs. I'm a strong supporter of science and technology, and believe they have the potential for incredible good—to improve lives, to save life, to conquer disease. Research offers hope that millions of our loved ones may be cured of a disease and rid of their suffering. I have friends whose children suffer from juvenile diabetes. Nancy Reagan has written me about President Reagan's struggle with Alzheimer's. My own family has confronted the tragedy of childhood leukemia. And, like all Americans, I have great hope for cures.

I also believe human life is a sacred gift from our Creator. I worry about a culture that devalues life, and believe as your President I have an important obligation to foster and encourage respect for life in America and throughout the world. And while we're all hopeful about the potential of this research, no one can be certain that the science will live up to the hope it has generated.

Eight years ago, scientists believed fetal tissue research offered great hope for cures and treatments—yet, the progress to date has not lived up to its initial expectations. Embryonic stem cell research offers both great promise and great peril. So I have decided we must proceed with great care.

As a result of private research, more than 60 genetically diverse stem cell lines already exist. They were created from embryos that have already been destroyed, and they have the ability to regenerate themselves indefinitely, creating ongoing opportunities for research. I have concluded that we should allow federal funds to be used for research on these existing stem cell lines, where the life and death decision has already been made.

25 Leading scientists tell me research on these 60 lines has great promise that could lead to breakthrough therapies and cures. This allows us to explore the promise and potential of stem cell research without crossing a fundamental moral line, by providing taxpayer funding that would sanction or encourage further destruction of human embryos that have at least the potential for life.

I also believe that great scientific progress can be made through aggressive federal funding of research on umbilical cord placenta, adult and animal stem cells which do not involve the same moral dilemma. This year, your government will spend $250 million on this important research.

I will also name a President's council to monitor stem cell research, to recommend appropriate guidelines and regulations, and to consider all of the medical and ethical ramifications of biomedical innovation. This council will consist of leading scientists, doctors, ethicists, lawyers, theologians and others, and will be chaired by Dr. Leon Kass, a leading biomedical ethicist from the University of Chicago.

This council will keep us apprised of new developments and give our nation a forum to continue to discuss and evaluate these important issues. As we go forward, I hope we will always be guided by both intellect and heart, by both our capabilities and our conscience.

I have made this decision with great care, and I pray it is the right one.

30 Thank you for listening. Good night, and God bless America.

END 8:12 P.M. CDT

Mapping the Text

1. Make a list of issues that President Bush identifies related to stem-cell research. Organize your list by the issues that you think are priorities. What conclusions do you draw from this cluster about appropriate actions or responses?
2. President Bush's statement is a policy statement. Do you agree or disagree with his position? In your explanation, cite specific points from the statement and offer reasons for your support or lack of support.

Writing to Inquire

1. Write an essay in which you choose a portion of President Bush's speech as the springboard for presenting your own point of view about stem-cell research.

The Coming Plague

LAURIE GARRETT

Laurie Garrett is a medical and science writer for *Newsday,* based in New York City. A native of Los Angeles, Garrett studied biology as an undergraduate and was pursuing a PhD in bacteriology and immunology when she started reporting on science news for a local radio station. Her reporting hobby soon became a full-time career in journalism, and Garrett abandoned her academic research to work as a science reporter. Garrett has written for many publications, including *Esquire, Vanity Fair,* and the *Washington Post;* she is the only writer ever to have been awarded all three of the major awards in journalism: the Peabody, Polk, and Pulitzer prizes. Garrett is the author of two major books: *Betrayal of Trust: The Collapse of Global Public Health* (2000); and *The Coming Plague: Newly Emerging Diseases in a World Out of Balance* (1994), from which the excerpt below is taken.

By the time my Uncle Bernard started his medical studies at the University of Chicago in 1932 he had already witnessed the great influenza pandemic of 1918–19. He was seven years old when he counted the funeral hearses that made their way down the streets of Baltimore. Three years earlier Bernard's father had nearly died of typhoid fever, acquired in downtown Baltimore. And shortly after, his grandfather died of tuberculosis.

In his twelfth year Bernard got what was called "summer sickness," spending the long, hot Maryland days lying about the house, "acting lazy," as his mother put it. It wasn't until 1938, when he volunteered as an X-ray guinea pig during his internship at the University of California's medical school in San Francisco, that Uncle Bernard discovered that the "summer sickness" was actually tuberculosis. He had no doubt acquired consumption from his grandfather, survived the disease, but for the rest of his life had telltale scars in his lungs that were revealed by chest X rays.

It seemed that everybody had TB in those days. When young Bernard Silber was struggling his way through medical studies in Chicago, incoming nursing students were routinely tested for antibodies against TB. The women who came from rural areas always tested negative for TB when they started their studies. With equal certainty, they all tested TB-positive after a year on the urban hospital wards. Any ailment in those days could light up a latent TB infection, and tuberculosis sanitariums were overflowing. Treatment was pretty much limited to bed rest and a variety of hotly debated diets, exercise regimens, fresh air, and extraordinary pneumothorax surgical procedures.

In 1939 Uncle Bernard started a two-year residency in medicine at Los Angeles County Hospital, where he met my Aunt Bernice, a medical social worker. Bernice limped and was deaf in one ear, the results of a childhood bacterial infection. When she was nine, the bacteria grew in her ear, eventually infecting the mastoid bone. A complication of that was osteomyelitis, which left her right leg about an inch shorter than her left, forcing Bernice to walk knock-kneed to keep her balance. Shortly after they met, Bernard got a nasty pneumococcal infection and, because he was a physician, received state-of-the-art treatment: tender loving care and oxygen. For a month he languished as a patient in Los Angeles County Hospital, hoping he would be among the 60 percent of Americans who, in the days before antibiotics, survived bacterial pneumonia.

5 Bacterial infections were both common and very serious before 1944, when the first antibiotic drugs became available. My Uncle Bernard could diagnose scarlet fever, pneumococcal pneumonia, rheumatic fever, whooping cough, diphtheria, or tuberculosis in a matter of minutes with little or no laboratory support. Doctors had to know how to work quickly because these infections could escalate rapidly. Besides, there wasn't much the lab could tell a physician in 1940 that a well-trained, observant doctor couldn't determine independently.

Viruses were a huge black box in those days, and though Bernard had no trouble differentiating between German measles, influenza, St. Louis encephalitis, and other viral diseases, he had neither treatments nor much of an understanding of what these tiniest of microbes did to the human body.

Uncle Bernard was introduced to tropical medicine during World War II, when he served in the Army Medical Corps at Guadalcanal and other battlefields of the Pacific. That's when he learned firsthand about diseases of which he'd heard very little in medical school: malaria, dengue (breakbone fever), and a variety of parasitic diseases. Quinine did a good job of curing malaria, but there was little he could do for GIs afflicted with the other tropical organisms that were rife in the Pacific theater.

Two years into the war the Army issued its first meager supplies of penicillin, instructing physicians to use the precious drug sparingly, in doses of about 5,000 units (less than a third of what would be considered a minimal penicillin dose for minor infections in 1993). In those early days before bacteria became resistant to antibiotics, such doses were capable of performing miracles, and the Army doctors were so impressed with the powers of penicillin that they collected the urine of patients who were on the drug and crystallized excreted penicillin for reuse on other GIs.

Years later, when I was studying immunology in graduate school at UC Berkeley, Uncle Bernard would regale me with tales of what sounded like medicine in the Dark Ages. I was preoccupied with such things as fluorescence-activated laser cell sorters that could separate different types of living cells of the immune system, the new technology of genetic engineering, monoclonal antibodies, and deciphering the human genetic code.

"I always liken the production of antibiotics to the Internal Revenue Service," Uncle Bernard would say when I seemed less than interested in the pre-antibiotic plights of American physicians. "People are always looking for loopholes, but as soon as they find them, the IRS plugs them up. It's the same way with antibiotics—no sooner have you got one than the bacteria have become resistant."

During the summer of 1976 I had reason to reconsider much of my Uncle Bernard's wisdom. As I tried to make sense of my graduate research project at Stanford University Medical Center, the news seemed overfull of infectious disease stories. The U.S. government was predicting a massive influenza epidemic that some said would surpass that of 1918—a global horror that claimed over 20 million lives. An American Legion group met in a hotel in Philadelphia on the Fourth of July, and something made 182 of them very sick, killing 29. Something else especially strange was going on in Africa, where, according to garbled press accounts of the day, people were dying from a terrifying new virus: in Zaire and the Sudan, something called Green Monkey Virus, or Marburg, or Ebola, or a mix of all three monikers was occupying the urgent attention of disease experts from all over the world.

In 1981 Dr. Richard Krause of the U.S. National Institutes of Health published a provocative book entitled *The Restless Tide: The Persistent Challenge of the Microbial World*,[1] which argued that diseases long thought to have been defeated could return to endanger the American people. In hearings a year later before the U.S. Congress, Krause was asked, "Why do we have so many new infectious diseases?"

"Nothing new has happened," Krause replied. "Plagues are as certain as death and taxes."[2]

But the shock of the AIDS epidemic prompted many more virus experts in the 1980s to ponder the possibility that something new was, indeed, happening. As the epidemic spread from one part of the world to another, scientists asked, "Where did this come from? Are there other agents out there? Will something worse emerge—something that can be spread from person to person in the air?"

15 The questioning grew louder as the 1980s dragged on. At a Rockefeller University cocktail party, a young virologist named Stephen Morse approached the institution's famed president, Nobel laureate Joshua Lederberg, and asked him what he thought of the mounting concern about emerging microbes. Lederberg characteristically responded in absolute terms: "The problem is serious, and it's getting worse." With a sense of shared mission, Morse and Lederberg set out to poll their colleagues on the matter, gather evidence, and build a case.

By 1988 an impressive group of American scientists, primarily virologists and tropical medicine specialists, had reached the conclusion that it was time to sound an alarm. Led by Morse and Lederberg of Rockefeller University, Tom Monath of the U.S. Army's Medical Research Institute of Infectious Diseases, and Robert Shope of the Yale University Arbovirus Research Unit, the scientists searched for a way to make tangible their shared concern. Their greatest worry was that they would be perceived as crybabies, merely out to protest shrinking research dollars. Or that they would be accused of crying wolf.

On May 1, 1989, the scientists gathered in the Hotel Washington, located across the street from the White House, and began three days of discussions aimed at providing evidence that the disease-causing microbes of the planet, far from having been defeated, were posing ever-greater threats to humanity. Their gathering was co-sponsored by the National Institutes of Allergy and Infectious Diseases, the Fogarty International Center, and Rockefeller University.

"Nature isn't benign," Lederberg said at the meeting's opening. "The bottom lines: the units of natural selection—DNA, sometimes RNA elements—are by no means neatly packaged in discrete organisms. They all share the entire biosphere. The survival of the human species is *not* a preordained evolutionary program. Abundant sources of genetic variation exist for viruses to learn new tricks, not necessarily confined to what happens routinely, or even frequently."

University of Chicago historian William McNeill outlined the reasons *Homo sapiens* had been vulnerable to microbial assaults over the millennia. He saw each catastrophic epidemic event in human history as the ironic result of humanity's steps forward. As humans improve their lots, McNeill warned, they actually *increase* their vulnerability to disease.

20 "It is, I think, worthwhile being conscious of the limits upon our powers," McNeill said. "It is worth keeping in mind that the more we win, the more we drive infections to the margins of human experience, the more we clear a path for possible catastrophic infection. We'll never escape the limits of the ecosystem. We are caught in the food chain, whether we like it or not, eating and being eaten."

For three days scientists presented evidence that validated McNeill's words of foreboding: viruses were mutating at rapid rates; seals were dying in great plagues as the researchers convened; more than 90 percent of the rabbits of Australia died in a single year following the introduction of a new virus to the land; great influenza pandemics were sweeping through the animal world; the Andromeda strain nearly surfaced in Africa in the form of Ebola virus; megacities were arising in the developing world, creating niches from which "virtually anything might arise"; rain forests were being destroyed, forcing disease-carrying animals and insects into areas of human habitation and raising the very real possibility that lethal, mysterious microbes would, for the first time, infect humanity on a large scale and imperil the survival of the human race.

As a member of a younger generation trained in an era of confident, curative medicine and minimal concern for infectious diseases, I experienced such discussion as the stuff of Michael Crichton novels rather than empiric scientific discourse. Yet I and thousands of young scientists also reared in the post-antibiotic, genetic engineering era had to concede that there was an impressive list of recently emergent viruses: the human immunodeficiency virus that caused AIDS, HTLV Types I and II which were linked to blood cancers, several types of recently discovered hepatitis-causing viruses, numerous hemorrhage-producing viruses discovered in Africa and Asia.

In February 1991 the Institute of Medicine (IOM), which is part of the U.S. National Academy of Sciences, convened a special panel with the task of exploring further the questions raised by the 1989 scientific gathering and advising the federal government on two points: the severity of the microbial threat to U.S. citizens and steps that could be taken to improve American disease surveillance and monitoring capabilities. In the fall of 1992 the IOM panel released its report, *Emerging Infections: Microbial Threats to Health in the United States*,[3] which concluded that the danger of the emergence of infectious diseases in the United States was genuine, and authorities were ill equipped to anticipate or manage new epidemics.

"Our message is that the problem is serious, it's getting worse, and we need to increase our efforts to overcome it," Lederberg said on the day of the report's release.

After the release of the report, the U.S. Centers for Disease Control and Prevention in Atlanta began a soul-searching process that would, by the spring of 1994, result in a plan for heightened vigilance and rapid response to disease outbreaks. The slow response to the emergence of HIV in 1981 had allowed the epidemic to expand by 1993 to embrace 1.5 million Americans and cost the federal government more than $12 billion annually in research, drug development, education, and treatment efforts.

The CDC was determined that such a mistake would not be repeated.

But there were dissident voices in 1993 who protested both the American scientific community's often narrow emphasis on viruses and its focus on threats posed solely to U.S. citizens. Disease fighters like Joe McCormick, Peter Piot, David Heymann, Jonathan Mann, and Daniel Tarantola argued forcefully that microbes had no respect for humanity's national borders.

Furthermore, they said, in much of the world the most dangerous emerging diseases were not viral, but bacterial or parasitic. A far larger view was needed, they argued.

Other critics stressed that a historical perspective on mankind's bumbling, misguided attempts to control the microbes would reveal that much of the fault lay with the very scientific community that was now calling for vigilance. What seemed to make sense as microbe control action, viewed from the academic and government offices of the world's richest country, argued the likes of Uwe Brinkmann, Andrew Spielman, and Isao Arita, could prove disastrous when executed in the planet's poorer nations.

The critics charged that Americans, by virtue of their narrow focus on the appearance of disease within the United States, were missing the real picture. It was a picture captured in the sight of a little Ndbele girl wrapped in a green *kanga.* She lay on the hardened clay floor of a health care clinic outside Bulawayo, Zimbabwe. Her mother sat beside her, casting beseeching looks at every stranger who entered the two-room clinic. The four-year-old girl cried weakly.

"That is measles," said the clinic director, pointing a stern finger at the child. The director led an observer outside to show the local innovations in toilet hygiene and efforts to increase the protein content of village children's diets.

When he returned an hour later to the wattle-clay clinic, the mother was rocking back and forth on the balls of her feet, tears silently streaming down her face; the child's soft crying had ceased. A few hours later the mother and her husband placed across bicycle handlebars a rolled straw mat containing their little girl's body and, staring blankly at the horizon, forlornly walked the bike down the red clay road.

At a time when mothers of the world's wealthiest nations arranged to have their children "immunized" by deliberately exposing the youngsters to measles, mumps, even chicken pox, these diseases were forcing parents in some of the world's poorest nations to find ways to cope with the expected deaths of more than half their children before the age of ten.

The long list of vaccines and prescription drugs that American physicians urged their patients to take before traveling south of Tijuana was ample testimony to the health impact of the world's wide gulf in wealth and development. In the 1970s Americans and Europeans who were distressed by the poverty of the Southern Hemisphere poured money into the poorest countries for projects intended to bring their populations into "the modern age." The logic of the day was that the health status of a population would improve as the society's overall structure and economy grew to more closely resemble those of the United States, Canada, and Western Europe.

But by 1990 the world's major donor institutions would be forced to conclude that modernization efforts seemed only to have worsened the plight of the average individual in the Third World, while enhancing the power, wealth, and corruption of national elites and foreign-owned institutions. Bucolic agricultural societies were transformed in the space of a single generation into countries focused around one or more vast urban centers that grew like ghastly canker sores over the landscape, devouring the traditional lifestyles and environments of the people and thrusting young job seekers into sprawling semi-urban slums that lacked even a modicum of proper human waste disposal or public health intervention.

In the industrialized free market world of the 1970s, people at all societal strata became increasingly conscious of the link between environmental pollution and personal health. As the dangers of pesticide misuse, lead paint, asbestos fibers, air pollution, and adulterated foods became apparent, residents of the world's wealthiest countries clamored for regulations to curb contamination of the environment and the food supply.

With the discovery of Earth's ozone holes, the world's scientists initiated a debate about global responsibility for preventing further pollution destruction of the planet's protective gaseous layer. Similarly, marine biologists argued with increasing vehemence that all the nations of the world shared responsibility for the sorry state of Earth's oceans and the near-extinction or endangerment of its fish, coral, and mammal populations. Conservationists turned their attention to global wildlife protection. And biologists like Harvard's E. O. Wilson and the Smithsonian's Thomas Lovejoy warned of a global mass flora and fauna extinction event that would rival that of the great Cretaceous period dinosaur die-off.

Citing the fossil evidence for five great extinction events in Earth's ancient history, Wilson asked how much more environmental destruction at man's hand the world could tolerate: "These figures should give pause to anyone who believes that what *Homo sapiens* destroys, Nature will redeem. Maybe so, but not within any length of time that has meaning for contemporary humanity."[4]

As humanity approached the last decade of the twentieth century, the concept of a Global Village—first elucidated in the 1960s by Canadian philosopher Marshall McLuhan as a description of the sense of worldwide interconnectedness created by mass media technology—had clearly entered mass consciousness in the context of Earth's ecology. Environmentalists were thinking on the macro level, plotting ways to change the whaling policies of places as disparate as Japan, Alaska, Russia, and Norway. The World Bank decided to include ecological concerns in its parameters for issuing loans to developing countries. The Chernobyl nuclear accident proved, in the eyes of many scientists, that it was folly to consider toxic risk control a problem whose solutions were always constrained by issues of national sovereignty.

And in 1992 the United States elected a Vice President who espoused an ambitious global Marshall Plan to protect the environment. Albert Gore warned that nothing short of a massive worldwide shift in human perspective, coupled with elaborate systems of international regulation and economic incentives, would be adequate to ensure the survival of the planet's ecology. And he adopted the rhetoric of critical environmentalists, saying, "Those who have a vested interest in the status quo will probably continue to stifle any meaningful change until enough citizens who are concerned about the ecological system are willing to speak out and urge their leaders to bring the earth back into balance."[5]

40 At the macro level, then, a sense of global interconnectedness was developing over such issues as economic justice and development, environmental preservation, and, in a few instances, regulation. Though there were differences in perspective and semantics, the globalization of views on some issues was already emerging across ideological lines well before the fall of the Berlin Wall. Since then it has sped up, although there is now considerable anxiety expressed outside the United States about American domination of the ideas, cultural views, technologies, and economics of globalization of such areas as environmentalism, communication, and development.

It wasn't until the emergence of the human immunodeficiency virus, however, that the limits of, and imperatives for, globalization of health became obvious in a context larger than mass vaccination and diarrhea control programs. From the moment it was discovered in 1981 among gay men in New York and California, AIDS became a prism through which the positive lights by which societies hoped to be viewed were fractured into thousands of disparate and glaring pieces. Through the AIDS prism it was possible for the world's public health experts to witness what they considered to be the hypocrisies, cruelties, failings, and inadequacies of humanity's sacred institutions, including its medical establishment, science, organized religion, systems of justice, the United Nations, and individual government systems of all political stripes.

If HIV was our model, leading scientists concluded, humanity was in very big trouble. *Homo sapiens* greeted the emergence of the new disease first with utter nonchalance, then with disdain for those infected by the virus, followed by an almost pathologic sense of mass denial that drew upon mechanisms for rationalizing the epidemic that ranged from claiming that the virus was completely harmless to insisting that certain individuals or races of people were uniquely blessed with the ability to survive HIV infection. History, they claimed, would judge the 1980s performance of the world's political and religious leaders: would they be seen as equivalent to the seventeenth-century clerics and aristocracy of London who fled the city, leaving the poor to suffer the bubonic plague; or would history be more compassionate, merely finding them incapable of seeing the storm until it leveled their homes?

Over the last five years, scientists—particularly in the United States and France—have voiced concern that HIV, far from representing a public health aberration, may be a sign of things to come. They warn that humanity has learned little about preparedness and response to new microbes, despite the blatant tragedy of AIDS. And they call for recognition of the ways in which changes at the micro level of the environment of any nation can affect life at the global, macro level.[6]

Humanity's ancient enemies are, after all, microbes. They didn't go away just because science invented drugs, antibiotics, and vaccines (with the notable exception of smallpox). They didn't disappear from the planet when Americans and Europeans cleaned up their towns and cities in the postindustrial era. And they certainly won't become extinct simply because human beings choose to ignore their existence. . . .

What is required, overall, is a new paradigm in the way people think about disease. Rather than a view that sees humanity's relationship to the microbes as a historically linear one, tending over the centuries toward ever-decreasing risk to humans, a far more challenging perspective must be sought, allowing for a dynamic, nonlinear state of affairs between *Homo sapiens* and the microbial world, both inside and outside their bodies. As Harvard University's Dick Levins puts it, "we must embrace complexity, seek ways to describe and comprehend an ever-changing ecology we cannot see, but, nonetheless, by which we are constantly affected."

Now in his eighties and retired from the daily practice of medicine, my Uncle Bernard wonders how many American physicians today would recognize a case of malaria, diphtheria, rheumatic fever, tuberculosis, or typhus without needing the guiding advice provided by time-consuming laboratory diagnostic analysis. He doubts whether most physicians in the industrialized world could diagnose an old scourge, like yellow fever or dengue fever, much less spot an entirely new microbe. As he and the rest of the pre-antibiotic era physicians of the developed world retire and age, Bernard asks if doctors of the year 2000 will be better or worse equipped to treat bacterial pneumonia than were physicians in his pre-antibiotic days.

Preparedness demands understanding. To comprehend the interactions between *Homo sapiens* and the vast and diverse microbial world, perspectives must be forged that meld such disparate fields as medicine, environmentalism, public health, basic ecology, primate biology, human behavior, economic development, cultural anthropology, human rights law, entomology, parasitology, virology, bacteriology, evolutionary biology, and epidemiology.

The Coming Plague tells the stories of men and women who struggled to understand and control the microbial threats of the post–World War II era. As these disease vanquishers retire, the college laboratories and medical schools grow full of youthful scientific energy, but it is not focused on the seemingly old-fashioned, passé tasks that were invaluable in humanity's historic ecological struggles with the microbes. As we approach the millennium, few young scientists or doctors anywhere in the world can quickly recognize a tiger mosquito, *Peromyscus maniculatus* mouse, pertussis cough, or diphtherial throat infection.

The skills needed to describe and recognize perturbations in the *Homo sapiens* microecology are disappearing with the passing of the generations, leaving humanity, lulled into a complacency born of proud discoveries and medical triumphs, unprepared for the coming plague.

Notes

[1]R. M. Krause, Washington, D.C.: National Foundation for Infectious Diseases, 1981.
[2]R. M. Krause, Foreword to S. S. Morse, ed., *Emerging Viruses* (Oxford, Eng.: Oxford University Press, 1993).
[3]J. Lederberg, R. E. Shope, and S. C. Oaks, Jr., Washington, D.C.: National Aoademy Press, 1992.
[4]E. O. Wilson, *The Diversity of Life* (Cambridge, MA: Harvard University Press, 1992). 31.
[5]A. Gore, *Earth in the Balance* (New York: Houghton Mifflin, 1992).
[6]J. Lederberg, "Medical Science, Infectious Disease, and the Unity of Mankind," *Journal of the American Medical Association 260* (1988): 684–85; and Institute of Medicine, *Emerging Infections: Microbial Threats to Health in the United States* (Washington, D.C.: National Academy Press, 1992).

Mapping the Text

1. Garrett uses the figure of her Uncle Bernard to tell a story about changes in perceptions and attitudes about disease over the last century. What story or lesson does Garrett derive from her uncle's story? How has her own experience been different from his? What point is she making about changes in medicine and social attitudes toward infectious disease?
2. In what ways, according to Garrett, did the growing awareness of AIDS as a global crisis affect perceptions and practice in medical research? What new questions and issues did AIDS pose for virus research? How does Garrett characterize this shift? What kind of action and response is Garrett calling for in this essay?
3. Garrett uses a particular image as a rhetorical strategy in this essay: "a picture captured in the sight of a little Ndbele girl wraped in a green *kanga*" (p. 492). What argument is she trying to make with this image? What other types of evidence does she use to support her claims? Can you imagine counterarguments that might be made in response to Garrett's claims? How is Garrett using this image to provoke a response?
4. Near the end of this essay, Garrett calls for "a new paradigm in the way people think about disease" (p. 495). How would you describe this "new paradigm"? How is it, or how will it be, different from current paradigms? What kinds of questions and issues would such a paradigm present for medical and scientific research? In what sense does Garrett's argument for a new paradigm function as a call to action?

Writing to Inquire

1. Do some research on the "great influenza pandemic of 1918–19" referred to by Garrett. What impact did this disease crisis have on history? What can we learn from it about the social impact of disease in modern society? Write a descriptive account of this historical epidemic, based on your research, in which you draw implications for an audience of contemporary readers who may not be aware of the magnitude of the flu epidemic in those years.
2. Garrett's essay offers a cautionary tale for current and future medical practice and research. Do you think anything has changed since this essay was published in 1994? Choose one of the issues or diseases covered by Garrett and do some exploratory research to inquire into the impact of Garrett's warnings. Have other writers made similar arguments? How has medical research responded to these concerns?
3. Garrett seems to imply that a new perspective is needed in medical research on infectious diseases. How might medical schools adapt to promote this new perspective? Write an argument calling for changes in medical training and education, or in public and institutional policies related to medical training.

INQUIRY: HOW DOES AN INDIVIDUAL'S PERSONAL STATE OF HEALTH BECOME AN ISSUE FOR PUBLIC DECISION MAKING?

1. When you think about the terms *health* and *well-being,* what comes to your mind? Make a list of your hopes and fears about health. How is your list affected by your knowledge and understanding of specific illnesses and ailments? What are your sources of information about illness? On what basis do you consider these sources credible? How prepared do you feel to face the hopes and fears on your list?
2. What does it mean when a health issue becomes a *public* health issue? What are the advantages and disadvantages of being labeled a *public* concern? Using one of the instances of disease or disability presented in this chapter, what public money, time, or attention has been granted to the problem, and with to effect?
3. Consider issues such as euthanasia, harvesting body parts, and various ordinary and extraordinary options for health and long life that have become available with advances in technology. What are the

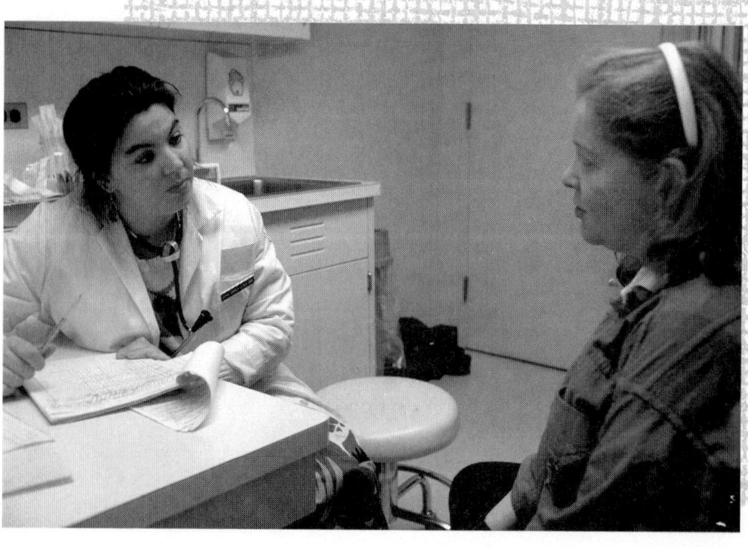

What role does language play in the treatment of illness? How are doctors and patients identified in exchanges like the one pictured here? What rights and responsibilities do both participants have in this process?

problems and concerns that arise? What are the implications for personal, social, and public decision making?

4. Consult library or Internet sources to gather information about federal funding for health care. When did public support for health care begin? To whom has it been available over time? What are the contemporary concerns about health care funding?
5. Choose a disease you would like to know more about and explore it. Include in your exploration attention to whether the disease receives federal support for research and the identification of therapies.
6. Under what conditions do you think an individual's private health problems become a public concern? Why? How would you develop and present your position in a persuasive essay?

CHAPTER 7

Digital Frontiers

We live in an age where science and technology abound as evidence of incredible human ingenuity and imagination. Throughout human history, we have focused energy on coming to know and understand more about the world, and, in cyclical fashion, the knowledge that we have gained has helped us create even more effective scientific and technological responses to the world. Our capacity is rapidly growing to alter the conditions of life, to make a critical difference in the quality of life, and to gain greater control over the material world, including the physical environment and, indeed, our own bodies. We can do more better, faster, and easier, and with greater comfort and confidence; we think of the universe as systematic, reasonable, knowable, even manageable, rather than mysterious. Despite moments of doubt and concern about the ethics of some of these developments, we tend to think of science and technology as assets rather than liabilities, as reasons for hope and great expectation.

The title of Chapter 7, "Digital Frontiers," is meant to signal the newness of the cultural and social landscapes that digital technologies have opened for us. It also alludes to the long history of frontiers, both literal and metaphorical, in the American imagination. Like the literal frontiers of the American West, some of which are described in earlier chapters, the digital frontiers of contemporary technology carry forth the thread of "new homes" and keep before us the need to remake ourselves on and in these new frontiers. This theme of digital frontiers sets in place a framework that helps identify the frontiers we are paying attention to, four of which are key themes in Chapter 7: the need for new language to discuss and envision the territory on the digital fronter; the process of making and remaking identities in this new landscape; the need to consider social, public, and ethical issues that emerge in and around new technologies; and the need to consider the benefits and consequences for all of us.

The selections in Chapter 7 focus on computers as just one dimension of the broad array of sciences and technologies that surround us. This choice underscores the idea that amid our extraordinary possibilities, we still remain human and face the ongoing challenges of incorporating tools, complex and simple, into the fabric of our daily lives. These selections continue to raise questions, as readings in earlier chapters have, about identity and relationships, about social and public responsibility, about ethical action. With these selections, however, the focus shifts toward the context. We live in a highly technological world in which computers are ubiquitous. What does their presence in our lives mean?

FRAMING THE TOPIC

Framing Conversations about Technology

BONNIE A. NARDI AND VICKI L. O'DAY

Bonnie A. Nardi is an anthropologist and researcher at Agilent Laboratories. She has lived and studied in Papua New Guinea and Western Samoa and has investigated the technological habits of spreadsheet users, brain surgeons, reference librarians, and American teenagers. More recently, Nardi has been conducting research on social networks in the workplace. Her publications include *A Small Matter of Programming: Perspectives on End User Computing* (1993), and *Context and Consciousness: Activity Theory and Human-Computer Interaction* (1996). Vicki O'Day, formerly a researcher at the Xerox Palo Alto Research Center, is a graduate student in anthropology at the University of California at Santa Cruz. The selection below is a chapter (with occasional ellipses) from a book-length work entitled *Information Ecologies: Using Technology with Heart* (1999).

The seventy-year-old film *Metropolis* is a reminder that our current questions and concerns about technology have a long history. Many of the particular technologies we experience now are fairly new—voicemail, cellular phones, the Internet, and many more. But the challenge of responding well to technological change goes back at least to the invention of the earliest machines.

There is no question about the imaginative appeal of technology, not just in the cityscape of Metropolis but in our own world today. With the help of technology, we can understand genetic structure, take pictures of stars being born, and perform in utero surgery to save the life of an unborn baby. These are accomplishments that give us a sense of wonder and appreciation for human inventiveness. They celebrate our abilities and extend our connections with the natural world.

When we adopt new technologies, we face uncertainty about how our quality of life may change. The development of new technology affects the nature of work, school, family life, commerce, politics, and war. We might expect that anything with such profound influence on the way we live would be subject to considerable scrutiny and debate. But most of us don't see ourselves as influential participants who can offer informed opinions about the uses of technology. On the contrary, new technologies tend to be mystifying. They resist our attempts to get a grip on what they do and how they work.

As long as we think we do not have enough expertise to engage in substantive discussions about technology, we are effectively prevented from having an impact on the directions it may take. But there *are* opportunities for discussion and intervention in the process of technological growth and change, and it is important to take advantage of them. We believe that the lack of broad participation in conversations about technology seriously impoverishes the ways technologies are brought into our everyday lives. Our aim is to show how more people can be more fully engaged in important discussions and decisions about technology.

5 . . . Our perspective comes from our experience as researchers in Silicon Valley and as users and consumers of technology. We, Bonnie Nardi and Vicki O'Day, have been trained in (respectively) anthropology and computer science. We have each crossed boundaries into the other's discipline during our years of working in industrial research labs, including those at Hewlett-Packard, Apple Computer, and Xerox. Both of us have designed and implemented computer software, and both of us have conducted empirical studies of how people use technology.

Our empirical studies are ethnographic studies, which means that we go out into the "field" to study situations in which people are going about their business in their own ways, doing whatever they normally do. For us, the field has included offices, libraries, schools, and hospitals. We observe everyday practices and interview people in their own settings over a period of time, to learn more about the complicated and often surprising workings of a particular environment. We bring the insights we develop from ethnographic studies to help in the design of technological tools that will be a good fit for the people who use them.

We consider ourselves critical friends of technology. We want to see more examples of good, useful applications of technology out in the world, like those we have seen in some of our studies. But as we do our fieldwork, read the newspapers, and watch the developments around us, we are sometimes troubled by what we see. Technical developments in everything from telephone menus to cloning and genetic engineering have potentially disturbing effects.

We have noticed that people seem to distance themselves from a critical evaluation of the technologies in their lives, as if these technologies were inevitable forces of nature rather than things we design and choose. Perhaps some of this lack of critical attention is due to the sheer excitement at the novelty and promise of new technology, which makes it easy to move ahead quickly and without reflection. For example, NetDays focused on wiring public schools for Internet access were carried out with good intentions, but we have seen that some of our local schools have had a difficult time coping with the new technology once they have it.

We are troubled when people ignore the human intentionality and accountability behind the use of technological tools. For example, when one of us recently forgot to pay a credit card bill and saw her credit card temporarily disabled as a result, she called her bank to ask it to accelerate the process of turning the card back on. She assumed that a twenty-year history as a good customer would make a difference. The response from each of the three customer service people she talked to was the same: "You know, you're dealing with a computer here." Well, not exactly. We are also dealing with people who solve problems and make decisions, or we should be. Human expertise, judgment, and creativity can be supported, but not replaced, by computer-based tools.

10 Many people have misgivings about technology, but most of the time we do not express them. Our own specific concerns are unimportant in this discussion. What is important is that each of us develop and use our own critical sensibilities about the technologies that affect us. . . .

For all of our readers, what we hope to accomplish is a shift in perception. To explain what we mean, we can use visual perception as an analogy. Psychologists have studied the way people see, and recent research suggests that there is no conscious perception of the visual world *without paying attention to it.* That is, you can't see what is in your field of view unless you are prepared to notice and process what your eye takes in. According to Arien Mack and Irvin Rock, who have carried out research in this area, we are subject to "inattentional blindness" when we are not ready to pay attention to something in our field of view.[1]

This language about visual perception and inattentional blindness resonates with our experience as researchers who study technology in use. Sometimes we have seen different things in settings we have studied than other technologists or even some of the participants themselves have seen. We believe that to some extent, this is because we were prepared to see and pay attention to different things. We were looking for a multiplicity of viewpoints in the settings we studied, the hidden side effects of technology, people's values and agendas as they deployed technology, the resources they brought to bear in getting their work done, the actual work practices that accomplished the goals of the work, and the social interactions that affected work and technology use.

In other words, some of what goes on in any setting is invisible unless you are open to seeing it. We have noticed two blind spots people seem to have in considering work settings: informal practices that support work activities and unobtrusive work styles that hide valuable, skilled contributions.[2]

In any work setting, there are commonly accepted accounts of the regular and sensible ways things get done. They come in the form of written procedures, job descriptions, organizational charts, project planning documents, training materials, and more. While these descriptions are useful in helping people coordinate and carry out their work, they do not always reflect the whole picture of the way things get done. They capture the work activities, roles, and relationships that are most visible, but not the informal practices that may be just as important.

15 For example, informal collaboration among co-workers is common but little discussed. An individual might own the responsibility for a particular

task, but behind this formal responsibility there are many informal consultations and small communications with co-workers that help get the task done. In engineering work groups we studied, engineers asked one another for help in using complicated computer-aided design tools, although coaching was not in anyone's job description.

Sometimes work is invisible because workers are intentionally unobtrusive in their activities. In our research in corporate libraries, for example, we have seen that reference librarians usually carry out their highly technical and skilled search activities behind the scenes, so much so that their own clients are largely unaware of what they do. Since clients may not understand what librarians are doing, they may think that automated services can replace librarians. If they looked at the actual work, they would understand that automated services cannot perform the same tasks.

When new technologies are adopted into a work setting, they usually affect the informal activities and unobtrusive activities as well as the formal ones. As we plan the introduction of new technologies or the modification of existing technologies, it is useful to shift our perception and become aware of aspects of work that are usually invisible.

Though we are all subject to inattentional blindness, we can try to be more aware of informal and unobtrusive activities. By preparing to see between and behind the formal, well-advertised roles and processes, we can enlarge our vision. And if we learn to see our own settings differently, we will also be able to see different possibilities for discussion and local action.

The Rhetoric of Inevitability

To achieve a shift in perception and prepare for conversations for action, we must look beyond some of the common rhetoric about technology. As we read and listen to what designers and technology commentators have to say, we are struck by how often technological development is characterized as *inevitable.* We are concerned about the ascendance of a rhetoric of inevitability that limits our thinking about how we should shape the use of technology in our society.

20 Some commentators welcome the "inevitable" progress of technology—that is the view of the technophiles, who see only good things in future technological developments. Some decry the inexorable advance of technology—that is the view of dystopians, who wish we could turn our backs on the latest technologies because of their intrusive effects on our social experience.

There are more possibilities for action than these extremes suggest. But to see past this pervasive rhetoric, we first need to bring it clearly into view, so we can recognize it, sensitize ourselves to it, and then move forward to a more fruitful position.

To consider just one of many examples of the rhetoric of inevitability, in an article in *Beyond Calculation: The Next Fifty Years of Computing,* Gordon

Bell and Jim Gray of Microsoft assert that "by 2047. . . all information about physical objects, including humans, buildings, processes and organizations, will be online. This is both desirable and inevitable."[3] It is instructive to read those two sentences aloud.

Humans are *objects.* We are in the same category as buildings. In this formulation, any special considerations we might have simply because we are humans (such as rights to privacy) are obliterated. The authors declare that creating a world in which people are objects in a panoramic electronic database is "both desirable and inevitable."

The authors use their authority as virtuoso engineers to tell us what they believe to be inevitable and to suggest how we should feel about it. Bell and Gray's article is not an anomaly. It is one example of many books and articles in which experts describe how technology will be used in the future with a sense of certainty, both about the technology itself and our own acceptance of the benefits it will bring to us.[4]

Bell and Gray state, "Only the human brain can process and store information more easily, cheaply and rapidly [than a computer]." The human brain is formulated here as cheap information storage. By reducing people's intellects to simple computation and storage capabilities, our goals and intentions and opinions are rendered invisible and uninteresting. We are concerned about the way the corporate mind is reaching into the future to define us as physical objects about whom any data can be stored online. Through the rhetoric of inevitability we are being declared nonplayers in the technical future. We are bargain basement commodities.

Another example of the rhetoric of inevitability can be found in the discussions of cloning people, which have featured inevitability as a constant refrain. Immediately after the story about the successful cloning of sheep in Scotland appeared in the newspapers in February 1997, a U.S. government spokesperson said, "Should we stop scientific development in these areas because the capacity [to clone humans] might become available? I don't think that's reasonable, or even possible. I just think that's one of the costs that come along with scientific discovery, and we have to manage it as well as we can. But it's awfully hard to stop it."[5]

The author of these remarks was Harold Shapiro, the chair of the National Bioethics Advisory Commission appointed by President Clinton. Surely someone appointed as a representative of the people's interests to advise the government on the ethics of biotechnology should take a little more time before declaring cloning technology inevitable. Is it not appropriate to have a public conversation about this far-reaching, controversial technology? Here the rhetoric of inevitability protects a scientific establishment that wants to be free of considerations of how its activities might affect the rest of society.

Shapiro was joined by Eric Juengst, a bioethicist at Case Western Reserve University, in declaring that banning future research is like "trying to put a genie back in its bottle."[6] The rhetoric of inevitability reaches a nadir in Juengst's comment: "Do we want to outlaw it [cloning] entirely? That means of course only outlaws will do cloning."

There must be a better argument to be made about the implications of cloning than that only outlaws will clone if we make it illegal. Let's throw away all our laws, in that case! This is a sad logic, especially from someone described as in the newspaper as "one of the nation's leading biomedical ethicists."

30 Fortunately, the cloning discussion has been more polyphonic than many other technology discussions. In a story about cloning in the *San Jose Mercury News*, our local newspaper, it was reported that in 1973 the scientific community declared a moratorium on research in which DNA from one species was moved to another species, because there was popular concern about mutant strains of bacteria escaping from laboratories and infecting the entire world. In 1974, scientists urged the federal government to regulate all such DNA technology. Strict guidelines followed. They have been relaxed as the scientific community has taken time to sort through the issues and as public understanding has grown, but the regulations are widely regarded as responsible and socially beneficial steps to have taken at that time.[7]

Margaret McLean, director of biotechnology and health care ethics at the Markkula Center for Applied Ethics at Santa Clara University, wrote of the cloning debate, "We ought to listen to our fears." She noted that Dolly the sheep seems to be growing old before her time, possibly due to the aged genetic material from which she was cloned. McLean discussed concerns with attempts to overcontrol a child's future by controlling its genes, by setting expectations that a cloned child might find emotionally unbearable. She argued that we should consider our misgivings and give voice to them. McLean takes on the issue of inevitability squarely, declaring, "I, for one, believe that the possible is not the inevitable."[8]

The developer of the cloning technique himself, Ian Wilmut, voiced opposition on ethical grounds to applying the technology to people. There are already laws in some European countries that ban the cloning of human beings.

We hope that our readers will develop active antennae for sensing the rhetoric of inevitability in all the media that surround us. The cloning discovery and the variable responses to it show that there is not a single story to be told about any technology. Those who declare a technical development "inevitable" are doing so by fiat.

Conversational Extremes: Technophilia and Dystopia

Conversations about technology are often positioned at one of two extremes: uncritical acceptance or condemnation. Writers of both technophile and dystopic works often assume that technological change is inevitable—they just feel very differently about it.[9]

35 These two positions stake out the ends of the continuum, but they leave us with poor choices for action. We want to claim a middle ground from which we can carefully consider the impact of technologies without rejecting them wholesale.

Nicholas Negroponte's book *Being Digital* is a shining example of the work of a technophile. Negroponte, director of the MIT Media Lab in Cambridge, Massachusetts, populates a new and forthcoming Utopia with electronic butlers, robot secretaries, and fleets of digital assistants.[10] In Negroponte's world, computers see and hear, respond to your every murmur, show tact and discretion, and gauge their interactions according to your individual predilections, habits, and social behaviors. Negroponte's lively future scenarios in which digital servants uncomplainingly do our bidding are always positive, unproblematic, and without social costs. There are some important pieces missing from this vision, though it is certainly engagingly presented.

Technological tools and other artifacts carry social meaning. Social understanding, values, and practices become *integral aspects* of the tool itself. Perhaps it's easiest to see this clearly by looking at examples of older and more familiar developments, such as the telephone. The telephone is a technological device. It is a machine that sits on a desk or is carried around the house, and it has electronic insides that can be broken. But most of us probably don't think of a telephone as a machine; instead, we think of it as a way of communicating. There is an etiquette to placing a call, answering the phone, taking turns in conversation, and saying good-bye, which is so clear to us that we can teach it to our children. There are implicit rules about the privacy of telephone conversations; we learn not to eavesdrop on others and to ignore what we may accidentally overhear. These conventions and practices are not "designed in" and they do not spring up overnight. They were established by people who used telephones over time, as they discovered what telephones were good for, learned how it felt to use them, and committed social gaffes with them.

Negroponte's scenarios are missing a sense of each technology's evolving social meaning and deep integration into social life. Though these social meanings can't be engineered (as the histories of earlier technologies have shown), we must understand that social impacts are crucially important aspects of technological change. We should be paying attention to this bigger picture, as it emerges from its fuzzy-grained beginnings in high-tech labs to saturate our houses, schools, offices, libraries, and hospitals. It is not enough to speculate about the gadgets only in terms of the exciting functions they will perform.

When we turn to writings in the dystopic vein, we find that concerns with the social effects of technology *are* voiced. But the concerns are met with a big bucket of cold water—a call to walk away from new technologies rather than use them selectively and thoughtfully.

40 A recent best-seller in this arena was Clifford Stoll's *Silicon Snake Oil.*[11] Stoll is an astronomer and skilled computer programmer who is well known for his remarkable success in tracking down a group of West German hackers who broke into the Lawrence Berkeley Laboratory computers in 1986. In *Silicon Snake Oil,* Stoll shares his concerns about the hype surrounding the Internet for everyday use. He suggests that consumers are being sold a bottle of snake oil by those promoting the Internet and other advanced technologies. In the rush to populate news groups, chat rooms, and online bookstores in a search for community, we may find ourselves trading away the most basic building blocks for community that we already have—our active participation in local neighborhoods, schools, and businesses.

This is not an unreasonable fear. Another technology, the automobile, transformed the landscape of cities, neighborhoods, and even houses in ways that profoundly affect the rhythms and social networks of daily life. In the suburban Silicon Valley neighborhood where both of us live, each ranch-style house is laid out with the garage in front, making it the most prominent feature of the house to neighbors or passersby. The downtown shops are a long walk away on busy roads that are not meant for pedestrian traffic. Most people routinely drive many miles to get to work. We can be reminded of what our driving culture costs us by walking for awhile in a town or neighborhood built before cars—though this is not an easy exercise for Californians and other Westerners. In these earlier neighborhoods, there are mixtures of houses, apartments, and small shops, all on a scale accessible to people walking by, not shielded from the casual visitor by vast parking areas.

While we share Stoll's belief that the introduction of new technologies into our lives deserves scrutiny, we do not believe that it is reasonable or desirable to turn our backs on technology. It is one thing to choose not to use automated tools for the pure pleasure of doing something by hand—to create beautiful calligraphy for a poem instead of choosing from twenty or thirty ready-made fonts, or to play Monopoly (an activity advocated by Stoll) instead of Myst (a computer game with beautiful graphics). But sometimes the computer is exactly the right tool for the job, and sometimes it is the *only* tool for the job.

The issue is not whether we will use technologies, but which we will choose and whether we will use them well. The challenge now is to introduce some critical sensibilities into our evaluation and use of technology, and beyond that, to make a real impact on the kinds of technology that will be available to us in the future.

Stoll and Negroponte seem to be diametric opposites. Stoll says faxing is fine; Negroponte offers a withering critique. Stoll asserts that people don't have time to read email; according to Negroponte, Nobel prize winners happily answer the email of schoolchildren. Stoll tells schools to buy books; Negroponte says computers make you read more and better. But both Negroponte and Stoll are in agreement on one crucial point: the way technology is designed and used is beyond the control of people who are not technology experts. Negroponte asserts that being digital is inevitable, "like a force of nature." What Mother Nature fails to provide will be taken care of by the engineers in the Media Lab. And Stoll describes the digital promises as snake oil—not home brew. Neither Stoll nor Negroponte offers scenarios in which citizens have a say in how we want to shape and use technology.

A Different Approach

45 Our position in this public conversation about technology lies between the positions exemplified by Stoll and Negroponte in some ways, and completely outside their construction of the argument in others. We share Negroponte's enthusiasm for and fascination with cutting-edge technology development. We share Stoll's concerns about the social impact of technology. But to shun digital technology as Stoll advocates is to miss out on its benefits. Neither does it seem wise to sit back passively waiting for the endless stream of amazing gadgets that Negroponte hypothesizes. It is not necessary to jump on the digital bandwagon. It is dangerous, disempowering, and self-limiting to stick our heads in the sand and pretend it will all go away if we don't look. We believe that much more discussion and analysis of technology and all its attendant issues are needed.

Some of this discussion is fostered by political action books, such as Richard Sclove's *Democracy and Technology.*[12] Sclove argues for grassroots political action to try to influence official governmental policies on technology. He writes, "[i]t is possible to evolve societies in which people live in greater freedom, exert greater influence on their circumstances, and experience greater dignity, self-esteem, purpose, and well-being."

We are in passionate agreement with this statement. At the same time, we recognize that politics per se—national, regional, or local policy advocacy—is not for everyone. There are other ways to engage with technology, especially at the local level of home, school, workplace, hospital, public library, church, and community center. We all have personal relationships with some of these institutions. We can influence them without having to change broad governmental policy, though that might happen in some cases. . . .

Notes

[1] Arien Mack and Irvin Rock, *Inattentional Blindness* (Cambridge, MA: MIT Press, 1998).

[2] The issue of invisible work is explored at length in *Computer-supported Cooperative Work—A Journal of Collaborative Computing* 8, nos. 1–2 (May 1998), with guest editors Bonnie Nardi and Yrjö Engeström.

[3] Gordon Bell and James N. Gray, "The Revolution Yet to Happen," in *Beyond Calculation: The Next Fifty Years of Computing,* ed. Peter J. Denning and Robert M. Metcalfe (New York: Springer-Verlag, 1997).
[4] See also Michael Dertouzos, *What Will Be: How the New World of Information Will Change Our Lives* (San Francisco: Harper San Francisco, 1997).
[5] "Cloning procedure could bring unthinkable within reach," *San Jose Mercury News,* 24 February 1997.
[6] "Cloning procedure could bring unthinkable within reach," *San Jose Mercury News,* 24 February 1997.
[7] "Cloning procedure could bring unthinkable within reach," *San Jose Mercury News,* 24 February 1997.
[8] Margaret R. McLean, "Just because we can, should we?" *San Jose Mercury News,* 18 January 1998.
[9] Dystopic visions include Jerry Mander, *In the Absence of the Sacred* (San Francisco: Sierra Club Books, 1991); Sven Birkerts, *The Gutenberg Elegies: The Fate of Reading in an Electronic Age* (New York: Fawcett Books, 1995); and Neil Postman, *Technopoly* (New York: Vintage Books, 1993). Technophilia is well represented across the mass media in old-line publications such as *Time* and newer outlets such as *Wired.*
[10] Nicholas Negroponte, *Being Digital* (New York: Knopf, 1995).
[11] Clifford Stoll, *Silicon Snake Oil: Second Thoughts on the Information Highway* (New York: Doubleday, 1995).
[12] Richard Sclove, *Democracy and Technology* (New York: Guilford Press, 1995).

Mapping the Text

1. Nardi and O'Day argue that "more people can be fully engaged in important discussions and decisions about technology." How do they support this argument? What rhetorical tools do they offer readers to help them engage in meaningful debate about technology? How convincing do you find their argument?
2. What do Nardi and O'Day mean when they talk about "the rhetoric of inevitability"? Where do you find examples of this rhetoric in your current reading? Can you offer any counterexamples? What is the social and cultural effect of the rhetoric of inevitability? How do these authors propose that we respond to it?
3. Identify the "two conversational extremes" characterized by Nardi and O'Day. Look for examples of each rhetorical extreme in recent media coverage of technology. Do you agree that the rhetoric of technology tends to be "positioned at one of two extremes," as these authors claim? Why or why not? Find an example of an article or essay that moves closer to the middle ground called for in this article, and offer a brief analysis of your selection for your class or group members.

Writing to Inquire

1. Nardi and O'Day propose a framework for studying technology use in workplace settings. How would you summarize their methods? How does their approach capture the "invisible" aspects of work? What are these

invisible aspects? Based on their approach, carry out your own ethnographic study of technology use in a school or workplace setting to which you have access. Write an essay to describe the ways you observe people using and talking about technology and related issues in that setting.

2. Find a recent news story or magazine article dealing with the emergence of a particular new technology. Using the rhetorical frameworks established by Nardi and O'Day, analyze the rhetoric of that story or article, and develop an argument about how well it does or does not fit their proposed framework.

http://www.when_is_enough_enough?.com

Paul De Palma

Paul De Palma is a professor of mathematics and computer science at Gonzaga University in Spokane, Washington, where he teaches courses ranging from computer programming to studies in artificial intelligence. De Palma has published numerous articles, and his work has appeared in publications such as *The American Scholar, The Journal of Mathematics and Science Teaching,* and *Charter.* This essay, "http://www.when_is_enough_enough?.com," has appeared in three anthologies, including *Best American Science and Nature Writing* (2000).

In the misty past, before Bill Gates joined the company of the world's richest men, before the mass-marketed personal computer, before the metaphor of an information superhighway had been worn down to a cliché, I heard Roger Schank interviewed on National Public Radio. Then a computer science professor at Yale, Schank was already well known in artificial intelligence circles. Because those circles did not include me, a new programmer at Sperry Univac, I hadn't heard of him. Though I've forgotten the details of the conversation, I have never forgotten Schank's insistence that most people do not need to own computers.

That view, of course, has not prevailed. Either we own a personal computer and fret about upgrades, or we are scheming to own one and fret about the technical marvel yet to come that will render our purchase obsolete. Well, there are worse ways to spend money, I suppose. For all I know, even Schank owns a personal computer. They're fiendishly clever machines, after all, and they've helped keep the wolf from my door for a long time.

It is not the personal computer itself that I object to. What reasonable person would voluntarily go back to a typewriter? The mischief is not in the computer itself, but in the ideology that surrounds it. If we hope to employ computers for tasks more interesting than word processing, we must devote some attention to how they are actually being used, and beyond that, to the remarkable grip that the idol of computing continues to exert.

A distressing aspect of the media attention paid to the glories of technology is the persistent misidentification of the computing sciences with microcomputer gadgetry. This manifests itself in many ways. Once my seatmate on a plane learns that I am a computer science professor, I'm expected to chat about the glories of the new DVD-ROM as opposed to the older CD-ROM drives; or about that home shopping channel for the computer literate, the World Wide Web; or about one of the thousand other dreary topics that fill *PC Magazine* and your daily paper, and that by and large represent computing to most Americans. On a somewhat more pernicious level, we in computer science must contend with the phenomenon of prospective employers who ask for expertise in this or that proprietary product. This has had the effect of skewing our mission in the eyes of students majoring in our field. I recently saw a student résumé that listed skill with Harvard Graphics but neglected to mention course work in data communications. Another recent graduate in computer science insisted that the ability to write Word Perfect macros belonged on her résumé.

5 This is a sorry state. How we got there deserves some consideration.

A few words of self-disclosure may be in order. What I have to say may strike some as churlish ingratitude to an industry that has provided me with a life of comparative ease for nearly two decades. The fact is that my career as a computer scientist was foisted upon me. When I discovered computers, I was working on a doctorate in English at Berkeley and contemplating a life not of ease but of almost certain underemployment. The computer industry found me one morning on its doorstep, wrapped me in its generous embrace, and has cared for me ever since. I am paid well to puzzle out the charming intricacies of computer programs with bright, attentive students, all happy in the knowledge that their skills will be avidly sought out the day after graduation. I can go to sleep confident that were tenure to be abolished tomorrow, the industry would welcome me back like a prodigal son.

Yet for all its largesse, I fear the computer industry has never had my full loyalty. Neither did English studies, for that matter, but this probably says more about those drawn to the study of texts than about me. My memories of the time I spent in the company of the "best which has been thought and said" are hazy, perhaps because the study of literature is not so much a discipline as an attitude. The attitude that dominated all others when I was a student, that sustained my forays into the Western Americana of the Bancroft Collection, is that there is no text so dreary, so impoverished, so bereft of ideas that it does not cry out to be examined—deconstructed, as a graduate student a few years my junior might have said. But the text I now propose to examine, impelled, as it were, by early imprinting in the English department, goes beyond words on a page.

From an article here and a TV program there, from a thousand conversations on commuter trains and over lunch and dinner, from the desperate scrambling of local politicians after software companies, the notion that prosperity follows computing, like the rain that was once thought to follow the settler's plow, has become a fully formed mythology.

In his perceptive little book *Technopoly,* Neil Postman argues that all disciplines ought to be taught as if they were history. That way, students "can begin to understand, as they now do not, that knowledge is not a fixed thing but a stage in human development, with a past and a future." I wish I'd said that first. If all knowledge has a past—and computer technology is surely a special kind of knowledge—then all knowledge is contingent. The technical landscape is not an engineering necessity. It might be other than it is. Our prospective majors might come to us, as new mathematics or physics majors come to their professors, because of an especially inspiring high school teacher, because of a flair for symbol manipulation, or even because of a (dare I use the word?) curiosity about what constitutes the discipline and its objects of study—not simply because they like gadgets and there's a ton of money to be made in computing.

10 The misidentification of computer science with microcomputer gadgetry is a symptom of a problem that goes far beyond academe. Extraordinary assertions are being made about computers in general and microcomputers in particular. These assertions translate into claims on the American purse—either directly, or indirectly through the tax system. Every dollar our school districts spend on microcomputers is a dollar not spent reducing class size, buying books for the library, reinstating art programs, hiring school counselors, and so on. In fact, every dollar that each of us spends outfitting ourselves with the year's biggest, fastest microcomputer is a dollar we might have put away for retirement, saved for our children's education, spent touring the splendors of the American West, or even chosen not to earn. In the spirit of Neil Postman, then, I'd like to speculate about how the mythology of prosperity through computing has come to be and, in the process, suggest that like the Wizard of Oz, it may be less miraculous than it looks.

The place to begin is the spectacular spread of microcomputers themselves. By 1993 nearly a quarter of American households owned at least one. Four years later, the *Wall Street Journal* put this figure at over 40 percent. For a home appliance that costs at least $1,000, probably closer to $2,000, this represents a substantial outlay. The home market, as it turns out, is the smaller part of the story by far. The Census Bureau tells us that in 1995, the last year for which data are available, Americans spent almost $48 billion on small computers for their homes and businesses. This figure excludes software, peripherals, and services purchased after the new machines were installed.

The title of an article in the *Economist*—"Personal Computers: The End of Good Times?"—hints at the extraordinary world we are trying to understand. In it we learn that annual growth in the home computer market slowed from 40 percent in 1994 to between 15 percent and 20 percent in 1995. By the fall of 1998, market analysts were predicting 16 percent growth in the industry as a whole for the current year. Those of us involved in other sectors of the economy can only look on in astonishment. When a 20 percent, or even 16 percent, growth rate—well over five times that of the economy as a whole—is "the end of good times," we know we're in the presence of an industry whose expectations and promises have left the earth's gravitational pull.

To put some flesh on these numbers, let's try a thought experiment. The computer on my desk is about 16 inches by 17 inches. The Census Bureau tells us that the microcomputer industry delivered over 18 million machines in 1994, the year when, according to the *Economist,* good times ended. Of these, perhaps a third went to the home market, the balance to business. At the 40 percent growth rate in the home market cited for that year and the more modest 16 percent growth rate for the business market, the boys in Redmond and Silicon Valley will have covered the United States' 3,679,192 square miles with discarded microcomputers well before my daughter, who is now thirteen, begins to collect Social Security.

Fabulous as they seem, these figures come from only part of the industry. Microcomputers do not define computing, despite their spectacular entry on the scene. The standard story goes like this: There was once a lumbering blue dinosaur called IBM that dominated the computer industry. In due course, smaller, more agile, and immensely more clever mammals appeared on the scene. The most agile and clever of these was Microsoft, which proceeded to expand its ecological niche and, in so doing, drove the feeble-minded IBM to the brink of extinction.

15 The business history in this story is as faulty as its paleontology. IBM may be lumbering and blue, but in 1997 its sales were nearly $78 billion. Compare that with Microsoft's $9 billion. The real story is not in the sales volumes of the two companies but in their profit margins. In 1997 IBM's was 7.7 percent, while Microsoft's was a spectacular 28.7 percent. This almost mythical earning capability is expressed best in *Forbes*'s annual list of very rich Americans. We don't hear much about IBM billionaires these days, but Microsoft fortunes are conspicuous in the *Forbes* list, with Bill Gates's $51 billion, Paul Allen's $21 billion, and Steven Ballmer's $10.7 billion. These fortunes were accumulated in less than twenty years from manufacturing a product that requires no materials beyond the inexpensive medium it is stored on—not so different from a pickle producer, whose only cost, after the first jar comes off the line, is the jar itself. It's a tale of alchemical transmutation if ever there was one. Is it really a surprise that most people don't know that IBM is still a very successful company or that computer science does not begin and end with Windows 98?

This joyous account of fortunes waiting to be made in the microcomputer industry has a dark side. Just as Satan is the strongest character in *Paradise Lost,* as C. S. Lewis observed, so is popular fascination with computers due as much to the dark side as to the light. Despite generally good economic news for the past few years, Americans seem gloomy about their prospects. Our brave new world, paved over with networked computers from sea to shining sea, may well be one in which we are mostly unemployed or have experienced a serious decline in living standards. Computers, if not always at the center of the problem, are popularly thought to have been a major contributing factor.

Look at the substantial decline in manufacturing as a segment of the workforce in the United States. Between 1970 and 1996 (the last year for which data are available), the number of Americans employed increased by about 50 million. During this same period, the number of manufacturing jobs declined by about 200,000. The culprit here is often thought to be computer technology, through assembly line robots or through U.S.-owned (or U.S.-contracted) manufacturing facilities in-developing countries. Asia and Latin America, of course, would have less appeal to American corporations without worldwide data communications networks.

This analysis of the decline in manufacturing employment is perhaps more appealing than true. I will return to the relationship between computers and productivity. For now it's enough to observe that most people believe there is such a relationship. So if the money to be made in the computer industry is not sufficient inducement to vote for the next school bond issue that would outfit every classroom in your city with networked computers, then the poverty your children will certainly face without such a network should do the trick. With those staggering Microsoft fortunes in the background and the threat of corporate retrenchment in the foreground, I suppose I'm naive to expect the strangers I chat with on planes to know that the computing sciences are more like mathematics and the physical sciences than like desktop publishing—or, for that matter, like the rush to the Klondike goldfields.

The emergence of the microcomputer as a consumer item in the past decade and a half has prompted a flood of articles in the educational literature promoting what has come to be called "computer literacy." In its most basic sense, this term appears to refer to something like a passing familiarity with microcomputers and their commercial applications, rather like the ability to drive a car and know when to get the oil changed. Sadly, the proponents of computer literacy have won the high ground by virtue of the term itself. Who would argue with literacy? It is, after all, one of the more complex human achievements. Not only is literacy a shorthand measure of a country's economic development, but as the rhetorician Walter J. Ong has long argued, once a culture becomes generally literate, its modes of conceptualization are radically altered. Literacy—like motherhood and apple pie in the America of my youth—is unassailable.

20 But what about the transformative nature of literacy? I am fully aware that similar claims have been made about computers—namely, that computers, like writing, will alter our modes of conceptualization. Maybe so, but not just by running Microsoft Office. I've developed a rule of thumb about claims of this sort: If the subject matter is computers and the tense of the claim is future (and, therefore, its truth-value cannot be ascertained), look at the subtext. Is the claimant a salesman in disguise? To recognize the nonsense in the claim that computers will transform the way we think, we need only indulge in some honest self-examination. I would give up my word processor with great reluctance. This doesn't mean that my neuronal structure is somehow fundamentally different from what it was when I was writing essays similar to this one on my manual Smith Corona. It does mean that the computer industry is a smidgen richer because of my contribution. It also means, as was recently pointed out to me, that it is a good bit easier to run on at great length on a computer than on a typewriter.

Not surprisingly, the number of articles addressing computer literacy in the educational literature has kept pace with microcomputer developments. ERIC is a database of titles published in education journals. When I searched ERIC using the keywords *computer literacy* and *computer literate,* I found 97 articles for the years 1966–1981, or an average of about 6 per year. The decade from 1982 to 1991 produced 2,703 hits, or about 270 per year. At first glance the production of articles since 1991 shows welcome signs of dropping off. But the Internet has come to the rescue of both the microcomputer industry and its prognosticators. When I add the terms "Internet," "World Wide Web," and "information superhighway" to the mix (subtracting for duplicates), the total rises to an astonishing 4,680 articles from 1992 through the first half of 1998. This works out to about 720 articles per year. The bulk of the recent articles, of course, are full of blather about the so-called information superhighway and how all those school districts that cannot give every child access to it will be condemning the next generation to lives of poverty and ignorance.

Since computer literacy advocates are eloquent on the benefits of computers in our schools (and equally eloquent on the grim fate that awaits those students not so blessed), a brief look at how microcomputers are actually used in primary and secondary schools is in order. Microcomputers are now a solid presence in American education. The U.S. Census Bureau put the number at nearly 7 million in 1997, or just over 7 students per machine, compared with 11 students per machine in 1994 and 63 per machine a decade earlier. Picture a classroom richly endowed with computers. Several students are bent over a machine, eyes aglow with the discoveries unfolding on the screen. Perhaps there is a kindly teacher in the portrait, pointing to some complex relationship that the computer has helped the budding physicists, social scientists, or software engineers to uncover. If this is the way you imagine primary and secondary school students using computers, you are dead wrong. Several important studies have concluded that primary and secondary school students spend more time mastering the intricacies of word processing than they do using computers for the kinds of tasks that we have in mind when we vote for a bond issue.

Programming, in fact, was the one area that school computer coordinators saw decline over previous years. I would be the first to acknowledge that programming does not define computer science. This simple fact is what makes the endless discussion of programming languages in computer science circles so tedious. Nevertheless, if computer science does not begin and end with programming, neither will it give up its secrets to those who cannot program. I greet the news that high school students do not program our millions of microcomputers as an English professor might greet the news that the school library is terrific but the kids don't read. Here is a puzzle worth more than a moment's thought. There is an inverse relationship between the availability of microcomputers to primary and secondary school students and the chance that those students will do something substantial with them. I am not saying that the relationship is causal, but the association is there. Draw your own conclusions.

Though the jury is still out on the potential educational benefits of computing, we all agree that skill with computers is necessary for success in business. Even here there's a problem. Recent studies have assembled evidence that should give computer enthusiasts some sleepless nights. It appears that most businesses would be better off had they taken all that money they spent on computer technology and put it into bonds at market rates. This investment has been substantial, as anyone knows who has seen the piles of unopened software, the manuals still in their shrink-wrapped plastic, and the stacks of obsolete hardware accumulating in storerooms around the country. By 1995 it had totaled over $4 trillion. This sum, it should be noted, excludes the public money involved in training (and employing) academic computer scientists and engineers.

25 It also excludes another hidden expenditure. The time employees spend rearranging icons on their screens, the time they spend wondering why their spreadsheets will not recognize their printers—in fact, all those minutes here and hours there spent fiddling with hardware and software—is time they do not spend on the tasks they are being paid to perform.

Let me tell a story. I have been a computer science professor for seven years. Before that I spent a decade working for some of the largest firms in the computer industry. I am, by any reasonable measure, computer literate. One recent Sunday afternoon I thought I might pop into my office, copy this essay to a floppy disk, and work on it at home, where I was also caring for a child with chicken pox. In other words, I took the microcomputer industry up on its central promise: workers will be liberated from the tyranny of place. Able to function as parents and workers simultaneously, we will prosper along with our employers.

Here's what really happened. I promised my wife I'd be gone no more than thirty-five minutes, twenty-five for the drive to and from the university, ten to copy the file. As it happens, I am the last remaining member of the professional middle class without Microsoft Windows running at home. What I have is a 286 IBM clone running DOS and WordPerfect 5.1, equipment my last employer gave me when I left seven years ago. This setup was well on its way toward obsolescence when I acquired it. Were my students to learn that I wrote with a quill pen by the light of an oil lamp, they would think me hardly less quaint.

However, my reluctance to part with hard-earned money for a shiny new computer that I would use only as an abundantly out-fitted typewriter did pose a small challenge. I would have to get the file from my office computer, a fancy Pentium workstation (courtesy of my current employer), to run on my ever-faithful home machine. Not a problem, I thought. I can easily transform the Microsoft Word file in my office to ASCII text, copy it to a $5\frac{1}{4}$-inch floppy disk, and read it into WordPerfect at home.

As we have all come to know, painfully at first and finally with resignation, when the subject is personal computers, things are not always as promised. (It has occurred to me more than once that the computer industry should have the honor of Iago and display these words boldly on every screen: "I am not what I am.") First I learned that my document was infected with the Word macro virus. No matter how I tried, Word would not let me transform it from a template (a term known to all Word users, happily ignored by most) to a text file. So I called a colleague who gave me what is known in the computer industry as a "workaround." A workaround is what you do when your machine is not running the way the manufacturer promised. By analogy, a workaround for faulty automobile brakes might be to open the door and drag your feet. In any case, my colleague is a clever fellow and the workaround did allow me to work around the handiwork of the disgruntled Microsoft employee who had infected Word with the virus. Having transformed my essay into a generic text file, I was ready to copy it to a floppy and return home, safe in the knowledge that I could be both productive and parental.

30 Unfortunately, our former systems administrator, for reasons that must have made eminent sense to him, had disabled my A drive. But as I said earlier, I am computer literate. Though annoying, a disabled drive is not catastrophic. I need only invoke a special setup routine to let Windows knows that, in fact, there is a $5\frac{1}{4}$-inch floppy drive on my machine. But since this machine is a castoff from our department's lab, the systems administrator had, wisely, password-protected the setup routine. He had also, in the meantime, decamped for the vastly more remunerative pastures

of the computer industry. In a word, he was unavailable and so was my machine. I returned home, nearly two hours after I had left, to an unhappy wife and a sicker child—and without the file.

This is not an isolated story. Anyone who has dealt with a microcomputer has a store of similar tales. There is another story here as well. Even if one is inclined to stick with the tried and true, the computer industry—and its minions across the land—will not permit it. By the time this article goes to press, the last computer in my department with a drive that accommodates $5^{1}/_{4}$-inch diskettes will have gone to wherever old computers go. My well-worn and well-loved 286 will then be an island cut off from the main, and I, its single inhabitant, will speak a language that is fast becoming extinct.

The price of computing equipment has dropped dramatically in recent years. For under $2,000 you can buy a microcomputer that processes millions of instructions per second and is equipped with a stunningly large memory and disk space. At that price we can all be equipped at the office, and most of us will choose to be equipped at home. As it happens, that $2,000 (plus a bit more for networking components) is the smallest slice of the great pie of microcomputer costs. The *Economist* cites a study by the Gartner Group, a respected consulting firm, that puts the annual cost of a microcomputer connected to a network at $13,200. Of this, only 21 percent goes to the purchase of hardware and software. Administrative costs absorb 36 percent. We have to pay all those people who come to our rescue, after all. This figure alone should slow down the headlong rush to outfit every desk on the planet with a microcomputer.

That administration costs more than the machine itself is not the biggest surprise. Recall my story. Just how much was my two hours worth? On the average, 43 percent of the cost of a microcomputer is consumed in what Gartner calls "end-user operations." Just what are end-user operations? They are all those things one does with a computer in order to do the things one gets paid to do. This includes rearranging icons, coaxing disk drives into action, loading and setting up software, avoiding viruses, listening to Microsoft's music as you wait helplessly on hold for advice from someone in technical support who probably knows less than you do, and so on.

Though the Gartner Group has done us the service of quantifying those long hours spent mastering yet another Microsoft user interface, the effect of that time on worker productivity has been known for some years now. Many studies, including some done by the National Research Council and by Morgan Stanley, the New York investment bank, fail to indicate any correlation between productivity growth and information technology expenditures. Distressingly, the opposite appears to be true. As Thomas Landauer has pointed out in *The Trouble with Computers,* those industries that invested most heavily in information technology, with the exception of communications, seem to have the most sluggish productivity growth rates. Though one still could argue that schools and colleges should continue to teach courses in microcomputer literacy because microcomputer usage has grown like a fungus after a heavy rain, our time might be more profitably spent breaking the bad news to the public that pays the bills. In the process, we might also come to understand how a machine so patently clever as the microcomputer could have done the business world (outside of the computer industry itself) so little good.

35 Given the several thousand articles on computer literacy and the emerging inverse relationship between productivity growth and computer expenditures, it seems reasonable to ask just who does benefit from the computer literacy movement—and who pays for it. The commonsense answer is, Students benefit. Well, common sense is right, but, as usual, only partially so. Students, of course, are served by learning how to use microcomputers. But the main beneficiaries are the major producers of hardware and software. The situation is really quite extraordinary. Schools and colleges across the country are offering academic credit to students who master the basics of sophisticated consumer products. Granted that it is more difficult to master Microsoft Office than it is to learn to use a VCR or a toaster oven, the difference is one of degree, not of kind.

The obvious question is why the computer industry itself does not train its customers. The answer is that it doesn't have to. Schools, at great public expense, provide this service to the computer industry free of charge. Not only do the educational institutions provide the trainers and the setting for the training, they actually purchase the products on which the students are to be trained from the corporations that are the primary beneficiaries of that training. The story is an old but generally unrecognized one in the United States: the costs are socialized, while the benefits are privatized.

I have described a bleak landscape in this essay. Let me summarize my observations:

Schools and universities purchase products from the computer industry to offer training that benefits the computer industry.

These purchases are both publicly subsidized through tax support and paid for by students (and their parents) themselves.

40 The skill imparted is at best trivial and does not require faculty with advanced degrees in computer science—degrees acquired by and large through public, not computer industry, support.

As the number of microcomputers in our schools has grown, the chance that something interesting might be done with them has decreased.

The stunning complexity of microcomputer hardware and software has had the disastrous effect of transforming every English professor, every secretary, every engineer, every manager into a computer systems technician.

For all the public subsidies involved in the computer literacy movement, the evidence that microcomputers have made good on their central promise—increased productivity—is, at the very least, open to question.

If my argument is at least partially correct, we should begin to rethink computing. The microcomputer industry has been with us for a decade and a half. We have poured staggering sums down its insatiable maw. It is time to face an unpleasant fact: the so-called microcomputer revolution has cost much more than it has returned. One problem is that microcomputers are vastly more complex than the tasks ordinarily asked of them. To write a report on a machine with a Pentium II processor, sixty-four megabytes of memory, and an eight-gigabyte hard disk is like leasing the space shuttle to fly from New York to Boston to catch a Celtics game. Though there are those who wouldn't hesitate to do such a thing if they could afford it (or get it subsidized, which is more to the point), we follow their lead at great peril. The computer industry itself is beginning to recognize the foolishness of placing such computing power on every office worker's desk. Oracle, the world's premier manufacturer of database management systems; Sun Microsystems, a maker of powerful and highly respected engineering workstations; and IBM itself are arguing that a substantially scaled down network computer, costing under $1,000, would serve corporate users better than the monsters necessary to run Microsoft's products.

45 Please don't misunderstand. This is not a neo-Luddite plea to toss computers out the window. I am, after all, a computer science professor, and I am certainly not ready (as the militias in my part of the country put it) to get off the grid. Further, the social benefits of computing—from telecommunications to business transactions to medicine to science—are well known. This essay is simply a plea to think reasonably about these machines, to recognize the hucksterism in the hysterical cries for computer literacy, to steel ourselves against the urge to keep throwing money at Redmond and Silicon Valley.

Putting microcomputers in their place will also have a salutary effect on my discipline. We in computer science could then begin to claim that our field—like mathematics, like English literature, like philosophy—is a marvelous human creation whose study is its own reward. To study computer science calls for concentration, discipline, even some amount of deferred gratification, but it requires neither Windows 98, nor a four-hundred-megahertz Pentium II processor, nor a graphical Web browser. Though I am tempted, I will not go so far as to say that the introductory study of computer science requires no computing equipment at all (though Alan Turing did do some pretty impressive work without a microcomputer budget). We do seem, however, to have confused the violin with the concerto, the pencil with the theorem, and the dancer with the dance.

I am afraid that we in computing have made a Faustian bargain. In exchange for riches, we are condemned to a lifetime of conversations about the World Wide Web. An eternity in hell with Dr. Faustus, suffering the torments of demons, would be an afternoon in the park by comparison.

References and Further Reading

Bennet, R.; Cavanagh, J. *Global Dreams.* NY: Simon & Schuster; 1995.

Does a nice job of discussing the global economy.

Landauer, T. *The Trouble with Computers: Usefulness, Usability, and Productivity.* Cambridge: MIT Press; 1995.

My source for productivity data. More recent statistics are slightly more optimistic than Landauer. Nevertheless, claims of productivity gains through computing have been around for three decades or more. That computers are finally—and tentatively—making good on these claims shows that they have long been overstated.

Ong, W.J. *The Presence of the Word.* New Haven: Yale University Press; 1967.

A scholarly discussion of genuine, as opposed to computer, literacy.

Postman, N. *Technopoly.* NY: Vintage; 1993.

An irreverent look at technology.

Rifkin, J. *The End of Work.* NY: G.P. Putnam's Sons; 1995.

One of the many books that claims that computers will put us out of work.

Weighing the Case for the Network Computer. *The Economist* 1/18/97: 61–62; 1997.

Provides numbers to support what I had long suspected, namely, that once you assign a cost to the time it takes to keep the computer on your desk running, the computer begins to seem like a less attractive investment.

Mapping the Text

1. Create an outline for Paul De Palma's essay, then explain how he answers the question posed by his title: When is enough enough? What is the focus of his concern?
2. Write a narrative of your first memory of using a computer. Think about the difference between that first experience and wherever you are now with computer technology. What effect have computers had on your life? What is the same? What is different? How did you think of computers in the beginning? How do you think of them now?

Writing to Inquire

1. Search library and other sources for information about the funding of technology in K–12 classrooms. What conclusions do you draw from the information you gathered? How has schooling been affected over the last few years by computer technology?
2. Write an essay in which you support or disagree with De Palma.

READINGS FOR INQUIRY AND EXPLORATION

Identity in the Age of the Internet

SHERRY TURKLE

Sherry Turkle is Professor of the Sociology of Science in the Program in Science, Technology, and Society at the Massachusetts Institute of Technology (MIT). Turkle also directs the MIT Initiative on Technology and Self, and she is a licensed clinical psychologist. Her works include numerous articles as well as *Psychoanalytic Politics: Jacques Lacan and Freud's French Revolution* (1978) and *The Second Self: Computers and the Human Spirit* (1984). "Identity in the Age of the Internet" is an excerpt from her most recent book, *Life on the Screen: Identity in the Age of the Internet* (1995). One of her most recent projects involved studying the relationships between children and their cyberpets, such as furbys, tamagotchis, and gigapets.

French Lessons

In late 1960s and early 1970s, I lived in a culture that taught that the self is constituted by and through language, that sexual congress is the exchange of signifiers, and that each of us is a multiplicity of parts, fragments, and desiring connections. This was the hothouse of Paris intellectual culture whose gurus included Jacques Lacan, Michel Foucault, Gilles Deleuze, and Félix Guattari.[1] But despite such ideal conditions for learning, my "French lessons" remained merely abstract exercises. These theorists of poststructuralism and what would come to be called postmodernism spoke words that addressed the relationship between mind and body but, from my point of view, had little or nothing to do with my own.

In my lack of connection with these ideas, I was not alone. To take one example, for many people it is hard to accept any challenge to the idea of an autonomous ego. While in recent years, many psychologists, social theorists, psychoanalysts, and philosophers have argued that the self should be thought of as essentially decentered, the normal requirements of everyday life exert strong pressure on people to take responsibility for their actions and to see themselves as intentional and unitary actors. This disjuncture between theory (the unitary self is an illusion) and lived experience (the unitary self is the most basic reality) is one of the main reasons why multiple and decentered theories have been slow to catch on—or when they do, why we tend to settle back quickly into older, centralized ways of looking at things.

Today I use the personal computer and modem on my desk to access MUDs. Anonymously, I travel their rooms and public spaces (a bar, a lounge, a hot tub). I create several characters, some not of my biological gender, who are able to have social and sexual encounters with other characters. On different MUDs, I have different routines, different friends, different names. One day I learned of a virtual rape. One MUD player had used his skill with the system to seize control of another player's character. In this way the aggressor was able to direct the seized character to submit to a violent sexual encounter. He did all this against the will and over the distraught objections of the player usually "behind" this character, the player to whom this character "belonged." Although some made light of the offender's actions by saying that the episode was just words, in text-based virtual realities such as MUDs, words *are* deeds.

Thus, more than twenty years after meeting the ideas of Lacan, Foucault, Deleuze, and Guattari, I am meeting them again in my new life on the screen. But this time, the Gallic abstractions are more concrete. In my computer-mediated worlds, the self is multiple, fluid, and constituted in interaction with machine connections; it is made and transformed by language; sexual congress is an exchange of signifiers; and understanding follows from navigation and tinkering rather than analysis. And in the machine-generated world of MUDs, I meet characters who put me in a new relationship with my own identity.

5 One day on a MUD, I came across a reference to a character named Dr. Sherry, a cyberpsychologist with an office in the rambling house that constituted this MUD's virtual geography. There, I was informed, Dr. Sherry was administering questionnaires and conducting interviews about the psychology of MUDs. I suspected that the name Dr. Sherry referred to my long career as a student of the psychological impact of technology. But I didn't create this character. I was not playing her on the MUD. Dr. Sherry was (she is no longer on the MUD) a derivative of me, but she was not mine. The character I played on this MUD had another name—and did not give out questionnaires or conduct interviews. My formal studies were conducted offline in a traditional clinical setting where I spoke face-to-face with people who participate in virtual communities. Dr. Sherry may have been a character someone else created as an efficient way of communicating an interest in questions about technology and the self, but I was experiencing her as a little piece of my history spinning out of control. I tried to quiet my mind. I told myself that surely one's books, one's intellectual identity, one's public persona, are pieces of oneself that others may use as they please. I tried to convince myself that this virtual appropriation was a form of flattery. But my disquiet continued. Dr. Sherry, after all, was not an inanimate book but a person, or at least a person behind a character who was meeting with others in the MUD world.

I talked my disquiet over with a friend who posed the conversation-stopping question, "Well, would you prefer it if Dr. Sherry were a bot trained to interview people about life on the MUD?" (Recall that bots are computer programs that are able to roam cyberspace and interact with characters there.) The idea that Dr. Sherry might be a bot had not occurred to me, but in a flash I realized that this too was possible, even likely. Many bots roam MUDs. They log onto the games as though they were characters. Players create these programs for many reasons bots help with navigation, pass messages, and create a background atmosphere of animation in the MUD. When you enter a virtual café, you are usually not alone. A waiter bot approaches who asks if you want a drink and delivers it with a smile.

Characters played by people are sometimes mistaken for these little artificial intelligences. This was the case for Doug's character Carrot, because its passive, facilitating persona struck many as one a robot could play. I myself have made this kind of mistake several times, assuming that a person was a program when a character's responses seemed too automatic, too machine-like. And sometimes bots are mistaken for people. I have made this mistake too, fooled by a bot that flattered me by remembering my name or our last interaction. Dr. Sherry could indeed have been one of these. I found myself confronted with a double that could be a person or a program. As things turned out, Dr. Sherry was neither; it was a composite character created by two college students who wished to write a paper on the psychology of MUDs and who were using my name as a kind of trademark or generic descriptor for the idea of a cybershrink.[2] On MUDs, the one can be many and the many can be one.

So not only are MUDs places where the self is multiple and constructed by language, they are places where people and machines are in a new relation to each other, indeed can be mistaken for each other. In such ways, MUDs are evocative objects for thinking about human identity and, more generally, about a set of ideas that have come to be known as "postmodernism."

These ideas are difficult to define simply, but they are characterized by such terms as "decentered," "fluid," "nonlinear," and "opaque." They contrast with modernism, the classical world-view that has dominated Western thinking since the Enlightenment. The modernist view of reality is characterized by such terms as "linear," "logical," "hierarchical," and by having "depths" that can be plumbed and understood. MUDs offer an experience of the abstract postmodern ideas that had intrigued yet confused me during my intellectual coming of age. In this, MUDs exemplify a phenomenon we shall meet often in these pages, that of computer-mediated experiences bringing philosophy down to earth.

10 In a surprising and counter-intuitive twist, in the past decade, the mechanical engines of computers have been grounding the radically nonmechanical philosophy of postmodernism. The online world of the Internet is not the only instance of evocative computer objects and experiences bringing postmodernism down to earth. One of my students at MIT dropped out of a course I teach on social theory, complaining that the

writings of the literary theorist Jacques Derrida were simply beyond him. He found that Derrida's dense prose and far-flung philosophical allusions were incomprehensible. The following semester I ran into the student in an MIT cafeteria. "Maybe I wouldn't have to drop out now," he told me. In the past month, with his roommate's acquisition of new software for his Macintosh computer, my student had found his own key to Derrida. That software was a type of hypertext, which allows a computer user to create links between related texts, songs, photographs, and video, as well as to travel along the links made by others. Derrida emphasized that writing is constructed by the audience as well as by the author and that what is absent from the text is as significant as what is present. The student made the following connection:

> Derrida was saying that the messages of the great books are no more written in stone than are the links of a hypertext. I look at my roommate's hypertext stacks and I am able to trace the connections he made and the peculiarities of how he links things together. . . . And the things he might have linked but didn't. The traditional texts are like [elements in] the stack. Meanings are arbitrary, as arbitrary as the links in a stack.

"The cards in a hypertext stack," he concluded, "get their meaning in relation to each other. It's like Dorrida. The links have a reason but there is no final truth behind them."[3]

Like experiences on MUDs, the student's story shows how technology is bringing a set of ideas associated with postmodernism—in this case, ideas about the instability of meanings and the lack of universal and knowable truths—into everyday life. In recent years, it has become fashionable to poke fun at postmodern philosophy and lampoon its allusiveness and density. Indeed, I have done some of this myself. But through experiences with computers, people come to a certain understanding of postmodernism and to recognize its ability to usefully capture certain aspects of their own experience, both online and off.

In *The Electronic Word,* the classicist Richard A. Lanham argues that open-ended screen text subverts traditional fantasies of a master narrative, or definitive reading, by presenting the reader with possibilities for changing fonts, zooming in and out, and rearranging and replacing text. The result is "a body of work active not passive, a canon not frozen in perfection but volatile with contending human motive.[4] Lanham puts technology and postmodernism together and concludes that the computer is a "fulfillment of social thought." But I believe the relationship is better thought of as a two-way process. Computer technology not only "fulfills the postmodern aesthetic" as Lanham would have it, heightening and concretizing the postmodern experience, but helps that aesthetic hit the street as well as the seminar room. Computers embody postmodern theory and bring it down to earth.

As recently as ten to fifteen years ago, it was almost unthinkable to speak of the computer's involvement with ideas about unstable meanings and unknowable truths.[5] The computer had a clear intellectual identity as a calculating machine. Indeed, when I took an introductory programming course at Harvard in 1978, the professor introduced the computer to the class by calling it a giant calculator. Programming, he reassured us, was a cut and dried technical activity whose rules were crystal clear.

These reassurances captured the essence of what I shall be calling the modernist computational aesthetic. The image of the computer as calculator suggested that no matter how complicated a computer might seem, what happened inside it could be mechanically unpacked. Programming was a technical skill that could be done a right way or a wrong way. The right way was dictated by the computer's calculator essence. The right way was linear and logical. My professor made it clear that this linear, logical calculating machine combined with a structured, rule-based method of writing software offered guidance for thinking not only about technology and programming, but about economics, psychology, and social life. In other words, computational ideas were presented as one of the great modern metanarratives, stories of how the world worked that provided unifying pictures and analyzed complicated things by breaking them down into simpler parts. The modernist computational aesthetic promised to explain and unpack, to reduce and clarify. Although the computer culture was never monolithic, always including dissenters and deviant subcultures, for many years its professional mainstream (including computer scientists, engineers, economists, and cognitive scientists) shared this clear intellectual direction. Computers, it was assumed, would become more powerful, both as tools and as metaphors, by becoming better and faster calculating machines, better and faster analytical engines.

From a Culture of Calculation toward a Culture of Simulation

15 Most people over thirty years old (and even many younger ones) have had an introduction to computers similar to the one I received in that programming course. But from today's perspective, the fundamental lessons of computing that I was taught are wrong. First of all, programming is no longer cut and dried. Indeed, even its dimensions have become elusive. Are you programming when you customize your wordprocessing software? When you design "organisms" to populate a simulation of Darwinian evolution in a computer game called SimLife? Or when you build a room in a MUD so that opening a door to it will cause "Happy Un-Birthday" to ring out on all but one day of the year? In a sense, these activities are forms of programming, but that sense is radically different from the one presented in my 1978 computer course.

The lessons of computing today have little to do with calculation and rules; instead they concern simulation, navigation, and interaction. The very image of the computer as a giant calculator has become quaint and dated. Of course, there is still "calculation" going on within the computer, but it is no longer the important or interesting level to think about or interact with. Fifteen years ago, most computer users were limited to typing commands. Today they use off-the-shelf products to manipulate simulated desktops, draw with simulated paints and brushes, and fly in simulated airplane cockpits. The computer culture's center of gravity has shifted decisively to people who do not think of themselves as programmers. The computer science research community as well as industry pundits maintain that in the near future we can expect to interact with computers by communicating with simulated people on our screens, agents who will help organize our personal and professional lives.

On my daughter's third birthday she received a computer game called The Playroom, among the most popular pieces of software for the preschool set. If you ask for help, The Playroom offers an instruction that is one sentence long: "Just move the cursor to any object, click on it, explore and have fun." During the same week that my daughter learned to click in The Playroom, a colleague gave me my first lesson on how to use the World Wide Web, a cyberconstruct that links text, graphics, video, and audio on computers all over the world. Her instructions were almost identical to those I had just read to my daughter: "Just move the cursor to any underlined word or phrase, click on it, explore, and have fun." When I wrote this text in January 1995, the Microsoft corporation had just introduced Bob, a "social" interface for its Windows operating system, the most widely used operating system for personal computers in the world.[6] Bob, a computer agent with a human face and "personality," operates within a screen environment designed to look like a living room that is in almost every sense a playroom for adults. In my daughter's screen playroom, she is presented with such objects as alphabet blocks and a clock for learning to tell time. Bob offers adults a wordprocessor, a fax machine, a telephone. Children and adults are united in the actions they take in virtual worlds. Both move the cursor and click.

The meaning of the computer presence in people's lives is very different from what most expected in the late 1970s. One way to describe what has happened is to say that we are moving from a modernist culture of calculation toward a postmodernist culture of simulation.

The culture of simulation is emerging in many domains. It is affecting our understanding of our minds and our bodies. For example, fifteen years ago, the computational models of mind that dominated academic psychology were modernist in spirit: Nearly all tried to describe the mind in terms of centralized structures and programmed rules. In contrast, today's models often embrace a postmodern aesthetic of complexity and decentering. Mainstream computer researchers no longer aspire to program intelligence into computers but expect intelligence to emerge from the interactions of small subprograms. If these emergent simulations are "opaque," that is, too complex to be completely analyzed, this is not necessarily a problem. After all, these theorists say, our brains are opaque to us, but this has never prevented them from functioning perfectly well as minds.

20 Fifteen years ago in popular culture, people were just getting used to the idea that computers could project and extend a person's intellect. Today people are embracing the notion that computers may extend an individual's physical presence. Some people use computers to extend their physical presence via real-time video links and shared virtual conference rooms. Some use computer-mediated screen communication for sexual encounters. An Internet list of "Frequently Asked Questions" describes the latter activity—known as netsex, cybersex, and (in MUDs) TinySex—as people typing messages with erotic content to each other, "sometimes with one hand on the keyset, sometimes with two."

Many people who engage in netsex say that they are constantly surprised by how emotionally and physically powerful it can be. They insist that it demonstrates the truth of the adage that ninety percent of sex takes place in the mind. This is certainly not a new idea, but netsex has made it commonplace among teenage boys, a social group not usually known for its sophistication about such matters. A seventeen-year-old high school student tells me that he tries to make his erotic communications on the net "exciting and thrilling and sort of imaginative." In contrast, he admits that before he used computer communication for erotic purposes he thought about his sexual life in terms of "trying [almost always unsuccessfully] to get laid." A sixteen-year-old has a similar report on his cyberpassage to greater sensitivity: "Before I was on the net, I used to masturbate with *Playboy;* now I do netsex on DinoMUD[7] with a woman in another state." When I ask how the two experiences differ, he replies:

> With netsex, it is fantasies. My MUD lover doesn't want to meet me in RL. With *Playboy,* it was fantasies too, but in the MUD there is also the other person. So I don't think of what I do on the MUD as masturbation. Although, you might say that I'm the only one who's touching me. But in netsex, I have to think of fantasies she will like too. So now, I see fantasies as some thing that's part of sex with two people, not just me in my room.

Sexual encounters in cyberspace are only one (albeit well-publicized) element of our new lives on the screen. Virtual communities ranging from MUDs to computer bulletin boards allow people to generate experiences, relationships, identities, and living spaces that arise only through interaction with technology. In the many thousands of hours that Mike, a college freshman in Kansas, has been logged on to his favorite MUD, he has created an apartment with rooms, furniture, books, desk, and even a small computer. Its interior is exquisitely detailed, even though it exists only in textual description. A hearth, an easy chair, and a mahogany desk warm his cyberspace. "It's where I live," Mike says. "More than I do in my dingy dorm room. There's no place like home."

As human beings become increasingly intertwined with the technology and with each other via the technology, old distinctions between what is specifically human and specifically technological become more complex. Are we living life *on* the screen or life *in* the screen? Our new technologically enmeshed relationships oblige us to ask to what extent we ourselves have become cyborgs, transgressive mixtures of biology, technology, and code.[8] The traditional distance between people and machines has become harder to maintain.

Writing in his diary in 1832, Ralph Waldo Emerson reflected that "Dreams and beasts are two keys by which we are to find out the secrets of our nature. . . they are our test objects."[9] Emerson was prescient. Freud and his heirs would measure human rationality against the dream. Darwin and his heirs would insist that we measure human nature against nature itself—the world of the beasts seen as our forbears and kin. If Emerson had lived at the end of the twentieth century, he would surely have seen the computer as a new test object. Like dreams and beasts, the computer stands on the margins. It is a mind that is not yet a mind. It is inanimate yet interactive. It does not think, yet neither is it external to thought. It is an object, ultimately a mechanism, but it behaves, interacts, and seems in a certain sense to know. It confronts us with an uneasy sense of kinship. After all, we too behave, interact, and seem to know, and yet are ultimately made of matter and programmed DNA. We think we can think. But can *it* think? Could it have the capacity to feel? Could it ever be said to be alive?

25 Dreams and beasts were the test objects for Freud and Darwin, the test objects for modernism. In the past decade, the computer has become the test object for postmodernism. The computer takes us beyond a world of dreams and beasts because it enables us to contemplate mental life that exists apart from bodies. It enables us to contemplate dreams that do not need beasts. The computer is an evocative object that causes old boundaries to be renegotiated.

This book traces a set of such boundary negotiations. It is a reflection on the role that technology is playing in the creation of a new social and cultural sensibility. I have observed and participated in settings, physical and virtual, where people and computers come together.[10] Over the past decade, I have talked to more than a thousand people, nearly three hundred of them children, about their experience of using computers or computational objects to program, to navigate, to write, to build, to experiment, or to communicate. In a sense, I have interrogated the computers as well. What messages, both explicit and implicit, have they carried for their human users about what is possible and what is impossible, about what is valuable and what is unimportant?

In the spirit of Whitman's reflections on the child, I want to know what we are becoming if the first objects we look upon each day are simulations into which we deploy our virtual selves. In other words, this is not a book about computers. Rather, it is a book about the intense relationships people have with computers and how these relationships are changing the way we think and feel. Along with the movement from a culture of calculation toward a culture of simulation have come changes in what computers do *for* us and in what they do *to* us—to our relationships and our ways of thinking about ourselves.

We have become accustomed to opaque technology. As the processing power of computers increased exponentially, it became possible to use that power to build graphical user interfaces commonly known by the acronym GUI, that hid the bare machine from its user. The new opaque interfaces—most specifically, the Macintosh iconic style of interface, which simulates the space of a desktop as well as communication through dialogue—represented more than a technical change. These new interfaces modeled a way of understanding that depended on getting to know a computer through interacting with it, as one might get to know a person or explore a town.

The early personal computers of the 1970s and the IBM PC of the early 1980s presented themselves as open, "transparent," potentially reducible to their underlying mechanisms. These were systems that invited users to imagine that they could understand its "gears" as they turned, even if very few people ever tried to reach that level of understanding. When people say that they used to be able to "see" what was "inside" their first personal computers, it is important to keep in mind that for most of them there still remained many intermediate levels of software between them and the bare machine. But their computer systems encouraged them to represent their understanding of the technology as knowledge of what lay beneath the screen surface. They were encouraged to think of understanding as looking beyond the magic to the mechanism.

In contrast, the 1984 introduction of the Macintosh's iconic style presented the public with simulations (the icons of file folders, a trash can, a desktop) that did nothing to suggest how their underlying structure could be known. It seemed unavailable, visible only through its effects. As one user said, "The Mac looked perfect, finished. To install a program on my DOS machine, I had to fiddle with things. It clearly wasn't perfect. With the Mac, the system told me to stay on the surface." This is the kind of involvement with computers that has come to dominate the field; no longer associated only with the Macintosh, it is nearly universal in personal computing.

We have learned to take things at interface value. We are moving toward a culture of simulation in which people are increasingly comfortable with substituting representations of reality for the real. We use a Macintosh-style "desktop" as well as one on four legs. We join virtual communities that exist only among people communicating on computer networks as well as communities in which we are physically present. We come to question simple distinctions between real and artificial. In what sense should one consider a screen desktop less real than any other? The screen desktop I am currently using has a folder on it labeled "Professional Life." It contains my business correspondence, date book, and telephone directory. Another folder, labeled "Courses," contains syllabuses, reading assignments, class lists, and lecture notes. A third, "Current Work," contains my research notes and this book's drafts. I feel no sense of unreality in my relationship to any of these objects. The culture of simulation encourages me to take what I see on the screen "at (inter)face value." In the culture of simulation, if it works for you, it has all the reality it needs.

The habit of taking things at interface value is new, but it has gone quite far. For example, a decade ago, the idea of a conversation with a computer about emotional matters, the image of a computer psychotherapist, struck most people as inappropriate or even obscene. Today, several such programs are on the market, and they tend to provoke a very different and quite pragmatic response. People are most likely to say, "Might as well try it. It might help. What's the harm?"

We have used our relationships with technology to reflect on the human. A decade ago, people were often made nervous by the idea of thinking about computers in human terms. Behind their anxiety was distress at the idea that their own minds might be similar to a computer's "mind." This reaction against the formalism and rationality of the machine was romantic.

I use this term to analogize our cultural response to computing to nineteenth century Romanticism. I do not mean to suggest that it was merely an emotional response. We shall see that it expressed serious philosophical resistance to any view of people that denied their complexity and continuing mystery. This response emphasized not only the richness of human emotion but the flexibility of human thought and the degree to which knowledge arises in subtle interaction with the environment. Humans, it insists, have to be something very different from mere calculating machines.

In the mid-1980s, this romantic reaction was met by a movement in computer science toward the research and design of increasingly "romantic machines." These machines were touted not as logical but as biological, not as programmed but as able to learn from experience. The researchers who worked on them said they sought a species of machine that would prove as unpredictable and undetermined as the human mind itself. The cultural presence of these romantic machines encouraged a new discourse; both persons and objects were reconfigured, machines as psychological objects, people as living machines.

But even as people have come to greater acceptance of a kinship between computers and human minds, they have also begun to pursue a new set of boundary questions about things and people. After several decades of asking, "What does it mean to think?" the question at the end of the twentieth century is, "What does it mean to be alive?" We are positioned for yet another romantic reaction, this time emphasizing biology, physical embodiment, the question of whether an artifact can be a life.[11]

These psychological and philosophical effects of the computer presence are by no means confined to adults. Like their parents, and often before their parents, the children of the early 1980s began to think of computers and computer toys as psychological objects because these machines combined mind activities (talking, singing, spelling, game playing, and doing math), an interactive style, and an opaque surface. But the children, too, had a romantic reaction, and came to define people as those emotional and unprogrammable things that computers were not. Nevertheless, from the moment children gave up on mechanistic understandings and saw the computer as a psychological entity, they began to draw computers closer to themselves. Today children may refer to the computers in their homes and classrooms as "just machines," but qualities that used to be ascribed only to people are now ascribed to computers as well. Among children, the past decade has seen a movement from defining people as what machines are not to believing that the computational objects of everyday life think and know while remaining "just machines."

In the past decade, the changes in the intellectual identity and cultural impact of the computer have taken place in a culture still deeply attached to the quest for a modernist understanding of the mechanisms of life. Larger scientific and cultural trends, among them advances in psychopharmacology and the development of genetics as a computational biology, reflect the extent to which we assume ourselves to be like machines whose inner workings we can understand. "Do we have our emotions," asks a college sophomore whose mother has been transformed by taking antidepressant medication, "or do our emotions have us?" To whom is one listening when one is "listening to Prozac"?[12] The aim of the Human Genome Project is to specify the location and role of all the genes in human DNA. The Project is often justified on the grounds that it promises to find the pieces of our genetic code responsible for many human diseases so that these may be better treated, perhaps by genetic reengineering. But talk about the Project also addresses the possibility of finding the genetic markers that determine human personality, temperament, and sexual orientation. As we contemplate reengineering the genome, we are also reengineering our view of ourselves as programmed beings.[13] Any romantic reaction that relies on biology as the bottom line is fragile, because it is building on shifting ground. Biology is appropriating computer technology's older, modernist models of computation while at the same time computer scientists are aspiring to develop a new opaque, emergent biology that is closer to the postmodern culture of simulation.[14]

Today, more lifelike machines sit on our desktops, computer science uses biological concepts, and human biology is recast in terms of deciphering a code. With descriptions of the brain that explicitly invoke computers and images of computers that explicitly invoke the brain, we have reached a cultural watershed. The rethinking of human and machine identity is not taking place just among philosophers but "on the ground," through a philosophy in everyday life that is in some measure both provoked and carried by the computer presence.

We have sought out the subjective computer. Computers don't just do things for us, they do things to us, including to our ways of thinking about ourselves and other people. A decade ago, such subjective effects of the computer presence were secondary in the sense that they were not the ones being sought.[15] Today, things are often the other way around. People explicitly turn to computers for experiences that they hope will change their ways of thinking or will affect their social and emotional lives. When people explore simulation games and fantasy worlds or log on to a community where they have virtual friends and lovers, they are not thinking of the computer as what Charles Babbage, the nineteenth-century mathematician who invented the first programmable machine, called an analytical engine. They are seeking out the computer as an intimate machine.

Notes

[1] I immersed myself in these "French lessons," first in the aftermath of the May 1968 student revolt, a revolt in which Lacan and Foucault became intellectual heroes. Later, in 1973–74, the immersion continued while I studied the intellectual fallout of that failed revolution. That fallout included a love affair with things Freudian and an attack on unitary models of self. While followers of Lacan relied on reinterpretations of Freud that challenged models of a centralized ego, Deleuze and Guattari proposed more radical views that described the self as a multiplicity of desiring machines. See Gilles Deleuze and Félix Guattari, *Anti-Oedipus: Capitalism and Schizophrenia,* trans. Robert Hurley, Mark Seem, and Helen R. Lane (Minneapolis: University of Minnesota Press, 1983).

[2] Jill Serpentelli, "Conversational Structure and Personality Correlates of Electronic Communication," unpub. ms., 1992.

[3] The student's association of Derrida and hypertext may be unsophisticated, but it is far from outlandish. See, for example, George P. Landow, *Hypertext: The Convergence of Critical Theory and Technology* (Baltimore: Johns Hopkins, 1992), pp. 1–34; and in George P. Landow and Paul Delany, eds., *Hypermedia and Literary Studies* (Cambridge, Mass: MIT Press, 1991).

[4] Richard A. Lanham, *The Electronic Word: Democracy, Technology, and the Arts* (Chicago: The University of Chicago Press, 1993), p. 51. George Landow sees critical theory and technology in the midst of a "convergence." See Landow, *Hypertext.*

[5] I say almost unthinkable because a small number of postmodern writers had begun to associate their work with the possibilities of computer technology. See, in particular, Jean-François Lyotard, *The Postmodern Condition: A Report on Knowledge,* trans. Geoff

Bennington and Brian Massumi (Minneapolis: University of Minnesota Press, 1984).
[6] *The Wall Street Journal,* 3 January 1995: A3, A4, and *The Wall Street Journal,* 10 January 1995: B1, B3.
[7] Here I have changed the name of the MUD (there is to my knowledge no DinoMUD) to protect the confidentiality I promise all informants. I use the real name of a MUD when it is important to my account and will not compromise confidentiality. See "A Note on Method."
[8] See, for example, Donna Haraway, "A Manifesto for Cyborgs: Science, Technology, and Socialist Feminism in the 1980s," *Socialist Review* 80 (March–April 1985): 65–107.
[9] The quotation is from a journal entry by Emerson in January 1832. The passage reads in full, "Dreams and beasts are two keys by which we are to find out the secrets of our nature. All mystics use them. They are like comparative anatomy. They are our test objects." See Joel Porte, ed., *Emerson in His Journals* (Cambridge, Mass.: Belknap Press, 1982), p. 81.
[10] See "A Note on Method."
[11] In a recent review of the place of genetics in contemporary popular culture, Dorothy Nelkin and Susan Lindee have said: "DNA has taken on the social and cultural functions of the soul." See their *The DNA Mystique: The Gene as a Cultural Icon* (San Francisco and New York: W. H. Freeman, 1995), p. 42.
[12] Peter Kramer, *Listening to Prozac: A Psychiatrist Explores Mood-Altering Drugs and the New Meaning of the Self* (New York: Viking, 1993).
[13] Nelkin and Lindee's *The DNA Mystique* documents the degree to which genetic essentialism dominates American popular culture today.
[14] Evelyn Fox Keller, "The Body of a New Machine: Situating the Organism Between Telegraphs and Computers," *Perspectives on Science* 2, no. 3 (1994): 302–23.
[15] For a view of this matter from the perspective of the 1980s, see Sherry Turkle, *The Second Self: Computers and the Human Spirit* (New York: Simon & Schuster, 1984).

Mapping the Text

1. In "Identity in the Age of the Internet," Sherry Turkle states, "The computer had a clear intellectual identity as a calculating machine. Indeed, when I took an introductory programming course at Harvard in 1978, the professor introduced the computer to the class by calling it a giant calculator. Programming, he reassured us, was a cut and dried technical activity whose rules were crystal clear." Discuss your views about whether the computer remains "a giant calculator," citing evidence from your own experiences with computers that supports your views.
2. Turkle makes a distinction between the world of calculation and the world of stimulation. Explain this distinction. Then explain whether you consider her examples of both worlds helpful in making this point.
3. Review Turkle's essay and choose a passage that you think best captures her point. Explain why you think this passage is a good choice.
4. In discussing computers and the Internet in the ways that she does, what impression of herself as the writer of this essay does Turkle present? Describe the person/personality that comes through as she speaks.

Writing to Inquire

1. Make a list of the terms in this essay that seem to be computer-related—terms that have gained particular meaning because of the way they are perceived in this arena. How do you think computer-related territory is affecting our use of language? How do you think that computers are affecting our sense of identity—as individuals, as a society?
2. Write a narrative about your experiences as a user of computer technologies. How has your identity been shaped or reshaped by this technology? How do you interact with your friends and family? Does technology play a role in those interactions? To what extent do you think Turkle's analysis applies to your sense of self?

Space Is Numeric

ELLEN ULLMAN

Ellen Ullman has worked for over fifteen years in software development as a programmer, engineer, and consultant. She is a consulting editor for *Byte* magazine and a contributing author for *Red Herring,* a business and technology magazine. She has also served as a technology commentator for National Public Radio. The selection below is excerpted from Ullman's book, *Close to the Machine: Technophilia and its Discontents* (1997). This book and her other writings create a memoir that displays both her critique and her love of computer technologies.

I have no idea what time it is. There are no windows in this office and no clock, only the blinking red LED display of a microwave, which flashes 12:00, 12:00, 12:00, 12:00. Joel and I have been programming for days. We have a bug, a stubborn demon of a bug. So the red pulse no-time feels right, like a read-out of our brains, which have somehow synchronized themselves at the same blink rate.

"But what if they select all the text and—"

"—hit Delete."

"Damn! The NULL case!"

5 "And if not we're out of the text field and they hit space—"

"—yeah, like for—"

"—no parameter—"

"Hell!"

"So what if we space-pad?"

10 "I don't know. . . . Wait a minute!"

"Yeah, we could space-pad—"

"—and do space as numeric."

"Yes! We'll call SendKey(space) to—?

"—the numeric object."

"My God! That fixes it!"

"Yeah! That'll work if—"

"—space is numeric!"

"—if space is numeric!"

We lock eyes. We barely breathe. For a slim moment, we are together in a universe where two human beings can simultaneously understand the statement "if space is numeric!"

Joel and I started this round of debugging on Friday morning. Sometime later, maybe Friday night, another programmer, Danny, came to work. I suppose it must be Sunday by now because it's been a while since we've seen my client's employees around the office. Along the way, at odd times of day or night that have completely escaped us, we've ordered in three meals of Chinese food, eaten six large pizzas, consumed several beers, had innumerable bottles of fizzy water, and finished two entire bottles of wine. It has occurred to me that if people really knew how software got written, I'm not sure if they'd give their money to a bank or get on an airplane ever again.

What are we working on? An artificial intelligence project to find "subversive" talk over international phone lines? Software for the second startup of a Silicon Valley executive banished from his first company? A system to help AIDS patients get services across a city? The details escape me just now. We may be helping poor sick people or tuning a set of low-level routines to verify bits on a distributed database protocol—I don't care. I should care; in another part of my being—later, perhaps when we emerge from this room full of computers—I will care very much why and for whom and for what purpose I am writing software. But just now: no. I have passed through a membrane where the real world and its uses no longer matter. I am a software engineer, an independent contractor working for a department of a city government. I've hired Joel and three other programmers to work with me. Down the hall is Danny, a slim guy in wire-rimmed glasses who comes to work with a big, wire-haired dog. Across the bay in his converted backyard shed is Mark, who works on the database. Somewhere, probably asleep by now, is Bill the network guy. Right now, there are only two things in the universe that matter to us. One, we have some bad bugs to fix. Two, we're supposed to install the system on Monday, which I think is tomorrow.

"Oh, no, no!" moans Joel, who is slumped over his keyboard. "No-*o-o-o.*" It comes out in a long wail. It has the sound of lost love, lifetime regret. We've both been programmers long enough to know that we are at *that place.* If we find one more serious problem we can't solve right away, we will not make it. We won't install. We'll go the terrible, familiar way of all software: we'll be late.

"No, no, no, no. What if the members of the set start with spaces. Oh, God. It won't work."

He is as near to naked despair as has ever been shown to me by anyone not in a film. Here, in *that place,* we have no shame. He has seen me sleeping on the floor, drooling. We have both seen Danny's puffy white midsection—young as he is, it's a pity—when he stripped to his underwear in the heat of the machine room. I have seen Joel's dandruff, light coating of cat fur on his clothes, noticed things about his body I should not. And I'm sure he's seen my sticky hair, noticed how dull I look without make-up, caught sight of other details too intimate to mention. Still, none of this matters anymore. Our bodies were abandoned long ago, reduced to hunger and sleeplessness and the ravages of sitting for hours at a keyboard and a mouse. Our physical selves have been battered away. Now we know each other in one way and one way only: the code.

Besides, I know I can now give him the pleasure of an order which is rare in any life: I am about to save him from despair.

"No problem," I say evenly. I put my hand on his shoulder, intending a gesture of reassurance. "The parameters *never* start with a space."

It is just as I hoped. His despair vanishes. He becomes electric, turns to the keyboard and begins to type at a rapid speed. Now he is gone from me. He is disappearing into the code—now that he knows it will work, now that I have reassured him that, in our universe, the one we created together, space can indeed be forever and reliably numeric.

The connection, the shared thought-stream, is cut. It has all the frustration of being abandoned by a lover just before climax. I know this is not physical love. He is too young, he works for me; he's a man and I've been tending toward women; in any case, he's too prim and business-schooled for my tastes. I know this sensation is not *real* attraction: it is only the spillover, the excess charge, of the mind back into the abandoned body. *Only.* Ha. This is another real-world thing that does not matter. My entire self wants to melt into this brilliant, electric being who has shared his mind with me for twenty seconds.

Restless, I go into the next room where Danny is slouched at his keyboard. The big, wire-haired dog growls at me. Danny looks up, scowls like his dog, then goes back to typing. I am the designer of this system, his boss on this project. But he's not even trying to hide his contempt. Normal programmer, I think. He has fifteen windows full of code open on his desktop. He has overpopulated his eyes, thoughts, imagination. He is drowning in bugs and I know I could help him, but he wants me dead just at the moment. I am the last-straw irritant. *Talking:* Shit! What the hell is wrong with me? Why would I want to *talk* to him? Can't I see that his stack is overflowing?

"Joel may have the overlapping controls working," I say.

"Oh, yeah?" He doesn't look up.

"He's been using me as a programming dummy," I say. "Do you want to talk me through the navigation errors?" Navigation errors: bad. You click to go somewhere but get somewhere else. Very, very bad.

"What?" He pretends not to hear me.

"Navigation errors. How are they?"

35 "I'm working on them." Huge, hateful scowl. Contempt that one human being should not express to another under any circumstances. Hostility that should kill me, if I were not used to it, familiar with it, practiced in receiving it. Besides, we are at *that place.* I know that this hateful programmer is all I have between me and the navigation bug. "I'll come back later," I say.

Later: how much later can it get? Daylight can't be far off now. This small shoal of pre-installation madness is washing away even as I wander back down the hall to Joel.

"Yes! It's working!" says Joel, hearing my approach.

He looks up at me. "You were right," he says. The ultimate one programmer can say to another, the accolade given so rarely as to be almost unknown in our species. He looks right at me as he says it: "You were right. As always."

This is beyond rare. *Right:* the thing a programmer desires above, beyond all. *As always:* unspeakable, incalculable gift.

40 "I could not have been right without you," I say. This is true beyond question. "I only opened the door. You figured out how to go through."

I immediately see a certain perfume advertisement: a man holding a violin embraces a woman at a piano. I want to be that ad. I want efficacies of reality to vanish, and I want to be the man with violin, my programmer to be the woman at the piano. As in the ad, I want the teacher to interrupt the lesson and embrace the student. I want the rules to be broken. Tabu. That is the name of the perfume. I want to do what is taboo. I am the boss, the senior, the employer, the person in charge. So I must not touch him. It is all taboo. Still—

Danny appears in the doorway.

"The navigation bug is fixed. I'm going home."

"I'll test it—"

45 "It's fixed."

He leaves.

It is sometime in the early morning. Joel and I are not sure if the night guard is still on duty. If we leave, we may not get back up the elevator. We leave anyway.

We find ourselves on the street in a light drizzle. He has on a raincoat, one that he usually wears over his too-prim, too-straight, good-biz-school suits. I have on a second-hand-store leather bomber jacket, black beret, boots. Someone walking by might wonder what we were doing together at this still-dark hour of the morning.

"Goodnight," I say. We're still charged with thought energy. I don't dare extend my hand to shake his.

50 "Goodnight," he says.

We stand awkwardly for two beats more. "This will sound strange," he says, "but I hope I don't see you tomorrow."

We stare at each other, still drifting in the wake of our shared mind-stream. I know exactly what he means. We will only see each other tomorrow if I find a really bad bug.

"Not strange at all," I say, "I hope I don't see you, either."

I don't see him. The next day, I find a few minor bugs, fix them, and decide the software is good enough. Mind-meld fantasies recede as the system goes live. We install the beginnings of a city-wide registration system for AIDS patients. Instead of carrying around soiled and wrinkled eligibility documents, AIDS clients only have to prove once that they are really sick and really poor. It is an odd system, if I think of it, certifying that people are truly desperate in the face of possible death.

55 Still, this time I'm working on a "good" project, I tell myself. We are *helping* people, say the programmers over and over, nearly in disbelief at their good fortune. Three programmers, the network guy, me—fifty-eight years of collective technical experience—and the idea of helping people with a computer is a first for any of us.

Yet I am continually anxious. How do we protect this database full of the names of people with AIDS? Is a million-dollar computer system the best use of continually shrinking funds? It was easier when I didn't have to think about the real-world effect of my work. It was easier—and I got paid more—when I was writing an "abstracted interface to any arbitrary input device." When I was designing a "user interface paradigm," defining a "test-bed methodology." I could disappear into weird passions of logic. I could stay in a world peopled entirely by programmers, other weird logic-dreamers like myself, all caught up in our own inner electricities. It was easier and more valued. In my profession, software engineering, there is something almost shameful in this helpful, social-services system we're building. The whole project smacks of "end users"—those contemptible, oblivious people who just want to use the stuff we write and don't care how we did it.

"What are you working on?" asked an acquaintance I ran into at a book signing. She's a woman with her own start-up company. Her offices used to be in the loft just below mine, two blocks from South Park, in San Francisco's Multimedia Gulch. She is tall and strikingly attractive; she wears hip, fashionable clothes; her company already has its first million in venture-capital funding. "What are you working on," she wanted to know, "I mean, that isn't under non-D?"

Under non-D. Nondisclosure. That's the cool thing to be doing: working on a system so new, so just started-up, that you can't talk about it under pain of lawsuit.

"Oh, not much," I answered, trying to sound breezy. A city-wide network for AIDS service providers: how unhip could I get? If I wanted to do something for people with AIDS, I should make my first ten million in stock options, then attend some fancy party where I wear a red ribbon on my chest. I should be a sponsor for Digital Queers. But actually working on a project for end users? Where my client is a government agency? In the libertarian world of computing, where "creating wealth" is all, I am worse than uncool: I am aiding and abetting the bureaucracy, I am a net consumer of federal taxes—I'm what's wrong with this country.

60 "Oh, I'm basically just plugging in other people's software these days. Not much engineering. You know," I waved vaguely, "*plumbing* mostly."

My vagueness paid off. The woman winked at me. "Networks," she said.

"Yeah. Something like that," I said. I was disgusted with myself, but, when she walked away, I was relieved.

The end users I was so ashamed of came late in the system development process. I didn't meet them until the software was half-written. This is not how these things are supposed to go—the system is not supposed to predate the people who will use it—but it often goes that way anyhow.

The project was eight months old when my client-contact, a project manager in a city department, a business-like woman of fifty, finally set up a meeting. Representatives of several social-service agencies were invited; eight came. A printed agenda was handed around the conference table. The first item was "Review agenda." My programmer-mind whirred at the implication of endless reiteration: Agenda. Review agenda. Agenda. Forever.

65 "Who dreamed up this stuff?" asked a woman who directed a hospice and home-care agency. "This is all useless!" We had finally come to item four on the agenda: "Review System Specifications." The hospice director waved a big stack of paper—the specifications arrived at by a "task force"—then tossed it across the table. A heavy-set woman apparently of Middle-Eastern descent, she had probably smoked a very large number of cigarettes in the course of her fifty-odd years on earth. Her laugh trailed off into a chesty rumble, which she used as a kind of drum roll to finish off her scorn.

The other users were no more impressed. A black woman who ran a shelter—elegant, trailing Kente cloth. She arranged her acres of fabric as some sort of displacement for her boredom; each time I started talking, I seemed to have to speak over a high jangle of her many bracelets set to play as she, ignoring me with something that was not quite hostility, arranged and rearranged herself. A woman who ran a clinic for lesbians, a self-described "femme" with hennaed hair and red fingernails: "Why didn't someone come talk to us first?" she asked. A good question. My client sat shamefaced. A young, handsome black man, assistant to the hospice director, quick and smart: he simply shook his head and kept a skeptical smile on his face. Finally a dentist and a doctor, two white males who looked pale and watery in this sea of diversity: they worried that the system would get in the way of giving services. And around the table they went, complaint by complaint.

I started to panic. Before this meeting, the users existed only in my mind, projections, all mine. They were abstractions, the initiators of tasks that set off remote procedure calls; triggers to a set of logical and machine events that ended in an update to a relational database on a central server. Now I was confronted with their fleshly existence. And now I had to think about the actual existence of the people who used the services delivered by the users' agencies, sick people who were no fools, who would do what they needed to do to get pills, food vouchers, a place to sleep.

I wished, earnestly, I could just replace the abstractions with the actual people. But it was already too late for that. The system pre-existed the people. Screens were prototyped. Data elements were defined. The machine events already had more reality, had been with me longer, than the human beings at the conference table. Immediately, I saw it was a problem not of replacing one reality with another but of two realities. I was there at the edge: the interface of the system, in all its existence, to the people, in all their existence.

I talked, asked questions, but I saw I was operating at a different speed from the people at the table. Notch down, I told myself. *Notch down.* The users were bright, all too sensitive to each other's feelings. Anyone who was the slightest bit cut off was gotten back to sweetly: "You were saying?" Their courtesy was structural, built into their "process." I had to keep my hand over my mouth to keep from jumping in. Notch down, I told myself again. *Slow down.* But it was not working. My brain whirred out a stream of logic-speak: "The agency sees the client records if and only if there is a relationship defined between the agency and the client," I heard myself saying. "By definition, as soon as the client receives services from the agency, the system considers the client to have a relationship with the provider. An internal index is created which represents the relationship." The hospice director closed her eyes to concentrate. She would have smoked if she could have; she looked at me as if through something she had just exhaled.

I took notes, pages of revisions that had to be done immediately or else doom the system to instant disuse. The system had no life without the user, I saw. I'd like to say that I was instantly converted to the notion of real human need, to the impact I would have on the working lives of these people at the table, on the people living with AIDS; I'd like to claim a sudden sense of real-world responsibility. But that would be lying. What I really thought was this: I must save the system.

I ran off to call the programmers. Living in my hugely different world from the sick patients, the forbearing service providers, the earnest and caring users at the meeting, I didn't wait to find a regular phone. I went into the next room, took out my cell phone, began punching numbers into it, and hit the "send" button: "We have to talk," I said.

By the time I saw Joel, Danny, and Mark, I had reduced the users' objections to a set of five system changes. I would like to use the word "reduce" like a cook: something boiled down to its essence. But I was aware that the real human essence was already absent from the list I'd prepared. An item like "How will we know if the clients have TB?"—the fear of sitting in a small, poorly ventilated room with someone who has medication-resistant TB, the normal and complicated biological urgency of that question—became a list of data elements to be added to the screens and the database. I tried to communicate some of the sense of the meeting to the programmers. They were interested, but in a mild, backgrounded way. Immediately, they seized the list of changes and, as I watched, they turned them into further abstractions.

"We can add a parameter to the remote procedure call."

"We should check the referential integrity on that."

"Should the code be attached to that control or should it be in global scope?"

"Global, because this other object here needs to know about the condition."

"No! No globals. We agreed. No more globals!"

We have entered the code zone. Here thought is telegraphic and exquisitely precise. I feel no need to slow myself down. On the contrary, the faster the better. Joel runs off a stream of detail, and halfway through a sentence, Mark, the database programmer, completes the thought. I mention a screen element, and Danny, who programs the desktop software, thinks of two elements I've forgotten. Mark will later say all bugs are Danny's fault, but, for now, they work together like cheerful little parallel-processing machines, breaking the problem into pieces that they attack simultaneously. Danny will later become the angry programmer scowling at me from behind his broken code, but now he is still a jovial guy with wire-rimmed glasses and a dog that accompanies him everywhere. "Neato," he says to something Mark has proposed, grinning, patting the dog, happy as a clam.

"Should we modify the call to AddUser—"

"—to check for UserType—"

"Or should we add a new procedure call—"

"—something like ModifyPermissions."

"But won't that add a new set of data elements that repeat—"

"Yeah, a repeating set—"

"—which we'll have to—"

"—renormalize!"

Procedure calls. Relational database normalization. Objects going in and out of scope. Though my mind is racing, I feel calm. It's the spacey calm of satellites speeding over the earth at a thousand miles per second: relative to each other, we float. The images of patients with AIDS recede, the beleaguered service providers are forgotten, the whole grim reality of the epidemic fades. We give ourselves over to the sheer fun of the technical, to the nearly sexual pleasure of the clicking thought-stream.

Some part of me mourns, but I know there is no other way: human needs must cross the line into code. They must pass through this semipermeable membrane where urgency, fear, and hope are filtered out, and only reason travels across. There is no other way. Real, death-inducing viruses do not travel here. Actual human confusions cannot live here. Everything we want accomplished, everything the system is to provide, must be denatured in its crossing to the machine, or else the system will die.

Mapping the Text

1. Describe the style and voice of Ullman's writing. How does she use language to create a sense of drama and suspense? Although this is a nonfiction work, it displays many of the genre characteristics of fiction. Find several passages that work effectively for you and describe the stylistic devices and tools Ullman uses to create this effect.
2. What kind of ethos or persona does Ullman develop in this selection? Does her insider status as a programmer give her words special weight or authority? Why or why not?
3. What conclusions or lessons does Ullman draw about the impact of computer technologies? How do software engineers see the world? In what way is their vision or perspective embodied in the technologies they create?
4. What ethical dilemmas does Ullman confront in her work? How does working on an AIDS database change her view of technology and its effects? Does she offer any possible solutions to these dilemmas?

Writing to Inquire

1. Write a brief essay to describe your own experiences as a user of a specific piece of software or technology. How do you think the designers of that software understood you as a user? as a person? If you have worked to design or program software, you may want to write from the perspective of the designer; describe your own image of the person you assumed would be using your software when it was completed.
2. Interview a computer science professor or graduate student, using Ullman's essay as a starting point and framework for discussion. Try to find out how typical her experiences are and whether or not her generalizations about computer engineers and software designers are accurate.

The Next Brainiacs

JOHN HOCKENBERRY

John Hockenberry, a veteran broadcast journalist, has served as a reporter for National Public Radio, as a national and international correspondent for ABC News and for their news magazine, *Day One,* and since 1996 as a correspondent for *Dateline NBC.* He has written for the *New York Times,* the *Columbia Journalism Review, Modern Maturity,* the *Washington Post, ID* magazine, and

New Yorker magazine. Hockenberry's broadcasting awards include the 1984 and 1985 Champion Tuck Business Reporting Awards, the 1985 Benton Fellowship in broadcast journalism, the 1987 Unity in Media Award, and the first Peabody Award in 1987 for a profile of a young man who was permanently injured in a drive-by shooting. In addition, Hockenberry has written several books, including *Moving Violations: War Zones, Wheelchairs, and Declarations of Independence* (1996) and *A River Out of Eden: A Novel* (2001). In the essay below, Hockenberry takes an insightful look at the intimate relationships between technology and people who have disabilities and how this relationship can shift our basic view of what it means to be human.

When you think disability, think zeitgeist. I'm serious. We live at a time when the disabled are on the leading edge of a broader societal trend toward the use of assistive technology. With the advent of miniature wireless tech, electronic gadgets have stepped up their invasion of the body, and our concept of what it means and even looks like to be human is wide open to debate. Humanity's specs are back on the drawing board, thanks to some unlikely designers, and the disabled have a serious advantage in this conversation. They've been using technology in collaborative, intimate ways for years—to move, to communicate, to interact with the world.

When you think disability, free yourself from the sob-story crap, all the oversize shrieking about people praying for miracles and walking again, or triumphing against the odds. Instead, think puppets. At a basic level, physical disability is really just a form of puppetry. If you've ever marveled at how someone can bring a smudged sock puppet to life or talked back to Elmo and Grover, then intellectually you're nearly there. Puppetry is the original brain-machine interface. It entertains because it shows you how this interface can be ported to different platforms.

If puppetry is the clever mapping of human characteristics onto a nonhuman object, then disability is the same mapping onto a still-human object. Making the body work regardless of physical deficit is not a challenge I would wish on anyone, but getting good at being disabled is like discovering an alternative platform. It's closer to puppetry than anything else I can think of. I should know: I've been at it for 25 years. I have lots of moving parts. Two of them are not my legs. When you think John Hockenberry, think wheelchair. Think alternative platform. Think puppet.

Within each class of disability, there are different forms of puppetry, different people and technologies interacting to solve various movement or communication problems. The goal, always, is to project a whole human being, to see the puppet as a character rather than a sock or a collection of marionette strings.

5 When you meet Johnny Ray, it's a challenge to see the former drywall contractor and amateur musician trapped inside his body, but he's there. Ray, a 63-year-old from Carrollton, Georgia, suffered a brain-stem stroke in 1997, which produced what doctors call "locked-in syndrome": He has

virtually no moving parts. Cognitively he's intact, but he can't make a motion to deliver that message or any other to the world.

Getting a puppet with no moving parts to work sounds like a task worthy of the Buddha, but a pioneering group of neuroscientists affiliated with Emory University in Atlanta has taken a credible stab at it. In a series of animal and human experiments dating back to 1990, Philip Kennedy, Roy Bakay, and a team of researchers have created a basic but completely functional alternative interface using electrodes surgically implanted in the brain. In 1996, their success with primates convinced the FDA to allow two human tests. The first subject, whose name was withheld to protect her privacy, was a woman in the terminal stages of ALS (Lou Gehrig's disease); she died two months after the procedure. The second was Johnny Ray.

Kennedy, who invented the subcranial cortical implant used in these operations, wanted to create a device that could acquire a signal from inside the brain—a signal robust enough to travel through wires and manipulate objects in the physical world. Making this happen involved creating new access points for the brain, in addition to the natural ones (defunct in Ray's case) that produce muscle motion. Bakay has since moved to Rush-Presbyterian-St. Luke's Medical Center in Chicago, where he's part of an institute devoted entirely to alternative brain-body interfaces. The soft-spoken doctor wouldn't describe anything he does as show business, but to me the results of his work sound like a real-world version of the nifty plug Neo/Keanu sported in *The Matrix.*

"We simply make a hole in the skull right above the ear, near the back end of the motor cortex, secure our electrodes and other hardware to the bone so they don't migrate, and wait for a signal," Bakay says. The implant is an intriguing hybrid of electronics and biology—it physically melds with brain tissue.

"We use a small piece of glass shaped like two narrow cones into which a gold electrical contact has been glued," Bakay says. "The space in the cones is filled with a special tissue culture, and the whole thing is placed inside the motor cortex." The tissue culture is designed to "attract" brain cells to grow toward the contact. When brain cells meet gold, the electrical activity of individual cells is detectable across the electrode. Gold wires carry signals back out of the skull, where they are amplified. This produces a far more sensitive and usable signal than you get from surface technology like the taped-on electrodes used in EEGs.

10 To get a broad sense of what the patient's brain is doing, neurologists perform magnetic resonance imaging and compare changes in the motor cortex with voltages monitored through the electrodes. Then the doctors get really clever. The patient is encouraged to think simple thoughts that correspond to distinct conditions and movements, like hot/cold or up/down. Gradually, the doctors extract and codify electrical patterns that change as a patient's thoughts change. If a patient can reproduce and trig-

ger the signal using the same thought patterns, that signal can be identified and used to control, say, a cursor on a computer screen. The technique is very crude, but what Bakay and his colleagues have demonstrated is a truly alternative brain-body interface platform.

Ray's implant was installed in 1998, and he survived to start working with the signals, which were amplified and converted to USB input for a Dell Pentium box. In the tests that followed, Ray was asked to think about specific physical motions—moving his arms, for example. Kennedy and Bakay took the corresponding signal and programmed it to move the cursor. By reproducing the same brain pattern, Ray eventually was able to move the cursor at will to choose screen icons, spell, even generate musical tones.

Mapping the Text

1. In "The Next Brainiacs," John Hockenberry discusses the "specs" of humanity. What are the specs of humanity? How is Hockenberry suggesting that technology collaborates in changing those specs? How does this view of collaborations between humans and machines affect, or even alter, typical views of disability?
2. When we think of merging humans with technology, we often think about media images of cyborgs. Do you consider such images science fiction or science? On what evidence do you base your view?

Writing to Inquire

1. Think about disabilities with which you are familiar. Choose one as the focus of exploration. Search library and other sources to identify technologies that have been used over time to enhance human "specs." Report to the class on your findings.

The Good Deed

SUSAN MCCARTHY

Susan McCarthy is a freelance writer working out of the San Francisco area whose essays appear regularly in several publications, including *Salon.com* and *Wired.* Among her other publications are *Ethnobotany and Medicinal Plants Bibliography: July 1991–July 1992* (1993); *When Elephants Weep: The Emotional Lives of Animals* (1996), coauthored with Jeffrey Moussaieff Masson; and *Caesar Rodney: American Patriot* (2001).

No one's more wired than Vanessa Gonzalez. A poised 13-year-old in T-shirt, shorts, pink socks, and a charm bracelet, she's a VR expert who's mastered Starbright World, a 3-D virtual Eden with real-time videoconferencing.

She's navigating Starbright World now, via a Pentium-based workstation. Around the screen is a whimsical frame with pictures of wooden Tinkertoys and the logos of Starbright's corporate partners. A small videocamera is perched to the right of the monitor. Vanessa wears a headset, and conversations are audible throughout the room. The sound quality isn't great, but the speech is clear.

Vanessa's hair is fuzz-short because of chemotherapy she's getting for osteosarcoma, and she's hooked to an IV pole with three drip bags—two clear and one yellow. A monitor on the IV flashes numbers: 10.0, 13.0, 7.4. Before Vanessa has settled at the Starbright terminal the monitor beeps, and she checks it calmly. "I need to get plugged in," she says.

The Starbright Pediatric Network, which includes Starbright World, aims to connect children who are hospitalized for long periods or must return repeatedly. It links children like Vanessa in Palo Alto, California, with others in Pittsburgh, New York, Dallas, and elsewhere, who come for chemotherapy, for organ transplants, or with chronic illnesses like cystic fibrosis.

5 Vanessa is sitting in a small windowless "rec-tech room" at the Lucile Salter Packard Children's Hospital at Stanford University. Although ultimately there will be Starbright stations that can be wheeled to children's beds, for now the necessary DS3 (equivalent to T3) wiring has been installed only here and in the main playroom.

Vanessa, represented in Starbright World by a helicopter, is "just churning around" until—in Cave World—she meets a fish, denoting a user at a Pittsburgh hospital. In text, they agree to switch to videoconferencing. The Pittsburgh fish turns out to be Rachel, who's 17. (Names and other identifying details of children at the Pittsburgh hospital have been changed.) Asthma has put Rachel in the hospital. The screen shows her sitting slouched in the playroom. In a corner of the screen, a smaller image shows Vanessa, as Pittsburgh sees her. "What are you guys doing?" Rachel asks. "Anything exciting?"

"No. Not really."

"It sounds like a normal hospital."

"Very," says Vanessa dryly.

10 A child using Starbright World these days is often ringed by observers—product developers, medical experts, hospital public relations people, parents, and reporters like me. Still in beta testing, Starbright is courting publicity. So are the four corporate partners who have made this broad-bandwidth network possible—Intel Corp. is contributing workstations and its ProShare Video System 1.9; UB Networks Inc. is supplying local-area networking; Sprint Communications Co. is providing DS3 lines; and Worlds Inc. is contributing the virtual reality space.

The kids navigate one of the most advanced video networks on the planet—an unequalled package bundling real-time videoconferencing with a series of real-time multiuser 3-D virtual worlds. The kids get top-of-the-line Pentium machines (32 megs of RAM) with ATM lines (133 bps or more). As the project brings diverse state-of-the-art technologies together, the corporate partners are avidly watching this almost perfect—if costly—test arena for broadband networking.

Always hovering nearby are "child life" specialists, hospital employees whose job it is to make patients' lives more tolerable and who act as educators, helping children and their families adapt to hospital life and medical procedures. At hospitals with Starbright World, child life specialists also become technical support people. For them, Starbright promises a way to lure depressed children out of their rooms, to show a child with a rare disease that there are others in a similar condition, or to make some part of hospital life an exciting and enviable experience.

This multimillion-dollar project was organized by Starbright, a self-styled "entrepreneurial charity" that is a sibling foundation to Starlight, a conventional charity granting wishes to critically ill children. Starlight's co-founder, Peter Samuelson, is a Hollywood producer *(Revenge of the Nerds, Tom & Viv)* who had begun to feel that Starlight left sick kids miserably entertained. He describes visiting one hospital and asking a nurse how a boy in traction could change channels on the black-and-white wall-mounted TV. "We have a remote control," replied the nurse, fetching a 10-foot-long bamboo pole. Samuelson says, "The poor kid was supposed to lie in bed and poke the button with it!"

Samuelson reacted by starting two programs: Starlight Express, media rooms installed in pediatric hospitals, and Starlight Express Fun Centers, VCR-PC-laserdisc-videogame combos on carts that slide over a child's bed and that have been distributed to more than 1,000 hospitals.

15 Off-the-shelf software used in those two programs "was having a very good effect on the kids," Samuelson says, but "I began to wonder what would happen if we made software focused on kids' needs." He enlisted the help of Steven Spielberg, the 300-pound gorilla of the entertainment industry, who agreed to chair the new Starbright Foundation and made a seven-figure donation.

Out of their ambition—to combine Southern California's entertainment industry with pediatric medicine and new interactive technologies—came the remarkable combination of benevolence and marketing that is the Starbright Pediatric Network.

The corporate partners get a chance to test-market new technology on a real-world population in an unquestionably philanthropic way. Some are deploying technologies previously restricted to business markets. (Will *children* accept them?) They are forming valuable alliances with the other corporate partners and with the entertainment industry. Thus, Worlds Inc. program manager Kevin Ugarte remarks, though some think it's insane for a start-up like Worlds to invest in a huge project like Starbright, the program not only connects the company with bigger corporate players and lets it learn to work with children, but also acts as an intense idea generator.

In addition, all those who actually go into the hospitals seem deeply struck by the human value of the endeavor, almost startled by the genuineness of the Good Deed.

As for the children, they get a break from the grimness and tedium of institutional routine. And they communicate with other sick kids in powerful, unprecedented ways.

20 Rachel and Vanessa decide to go back into virtual reality and explore Cave World. Instead of talking through text, they carry the audio with them, a favorite technique. They go into Tropical World, a gorgeous land of palms, low mountains, and pools. Entering a rainbow, they whiz to Sky World: flocks of high-heaped cumulus, one holding a classic Mad King Ludwig castle. Colette Case, a child life specialist at Vanessa's end of the line, suggests they visit the Build Your Own Zone, where users can create structures. They descend into the BYOZ through a tornado, but can't find each other visually.

"We're gonna fly above and see if we can see you guys," says Rachel. "What are you near?"

"I'm by the wall with flames of fire on it," says Vanessa.

But the BYOZ is such a tumult of walls, midair waterfalls, big-eyeballed plants, cubes, and staring green aliens, that it's not easy to locate the wall of flames.

Finally they cut the connection, meet in Tropical World, and go through a gold sliding door to arrive back in Cave World, a mysterious dim green streaky maze. Rachel remarks, "I've never really been in the cave. This girl Marie, like she's always in the cave. Oh wait, here's Marie!" Marie walks up to the terminal in the Pittsburgh playroom, and Rachel points to—and introduces—the helicopter on the screen. "This is Vanessa—in California."

25 Shortly after joining Starbright's board, Lee Rosenberg, a senior vice president at the William Morris Talent Agency and a founder of Triad Artists, arranged a large lunch meeting in 1993 for pediatric specialists, members of the entertainment industry, and representatives of companies like Brøderbund and Microsoft. It was designed as a brainstorming session to find solutions to emotional and physical problems confronting critically ill children.

The brainstormers came up with 25 projects. Seven, with various corporate partners, are in development, including Starbright, which has raised several million dollars. General Norman Schwarzkopf was drafted to head a campaign to raise US$60 million more.

Everyone has agreed *not* to specify how much Starbright costs: "multimillions" is all they'll say. It's obviously not cheap. The more than 100 high-end PCs supplied by Intel, for example, retail for around $6,000 each. Worlds Inc. has devoted up to eight people at a time to Starbright. Sprint is supplying and maintaining seven DS3 connections, more than any of their corporate customers have.

Vanessa, Rachel, and Marie switch back to videoconferencing. They go through introductions. Marie, 14 in a few days, is there from Vermont because "my liver numbers went up. As you can probably see, I'm a little bit yellow." She sounds weary. "They're probably going to do a transplant." An ebullient 12-year-old, Emma, squeezes in next to Marie. She doesn't want to talk about illness, though she does want to know how long Vanessa's been in.

"This is my second day so far."

30 "This is my first day here," says Emma. "I come here a lot though."

"Me too."

Starbright fundraisers didn't simply ask for big donations, they asked for the creation of an unprecedented network and specified what they thought would help sick children. The corporations they approached hesitated. "We knew that Spielberg was capable of having a great dream; we just didn't know if his dream was implementable," says Avram Miller, Intel's vice president for business development, a unit formed to seek out new markets for Intel processors.

Roel Pieper, CEO of Tandem Computers Inc., parent company to UB Networks, agrees. "It was a risky endeavor. We didn't know if we could get all the ATM technology to work, we didn't know if we could get sufficient performance for the ProShare videoconferencing, we didn't know if we could get sufficient acceptance from the children on the 3-D graphics."

But the project had great allure for the corporate partners. It's R&D with an unbeatable PR angle. While such a partnership *could* happen in the strictly for-profit world, Miller says corporations alone would be unlikely to tackle a project with sick kids.

35 "It's the kind of thing that Steven Spielberg, who is a storyteller and has a relationship with children, can do," he says. "If we proposed this, we would have been viewed as being very invasive. A bunch of geeks, people in white coats (although I don't think any of us have white coats), not really caring about the kids, but wanting to instrument the kids and treat them like objects. I don't say we *would,* but I think that's how we would have been perceived."

Steven Spielberg, content provider extraordinaire, lured the sponsors, lured the big donors, lured the reporters. Just his name has lured the shy kids online, as child life specialists hold out the prospect that kids might run into Spielberg—in the form of his avatar, E. T. ("Running into Spielberg" is no mean feat: weeks of calling didn't get *Wired* an interview.)

The director's own Starbright experience drives home the cost of this technology. He only got a Starbright terminal in March. Since a DS3 line would have cost perhaps $50,000 to install and $7,000 to $8,000 a month to run, an ISDN line was installed in Spielberg's office. He gets 7 to 8 video fps, instead of 15, and a quarter-second delay, but all features offered to kids are there.

This compromised rig is itself a bit of a beta test: it may show whether Starbright's projected Phase 2, in which Starbright kids will get access from home, probably over ISDN lines, will work.

Half a dozen hospitals are participating in Phase 1: Lucile Packard, Mount Sinai Hospital in New York, Children's Hospital of Pittsburgh, and hospitals in LA and Washington, DC. (As this article went to press, a Boston hospital had dropped out of the program, and Children's Medical Center of Dallas went online.) As new hospitals are added, Starbright looks for more donors.

40 Emma, Marie, and Vanessa turn to the subject of hospital playrooms and activities. "A lot of crazy stuff goes on here," says Emma enthusiastically. "Somebody sent us these!" She jams a figurine against the screen. "It's made from a peanut and it's got a top hat on. Isn't it neat? I'm all the way in Pittsburgh and you're all the way in California. Is it dark there yet?"

"No."

"We're going to show you Rachel painting the windows," declares Emma, a media natural. She rips the videocamera from its Velcro mount and carries it around, showing Rachel standing on a chair painting snowflakes. "She said Hi! Rachel, don't fall off! She said she's already in the hospital!"

Children in isolation during bone-marrow transplants give perhaps the most striking example of the sorrowful conditions Starbright is meant to alleviate. They live in a small, sanitary room for four to eight weeks, seeing few, certified-healthy visitors. Their strength is low and their spirits are apt to be lower. Severe mouth sores make it painful to talk on the phone. Child life workers on transplant wards ache to get isolation rooms wired.

Such patients got Starbright its highest-profile fundraiser: when Norman Schwarzkopf was first approached by Samuelson and Spielberg to raise money for Starbright, he declined. Though he'd worked with camps for sick children, he was involved in so many charities that he didn't want to take on another. Then, after a fundraiser at a Florida hospital, he visited the children's ward. In the transplant unit he found Heather, a child he knew from one of the camps. "She was lying there in the bed in the fetal position, totally isolated from the entire world, with no companionship whatsoever," Schwarzkopf says. "What she wanted to talk about was camp and the one time when she'd been allowed to just be a kid. I suddenly realized that if we could have Starbright World in that room with her, she wouldn't be isolated, she'd be able to escape. So I called up Starbright and said 'OK. Where do you want me to start?'"

45 Emma, Marie, and Vanessa discuss birthdays and favorite authors and then happen on the subject of brothers—how many, how old, how tolerable. Marie and Vanessa have serious complaints, and Emma joins in—just to be companionable. When Marie says that brothers are always in your face, Vanessa answers emphatically, "Tell me about it. It's true. They never leave you alone."

"They're always in your business," says Emma.

"And they never come see you in the hospital!" exclaims Marie. "They always have excuses."

This produces heated discussion. "My brother comes every night," says Vanessa. "Except he comes and he doesn't spend any time in the room, he's always outside playing."

Later, after the kids in Pittsburgh—in a later time zone—say good night and log off, Vanessa's younger brother arrives. He asks to see Starbright, and they sit at adjacent stations. She shows him how to enter Tropical World and take the rainbow to Sky World.

"It's cool," he says, authoritatively. "Neat graphics."

Both Palo Alto workstations are represented in VR by an avatar in the form of a helicopter. (Later, kids will have individual avatars.) "That's me?" asks Vanessa's brother. "I don't get it. Oh. . . we're *connected?* I can see you?"

They explore Cave World, hunting for a huge stone face whose square mouth is a door that takes two people to open—so Vanessa has never been through. The environments are designed to foster cooperation, as Worlds producer Tamiko Thiel explains: "A lot of the therapeutic work with these kids is to get them to come out of their shells, come out of their concern with themselves and their sickness and start socializing again."

Together Vanessa and her brother open the door and come out in the sky.

Videoconferencing is the first thing many kids want to try. Colette Case, a buoyant young woman with short dark hair who is the Starbright coordinator at Stanford, says she's astounded by the children's candor in videoconferencing. "They tell each other just everything. We sit there in awe." But when she asks Vanessa, "Do you think you guys would talk differently if there weren't people watching you?" Vanessa gazes at Case and slowly nods, nods, nods.

The corporate partners are eager to see *how* they use it. For decades, videoconferencing has been just around the corner, yet its use is confined to the business market. (Picture phones were just too expensive.) But now, they say, it's *really* around the corner. PCs make the difference, says Miller. Instead of buying a new system, users will need software and a $50 camera for their PCs. "By the end of the decade, it will become unusual not to be able to communicate in some form of video communication from your office. It's going to be explosive." (ProShare 1.9 now retails for around $1,000.)

Robba Benjamin, president of Sprint's multimedia unit, agrees. "The features and functionality that we're giving the Starbright children are the basic features and functionality of the 21st-century phone." Starbright, as a test market, provides a way for Sprint to explore new markets, to look not at productivity in a business setting, but at what people like to do, at uses they consider improvements in their lives.

Yet one of the important features of Starbright is that kids *don't* have to be seen. In fact, some kids refuse the option. One child who was hooked to an oxygen tank said he preferred not to be seen.

Pieper of Tandem Computers wants to examine the possibilities of a network without ProShare, to find out whether video is critical or a frill. It's a key question. Ordinary phone lines would suffice for the virtual worlds and for text and voice communication, while ProShare takes a lot of bandwidth to give decent video quality. ProShare is why Starbright runs over DS3 lines (equivalent to 672 voice telephone lines), and why it costs so much. "You've got people who believe that the real issue of getting a network to become a conferencing system is voice-driven, and the other group that says it has to be image-driven," says Pieper about the marketing issues Starbright is meant to illuminate. "We don't know. We truly don't know."

Justin Lamarche is in the BYOZ when he meets a blue bear in a green T-shirt and shades. The avatar represents Susan Prosser, who does tech support for Worlds out of Seattle.

60 Prosser and Justin know each other well. Justin's 12, wearing a black motorcycle T-shirt and purple shorts. The effects of chemotherapy show in his shorter-than-crewcut hair. He is at Children's Hospital in Boston and will soon go into isolation for a transplant. A rare smile reveals his tremendous dimples. Prosser and Justin communicate in text superimposed on their avatars. They agree to head for Tropical World, where Prosser saw a Pittsburgh fish and a green car, the avatar for New York's Mount Sinai Hospital.

The trip from BYOZ to Tropical World takes time, because in the transition between worlds, there's a pause while the new one is loaded into memory. As Justin travels, he and his child life specialist, Paula Johnson-Grenier, discuss a drag race he just ran with some other kids. Johnson-Grenier has a serious demeanor and honey-blond hair. She is insisting, in the nicest possible way, that Justin ought to confess to cheating.

"I just pressed a little Alt," says Justin, with what looks like pleasurable reminiscence. Two nurses in hospital blues appear in response to a fit of beeps from Justin's IV monitor. Justin questions them. "You going to hang my bag now? I have to go back to my room or can you do it here?"

A nurse replies sympathetically, "I think I can do it here—are you busy?"

"Yeah. We're too busy to talk to blue coats around here. We only talk to white coats," he teases.

65 "Snob!" she exclaims.

Justin returns to discussing the race.

"I kicked their butts!"

Starbright World isn't meant to be a snap to navigate. "You can either take the time to explore it yourself or you can ask some other kid and say, 'Hey, show me around,'" explains Thiel. "That's different from existing computer tools, where the whole idea is to be able to do something faster and easier."

Indeed, the most popular place in Starbright World, the BYOZ, is also the hardest to navigate, the chewiest—and the one that grants users the most control and most clearly bears the traces of their presence. In the BYOZ, you can move things, build things, or heap things up, and everyone can see what you've done.

70 At first, two tricks got kids out of the BYOZ—using a portal in a checkerboard pavilion, or going to desktop level. Then a kid at Stanford found out how to move—and hide—the portal, leaving other users to make baffled runs at the place it used to be. Another kid went to the desktop and started changing things at the pixel level. Next version, desktop access was cut off and the portal was nailed down.

Thiel says some media people are so smitten by videoconferencing they ask if virtual worlds are necessary. "'Couldn't they just have the videoconference and that would be the same thing?' The answer really is No. It's pretty weird if you just all of a sudden telephone someone that you don't know and start talking to them. You need some sort of context, some sort of shared experience."

She tells of watching two boys using the system, "an older, bigger, really sort of bullying kid and another, much smaller, very quiet kid. The older kid said, 'OK, you know the space better, how about if you show me around?'" She gloats a nerdly gloat. "The younger, quieter kid was the expert!"

"Always, the fear is that giving kids (or adults) computers will make them retreat into themselves and become less human," Thiel says. "The Starbright space has been designed to socialize kids."

By the rainbow in Tropical World, the Pittsburgh fish hangs in midair, pouting powder-blue lips. It faces the Mount Sinai car, which races its wheels. Justin calls them, but gets no reply. The bear—Prosser—sends a message to Justin, suggesting they switch to video.

When they do, Justin says with apparent sincerity, "I think you should fix your hair, it's sticking up." Prosser runs a startled hand over her hair and blanks the screen, undoubtedly discovering that her hair is fine. Justin snickers.

The picture returns, and Justin describes a sign reading "HI BOSTON" that he and Johnson-Grenier built in the BYOZ, which Prosser wants to see.

"It's over by the racetrack. When you first come out of the rainbow you should see it. It has big letters."

Justin abruptly hangs up to try to get through to New York. Later, he finds Prosser again in the BYOZ, and she types, "so where is this sign you spoke of"

"do you want to see the sign brat" He turns to Johnson-Grenier and asks, "I'm getting better at typing, huh?"

Justin agrees to show Prosser the sign if she begs.

"please oh please show me the sign Please mr Pony sir"

"well all right brat"

They set out, and Justin exclaims to Johnson-Grenier, "Let's try to lose her!"

Justin changes his style depending on who he's talking to, Johnson-Grenier says. He teases people his own age, eases off with younger kids. Starbright has discussed having monitors in case one kid harasses another. "But they're all pretty sensitive to what other kids are going through, because they're going through the same thing," says Ugarte. "I've never witnessed a malicious moment."

"I came into it with a somewhat idealistic idea of what we were going to do and have been brought down to earth," Ugarte adds. What brought him to earth? "The day-to-day things that these kids go through and how amazingly they cope with them. We're giving them another tool to help them cope. But we're not saving these kids. These kids are saving themselves with everything they can."

One small study conducted at a Los Angeles hospital measured the pain medication taken by children who used Starlight Express Fun Centers. The children were patients who could self-administer small doses by pressing a button on a pump. The study, which Starbright points to with pride, found that children not only used less medication when using the Starlight Express trolleys to watch videos or play games, but also used less in the periods immediately before and after using the trolleys. The first decrease is thought to be due to anticipation, the second to a lingering distraction effect. Starbright representatives, from Samuelson to Schwarzkopf, say the drop in pain medication use was between 50 and 80 percent, depending on how the data are interpreted.

The children said they preferred controlling their pain with videogames to using medication, which usually has disorienting effects and may depress the immune system. (While it's rare in children, the medicine can also be addictive.)

Unfortunately, the Starlight Express study is not an impressive model. It looked at only 28 children, and there was no control group. Because of limited availability of the trolleys, the kids could use them no more than two hours a day, and the study didn't look for a decrease in the total amount of medication.

When Starbright Worlds gets out of beta, a massive medical research program—to include control groups and to be much larger—will look at its effects on use of medication, length of hospital stay, and frequency of "positive outcome," according to Dr. Mel Marks, who oversees the health applications and research component of the Starbright Foundation.

90 "These major investments in technology and resources are going to have to be justified extremely carefully by the most rigorous measures of outcome," Marks says. "We want to be careful not to divert millions of dollars to what is right now an experimental technique."

What if Starbright can't show health benefits? "We have Apple computers now, where the children can do their schoolwork or play games," says child life specialist Johnson-Grenier. "I could never claim it decreases their use of nausea medicine or something, but I certainly think it makes their stay in the isolation room better."

Asked about the importance of measurable health benefits, Schwarzkopf exclaims, "I don't *care* whether there are measurable benefits!" Calming, he reviews the hoped-for advantages, but adds, "I gotta tell you, all that sounds good, but as far as I'm concerned, if we can just cause one child to be relieved from the terrible suffering that they're going through, it's worth every nickel."

In Justin's HI BOSTON sign, each letter is on a separate block, each in a different typeface.

"I like this sign," Prosser types.

95 Paula Johnson-Grenier warns Justin that it's time to log off. As a nurse takes his blood pressure, he finds Susan Prosser's bear avatar in the BYOZ and types "brat are you going to be here tomorrow"

"maybe maybe not depends on how nice you are to me"

"do you want me to beg" He turns to us. "Watch what I say if she says yes!"

"It may help" Prosser responds.

"i forgot my standreds are to hi" he grins enormously and types, "brat"

100 Urgently struck by an idea, Justin tells Johnson-Grenier he'll pretend to be her. "this is paula what time do you want to talk tomorrow and work some kinks" he types.

"I am flexible what's better for you" comes the reply.

After consulting Johnson-Grenier, he types, "200–400 500–800"

"ok I'll be hanging around the tropical world" types Prosser.

"see you then brat"

Mapping the Text

1. What does this narrative suggest about social relationships and healing? What role(s) does technology play between the two? What is the significance of the economic implications?
2. McCarthy conveys much of her message through the eyes, voices, and experiences of the children. What is the impact of this choice?

Writing to Inquire

1. Susan McCarthy begins this essay with a reference to Steven Spielberg and the Starbright World. Use library and other resources to gather information on both. Who is Steven Spielberg? What is the Starbright Foundation?
2. Write an essay in which you account for the impact of technology in this environment.

"Is This the Party to Whom I Am Speaking?" Women, Credibility, and the Internet

LAURA GURAK

Laura Gurak is an associate professor at the University of Minnesota in the Department of Rhetoric and director of the Center for Internet Studies. Her research is in the areas of computer-mediated communication, social aspects of computing, and intellectural property and electronic texts. She has written numerous articles and essays on technology and received the Outstanding Article of the Year Award in 1992 from the journal *Technical Communication.* Her books include *Persuasion and Privacy in Cyberspace: The Online Protests over Lotus MarketPlace and the Clipper Chip* (1997) and the forthcoming *Cyberliteracy: Navigating the Online World with Presence.* In the essay below, Gurak discusses issues related to truth and identity on the Internet.

Most people have by now seen the famous *New Yorker* cartoon of two dogs sitting at the computer. Remarking on the way online technology can be used to mask identity, one canine says to the other, "On the Internet, no one knows you're a dog."

In truth, on the Internet, there is a lot we don't know about what comes streaming onto our computer screens. No one knows who the author of a Web page really is; no one knows if information is accurate or not: no one knows if a site is the official one or a parody site; no one knows for sure if an email message is really coming from a person, a robot, or a person masquerading as someone else. In essence we have lots of information, pictures and sound on the Internet but little by way of how to judge the credibility of what we see.

A Minnesota-based Web page provides one example. This site about the city of Mankato displays a photograph of a beach with a swimmer relaxing in the warm sun. It lures Web surfers to visit the beaches of its lovely lakes:

> Mankato, Minnesota is truly a wonderland. Tucked into the Emerald Green Valley in Southern Minnesota, it is the hidden vacation Mecca of scores of knowing Midwesterners. Mankato has everything thanks to a freak of nature: the Farr/Sclare Fissure. This fissure in the earth's crust takes water seeping through the earth, heats it to well over 165 degrees, and sends it back up to the surface in steam pits and boil holes. The heat from these pits and holes heats the valley air to such an extent that the winter temperature in many Mankato neighborhoods has never dropped below a balmy 70 degrees!!!! Come enjoy our winters! Let's "Make it Mankato"!! (www.lme.mankato.msus.edu/mankato/mankato.html)

Trouble is, there is no such thing as the "Farr/Sclare Fissure." Mankato gets as cold as the rest of the state. Yet the site drew viewers from around the world, many of whom requested more information on lodging and travel. Soon the site had to include at the top of its page a link to a disclaimer informing Web surfers that Mankato was no place to surf the waves in December!

Another example are email hoaxes. From cellular phones that might make gas pumps explode to virus email messages that will crash your computer to sick children in need of greeting cards, rumors and hoaxes abound on the Internet. Anyone with an email account quickly notices that certain messages regularly make the rounds. Hoaxes asking you to send a card to a dying child or save box tops from cereal so that a family won't starve are popular. So are messages about deadly computer viruses that will wipe out your hard disk. These messages come disguised in language that makes them seem credible, but they are almost always false. In addition, humorous messages—workplace humor, political jokes, not-so-funny puns—from your brother, your distant cousin, or a friend you have not seen in years may also appear in your email box, prefaced by a long list of others who've also been forwarded this message.

5 So: what does this issue have to do with women? A great deal, it turns out, if you begin to consider the issues in detail. There has already been a wealth of discussion—both in the popular press and in the research community—about women and the Internet more generally, with topics including how women are displayed (pornographic images abound in cyberspace), whether women have equal access (no, though it's getting better), whether girls get as much computer time as boys (no), whether or not women need "a room of their own" by way of women-oriented Web sites (maybe, though some would argue this is just another way of isolating women, and whether Deborah Tannen-style communication patterns also happen in online discussions (turns out they do, and then some). What we have not heard as much about is the more complicated confluence of credibility. Internet communication and issues relevant to women.

First, let's back up. If you examine the history of the Internet, you quickly come to see that cyberspace is gendered space. No technologies are value-neutral. They carry the marks of their makers and the ethos of the culture in which they arise. And though marketing hype by telecommunications companies would have us believe that "there is no gender on the Internet" (in the words of an MCI commercial in the late 1990s), the Internet was originally developed by almost exclusively male scientists and engineers in the late 1950s as a Department of Defense technology. Even today, science and engineering fields, including the all-powerful computer science (the heartbeat of Internet development), are dominated by men.

The history of Internet development is decidedly male; gender bias is built into the fibers and cables, into the protocols and switches, and into the subsequent computer culture and language habits that arose in these spaces—just look at some of the commands of early operating systems: "kill," "abort" and so on. Thus, it is no surprise that as Internet use became more widespread, from the late 1980s to the mid 1990s, certain gendered interactions began to occur.

The first of these, which will bring us back to a discussion of credibility, is flaming, the angry, vitriolic style of communication that is common in email messages. Linguist Susan Herring, who is well known for her studies of gender online, has made the case that flaming is in some part a gendered style of communicating. In one study of an academic mailing list she noted that men participated more than women, and that when women did contribute, their language was attenuated and meek, while men's language was assertive and imperative. Men made more statements, whereas women asked more questions. Men were more sarcastic and self-promoting, while women often asked supportive questions and made apologies for themselves and their thoughts. When people—both men and women—find themselves involved in communication that so dramatically heightens gendered styles, they begin to question the usefulness and credibility of the information they receive.

Another issue is privacy. Many ecommerce companies have learned that customers need to understand how their personal information is being used before they will find a site credible (and, therefore, make a purchase). Companies create "privacy protection statements" to assure visitors that the site takes seriously the protection of personal data. And while this sort of attention to online privacy (which many—myself included—believe is still rather inadequate) is a good thing, legal scholar Anita L. Allen argues that when it comes to women, too much privacy can also be a problem. Women, she notes, have long fought to overcome concepts of privacy that have kept them in second-class status; she argues that "a traditional predicament of American women was too *much* of the wrong kinds of privacy," including social mores like modesty, chastity, and domestic isolation, as well as too *little* privacy when it came to individual privacies and private choice.

10 On the Internet, she notes, women "face special privacy problems" for many of the same reasons they do in real life. Private images of women can be easily displayed to the entire world by anyone with an Internet account; electronic consumer data can be collected and resold, making women just another category of marketing campaigns; women—as many commentators note—are more frequently than men targets of electronic harassers, stalkers and just plain creeps. When a technology interferes with women's privacy in these ways, it will not be a credible technology and women will not trust it. But the trouble is that while some forms of cyberspace privacy invasions are overt (e.g., online harassment), others are not even noticeable (systems that sell your personal data based on income or gender; Web sites that collect keystrokes and site visit information without telling you).

Then there is the issue of identity. On many real-time chat sites and email systems, male participants can log in as females, females can easily assume the character of a male, and both men and women can participate as an "it" or other neuter gender. As the *New Yorker*'s dogs noted, it's often hard to know who is doing the talking. In one famous case, a man tricked a group of women into thinking that he was "Joan," a lonely house-bound woman with no friends other than her virtual ones. After others on the list got to know Joan, offering support and sharing intimate secrets, she was revealed to be an able-bodied man who had assumed this identity in order to see "what it felt like to be female." List participants were extremely angry at this deception, which is usually played out by men toward women. "From my earliest effort to construct an online persona," notes Sherry Turkle, "it occurred to me that being a virtual man might be more comfortable than being a virtual woman." One of the most obvious ways in which all humans assess credibility is by knowing who the speaker or author is. In a space where men can become women and then use this identity-skewing to harass, target and get women to open up to them, we begin to realize that we can not trust online interactions.

One example of how issues about identity and authorship play out occurs when women (or men) use the Web to seek out medical information. Especially in the case of women's health, long recognized as lacking the same funding and visibility as many male health concerns, we become vulnerable to Web sites that may appear credible. After all, anyone with a computer and the right software can make a site that appears valid by using the right colors, the right fonts, the right links to other sites and so on. In a recent study here at the University of Minnesota, my graduate students and I at the Internet Studies Center (www.isc.umn.edu) discovered that women often take the lead in researching medical information on the Internet, both for themselves and for their families and friends. Given the lack of gatekeeping that is an essential part of Internet communication, we must be ever on the alert for information that is credible and information that is not.

How do we take an activist stance in dealing with the troublesome issues related to women, credibility, and the Internet? In my forthcoming book, I suggest what I call "cyberliteracy" as a way to become aware of how we intersect with this new media. I articulate two key operating concepts that make the Internet function. These are speed and reach, and each brings with it us own set of implications. Speed, for example, invites people to post messages without thinking. Reach has implications for credibility also, because people are often seduced into publishing something that may not be completely accurate but will reach millions of people in seconds. The combination of these factors makes. Internet communication extremely powerful. Speed and reach also change how we think about social conditions, including gender. We must learn to "read" Internet texts with a critical eye.

For example, to return to the issue of medical information on the Web: Recently, I learned that my sister's two-month-old son, who already went through surgery when he was just four days old, was now suffering from a case of bronchiolitis. Being the Internet researcher for the family, I went to my favorite search engine and typed in this term. Naturally, I found numerous hits, and so now my job was to determine which of these might be credible and useful. The first site on the list was the Children's Hospital of Iowa's "Virtual Children's Hospital" (www.vh.org). The article was written by an M.D. and peer reviewed and the content seemed balanced and sensible. In other cases, medical information may be out of balance, representing, let's say, the views of pharmaceutical companies that sponsor the sites, or the worst-case scenarios of the people who post messages. And while the latter may be helpful for patients and their families by way of sharing information and finding comfort, they and other sites may not be the best sources of balanced information. You might think this is obvious, but you'd be surprised how normally cautious, even sceptical people sometimes forget the phrase "caveat emptor" when they are wandering around the speedy spaces of the Internet.

We can move to make cyberspace more credible by becoming part of the scene. Barbara Warnick, while noting the sexism of computer culture, observes that women are increasingly more comfortable with the Web and are in fact building their own sites, "constructing welcoming places where invitational discourse becomes truly inviting." Cyberliteracy requires us to acknowledge the gendered nature of the Internet and to take action. We can construct sites that defy this trend, create new role models for girls and women, and recognize that there is no utopia in cyberspace. Fact and fiction blur together in ways we are only now beginning to recognize. For women, who are the target of much pressure to get themselves online (mainly for our personal data and our money, notes legal scholar Ann Bartow), it is important to embrace this special form of critical literacy while there is still time.

Note: The title of this essay is the famous line by Lily Tomlin as her character Ernestine the telephone operator. Phrase used here for purposes of scholarly criticism, which is covered by fair use doctrine under US Copyright law.

References

Allen, Anita L. "Gender and privacy in cyberspace," *Stanford Law Review* 52 (May, 2000): 1175–1200.

Bartow, Ann. "Our data, ourselves: privacy, propertization, and gender," *University of San Francisco Law Review* 34.4 (Summer, 2000): 633–704.

Gurak, Laura J. *Cyberliteracy: Navigating the Internet with Awareness.* New Haven: Yale University Press, forthcoming, 2001. Available for preview at www.rhetoric.umn.edu/cyberliteracy.

Herring, Susan. "Gender and democracy in computer-mediated communication," *Electronic Journal of Communication* 3,2 (1993): 1–12.

Internet Studies Center, University of Minnesota. www.isc.umn.edu.

Turkle, Sherry. *Life on the Screen: Identity in the age of the Internet.* New York: Simon and Schuster, 1995.

Van Gelder, Lindsay. "The strange case of the electronic lover," in Gary Gumpert and Sandra L. Fish (Eds.), *Talking to strangers: Mediated therapeutic communication.* (Norwood: NJ: Ablex, 1990).

Warnick, Barbara. "Masculinizing the feminine: Inviting women online ca. 1997," *Critical Studies in Mass Communication* 16.1 (1999): 1–19.

Mapping the Text

1. Outline the problems in Internet communications that Laura Gurak identifies in this essay. Do you find her views reasonable and credible? Why?

2. Gurak also proposes solutions. Outline the solutions. What do you think she means by "cyberliteracy"? What does she suggest it would take for a person to be cyberliterate?
3. What is Gurak's purpose in writing this essay? Who is her intended audience? What types of appeals does she use to address this audience? In your view, were her choices reasonable, appropriate, effective? Explain.

Writing to Inquire

1. Gurak asks, "How do we take an activist stance in dealing with the troublesome issues related to women, credibility, and the Internet?" What are the issues Gurak identifies related to women, to credibility, to the Internet? Do you agree with her that we should take an activist stance? Explain.

Women and Children First: Gender and the Settling of the Electronic Frontier

LAURA MILLER

Laura Miller is a journalist and critic who has contributed to the *San Francisco Examiner, Harper's Bazaar,* and *GirlJock.* She is a contributing editor for *San Francisco Weekly.* The selection below is taken from a collection of essays entitled *Resisting the Virtual Life: The Culture and Politics of Information* (1995).

When *Newsweek* (May 16, 1994) ran an article entitled "Men, Women and Computers," all hell broke out on the Net, particularly on the on-line service I've participated in for six years, The Well (Whole Earth 'Lectronic Link). "Cyberspace, it turns out," declared *Newsweek*'s Nancy Kantrowitz, "isn't much of an Eden after all. It's marred by just as many sexist ruts and gender conflicts as the Real World. . . . Women often feel about as welcome as a system crash." "It was horrible. Awful, poorly researched, unsubstantiated drivel," one member wrote, a sentiment echoed throughout some 480 postings.

However egregious the errors in the article (some sources maintain that they were incorrectly quoted), it's only one of several mainstream media depictions of the Net as an environment hostile to women. Even women who had been complaining about on-line gender relations found themselves increasingly annoyed by what one Well member termed the "cyberbabe harassment" angle that seems to typify media coverage of the issue. Reified in the pages of *Newsweek* and other journals, what had once been the topic of discussions by insiders—on-line commentary is informal, conversational, and often spontaneous—became a journalistic "fact" about the Net known by complete strangers and novices. In a matter of months, the airy stuff of bitch sessions became widespread, hardened stereotypes.

At the same time, the Internet has come under increasing scrutiny as it mutates from an obscure, freewheeling web of computer networks used by a small elite of academics, scientists, and hobbyists to. . . well, nobody seems to know exactly what. But the business press prints vague, fevered prophecies of fabulous wealth, and a bonanza mentality has blossomed. With it comes big business and the government, intent on regulating this amorphous medium into a manageable and profitable industry. The Net's history of informal self-regulation and its wide libertarian streak guarantee that battles like the one over the Clipper chip (a mandatory decoding device that would make all encrypted data readable by federal agents) will be only the first among many.

Yet the threat of regulation is built into the very mythos used to conceptualize the Net by its defenders—and gender plays a crucial role in that threat. However revolutionary the technologized interactions of on-line communities may seem, we understand them by deploying a set of very familiar metaphors from the rich figurative soup of American culture. Would different metaphors have allowed the Net a different, better historical trajectory? Perhaps not, but the way we choose to describe the Net now encourages us to see regulation as its inevitable fate. And, by examining how gender roles provide a foundation for the intensification of such social controls, we can illuminate the way those roles proscribe the freedoms of men as well as women.

5 For months I mistakenly referred to the EFF (an organization founded by John Perry Barlow and Lotus 1-2-3 designer Mitch Kapor to foster access to, and further the discursive freedom of, on-line communications) as "The Electronic Freedom Foundation," instead of by its actual name, "The Electronic Frontier Foundation." Once corrected, I was struck by how intimately related the ideas "frontier" and "freedom" are in the Western mythos. The *frontier,* as a realm of limitless possibilities and few social controls, hovers, grail-like, in the American psyche, the dream our national identity is based on, but a dream that's always, somehow, just vanishing away.

Once made, the choice to see the Net as a frontier feels unavoidable, but it's actually quite problematic. The word "frontier" has traditionally described a place, if not land then the limitless "final frontier" of space. The Net, on the other hand, occupies precisely no physical space (although the computers and phone lines that make it possible do). It is a completely bodiless, symbolic thing with no discernable boundaries or location. The land of the American frontier did not become a "frontier" until Europeans determined to conquer it, but the continent existed before the intention to settle it. Unlike land, the Net was created by its pioneers.

Most peculiar, then, is the choice of the word "frontier" to describe an artifact so humanly constructed that it only exists as ideas or information. For central to the idea of the frontier is that it contains no (or very few) other people—fewer than two per square mile, according to the nineteenth-century historian Frederick Turner. The freedom the frontier promises is a liberation from the demands of society, while the Net (I'm thinking now of Usenet) has nothing but society to offer. Without other people, news groups, mailing lists, and files simply wouldn't exist and e-mail would be purposeless. Unlike real space, cyberspace must be shared.

Nevertheless, the choice of a spatial metaphor (credited to the science-fiction novelist William Gibson, who coined the term "cyberspace"), however awkward, isn't surprising. Psychologist Julian Jaynes has pointed out that geographical analogies have long predominated humanity's efforts to conceptualize—map out—consciousness. Unfortunately, these analogies bring with them a heavy load of baggage comparable to Pandora's box: open it and a complex series of problems have come to stay.

The frontier exists beyond the edge of settled or owned land. As the land that doesn't belong to anybody (or to people who "don't count," like Native Americans), it is on the verge of being acquired; currently unowned, but still ownable. Just as the ideal of chastity makes virginity sexually provocative, so does the unclaimed territory invite settlers, irresistibly so. Americans regard the lost geographical frontier with a melancholy, voluptuous fatalism—we had no choice but to advance upon it and it had no alternative but to submit. When an EFF member compares the Clipper chip to barbed wire encroaching on the prairie, doesn't he realize the surrender implied in his metaphor?

10 The psychosexual undercurrents (if anyone still thinks of them as "under") in the idea of civilization's phallic intrusion into nature's passive, feminine space have been observed, exhaustively, elsewhere. The classic Western narrative is actually far more concerned with social relationships than conflicts between man and nature. In these stories, the frontier is a lawless society of men, a milieu in which physical strength, courage, and personal charisma supplant institutional authority and violent conflict is the accepted means of settling disputes. The Western narrative connects pleasurably with the American romance of individualistic masculinity; small wonder that the predominantly male founders of the Net's culture found it so appealing.

When civilization arrives on the frontier, it comes dressed in skirts and short pants. In the archetypal 1939 movie *Dodge City,* Wade Hatton (Errol Flynn) refuses to accept the position of marshal because he prefers the footloose life of a trail driver. Abbie Irving (Olivia de Haviland), a recent arrival from the civilized East, scolds him for his unwillingness to accept and advance the cause of law; she can't function (in her job as crusading journalist) in a town governed by brute force. It takes the accidental killing of a child in a street brawl for Hatton to realize that he must pin on the badge and clean up Dodge City.

In the Western mythos, civilization is necessary because women and children are victimized in conditions of freedom. Introduce women and children into a frontier town and the law must follow because women and children must be protected. Women, in fact, are usually the most vocal proponents of the conversion from frontier justice to civil society.

The imperiled women and children of the Western narrative make their appearance today in newspaper and magazine articles that focus on the intimidation and sexual harassment of women on line and reports of pedophiles trolling for victims in computerized chat rooms. If on-line women successfully contest these attempts to depict them as the beleaguered prey of brutish men, expect the pedophile to assume a larger profile in arguments that the Net is out of control.

In the meantime, the media prefer to cast women as the victims, probably because many women actively participate in the call for greater regulation of on-line interactions, just as Abbie Irving urges Wade Hatton to bring the rule of law to Dodge City. These requests have a long cultural tradition, based on the idea that women, like children, constitute a peculiarly vulnerable class of people who require special protection from the elements of society men are expected to confront alone. In an insufficiently civilized society like the frontier, women, by virtue of this childlike vulnerability, are thought to live under the constant threat of kidnap, abuse, murder, and especially rape.

15 Women, who have every right to expect that crimes against their person will be rigorously prosecuted, should nevertheless regard the notion of special protections (chivalry, by another name) with suspicion. Based as it is on the idea that women are inherently weak and incapable of self-defense and that men are innately predatory, it actually reinforces the power imbalance between the sexes, with its roots in the concept of women as property, constantly under siege and requiring the vigilant protection of their male owners. If the romance of the frontier arises from the promise of vast stretches of unowned land, an escape from the restrictions of a society based on private property, the introduction of women spoils that dream by reintroducing the imperative of property in their own persons.

How does any of this relate to on-line interactions, which occur not on a desert landscape but in a complex, technological society where women are supposed to command equal status with men? It accompanies us as a set of unexamined assumptions about what it means to be male or female, assumptions that we believe are rooted in the imperatives of our bodies. These assumptions follow us into the bodiless realm of cyberspace, a forum where, as one scholar put it "participants are washed clean of the stigmata of their real 'selves' and are free to invent new ones to their tastes." Perhaps some observers feel that the replication of gender roles in a context where the absence of bodies supposedly makes them superfluous proves exactly how innate those roles are. Instead, I see in the relentless attempts to interpret on-line interactions as highly gendered, an intimation of just how artificial, how created, our gender system is. If it comes "naturally," why does it need to be perpetually defended and reasserted?

Complaints about the treatment of women on line fall into three categories: that women are subjected to excessive, unwanted sexual attention, that the prevailing style of on-line discussion turns women off, and that women are singled out by male participants for exceptionally dismissive or hostile treatment. In making these assertions, the *Newsweek* article and other stories on the issue do echo grievances that some on-line women have made for years. And, without a doubt, people have encountered sexual come-ons, aggressive debating tactics, and ad hominem attacks on the Net. However, individual users interpret such events in widely different ways, and to generalize from those interpretations to describe the experiences of women and men as a whole is a rash leap indeed.

I am one of many women who don't recognize their own experience of the Net in the misogynist gauntlet described above. In researching this essay, I joined America Online and spent an hour or two "hanging out" in the real-time chat rooms reputed to be rife with sexual harassment. I received several "instant messages" from men, initiating private conversations with innocuous questions about my hometown and tenure on the service. One man politely inquired if I was interested in "hot phone talk" and just as politely bowed out when I declined. At no point did I feel harassed or treated with disrespect. If I ever want to find a phone-sex partner, I now know where to look but until then I probably won't frequent certain chat rooms.

Other women may experience a request for phone sex or even those tame instant messages as both intrusive and insulting (while still others maintain that they have received much more explicit messages and inquiries completely out of the blue). My point isn't that my reactions are the more correct, but rather that both are the reactions of women, and no journalist has any reason to believe that mine are the exception rather than the rule.

20 For me, the menace in sexual harassment comes from the underlying threat of rape or physical violence. I see my body as the site of my heightened vulnerability as a woman. But on line—where I have no body and neither does anyone else—I consider rape to be impossible. Not everyone agrees. Julian Dibble, in an article for *The Village Voice,* describes the repercussions of a "rape" in a multiuser dimension, or MUD, in which one user employed a subprogram called a "voodoo doll" to cause the personae of other users to perform sexual acts. Citing the "conflation of speech and act that's inevitable in any computer-mediated world," he moved toward the conclusion that "since rape can occur without any physical pain or damage, then it must be classified as a crime against the mind." Therefore, the offending user had committed something on the same "conceptual continuum"

as rape. Tellingly, the incident led to the formation of the first governmental entity on the MUD.

No doubt the cyber-rapist (who went by the nom de guerre Mr. Bungle) appreciated the elevation of his mischief-making to the rank of virtual felony: all of the outlaw glamour and none of the prison time (he was exiled from the MUD). Mr. Bungle limited his victims to personae created by women users, a choice that, in its obedience to prevailing gender roles, shaped the debate that followed his crimes. For, in accordance with the real-world understanding that women's smaller, physically weaker bodies and lower social status make them subject to violation by men, there's a troubling notion in the real and virtual worlds that women's minds are also more vulnerable to invasion, degradation, and abuse.

This sense of fragility extends beyond interactions with sexual overtones. The *Newsweek* article reports that women participants can't tolerate the harsh, contentious quality of on-line discussions, that they prefer mutual support to heated debate, and are retreating wholesale to women-only conferences and newsgroups. As someone who values on-line forums precisely because they mandate equal time for each user who chooses to take it and forestall various "alpha male" rhetorical tactics like interrupting, loudness, or exploiting the psychosocial advantages of greater size or a deeper voice, I find this perplexing and disturbing. In these laments I hear the reluctance of women to enter into the kind of robust debate that characterizes healthy public life, a willingness to let men bully us even when they've been relieved of most of their traditional advantages. Withdrawing into an electronic purdah where one will never be challenged or provoked, allowing the ludicrous ritual chest-thumping of some users to intimidate us into silence—surely women can come up with a more spirited response than this.

And of course they can, because besides being riddled with reductive stereotypes, media analyses like *Newsweek*'s simply aren't accurate. While the on-line population is predominantly male, a significant and vocal minority of women contribute regularly and more than manage to hold their own. Some of The Well's most bombastic participants are women, just as there are many tactful and conciliatory men. At least, I think there are, because, ultimately, it's impossible to be sure of anyone's biological gender on line. "Transpostites," people who pose as member of the opposite gender, are an established element of Net society, most famously a man who, pretending to be a disabled lesbian, built warm and intimate friendships with women on several CompuServe forums.

Perhaps what we should be examining is not the triumph of gender differences on the Net, but their potential blurring. In this light, *Newsweek*'s stout assertion that in cyberspace "the gender gap is real" begins to seem less objective than defensive, an insistence that on-line culture is "the same" as real life because the idea that it might be different, when it comes to gender, is too scary. If gender roles can be cast off so easily, they may be less deeply rooted, less "natural" than we believe. There may not actually be a "masculine" or "feminine" mind or outlook, but simply a conventional way of interpreting individuals that recognizes behavior seen as in accordance with their biological gender and ignores behavior that isn't.

25 For example, John Seabury wrote in the *New Yorker* (June 6, 1994) of his stricken reaction to his first "flame," a colorful slice of adolescent invective sent to him by an unnamed technology journalist. Reading it, he begins to "shiver" like a burn victim, an effect that worsens with repeated readings. He writes that "the technology greased the words. . . with a kind of immediacy that allowed them to slide easily into my brain." He tells his friends, his coworkers, his partner—even his mother—and, predictably, appeals to CompuServe's management for recourse—to no avail. Soon enough, he's talking about civilization and anarchy, how the liberating "lack of social barriers is also what is appalling about the net," and calling for regulation.

As a newcomer, Seabury was chided for brooding over a missive that most Net veterans would have dismissed and forgotten as the crude potshot of an envious jerk. (I can't help wondering if my fellow journalist never received hate mail in response to his other writings; this bit of e-mail seems comparable, par for the course when one assumes a public profile.) What nobody did was observe that Seabury's reaction—the shock, the feelings of violation, the appeals to his family and support network, the bootless complaints to the authorities—reads exactly like many horror stories about women's trials on the Net. Yet, because Seabury is a man, no one attributes the attack to his gender or suggests that the Net has proven an environment hostile to men. Furthermore, the idea that the Net must be more strictly governed to prevent the abuse of guys who write for the *New Yorker* seems laughable—though who's to say that Seabury's pain is less than any woman's? Who can doubt that, were he a woman, his tribulations would be seen as compelling evidence of Internet sexism?

The idea that women merit special protections in an environment as incorporeal as the Net is intimately bound up with the idea that women's minds are weak, fragile, and unsuited to the rough and tumble of public discourse. It's an argument that women should recognize with profound mistrust and resist, especially when we are used as rhetorical pawns in a battle to regulate a rare (if elite) space of gender ambiguity. When the mainstream media generalize about women's experiences on line in ways that just happen to uphold the most conventional and pernicious gender stereotypes, they can expect to be greeted with howls of disapproval from women who refuse to acquiesce in these roles and pass them on to other women.

And there are plenty of us, as The Well's response to the *Newsweek* article indicates. Women have always participated in on-line communications, women whose chosen careers in technology and the sciences have already marked them as gender-role resisters. As the schoolmarms arrive on the electronic frontier, their female predecessors find themselves cast in the role of saloon girls, their willingness to engage in "masculine" activities like verbal aggression, debate, or sexual experimentation marking them as insufficiently feminine, or "bad" women. "If that's what women on line are like, I must be a Martian," one Well woman wrote in response to the shrinking female technophobes depicted in the *Newsweek* article. Rather than relegating so many people to the status of gender aliens, we ought to reconsider how adequate those roles are to the task of describing real human beings.

Mapping the Text

1. How does Miller make use of the metaphor of the frontier alluded to in her title? How does she describe gender relations on the Net? How are they different from gender relations "in real life"? How are they similar?
2. How are women and children typically portrayed in mainstream media accounts of Internet culture, according to Miller? What are the possible consequences of the language and imagery used in mainstream accounts? Why?
3. How does Miller draw on her own experience to construct an alternative account of women's experience in cyberspace? How is her experience different from the way women are often portrayed in media accounts? What are the consequences of this difference?

Writing to Inquire

1. Conduct your own study of gender relationships in a particular online community. You may want to choose a chat room, gaming site, or other virtual community. Write an essay to describe the way women and men are perceived in this online space, paying particular attention to the use of language and online persona.

Commodifying Human Relationships

JEREMY RIFKIN

Jeremy Rifkin is the founder and president of the Foundation on Economic Trends. An activist, writer, and teacher, he is the author of 15 books, most of which examine the relationships between science, technology, the economy, and the environment. His recent publications include *Beyond Beef: The Rise and Fall of the Cattle Culture* (1993); *The End of Work* (1995); *The Biotech Century: Harnessing the Gene and Remaking the World* (1999); and *The Age of Access* (2000). The range of his interests is considerable, but his voice in public conversations about cloning, genetics, and biomedical engineering has been particularly important.

One person's idea of utopia is often another's dystopian nightmare. Think of waking up one day only to find out that every aspect of your being has become a purchased affair, that your life itself has become the ultimate shopping experience.

The distinguishing characteristic of modern capitalism is the expropriation of various facets of life into commercial relationships. Land, human labor, production tasks, and social activities that once took place in the home all have been absorbed into the market and made into commodities. Still, as long as commerce was bound to discrete transactions between sellers and buyers, the commodification process itself was limited in time and space to either the negotiation and transfer of goods or the time elapsed in the performance of services. All other time still was free of the market and not beholden to market consideration. In the emerging cyberspace economy, network forces pull all remaining free time into the commercial orbit, making each institution and individual a captive of an all-pervasive "commerciality."

The Age of Access is defined, above all else, by the increasing commodification of all human experience. Commercial networks of every shape and kind weave a web around the totality of human life, reducing every moment of lived experience to a commodified status. In the propertied era of capitalism, the emphasis was on selling goods and services. In the cyberspace economy, the commodification of goods and services becomes secondary to the commodification of human relationships. Holding clients' and customers' attention in the new fast-paced, ever changing network economy means controlling as much of their time as possible. By shifting from discrete market transactions that are limited in time and space to commodification of relationships that extend open-endedly over time, the new commercial sphere assures that more and more of daily life is held hostage to the bottom line.

One need only open up the pages of any of the countless books being churned out by marketing and management consultants, economists, forecasters, and futurists to learn that success in the new era will belong to those who are able to make the transition from a production to a marketing perspective and from the notion of making sales to establishing relationships. In their book *Blur: The Speed of Change in the Connected Economy,* Stan Davis and Christopher Meyer point out that in the old economy, "the idea is to inspire repeat purchases, as a string of discrete transactions." In the new economy, however, the goal of every company is "to establish ongoing relationships between themselves and their customers."[1] In *The One to One Future,* marketing consultants Don Peppers and Martha Rogers write that "no matter how creative and innovative your firm is, the only software genuinely worth having is the *customer relationship.*"[2] Peppers and Rogers add, "all your products are ephemeral. Only your customers are real."[3]

The Customer Is the Market

5 In the industrial economy, with its emphasis on mass production and the sale of goods, securing a share of the market was utmost in the minds of every entrepreneur. In the Age of Access, with its emphasis on selling specialized services and providing access to expertise of all kinds, the role played by suppliers changes markedly, says Wim Roelandts of Hewlett-Packard. "We are shifting from being box sellers," says Roelandts, "to becoming trusted advisors."[4]

The new idea in marketing is to concentrate on share of customer rather than share of market. Peppers and Rogers argue that in the network economy, "you will not be trying to sell a single product to as many customers as possible. Instead, you'll be trying to sell a single customer as many products as possible—over a long period of time, and across different product lines."[5]

When businesses talk about letting go of the idea of selling products one at a time to as many customers as possible and, rather, concentrating on establishing a long-term relationship with each individual customer, what they're really focusing on is the potential of commodifying a person's entire lifetime of experiences. Marketing specialists use the phrase "lifetime value" (LTV) to emphasize the advantages of shifting from a product-oriented to an access-oriented environment where negotiating discrete market transactions is less important than securing and commodifying lifetime relationships with clients. Automobile dealer Carl Sewell estimates, for example, that each new customer that comes through the door of a Cadillac dealership represents a potential lifetime value of more than $322,000. The figure is a projection of the number of automobiles the customer is likely to purchase over his or her lifetime as well as the services those automobiles will require over their lifetimes. Mark Grainer, chairman of the Technical Assistance Research Programs Institute (TARP), estimates that the average "loyal" customer of a supermarket is worth more than $3,800 a year.[6] The key is to find the appropriate mechanism to hold on to the customer for life.

To calculate the LTV of a customer, a firm projects the present value of all future purchases against the marketing and customer-service costs of securing and maintaining a long-term relationship. Credit card companies, magazines, and mail-order catalogs, which rely on subscriptions and memberships, have long used LTV cost-accounting projections. Now the rest of the economy is beginning to follow suit.

The commercial potential of capturing a share of customer is directly proportional to the projected duration of his or her consumer lifetime. For that reason, many companies make every effort to capture customers at a very early age to optimize their potential LTV. Hyatt Hotels features its Camp Hyatt and a special newsletter aimed at its youngest LTV customers. A&P provides children's shopping carts to accustom youngsters to making their own selections in the store. Delta Airlines has its Fantastic Flyer club for kids.[7]

10 Peppers and Rogers offer a good hypothetical example of how relationship marketing based on LTV might work in practice. Suppose a diaper service were to provide you with all of the disposable diapers you need for your baby for a subscription fee. Rather than purchasing each diaper as a discrete transaction in the store, you will be getting unlimited access to diapers for as long as the baby requires them. Such companies already exist around the United States. But relationship marketing doesn't stop there. The same firm that contracts with you to provide disposable diapers might also contract, on a subscription basis, to provide you with toys, baby food, formula, and baby clothes. And why stop there? Once establishing a comprehensive service relationship, why not extend it through adolescence and into the teenage years—in other words, why not maximize LTV? Say Peppers and Rogers:

> *To the extent that you can maintain that relationship and nurture it over time, you could, over the years, sell toys for older children, school clothing and school supplies, family vacations, video games, compact discs, and even financial services to a family planning ahead for college expenses.*[8]

Determining a person's LTV is made possible with the new information and telecommunications technologies of the network economy. Electronic feedback loops and barcodes allow companies to receive continuously updated information on clients' purchases, giving them detailed profiles on customers' lifestyles—their dietary choices, wardrobes, states of health, recreational pursuits, and travel patterns. With appropriate computer modeling techniques, it is possible to use this mass of raw data on each individual to anticipate future desires and needs and map out targeted marketing campaigns to lure customers into long-term commercial relationships.

Many in the information sciences are suggesting even that the new technologies be thought of as relationship technologies, or R-technologies, rather than information technologies. "We need to turn away from the notion of technology managing information and toward the idea of technology as a medium of relationships," says Michael Schrage of the MIT Sloan School's Center for Coordination Science.[9] French economist Albert Bressand says that R-technology is an appropriate way to describe the new technologies because "relations rather than material products are what is processed in these machines."[10]

What is becoming clear to management and marketing experts, and a growing number of economists, is that the new computer software and telecommunications technologies allow for the establishment of rich webs of interconnections and relationships between suppliers and users, creating the opportunity to quantify and commodify every aspect of a person's lived experience in the form of a long-term commercial relationship. Says

Bressand, "The time has come to shift from the engineering approach of information technology, which was totally warranted at the beginning, to the human and relationship approach."[11]

In marketing circles, using R-technologies to commodify long-term commercial relationships is called "controlling the customer." Continuous cybernetic feedback allows firms to anticipate and service customers' needs on an ongoing open-ended basis. By turning goods into services and advising clients on upgrades, innovations, and new applications, suppliers become an all-pervasive and indispensable part of the experiential routines of customers. To borrow a Hollywood term, companies serve as "agents," performing a range of services. The goal is to become so embedded in the life of the customer as to become a ubiquitous presence, an appendage of the customer's very being, operating on his behalf in the commercial sphere.

Agents in the new schema are "systems integrators," a phrase coined by Robert C. Blattberg, professor of retailing at the Kellogg Graduate School of Management, and Rashi Glazer. They coordinate an increasing share of the commercial life of their clients.[12] In a sense, agents serve as go-betweens. They manage the continuous flow of information between the global economy and the end-use clients. Their function is a marketing one—to find the most effective way of establishing, maintaining, and enhancing relationships with clients.

Of course, the kinds of relationships these technologies conjure up are, by their very nature, one-sided. Despite the fact that the Internet and cyberspace give a modicum of counter-surveillance power back to the individual consumer and allow for interactivity, the company knows far more about the customer than he or she will ever glean about the company. The algebra of the new electronic marketplace still favors the corporate players.

Firefly, a start-up company now owned by Microsoft, is a cyberspace music vendor that uses software initially designed at the MIT media lab. Its 3 million registered users rank their preferences among hundreds of musical groups and composers. Firefly then makes recommendations of what other music the users might like based on the rankings of other customers with similar musical interests. In this instance, the participants willingly provide data about themselves in return for access to information of value to them. However, the great bulk of information generated each day about the buying patterns and lifestyles of millions of customers is collected and often sold to third parties for solicitation purposes without any consensual agreement by those whose information is being expropriated.

Critics of the indiscriminate use of R-technology argue that potential customers ought to be compensated by any firm using personal data about them for commercial purposes. James Rule, a sociologist at the State University of New York at Stony Brook, proposes that each person has a right to

> *withhold, sell or give away rights to commercial sale or exchange of information about himself or herself. . . . Everyone consenting to any release of personal information would retain a data rights agent, who would establish a computerized account for each client. Every time an organization sold or traded its mailing list, it would be legally obliged to collect royalties for the individuals concerned.*[13]

In the old industrial economy, each person's own labor power was considered a form of property that could be sold in the marketplace. In the new network economy, selling access to one's day-to-day living patterns and life experiences, as reflected in purchasing decisions, becomes equally coveted and a much sought-after intangible asset.

The Shift from a Production to a Marketing Perspective

20 The shift in emphasis from manufacturing and selling products to establishing and maintaining long-term commercial relationships brings the marketing perspective to the forefront of commercial life. The production imperative, which reigned supreme in the industrial era, is increasingly viewed as a back-office function of marketing. When even goods become platforms for managing services, and services become the primary engine driving global commerce, then establishing relationships with end users is critical. Marketing in the new network economy becomes the central framework, and controlling the customer becomes the goal of commercial activity.

Controlling the customer is the final stage in a long commercial journey marked by the increasing wresting away of both ownership and control of economic life from the hands of the masses and into the arms of corporate institutions. Recall that in the early stages of a production-oriented capitalism, economic tasks in the home and craft shops were spirited away and placed in factories by capitalist entrepreneurs. By assuming ownership and control over the tools of production, the capitalists were able to make previously self-sufficient families and artisans dependent on a wage system to secure their livelihoods and survival. Workers were further stripped of any last vestige of control over the production function with the introduction of division of labor and the assembly line in the early decades of the twentieth century. Frederic Taylor introduced his principles of scientific management to the factory floor and front office, revolutionizing the organization of production. Using a stopwatch, Taylor timed every movement of the workers with an eye toward improving their efficiency. The goal was to gain near total control over the worker in the production process.

Today, as the marketing perspective gains ascendancy and commodifying relationships with consumers becomes the essential business of business, controlling the customer takes on the same kind of import and urgency as controlling the worker did when the manufacturing perspective prevailed. If the stopwatch and assembly line provided the technological means to control the worker, cybernetic feedback loops and barcodes provide the technical means to control the customer. In the new century, organizing consumption becomes as important as organizing production was in the last century. The idea is to make the totality of one's experience dependent on commercial agents. Although the end user is engaged in the process, he or she becomes ever more reliant on intermediaries who serve his or her needs. Controlling the customer means exactly that—being able to hold and direct his or her attention and manage the minuscule details of each person's life experiences. The commercial agents assume the role of caretaker.

In the industrial economy, discrete market transactions and the transfer of property between seller and buyer afforded the customer a high degree of control over each consumption decision. In the Age of Access, however, customers risk slowly losing control over the process as short-term market decisions give way to long-term commercial relationships with trusted intermediaries, and the purchase of goods gives way to the contracting of a range of services that extend to virtually every aspect of one's lived experience. The customer becomes mobilized and embedded within a dense web of ongoing commercial relationships and may become totally dependent on commercial forces that he or she little understands and over which he or she has less and less control. In some ways, the new commercial dependency shares much in common with the kind of social dependency that arose under the welfare regimes of the post–World War II era. As democratic governments entered into expanding social service relationships with their citizenry, the democratic impulse that gave rise to these social compacts soon got lost in the growing dependency of large numbers of people on the very government services they had supported.

For example, consider financial planning. Many investment companies have begun to make the transition from simply trading stocks and bonds and managing customer portfolios to becoming a full-service provider—a systems integrator. Clients are looking to companies like Merrill Lynch to help them create customized investment packages for their specific needs and goals. Some financial institutions are becoming customer agents, providing complete financial planning services that include yearly business plans, personal budgeting plans, retirement income plans, estate planning, tax and accounting services, legal assistance, and other services. The idea is to bring the client into an all-encompassing relationship with an agent. The financial institution handles every aspect of the client's financial dealings for a lifetime and beyond. The client gains access to specialized expertise and trusted advisors who act on his behalf, often as his agent, surrogate, or advocate.

25 In the Age of Access, while the clients make the ultimate choice to enter into or leave these long-term, multifaceted relationships, the complexity of the services rendered and the expertise needed to perform those services can become difficult to understand and even baffling after a while—

especially if the customer cedes those tasks over to a third party early on. Not ever having to be personally engaged in the details of these services, the client often remains untutored and ignorant of the forces at work and may become increasingly dependent on the "expert" agents over time to manage his or her affairs. The agents, in turn, become the gatekeepers controlling the many channels of supply and distribution that connect each consumer to the global marketplace and the outside world.

It's no wonder that so many firms are making the leap from manufacturer and producer to agent and distributor. Once again, we see that in the Age of Access, controlling the customer is far more important than controlling the product. The product, after all, is just part of the services that make up the relationship with the client.

Medco Containment Services is a good example of a company whose sole mission is gaining access to and control over the customer. Medco is the largest mail-order drug distributor in the United States. The company has successfully positioned itself between the major pharmaceutical companies and the nation's leading health maintenance organizations (HMOs). Medco offers one-stop shopping for all pharmaceutical products and purchases and distributes drugs from all the leading pharmaceutical companies. Its buyers search for the best prices and guarantee their customers dollar-specific savings. In return for the savings, customers agree to let Medco "have a say in how customers manage their diagnosis, treatment, and home-health aftercare of each drug's patients," virtually ensuring that more drugs will get sold.[14] Medco has become, for all intents and purposes, the gatekeeper between the end users—HMOs—and the nation's pharmaceutical companies by virtue of the access it enjoys with the customers.

The drug companies found themselves increasingly at the mercy of Medco in recent years because of the control it exercised over customers' preferred drug lists. Merck decided that the best way to fend off the threat was to acquire Medco, which it did. Even after the acquisition, Medco continues to require Merck to discount its prices if it wants to have its products distributed through Medco channels. By the end of the year 2000, Merck estimates that 80 percent of its drug business will be through Medco. "When that happens," says sales consultant Mack Hannan, "Merck's 5,500 sales representatives at the time of Medco's acquisition will no longer be needed to call on individual practice physicians, doctors' groups, and hospitals."[15] Merck's sales force will likely disappear. The drug company will become what Hannan calls a tier-two supplier, and Medco, because it controls the gateway to the customer, will triumph.

Like Amazon.com and Nike, Medco is a pure marketing mechanism, freed up from the burdens of owning factories and having to invest in expensive and time-consuming research and development. Virtually propertyless, its prime asset is access to customers and its ability to forge long-term commercial relationships with end users. That's all it needs in a network economy, where the marketing perspective takes precedence over the manufacturing mode.

The evolution of marketing has as much to do with saturated consumer demand as with the new information and communications technologies that make possible a seamless one-to-one relationship between firms and customers. Innovations in manufacturing processes, especially in the post–World War II era, greatly expanded the flow of new goods into the marketplace. In the early years after the war, pent-up demand was sufficient to absorb virtually every item that came off the assembly line. The Great Depression and war years had slowed the production stream to a trickle. Anxious to make up for lost time and the years of going without the necessities and luxuries of life, the GI generation went on a buying spree. The migration to the suburbs, the creation of the highway culture, and the proliferation of shopping malls all became magnets for consumption. In the 1950s it was a seller's market. Manufacturing was king, and the corporate eye was fixed almost exclusively on the costs of production and distribution. With consumers buying as fast as the products could be made, there was little need to worry about developing long-term relationships with customers. Cash registers were ringing away. Discrete market transactions appeared sufficient, and repeat business seemed assured.

By the 1960s, however, consumer markets were becoming overrun with goods. Most families had two automobiles parked in their garages, washers and dryers humming away in their laundry rooms, and color televisions blaring in virtually all the rooms of their houses. Companies began to face a new reality: overproduction against falling consumer demand. The question was no longer how to produce fast enough to keep up with the consumer market but rather how to capture and hold the attention of the consumer long enough to make him or her a loyal, long-term customer.

One of the first to catch the significance of the shift from a production to a marketing prospective was Peter Drucker, the father of modern business management practices. He wrote:

> *The customer is the foundation of a business and keeps it in existence. He alone gives employment. And it is to supply the customer that society entrusts wealth-producing resources to the business enterprise. . . . Because it is its purpose to create a customer, any business enterprise has two—and only these two—basic functions: marketing and innovation. . . . Marketing is the distinguishing, the unique function of the business. . . . It is the whole business seen from the point of view of the final result, that is, from the customer's point of view. Concern and responsibility for marketing must therefore permeate all areas of the enterprise.*[16]

Business consultants began to urge their corporate clients to spend less time focusing on production and more on marketing if they wanted to capture market share. In a landmark article entitled "Marketing Myopia," Theodore Levitt, professor emeritus at the Harvard Business School, argued that companies are too concerned with the products they produce and not concerned enough with the customers they serve. He argued that businesses should develop their business plans from the customer end backward rather than the production end forward. The goal of business, he suggested, is to capture customers, not simply produce goods and services.[17] All of the new voices in marketing and management share a common sentiment—that the emphasis on building long-term customer relationships is far more important to a company's success than the more narrow objective of making discrete sales transactions.

While the shift from a seller's to a buyer's market hastened the transition from a production to a marketing orientation and the new information technologies of the network economy made possible the commodification of an ongoing lifetime relationship with customers, it was technological change in the production process in the 1980s and 1990s that guaranteed the ultimate ascendancy of the marketing perspective and the relegation of production to a function of the marketing process.

35 The new ability to customize production to the needs of each customer made it necessary for business operations to begin at the customer end and work backward toward the factory floor in the commercial process. Instead of suppliers mass-producing products and then creating markets to distribute them, consumers increasingly inform suppliers of their unique individual needs, which are then produced to their specifications.

The change from mass production to mass customization began in earnest in the 1980s. With consumer markets saturated, many suppliers of mass-produced goods found themselves with too much excess capacity and bloated inventories. Because so many suppliers were in each field and there was so little to differentiate the products of one company from another, the only way to stay ahead of the competition was to slash prices and lower profit margins. The steady decline in sales volume and profits convinced some companies that they had to radically change their direction if they were to survive. By differentiating their product offerings from their competitors', these companies hoped they could secure a larger share of the market and stay competitive. They began experimenting with new ways of organizing production in an effort to customize goods to each buyer. Production processes were revolutionized with the introduction of modular equipment, giving manufacturers the ability to tailor products to the customized needs of each client.

Motorola was one of the leaders in the new field of mass customization. Motorola was suffering declining sales in the face of intense competition from Japanese manufacturers. Hardest hit was Motorola's pager division. Japanese firms were selling high-quality pagers on the global market at half the price of the U.S. product. With other American manufacturers of pagers rapidly going out of business, Motorola decided that the only way to stay in the market would be to differentiate its product line and provide customers with the opportunity to customize their purchases. The company introduced its new line of pagers with hardware and software features that could be arranged in more than 29 million combinations. Any of the combinations could be produced with zero setup time and in lots of one. Meanwhile, manufacturing time was cut from more than five hours to less than twenty minutes. To capture and hold the customers, Motorola revamped its ordering process with the introduction of time- and cost-saving information technology. An order that used to take a month to process was reduced to an hour and a half.[18]

Bally Engineered Structures, a Pennsylvania-based company that specializes in manufacturing walk-in coolers, freezers, and cold-storage buildings, went through a similar conversion. Like Motorola, Bally was faced with market saturation and stiff competition, forcing it to drive down prices and lower profit margins. Bally retooled its manufacturing facilities in the 1980s by introducing modularized panels and accessories that could be customized to the design requirements of each of its customers. The new processes are so efficient that Bally can manufacture and deliver customized products four times faster than its competitors produce the older standardized products.[19]

Being able to customize goods to each customer's needs and desires gives firms a tremendous advantage over the competition. Because the new commercial process begins with the customer and works its way back to the production process, the structuring of the relationship between the firm and the consumer—the marketing function—is the critical factor. It determines the nature of the production. At the same time, the codesign of products creates a relationship between the company and end user that's more like that between a server and client than a seller and buyer. In short, customization comes to be regarded more as the contracting of a service.

New Kinds of Communities

R-technologies reach out to encompass the whole of a person's life experiences. The power of these marketing tools lies in the ability to create a comprehensive environment for organizing personal life and restructuring social discourse. Because they increasingly become a primary means by which people communicate with one another, R-technologies can be used to reconfigure the most fundamental categories of social existence. Already, in marketing circles the talk runs to ways of using R-technologies to create new kinds of communities made up of like-minded people who come together because of their shared interest in a particular commercial endeavor, activity, or pursuit. There's a growing awareness among management and marketing experts alike that establishing so-called "communities of interest" is the most effective way to capture and hold customer attention and create lifetime relationships. The companies become the gatekeepers to these newly defined communities and, for a price, grant customers access to these coveted new social arenas.

Marketing consultants Richard Cross and Janet Smith list several critical stages in the creation of communities of interest. Stage one is awareness bonding. The idea is to make the customer aware of your firm's product or service with the expectation of negotiating a first sale. Stage two is identity bonding. The customer begins to identify with your firm's product or service and incorporates it into his sense of self. It becomes one of the many ways he differentiates himself in the world. For example, driving a Cadillac or a VW Beetle serves as a social statement as much as a means of transportation. Stage three is relationship bonding, which we've explored above. The firm and the customer move from an arm's-length relationship to an interactive one. This is where R-technologies begin to play an important role. They help create what marketers call "customer intimacy." Hallmark's reminder service, for example, keeps a list in their electronic files of the important birthdays and anniversaries in your family and e-mails you a timely reminder along with suggestions of appropriate cards to send.[20]

Stage four is community bonding. The company brings its customers into relationships with one another based on their shared interest in the firm's products and services. The company's task is to create communities for the purpose of establishing long-term commercial relationships and optimizing the lifetime value of each customer. "This bond is extremely durable," say Cross and Smith. "To break it, competitors must actually disregard social ties among friends, colleagues, or family."[21]

The key to creating communities of interest is to plan events, gatherings, and other activities that bring customers together to share their common interest in your company's brand. Holiday Inn's Priority Club brings together between 500 and 1,000 of its most frequent guests, twice a year, at one of its resorts for a weekend of entertainment and recreation, peppered with several roundtable discussions with hotel management. The outings for Priority Club members include professional sports clinics, celebrity speakers, and special tours. The idea is to provide a time and place for club members to meet and form bonds of intimacy with one another and Holiday Inn executives. Members are encouraged to participate in focus-group discussions and "to share feelings and ideas with us," says Ken Pierce, vice president of frequency marketing for Holiday Inn.[22] Some of its 3.8 million members also are invited to become members of the company's many regional advisory boards. Priority Club members have proven to be loyal customers, spending, on average, 60 percent of their nights on the road at Holiday Inns.[23]

Backroads is an upscale tourist company that organizes bicycle and walking tours through some of the most scenic areas of the world. The company provides tents, prepares the food, and shuttles the guests to the various sites by van. The true value of the Backroads service, says authors Larry Downes and Chunka Mui in their book, *Unleashing the Killer App,* lies in "the quality of its network of customers, who pay, in part, for the opportunity to interact with and be entertained by *each other*. . . . We take such trips because we know that the company attracts like-minded individuals and we know that we'll make some new friends by the end of the trip."[24] Backroads, say Downes and Mui, is about "creating communities of value by valuing community."[25] Companies like Backroads will increasingly rely on R-technologies in the future to search out prospective customers based on their consumer profiles, lifestyles, and spending patterns. As software profiling becomes even more sophisticated, it will be possible to match the very specific lifestyle interests of prospective customers with particular trips, ensuring a more meaningful experience and the likelihood of creating effective community bonding among the guests.

45 Burger King Kids Club brings children together in a "community of interest." The club's 4 million members receive discounts on meals and a number of perks, including three age-directed magazines. A pen-pal club matches up Burger King Kids Club members. The company supplies the children with special Burger King stationery and pens. By 1994, the club was operating in more than twenty-five countries. The company is outspoken about the purpose of its Kids Club. Burger King's Michael Evans says, "We want to capture the hearts and minds of kids and keep them until they're 60."[26] In the meantime, sales of Burger King Kids Meals have tripled since the club was established in 1990.

The recreational vehicle (RV) industry boasts more than thirty manufacturer-sponsored RV clubs. Members are drawn together into a like-minded community by owning the same kind of RV. "It's a whole psychological study in customer bonding," says Warren MacKenzie of Foretravel, Inc.[27] MacKenzie adds that "our whole motivation in supporting the club is to develop a continuing loyalty to the product and the company." MacKenzie says, "We can almost pinpoint the percentage of sales that can be credited towards the club and the support of the club."[28]

Many of the RV clubs maintain their own park grounds or have reserved designated areas for their members in campgrounds. The Winnebago-Itasca Travelers Club, with its 14,000 members and 250 chapters, holds frequent rallies throughout the U.S. and Canada. Members receive a monthly magazine and perks, including road service, trip routing advice, insurance, product discounts, and even mail-forwarding service when they are on the road. The club accounts for more than 20 percent of the company's annual motor home sales.[29]

The transformation in the nature of commerce from selling things to commodifying relationships and creating communities marks a turning point in the way commerce is conducted. The commercial sphere is broadening its reach and deepening its penetration into virtually every aspect of human existence. In the twenty-first century, the economy becomes the arena where human beings live out much of their day-to-day experiences. In this new world, ownership of things, while important, is less important than securing commercial access to networks of mutual interests, webs of relationships, and shared communities. To belong, in the new era, is to be connected to the many networks that make up the new global economy. Being a subscriber, member, or client becomes as important as being propertied. It is, in other words, access rather than mere ownership that increasingly determines one's status in the coming age.

While there has been considerable public rift in recent years over the deregulation of government services and activities and their subsequent absorption into the commercial sphere, far less attention has been focused on the absorption of the personal sphere into the marketplace. The commodification of human relationships is a heady venture. Assigning lifetime values (LTVs) to people with the expectation of transforming the totality of their lived experience into commercial fare represents the final stage of capitalist market relations. What happens to the essential nature of human existence when it is sucked into an all-encompassing web of commercial relationships?

The growing shift from the commodification of space and goods to the commodification of human time and lived experience is everywhere around us. Every spare moment of our time is being filled with some form of commercial connection, making time itself the most scarce of all resources. Our fax machines, e-mail, voice mail, and cellular phones, our twenty-four-hour trading markets, instant around-the-clock ATM and online banking services, all-night e-commerce and research services, twenty-four-hour television news and entertainment, twenty-four-hour food services, pharmaceutical services, and maintenance services, all holler out for our attention. They worm their way into our consciousness, take up much of our waking time, and occupy much of our thoughts, leaving little respite.

When every endeavor is transformed into a commercial service, we run the risk of falling into a kind of temporal Malthusian trap. Although a day is limited and fixed to twenty-four hours, new kinds of commercial services and relationships are limited only by the entrepreneur's ability to imagine new ways of commodifying time. Already, even in the early stage of the transition to the Age of Access, the commodification of time is becoming saturated. Every institution and human being is being courted and connected to some form of commodified service or relationship. And while we have created every kind of labor- and time-saving device and activity to service one another's needs and desires in the commercial sphere, we are beginning to feel like we have less time available to us than any other humans in history. That is because the great proliferation of labor- and time-saving services only increase the diversity, pace, and flow of commodified activity around us.

The network-based economy does indeed increase the speed of connections, shorten durations, improve efficiency, and make life more convenient by turning everything imaginable into a service. But when most relationships become commercial relationships and every individual's life is commodified twenty-four hours a day, what is left for relationships of a noncommercial nature—relationships based on kinship, neighborliness, shared cultural interests, religious affiliation, ethnic identification, and fraternal and civic involvement? When time itself is bought and sold and one's life becomes little more than an ongoing series of commercial transactions held together by contracts and financial instruments, what happens to the kinds of traditional reciprocal relationships that are born of affection, love, and devotion? The fact that marketing professionals and corporations are seriously engaged in developing what they call long-term "customer intimacy" and are actively experimenting with a host of vehicles and venues for establishing deep "community bonding" is disturbing enough. What is more worrisome is that these large-scale efforts to create a surrogate social sphere tucked inside a commercial wrap are, for the most part, going unnoticed and uncritiqued, despite the broad and far-reaching potential consequences for society. When virtually every aspect of our being becomes a paid-for activity, human life itself becomes the ultimate commercial product, and the commercial sphere becomes the final arbiter of our personal and collective existence.

Notes

[1] Stanley M. Davis and Christopher Meyer, *Blur: The Speed of Change in the Connected Economy* (Oxford: Capstone Publishing Ltd., 1998), p. 48.
[2] Don Peppers and Martha Rogers, *The One to One Future: Building Relationships One Customer at a Time* (New York: Doubleday, 1993), p. 394.
[3] Ibid.
[4] Don Tapscott, *The Digital Economy: Promise and Peril in the Age of Networked Intelligence* (New York: McGraw-Hill, 1996), p. 245.
[5] Peppers and Rogers, *The One to One Future,* p. 15.
[6] Carl Sewell and Paul Brown, *Customers for Life: How to Turn That One-Time Buyer Into a Lifetime Customer* (New York: Doubleday/Currency, 1990).
[7] William H. Davidow and Michel S. Malone, *The Virtual Corporation: Structuring and Revitalizing the Corporation for the 21st Century* (New York: HarperCollins, 1992), p. 230; Hyatt Resorts, "Discover Camp Hyatt," <http://www.hyatt.com/resorts/camp/index.html.>]
[8] Peppers and Rogers, *The One to One Future,* pp. 45–46.
[9] Kevin Kelly, *New Rules for the New Economy: 10 Radical Strategies for a Connected World* (New York: Viking, 1998), pp. 118–19.
[10] Peter Schwartz, "R-Tech," *Wired* 4, no. 6 (June 1996), <http://www.hotwired.com/collections/virtual_communities/4.06-r_tech_pr.html.>
[11] Ibid.
[12] Robert C. Blattberg and Rashi Glazer, "*The Marketing Information Revolution,*" in Robert C. Blattberg, John D. Little, and Rashi Glazer, eds., The Marketing Information Revolution (Boston: Harvard Business School Press, 1994). p. 9.
[13] James Rule, "My Mailbox Is Mine," *Wall Street Journal,* August 15, 1990, p. A8.

[14] Mack Hanan, *Sales Shock! The End of Selling Products, the Rise of CoManaging Customers* (New York: AMACOM, 1996), p. 107.
[15] Ibid.
[16] Peter F. Drucker, *The Practice of Management* (Oxford: Butterworth-Heinemann, 1954, 1993), pp. 35–36.
[17] Theodore Levitt, "Marketing Myopia," *Harvard Business Review* 38 (July–August 1960): 45–56.
[18] B. Joseph Pine II, *Mass Customization: The New Frontier in Business Competition* (Boston: Harvard Business School Press, 1993), pp. 146–49.
[19] Ibid., pp. 141–45, 196–99.
[20] Richard Cross and Janet Smith, *Customer Bonding* (Lincolnwood, IL: NTC Business Books, 1995), pp. 56–59; Larry Downes and Chunka Mui, *Unleashing the Killer App: Digital Strategies for Market Dominance* (Boston: Harvard Business School Press, 1998), pp. 112, 116–18; Hallmark, "Reminder Service," <http://www.hallmark.com.>
[21] Cross and Smith, *Customer Bonding,* p. 190.
[22] Ibid., p. 162.
[23] Ibid., pp. 162–63.
[24] Downes and Mui, *Unleashing the Killer App,* p. 101.
[25] Ibid.
[26] Cross and Smith, *Customer Bonding,* pp. 121–22.
[27] Ibid., pp. 149, 153.
[28] Ibid., p. 154.
[29] Ibid., pp. 154, 156; Winnebago Industries, "Winnebago-Itasca Travelers Club," http://www.winnebagoind.com/witclub.htm; Winnebago Industries, "Member Benefits," http://www.winnebagoind.com/witbenefits.htm.

Mapping the Text

1. In this essay, Jeremy Rifkin uses the word *access* in a way that is different from what we might typically expect. He says, for example, "Marketing specialists use the phrase 'lifetime value' (LTV) to emphasize the advantages of shifting from a product-oriented to an access-oriented environment where negotiating discrete market transactions is less important than securing and commodifying lifetime relationships with clients. . . . The key is to find the appropriate mechanism to hold on to the customer for life." What does *access* mean in this context? How many questions can you raise about this passage?
2. How does Rifkin fit technology into this context?
3. Explain the "evolution" of marketing that Rifkin describes. What sorts of communities does he assert are created by this evolution? What are the implications of their existence? How does technology enable these communities?

Writing to Inquire

1. Go through Rifkin's essay and make a list of each word about which you need clarification or information. Search reference sources for these terms, then reconsider the essay. Are you now better able to understand Rifkin's ideas? How so?

CALLS TO ACTION AND RESPONSE

The Digital Citizen

JON KATZ

Jon Katz is a media critic and writer whose essays have appeared in publications such as the *New York Times, Rolling Stone,* and *Wired.* He is perhaps best known for his controversial work on "geek life," work that touched on the relationship between teen social hierarchies and school violence. In addition to his many articles, editorials, and columns published on his personal web page, Slashdot, and in print magazines, Katz has also written several books. Among them are *Fathers' Club* (1997); *Media Rants: Postpolitics in the Digital Nation* (1997); *Death Row* (1998); *Running to the Mountain: A Journey of Faith and Change* (1999); *Running to the Mountain: A Midlife Adventure* (2000); and *Geeks: How Two Lost Boys Rode the Internet Out of Idaho* (2001).

Since 1992, as a writer for both *Wired* and its online cousin, *HotWired,* I have been tracking the emergence of a new political ethos that I have seen developing in cyberspace. Over the years, as I explored the Web and exchanged email with countless people all over the world, I felt I was witnessing the birth of a new political sensibility that lies beyond the tired rhetorical combat of Democrats and Republicans.

In April of this year, I sketched the outlines of this sensibility in an essay called "Birth of a Digital Nation" (see *Wired* 5.04, page 49). In that article, I described the primordial stirrings of a new "postpolitical" community that blends the humanism of liberalism with the economic vitality of conservatism. I wrote that members of this group consistently reject both the interventionist dogma of the left and the intolerant ideology of the right. Instead, I argued, Digital Citizens embrace rationalism, revere civil liberties and free-market economics, and gravitate toward a moderated form of libertarianism. But without real leaders or a clearly defined agenda, I remarked, they seemed unable to channel their abundant energy and knowledge in meaningful directions.

"Can we build a new kind of kind of politics?" I asked. "Can we construct a more civil society with our powerful technologies? Are we extending the evolution of freedom among human beings? Or are we nothing more than a great, wired babble pissing into the digital wind?" These ideas triggered an electronic outpouring, as thousands of Internet users responded to the article by emailing me. Representatives of both major political parties, media organizations, and corporate and educational groups offered me piles of money to speak to them about this emerging consciousness. Yet I declined all these offers because I saw the "Birth of a Digital Nation" piece as merely a signpost pointing toward the early stirrings of a nascent political community. The article reflected my own observations, but I couldn't really confirm that those observations were true.

Others, however, were eager to test my hypotheses. A few months after my article was published, *Wired* teamed up with Merrill Lynch Forum to develop a survey that would examine the attitudes and beliefs of individuals who are at the leading edge of the digital revolution. The two companies then recruited Frank Luntz—an Arlington, Virginia, pollster and political strategist who has worked with House Speaker Newt Gingrich, New York mayor Rudolph Giuliani, and Canada's Reform Party—to conduct the survey and analyze the findings.

5 The survey was designed without any input from me, and I learned of its existence just two weeks before the results were compiled. The findings themselves were revealed to me during my first-ever videoconference, as I sat in *Wired*'s Manhattan office watching Frank Luntz address the Wired Ventures hierarchy in a San Francisco conference room. It was an unnerving experience, largely because writers rarely have their speculations subjected to rigorous and thorough analysis.

It turns out the "Digital Nation" piece was right and wrong.

The survey reveals there is indeed a distinct group of Digital Citizens. As I suggested, they're knowledgeable, tolerant, civic-minded, and radically committed to change. Profoundly optimistic about the future, they're convinced that technology is a force for good and that our free-market economy functions as a powerful engine of progress. But among the survey's many powerful findings, one in particular caught me by surprise: where I had described them as deeply estranged from mainstream politics, the poll revealed that they are actually highly participatory and view our existing political system positively, even patriotically.

In fact, Digital Citizens love their political system more than the system loves them. Almost all conventional wisdom about digital culture—especially as conveyed in recent years by journalists, politicians, intellectuals, and other fearful guardians of the existing order—is dead wrong. The Internet, it turns out, is not a breeding ground for disconnection, fragmentation, paranoia, and apathy. Digital Citizens are not alienated, either from other people or from civic institutions. Nor are they ignorant of our system's inner workings, or indifferent to the social and political issues our society must confront. Instead, the online world encompasses many of the most informed and participatory citizens we have ever had or are likely to have.

Meet the Model Citizens

To develop a profile of this rising group, Luntz researchers polled 1,444 randomly selected Americans and divided them into four categories based on how often they use email and the extent to which they have access to a laptop, a cell phone, a beeper, and a home computer. The "Superconnected" use email at least three days a week and use all four of the target technologies. The "Connected" also exchange email at least three days a week, but they have access to only three of the other four communication tools. The "Semiconnected" use at least one but not more than four of the technologies. Obviously, the "Unconnected" use none of these resources.

By this methodology, the survey shows that Digital Citizens—Connected and Superconnected Americans—constitute 8.5 percent of the overall population. The survey also reveals that the more connected we are, the more democratic we are, the more likely we are to vote, the more we know about our political system, and the more faith we are likely to have in it.

Digital Citizens are extremely knowledgeable about the world around them. Compared with their Unconnected compatriots, Connected Americans are almost twice as likely to know that William Rehnquist is the chief justice of the United States. Likewise, while only 48 percent of Unconnected Americans could name the Speaker of the House of Representatives, 79 percent of the Connected properly identified him as Newt Gingrich. Remarkably, the Speaker enjoys even greater name recognition than several pop culture icons—only 62 percent of the Connected could come up with the first name of the TV character known as Seinfeld.

Despite the national lament that technology undermines literacy, Connected Americans are also more likely to spend time reading books than any other segment of the population broken down in this survey. Seventy percent of the Connected say they spend 1 to 10 hours reading a book during a typical week; another 16 percent read for 11 to 20 hours a week.

Far from being distracted by technology, Digital Citizens appear startlingly close to the Jeffersonian ideal—they are informed, outspoken, participatory, passionate about freedom, proud of their culture, and committed to the free nation in which it has evolved. An astounding 57 percent of Connected Americans have "a lot of confidence" in democracy, compared with 48 percent of the total population and only 42 percent of the Unconnected. The Connected are also more inclined to translate their views into political action—nearly 60 percent say they "always" vote in national, state, and local elections. Yet even if they brim with confidence in American ideals, the Connected are less enthralled with the institutions that carry them out. Although 46 percent of Connected Americans express "some confidence" in the two-party system, only 29 percent say they have "a lot of confidence" in it. In other areas—such as their level of confidence in the legal system, the courts, the police, the military, and US schools—Connected and Unconnected Americans are virtually indistinguishable.

These facts put the lie to much of contemporary political discourse and mainstream journalism, which together disseminate countless tales of perversion, porn, hatemongering, violence, addiction, and other perils that are said to flow from the online world. And while some of these dangers are real, the tales themselves are usually presented in such sensationalistic detail as to suggest that they are unavoidable realities of online life—rather than as the comparatively rare, though tragic, occurrences they actually are. More important, the common stereotype of the Internet as a haven for isolated geeks who are unaware of important events occurring outside their cavelike bedrooms can now be exploded as an inaccurate myth. The same goes for the caricature of technology as a civic virus that breeds disaffection from politics. If anything, the survey shows that political dissatisfaction does not stem from staring at computer screens, but from avoiding them.

15 The less connected people are, the more ignorant of and alienated from politics they are likely to be. In fact, the Unconnected are far more likely to embrace all the negative attitudes toward politics so commonly attributed to the Connected. Nevertheless, Digital Citizens have gotten a bad rap—denounced by moral and intellectual guardians on both the left and right, reviled in contemporary politics and culture, and assaulted by V-chips, the Communications Decency Act, privacy-busting encryption rules, and other crude attempts at technological regulation. To this day, the patriotic fervor of Digital Citizens has gone unrequited.

Change Is Good

It makes sense that Digital Citizens view their political system with affection. They are poised to lead it and prosper from it. They stand out from the rest of the population in their positive attitudes about the future and their eagemess to embrace change. They feel optimistic and in control. They are the most future-oriented people in the country.

Americans are bitterly divided about whether technology is good or bad, whether it elevates our lives or corrodes our values. Many intellectual and journalistic leaders see technology as a dangerous, out-of-control force that has an immoral impact on society. Digital Citizens have a different response, viewing technology with caution, but rarely with fear. They understand quite well—better, surely, than anybody—that technology has limits, and that it can bring unforeseen consequences in addition to its many benefits. Although only 24 percent of Unconnected Americans subscribe to the belief that technological breakthroughs will leave them with less free time in the future, for example, the Connected are even more skeptical—37 percent are convinced that new technology translates into less free time.

For the Connected, technology is seen not as a cure-all, but as a powerful tool for individual expression, democratization, economic opportunity, community, and education. Their familiarity with technology has helped create what may be the most confident and optimistic segment of our political culture. For Digital Citizens, as for the world beyond, stasis is simply not an imaginable option.

Change is inevitable, and Connected Americans view it as a force that they can master. Among the Connected, almost seven in ten feel they control change, while only 19 percent think change controls them. In the US population as a whole, just 52 percent say they control change; a third say it controls them. The statistics are even more bleak among the Unconnected, with 40 percent saying they control change and another 40 percent believing that it controls them.

In recent years, pollsters and politicians have reacted with increasing alarm to what they call "the loss of intergenerational optimism and hope." But the Connected segment of the American population suffers no such malaise. By more than two to one—66 percent to 24 percent—Connected Americans believe their children and the next generation of Americans will enjoy a better quality of life than they have. In comparison, a much slimmer majority of the Unconnected—53 percent—think their children's quality of life will surpass their own, while 37 percent of them believe it will not.

The technological chasm that divides those who feel in control of a rapidly changing world and those who feel at its mercy is one of the most politically and economically significant findings of the Digital Citizen survey. For years our political culture has pandered almost exclusively to the latter group—a constituency that is more fearful than curious, more anxious to halt change than embrace it. This pandering, the survey suggests, is a profound mistake. Connected Americans are not only comfortable with change—they relish it. And if technology is indeed transforming the world, its economies, and its politics, they are more eager than anyone to join the process.

Apart from the Crowd

Politicians would do well to transcend their current obsession with dirty pictures on the Internet and start talking and listening to this vibrant, new community. A vast, well-educated, communicative, intensely political constituency remains up for grabs. And increasingly they consider themselves a distinct political entity—39 percent of Connected Americans say they consider themselves members of a "Digital Nation." The Connected constitute a distinct political subculture. They see the world as being driven by decentralized growth and opportunity, rather than a fixed ideology imposed by a central authority. In their eyes, Bill Gates has about as much influence over the fate of the nation as Bill Clinton. By a margin of 58 to 33 percent, most Americans say the president has a greater overall impact on the country than the founder of Microsoft. But the Connected are almost equally divided as to which man will affect the country more.

This should come as no surprise. As Connected Americans have watched Bill Gates become a billionaire, his company has grown into one of the most powerful forces on the planet. They've watched as Gates's corporate culture has quickly—and sometimes ruthlessly—reinvented, expanded, and equipped the world in which we live. By comparison, government seems nearly paralyzed, mired in squabbles and sadly bereft of creativity as Republicans and Democrats endlessly lock horns—often at the expense of the public and its needs.

But the real significance of this finding goes beyond Gates and Clinton themselves. It suggests that for Digital Citizens, entrepreneurs and companies are seen as more effective agents of change than conventional politicians. For this reason, I dissent somewhat from the findings of the Digital Citizen pollsters. Despite the general satisfaction many Connected Americans expressed with the two-party system, the countless online discussions about politics that I've had over the years have convinced me that technologically savvy Americans feel endemic disenchantment with the way our civic institutions perform. Affection for the two-party system aside, I believe the two political cultures are on a collision course. The Digital Citizens' rationalism, knowledge, belief in the free exchange of information, and passion for change are all antithetical to the political culture of Washington. And as they grow in strength and number, it seems to me that Digital Citizens will inevitably take a tougher look at political institutions which seem trapped in antediluvian models of communication and problem solving. This may make our current crop of political leaders nervous, but in the long run I'm convinced that the US has nothing to fear from Digital Citizens—they are deeply democratic and relatively prosperous, and thus more likely to work within the system instead of trying to overthrow it.

25 Furthermore, this is an inherently tolerant group—the first generation to truly embrace diversity as a healthy, positive aspect of American life. If there is any segment of the American population that couldn't care less about gender, national origin, skin color, or sexual orientation, it is Digital Citizens. According to the survey, 79 percent of them believe that a diverse workforce is more productive than one in which workers share the same background. Unconnected citizens are far less certain about the virtues of diversity, with only 49 percent favoring diverse backgrounds, while 32 percent say shared backgrounds lead to greater productivity. If Connected Americans occupy greater positions of economic and political influence in the coming decades, then the cherished goal of equal opportunity for all—an American ideal that has been much discussed but only sporadically realized—could become a far more common reality in the fabric of our lives.

Connected and Free

Digital Citizens are markedly libertarian—they have much more confidence in the ability of business and individuals to solve problems than in government. Strong majorities of both the Connected and the Superconnected—55 and 59 percent respectively—believe that Internet users should be allowed to police themselves rather than be subjected to regulation by the federal government. Perhaps because so many of the Connected live, work, play, and communicate in a culture with few taboos and restrictions, they value freedom of thought much more than the Unconnected.

Digital Citizens' political values draw heavily from the humanism and social tolerance of the left, but they dispute the view that government is both primarily responsible for and effective at confronting and solving social problems—a cornerstone of both the Democratic Party and the ideology we've come to call liberalism. Personal responsibility is a powerful idea in the online world—a notion that meshes closely with the survey's findings that Connected Americans believe in democracy, but not necessarily in the ability of government to solve social problems. Their passion for individual responsibility and market forces suggests the ideology of the right. More than 90 percent of them expressed confidence in the workings of the free market.

But they are not "uppercase" Libertarians. When asked to choose, slightly more Connected Americans label themselves as Republicans than as Democrats, but many choose neither. Nineteen percent describe themselves as "strong" Republicans, and 21 percent say they are "weak" Republicans. In the same group, 15 percent see themselves as strong Democrats, and 18 percent as weak Democrats. Meanwhile, 20 percent of the Connected prefer to call themselves independent.

This is a group that thinks for itself and decides issues one by one, instead of following a strict ideology or platform. In a nod to conservatives, nearly half of Connected Americans believe the Social Security system requires "truly major reform," and more than three-quarters support the death penalty. But in sympathy with liberals, more than half believe it's possible to cut military spending by a third and still maintain current levels of national security, and an amazing 71 percent support the legalization of marijuana for medical use.

Connected Americans are also family-centered, with strong connections to other people—56 percent of them would agree to give up a day's pay each week if that meant they could spend one more day at home with friends and family. Despite their technological savvy, Connected Americans still prefer the familiarity of a human voice: overwhelmingly, they said they would prefer to relate good news to friends and family via telephone rather than via email.

The postpolitical flexibility of the Digital Citizen is rationalist, largely fact-driven, and more concerned with perceived truths than traditional labels. If evidence suggests that the Social Security system needs reform, Connected Americans support reform. If medical evidence suggests marijuana would help reduce suffering among the terminally ill, then they support its limited legalization despite the countervailing drone of political and religious rhetoric. What Digital Citizens reject, the survey suggests, isn't civics or two-party politics, but rigidly formalized authority. This new culture represents a political community with a strong sense of adventure and exploration. Its members want politicians to be smart and tell the truth, and they have little admiration for those who blindly adhere to party platforms or stiffly parrot what their political handlers tell them.

The Media Myth

Connected Americans report that they still get the bulk of their news from newspapers and cable television instead of relying on the Internet. But they have little regard for either TV or print journalism. A measly 13 percent of Connected Americans say they have "a lot of confidence" in TV and newspapers, with a further breakdown showing that TV is trusted even less than newspapers. In substantial numbers, Connected Americans view conventional media as sometimes inaccurate and routinely too sensational. But in a challenge to the ubiquitous characterization of the Internet as an unfiltered blur of unreliable data, they trust the Internet more than any other medium—22 percent say they have a lot of confidence in the information they find online.

If Connected Americans are suspicious of traditional media, that may be because mainstream media has consistently treated them as either dangerous sociopaths to be controlled or commercial targets to be exploited. The US is obsessed with the idea of being connected, but now we know a lot more about who the Connected really are:

- Digital Citizens are young, but they are no longer youths. There are more Connected Americans in their 40s than in their 20s. Only 11 percent are over the age of 55.
- The gender gap has largely closed. Connected Americans are 52 percent male and 48 percent female.
- They are also 87 percent white, 5 percent black, and 4 percent Hispanic; 58 percent live in the suburbs, 28 percent live in cities, and 13 percent live in rural areas.
- They are better educated than the population as a whole. More than half of Connected Americans are college graduates, as opposed to 16 percent of Unconnected Americans. Still, a startling 43 percent of the Connected never graduated from college.
- The majority of Connected Americans earn between US$30,000 and $79,999 per year; 12 percent earn more than $80,000 a year. Among the Unconnected, only 8 percent earn more than $50,000. The Connected are comfortable, but solidly middle-class.
- Connected people not only believe in the free-market system, they are part owners of it—82 percent own stocks, bonds, or mutual funds.

Surprise, Surprise

Many of these characteristics seem predictable to those us who are already familiar with this culture. But the patriotic feelings Digital Citizens reserve for the existing political system came as a big surprise to me. I am happy to have been wrong, but I remain puzzled by the incongruity of my own experience and the survey results. The best explanation I can offer is that Connected Americans have a deep stake in democracy and a political system that they believe to be inherently workable—even if they aren't overjoyed by the current politicians who administer it.

35 After all, Connected people are poised to prosper in an era of great technological change. It may be in their best interest to ride the boat, rather than to rock it. I might have anticipated this. The Digital Citizens I've come to know are brainy, quarrelsome, and skeptical—but at heart, they are profoundly idealistic. They are proud of their new nation and culture, eager to explain, defend, and preserve it—and frequently called upon to do all three.

There were other surprises. While there are thousands of Web sites devoted to spirituality and religion, I've seen little in the online world to make me believe that Digital Citizens readily embrace institutions like organized religion and incorporate prayer into their daily lives. Yet roughly a third of the Connected surveyed say they attend religious ceremonies an average of four times a month—almost precisely the same percentage as the Unconnected. Fifty-six percent of the Connected (like 59 percent of the Unconnected) pray at least once a day. I suspect the poll was picking up a trend that other surveys have also found about younger Americans: they have a deep spiritual—as opposed to religious—bent. With that possible distinction in mind, I remain convinced that this group is allergic to preaching and piety, whether it comes from the White House or the Vatican.

My other concern about this survey has to do with the manner in which it defined and identified the select group of individuals known as Digital Citizens. By linking connectedness so closely to five specific technologies—email, laptops, personal computers, pagers, and cell phones—there seems to be a risk of excluding many people who simply don't have the money or the need for all this high-tech machinery. I don't use all that stuff myself, nor do many of the online people I know. But using broader criteria—such as participation in digital forums on the Web or Usenet—Digital Citizens might prove to be even larger than that the 8.5 percent of the United States population uncovered by this survey. To me, being connected is about community, and not about hardware.

In fact, the whole notion of connectedness has become so mired in posturing, paranoia, and propaganda that it has lost much of its meaning. Certain political and intellectual élites hate the idea of connectedness, in part because it threatens their longstanding primacy over the control of ideas and social agendas. But the tone of the rhetoric coming from Digital Citizens hasn't helped either—it has often been so shrouded in technobabble and arrogance that it has taken on an élitism of its own. It may not be pretty, but such attitudes are perhaps inevitable in a culture that is both new and revolutionary.

Despite these qualms, the survey gets to the heart of what being connected is all about. Ultimately, it's not about gadgetry, hipness, or cultural domination. It's much more about giving individuals a taste of democracy, helping them create new kinds of communities, and reconnecting them with the institutions that shape their daily lives. It's about sharing knowledge and information, and spreading ideas and prosperity. These are the core values and goals of Digital Citizens.

40 The survey's findings are in many ways a scathing indictment of the lazy, reactionary manner in which many contemporary institutions have resisted change, demeaned and patronized the young, and struggled to preserve their own power. Many of these critics remind me of the hoary old men in the Kremlin who hung on for dear life during the dying days of communism, shrouding their self-interest in gaseous talk of preserving a culture and a civilization. But in the process, US leaders have alienated a culture whose patronage and confidence they could dearly miss in the years ahead.

For educators, the survey suggests the need for some radical rethinking about the interaction between education and technology. The Internet is not, after all, something that children need to be protected from. Rather, they urgently need access to it. Clearly, there is now evidence that technology promotes democracy, citizenship, knowledge, literacy, and community. But to cultivate these virtues, our educational system needs to learn how to accommodate a culture that is interactive, knowledgeable, participatory, and frequently restless.

For our political system, the implications of this survey are both urgent and obvious: it's time to move discussion about the Net and other new technologies beyond the current obsession with the evil they might cause and toward a focus on the truly revolutionary opportunities they create. But it remains unclear who will speak to this booming and powerful new culture to help it establish a meaningful agenda. Politicians like Al Gore, Bill Clinton, and Newt Gingrich have all made noises about embracing new technology, yet they are so far removed from the core values of Digital Citizens that their pronouncements inevitably seem hollow and opportunistic. If they can be led at all, leadership for the Digital Citizens might have to come from within. For now, however, they exist as a wondrous, but orphaned, movement in waiting.

Ours is a cynical world. In our smarty-pants media culture, idealism is out of style. Still, the question demands consideration: If Digital Citizens emerge as a powerful force in the 21st century, what might they build?

I am no utopian, but if I allow myself to dream along those lines, I envision a new style of politics—less confrontational, more fact-driven, more responsive and agile. This politics might be practiced in a pluralistic and diverse world in which cultural differences are debated and celebrated, while garden-variety bigotry and horrors like the Bosnian slaughter are consigned, like smallpox, to the ash heap of history. It is a world in which the future is embraced, not dreaded.

45 I've always seen the significance of the Internet as having much more do with the Enlightenment than the dawn of a New Millennium. Like the brave philosophers of the 18th century, Digital Citizens are united by an ambitious vision, much like the one historian Peter Gay described in his book The Enlightenment as "a program of secularism, humanity, cosmopolitanism, and freedom, above all, freedom in its many forms—freedom from arbitrary power, freedom of speech, freedom of trade, freedom to realize one's talents, freedom of aesthetic response, freedom, in a word, of moral man to make his own way in the world."

What finally emerges both from my own experience and the survey is a powerful feeling that we are, in fact, part of a political movement that will be much bigger than us. We are a political nation, citizens of reason with common values, struggling to come together in common cause.

Meanwhile, the questions I asked last spring remain: "Can we build a new kind of politics? Can we construct a more civil society with our powerful technologies? Are we extending the evolution of freedom among human beings?"

When I wrote that, my best answer was that I honestly couldn't say. But after poring over the Digital Citizen survey, I think that, just maybe, we can.

Mapping the Text

1. In "The Digital Citizen," Jon Katz says "Digital Citizens embrace rationalism, revere civil liberties and free-market economics, and gravitate toward a moderated form of libertarianism. But without real leaders of a clearly defined agenda, . . . they seemed unable to channel their abundant energy and knowledge in meaningful directions."
   - Do you agree with the idea that there should be rights, privileges, and responsibilities of digital citizenship?
   - Make a list of the values and characteristics Katz presents in this essay. Who does Katz indicate a digital citizen is? Do you agree with this characterization?
   - What is the relationship between leadership (and its ability to define a meaningful agenda) and meaningful action?
2. What message do you think Katz intends to convey through this essay?
3. What action does Katz call for in this essay?

Writing to Inquire

1. Katz talks about "civil society." How do you define this term? How do you think technology hinders or enables such a society?

Racial Digital Divide

LOGAN HILL

Logan Hill is an editorial assistant at *New York* magazine who has written several essays about race and technology. In the selection below, dated April 26, 1999, Hill discusses differences in access, availability, and the mastery of technology based on race and income.

Record numbers of students are going online, according to UCLA's annual survey of college freshmen released this past January. But this new battery of Internet statistics—the latest in a field updated as rapidly as software—confirms that a digital divide persists between the races. Of the freshmen surveyed at private universities, 90.2 percent reported using the Internet for schoolwork, but just 77.6 percent of students at traditionally black public colleges said the same. The study reveals that this problem is linked to the lack of computer access at public high schools, which 92.2 percent of the respondents from black public colleges attended, compared with less than two-thirds of the students surveyed at private universities.

Unfortunately, the press garbled these results. First, the *New York Times*'s William Honan exaggerated the racial divide, reporting that the UCLA researchers found a "great disparity in computer mastery between students entering elite private colleges, 80.1 percent of whom say they use computers regularly, and those attending traditionally black public institutions, 41.1 percent of whom say that." These statistics actually refer to the percentage of students who use e-mail, not computers. The gap in scholastic Internet usage is significant (12.6 percentage points) but not inexplicably huge, while the e-mail discrepancy indicates that minority students, who are less likely to own PCs, are also less likely to have their own e-mail accounts or free time for nonessential computing at overburdened public terminals.

Honan's relatively benign conflation of these statistics soon mutated into a different and more troubling story. On January 25, *Slate* columnist Scott Shuger, dubbed a "cool cat" by William F. Buckley Jr. and recently wedged between Maureen Dowd and Matt Drudge as one of *Newsweek*'s "20 Stars of the New News," sent out his site's widely read "Today's Papers" e-mail brief. Shuger summarized the *Times*'s coverage but appended the following advice: "Before too much redistributive social policy gets made around such results, it might be good to add a question to the survey: 'Do you have a luxury sound system or a car less than two years old, or a luxury sound system in that car?'" Having stumbled upon such stereos—and students—at Freaknik, a spring break party for black college students in Atlanta, Shuger concluded that "computer/Internet paucity. . . may be a function of [black students'] own interests and choices rather than that of affordability."

The *Times* granted Shuger three paragraphs of blustering self-defense (and just two words of quoted criticism) the following week, excusing him as a groggy nocturnal Web reporter. But logic like Shuger's is far from innocuous. In its report "The Myth of an Emerging Information Underclass," the Cato Institute opined that "the fact that people do not log on does not necessarily imply that they cannot afford to do so. They may simply have other priorities." Last year, a combination of such cyberculture-of-poverty arguments and hysteria over a "Gore Tax" led Congress to slash the VP's Internet access program from $2.5 billion to nearly half that.

5 Advocates like B. Keith Fulton, director of technology programs and policy for the National Urban League, have little patience for such speculation. In predominantly white classrooms, Fulton points out, students are three times more likely to have Internet access than students in mostly minority classrooms. He says, "People like [Shuger] are not held accountable. They aren't out there working on studies, so they make a stereotyped comment and it gets attention. But we can train 1,400 people in an LA computer center, they can earn $31 million in salaries, and nobody talks about that." Fulton and the organizers of more than 250 community technology centers across the country (see www.ctcnet.org for more information) help provide computers, training and resources to minorities through schools, libraries and public centers.

The racial digital divide is real and cannot simply be attributed to income, as corroborated by a series of federal studies. With historically inferior technology access, minorities have been discouraged from computer education, recreation and professions. Currently, African-Americans and Latinos compose 22 percent of the Silicon Valley area's population, but only 4 percent of employees at its major firms are African-American, and just 8 percent are Latinos—and many work in service or support positions.

These stark numbers result from a systemic denial of training as well as access, which is bad news for techno-optimists who foresee democracy flourishing as every television set becomes an Internet node. Even as the Internet becomes more accessible, a skills gap will persist unless public schools are able to offer equitable teaching and other resources. Studies by the National Science Foundation and Vanderbilt University have found that even minority students who are able to surf do not receive the same levels of practical computer training that would allow them to share in the economic benefits of the high-tech boom.

Smaller class size and higher teacher pay might well do more to improve heavily minority schools than a blueberry iMac, but teachers can't even begin to impart technological knowledge until they have computers and support. Linda Sax, director of the UCLA survey, says that although "nearly everyone's misinterpreted something" about the study, it nonetheless offers some reason for hope in this regard: "Our survey shows that minority students are using the computers at school. That's excellent. That's working." But, she adds, African-American students own fewer computers, and "there won't be equity [in access] until every student has their own computer." Ramon Harris, who directs the Executive Leadership Foundation's Transfer Technology Project, a program that works to enhance computer course programs at traditionally black colleges, has the same goal in mind. He says, "Universal computing access is necessary and should be subsidized like a utility. Like water. Like light. It's that simple."

Mapping the Text

1. In this essay, Logan Hill suggests there is a body of technological knowledge and experience that contemporary students should have. What, in your view, is this knowledge and experience? In looking back over your own computer access, training, and experience, do you consider yourself adequately prepared to meet contemporary challenges?
2. What do you think Hill's purpose was in writing this essay? Who is his intended audience? What do you think he would like to see happen?
3. Hill raises some questions in this essay about the uses and interpretations of data. What does he see as the problem? What does his discussion suggest readers should do?

Writing to Inquire

1. Go to your library and read the *New York Times* article to which Hill refers. See if you can find other articles in newspapers and magazines that discuss this issue. Form your own opinion, taking into account the information that you have gathered. Assuming that there is some consensus on the actual existence of a racial digital divide, what conditions seem to create it? What consequences result? What message do you take away from this situation?

INQUIRY: HOW DOES TECHNOLOGY AFFECT OUR WAYS OF OPERATING AS CITIZENS?

1. Given what you have learned and experienced about the world of computers, describe the culture of cyberspace.
2. Review the selections in this chapter. What do you see the impact of technology to be on the way human beings form identities in this medium?
3. What difference do race, gender, age, socioeconomic status, political beliefs, etc., make in the ways that people participate in this world?
4. What do the increasing opportunities of this technology suggest about education and training?
5. What, in your view, are the pressing issues of the cyberworld?
6. What social, political, and ethical issues do you associate with computer technology? What are the benefits? What are the consequences? What is gained? What, if anything, is lost?
7. Should there be codes of conduct in the uses of Internet or digital communication?
8. What is the impact of the cyberworld on health and wellness, on our ability to shape our environment and enhance our physical abilities?

What differences do race and age make in the ways we interact with technology? What kind of social frontiers are being opened by new technologies?

Credits

TEXT ACKNOWLEDGMENTS

Sherman Alexie, "Indian Education" from *The Lone Ranger and Tonto Fistfight in Heaven*. Copyright © 1993 by Sherman Alexie. Used by permission of Grove/Atlantic, Inc.

Paula Gunn Allen, "Taking a Visitor to See the Ruins" from *Skin and Bones: Poems 1979-87*. Copyright © 1988 by Paula Gunn Allen. Reprinted with the permission of West End Press, Albuquerque, New Mexico.

Maya Angelou, "Phenomenal Woman" from *And Still I Rise*, copyright © 1978 by Maya Angelou. Used by permission of Random House, Inc.

Gloria Anzaldúa, "The Homeland, Aztlán" from *Borderlands/La Frontera: The New Mestiza*. Copyright © 1987, 1999 by Gloria Anzaldúa. Reprinted by permission of Aunt Lute Books.

Michael Bèrubè, "Introduction" to *Life As We Know It*, copyright © 1996 by Michael Bèrubè. Used by permission of Pantheon Books, a division of Random House, Inc.

Carlos Bulosan, "My Education" from *On Becoming Filipino*, edited by E. San Juan, Jr., Temple University Press, pages 124-130. Reprinted by permission.

Abena Busia, "Migrations" from *Testimonies of Exile*, copyright © 1990. Reproduced with the permission of Africa World Press, Trenton, New Jersey.

Rachel Carson, "The Obligation to Endure" from *Silent Spring*. Copyright © 1962 by Rachel L. Carson. Reprinted by permission of Houghton Mifflin Company. All rights reserved.

Diego Castellanos, "A Polyglot Nation" from *The Best of Two Worlds: Bilingual-Bicultural Education in The U.S.*, New Jersey State Department of Education, 1983. Reprinted by permission of the author.

Kim Chernin, "Confessions of an Eater" from *The Obsession: Reflections on The Tyranny of Slenderness*. Copyright ©1981 by Kim Chernin. Reprinted by permission of HarperCollins Publishers Inc.

Sandra Cisneros, "Eleven" from *Woman Hollering Creek*. Copyright © 1991 by Sandra Cisneros. Published by Vintage Books, a division of Random House, Inc., New York and originally in hardcover by Random House, Inc. Reprinted by permission of Susan Bergholz Literary Services, New York. All rights reserved.

The Combahee River Collective, "A Black Feminist Statement," copyright © 1995 *Words Of Fire: An Anthology of African-American Feminist Thought* edited by Beverly Guy-Sheftall. Reprinted by permission of The New Press. (800) 233-4830

Paul de Palma, "http://www.when_is_enough_enough?.com" from *The American Scholar*, Volume 68, No. 1, Winter 1999. Copyright © 1999 by Paul de Palma. Reprinted by permission of The American Scholar and the author.

Mary Crow Dog, from *Lakota Woman* copyright © 1990 by Mary Crow Dog and Richard Erdoes. Used by permission of Grove/Atlantic, Inc.

Elliot N. Dorff, "Visiting the Sick" from *Matters of Life and Death*, pp. 255-263. Copyright 1998 © by Elliot N. Dorff, The Jewish Publication Society. Used by permission.

Tony Earley, "The Quare Gene: What Will Happen to the Secret Language of the Appalachians." Reprinted by permission of Gordon Kato Agency. Copyright © 1988 by Tony Earley. Originally published in *The New Yorker*.

Ralph Waldo Emerson, "The American Scholar" from *Selections From Ralph Waldo Emerson: An Organic Anthology*, edited by Stephen E. Whicher, copyright 1957 by Houghton Mifflin Company.

Nikky Finney, "Fishing Among the Learned" reprinted by permission of the author.

Dave Foreman, "Putting the Earth First" from *Confessions of an Eco-Warrior*, copyright © 1991 by Dave Foreman. Used by permission of Harmony Books, a division of Random House, Inc.

Laurie Garrett, excerpts from Introduction from *The Coming Plague: Newly Emerging Diseases in a World Out of Balance*. Copyright © 1994 by Laurie Garrett. Reprinted by permission of Farrar, Straus and Giroux, LLC.

John Gehring, "Not Enough Girls" from *Education Week*, Volume 20, Issue 35, May 10, 2001. Reprinted with permission from Education Week.
David Gergen. "A Moment to Step Up" from *U.S. News & World Report*, 2/26/01. Copyright 2001 U.S. News & World Report, L.P. Reprinted with permission.
Myra Vanderpool Gormley, "Genealogy: Quacks, Cures, and Ancestors" from *Colonial Homes*, August 1977, pages 26-27. Reprinted by permission of the author.
Laura Gurak, "Is This the Party to Whom I Am Speaking?," copyright © 2001 by Laura J. Gurak. Reprinted by permission of the author.
Shirley Brice Heath, excerpted from "A National Language Academy? Debate in the New Nation" from *International Journal of The Sociology of Language 11*, 1976. Reprinted by permission of the author.
Nels P. Highberg, "What I Did on My Summer Vacation" reprinted by permission of the author.
Logan Hill, "Racial Digital Divide" reprinted with permission from the April 26, 1999 issue of *The Nation*.
John Hockenberry, "The Next Brainiacs" copyright © 2001 by John Hockenberry. Reprinted by permission of John Hockenberry and the Watkins/Loomis Agency. Originally published in *Wired*.
Douglas R. Hofstadter, excerpts from "Analogy as the Core of Cognition" in *The Best American Science Writing* (Guest Editor: James Gleick, Series Editor: Jesse Cohen, The Ecco Press.) By permission of Douglas R. Hofstadter.
Linda Hogan, "The Alchemists" from *The Book of Medicines*. Copyright © 1993 by Linda Hogan. Reprinted with the permission of Coffee House Press, Minneapolis.
bell hooks, "Homeplace: A Site of Resistance" from *Yearning: Race, Gender, Politics*. Reprinted by permission of South End Press.
bell hooks, "Learning in the Shadow of Race and Class" (as adapted for *The Chronicle of Higher Education*, 11/17/00) from *Where We Stand: Class Matters*. Reproduced by permission of Routledge, Inc., part of The Taylor & Francis Group.
Langston Hughes, "I, Too, Sing America" from *The Collected Poems of Langston Hughes*, copyright © 1994 by The Estate of Langston Hughes. Used by permission of Alfred A. Knopf, a division of Random House, Inc.
June Jordan, "For My American Family: A Belated Tribute to a Legacy of Gifted Intelligence and Guts" from *Technical Difficulties: African-American Notes of The State of The Union*, 1992. Reprinted by permission of the author.
June Jordan, excerpt from "Free Flight" in *Passion: New Poems 1977-1980*. Copyright © 1980 by June Jordan. Used by permission of the June M. Jordan Literary Estate.
Jon Katz, "The Digital Citizen," copyright © 1997 by Jon Katz. Reprinted by permission of Sterling Lord Literistic, Inc. Originally published in *Wired*.
Jamaica Kincaid, excerpt from *A Small Place*, copyright © 1988 by Jamaica Kincaid. Reprinted by permission of Farrar, Straus and Giroux, LLC.
Barbara Kingsolver, "The Memory Place" from *High Tide in Tucson: Essays From Now Or Never*. Copyright © 1995 by Barbara Kingsolver. Reprinted by permission of HarperCollins Publishers Inc.
Maxine Hong Kingston, excerpts from *China Men*, copyright © 1977, 1978, 1979, 1980 by Maxine Hong Kingston. Used by permission of Alfred A. Knopf, a division of Random House, Inc.
Jonathan Kozol, "Other People's Children: North Lawndale and the South Side of Chicago" from *Savage Inequalities*, copyright © 1991 by Jonathan Kozol. Used by permission of Crown Publishers, a division of Random House, Inc.
Michael Lassell, "How to Watch Your Brother Die" from *Decade Dance*, copyright © 1990 by Michael Lassell. Reprinted by permission of the author.
Friedrich Leipzig, excerpt from *Ellis Island Interviews: In Their Own Words* by Peter Morton Coan. Copyright © 1997 by Peter Morton Coan. Reprinted by permission of Facts On File, Inc.
Rae Lewis-Thornton, "Facing AIDS" from *Essence*, Copyright December, 1994. Reprinted with the author's permission.
Barry Lopez, "Landscape and Narrative" from *Crossing Open Ground*. Reprinted by permission of Sterling Lord Literistic, Inc. Copyright © 1988 by Barry Holstun Lopez.
Audre Lorde, from *The Cancer Journals, Special Edition*. Copyright © 1997 by Audre Lorde Estate. Reprinted by permission of Aunt Lute Books.

Susan McCarthy, "The Good Deed," copyright © 1996 Conde Nast Publications Inc. All rights reserved. Reprinted with permission of *Wired*.
Mary Jane Megquier, excerpts of letter from Mary Jane Megquier to Angeline (Megquier) Gilson, June 30, 1850, MQ 22. This item is reproduced by permission of The Huntington Library, San Marino, California.
Dr. Menninger, reprinted from *Dear Dr. Menninger: Women's Voices From the Thirties*, edited by Howard J. Faulkner and Virginia D. Pruitt, by permission of the University of Missouri Press. Copyright © 1997 by the Curators of the University of Missouri.
Laura Miller, "Women and Children First: Gender and the Settling of the Electronic Frontier" from *Resisting The Virtual Life* edited by James Brook and Iain A. Boal, copyright © 1995 by Laura Miller. Reprinted by permission of City Lights Books.
Toni Morrison, excerpts from *Jazz* reprinted by permission of International Creative Management, Inc. Copyright © 1992 by Toni Morrison.
Shoba Narayan, "The God of Small Feasts" from *Gourmet*, January 2000. Reprinted by permission of the author.
Bonnie A. Pardi and Vicki L. Oday, "Framing Conversations about Technology" from *Information Ecologies: Using Technology With Heart*, copyright © 1999 by Massachusetts Institute of Technology. Reprinted by permission of The MIT Press.
Bill Piatt, "The Confusing State of Minority Language Rights" in "Toward Domestic Recognition of a Human Right to Language" from *Houston Law Review 23* (1986). Reprinted by permission of Houston Law Review.
Dudley Randall, "The Melting Pot," published by permission of the Dudley Randall Estate.
Jeremy Rifkin, "Commodifying Human Relationships" from *The Age Of Access*, copyright © 2000 by Jeremy Rifkin. Used by permission of Jeremy P. Tarcher, a division of Penguin Putnam Inc.
Oliver Sacks, "Hands" reprinted with permission of Simon & Schuster Adult Publishing Group from *The Man Who Mistook His Wife For a Hat and Other Clinical Tales*. Copyright © 1970, 1981, 1983, 1984, 1985 by Oliver Sacks.
Carl Sandburg, "Chicago" from *Chicago Poems*, copyright 1916 by Holt, Rinehart and Winston and renewed 1944 by Carl Sandburg. Reprinted by permission of Harcourt, Inc.
Judy Scales-Trent, "Affirmative Action and Stigma: The Education of a Professor" from *Notes of a White Black Woman: Race, Color, Community* (University Park, the Pennsylvania State University Press, 1995), pages 117-125. Copyright © 1995 by The Pennsylvania State University. Reproduced by permission of the publisher.
Lillian Schlissel, from *Women's Diaries of the Westward Journey*, copyright © 1983 by Schocken Books. Used by permission of Schocken Books, a division of Random House, Inc.
Sarah Schulman, "AIDS and the Responsibility of the Writer" from *My American History: Essays 1981-1994*, copyright © 1994 by Sarah Schulman. Reproduced by permission of Routledge, Inc., part of The Taylor & Francis Group.
Bret Silverstein and Deborah Perlick, from *The Cost Of Competence: Why Inequality Causes Depression, Eating Disorders, And Illness in Women*, copyright © 1995 by Oxford University Press, Inc. Used by permission of Oxford University Press, Inc.
David Barton Smith, excerpts from *Health Care Divided: Race And Healing A Nation* (Ann Arbor: The University of Michigan Press, 1999). Reprinted by permission of the publisher.
Monica Sone, from *Nisei Daughter*, copyright © 1953 by Monica Sone; copyright © renewed 1981 by Monica Sone. By permission of Little, Brown and Company, (Inc.).
Kenneth S. Stern, "Battling Bigotry on Campus" (as published in *USA Today Magazine*, March 1992). Reprinted by permission of the author.
Students for a Democratic Society, excerpts from "The Port Huron Statement of the Students for a Democratic Society," 1961. Reprinted by permission of Charles H. Kerr Publishing Company, Chicago, IL.
Luci Tapahanso, "Just Past Shiprock" from *S·anii Dahataal: The Women Are Singing*, © 1993 Luci Tapahanso. Reprinted by permission of the University of Arizona Press.
Studs Terkel, "C.P. Ellis" from *American Dreams*. Reprinted by permission of Donadio & Olson, Inc. Copyright © 1980 by Studs Terkel.
Henry David Thoreau, "Where I Lived, and What I Lived For" from *The Selected Works Of Thoreau* by Walter Harding. Copyright © 1975 by Houghton Mifflin Company. Reprinted by permission of Houghton Mifflin Company. All rights reserved.

Sherry Turkle, reprinted with the permission of Simon & Schuster Adult Publishing Group from *Life on the Screen: Identity in the Age of the Internet*. Copyright © 1995 by Sherry Turkle.
Ellen Ullman, "Space is Numeric" from *Close To The Machine*, copyright © 1997 by Ellen Ullman. Reprinted by permission of City Lights Books.
Barbara Vobejda, "The Changing Face of America" from *The Washington Post National Weekly Edition*, © 1991, The Washington Post. Reprinted with permission.
Rebecca Walker, excerpts from *Black, White And Jewish*, copyright © 2001 by Rebecca Walker. Used by permission of Riverhead Books, a division of Penguin Putnam, Inc.
Terry Tempest Williams, "The Clan of One-Breasted Women" from *Refuge: An Unnatural History of Family and Place*, copyright © 1991 by Terry Tempest Williams. Used by permission of Pantheon Books, a division of Random House, Inc.
Tim Wise, "Blinded by the White: Crime, Race, and Denial in America" by Tim Wise, an anti-racist essayist, activist and educator. Reprinted by permission of the author.
Samantha Dunaway, "Melting into Canaan" Reprinted by permission of the author.
Arlene Mestas, "My Name Is. . . " Reprinted by permission of the author.

PHOTO ACKNOWLEDGMENTS

Chapter 1: © VCL/Getty Images
Chapter 2: © Bettman/Corbis
Chapter 3: © Mark Hormel/Getty Images
Chapter 4: © Phil Degginger/Getty Images
Chapter 5: © Michael Pole/Corbis
Chapter 6: © Robert Brenner/Photo Edit
Chapter 7: © Digital Vision/Getty Images

Index